THE DREAM FACTORY

BY TOM WHEELER

ISBN: 978-1-4234-3698-0

Published by:
Hal Leonard Corporation
7777 W. Bluemound Road
P.O. Box 13819
Milwaukee, WI 53213

Library of Congress Cataloging-in-Publication Data

Wheeler, Tom (Thomas Hutchin)
The dream factory - Fender Custom Shop / by Tom
Wheeler. – 1st ed.
p. cm.
Includes index.
ISBN 978-0-634-05613-0
1. Fender Musical Instruments–History. 2.Guitars –History. I.Title.
ML1015.G9W53 2007
787.87'1973–dc22
2007015680

Printed in China through Colorcraft Ltd, Hong Kong

First Edition

Visit Hal Leonard Online at **www.halleonard.com**

VINT FRETS
.900
890
R-9
ROBERT CRAY
R-7
.980
.970
CLAPTON
9½R
.920
.830
910
Fender STRATOCASTER
LENNY SRV
JEFF BECK
SAMPLE
.850
R-9

THE DREAM FACTORY

TABLE OF CONTENTS

Jazzmaster "prototype," Chap. 29

ABOUT THE AUTHOR

Tom Wheeler

After freelancing for *Rolling Stone*, Tom served as the Editor in Chief of *Guitar Player* and the founding Editorial Director of *Bass Player*. His first hardcover encyclopedia, *The Guitar Book: A Handbook for Electric and Acoustic Guitarists* (foreword by B.B. King), was published by Harper & Row in various languages.

His next book, *American Guitars: An Illustrated History* (foreword by Les Paul) was called by one retail catalog "the best book ever written about guitars." His 2004 book, *The Stratocaster Chronicles* (foreword by Eric Clapton), was named Book of the Year by *Vintage Guitar Magazine*. Tom also wrote *The Soul of Tone: Celebrating 60 Years of Fender Amps* (foreword by Keith Richards).

He has interviewed Muddy Waters, B.B. King, Chuck Berry, Eric Clapton, Les Paul, Leo Fender, Ted McCarty, Keith Richards, and many others. He co-edited Richard Smith's *Fender: The Sound Heard 'Round The World*, and also wrote the foreword. He was a consultant to the Smithsonian Institution and to the publishers of *The Guitar Collection: An Elite Gathering of 150 Exceptional Guitars*. He wrote the foreword for *The PRS Guitar Book* and contributed chapters to *Gibson Guitars, 100 Years of an American Icon; The Electric Guitar; Electric Guitars of the Fifties;* and *Electric Guitars of the Sixties;* among others.

Tom has been interviewed by *The New York Times, The Chicago Tribune, The Wall Street Journal, U.S. News & World Report*, Irish Public Radio, American Public Radio, MTV, NPR, the BBC, and CNN. He appears in the Smithsonian Channel's documentary *Electrified: The Guitar Revolution,* serves on Fender's Hall of Fame Selection Committee, and was the writer and host of informational videos for Fender and Guild. He holds a Juris Doctor degree from the Loyola School of Law, is currently a professor at the University of Oregon's School of Journalism and Communication, and gigs regularly with soul singer Deb Cleveland.

Dan Smith

Dedicated to Dan Smith and to the memory of Freddie Tavares.

Freddie Tavares

ACKNOWLEDGEMENTS

This was supposed to be the easy one. After spending two years on *The Stratocaster Chronicles* and another two on *The Soul of Tone*, I thought writing a history of the Custom Shop would go relatively quickly. After all, Fender's been making Stratocasters for more than 50 years, amplifiers for more than 60. The Custom Shop has been around for a bit longer than two decades, so I expected to write one of my shorter books, not the longest one ever. But as is often the case, the more I learned, the more I realized I didn't know. Every door seemed to lead into a room with three other doors, but that's fine. The joy of doing these projects comes more from new discoveries than from sharing what I thought I already knew. In any case, the deeper I got, the more I relied on the expertise of others.

Working with Art Director Richard Slater is a blessing. He's a guitar player, so aside from his formidable design skills he thoroughly understands what guitars are all about. He gets it, and he's the reason this book is laid out so creatively and so beautifully. Time and again he put in the extra hours, painstakingly refining chapters that already would have passed muster at other publishers. Brad Smith has been my editor for several years now, an enthusiastic supporter and collaborator in these projects. I often say my partnership with Hal Leonard is the best writer/publisher relationship I've ever heard of.

Some four decades ago, Jimi Hendrix called Billy Gibbons "America's best young guitar player." Since then, Billy has endeavored not only to live up to Jimi's accolade but also to explore and to celebrate the multicultural roots of American rock and blues. Eric Clapton once said: "When I first started going to Texas, I'd hang out, and the only thing that was on the jukeboxes in Texas was ZZ Top [laughs]. And then I'd put the money in and I'd hear it, and my world changed. And then I got to meet Billy and realized that he's another very, very serious archivist type, musicologist type guy. I mean, these are *scholars*, you know. All that stuff they do is great and everything, but it's built on a really strong foundation." For all these reasons, and because Billy Gibbons has been an avid patron of the Custom Shop since the facility opened its doors, he was the perfect choice to write the foreword for this book. I am honored to have his soulful and insightful essay. *So good!*

Many of the Custom Shop's Master Builders contributed hours of their time. J. Black and John Page not only agreed to be interviewed (repeatedly), but they also answered what must have been a hundred or more e-mails each. They read several sections of the manuscript, lent boxes of photos and memorabilia, and offered many suggestions and insights. My old friend Dan Smith has a deeper perspective of the inner workings of Fender than anyone I know, and I very much appreciate his generous support and wise counsel. Mike Eldred offered advice, guidance, and information over a period of three years, and he was essential to my efforts to chronicle the shop's second decade.

All of the current Master Builders and most of the former ones shared their recollections and patiently explained their techniques and the details of many of their guitars. Several other current and former employees may not have Master Builder decals, but they have been essential to the shop's operation and were equally helpful. More than two dozen Senior Master Builders, Master Builders, other craftspeople, R&D engineers, apprentices, shop foremen, and managers sat through multiple in-person interviews, took my calls, responded in depth to what must have seemed like a never-ending stream of e-mails, and read portions of the manuscript. These generous souls include Gene Baker, George Blanda, Duane Boulanger, Scott Buehl, Mike Bump, John Cruz, Art Esparza, Ralph Esposito, Brett Faust, Greg Fessler, Brian Fields, Chris Fleming, Dennis Galuszka, Scott Grant, Alex Nicholas, "Red" Dave Nichols, Alex Perez, Mike Ponce, Louis Salgado, Yuriy Shishkov, Jason Smith, Stephen Stern, Fred Stuart, John Suhr, Paul Waller, Abigail Ybarra, and especially Mark Kendrick, Todd Krause, and Michael Stevens.

Steve Pitkin's dazzling photos are familiar to owners of various Custom Shop calendars and readers of Richard Smith's fine book *Fender Custom Shop Guitar Gallery*. It's been a pleasure working with Steve, reprinting some of his older images and displaying dozens of others taken after Richard's book appeared back in 1996. (Steve also created some of the composite images you'll see in these pages; Richard Slater created others.) Thanks also to the other photographers whose work appears here, especially Dave Maddux and Matt York.

Many current and former Fender executives, media professionals, marketers, managers, salesmen, road reps, artist reps, and administrators also lent a hand, and I'm grateful for their efforts. Thanks to Rose Bishop, Bruce Bolen, Del Breckenfeld, Joe Carducci, Bill Cummiskey, Keith Davis, JD Dworkow, Dina Elias, Jason Farrell, Mike Geohegan, John Grunder, Ken Helman, Paul Jernigan, Beth McReynolds, Bill Mendello, Chris Puffe, Joe Reynoso, Rich Siegle, Chris Suffolk, and especially Mike Lewis and Richard McDonald.

Some of the shop's most striking instruments have been created in partnerships with woodcarvers, leatherworkers, jewelers, pinstripers, pearl-inlay specialists, and other artists. Their stories enrich the text, and their artworks dazzle. Thanks to George Amicay, Kit Carson, Nevena Christie, Jim Doody, Peter Kellett, Barry and Jan Lowe, Dave Newman, Sara Ray, Joe Wood, and especially Pamelina H.

Thanks also to Richard Ash at Sam Ash Music, author Tony Bacon, Matt Baker at Action Music, "Burst Brothers" David Belzer and Drew Berlin at Guitar Center, Lawrence Berndt at Berndt Woods, Caroline Brass and David Brass at Fretted Americana Inc., Jim Campilongo, John Carruthers at Carruthers Guitars, Vince Cunetto at Vinetto, Jerry Donahue, Seymour Duncan, Travis Egnor and George Gruhn at Gruhn Guitars, Dustin Jack, Stan Jay at Mandolin Bros., Nicole Julius at Hal Leonard, Phil Kubicki, Joslyn M. Maki, Adrian Ashton at Mansons Guitar Shop, Rene Martinez, Steve Mesplè at Wildwood Guitars, Dan Milligan, Takashi Nonomura and Atsushi Ohata at Yamano Music, Bob November at McKenzie River Music, James Peterson, Mark Pollock at Transpecos Guitars, Chuck Riley at Rumble Seat Music, Alan Rogan, Marty Schulte at Spruce Hill Guitars, Evan Skopp at Seymour Duncan, G.E. Smith, Steve Soest at Soest Guitar Repair, Justin Spargo, Alice Stevens, Steve Stevenson, Matt Tapp, Phil Taylor, Jimmy Wallace at Jimmy Wallace Guitars, Tom Watson at Modern Guitars Magazine, Sunny and the gang at Café Vero, and especially Lee Dickson.

Thanks to transcribers Melissa Bennett, Nick DeMarino, Christina Diamond, Elizabeth Dow, Jasmine DuVall, Meghan Hilliard, Maddy Lewis, Katrina Nattress, Rebecca Taylor, Aaron Thayer, and Joe Wheeler. Thanks also to proofreaders Lea Artz, Emilee Booher, Cate Foss, Randianne Leyshon, Christina O'Connor, Sarah Payne, Rebecca Sedlak, Kathryn Stephenson, and Chris Wig.

I am fortunate to count among my friends several lifelong Fender aficionados who are knowledgeable and eminently sensible. I can always call on them, and their insights are invariably helpful. I am indebted to Ritchie Fliegler, a former Senior Vice President of Fender and a partner at Fearless Marketing LLC/TMBPartners; Richard Smith, author of *Fender: The Sound Heard 'Round The World* and the aforementioned *Fender Custom Shop Guitar Gallery*; and John Peden, who raised the photography of guitars to an art form.

Most of all, I will be forever grateful to Anne for her encouragement and unwavering support over the three years it took me to research and write this thing.

— Tom Wheeler

Travel Master Esquire, Chap. 25

A sharp-dressed man with one of his favorite guitars, a Team Built Custom Shop Esquire. The snake-and-bone piece was handcrafted by the late master silversmith Gabor.

FOREWORD

Phoenix Rising

by Billy F Gibbons

Let's turn back the pages for a moment. There was a time, not so long ago, when very few players could order a guitar with specific requests for some "this's and that's," with "non-catalog" specs and parts. And, for a period of some years there, the guitars coming from the great marques required perhaps some "spiffing up" to shake out the bugs and get them in good working order. Presently, it's good news … Good news! In recent years, I see Fender in particular as Phoenix rising. They hold the aim of "we will deliver for you," and the Custom Shop is at the forefront of making it happen.

For many years, if a guy tried out a new guitar and said, no, I want it that way, the goliaths of the industry just wouldn't have it. It's not that Fender didn't want to do it, but they were trying to stay one step ahead of the hounds and survive in the business, and truth is, there was little time to engage in the luxury of veering off the production-line standard. There were some exceptions. Every time you think you've seen it all, go to a guitar show gathering and there's some one-of-a-kind Fender, with a custom paint job or whatever it might be and, of course, there is no record of it. But such things are few and far between.

The good news is, the sweet pie has gotten sweeter, and today we have a legion of dedicated professionals who understand the value of so many different elements that go into making a great guitar on Monday for the Monday customer, and then maybe something completely different with the guitar they make for the Tuesday customer or the Wednesday customer.

One of the things the Fender Custom Shop did was develop a great allegiance between companies and players. Presently, we are in the sweet spot of time, knowing that the shop is tending to the most finite of details, tiny things that were long overlooked or treated in some laissez-faire, cavalier manner. The demands for the guitars' particulars are coming from the right place, the place they deserve to come from — the street, and the guys and gals who play 'em. For this connection we owe much to Fender's Master Builders.

In the early days of the shop, Michael Stevens, Larry Brooks, John Page and the other guys cherished and relished an American treasure, the history and lore of Fender. Page and Stevens were stridently focused, although they were flying blind in one sense. They knew resurrecting an entire company brand and image with guitar-building perfection required passionate people, loads of time, and lots of dedicated effort. And they could think of nothing better!

It's a tricky story we are telling here. It's like Howlin' Wolf said about the blues — *"What do you mean, we're bringing it back? It ain't never left!"* And in a certain way, that resonates with me when I think of Fender. The love and respect for Fender's original vision never went away, at least among the players out there who used those instruments every day, and it came alive in the Custom Shop.

The shop had humble beginnings. They had very little in the way of resources. What they did have was energy … a fierce pride. Stevens and Page assumed the reins of custodianship, to preserve and maintain the tradition. It required a bit of wrangling to get things into proper place, so that the instruments, as Leo Fender had envisioned them, could once again fall into the hands of the unsuspecting. Slowly but surely, the impetus that was so humbly kicked into motion in the late 1980s brought about a familial thing, a true Custom Shop family with a commitment to creating top-drawer gear.

Mike Eldred, the real Fender "in house" ace, maintains a respect for the past and drives the shop from "doors open" 'til the time doors close every day. Everyone involved enjoys picking up the torch, picking up the pace. Fender builders are focused on perfecting the best of the best. Eldred and all of the Fender team — I love 'em. Eccentric, serious players, and a bonus to have a Fender in hand! "El Dred" and his compadres in the shop and Fender marketing are artistically "on it" and totally committed to maintaining the ultimate of the Fender legacies. This is Fender at its finest.

And dig ... the Master Builders are not afraid to step out and try something different — it's as simple as maintaining that "Leo" tradition. Have you seen La Cabronita Especial? I am totally all about that guitar. Simple, simple, simple. It doesn't even have Leo's infamous "hot dog" control plate. Sometimes the shop will take a step into the unknown, but at no point do we find that Leo's visionary creation has been compromised.

Here's an example that goes way back. I dropped by the shop one time with a few boxes of Krispy Kremes for the guys and saw a hardtail Strat that Chris Fleming had made. This sparked a discussion that resulted in three "El Cabron" guitars — a soft-V Tele neck on a white blonde Strat body, one pickup, a gold aluminum pickguard. I still have those guitars in stock. Now, this touches upon a key point. If someone went in and said, "OK, make me a Vox Phantom teardrop with a Strat neck," well, that ain't gonna happen. Everything goes back to square one, upholding the legacy ... and the custodians of Leo's vision are strident in maintaining it. The Master Builders don't step out of bounds. Back in the day, Fender never made a one-pickup Strat with a Tele neck, but when you see this thing, you might say, "I never knew Fender made something like this" ... but you won't have to ask, "What is it?" You'll know exactly what it is: This could only be a Fender.

Even if what the Custom Shop customer wants is a wall hanging, it is still a true taste of Fender. Take something like the red Bonecaster, a serious work of art in every sense where the drama of the artistic expression is unleashed. And, the instrument maker's vision is wide open as well. That guitar would sit comfortably in a gallery of fine contemporary art, but let me tell you, it doesn't cross the line. There is no disturbance of playability. It feels great and sounds great. The shop would never let a guitar out the door if it didn't pass the Fender firing line of quality control and function.

I'll give you another example. I was studying silversmithing for a time, and a gang of us were understudies of a guy from Hungary who went by one name, Gabor. He passed away some years ago, and I am at a loss for words to explain what a character and artist this man was. He made me a snake-and-bone piece like one I had admired on his leather jacket. I thought maybe I could get the Custom Shop guys to humor me and make a guitar around it. Gabor, god rest his soul, knew I liked to have a backup, so he cast two of 'em. I brought them to the shop, and this is when I realized how serious they were — not just about the standard Teles and Strats but everything they do. I wanted that thing under the strings, but they wanted to make sure that this big, heavy piece in no way impeded the functionality, so they figured out a way to actually rout a channel so the piece would lay flush for total playability.

These benefits of the Custom Shop identify the shop's "in house" guitars. They maintain the true Fender line. They influence an entire industry, really. Some of the techniques and standards pioneered or resurrected in the shop are now production-line essentials. Check out the Mexican-factory Esquire, with that crazy, milky, see-through finish, one pickup, a maple neck. The finish is accurate, the frets are set correctly, the intonation is right. Take it out on the bandstand for a couple of months; go ahead. Simply ain't gonna be an issue! Well, so much of this goes back to Stevens and Page and now Fender's Master Builders and everything they have — the knowledge, the tradition, the discoveries.

Bottom line: In order to make vintage for tomorrow, you got to make it good today. The Fender Custom Shop has seen fit to ensure that what reaches your hands is certain to satisfy. Now, learn to play what you want to hear... Rock on...!

Created for Billy Gibbons, the Bonecaster Esquire brims with righteous mojo. (The volume knob evokes Billy's Nudu hat, a ceremonial item with distinctive "fringles" worn by the Bamileke tribe of Western Cameroon.) Bonecaster details: Chap. 25.

INTRODUCTION

The Third Guy

"Three guys, side by side, digging ditches. Ask them, 'What are you making?' First guy says, 'I'm making a ditch.' Second guy, 'I'm making five-fifty an hour.' The third guy says, 'I'm making a cathedral to God.' At the Fender Custom Shop, we're the third guy. I don't care if it sounds corny or whatever. That's who we are."

The speaker is Mike Eldred, Director of Sales and Marketing for Fender's Custom Shop, a place where commitment to a guitar's function, practicality, and commercial potential is fused with a passion for craft and attaining the highest artistic standards. "This isn't just about making money or selling instruments," Mike explains. "We could go to a lot less trouble and still sell guitars and make money. This is something else. This is about expressing yourself, about developing your craft to the highest level, and advancing that craft for the whole industry. It's about working one on one with a particular player to make his dreams come true, whether it's Eric Clapton or the guy down the street playing in his living room."

The ultimate question

What if? When it comes to sparking the imagination, it's the ultimate question. What if man could fly? What if man could walk on the moon? What if man could have a surf green Stratocaster with a Tele neck and lipstick pickups and jumbo frets and a moto pickguard? *What if?*

Probably every player has at one time or another dreamed up his or her ideal guitar — perhaps sketching the thing on college-ruled paper during history class or on a bottle-ringed napkin at a pizza-joint gig. It might have been some classic model that hasn't been made for decades, or a never-before-seen instrument with a unique combo of features. Fender's Custom Shop, aptly nicknamed the Dream Factory, was founded to make those dreams come true. And if your ideal guitar is just some murky vision whose details have yet to come into focus, you can find co-dreamers in the shop who will guide you through the process.

Like many of us, the shop's early bosses and builders asked the same, what-if question. What if instead of limiting ourselves to selling one unique guitar at a time we designed our own models, distinguished them from the factory's guitars, and sold *hundreds* of them? What if we partnered with graphic designers, inlay specialists, jewelers, smiths, leatherworkers and others to create art objects that doubled as musical instruments? What if the processes we perfected in the shop could migrate over to the factory and even to our affiliates in Mexico and Japan, raising the quality of all Fender instruments and enhancing the reputation of Fender's entire global enterprise? *What if?*

The Custom Shop collaborates with Fender departments, Fender dealers, and Fender players all over the world to bring these lofty imaginings down to earth. The result: a collection of instruments not only manifesting the highest standards of quality but also appealing to every taste and style, from Nudie suits to nipple rings.

Expanding visions

The Custom Shop opened in early 1987 as a two-man specialty operation. Before the year was out, it was overwhelmed with orders for unique one-offs and for more or less authentic repros of vintage Fenders. The first customers were previous clients of the shop's inaugural builders, Michael Stevens and John Page, but requests soon flooded in from artists, avid amateurs and professionals, collectors, retail chains, individual stores, distributors, and Fender marketing.

As demand increased, it became increasingly clear that the shop must not only expand its workforce and floor space but also reconsider its very mission. A victim of its own success, it grew so rapidly that its builders and Fender in general could hardly keep up. In one respect, the tale of the shop's first several years is one of a guitar-building enterprise desperately playing catch-up to its own rapidly evolving vision.

Left, a study in gold leaf, the 2005 Master Salute Stratocaster

what if?

The bigger picture

The Custom Shop is often portrayed as a semi-freestanding facility within the Fender organization, and the characterization is reasonably accurate as far as it goes. Certainly, the shop's guitars do indeed have their own standards, tolerances, and high levels of handwork. But the shop's public image, official functions, and jawdropper one-off instruments tell only a part of the story, and not necessarily the most interesting part. In 1985, the company's new owners acquired little more than the Fender name, patents, production equipment, and a small store of leftover instruments. For years the working atmosphere was frenzied, as Fender set up a new factory, rebuilt its work force, and struggled to regain its once-envied reputation.

The Custom Shop was born into this high-stakes, pressure-cooker environment. Not surprisingly, corporate niceties such as organizational charts and job descriptions were ignored as employees collaborated across departmental lines and worked overtime to get the guitars out the door. The interplay among the shop and other departments was constant and complex; official boundaries were at times virtually nonexistent. (R&D people were even pictured as members of the Custom Shop crew.) As R&D guru George Blanda puts it, "The cross-pollination went every which way."

So the Custom Shop is hardly a mere adjunct to Fender. It's a cornerstone, supporting any number of activities. Its builders have designed guitars that are then built not only in the shop but also in the main California factory, in Mexico, and in Japan. Some of the artists whose signature Fenders are built in the main factory have their personal guitars crafted in the Custom Shop. Some models were initially offered through the shop and migrated to the factory; others were first issued from the factory and then reborn in upgraded forms in the Custom Shop. Time and again, production techniques perfected in the shop filtered over to the main facility, helping to boost the quality of all Fender instruments.

Custom Shop people both taught and learned from their colleagues on the main line. Many Custom Shop instruments, particularly in the early years, were assembled in part from factory components. For some guitars, certain production stages were completed in the shop, others in the factory. Until the shop finally received its own paint facility, most or all Custom Shop guitars were painted in the factory. As J. Black says in these pages, "The shop wasn't a separate institution. It was a moving, flowing process, never in stone . . . We worked with the factory people all the time, and they helped us all the time as well. Don't kid yourself — if it weren't for manufacturing, we could not have built one-offs."

There's more. When the shop introduces a new model, it doesn't do so in a vacuum. How does its '54 Strat differ from the factory's version? What about quality control in the shop vs. the factory? Is the $2,500 Telecaster really better than the $800 Tele? Well, yes, but how so? To what extent do the prices and marketing of Custom Shop guitars and factory guitars affect each other? These issues are constantly addressed internally, and one goal of this book is to explore the ways in which the shop's builders and products are indeed separate from those of the factory, as well as the ways in which the shop and other departments are inextricably entwined.

Accounts of the Custom Shop that fail to consider the larger story of the post-buyout Fender are necessarily fragmentary and incomplete. The late William Schultz, rightly credited as the man who saved Fender, set the wheels in motion. This author sees the story of the Custom Shop as being inseparable from the tale of Fender's Third Age, the era of Bill Schultz and his corporate heirs. It was Schultz who insisted that Fender look beyond its traditional instruments, who chafed at seeing competitors sell custom-built guitars for thousands of dollars, and who refused to accept the limitations of Fender's role as the builder of durable tools for working musicians. He told videographer Dennis Baxter: "People laughed when I said I was going to open a custom shop . . . but a Fender is a top-of-the-line product. It can be used anywhere. It can be a collectible. It can be used with a top artist." It was in the Custom Shop where this vision would be realized in wood and wire, metal and plastic.

The hands of a Master Builder: John Cruz tests the action on his prototype of the Yngwie Malmsteen Tribute Strat, with Yngwie's original guitar in the background.

As we will see, the efforts of Custom Shop builders were also essential in reconnecting Fender to its roots in the First Age, the Leo Fender era. During a period when the factory was incapable of rendering authentic, detailed reissues of Fender's classic guitars and basses, Custom Shop workers brought with them an abiding respect for pre-CBS instruments. As employees who vociferously championed the vintage cause within the organization, they saw themselves as true keepers of the Fender flame.

The vanguard

As Fender responded to shifting trends and evolving markets, time and again it was the Custom Shop at the forefront of these efforts, serving as Fender's first-response unit to many challenges. For the first several years, many people outside the company never drew the sharp distinctions we make today regarding the shop's identity. Former salesman John Grunder: "In the late '80s, a clear picture of the shop had yet to come into focus. When I took Custom Shop guitars to dealers and players, the reactions were not so much a recognition of any sort of separation between the shop and factory. The sentiment was simply, Fender is back; Fender is beginning its slow recovery from the CBS era. People were rabid, just so excited. They hadn't played a great new Fender in a long time. At first, the big news wasn't that these guitars came from a Custom Shop. The big news was that they said *Fender* on the headstock."

Rivalries and teamwork

Whatever the public perceptions might have been, the shop strove to develop an identity distinct from that of its parent corporation. First of all, its craftspeople have always been acknowledged as the best of the best, some even worthy of the title Master Builder; any time a factory worker relocates to the shop, it is rightly considered a promotion, a step up. The shop furthered its culture of autonomy with its own catalogs and trade show displays. The dazzling guitars drew loads of media attention. The operation seemed to be a seat-of-the-pants/hang-loose type of deal, more casual and fun than the atmosphere in a typical factory. The ragtag, happy-go-lucky attitude sometimes entailed a lack of communication with other departments, so while internal relationships were marked by collaboration, they also entailed frequent, sometimes heated, debates.

Still, the frustrations and resentments were small compared to the triumphs. Veterans in all corners of the company — R&D, the factory, the Custom Shop, and Fender marketing — recall the shop's first decade with pride and affection. R&D's Senior Master Builder, Mike Bump, explains: "The way we all helped each other out, that's how everybody got good, I think. We all had our specialties. I might be making Kubicki necks during the first three weeks of the month, but then during that last week I might do assembly, make bridges, dress necks, tune test, or just pack guitars for shipping. This forced all of us to expand our skills beyond our original specialties. Everybody pitched in and helped everybody else, to make sure we got our numbers out, and I really think that's how we all became good builders. We learned a lot of different things, and those were some fun times."

Do the Custom Shop shuffle

Trying to keep track of Custom Shop series names is about as effortless as copying that first Mahavishnu album by ear. Some of the early literature lumped Custom Shop and production instruments in the same group, with inevitably confusing results. Some model names can be misleading; for example, the late-'90s "Relic Jazz Bass" was actually available in all three Time Machine finishes, not just the Relic. In the late '90s, while all guitars in the official "Master Built" series were indeed Master Built instruments, other Master Built instruments were excluded from it. Not all Showmasters were in the Showmaster series. Not all Limited Edition guitars were in the Limited Edition series. Sometimes "Signature" was part of the name of a model that might not have been in the official Signature category. Sometimes guitars were billed as "New!" years after their appearance. Some guitars were shuffled from one series to another. In 2009, the Classic S-1 Telecaster and Classic HBS-1 Stratocaster were listed in both the Time Machines and the Special Editions. Around that same time, the Strat Pro moved from the Custom Classics to the Special Editions, the Bass VI from the Limited Releases to the Special Editions, the Telecaster Thinline from the Time Machines to the Special Editions, and . . . .

Here's a suggestion: Let's fix ourselves a tray of piña coladas and forget about such anomalies. It's a certainty that not even a full-time sales employee could recite from memory the lifespan of every Custom Shop series since,

Chris Fleming: "In the mid 2000s, I had the idea to fully wrap a guitar with hand-tooled western saddle leather. I worked with Bill Silverman, of El Dorado Guitar Accessories, in Pasadena. They made the covering and also engraved the metal parts to match the rose motif. It was one of a kind at the time. I subsequently made another for the European market. It's the kind of design you either love or hate. The cowboy/country crowd loved it. By the way, the guitar plays and sounds great."

say, 2000 (let alone since the founding of the shop in 1987), along with the instruments in every series, plus every example of a single instrument's being assigned to more than one series at a time, plus every relocation from one series to another, plus all the other flukes and quirks.

Fender, like its rivals, must constantly adjust to shifts in the marketplace, and given the exhaustive number of feature combinations and the iconic stature of so many Fenders, it's no wonder that some models combine aspects of different series. It is important to grasp the fundamental distinctions — factory vs. Custom Shop, Team Built vs. Master Built, Tributes vs. signature models, Relic vs. N.O.S., Set-Necks vs. bolt-ons, etc. But while this book provides scores if not hundreds of details regarding various series, the author cautions not to expect airtight consistency in Fender nomenclature. Besides, a model's individual specs are more important than its (perhaps temporary) location in this or that series.

A focus on certain models

The Custom Shop's Master Builders have crafted hundreds of different models over the years. While all are noteworthy in one respect or another, some are more important by virtue of their effect on the shop's operation, or their effect on how the shop was perceived by the public or by Fender itself. Therefore, some guitars are documented here much more extensively than others, particularly if they marked a leap in the shop's evolution or some new strategy. Examples include the Set-Neck models, dozens of the "art" guitars, artist signature models, Relics, Time Machines, Team Builts, Tributes, Limited Editions, etc.

A prime example: The Eric Clapton Signature Stratocaster was designed before the shop was founded. It was intended from the outset to be a factory guitar rather than a Custom Shop product, and yet it is profiled in depth in these pages, for several reasons. Eric Clapton's association with the Custom Shop is long and deep, and the shop's involvement in refining the Signature model was essential. The tale of the Clapton Strat reveals much about the inner workings of the Custom Shop, despite the model's official status as a "factory" guitar. In fact, all of the early "factory" artist guitars were developed and perfected in the Custom Shop, another example of why the story of the shop is very much a story of the entire Fender organization.

Into the future

Unlike its sometimes inconsistent and vague efforts of the early period, Fender has endeavored in recent years to draw sharp distinctions between its Custom Shop instruments, U.S. factory instruments, and imports. Internally, however, under the direction of Mike Eldred, Richard McDonald, and their colleagues, Fender's departments are more cooperative and integrated than ever. "My thing is, whatever we're doing in the shop gets translated over to the factory so that everybody benefits," says Mike Eldred. "Everything we do in the Custom Shop should benefit the first-time Fender buyer. That's my opinion, and I think that is the opinion of the majority of the guys in the shop now. They get that."

The little Custom Shop crew of 1987 and 1988 made many one-off guitars; as the shop grew, its managers initiated the custom option approach, followed by the "price sheet" and official catalogs. A more recent shift has been replacing cataloged models with limited collections. Mike Eldred: "You might have to move fast to get one. They are limited either by the number of pieces — maybe 200, maybe only 10 — and sometimes they are limited by the time they're available. They might be available for one year, or even less if they sell out quickly. This makes them even more desirable and collectible, and it gives us a chance to experiment with all sorts of short-term approaches to serve that Custom Shop customer, no matter how picky or discriminating he is."

In the coming years, musical tastes will shift in unpredictable ways, and the global economy will cycle through various trends. Whatever challenges Fender may face, its Custom Shop will continue to harness the talents and passions of some of the world's most creative craftspeople. Somewhere inside the Dream Factory, the spirit of the Third Guy will continue to ponder — *What if?*

Yuriy Shishkov's stunning peacock Tele has a body of aged ash. Yuriy chose rare redwood burl for the top cap because its striking bird's-eye patterns resemble the "eyes" of a peacock's feather. High-grade diamonds, rubies, emeralds, sapphires, and amethysts are mounted in solid gold settings, and the inlays are mother of pearl and gold and blue abalone. Yuriy adds: "The flat sterling silver wire is hammered into a hand-carved channel, a technique used for centuries in decorative firearms embellishments. The wire fits perfectly, without adhesives. The gun-stock varnish was applied, rubbed, and buffed by hand, the finishing process alone taking a full week."

Fender

CHAPTER ONE

1

Seeds and Roots

Origins of the Custom Shop Concept

Let's go all the way back in time to an era when Fender was a tiny company with few employees, scant inventory, and no great prospects for success.

1946?

No, 1985. In March of that year, Fender's parent corporation, CBS, sold the company to a team of investors headed by Fender President William Schultz. Other key figures were Bill Mendello, who would serve as Fender's Executive Vice President, Chief Financial Officer, Chief Operating Officer, President, and Chief Executive Officer; and Kurt Hemrich, a Senior Vice President responsible for Operations and, later, Fender's manufacturing facilities in Corona, California, and Ensenada, Mexico.

A former executive at Yamaha, Schultz had been recruited by CBS four years earlier to turn around the fortunes of a once prestigious company whose reputation had long suffered from cost cutting, mismanagement, and compromises to the quality of its guitars and amplifiers. Once renowned for the value and reliability of its Stratocasters, Telecasters, Twins, and Super Reverbs, Fender now reeled under a stigma of building boat-anchor guitars and tinny sounding, failure-prone amplifiers. That reputation reflected only part of the story, but with vintage consciousness on the rise, the word on the street was, if you want a good Fender, get an old one from the '50s or early '60s — assuming you can find one, and assuming you can afford it. "Pre-CBS" was among the earliest buzzwords of the emerging vintage lexicon.

Evoking iconic automotive designs, the sleek, ultra-cool Rocketcaster (Chap. 11) was built by George Blanda, who was hired in October 1985 to head up Fender's new Custom Shop.

Dan Smith was another Yamaha veteran who in 1981 joined the CBS Fender team as director of marketing for electric guitars. He remembers, "When I worked at Yamaha, I traveled around and talked to dealers all the time, and I knew Fender's reputation was in the toilet. I was trying to get people interested in our Yamaha SG 2000 guitars, but all they could talk about was how crappy Fender and Gibson had become. Prior to that, I'd had a repair shop and could see how bad the stuff was. In fact, I used to charge more money to work on a Fender. A lot of stuff they made in the '70s was terrible. There was a good guitar here and there, but enough of it was crap that their reputation really suffered."

During the CBS era, Fender's reputation was sometimes tarnished by substandard quality control. One example was 1979's 25th Anniversary Stratocaster, notorious for its flake-prone paint job (note the body's bottom edge).

Resurrection strategy

Despite this albatross, Schultz and his team had begun to reverse the company's declining reputation during the sunset of the CBS regime. Dan Smith spearheaded Fender's first reissue projects in 1982, and their quality and relative vintage authenticity went a long way toward re-burnishing Fender's halo. Dan Smith: "Those first reissues were huge. They helped to get our reputation back. Some people were actually surprised when CBS put us up for sale, because they thought things had gotten better. At least we had brokered a lot of good will from 1981 to 1984, at the tail end of CBS." Among the new Fender's meager assets, that residual goodwill would prove crucial as Bill Schultz set about rebuilding the company he had run for four years and now co-owned.

In the buyout of '85, Schultz acquired the Fender name and patents, some office space, extensive production equipment, and a small store of leftover inventory, but that was about it. He had no new designs, no factory, no R&D (Research & Development) department, and no substantial work force. What he did have was a hard-charging personality, a knack for motivating the hell out of his employees, a rep for ethical but hard-nosed business decisions, and one more thing — an unshakeable faith in the legacy of Leo Fender.

His principal strategy was a carryover from CBS: Fender would continue importing fine guitars manufactured in Japan by Fuji-Gen Gakki. Only the relatively exclusive Vintage Series would be built in America. In other words, Japan would produce the mainstream guitars and basses, historically the company's bread and butter, and from then on, made-in-America Fenders would be the exceptions, not the rule.

But there was one more idea that had been back-burnered for years and would soon come to the fore: As a sideline of sorts, Fender would at some point establish a modest domestic facility to produce a few high-end instruments for famous artists.

As we will see, things turned out differently. The little shop that was intended to build a few special guitars for

William Schultz, rightly credited as the man who saved Fender. He thought that an in-house team of elite craftsmen could help restore his company's reputation by building custom guitars for celebrated players.

favored clients would ultimately evolve into a prestigious entity in its own right, a large, semi-freestanding facility renowned for making some of the most stunning and desirable electric guitars the world has ever seen. For the inheritors of the Fender legacy, its success would exceed their plans, their predictions, even their dreams. They called it the Custom Shop.

Reviving an old idea

The limited-production/high-end concept was not new. Before Dan Smith and Bill Schultz even came to Fender, they had discussed the idea at Yamaha. That company had its own stigma to deal with — being limited to building good-value, moderately priced guitars for people who couldn't afford something *really* good. To help them break into the professional market, Yamaha built signature models for prominent artists such as John Denver and David Lindley.

In those days Dan Smith had a proposal on the table of having a select artist committee whose members would be associated with unique models of Yamaha guitars. He brought a similar concept to Fender. Rather than having a Custom Shop per se, the idea was to have some sort of separate and independent operation limited to building special guitars for important artists, prestigious instruments that would elevate Fender's value in the marketplace.

Close relations with artists have always been vital to Fender's success. Here's the great Eldon Shamblin, from the Texas Playboys, with the gold '54 Stratocaster given to him by Leo Fender. A line of artist "signature" guitars would expand that tradition. The concept materialized in the Custom Shop, where Master Builders crafted guitars to order for individual players and developed cataloged artist models for the shop and factory.

Pre-shop customs

Of course, Fender was aware that Martin and Gibson had for years made one-of-a-kind pieces for famous artists or other well-heeled patrons. A custom-made guitar certainly had enormous appeal. It meant getting a unique instrument built especially for you. It meant exclusivity. Sadly, it often meant a slap-your-cheek price tag, too.

Fender had at least dabbled in custom finishes back in the vintage era, building a gold Strat for Eldon Shamblin, a Cimarron Red Stratocaster for Bill Carson, gold sparkle and silver sparkle Telecasters for Buck Owens and Don Rich, and a few other unique looking if otherwise basically stock instruments. (Some "special" Fenders weren't custom-ordered at all but were simply the results of Fender's using up leftover parts or covering up flaws with nonstock paints.)

Phil Kubicki worked for Fender from 1964 to 1971, the later years in R&D. As he explains: "An R&D department is already a custom shop of sorts. We built prototypes — many of them were never turned into regular products — and sometimes we'd build something special for an artist." Among Kubicki's most celebrated instruments were the first two rosewood Telecasters, one of which went to George Harrison. He played it in the film *Let It Be*, on the sessions for the *Get Back* LP, and also during the Beatles' last hurrah, the legendary concert on the Apple building's rooftop in London. Har-

These are Custom Shop recreations of guitars that helped put Fender on the map. Some employees felt that Fender's biggest asset — its legacy — was also a burden that limited its ability to explore new designs. For their part, the Master Builders eventually pursued dual strategies of vintage authenticity and innovation.

rison gave the guitar to his friend Delaney Bramlett, and it was later sold at auction.

Phil Kubicki also built two rosewood Stratocasters. He recalls, "We were going to pick the best one and give it to Jimi Hendrix, but then we got the news that he had passed away [September 18, 1970]. The word came down from management that we were to bring the guitar over to Fender headquarters. I dropped it off with the secretary at the front desk, and I've never seen it since. A few people over the years have wanted to think that they owned the 'Hendrix rosewood Strat,' but I have never authenticated one of those. That guitar disappeared."

Kubicki worked under the direction of Roger Rossmeisl, a German émigré and a veteran of both Gibson and Rickenbacker. Kubicki built Fender archtop guitars, including both the LTD (with carved tops and backs) and Montego models (with pressed tops and backs). While these models appeared in catalogs, they were rare. Phil Kubicki recalls that only 36 LTDs were made. He also worked on prototypes of a Fender Rocker guitar and a Mod bass, both of which were made of zebrawood, of all things, and are described by Kubicki as having Rossmeisl's trademark raised ridge (or "German carve") on the tops — "very un-Fender," as Kubicki puts it. He also helped build Fender's electric violin (Freddie Tavares made the pickups), as well as the Songwriter flat-top, which appeared in a flyer but was never manufactured; the prototype was given to singer Bobbi Gentry, of "Ode to Billy Joe" fame.

Phil Kubicki's last project was the semi-hollowbody Starcaster. Its ostensible purpose was to compete with Gibson's ES-335, but its less publicized function was to use up stacks of leftover body rims from Fender's unpopular Coronado models. A short-lived "Fender that didn't seem like a real Fender," it demonstrated how difficult it was for the company to expand beyond the designs rendered decades before by Leo Fender and his associates. Fender would continue to be challenged by such limitations when marketing its mainstream factory guitars; on the other hand, some sort of Custom Shop might be ideally suited as a laboratory/proving ground for testing outside-the-box designs.

The custom-instrument concept continued in the late '70s when John Page built one-off guitars for Fender artists in the R&D department. Elliot Easton of the Cars was one such customer. In an interview with videographer Dennis Baxter, Easton described a process that reflected one of the strategies the official Custom Shop would adopt years later: "It's one person building that guitar, so you can call and say, 'I have a little idea I would like to try.' You can get into it as deeply as you like — how many winds in the pickup, or what you want the body to weigh, the wood grain you want."

John Page: "There wasn't much structure in R&D in those days. It was very free-form, so we had room for all sorts of projects. We did lots of stuff for the Cars around '79. Ric [Ocasek] got a pink Jazzmaster or Jaguar, and then the other guys wanted matching instruments. At marketing's request, we also built a couple of Stratocasters for Frank Zappa. We asked him to send us a picture of him with a Strat, and he sent us a picture of him holding a Les Paul [laughs]. It was totally Frank." In the last year of the CBS era, Page recalls that he and several associates proposed that they start a Custom Shop as independent contractors, but given Fender's precarious financial position, and with CBS about to pull the plug, Bill Schultz was in no position to authorize such an arrangement.

Despite these sporadic, generally behind-the-scenes activities and despite CBS's mammoth production capacity, the Fender company of the '70s and mid '80s had no separate facility beyond its R&D department's model shop for building one-off guitars. It had no employees exclusively tasked with crafting such instruments, no arrangements with its dealers for distributing such instruments, and no system in place whereby regular customers could consult with builders one-on-one or choose from a list of special features (beyond custom colors and gold hardware) for the guitar of their dreams.

Bill Schultz vowed to change all that: "There's no limit as to where we can go with quality and playability."

Enough with the working man's guitar already

Schultz's no-limits attitude was all well and good, but how would the notion of a small, elite shop building fancy, expensive guitars one at a time fit in with Fender's stock in trade: practical, reasonably priced, factory-built guitars for working musicians? Keith Richards, whose affection for Telecasters is well known, once described the Fender esthetic as "the hardware store." Would Fender's own tradition prove to be a burden? The short answer: Yes. After all, if anything, the previous corporate attitude toward custom instruments had been not merely neutral but vociferously negative. Back in the summer of 1977, a CBS Vice President had exclaimed, "Do we create exotic instruments? *No!* Our products are the basic bread-and-butter heroes of the musical instrument field."

Dan Smith: "You know, it's hard to do something other than what you're known for. The kind of guitars we've always made, that's our strongest asset. But in a way, that kind of thing can be a handicap if you're trying to expand. People look at something new and say, 'Well, that's not Fender.' We had tried to sell some expensive things over the years, like those LTDs and the Montegos, but they weren't the right kinds of designs. They were very expensive, and they went over like a fart in a space suit [laughs]. They didn't do well. It wasn't Fender's area.

William Schultz intended to move Fender beyond its functional, "working man's guitar" reputation. But could he have dreamed of departures such as this one? The wood-burned, painted, and artificially aged "Tiki-Caster" was a collaboration between Master Builder Dennis Galuszka and artists Barry and Jan Lowe. Beginning in the early 1990s, high-profile "art guitars" would help to make the Custom Shop one of the most prominent facilities in the world.

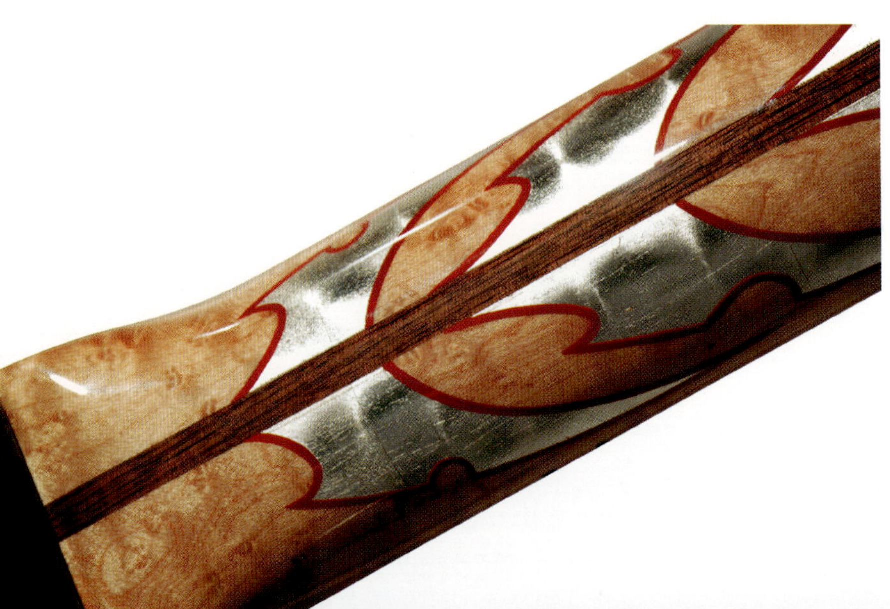

Guitars such as this one might have puzzled the company's founders, but radical graphics provided one more avenue into new markets. This twin-humbucker Strat was built by Senior Master Builder Todd Krause; artwork by Troy Lee Designs.

"Whenever I quoted the 'Fender is the working man's guitar' thing to Bill, it ticked him off every time. He'd read me an article and say, 'Gibson just sold some guitar for thousands of dollars, and Martin just built this or that special guitar — why can't we do that?' It irritated him, and he called me into his office and said, 'Hey, I'm tired of hearing this crap about *working man's guitar*' [laughs]. It always bugged him that other companies were selling high-end stuff. It was a big priority for him. But it was tough, because one of the cool things about Fender when I was a kid playing in bars was that you knew you could fight your way out of the joint with your guitar if you had to and still play it the next night, which wasn't something you could say about a Gibson or whatever. Fenders were tough."

Tough, indeed. One of the more common adjectives in early Fender literature was "rugged." Leo Fender was known for reinforcing and overbuilding everything from his factory to his yacht. This tough-as-nails esthetic carried over to his guitars' bolt-on, rock maple necks and his amplifiers' solid pine cabinets with virtually indestructible finger-jointed corners. But Bill Schultz reckoned that building a few expensive one-offs in a small California shop and also importing large quantities of affordable factory guitars were hardly mutually exclusive concepts. Why not do both? What's the problem?

Shortly after the Custom Shop's founding, a commitment to vintage authenticity took root, eventually culminating in instruments such as this recent, highly detailed LTD Limited Broadcaster.

First things first

Actually, the problems were numerous and complex. In the early '80s, while Schultz, Smith and others had at least discussed opening a Custom Shop, other priorities took precedence — convincing CBS to keep Fender's doors open, for starters. Dan Smith: "A lot of people didn't even think Fender was going to make it. That's how bad things had gotten in 1984 and 1985 at the tail end of CBS, despite some progress. You didn't find a lot of people betting on our horse in the race."

After the buyout, Schultz and Smith met with the principals of Heritage Guitar, located in Gibson's old Kalamazoo, Michigan, factory. They also traveled to LaSiDo, the large Canadian manufacturer. They didn't need much in the way of production facilities, or so they thought. Given the excellence of Fuji-Gen's guitars and the weakness of the yen relative to the dollar, Fender stuck with its plan to build only its Vintage Series instruments and import everything else. The thinking was, if Fender could show the world that it could craft vintage-style guitars to exacting, purist-approved standards, then that success might open some doors for the company to expand into new territories.

Back in 1983, Fender had signed a deal with renowned arch-top builder Jimmy D'Aquisto to design a series of high-end jazz guitars. This was one of the Schultz team's early efforts to demonstrate that the Fender brand could legitimately be applied to instruments beyond the "working man's guitar" concept. For the post-buyout Fender, however, the top priority was simply getting basic Strats, Teles, and basses into production. Exotic pursuits such as hand-carved arch-tops or custom-built one-offs would have to wait.

Thinking big

The reverence, nostalgia, and affection musicians still held for the Fender name helped to counter the lingering disappointments from the CBS debacle. Players and dealers alike were rooting for the new team. The Japanese product was selling, and confidence in the new Fender began to build. In the last year under CBS, the company had grossed an estimated 25 million dollars worth of business. Thanks in large measure to the quality of the imports (and the stewardship of Schultz and Mendello), the new, post-CBS Fender grossed an estimated 42 million dollars during its first year.

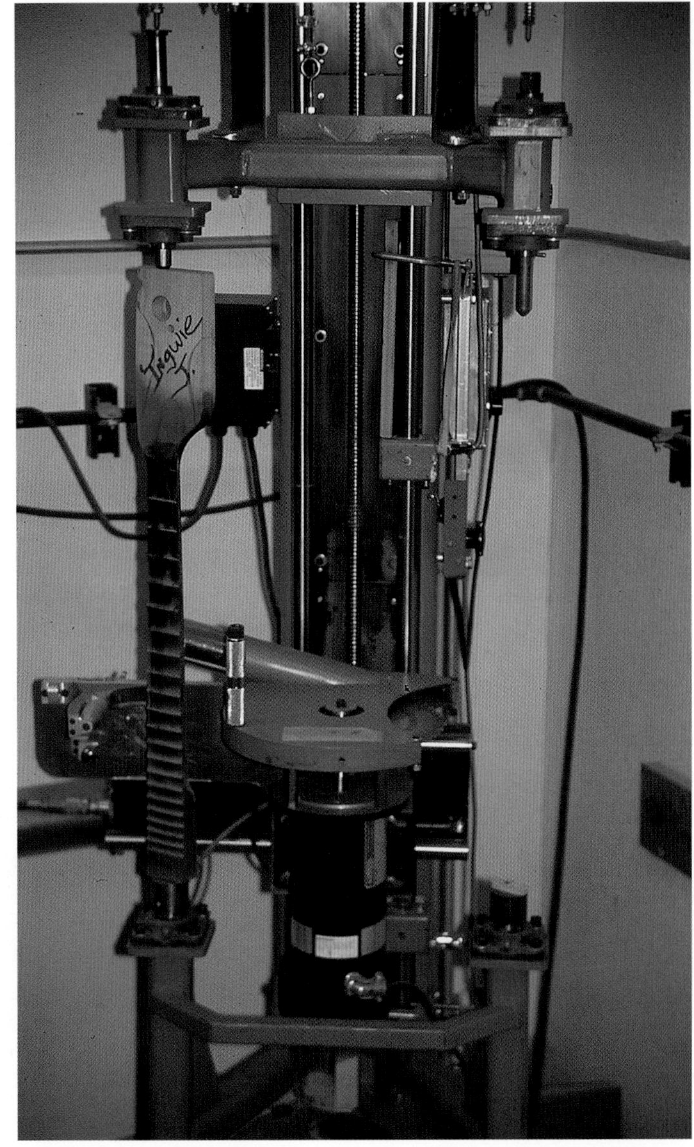

The shop's neck duplicator, devised by the ingenious John Carruthers. He likened its operation to a three-dimensional key duplicator.

That debut was impressive by any standard, even more so considering the hardships, and yet Bill Schultz was not one to rest on his laurels. Dan Smith: "I remember one meeting where he said, 'Look, we can be a really good 30 or 40 million dollar company, a small company that just makes a certain number of guitars a year. Or we can go on

One of these master neck templates would be mounted on the neck duplicator alongside a rough-cut neck blank.

to be what we should be, which is a large company that does everything well.' If you knew Bill, you knew he was not the kind of guy who was going to be a little 30 million dollar company [laughs]. So he was looking for all kinds of ways to expand.

"Bill told the story about how he started the Custom Shop, and I'm sure he believed he started it, because it sure wouldn't have happened without him. But the way he always told it was, 'Dan Smith came in and said Fender was the working man's guitar, and that really ticked me off, so I told him he better do something about it.' Well, the other companies had custom shops, but the thing holding us back was that we hadn't even opened our factory yet."

Aside from Dan Smith and Bill Schultz, credit for "starting" the Custom Shop has also been given to George Blanda, Bruce Bolen, and Michael Stevens. Moreover, John Page's contributions were essential; there would be no Custom Shop as we know it without him. As we will see, each of these gentlemen played a role. Phil Kubicki's comment — "An R&D department is already a custom shop of sorts" — would prove prophetic in a way. In fact, the first person brought in to Fender to direct the Custom Shop was promptly reassigned to R&D. The shop's first co-director was a Fender R&D veteran; in later years he would simultaneously head up the Custom Shop as well as R&D for all of Fender. To this day, the shop's Master Builders and R&D's designers and engineers work across departmental lines to stimulate ideas and to support each other.

George Blanda. Dan Smith called him "one of the best people who has ever built electric guitars."

John Carruthers and George Blanda

In October, 1985, seven months after the sale, Fender opened its new factory in Corona, California. By then, the Custom Shop idea had inched forward, from a vague wish to a firm commitment. Schultz announced that the shop would make guitars that demonstrated the highest levels of craft, sparked musicians' imaginations, and served the needs of the most discriminating artists. Furthermore, the shop itself would be a showcase displaying custom-built workbenches and arrays of hand tools sure to impress visitors. Key point: He didn't really mind if it didn't make money. It was all about showing players and dealers (and competitors, to be sure) that Fender's vision extended beyond the valuable yet limiting "working man's guitar" image.

Having written *Guitar Player* magazine's repair column for years and repaired and customized instruments for some of L.A.'s most acclaimed musicians, John Carruthers was one of the foremost repairmen in the country. He would go on to design several notable instruments and serve as a consultant to Ibanez, EMG, Yamaha, Musicians Institute, Fender, and others. Carruthers and Dan Smith went way back. In fact, as a consultant to Yamaha, it was Carruthers who had interviewed and hired Smith for his position at that company and recommended him for the Fender job as well. Smith remembers, "He was always there for me as a consultant with feedback and suggestions for both Yamaha and Fender. He's been one of my best friends in my life and a valuable resource, one of those amazing, multi-talented people who can go out in the morning and take wonderful photographs and then build you a Model T the same day."

John Carruthers: "I was one of the first four or five people hired by Bill Schultz when he took over at CBS Fender. I was a consultant, not an employee. They wanted me to be the director of the Custom Shop, but since I had established my business and had my own thing going, I decided not to do it. I did make a machine that got used at Fender. I called it a neck duplicator. You could put a neck you liked on one side, and it had a follower and then a cutter on the other side that would cut that second neck in the same shape, like a three-dimensional key machine. A lot of the artists I worked with had certain necks they liked, and I wanted to find a way to make a replica with fairly close tolerances in a relatively short time. I made the machine myself — two of them, actually, one for Fender and one for me."

John had helped Dan Smith, Freddie Tavares, and others on the reissues of '82, measuring many vintage Fenders, re-specing the reference standards, and helping to update or replace at least some of the worn-out tooling. Officially, his influence was felt more in the main factory than in the Custom Shop, but practically speaking there was a fair amount of crossover between the two entities, and he continued to provide valuable counsel as the Custom Shop concept came into focus. Carruthers would have been Dan Smith's first choice to head up the shop, but as noted he had his hands full with his own roster of professional clients. It would have made little sense for him to abandon his promising new venture to take over an enterprise with such an uncertain future, even if it did bear the Fender brand.

Smith then turned to designer, engineer, and guitar builder George Blanda. Based on the beauty and quality of a couple of Blanda's guitars, Dan had considered hiring him at CBS prior to the '85 buyout. In retrospect, it was a good thing for all concerned that Blanda hadn't come onboard back then, because he might well have been let go along with the scores of others who left in the turbulence of CBS Fender's last days.

But now the time seemed right. Smith had remembered Blanda's guitars and had held on to his business card. He sang his praises to Bill Schultz, who green-lighted Smith's proposal to tap Blanda as the director of a Custom Shop that had yet to progress beyond initial planning. George Blanda, who'd had his eye on Fender for years, quickly accepted, joining the Fender team in October '85.

He remembers, "I had a business building guitars, and prior to that I had a couple of years' experience working at Ax In Hand in DeKalb, Illinois, so I had seen a great many vintage guitars. Within a couple of months after the buyout, they weren't really sure what they were going to do, but they had determined that they were going to start a Custom Shop, and that would be a good place for me."

The former rival

Bruce Bolen had for years been a prominent industry figure, handling marketing, R&D, and quality control for Fender's principal competitor, Gibson. Paralleling Fender's own history in significant respects, Gibson had introduced many innovations, enjoyed a modern golden age in the '50s and early '60s, garnered a long list of famous endorsers, was acquired by a huge conglomerate in the 1960s, declined in the '70s and early '80s to the point of near-bankruptcy, and struggled to respond as its vintage guitars far eclipsed current models in prestige and dollar value. And again like

An essential aspect of the shop from the outset was the almost anything-goes creative freedom enjoyed by builders. John English is shown here putting the finishing touches on a rosewood Stratocaster (note the body's "sandwich" construction, with a thin, contrasting layer of wood between the top and bottom pieces).

Fender, the faltering company in Kalamazoo, Michigan, was purchased by a leaner, savvier group of investors in the mid '80s. As a wearer of many hats at Gibson during good times and bad, Bruce Bolen knew all about the ups and downs of the guitar business.

Dan Smith: "Bruce was leaving Gibson. Our companies were fierce competitors, but he and I liked each other and had gotten to be friends. I thought Bruce would be a great guy to come to Fender. I knew Bill Schultz was looking for a sales and marketing person, so I told Bruce to emphasize his sales and marketing experience when he was talking to Bill [laughs]."

Schultz's decision to hire his archrival's key executive — who was also the founder and for two years director of Gibson's successful Custom Shop — was typically far-sighted. Bruce Bolen arrived in California in 1986, just as the new Fender was getting off the ground. His influence would prove crucial to the development of Fender's own Custom Shop, not only in getting it up and running but also in fundamentally changing its vision and operation.

On the lookout

George Blanda's position as director of the Custom Shop was mostly a formality, simply because there wasn't much of an operation for him to direct. As he recalls, "I got in there and started working before the shop was even in place. For the first few months, the whole Custom Shop thing was kind of on-again and off-again, so I was a jack of all trades for a while." He remained in the Electronics R&D department in the new Fender company's first office building, in Brea, California, with a makeshift model shop right outside his door. During this period he built the Hank Marvin Stratocaster [p. 53], one of several contenders for the title of "first Fender Custom Shop guitar."

Before Fender could get around to allocating space for the Custom Shop's production area, George Blanda was reassigned to R&D. The reason? International monetary trends. The yen was rising in value — from about 250Y to the dollar in 1985 to only 125Y by mid 1986 — and when it became more expensive to import Japanese Fenders, the advantages of increasing domestic production were impossible to ignore. The plan for the Fender factory in 1985 had been to go from building seven or eight guitars a day to 150 a day, within five years. Fender would also establish its little Custom Shop, making just a few prestigious guitars a year. But now the message from dealers and players was changing: "Hey, we want *American* Fenders." The Japanese guitars were still good, but as they became more expensive, Dan Smith thought, well, if we can make American guitars that are competitively priced — not just the high-end or vintage stuff, but a broader product line — then we can *really* resurrect Fender's reputation.

Given increasing demands for American-made Fenders, designing the next generation of Stratocasters, Telecasters, and basses was a much higher priority than starting a little nonprofit Custom Shop. Dan Smith: "Bill said, 'We're gonna need a new person for R&D,' and I said, 'We already have somebody. George Blanda is one of the best people who has ever built electric guitars. There's no better person. George is the guy.'"

Blanda proved to be not only a fine builder but a mechanical engineer, draftsman, and innovative designer as well. Working in the Brea R&D office, he and Smith began to collaborate on what would become one of the biggest success stories in Fender's entire history, the American Standard series. It was designed in 1986 and unveiled to enthusiastic reviews at the January 1987 NAMM trade show. Bruce Bolen: "George is to be exalted, because the American Standard Strat just proved to be so important to Fender in getting back on its feet. That project was not so much Custom Shop work but rather prototyping in the model shop."

With Blanda up to his neck in research and development, Fender was once again on the lookout for someone to get the Custom Shop off the ground. They found him in Texas.

Custom Shop guitars are often personalized by the craftspeople who worked on them. Several of the Master Builders came to be known for their distinctive touches and gained personal followings among clients.

If there is a Fairy Godmother of Tone, it's Abigail Ybarra, crafter of Fender pickups. Longtime company veterans such as Abby Ybarra are revered in the shop and remain valued collaborators.

Certificate of Authenticity

Fender®

Fender® Custom Shop
-Tribute Series-
The Fender® Custom Shop Mary Kaye Tribute Stratocaster® Guitar

Kaye descended from Hawaiian royalty and was a direct descendent of Queen Liliuokalani, Hawaii 's last
ing monarch. With her band, The Mary Kaye Trio, Mary was hot property back in 1956. The Rock-N-Roll
sion had just happened and the band won many admirers, among them Elvis Presley and Sammy Davis Jr.
During the '50's and '60's, Mary and her band became a regular act on the Las Vegas strip.

Mary won the accolade of being the first female artist to break into the U.S Billboard chart
th 1959's "You Can't Be True, Dear"). Among her several album releases are, A Night in Las Vegas (1955),
on a Silver Platter (1956), You Don't Know What Love Is (1957), Kookie's Love Song (1958), Too Much (1958),
Jackpot (1959), On the Sunset Strip (1959), Up Front (1960), For the Record (1961), Our Hawaii (1962),
the Idle Poor Become the Idle Rich (1964) and Night Life (1966). As a female guitarist, Mary Kaye was unique
and so was a guitar she played. Mary helped this particular model become popular and has enjoyed a
long and successful career, both as a solo artist and as part of the Mary Kaye Trio.

The Fender Custom Shop Mary Kaye Tribute Stratocaster guitar features a select ash body with a thin,
hite Blonde nitrocellulose Closet Classic finish, a hard-rock maple neck and gold hardware. As an added feature,
e have installed a set of pickups that have been hand-wound by Abigail Ybarra on each of these Limited Edition
instruments. Abigail started working at Fender in 1956, and more likely than not,
wound the pickups found in most late-'50s Fender Stratocaster guitars.

"In the early '50s, Fender put out a Stratocaster, which was white ash wood with gold fittings. It didn't have a nar
n it – just Fender. We did some movies for Howard Koch at Paramount. I told Fender that we were doing the mo
they sent over the Stratocaster and I played it in the movie Cha Cha Cha Boom. There was a lot of publicity.
There was a particular picture with the three of us. I had the Stratocaster and Frankie (Mary's late partner,
Frankie Ross) had a Fender amplifier in front of him. The picture went around the world. Instead of custome
asking for a white guitar with gold fittings, they said – 'I want the guitar that Mary Kaye was playing.'
All of a sudden the guitar became known as the Mary Kaye Stratocaster." – Mary Kaye

The Fender Custom Shop is proud to acknowledge Mary Kaye's contribution to the success of the
Fender Stratocaster guitar with the Limited Release of this instrument,
which we believe is almost as beautiful as the person it was most often associated with!

Mary Kaye

Mary Kaye

This Limited Release instrument will be available from January 20th to December 31st 2005.

Fender Custom Shop
TRIBUTE SERIES

Fender Custom Shop • 311 Cessna Circle • Corona, California • 92880

CHAPTER TWO

2

Setting Up Shop

Mr. Stevens, Meet Mr. Page

Michael Stevens comes to town

Michael Stevens is a cowboy. Not a Hollywood cowboy, not a dude ranch cowboy, but a real one. His dad was a cowboy, too. Michael has been a calf roper, a trainer of Arabian horses, and a Texas ranch hand. He is a man for whom "rodeo" is a verb. Slim, soft-spoken, flinty-eyed and decked out in a tapered Western shirt, stovepipe jeans, a classic silver belt buckle, high-heeled leather boots, and the kind of black cowboy hat even city folks can appreciate, he cuts a distinctive figure, standing out like the real deal even on the streets of the west Texas town of Alpine, where he's lived since 1990. The former college art major is also an acclaimed guitar builder and repairman who over the years has served some of the electric guitar's most admired players: Stevie Ray Vaughan, Jimmie Vaughan, Eric Johnson, Albert King, Otis Rush, Hubert Sumlin, Lonnie Mack, Ray Benson, George Thorogood, Junior Brown (Stevens built both of Brown's "Guit-Steels"), and many others.

John Page, left, and Michael Stevens with serial no. 0001, a Strat/Esquire doubleneck. In the years to come, the impressive Certificate Of Authenticity would reflect the shop's evolution from a seat-of-the-pants operation to a more official entity. Also shown: Page's business card, a pin depicting the first logo, Michael Stevens's decal, and a drawing rendered by Danny Gatton and sent to Fred Stuart for the doubleneck pictured in Chap. 18.

Michael Stevens was raised on a quarter-horse ranch in Ohio, moved to Texas when he was about 20, and relocated to California not long after the Summer of Love. He recalls, "In late '67, I moved out there to Berkeley, from West Texas, which is where I'm from now. I was chasing a woman, and I ran into Larry Jameson. He was chasing the same woman, but he became a real friend, a partner and mentor."

Stevens acquired a 1946 Martin herringbone D-28. "I managed to split the peghead," he remembers. "I took it to Jon Lundberg, who was the best known repair guy around Berkeley, and he became a very good friend. Well, for 35 dollars, he said he'd fix it. I thought that was too much money [laughs], so I figured I'd try to fix it myself. People started asking me to fix things, and it happened really fast once the word got around.

Western duds all around: Michael Stevens in full regalia with an appropriate guitar, a Waylon Jennings Tele clad in hand-tooled leather.

"I was performing, playing lots of music. During the day, I was digging subway tunnels for BART [Bay Area Rapid Transit], making so much money. Anyway, Larry and I decided to go into business." Stevens and Jameson worked together at the original Guitar Resurrection in Oakland, but in 1974 Stevens went back to the horse trade. "I packed up all my stuff and drove back to Fort Worth and started training Arabians. I stopped repairing and decided I'd be a horseman for four or five years, but that was about the time the oil boom cut down. Money wasn't coming in as much. You'd be in the Hilton one weekend and back on the ranch the next weekend trying to figure out how you could afford to fix your boots. Lots of good horses, though, national champions."

Having relocated to Austin in 1978, Michael set up shop, started repairing guitars again, and soon found himself inundated with work. He built a Strat-style doubleneck for Christopher Cross, as well as a guitar of his own design which he called the Classic, sort of a smaller-bodied Gibson ES-335. He also crafted a 6-string bass for Roscoe Beck, who was playing with Robben Ford.

Michael Stevens: "Dan Smith and Robben were like father and son, and Dan became aware of my work and I guess he liked it. At some point in '86 he called and said, 'We'd like for you to consult because I've seen your [6-string] bass, and we'd like to get into that market.' We talked about possibly licensing my designs, and on the third phone call Dan said they'd be opening a Custom Shop, and might I be interested in doing that? And I said, 'Let's talk.'"

Dan Smith: "I saw Robben Ford every chance I got, so I was pretty familiar with that 6-string bass, and I saw some of Michael's guitars. They were Gibsonesque, but his building chops were and still are impeccable. He's just an unbelievable talent. He's a fantastic guy and a great builder and has a real good design sense. He was building Fender-style stuff as well, but mostly what he was known for were his LJ guitars [named after his friend Larry Jameson] and his downsized 335-type guitars. I was very impressed. The Custom Shop originally wasn't going to build a lot of guitars, and we didn't care if it made money. It was just going to make these beautiful, prestige sorts of instruments. That was perfect for a Michael Stevens type of guy."

Return of the son

John Page is an artist of much talent and little formal training. He grew up the rebellious child of an ultra-conservative preacher, sometimes chafing against the conventions of middle-class life in white-bread Whittier, California, home town of Richard Nixon. Almost like a character from early Dylan or Kerouac, he was a runaway, songwriter, surfer, maker of jewelry, slinger of fries and dogs at Pup 'n' Taco, and oil field janitor. Rock and roll (or "devil music," in the Page household) grabbed him by the throat and rearranged his priorities. As a teenager he began to play the instrument that would consume much of his adult life. He built his first guitar with a camping knife and a few other generic tools. It wound up in a Dumpster, but John Page was hooked.

He came to Fender in 1978 at age 21, buffing necks, working in the model shop, building prototypes, and ultimately designing and crafting guitars alongside the humble, affable and brilliant Freddie Tavares. Often described as Leo Fender's right-hand man, Freddie was perhaps the most esteemed of all the first-generation Fender employees. He treated John like a son.

A few weeks after the January '86 NAMM show, John wandered away from Fender to pursue a musical career, but after eleven months he returned. "I told Dan [Smith] I was looking to get back in. He said, 'Well, two possibilities — we could use you back in R&D, but we're also finally going to get the Custom Shop going.' See, we had been discussing the Custom Shop for years, all the way back to CBS."

Michael Stevens: "They told me you can have anybody you want for your assistant. There were several people they wanted me to interview, and they said this guy John Page used to work in R&D, and he left Fender for a while to go off and become a rock and roll singer and now he's back looking for a job. I talked to John and that was it. I wound up not even talking to the other guys. John knew his way around Fender, and I didn't know anything. I figured he would know the ropes, and I liked him. He's a jovial kind of funny guy. I figured we would work well together. So he came on within weeks of my arrival. He reported to me."

Page actually remembers reporting for duty at about the same time Stevens arrived, but this minor discrepancy is likely attributable to the fact that, as we will see, Stevens's "arrival," finding a site for the shop, and building the "first" Custom Shop guitars all entailed fits and starts, transitions, semantic nitpicking, and overlaps of various sorts.

John Page. Dan Smith said of him: "John wore every hat that you could possibly have for the Custom Shop. There was a lot of passion there, and he fought for what he believed in."

Seeking a home

For months, the Custom Shop was a concept without a home. Its little skeleton crew moved around like desert-dwelling nomads, pitching their tents and setting up shop wherever they could find room for a bench and a few tools.

Fender President and Chairman of the Board of Directors Bill Schultz and his investors had bought Fender in March of 1985. In mid-summer, the new company acquired office space at 1130 Columbia Street in Brea, not far from Fullerton, Fender's previous home. Not only was there no Custom Shop, there was no Fender factory at all. Fender's later CEO, Bill Mendello, was Executive Vice President, CFO, and a member of the Board of Directors at the time. He recalls that after the sale, Fender stayed in the old factory through July before moving the office to Brea. Fender did not retain any of the factory workers, nor did it do any manufacturing in Brea during that period. Once Schultz, Mendello, and their associates decided to manufacture at least some of Fender's guitars (rather than importing all

John and Michael with the banjo neck for 0002, a project that Michael brought with him to the shop. John Page: "On the right, in back, is our little Hegner table saw; that was the first tool we bought, and what you see here is almost the entire Custom Shop at first — tables and benches, a little saw, some hand tools. That's about it. The building was not even completed yet."

of them), they leased a facility in nearby Corona and hired key factory personnel. Bill Mendello: "Because we had purchased millions of dollars of raw materials and work in progress, as well as machinery and tooling, and also because we had to vacate the old Fender factory in July, we needed a place to move the inventory and machinery to ASAP. My memory is that we moved the inventory and equipment to the Corona facility in July but it took us two to three months before we had any finished guitars to ship. So it was late September or early October when the first Corona guitar was shipped."

The new factory was twenty-two miles or so east of Fullerton and just off the Riverside Freeway. It took up part of a single leased structure in a cluster of buildings bordered to the east and south by a curve in Pomona Road and to the west by Enterprise Court. Serving as both factory and warehouse, the 14,000 square foot building at 1163 Pomona Road was modest to say the least (by comparison, CBS Fender had occupied nearly a quarter-million square feet), so space was tight. The Sandak company, maker of sandals, owned the property and operated in the same building.

For a full year after opening the main factory, Fender was consumed with setting up limited production of a few basic models, re-establishing at least a rudimentary dealer base, and hiring staff. Soon to be the Custom Shop's official boss and Senior Design Engineer, Michael Stevens actually went on the payroll on December 1st, 1986, while still working out of his Austin home. "It took a while to set up in California," he explains, "so the first work for Fender was still back in Austin, getting Eric Johnson ready. He was already a customer of mine. He was so picky, they wanted me to set up his guitars. These were American Standard Stratocasters, so they sent me half a dozen bodies and necks and wiring harnesses. Eric didn't like the stock frets, so I re-fretted them right away. He wanted a flatter radius, a 12-inch, so I did that and a whole bunch of other things for him."

Richard Syarto, left, and Fred Stuart working on necks in the first Custom Shop building. Richard may be scalloping an early Yngwie Malmsteen neck.

Brea

After arriving in California (temporarily, at first), Michael Stevens joined John Page and worked for about three weeks or so alongside George Blanda in the little R&D facility's model shop in Brea, getting ready for the upcoming NAMM show in January, 1987. Fender's Eric Clapton Signature guitar project had been in the works for two years but details remained unsettled. Michael Stevens: "I assembled some prototype Clapton models [Chap. 5], most I recall from bodies that had been used before. I shaped

This is the very first shop, a long rectangular work space inside the main factory, looking from the rear toward the front door. Michael Stevens called it "the bowling alley." That's Fred Stuart, Richard Syarto and, way in the back, John Page. The storage mezzanine by the ladder was one of the early "expansion" projects.

some [Clapton] necks. The exact V for those necks had not been decided on yet, and a couple were radical, hard V shapes — like a Martin that Eric had, as I was told. George was not a Custom Shop person, officially. He was in R&D, but we worked a lot together and exchanged lots of ideas."

Once the January NAMM show was behind them, Fender finally allocated some space in the Pomona Road factory for the Custom Shop. Michael Stevens and John Page scouted the area, drew up plans, purchased hand tools, and ordered the equipment they thought they would need. At that point Michael went back to Texas to pack up and move. John oversaw the finishing of the shop, still a raw workspace in need of wiring, sheet rock, lighting, and air conditioning. While Stevens was collecting his things back in Austin, Page worked in the Brea office at a drawing table and a desk — "furiously," as Blanda remembers it — collaborating with Stevens on a tool list, coordinating the setup of the shop, and designing the Performer 5-string bass.

Note that the radically styled Performer was manufactured in Japan, not in the Custom Shop. It marks a very early example of what would become a Fender tradition — Custom Shop builders designing products to be manufactured by the Fender factory in Corona, Fuji-Gen Gakki in Japan or, later, Fender's plant in Ensenada, Mexico. Other early examples were Fender's first two artist signature guitars (both manufactured in the main factory), the Eric Clapton and Yngwie Malmsteen Stratocasters. George Blanda: "Michael and John did some Yngwie Malmsteen protos and some Clapton protos before we were in production. The Claptons were shown at three NAMM shows before we ever delivered a production unit, so these were very early in relation to the actual 1988 introduction. I believe the Yngwies were made as show samples and also for artist approval. I had measured and documented Yngwie's favorite necks only a couple weeks before and had given all of the specs to Stevens and Page when they took over the artist stuff. This was all moving very fast."

From Dan Smith's perspective, the first Custom Shop was there in Brea, simply because that's where George Blanda was stationed; he was the first Custom Shop hire, and he worked on Custom Shop guitars. Another point of view, however, was that there was no Custom Shop per se until Page and Stevens moved into their own place.

Page recalls that they might have built a guitar for David Gilmour in the Brea facility, although some might argue that such instruments as well as the prototype Malmsteens and Claptons were R&D/ model shop guitars, not true Custom Shop projects.

Richard Syarto working on necks at John Page's old bench in the second shop. (John Page: "Notice the Shell Pink accent lights!")

Bill Schultz: "Here's what *I* want."

Stevens returned to California in the middle of February, 1987. Before production could commence, his list of requirements needed attention. "I needed *exact* climate control, day and night. I also wanted our own separate wood stock, and a very specific set of tools. John had his requirements, too. He wanted a Hegner scroll saw, which turned out to be pretty nice for doing templates. We would be doing a lot of things by hand — cutting bodies and pickup holes and all sorts of things — so the tools had to be right.

"We went to Bill Schultz and said, 'Here's what we want,' and he said, 'OK, fine, now here's what *I* want. I want the premiere custom shop in the world. I want to deal with the world's greatest artists. I want to be able to build these artists *exactly* what they want. I want you to be able to hand them a guitar and have them go away smiling, no matter how discriminating they are. And if we can break even on this project, I'm happy.'"

John Page recalls that, at first, Schultz wouldn't approve of the climate control expenditures. "Then one day in the middle of summer, one of those 100 degree plus days in Corona, Bill was taking some of the Board of Directors through the shop. He came in and introduced them to Mike and me. I was in the middle of hand-rasping the back contour on a Strat body and was dripping sweat, even with my ultra-cool bandana/headband on. Bill said, 'Hey, we've got to get your air conditioning in here.' We ordered it the next day." John also insisted that the shop purchase a good pin router, a machine that compared to hand routers was better suited to a production approach.

John Page: "Bill's vision was simple. The charge he gave us was open-ended. The whole idea was almost a romantic thing. He wanted a couple of artisans out in the 'back 40,' woodchuckin' guitars the old-fashioned way. He knew it would reflect well on the whole operation. One of the first things we did, even before we'd finished building our benches, was to take over the Clapton project from Dan and George and move that forward, getting Clapton Signature models ready for the NAMM show."

Dan Smith: "Even in this little 14,000 square foot facility, Bill wanted a high-end shop that would be a showplace where you could bring people through on tours and say, we've got some artists here, and they're whittling trees into great guitars, or whatever [laughs]. We didn't care if it made money. It was all about prestige, getting high-profile artists, and making some beautiful things for NAMM. The idea was, this buzz and prestige would wash down to the rest of the line and allow us to build more expensive guitars that would be accepted."

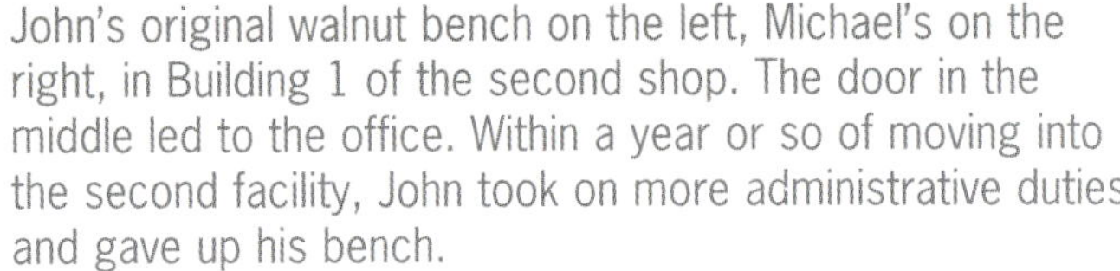

John's original walnut bench on the left, Michael's on the right, in Building 1 of the second shop. The door in the middle led to the office. Within a year or so of moving into the second facility, John took on more administrative duties and gave up his bench.

Second shop: To the left of the workbenches, the stairway led up to the mezzanine. The walls were adorned with Michael's cowboy guitar collection, and the wall adjacent to the stairway was lined with Plexiglas routing templates for factory bodies from the 1980s.

A garage band of brothers

Construction of the shop took another two months or more, so Stevens and Page worked out of Stevens's garage in Corona until April or May of 1987. Michael Stevens: "Bill Schultz wanted the Cadillac, the flagship, and we delivered. Fender had previously made those walnut Strats back in Fullerton [the Collector Series]. I hated them, but Fender still had pallets of walnut and stacks of ebony for fingerboards. I wouldn't let them sell the wood. At some point that came up, and I said, 'No! You've got more beautiful Gabon ebony here than anybody; just put it away and we'll take care of it later.' We used a lot of that walnut to build our first three workbenches." (Leo Fender, always one to make creative use of leftovers, would have approved.) The walnut benches were beautiful, with ebony plugs over the screw holes and black Formica tops. During this period the two compadres also used Stevens's pantograph device to redo by hand the contours for Stratocaster bodies.

John Page: "Bill told us to make it a showplace, and Mike took that to heart. He was on a mission. I thought this was so cool. I had worked in the corporate office environment of CBS for nine years, and now this Texas cowboy guy was saying, hey, let's go up to my garage and cut up some wood and build some stuff. I thought, great!"

It's official

A flyer dated May 15, 1987 was written by Dan Smith and labeled *Retail Price List: Fender Electric Guitar and Bass Custom Options.* It was accompanied by an open letter welcoming "Our Valued Fender Customer" to the "newly established Fender Custom Guitar Design and Manufacturing Facility." The flyer explained that Michael Stevens would head up the operation, assisted by John Page, formerly a Senior Design Engineer in Fender R&D. (Michael Stevens: "The first Master Builder was me, although the phrase had not been coined yet. My title was 'Senior Design Engineer.'") A month later, the Custom Shop was officially introduced to

A grinder on the left, a spindle sander on the right, two of the early power tools allocated to Custom Shop work (John Page: "On those clamps, Michael wanted the red handles").

Michael Stevens at his desk, surrounded and no doubt inspired by his personal collection of guitars, lap steels, and ukes.

the industry at the NAMM Expo in Chicago's McCormick Place convention center.

A "customized" item is a relative proposition (are we talking about slapping accessory-catalog hubcaps on a Buick Skylark — or building the Batmobile?). In Fender's initial offering, two types of instruments were specified. Some would be "based directly on pre-priced 'custom options,' utilizing component parts from our existing American-made product line and some parts that have been designed specifically for this program," while others would be "completely custom built instruments, crafted directly to your own specifications."

So right from the get-go, Fender was thinking about different levels or degrees of customizing. Of course, there are many points across the spectrum between a guitar that simply reshuffles standard components from the parts bin and another that requires a redesign from the ground up. Figuring out a practical way to make all these gradations available was a challenge that persists to this day.

The view from the mezzanine in the second shop, after its expansion in early 1989.

John Page doing what Elliot Easton told him he was born to do: building guitars.

A place of their own: Production facilities, 1987 – 1995

Pomona Road

Fender enlarged its Pomona Road facility in Corona by expanding into the building next door, which freed up a bit of space in the original location for the Custom Shop. After a couple of months or so in Stevens's garage, Michael and John finally moved into their own tiny production area in the late spring or early summer of 1987. It was a walled-off, approximately 850 square foot section of the factory with a couple of small, adjoining offices. Stevens remembers, "It was like a bowling alley, a skinny room with a little office in the front. It had big poles in the center, with stuff everywhere. I like everything neat and in rows, but it was fairly jumbled. We had to set our tools around the poles. It was cramped. We squeezed a lumber rack and all of our equipment in there and got to work, just the two of us. That's where it all started." Page had purchased a Hegner scroll saw for $1,850 at a wood-products show. At first, it was the one and only major tool installed in the Pomona Road shop. In late '87 or early '88, after Richard Syarto and Fred Stuart had come onboard, the shop's west-side wall was knocked out to gain a bit of extra space for Fred's work area.

That first facility would have been adequate had the shop's mission remained the same. It didn't.

Phase two

After a year or so in "Pomona One," Sandak left and Fender took over a third building in the complex as well as several bays, or suites, in a fourth. The Custom Shop vacated its original space, which reverted to the factory, and moved into two and a half suites — about 3,650 square feet — of the fourth building. This was a significant leap forward. Stevens and Page laid out the floor plan, which featured twin staircases going up to mezzanine areas and increased work space accompanied by a final assembly room, a mill, a lumber storage area, as well as additional office space.

Phase three

According to Page's records, the Custom Shop took over exclusive, full-scale manufacturing of Kubicki Factor basses in February, 1989 [Chap. 6]. To accommodate this new endeavor, the Custom Shop's "phase three" entailed an expansion into another suite at the north end of the fourth

Pomona Road building. The shop now occupied about 5,100 square feet in all.

Enterprise One

In October 1990, Fender acquired a nearby 9,500 square foot building on Enterprise Court, an L-shaped street that adjoined Pomona Road. Half of the new building, located at 135 Enterprise Court, provided space for the Custom Shop's rough wood mill and lumber storage; the other half was allocated for the factory's rough wood mill and storage and also the recently relocated R&D office. (John Page had taken over Fender R&D on September 13, 1989, practically doubling his responsibilities and facilitating a new role for the shop as Fender's proving ground and lab; Chap. 8.) The Custom Shop now occupied the suites in the fourth Pomona Road building as well as the new facility at 135 Enterprise.

Enterprise Two

The shop spread to another building at 1233 Enterprise, around the corner from 135 Enterprise. (Stephen Stern arrived in May 1993 and estimates that by then the shop had been in this new location for four months or so.) Like 135, the new location at 1233 provided about 9,500 square feet. In John Page's view, this was the Custom Shop's "Dream Factory." Why? "In a word, synergy," he says. "We were all pretty much in the same building, with very few walls. We were also physically separated from the factory, albeit only by a block or so. It allowed us to create our own environment, our own mood. It felt like we were growing up and becoming professional, standing on our own. As time went on we became completely 'satellite,' even with our own paint facility. We got to the point where we brought in raw lumber, made our own bodies and necks, painted and buffed them, assembled them, made our own pickups and even our own straps, all under our own roof. It made us proud of what our rag tag bunch had accomplished, and allowed us to promote and produce guitars by our own internal code of building. Our focus was quality and spirit. Management measured the shop and also my personal performance by quantity, efficiency, and profitability, but I tried to keep as much of that to myself as possible so the folks on the floor could just focus on quality."

Lewis Court

For a while, the shop occupied both Enterprise Court buildings. It then vacated the first one at 135, remained in the second one at 1233, and expanded yet again into a building on Lewis Court, right behind the 1233 Enterprise facility. Fender reported that by 1995, the Custom Shop's floor space had grown to a total of about 18,000 square feet spread over several sites. The little two-man team "woodchuckin'" guitars in a tiny space tucked away inside the Fender factory had faded into Fender's storied lore, as the shop's workforce now numbered about 50 employees.

Jason Davis, left, and Larry Brooks, as the shop was moving into new digs in Enterprise Two, the facility that John Page called "the Dream Factory."

Fender
STRATOCASTER
Fender
"ESQUIRE"
0001

CHAPTER THREE

3

First Guitars, Evolving Roles

The New Mandate: Deliver Product, Be Timely, and Make a Profit.

The reality of the early Custom Shop fit perfectly with Bill Schultz's original concept: Here were a couple of artists operating fairly independently in a showplace facility, renegade escapees from the nine-to-five corporate world hand-crafting dazzling guitars for elite clients, unburdened of typical pressures to generate profits.

That lasted about ten minutes. Even as the dust was settling (literally) in the shop's first Pomona Road facility, the seeds of fundamental change were already taking root. Soon the little shop found itself mired in a self-stoking cycle of shortcomings — getting up and running but then having too few orders to justify the overhead, then having too *many* orders but too few builders to fill them, then hiring additional builders but having no place to put them, then expanding the floor space but having too few orders to justify the increase in overhead, then . . . .

Several instruments may contend for the title of "first Custom Shop guitar," but as far as Michael Stevens is concerned, there is no contest. This is it, serial no. 0001. Michael Stevens: "It was the first order taken for the Custom Shop. I was told that it brought the highest dealer cost of any Fender to date. It was Fender's first doubleneck, not counting a not-for-sale, not-very-pretty 'plank' doubleneck they had in R&D for testing strings, and also the first Fender to have a Master Built decal. It was built and painted entirely by me, no line parts involved."

Dusty relics in Mecca

Aside from his official job description, Michael Stevens had another, more personal quest. "My unofficial job description, in my own mind, was this: Preserve Fender history. When I went there it was like Mecca to me. Most of the early crew left at 2:30 in the afternoon, so I kinda had the place to myself in the evenings, and I would find stuff in some dusty corner somewhere. I found the original or nearly original steel templates for just about everything. Some of them I didn't care about — I didn't care about a Bronco — but I found stuff all over that factory in nooks and crannies covered in dust, stuff that Leo and Freddie and those guys had used.

"I'd dig around some dusty corner late at night and I crawled into every cubby hole, every rat hole, looking for the old stuff. Like, I found the original Jazz Bass template. See, Fender was making none of the vintage basses when I got there. We were just about to make the James Jamerson bass, and I found a Jazz Bass template stamped *1965*, and I just about freaked out. So I started looking for *all* that stuff."

Cherry pickers

Michael Stevens wanted access to his own wood stock, and he got it. The factory crew typically received the wood shipments and then examined, organized, stacked, planed, and palleted the pieces. Neck blanks, for example, were stored before going to the fingerboard area, so Page and Stevens could cherry-pick desirable blanks from factory stock. They also were permitted to select particularly figured maple. Michael Stevens: "When those semi trucks came in, Page and I would get on top of the semi and hand the wood off the truck. We had a tape measure up there, and we got exactly what we wanted. We were especially on the lookout for wood that could be used for a one-piece body, unless it weighed a ton. Most players didn't want a six pound body. In the Custom Shop, we liked three pound bodies. They sounded better, although you can get them too light, too; if they're two and a half pounds the tone can wash out. So from about two and three quarters to three and a half or so, people pick it up and say, hey, nice guitar. We just wanted our guitars to be the best they could possibly be, and it all started with materials."

Team mates

Stevens and Page were a good team. Page knew a lot about the machinery, so he often worked with the tooling, and Stevens did much of the painting, neck shaping, fretting, and setup, particularly for Yngwie Malmsteen and other customers who liked super low actions. But they often traded tasks, overlapped their activities, and sometimes worked on the same guitar.

Mike often took his one-offs all the way through to completion, although sometimes John might do the bodies for him. While John did some of the bodies for second-generation Clapton prototypes, some of the 7-string guitars for Alex Gregory, and unique pieces for artists such as Elliot Easton and Cesar Rosas, it was Mike who more often took on the one-off projects and John who took responsibility for the "quantity" projects, such as limited runs for Yamano, Fender's Japanese distributor. Thanks to Page's years of factory experience, Stevens was able to learn from him and adapt quickly to the new and larger machinery the factory offered. Looking back, both builders agree that job descriptions were loose or non-existent; each builder stepped up and did whatever was necessary to build the best possible instrument on a case-by-case basis. That mindset would infuse the shop's working environment throughout its entire history.

John Page: "You know, Mike Stevens and I couldn't have been more different from each other. He's this tall, lanky, Texas cowboy, and I'm this stocky California surfer/ hippie guy, but I don't think I ever got so close to another person so quickly. We each had our talents, and had things the other guy didn't have. Building the guitars and thinking about the future was exciting, and we worked well together."

Within months of setting up the shop, however, that friendship would be strained by a change in the shop's mission, the expanding physical facility, shifting job descriptions, the complications of new hires and new systems, and pressures to increase production. Michael Stevens was a newcomer, not only to Fender but to corporate life in general. John Page, however, was a nine-year Fender veteran, so it was inevitable that the higher-ups would come to him with any demands for bigger numbers. John Page: "Mike's point of view was, 'Hey, I haven't even finished the showplace yet.' He was hanging up cowboy guitars on the wall and making a beautiful facility. It was really cool, but I was the one getting more of the pressure from the company side." This difference in management's perceptions of the two builders' roles would eventually result in a restructuring of the Custom Shop's hierarchy.

The "first" Custom Shop Guitar

What's with the quotation marks? Why qualify "first"? We'll qualify the word because Dan Smith, Michael Stevens, and John Page have different opinions. It's not a matter of who's right or wrong — they agree on the facts — but rather how you look at it. Which instruments might qualify? Should we count a guitar that was built by a Custom Shop person before there was any sort of Custom Shop to speak of? Guitars that were ordered before Page or Stevens arrived in Corona? Guitars that weren't custom-built from scratch but were simply mix-and-match jobs assembled from stock components? Guitars that were ordered by Fender marketing rather than dealers, distributors, artists, or other customers? What if Guitar A were ordered before Guitar B, but B shipped before A? Did B "come first"?

This author's view: The semantic nitpicking doesn't matter. The early days of the Custom Shop were marked by creativity and seat-of-the-pants inventiveness, sometimes frantic activity, more than a little stress, enthusiasm, and a dash of chaos thrown into the mix. What matters is that amid all the commotion, extraordinary guitars were built, and strong bonds were forged among builders and their customers and among the builders themselves.

The Hank Marvin Strat

Hank Marvin, lead guitarist for The Shadows, was the most influential electric guitarist in England prior to the ascendancy of the Beatles, the Rolling Stones, and the other bands that launched the British Invasion in 1964. For decades, England's best-known rockers would continue to cite his inspiration with respect to technique, tone, dreamy reverb, stage presence, and choice of instrument. In fact, his '59 Fiesta Red Stratocaster, serial no. 34346, is considered the first Strat to arrive in the UK. Shadows co-guitarist Bruce Welch told *Guitarist* magazine: " . . . no one had ever seen anything like it. It had that beautiful bird's-eye maple neck, the parts were all gold-plated, and of course it was that gorgeous pink color. But first of all, there was the tweed case — the tweed case with all that velvet inside — and when we opened it, it just took our breath away."

This '57-style Fiesta Red Stratocaster, serial no. 0161, was ordered in mid 1990 by the highly regarded guitar tech Alan Rogan at the behest of his employer at the time, John Entwistle, bassist with the Who. The idea was to capture, more or less, the look of Hank Marvin's iconic '59, the best known Fender in the UK. (Rogan also arranged for the shop to craft four additional maple-neck instruments for Entwistle, generally in the Mary Kaye style with white blonde finishes and gold hardware: a Precision Bass with a gold anodized pickguard, an unusual Jazz Bass with a reddish tortoiseshell pickguard, a '52-style Telecaster, and a Clapton-style Strat with Lace Sensors.) J. Black built all five of the Entwistle instruments. His personal logbook shows the same date for all five: 5/1/90. The red Strat (mis-identified in some sources as a '64) was sold at auction by Sotheby's on May 13, 2003, for £1,440. The auction notes specify that an alternate gold anodized pickguard was included in the tweed case. J. also made several guitars for Hank Marvin himself, all of which had Lace Sensors.

Fender's Artist Relations rep for the UK contacted Corona in 1985 with a proposal. George Blanda: "Hank Marvin was going to get some kind of lifetime achievement award over in England, and our AR guy felt we should do something. He brought the idea to us to build a guitar. We decided to re-create that red '59 Strat. I always liked The Shadows, and I knew who Hank Marvin was. I was hired in October of '85, and in December of '85 I started working on the guitar. It didn't take that much work because it was mainly a kind of assembly thing. We did have special paint for the body, and we had a neck made out of bird's-eye maple. The biggest issue was getting the gold-plated parts. We didn't have any in stock. We went to a plater [1928 Jewelry Co. in Burbank] who had been the gold plater for CBS. They wanted to know how many hundreds of units we wanted to do, so it was a little awkward because I just needed pieces for the one guitar. They were used to doing tens of thousands of parts or something, so we kind of treated the Marvin guitar parts as samples, and they came through and did a very nice job."

Fender's main Corona factory was only partially operational at the time, and there was no separate Custom Shop at all. It would be another year before Michael Stevens and John Page came on board. George Blanda: "In a way, the Hank Marvin guitar was the first Custom Shop guitar — before there even was a Custom Shop. It was fun to work on, but it was a fairly standard Strat, really."

Dan Smith: "My wife picked up the gold hardware, took it over to George — everything was very last minute. That's the first Custom Shop guitar. I don't care what anybody else says [laughs]. Fender built numerous 'custom' instruments pretty much from the very beginning, but there was no Fender Custom Shop until George was hired in October of 1985. Therefore, the Hank Marvin guitar represented the first custom guitar built by the first official Custom Shop builder. Bill Schultz considered it to be so at the time and made that known to Hank Marvin when we presented the guitar to him in London. I was standing next to Bill when he made the statement."

Michael Stevens's first Custom Shop guitars

You couldn't have scripted a more appropriate "first Fender Custom Shop guitar" than the Strat/Esquire doubleneck Mike Stevens built for his pal Jimmy Wallace in the summer of '87. It's a Fender through and through — all of Leo Fender's design principles are intact — and yet it's

On the Wallace doubleneck, note the bookmatched maple necks and the whammy bar's left-hand attachment, which keeps it out of the musician's way when playing the Esquire.

a bold departure from all the Fenders that came before it. It exudes craftsmanship of the highest order, and it bears distinctive touches that add to its beauty without compromising its function. (Bookmatched maple *necks?* Wow.)

A longtime mainstay of the Texas guitar scene, Jimmy Wallace is a guitarist with the Stratoblasters, a deeply knowledgeable collector, a former Fender dealer, and co-honcho of the annual Dallas International Guitar Festival. Jimmy Wallace: "Michael and I have known each other for something like 45 years, ever since I was about 19. He had made guitars for me before, and when I heard he was going to California to start the Custom Shop I asked if I could have the first one." As Stevens puts it: "When the Texas boys found out I was going to Fender, they jumped on board. It was like the situation with John and Elliott Easton. We both brought our contacts and some of the first orders along with us. Jimmy was first, and I got to decide the project. 'Something cool and unique' were the only guidelines."

To meet the "cool and unique" criteria, a doubleneck seemed ideal. Stevens had already built a Strat-style twin-neck guitar for Christopher Cross, and that design had been successful on all counts. Jimmy Wallace: "Mine was Fender's first doubleneck ever, so that made it really stand out as something unusual. I love Strats, and I play Esquires, too, so we decided some sort of hybrid was the way to go. I wanted something that wasn't just a showpiece. I still have that guitar, and it's not just cool looking and unusual. It's a phenomenal playing guitar. First of all, it's not that heavy. I've played it on lots of gigs and it sounds amazing."

The necks are penciled with the initials MS and the dates 6/18/87 and 6/19/87. The backs of both pegheads feature Michael's stamp; the Strat neck bears the instrument's serial number, 0001. Michael Stevens: "That guitar has bookmatched necks — the grain patterns are mirror images of each other — and the maple came from my own stash, as the shop had no fancy maple yet. I consider it to be Fender Custom Shop Number One."

Serial no. 0002 is, of all things, a banjo. Aside from Michael Stevens's other talents — horseman, poet, picker, guitar builder extraordinaire — he is also a songwriter and

Left: Serial no. 0002 was a banjo with a complicated pitch-changing mechanism.

Below: Michael Stevens believes Mark Pollock's no. 0003 to be Fender's first f-hole Telecaster with a bound body.

Above: A pearl-inlaid fingerboard highlighted no. 0004, a Lake Placid Blue doubleneck.

Left: Michael Stevens built 0005 for guitarist and pedal steeler Rob Stein, a previous client from Austin. It has a one-piece ash body. The finish is Aniline blue-green powder stain, with a dark grain filler. Other details include a bird's-eye neck, Sperzel tuners, a Graph Tech nut, an ebony board, a middle humbucker, a customized tremolo tailpiece, and custom switching that permits the added pickup combos of 1 plus 3 or all three. The tailpiece is ingenious. Stevens cut off part of a vintage Tele bridge plate to accommodate a stock American Standard Stratocaster tremolo.

Rob Stein reported in 2010: "I wanted a guitar with more tonal options and a tremolo, but I wanted it to still be a 'Tele.' Mike was the guy. As well as being really good at what he does, he understood the stuff that gives Teles, Strats, etc. their character better than anybody else I had met. This guitar has about a million miles on it by now, and it's still giving me what I want."

former bassist with the Austin Lounge Lizards, a much-loved band known for both their mastery and their spoofs of bluegrass, pop, and country. (They are perhaps the only band to have been deeply influenced by both Joneses — George and Spike.) Michael's fellow Lounge Lizard Tom Pittman ordered up a banjo while Michael was still based in Austin, and Michael brought the project to Pomona Road and "Fenderized" it. Serial no. 0002 is an electric instrument with a pitch-changing pedal mechanism, generally similar in concept to Phil Baugh's pedal-equipped electric guitar; the pitch changer was built by a former employee of the ZB steel guitar company.

Serial no. 0003 was a Telecaster built for Mark Pollock, another pillar of the tight-knit Texas guitar community. He played guitar with Freddie King, James Cotton, and countless others and for years owned Charley's Guitar Shop in Dallas, founded by the late Charley Wirz, the patron saint of the Texas vintage guitar scene. Mark is the proprietor of Transpecos Guitars, located in Michael Stevens's hometown of Alpine, and Jimmy Wallace's partner in the Dallas International Guitar Festival. Michael Stevens: "When I said I was going to Fender, Mark Pollock stuck up his hand and got Number Three, a Thinline Tele. I think Mark's guitar must be Fender's first f-hole Tele with a bound body — and multiple bound, to boot. I also did an early one for Billy Idol's guitarist, Mark Younger-Smith, a black one with single white binding; that was Fender's second bound Thinline."

Michael Stevens's fourth Custom Shop instrument was a Strat/Precision doubleneck. Michael doesn't recall the customer's name, but the man was a preacher. His initials were G.C., and his nickname, apparently, was Toot. The top knob is the Strat's volume control. The forward slider switch is a 3-way neck selector, and the rear slider is a 5-way for the Strat's three pickups. Front to back, the bottom three knobs are guitar tone, bass volume, and bass tone. Details include a left-hand American Standard vibrato, and inlays by Tom Ellis of Precision Pearl, Inc. in Austin. Stevens painted the beautiful Lake Placid Blue finish himself.

Mike Stevens: "After these first few guitars went out, John and I rat-holed some low serial numbers, put them

CUSTOM SHOP LOG

Work Order #	Serial #	Description:	Comments:	Customer	BUILDER Body	Neck	Assy	Setup	Date In	Date Out
0001		5700 Strat	5700 LPB/refinnish out of stock/add white plastic	Buddy Rogers Music	FOY/JP	FOY/JP	JP	Line	4-13-87	6-8-87
0002	—	'57 strat "Mary Kay"	57 blond w/Gold Hdw/Ash body	Fender Mktg	JP	Line	JP	Line	5-15-87	6-22-87
0003	—	62 P-Bass "Mary Kay"	62 P-Bass w/Gold Hdw/Ash body	Fender Mktg	JP	Line	JP	Line	5-15-87	6-22-87
0004	—	Strat Plus Graffitti Yellow	Strat Plus proto for NAMM show	Fender Mktg	Line	Line/JP	JP	Line	5-15-87	6-22-87
0005	—	Strat Plus Surf Green	Strat Plus proto for NAMM show	Fender Mktg	Line	Line/JP	JP	Line	5-15-87	6-22-87
0006	0007	Tele Thinline Foam Green	Alder back-Maple top birdseye neck/LH	Elliot Easton	JP	JP	JP	JP	2-27-87	8-10-87
0007	0008	57 strat 'Mary Kay)	57 strat Ash/blond birdseye neck/LH	Elliot Easton	JP	JP	JP	JP/MS	2-27-87	7-17-87
0008	V027263	57 Lefty SB Strat	LH/Gold Hdw 5 way Switch/SB	Friendly River	JP	JP	JP	Line	6-9-87	9-11-87
0009	V029027	62 strat Sea Foam	RH/Sea Foam Green/Peghead/Gold Hdw/5 way	Friendly River	Line	Line	JP	Line	6-9-87	8-20-87
0010	0016	57 Strat Blond	Blond/2p Ash/old dots 5 way/#2 neck/7-8 lbs	ALM	JP	RS	FS	DM	6-9-87	2-27-88
0011	0017	62 Strat Daphne	Daphne blue/Gold Hdw Ebony/dot old/#3 neck	ALM	Line	JP	JP	FS	6-9-87	10-7-87
0012	5203	52 Tele 2CSB	2CSB/52 U neck	Lee's Music	JP	JP	JP	Line	6-11-87	9-16-87
0013	0009	Tele Flamed 2CSB	Flamed maple top/bound Mahog back/flame neck	Fender Mktg	JP	PK	JP	MS	6-2-87	7-16-87

John Page's logbook begins with work order 0001, the controversial 5700 Strat refinished in Lake Placid Blue. "Line" refers to work performed in the main factory, often by top craftsmen who would soon join the Custom Shop crew. The Date In and Date Out notations along with the initials of John Page and Michael Stevens reveal several aspects of the shop's early operations. Note the entry for Elliot Easton's '57 Mary Kaye Strat, which left the shop on July 17, 1987; Page considers it the first Custom Shop guitar.

away to use for celebrities and such. In the early days, no Custom Shop serial numbers were ever used twice, but later there were Custom Shop production runs that started with their own series of numbers — the Anniversary Teles and Strats, for example, or the Gatton signatures, which were numbered starting with 0001.

"Our early orders had to be made by hand as no tooling was available. We did have some truss rods which I

Early patron Elliot Easton with work order 0006, serial no. 0007, a Tele Thinline built by John Page. It was one of the first orders to be taken by the shop, back in February, 1987.

altered later, because we wanted fat '50s-style necks, and the American Standard rod depth would not move the fat necks. The [American Standard] 12th-fret dot spacing was also wrong for older-style necks. Of course, there were no banjo necks laying around or any tooling at all for 0002."

The Page logbook

John Page's handwritten logbook notations were intended not to provide future historians with convenient data but rather to simply facilitate in-house record keeping. They cover only the shop's first sixteen months or so. The numbers assigned to work orders and the serial numbers applied to guitars are not always linked in sequence. For example, the first five work orders have no serial numbers at all; work order 0013 has a 0009 serial number, while the later work order 0026 has a lower 0006 serial number, to cite just a couple of examples. (Page's logbook is not the only repository of early documentation. The information in other builders' notebooks sometimes matches Page's notes; sometimes it varies.)

Furthermore, neither the work orders nor the serial numbers consistently match the chronology of incoming or outgoing orders. Finally, simply because some guitars take longer to build than others, a guitar ordered in January might leave the shop months after a guitar ordered in February or March; this inevitability sometimes blurs distinctions regarding whether one guitar was built "earlier" than another. Despite such gaps and ragged edges, Page's pages provide insights into the shop's earliest activities and also help us to understand why determining the "first" Custom Shop guitar is a matter debated by Fender veterans to this day.

John Page's first Custom Shop guitars

The Page log's earliest "date in" entries are for six orders received in February 1987. The two with the lowest serial numbers and work order numbers are left-handed models dated 2/27/87. Elliot Easton ordered a Telecaster Thinline in Foam Green, with an alder back, a maple top, and a bird's-eye maple neck. John Page built it, set it up, and logged it in as work order 0006 and serial number 0007.

The other 2/27/87 "date in" guitar was also ordered by Easton, a '57 Stratocaster reissue with a blonde ash body and a bird's-eye neck. John Page built it, and he and Michael Stevens set it up. It was assigned work order 0007, serial number 0008, and was logged as a Mary Kaye Strat. Easton's Mary Kaye left the factory on July 17, 1987, a month or so after work orders 0001 through 0005 had been delivered.

John Page: "Elliot and I had been friends since '79, so we spoke often. He is the one who encouraged me to return to Fender to do the Custom Shop gig, despite my disappointment in not being able to make my songwriting and recording career take off. He told me that the guitars I made for him back in my R&D days were the best guitars he had, and that people were born to do things. He was born to play guitars, and I was born to build them. When I told him I went back to Fender, he immediately started thinking about what he wanted."

Although these two back-to-back orders were received before the opening of the first Pomona Road shop, both guitars were built entirely in that facility. (Note also that they were received almost three months before the official announcement of the Custom Shop's opening.) The five Custom Shop instruments with lower work order numbers were all set up in the factory rather than the shop, and John Page calls them "just some things we built for Fender marketing or R&D."

Despite the 0001 serial number on the Wallace doubleneck, John Page considers the Easton Mary Kaye to be first Custom Shop guitar. "I mean first 'true' Custom Shop guitar, built from scratch," he explains, "as opposed to marketing's mix-and-match kind of stuff we had to do for shows, or the Japanese re-paint [see below]. I would say Elliot's Mary Kaye is the first one because it was the first one out the door. It shipped on July 17, 1987. In some of the photos Mike and I have, at the walnut workbench, you can tell that [the Page/Easton Mary Kaye and the Stevens/Wallace doubleneck] are both in the final stages of assembly, ready for set-up and ship. Based on what I see there, plus my memories and my log book, I would say Elliot's Mary Kaye Strat was the first custom-built guitar out of the shop, even though it was serial number 0008. Elliot's Thinline shipped on August 10, 1987. I would guess that the doubleneck shipped around then as well."

Cesar Rosas, Eric Johnson

The other orders received in February 1987 have no logbook notations regarding the day, just the month and year. All left the factory after Easton's two guitars. Of that group, the

CUSTOM SHOP LOG

Work Order #	Serial #	Description:	Comments:	Customer	BUILDER Body	Neck	Assy	Setup	Date In	Date Out
0014	0011	Lefty 57 Strat "Mary Kay"	LH / blond / Gold Hdw / Custom Neck	Cesar Rojas	JP	JP	JP	FS/JP	2-87	9-16-87
0015	0012	Lefty 52 Tele blond	LH / blond custom neck	Cesar Rojas	JP					
0016	0013	Lefty 57 strat 2csb	LH / 2CSB	Cesar Rojas	JP	JP	JP	JP	2-87	10-30-87
0017	0025	Lefty 62 JBass Antigua	Antigua matching pegbead Gold/ blockinlay/binding	Friendly River Music		JP			6-17-87	
0018	0050	57 strat "MaryKay"	Deep Contours / Ash Blond w/tint	Jacksonville Guitar Center	JP	MS/RS	MS	MS	6-17-87	3-18-88
0019	E422076	Lefty American Std	LH / rosewood / 568	Rockit Music	JP	JP	JP	Line	6-26-87	8-21-87
0020		(2) 57 strat blond	#4 Neck / Gold Hdw Blond/	Rockin Robin	CS/MS	MS	MS	MS	6-26-87	5-27-88
0021	V025639	Am Std RH Lace sensors	Am std / 768 / 62 V strat Neck / Lace sensors	Mound city music	Line	Line	JP	Line	6-26-87	7-23-87
0022	0022	Vintage Strat Volvo blue	basswood body	Eric Johnson	JP	MS	MS	MS	2-87	10-2-87
0023	0023	Amer Std Strat black	1pc Ash body	Eric Johnson	JP	MS	MS	MS	2-87	10-2-87
0024	0026	56 strat – blond	2pc Ash body birdseye neck 9½ rad	Jerry Donahue	MS	MS	MS	MS	7-6-87	10-7-87
0025		56 strat – 2C SB Birdseye	1 pc Alder V-neck exact vintage spec	Haight Ashbury Music					6-23-87	
0026	0006	Tele Teal Green Strat Neck	1 pc Ash body Birdseye/Ebony Neck Duncan P/U's	John Grunder	JP				6-29-87	

When the Custom Shop opened its doors, word traveled fast. Many of the early customers were acclaimed guitarists with vintage tastes, including Cesar Rosas, Eric Johnson, and Jerry Donahue. Work order 0026 (serial no. 0006) was John Grunder's "Grundercaster," a Teal Green Tele with a Strat neck.

two with the lowest work orders and serial numbers were built for Cesar Rosas of Los Lobos. They are serial numbers 0011 and 0013. Serial number 0012 was also built for Rosas, and although its "date in" entry is blank, we may assume that the order was received in 2/87, along with 0011 and 0013. All are lefty guitars, which means that, remarkably, the logbook's first five artist guitars were all left-handed instruments, two for Elliot Easton, three for Cesar Rosas. Rosas requested a '57 Mary Kaye Strat with a custom neck (serial number 0011), a blonde '52 Tele with a custom neck (0012), and a two-color sunburst '57 Strat (0013).

The final two guitars marked 2/27 were built for Eric Johnson. In these cases the work orders matched the serial numbers. Number 0022 was simply designated "Vintage Strat Volvo blue" and had a basswood body, while 0023 was a black American Standard Strat with a one-piece ash body. The bodies for both guitars were built by John Page. The necks, assembly, and setup were completed by Michael Stevens. Both guitars shipped on 10/2/87.

The only other instrument with a 2/87 "date in" was the Stevens/Pittman banjo, serial number 0002.

Everything changes

The orders for the Easton, Rosas, and Johnson guitars were the results of personal contacts with those artists. This was all well and good, but according to the plan announced on May 15, artist guitars, however prestigious, would account for only part of the shop's production. Custom Shop instruments would be available to anyone who could afford them, and from the company's point of view it was high time to get to work on orders from those *other* customers — Fender dealers, distributors, and non-celebrity players. There was a problem with such orders, however. There weren't any.

Bruce Bolen had had success at Gibson with its Custom Shop in Nashville, and he told Bill Schultz that a similar business could be a profit center for Fender as well. Dan Smith: "Bingo! That changed everything, really. The vision for the shop was altered permanently. Bruce was in charge of sales, so he was given the task of putting his money where his mouth was, so to speak." George Blanda: "I don't think anyone realized what the potential was for the Custom Shop as a profit-generating entity until Bruce came on board. I would guess that since Bruce sold the concept to

Bill, he would have been hounded constantly until it made a profit."

George Blanda's opinion is confirmed by Bruce Bolen's recollection of the first few months of 1987: "I had started the Custom Shop for Gibson in Nashville. We had a whole portion of the factory that was dedicated to it, and it was very successful. But now, at Fender, the situation was, we had hired the two guys and we had some nice benches, but there weren't any orders. There were sporadic one-of-a-kinds here and there, and we did have some artist business, but certainly not enough to justify the expenses. No one took grief like I did, because we had two fulltime guys out there on the payroll and floor space and overhead and costs — and no orders. My responsibility in those days was sales, so I know how many orders they had, or didn't have. I remember this vividly because I was the guy who was getting beat up over it, all the time. And in turn, I was trying to beat them up, to get some production going. It was a while before significant numbers of orders started to come in, not until mid summer, as I recall."

CUSTOM SHOP LOG

Work Order #	Serial #	Description:	Comments:	Customer	BUILDER Body	Neck	Assy	Setup	Date In	Date Out
0027	V027190	57 strat - black	V-neck	Luca Music	Line	JP	JP	Line	6-30-87	9-22-87
0028	V027441	52 Tele - LH	Stock Left Hand	Zapes Music	JP	JP	JP	Line	7-1-87	11-23-87
0029	5170	52 Esquire - Dakota Red	Rosewood - Binding Top & back	Biehoff Music	RS	CS	RS	SG	7-6-87	1-27-88
0030	E415608	Am Std Strat Ash	Natural finish	Pecknell Music	Line/JP	Line	JP	Line	7-6-87	10-29-87
0031	V027320	62 V Strat	Left Hand	Sater's Music	Line	JP/FS/Line	RS	Line	7-6-87	11-23-87
0032	0051	62 V Strat blue/Green	Flame Mpl/Ebony neck - abalone	McFadyen Music	RS	RS	RS	RS	7-13-87	4-29-88
0033		57 V Stret 2CSB	3C P/G #5 Neck	Sam Ash					7-17-87	
0034	V026314	62 Strat Daphne blue	Left Hand/60s neck	Friendly River	Line/JP	RS	RS	Line	7-14-87	3-31-88
0035	on back	3-57 LH strats V White 3-57 LH " blk 3-62 LH V white 3-62 LH blk	All stock L-H	Mannys	CS/Line	CS/Line	FS/RS	Line	7-21-87	11-23-87
0036	E449274	Am Std Strat Fiesta Red	1 pc Ash - sperzels clapton elec's	Heart of Texas	FS	Line	SG	SG	7-31-87	5-17-88
0037		53 Tele Natural	#1 U neck tint body	Charles Music Inc	Line/RS	RS	RS	SG/RS	7-31-87	3-25-88
0038	V025818	62 V Stret	Daphne blue stock	Guitar Showcase	Line	Line	JP	Line	8-3-87	9-24-87
0039	V029525	57 V Strat	Fiesta Red - Gold (like Hank Marvin's)	Sound Post	Line	Line	JP	FS	8-11-87	9-22-87

Work order 0035 was a milestone: four sets of guitars, each set consisting of three instruments with identical specs. In late 1987 and early 1988 we see the initials of relative newcomers Richard Syarto, Scott Grant, and Fred Stuart.

The problem had nothing to do with the quality of the early Custom Shop guitars, which by all accounts were fabulous. It was more a matter of timing and priorities. Bruce Bolen: "I inherited the Custom Shop at the time when they were moving into their first facility in Corona. In those days Fender itself wasn't breaking any sales records, but how could they? The sales guys really didn't have a whole lot to sell in the first place. It was tough to get normal production of Strats, even tougher to get Teles, and we hadn't even started on P Basses and J Basses. With the '57 and '62 vintage Strats, we were only building six or seven guitars a day, and I got stuck with the dubious job of deciding which of our dozen or so sales reps would get them. So it wasn't like any Custom Shop products were going to be added to a full line of Fender guitars and basses.

"To give you an idea, we didn't even have an American amplifier, not one, until we came out with the Champ 12. We were proud of it, and I went around the country showing it off to dealers. A good but very narrow line of guitars, and one little amp — this is the Fender we're talking about in [early] 1987. I was the one who issued the mailings to all the sales guys, made the calls to dealers, and took calls from dealers, trying to sell them on this new idea of a Fender Custom Shop, but you know what? It was like pulling teeth to get orders. Our sales guys didn't want to know about that. *Where are the Strats and Teles?* They simply wanted product that was easy to sell, that players and dealers were already familiar with, the bread-and-butter guitars, the path of least resistance."

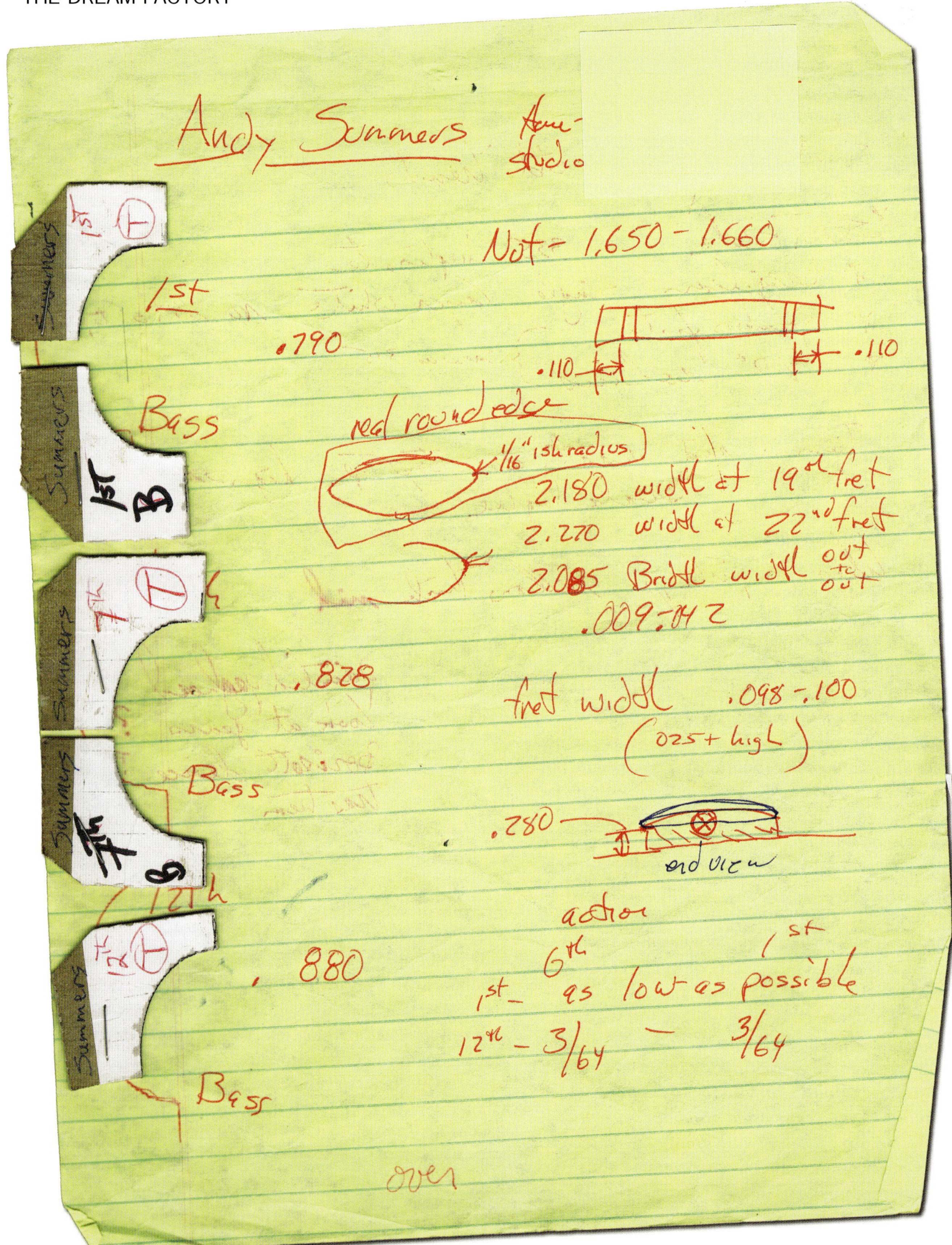
Andy Summers
studio
Nut - 1.650 - 1.660
1st
.790
.110
.110
Bass
real round edge
1/16"ish radius
2.180 width at 19th fret
2.270 width at 22nd fret
2.085 Bridge width out to out
.009-.042
.828
fret width .098-.100
(025+ high)
Bass
.280
end view
12th
action
6th
1st
1st as low as possible
12th - 3/64 - 3/64
.880
Bass
over
Summers 1st T
Summers 1st B
Summers 7th T
Summers 7th B
Summers 12th T

Order 0001

Page's logbook entries of early 1987 support Smith's and Bolen's recollections. No documented orders of any kind were received in March, not so surprising considering the shop hadn't even opened yet and Fender's official announcement was still a couple of months away. After a six-week dry spell following those late-February orders, Bruce Bolen forwarded to the Custom Shop a request from Buddy Roger's Music in Cincinnati. John Page remembers: "Bruce said, 'I've got a dealer who wants a 5700 Strat, but he wants it in Lake Placid Blue.' The 5700 was a model code for one of Fender's *imports*, so I said, 'Dude, that's not what we're about.' He said, 'I don't care, we're gonna do it.' So instead of building a custom guitar, the idea was to take a Japanese import and just refinish it. It was something they had to flip around, and the factory wasn't going to fill an order for one guitar, so we got tasked with it."

Bruce Bolen: "I asked John to strip the guitar and make it the color the dealer wanted. He looked at me like I'd lost my head. And I said, 'You gotta start someplace.' That was the very first [dealer] order ever taken for the Fender Custom Shop."

Having already started to work on his personal orders — custom guitars for the likes of Elliot Easton, Cesar Rosas, and Eric Johnson — John Page was less than thrilled with the idea of refinishing a Japanese Strat. Bruce Bolen: "There was dissention between a number of us. John Page and I didn't always agree on things. I've seen some things in print where I've been portrayed as just some suit who blew in and was demanding more and more production. To the extent that that was true, it was because I realized what could and could not be done. The fact is, we had hired people, allocated space for a factory, and were losing money."

John Page: "That 5700 was the first *official* piece we did, but I don't consider it a 'Custom Shop' guitar at all, because it was taking a guitar out of a box, stripping it, painting it, and putting it back together. First official guitar to leave? Yes. First guitar actually *built* in the Custom Shop? No. Elliot Easton's Mary Kaye was at least sort of a 'custom option' type thing, something we would actually go on to do. In fairness to Bruce, he was doing the best he could in a desperate situation. He had Bill Schultz climbing all over him, and we just had to start producing guitars."

Page's logbook shows work order 0001 — not to be confused with serial no. 0001 — coming in on April 13, 1987, and going out on June 8. The "Setup" column reads "line," meaning that after Page reassembled the guitar, it went back to the factory's regular production line for final tuning and setup. In the coming years, many Custom Shop guitars would follow that precedent, reflecting the skills of factory workers as well as the artists in the shop.

It's not so ironic that official order 0001 was the subject of contention. In fact, it was something of an omen. Stevens and Page reported at various times to Dan Smith or Bruce Bolen, each of whom had his own strategies for success. From day one, the conundrum of how to merge a small shop into a rapidly growing factory — one whose own challenges were numerous and fiendishly complicated — presented not only logistical obstacles but also something of an identity crisis. Bolen, Smith, Stevens, and Page had many intense discussions and more than a few heated arguments about the direction the shop would take, what it would stand for, what it would mean to Fender and to the guitar community.

The first dealer orders

The refinished import was the one and only order appearing in Page's logbook for April. There was nothing in early May. Then on May 15, 1987 — the same day Dan Smith's memo announced the opening of the shop — the sales department submitted work orders 0002 through 0005: a '57 Mary Kaye, a P Bass with Mary Kaye appointments, and two Strat Pluses, one in Graffiti Yellow, one in Surf Green. No other orders were logged for May. A June 2 entry specifies a Tele with a flame maple top. Although it was logged as a sales request, Page remembers the instrument as the shop's first "spec" guitar, meaning that it was conceived in the shop rather than built to order (Fender "speculated" that it could sell it later).

Left: Specs for an individual artist's instrument were often jotted down on notebook paper. This sheet specifies neck dimensions and other details of a custom guitar built for Andy Summers. Notes on the back specify a Strat body, a short scale (short for Fender, that is, duplicating a Gibson ES-335's), and a Brazilian rosewood fingerboard with a relatively flat 12" radius and jumbo frets. Also noted: "likes 61 pickup, mellow thick mid."

Finally, on June 9, the shop received orders for a lefty '57 sunburst Strat with gold hardware, a '62 Strat in Sea Foam Green, a '57 ash-bodied Strat in blonde, and a '62 Daphne Blue Strat with gold hardware and an ebony fingerboard. These four guitars — work orders 0008 through 0011 — were a little milestone of sorts, the Page log's first entries that came from dealers rather than from Fender sales or through personal contacts with artists. They took between two and a half months and eight and a half months to complete and ship.

Built for author Andre Duchossoir, this early Custom Shop Strat featured a highly figured maple neck, gold hardware, and a slanted middle pickup.

Dan Smith: "A lot of dealers backed off at first. Even though the prices weren't that high, the shop hadn't established itself yet, and the prices *seemed* high. So the dealers were shy, and Fender was shy because we didn't know if these Custom Shop guitars would be accepted." Varying perspectives yielded different reactions to the timing of these initial dealer orders. From the shop's point of view, they arrived early, scarcely three weeks after the official May 15 announcement and several weeks before the shop was even fully set up. From the view in the executive offices, however, they took forever.

Nine more instruments were ordered in June: a '52 Tele, a lefty '62 J Bass, a teal green Tele with a Strat neck, and six Strats.

Custom options

Aside from the one-of-a-kind guitars, many others were mix-and-match projects. They reflected the original May 15 document offering guitars "based directly on pre-priced 'custom options,' utilizing component parts from our existing American-made product line and some parts that have been designed specifically for this program." Fender was understandably pushing the custom option idea because of its potential for substantial production.

If a player wanted, say, a twin-neck guitar, of course it would have to be designed and built from scratch. But if he wanted a Stratocaster in Burgundy Mist with a matching headstock, a '50s style neck, a '60s style pickguard, and a mix of gold and nickel hardware — something the factory never offered and almost certainly one of a kind — the little Custom Shop crew could make it out of existing parts and supplies. Better yet, if a dealer wanted 20 or 30 of these mix-and-match instruments, or 20 or 30 vintage reissues, then production expenses per guitar would decline considerably, and efficiency (and profits) would go up.

Another little milestone: John Page's logbook shows work order 0035 coming from Manny's Music, the historic shop on New York's 48th Street. Dated 7/21/87, it's for a dozen lefty Strats: three each of the black '57s, white '57s, black '62s, and white '62s. The Manny's Strats from July '87 are the first examples in the Page logbook of what could be called "multiple orders" — several guitars with identical specs. All were collaborations between the shop ("CS" on the log entry) and the factory ("line" on the entry). Ten other instruments were ordered in July: a lefty '52 Tele, a natural-finish '53 Tele, a Dakota Red '52 Esquire, and seven Strats, including a blonde '56 for Jerry Donahue, soon to be a Custom Shop artist endorser.

Yamano

The next month would see yet another landmark: the first of many orders from Yamano Music, the Japanese distributor that would play a crucial role in the development and expansion of the shop (and for that matter, a crucial role in the resurrection of the entire Fender company). All were "multiples." Work orders 0040 through 0047 were for, in order: three Fiesta Red '57 Strats; 20 Candy Apple Red '62 Jazz Basses with matching red pegheads; 10 Lake Placid Blue '62 Jazz Basses with matching pegheads; 10 blonde, ash-bodied '57 Strats with gold parts; 10 blonde '52 Teles with rosewood fingerboards; 20 blonde '52 Teles with no. 4 necks; 30 black '57 Strats with no. 4 necks; and three blonde '57 Strats with gold parts.

All 106 instruments were ordered on 8/14/87, and all featured line (factory) bodies. The guitars all had line necks; the basses all had Custom Shop necks. All of the guitars went back to the line for setup. This collaboration between shop and factory allowed the small Custom Shop crew to complete about 76 instruments for Yamano by the end of 1987, the remainder by late May, 1988.

These early orders for multiples of a single model offered a glimmer of hope. After all, those beautiful walnut benches and the shop's initial equipment and materials all cost money. With the bills coming due, the mountain of orders left over from the Summer '87 NAMM show had to be addressed. It became increasingly clear that, however romantic, the notion of one craftsman building one guitar at a time for one client wasn't going to sustain the shop; as we will see, this fundamental realization would stimulate several reorganizations of both the work force and the product line in the coming years. While the shop would continue to offer one-off guitars for individuals right up to the present day, such efforts would have to be supplemented with increased emphasis on the more profitable custom option approach (or its descendants: the "price list" and later the Team Built program). Scott Grant was an early production coordinator for the shop. He explains: "We had certain numbers that we had to reach every month, and sometimes we just didn't have enough orders to do that. That was another advantage to the limited runs. We'd get together with [salesman] John Grunder and figure out what people would want, and then build some runs of 10 or 20 so we could meet the numbers Fender was requiring. Grunder would call dealers and sell them."

The custom option program served its purpose. It was a first step toward a semi-standard menu of choices for customers, and it provided a way for the crew to produce custom instruments with nowhere near the demands on resources required of one-off orders, particularly those with radically non-spec features or dimensions. Despite its success, the custom option scheme lasted only a year and a half or so. As we will see, it was replaced with more organized systems that better accommodated the ever increasing demand for Fender Custom Shop guitars.

Other logbook revelations

Many of the early guitars were completed in two or three months, some in seven or eight. A Fiesta Red American Standard Strat with Clapton electronics going to Heart of Texas Music in Austin took almost ten months; a blonde '57 Strat with gold hardware going to Rockin' Robin in Houston took eleven. From the shop's point of view this was to be expected — hey, building custom instruments takes time, sometimes lots of it. Still, Fender dealers were used to placing orders and receiving the instruments in four to six months, so for some of them the long delays took some getting used to. John Grunder: "The only part of my job that I didn't like — and this was the Chinese water torture part — was telling a dealer that guitar that I promised would be ready this month isn't ready, and it's not to be ready next month, either."

Of the first 30 Custom Shop orders appearing in the Page log, 23 of them were for vintage-style electric guitars or basses. The importance of the Custom Shop as a producer of vintage-style Fenders is further revealed by examining all 150 instruments listed in work orders 0001 through 0047 (remember, the sequence of work order numbers did not always parallel the chronology of actual orders or the production of instruments). Of those 150 instruments, almost all were vintage Strats, Teles, Jazz Basses, or Precision Basses. The only exceptions were the 5700 Lake Placid Blue

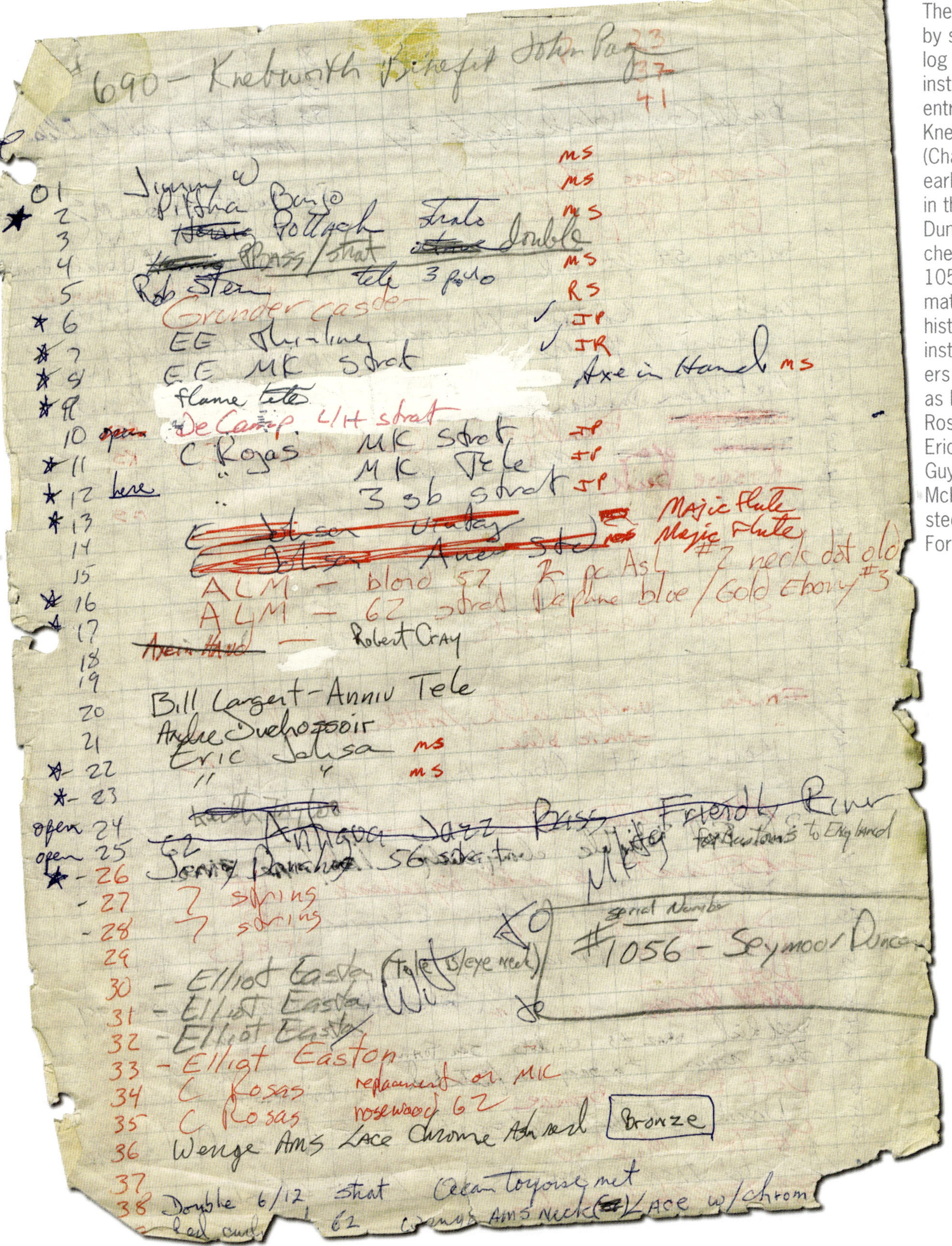

690 - Knebworth Benefit John Page

5 Rob Stern tele

6 Grindercaster

7 EE Thinline

8 EE MK strat — Axe in Hand

9 flame tele

10 DeCamp L/H strat

11 C Rosas MK strat

12 MK Tele

13 3 sb strat

Majic Flute

Majic Flute

ALM - blond 57

ALM - 62 strat Daphne blue / Gold Ebony #3

18 — Robert Cray

20 Bill Largent - Anniv Tele

21 Andre Duchossoir

22 Eric Johnson

Antigua Jazz Bass

Serial Number #1056 - Seymour Duncan

30 - Elliot Easton

31 - Elliot Easton

32 - Elliot Easton

33 - Elliot Easton

34 C Rosas replacement on MK

35 C Rosas rosewood 62

36 Wenge AMS Lace Chrome Ash neck — Bronze

37

38 Double 6/12 strat Ocean turquoise met Lace w/chrome

These notes were written by several builders and log the shop's first 90-plus instruments. You'll see entries for the unique Knebworth Telecaster (Chap. 11), several of the earliest guitars mentioned in this chapter, Seymour Duncan's translucent cherry Esquire — its 1056 serial number matching Jeff Beck's historic Esquire — plus instruments for key retailers and for artists such as Elliot Easton, Cesar Rosas, Robert Cray, Eric Johnson, Buddy Guy, Roscoe Beck, Duff McKagan, Yngwie Malmsteen, Arlen Roth, Robben Ford, and Steve Cropper.

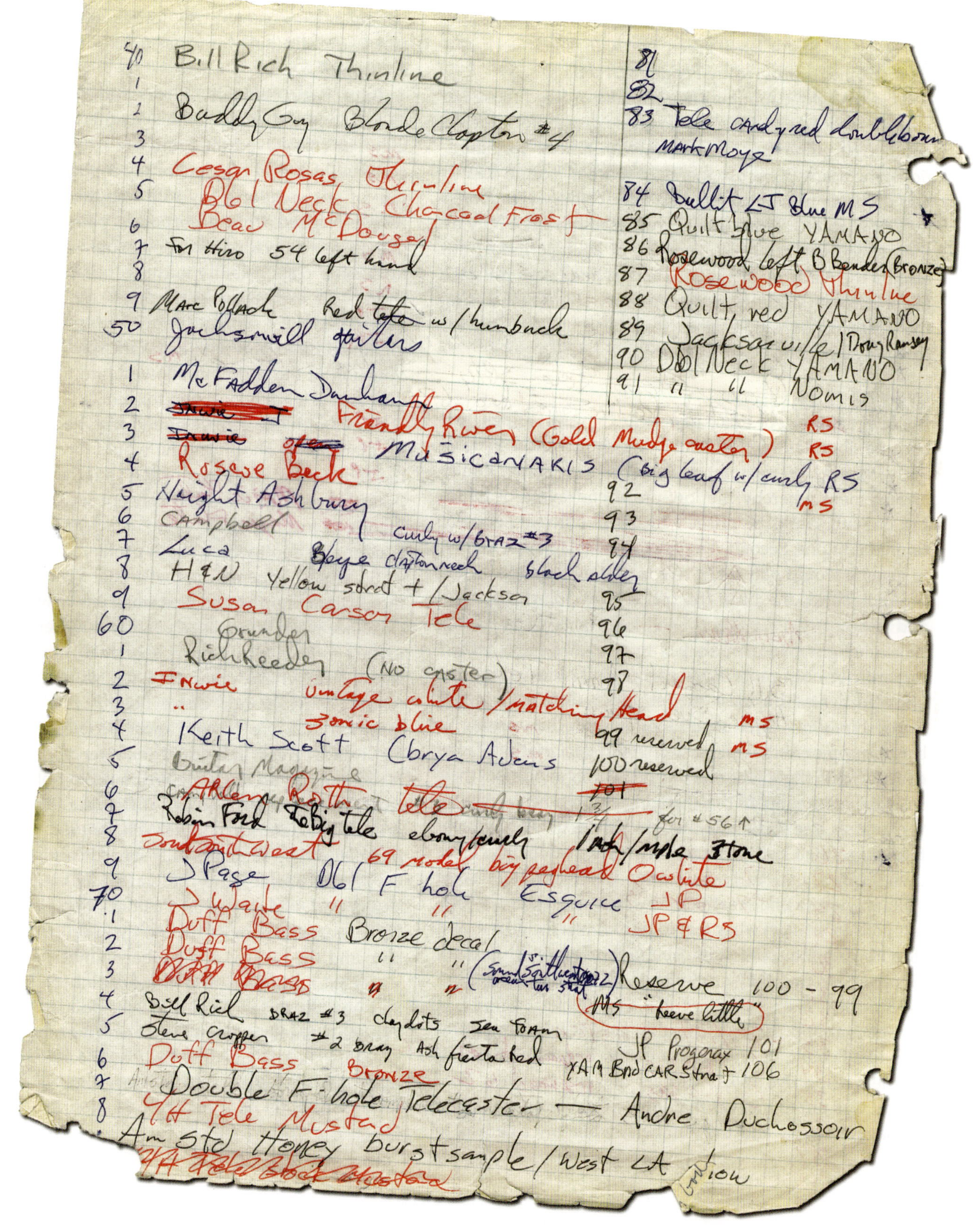

40 Bill Rich Thinline
1
2 Buddy Guy Blonde Clapton #4
3
4 Cesar Rosas Thinline
5 Dbl Neck Charcoal Frost
6 Beau McDougal
7 for Hiro 54 left hand
8
9 Marc Pollack Red tele w/humbuck
50 Jacksonvill guitars
1 McFadden Dunham
2 Friendly River (Gold Mudge caster) RS
3 MUSICANAKIS (big leaf w/curly RS
4 Roscoe Beck MS
5 Haight Ashbury
6 Campbell curly w/BRAZ #3
7 Luca Boyce claptonneck black alder
8 H&N Yellow strat +/Jackson
9 Susan Carson Tele
60 Grunder
1 Rich Reeder (NO caster)
2 Frwie vintage white/matching head
3 " sonic blue
4 Keith Scott Cbryan Adams
5 Guitar Magazine
6 Arlen Roth tele
7 Robin Ford Big tele ebony/curly
8 Southwest 69 model big peghead Owlite
9 J Page Dbl F hole Esquire JP
70 J Waite " " " JP&RS
1 Duff Bass Bronze decal
2 Duff Bass " "
3
4 Bill Rich BRAZ #3 claydots sea foam
5 Steve Cropper #2 BRAZ Ash fiesta red
6 Duff Bass Bronze
7 Double F-hole Telecaster — Andre Duchossoir
8 4H Tele Mustard
Am Std Honey burst sample/West LA

81
82
83 Tele candy red doublebound Mark Moyer
84 Bullit LJ blue MS
85 Quilt blue YAMANO
86 Rosewood left B Bender (Bronze)
87 Rosewood Thinline
88 Quilt red YAMANO
89 Jacksonville/Doug Ramsey
90 Dbl Neck YAMANO
91 " " NOMIS
92
93
94
95
96
97
98
99 reserved MS
100 reserved MS
for #56
Reserve 100 - 99
JP Progenax 101
YAM Bnd CAR Strat 106

Fender
Flamingo

CHAPTER FOUR

4

Building a Team

The Early Years

Help (you know I need somebody)

When Michael Stevens and John Page moved into Pomona Road, they suffered under the pressure of not having enough orders. But within a few months — particularly after Chicago's NAMM Expo in late June, 1987 — they had too many. As it turned out, the idea of having world-class builders create the Fender of your dreams appealed not just to well-off rock stars and other professionals but to hundreds and ultimately thousands of amateur and semi-pro guitarists. Once the word got out — *these new Fender guys can build pretty much anything you can dream up* — you could almost see the light bulbs clicking on over the heads of orthodontists and tax attorneys everywhere, guys who were settling in to their Relaxed Fit years but who'd played in rockin' frat party bands back at Michigan State or UCLA and now had enough dough in the bank (or maybe in junior's college fund) to indulge their weekend warrior instrument fantasies.

The fabulous Pink Flamingo is a metal-bodied one-off designed and built by Master Builder John English. Details: color anodizing by Peter Kellett, engraving by Ron Chacey, a highly figured flame maple neck with pink moto dots, and a headstock overlay similar to the one on the original Aloha Strat (Chap. 11). Note the unique aluminum knobs, switch tip, and pickup covers. The guitar resides in Peter Kellett's collection.

Michael Stevens: "Suddenly this whole idea of, 'Hey, I got some money and I'd like a Stratocaster with some unique features' — that all happened quickly. In fact, it already started by the time we finished getting our tools set up. [Note: John Page estimates that the process of "setting up the shop" took as long as six months.] I don't know what they told all those people, but we started trying to fill as many orders as we could and realized we had to adapt."

Not surprisingly, many of these guitars would be particularly labor-intensive. For example, John Page recalls that he and Michael likely spent more time on 7-string guitars for Alex Gregory [serial numbers 27 and 28 in the Page log book] than on any other early project. It entailed several weeks of time just interacting with Gregory, fine-tuning the drawings, and making the templates. That sort of time commitment was to be expected, but meanwhile, the orders on the desk were piling up. John Page: "We were just getting settled, and the pressure had already started. Bruce Bolen or Dan Smith would come in and say, look, we need 30 guitars a month, and if we don't get them, that's it, the Custom Shop will close down. Well, Mike thought he was coming to Fender to build a couple of guitars a month. He was great, still is, but he's one of those very meticulous builders who really takes his time. That's what you want, but it wasn't going to produce 30 guitars a month. He'd build a couple of one-offs, and the rest of it fell on me." Dan Smith: "Nothing happened that didn't come through Bill Schultz, so when Bruce and I would say those things, it was coming from Bill. Things like the Alex Gregory project were part of Fender's attempt to break into the big-hair, virtuoso rock market."

The good news was, out of the first couple of hundred orders, many were option guitars for Yamano — 20, 30, or more of one model. But the one-offs were a different story. There was no way Michael Stevens or John Page or any other individual could hand-build or even hand-assemble 30 finished, high-quality guitars every month.

Doubling the workforce — from two to four Richard Syarto, Fred Stuart

The situation had almost reached the breaking point when upper management recognized that the potential for the Custom Shop had quickly exceeded its original vision and gave John Page authority to hire some help. Before the end of the Custom Shop's first year, Richard Syarto joined the crew after coming out to California and reportedly hanging around the shop, hoping to get hired. Within a week or so after Syarto's arrival, Fred Stuart came over from Fender's production line, where he had been working since March 2. (Stuart estimates that he worked in production for five or six months, which would place his arrival, and Syarto's, in the summer or very early fall of 1987.) The crew had suddenly doubled from two to four. Fender management asked a reasonable question: Would production double as well?

Telecaster aficionado Fred Stuart was gifted and imaginative, a natural fit. With his work space well established in the main factory, he had already been helping out with Custom Shop projects during the somewhat chaotic transition period when Page and Stevens were moving from Michael's garage to Pomona Road. He had worked as a "tune tester" in the factory, one of the people at the end of the line who set up, tuned, and tested finished guitars. On many of the early Custom Shop orders, Page brought "line" necks and bodies from the factory to the shop, tweaked them, assembled them, matched them up the way the customers wanted, then took them back to Stuart for setup. So in these cases, Fender's main factory was involved at both the start and finish of Custom Shop projects. Another way to look at it: Future Master Builder Fred Stuart was already doing Custom Shop work before he became an official Custom Shop employee.

Michael Stevens was spending a lot of time making templates for different neck shapes and adapting tooling to recreate vintage-spec bodies and necks that Fender

Richard Syarto, in the second Pomona Road facility.

hadn't produced for years. Aside from those tasks, he was working almost exclusively on one-offs and typically carried those projects through to completion, so it was John Page who often called on Fred Stuart for help, particularly with final setup on limited-run guitars. "John never really liked doing the setup anyway," Stuart recalls. "I understand that. For me, to this day, final assembly and setup is the hardest part of guitar building. That's the point where you find out what's wrong [laughs], and then you have to fix it while the guitar is all put together and shiny and otherwise ready to pack up and ship."

At his new post in the Custom Shop, Stuart was tasked with what he calls "a lot of miscellaneous apprentice work" before he started designing and building guitars. For example, one of his first projects was to make a pin router tool that would accommodate a standard Strat body and carve out compartments for the preamp, battery, and output jack for the factory's long-delayed Eric Clapton model, which was originally designed to feature an extra switch.

Stuart remembers how cramped they were in that first shop. It had the pin router at one end and a couple of workbenches for Michael and John. Fred was stationed in a room that had a drafting table and not much else, and Richard Syarto set up his bench in an adjacent room. Fred Stuart: "Richard Syarto was there for a couple of years. He was a very accomplished and creative builder, and I learned a lot from him. He was a wonderful person, too. He built a lot of one-offs, and during that same period I started building one-offs myself." According to Page's records, Richard Syarto left Fender on April 20, 1989.

Even after Fender expanded the little Pomona Road facility by punching a hole in the wall and giving Stuart his own (tiny) space, the operation remained understaffed and underequipped.

Growing pains and cooperation

Some early orders couldn't be filled simply because the tooling was inadequate. The factory still had much of its old gear, including a few paper-feed hole-drillers and other machines that preceded the newer CNC (Computer Numeric Controlled) technology. Customers continued to be told they would have to wait.

Fred Stuart, with the "Liberace" guitar (Chap. 11).

The still-new Custom Shop had an ally in Doug Mills, recently hired as Fender's production supervisor. Michael Stevens recalls how Mills circulated among the factory crew and spent time in most or all of the positions, learning the various jobs on the factory floor and garnering admiration from fellow managers and workers alike. Fred Stuart: "Doug Mills started right after I did at Fender, possibly even the same week. He was running the plant, and he was a real good guy, one of the favorite people I've ever worked with. He was caught between the horns of a dilemma, because he was serving his bosses in the factory structure, and here we were in the Custom Shop making all sorts of additional requests for his resources. He did his best to help us out."

The Custom Shop craftsmen returned the favor on many occasions. For example, Stevens and Page sometimes took Strat bodies from the factory before they were run through the AB shaper, a useful machine but one that at the time was cutting body contours to the relatively bloated CBS specs ridiculed by vintage buffs. The Custom Shop's increasingly sophisticated clients wanted authentic '50s or '60s specs — sleeker bodies with properly rounded contours — which required hand-shaping with flat rasps. Mills turned to Stevens for samples of vintage-correct bodies, which Stevens hand-crafted in his home shop. Mills sent them to the AB shaper's manufacturer, who provided new blades that Stevens set up to render bodies much closer to the desired specs. This sort of cooperation helped foster bonds between Custom Shop and factory workers.

J. Black recounts the difficulty of producing special-order instruments during these early days, before there was any sort of organized production system. "John Grunder told me, 'I'm assembling artist guitars on the floor in Brea, Dan's telling me to do this, Bruce is telling me to do that. Then all of a sudden John Page and Mike Stevens show up, and they need some sales work, but I have to keep on doing outside sales, working with artists, doing some factory stuff, doing some Custom Shop stuff . . . ' So Grunder is doing artist relations, custom work, R&D, sales, all with these different bosses."

John Grunder: "I would try to gather pieces, the nicest body and nicest neck, and assemble them and take them down to Buddy Guy or whoever was playing in town. I used to call them 'rug guitars,' because I'd sit on the rug. I had a special piece of carpet so there wouldn't be any scratches. I would consume my drugs — Camels and coffee — and put these guitars together. We didn't really have a functioning shop at first. Once the shop was up and running I was fortunate enough to have people build these things for me, but that took a while."

Year one in review

At the end of the shop's first year, Fender's hard-charging President, Bill Schultz, was frustrated to say the least, because the little band in the Custom Shop was chronically behind on orders. Customers were told to expect delays of six months to a year, and Fender lost some customers who grew tired of waiting and gave up. This was acutely stressful for all parties — Schultz, Fender marketing, Fender sales, and the Custom Shop workers themselves. Everyone winced at the thought of lost orders, which of course meant a decrease in funds that could have gone not only to profits but also to hiring more Custom Shop craftspeople, expanding the floor space, and upgrading the tooling. Clearly, more helping hands were needed.

Building a team: The first four years

As noted, key figures at the dawn of the Custom Shop included Bill Schultz, Dan Smith, Bruce Bolen, George Blanda, Michael Stevens, John Page, and the sales reps and dealers. During the first several years a talented, passionate, and idiosyncratic crew of builders, apprentices, and other workers would join Stevens, Page, Syarto, and Stuart. Although officially a member of the R&D team, George Blanda continued to be a key Custom Shop collaborator.

John Grunder: Before coming to Fender in February 1986, John Grunder worked as a guitarist, music teacher, and music retailer in Butler, Pennsylvania. "My dream was to go out to California and go to work for Fender," he remembers. "When I started in sales, along with a little marketing and artist relations, it was

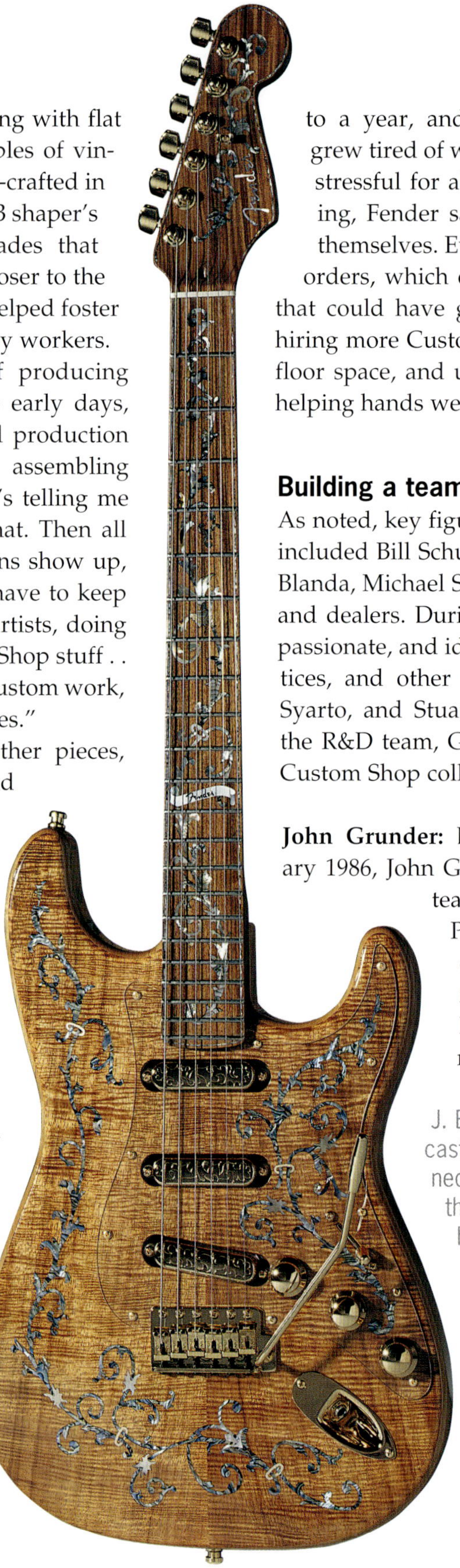

J. Black built the Tree Of Life Stratocaster, Larry Sifel inlaid the body and neck with abalone vines, and the two of them collaborated on the design. The body is flame koa on alder; the neck is pau ferro.

Right: The Robo-Caster: Steve Boulanger designed this guitar; he and John English built it and signed the back. It has a front and back of clear acrylic over a skeleton of gold-anodized, aircraft aluminum. Details include an ebony board on a figured maple neck.

Fender

Fueled on his drugs of choice — Camels and coffee — John Grunder is shown here doing what he did best, working the phones, drumming up support for the shop.

just the three of us — Mike Stevens, John Page, and myself. One other guy and I were handling national phone sales, backing up the regional reps, and I brought in artists to tell us exactly what they wanted. Getting something up and running, that's really the fun part, also the challenging part. Just getting off the ground seemed like a daily thing for us year after year, because we just grew and grew and grew. We were always at the start, always on the ground floor. My office was in Brea, so I'd drive out to Corona all the time. I'd wear a tie, which Page threatened to cut off every time I saw him.

"My nickname was Telecaster Jones, because I was jonesing for Teles so much. 'How many Telecasters does a guy need, John?' 'Just one . . . *more*.' I hot rodded them back home so I could get jazz sounds, blues sounds, and Strat sounds and not have to take a bunch of guitars to some dive where I was playing. My business cards actually said 'Telecaster Jones' on them. Bill Schultz said I had 'Fender' tattooed on my butt, I was so devoted."

John Grunder is remembered as "a hell of a salesman" by all of the builders from the early days. He not only sold guitars, but he also championed the very concept of a Fender Custom Shop at a time when many dealers were skeptical. Scott Grant called him "our point man to the outside world." J. Black: "John Grunder worked there a long time, but he was almost as much of a fan as he was an employee. He loved Fender and really was into his job, but his job was unique to him. He dealt with our best dealers and the public, one on one, in a way that was not noticed or understood by many around him." John Grunder: "Everybody had ideas about what the original Fender must have been like, and the Custom Shop was our opportunity to do it the way it might have been done in the old days, but even better. I won't use a high-minded word like 'design,' but I did get to make up all kinds of different guitars, as long as I could sell them."

Scott Grant came to Fender in 1977, a decade before the founding of the Custom Shop. He left in 1981 and returned

Below: Scott Grant. As Duane Boulanger said, "If you had a question or a problem, Scott was the guy you would go to on a daily basis, definitely a key figure."

to the factory in September, 1987. In mid year, 1988, he accepted John Page's invitation to join the Custom Shop team. "I was there before Art Esparza, so I think I was about the fifth employee, maybe the sixth," he recalls. "It was a tiny group. I was doing setup on guitars but soon got involved in the paperwork side of things. Eventually I became the lead for the whole shop. Maria Orduño reported to me. In 1989 or 1990 my official title became production supervisor." This task entailed the scheduling of products, prioritizing orders, tracking projects through stages toward completion, supervising apprentices, making sure the builders had the materials and components they needed, doing some final inspection, and along with Maria Orduño basically running the shop's day-to-day operation. In this regard, Scott Grant was John Page's right-hand man. John reports that without Scott, it would have been difficult to find any time at all to make plans for the shop beyond day-to-day operations. J. Black: "Scott was *the* key manager, with his hands in almost everything, but he did it as a friendly uncle, not a hard-nosed manager."

"Originally, we had a clipboard on the wall," Scott explains. "That was our system. The orders would go on the clipboard and the builders were free to pick and chose whatever they wanted. Well, some orders remained there for months, so we had to get a more realistic system. I came up with a bill of materials for each of the guitars, which is a listing of all the parts and assemblies. For example, a neck would be broken down into woods, truss rod, frets, tuners, fret markers, etc., and then all of those parts were numbered, inventoried, and stocked. It helped us to smooth out the operation and be a lot more efficient and responsive, especially as we got bigger."

Duane Boulanger: "If you had a question or a problem, Scott was the guy you would go to on a daily basis, definitely a key figure. If you wanted to make a guitar yourself or do something unusual or special, you'd ask Scott. There was no need to involve John Page on a daily basis unless it was an artist guitar or had something radical about it. If there was a dispute between the tune testers and Maria, Scott would make the call." Scott Grant left the shop in 2003. As we go to press, he assembles instruments at Suhr Guitars.

Art Esparza started at Fender on February 2, 1987, spent the better part of a year on the production line, and moved over to the shop to work on the Kubicki project [Chap. 6]. "I was the seventh employee of the Custom Shop," he recalls. "After working [for the Custom Shop] at Kubicki in Santa Barbara, I got back to Corona — we were still in the shop with the two staircases going up to the mezzanine — and they gave me my first management job. Suddenly I had about seven or eight people working under me. I apprenticed with J. Black for years, and then around '94 I got a title. They made me a Master Builder.

Art Esparza.

"Those early days were hectic. We were just trying to survive. But even in tough times, we pretty much knew we were going to be okay because the demand for our guitars was there." Specializing not only in Teles and Strats but also in Showmasters and hollowbody guitars, Art crafted instruments for Ernie Isley, Buddy Guy, and Eric Clapton, among others. He built the Strat-shaped and Tele-shaped

Ralph Esposito.

"Hollowcasters" for Sam Ash Music, the historic Manhattan retailer. During the late 1980s and early 1990s he mentored Dennis Galuszka, Jason Smith, Louis Salgado, Mike Ponce, John Cruz, and others. He left Fender on January 17, 2006. In October 2009, he joined the crew at James Trussart Custom Guitars in Los Angeles.

Ralph Esposito worked on the factory's night shift for several months before coming over to the shop to work on the Kubicki project with Mark Gould, Fred Stuart, and Art Esparza. "Fred and Art had gone to Santa Barbara to work with Phil Kubicki," he recalls, "while Mark and I stayed back to set up production. At that point my job was to assist Mark. He worked with me, along with others, until he took a gig playing bass with a Japanese band called Vow Wow. I then assumed the lead position until the Kubicki project was cancelled.

"It was very exciting and challenging at the time. I took on tasks that I saw a need for, just to keep things moving forward. One of my first tasks was organizing small parts. I was moved to an empty spot in the upstairs mezzanine near Mike Stevens and Fred Stuart where the floor was cluttered with boxes and bins full of parts. As well as being a performing musician, I had originally come from the automotive and graphic design industries, so I set up an automotive-style parts area and managed it for the builders." Ralph also decided to make and assemble pickguards rather than having to retrieve them from the production line. He wound pickups, sanded necks, tune tested, helped establish a purchasing department, collaborated with artists, and did CNC work. "Back in the day," he says, "everyone in the shop had an integral part of everything that went out. We were all involved." John Page: "Ralph can do everything. I could put him anywhere, on any task, perfect floater. Conventional management says, each worker has to do this job or that job, but with Ralph Esposito you might need him to do something different every day."

Scott Buehl: Charvel veteran Scott Buehl started shaping Custom Shop necks in late 1988 after working on Fender's production line for a year and a half. He graduated to several other tasks in short order — working on necks, making bodies, soldering electronics. "I think at that time Page wanted Mike Stevens to pump out high-end artist guitars, and he kind of gave me to Mike to help out. We built stuff for lots of artists. I still appreciate doing work for people like Jeff Beck or David Gilmour. Both of them came to us for special tremolo arms. I bent them up by hand. At one point I made some bodies for Pete Townshend, three Strats. I assume these were the first Custom Shop Strats that Pete played.

Multi-talented *über*-builder Scott Buehl.

Mike Bump, tap-toning a piece of wood destined for a guitar body.

"I don't really have a title. One of the guys here called me the '*über*-builder' a couple of years ago when I built some really crazy guitar, and then Mike Eldred got hold of it and that's been my name ever since. Rather than building guitars I'm mostly building tooling and machinery and writing programs for the CNC. I develop new processes for whatever we need."

Chris Fleming: "Scott Buehl is not an official Master Builder, but he is a *great* guitar builder. He is the shop engineer, doing all the machinist stuff, programming, and engineering stuff. He's a whiz at metalwork, just a really talented guy all around." J. Black: "Scott is one of those talented, gifted people who could work on cars, furniture, guitars, boats. He seemed to have his hands in lots of things, so they shifted him around. He's just a good character, really positive, and he works his ass off." Duane Boulanger: "Scott did many things, and he did them all well. He is a consummate builder, one of the best craftsmen I've ever met."

Year three, 1989, saw the arrivals of Mike Bump, the late John English, J. Black, "Red" Dave Nichols, and Jason Davis.

Mike Bump went to work in the factory on March 19. Starting in September, he came over to the shop to help with the Kubicki basses. "I also worked on the Set-Necks," he says, "and in late '92 I moved over to Custom Shop wood prep. I was in charge of all the bodies coming out of the shop until '97 — 'Red' Dave was handling the necks — and then I started to apprentice with Gene Baker." Mike worked closely with J. Black on various special projects, including several Stratocasters and Telecasters with highly figured tops. He also contributed to several special runs, such as anniversary projects for Guitar Center. He moved to Fender R&D in April, 1998 and became a Master Builder in early 2001. As we go to press, Mike Bump is R&D's model shop manager and a Senior Master Builder.

John English came to Fender back in 1970 and worked alongside legendary Fendermen such as Freddie Tavares and Bill Carson. He was interviewed by John Page on May 23rd, 1989 and started employment at the shop on June 5th.

John English.

J. Black.

Even among the Custom Shop's quirky crew, English was a particularly memorable and colorful character. "That guy was like my dad," says Dennis Galuszka. "I loved him to death and miss him terribly. He and I were very close, but of course everyone says they were close to John [laughs], because he just had that knack of making you feel good." Duane Boulanger: "I knew John English from the time I was five years old. He used to play in my brother Steve's band. I'd sit on his lap and he'd show me how to play drums. I actually learned a lot about guitars from John before I came to the shop, and of course I had my brother Steve to show me stuff, too. I remember John as being this really warm guy."

John English went on to build guitars for rock stars, a President (George W. Bush), even a King (Dick Dale). He was a vintage buff, and his work on the Relic guitars was particularly outstanding. Gene Baker: "He was a great guy, a really good soul. He loved to pass on a lot of Fender history and all the stories from the early days of the shop, like working on the LJs with Mike Stevens. He wanted to bring back a lot of the old-school stuff like the vintage details but felt like he had to fight tooth and nail to do that. He was very excited to see younger guys coming up and following in his footsteps." John English died on June 28, 2007.

J. Black arrived on Monday, June 19th and brought years of experience and an impressive list of clients with him. He recalls, "I was interviewing with Hamer and also thinking about Gibson when Page offered me a job in '89 – come to California, be a Master Builder, make two guitars a month. I thought that sounded good. When I got there, Michael Stevens was the only other Master Builder. John Page had a Master Builder decal, but he was also running the shop, as well as R&D. Richard Syarto had already left. The Kubicki project was in full swing, and that was the big thing in the Custom Shop at that time. Larry Brooks was the Artist Builder. Fred Stuart wasn't a Master Builder yet, but he was clearly of that stature, with incredible talent and incredible ideas. He could step outside the traditional things we have always done and yet still make it look traditional. Then when Alan Hamel came in, he and Fred supported each other in all sorts of creative projects."

Dan Smith: "While some of the guys were a little disorganized and scattered, J. Black is professional and businesslike. We desperately needed someone with a level head in there, and he was more dependable than anybody. He fostered the attitude that the shop guys should be working with the plant rather than being off on their own little island. He treated those guys in the plant with respect. To

Red Dave.

me, J. Black was responsible for turning the shop around in the mid '90s."

Gene Baker: "J. Black and Page made a lot of decisions together because J. was really good with organization and management as well as being such a great builder. Page was doing a lot of administrative stuff. You could say that J. was Page's ears and eyes on the floor. Fred Stuart: "Without a doubt, J. Black had the deepest knowledge of each person's talents in the shop. John was good at that too, of course, but he was increasingly buried in paperwork. J. could really size up a person's abilities, and match them to particular orders. A crazy assignment like an acoustic 12-string Tele, he'd bring it to me and I'd think, yeah, I'd love to do that. I flourished on that sort of thing."

John Grunder: "J. Black is one of my heroes, for a lot of reasons. We were way behind on orders, both with the Team Builts and the Master Builts, but when J. came on board, he grabbed the bull by the horns and took on more than his share of the load. Not only was he a great builder of one-offs, but he also had a lot of ideas about organizing the shop to make it work better, and he was diplomatic in suggesting improvements. He was organized and he took care of business. He's a hell of a guy. We'd have been in better shape if we'd had more guys like him."

Red Dave: John Page hired "Red" Dave Nichols on June 21st, 1989, two days after J. Black's arrival. "He was just out of high school," John remembers. "He went right into the Custom Shop, spent a lot of time in the wood shop, and eventually became the Custom Shop's wood guru dude. He was just brilliant when it came to selection and prep. I trusted him implicitly. He became my eyes when it came to selecting the perfect piece of wood for a particular project. Years later he became Freddie Tavares's grandson-in-law."

Lawrence Berndt is the founder of Yankee Veneer Corp., for many years a supplier of high-quality maple to the shop. He says: "When you are building guitars with that kind of quality, you get very, very picky about your materials. 'Red' Dave took me through their wood supplies and pointed out all of the things they did and didn't like. He was essential in communicating their needs and preferences."

Jason Davis joined the crew on August 6, 1989, and made a reputation for himself as a guy who had his own way of doing things, an exceptional builder

Jason Davis.

Artist Builder Larry Brooks.

who pushed, or at least nudged, the boundaries of Fender design. Duane Boulanger: "When you order a guitar from a Master Builder, you want a *Fender*, but Jason knew how to fudge that a little bit. He was very much into the '80s heavy metal thing, so he might do a compound radius or a flatter fingerboard. Maybe he wanted his guitars to play the way a Jackson might play. Some of his basses also were unconventional — multi-wood things, like Tobias might do."

Scott Buehl worked closely with Jason and knew him well. He found him to be naturally talented with his hands, exceptionally intelligent, and fearless when it came to implementing innovative ideas in wood and metal. "He was good at everything," Scott says. "He never had to try hard. He looked at a problem and saw the answer. He would boil down a process to its most efficient form in his head and then execute without a hitch. The things Duane said concerning Charvel/Jackson stem from the fact that in the '80s, Charvel had high standards, so when Jason or Todd or I would attempt to correct someone's process or dispute their standard of quality, we might bring up Charvel, only because they had proved that very high quality could be achieved in a production environment. Nobody wanted it to be Charvel; we just wanted to do the best job we could. Jason took pride in doing it right, and that was always his focus. He thought well outside the box and was doing things a couple steps beyond what anyone else did." Davis left the shop on March 5, 2004.

Larry Brooks joined Fender on February 5, 1990. He worked in — but officially not for — the Custom Shop. His title was "Artist Builder" or "Artist Relations Builder." All of the early Custom Shop builders crafted instruments for professional musicians and were therefore "artist builders," but Fender wanted a dedicated Master Builder more or less exclusively assigned to Artist Relations, or "AR" as it is known in-house. Although this person initially reported to that department's director, Mark Wittenberg, he worked alongside the shop's other craftsmen and on occasion took direction from John Page. Larry Brooks developed the factory's first SRV Strat and built guitars for Bonnie Raitt, Albert Collins, Buddy Guy, Eric Clapton, Jon Bon Jovi, Richie Sambora, and most of Fender's artist endorsers of the early 1990s.

Yasuhiko Iwanade is one of the foremost figures in Japan's guitar community, a guitarist, builder, renowned collector, repairman, historian, author of highly detailed books on both Gibson and Fender (*The Galaxy of Strats, The Fender Stratocaster, The Beauty of the 'Burst*), and President of Gibson Japan. According to John Page's datebook, he was interviewed for a job at Fender in December, 1989 and joined the crew shortly thereafter. He worked at the Custom Shop until the summer of 1993, and he profoundly influenced the builders in their quest to render authentic reissues.

Michael Stevens: "Yas beefed up the reverence and revived the interest for the old days, the old guitars, and the old guys that Fred [Stuart] and I so respected. He made the younger guys pay attention — *hey, this guy is from Japan and he knows more about American guitars than I do; maybe Michael and Fred are not so crazy!* Yas was also a *great* craftsman. I'm proud to be a friend of his."

John Page: "Yas spent years getting vast amounts of information on vintage Fenders — the location of every screw, every detail, everything about the wires, the covering on the wires. He spoke to Leo many times. When he came on board he looked at some of our 'vintage' pieces and said very diplomatically, 'You think these are right, but

J. Black, Larry Brooks (with a beautiful LJ), Yasuhiko Iwanade.

they are not right' [laughs]. And at first we were kind of pissed. *'Dude, what are you talking about, telling Fender we're not right?'* And he said, 'Well, you are *not right*.' And it was great, because although at first we took it as kind of a slap, we realized this was an opportunity for us to educate ourselves, so let's listen and let's learn." (For more on Yasuhiko Iwanade, see Chap. 7, Vintage Rising.)

Steve Boulanger: The year 1990 also saw the arrivals of Steve Boulanger in February, and Greg Fessler in March. By that time, the shop already employed several skilled craftspeople. What it needed most was someone who could bring its production techniques into the modern age. The late Steve Boulanger, or "Boley," was a musician, machinist, and craftsman. He was hired full-time on February 2 and took it upon himself to study computers and programming at night school. When it came to CNC technologies, he became the shop's guru, the person everyone turned to for help.

Gene Baker: "Boley and I spent a lot of time together. He appreciated being treated with respect, and if you did that, he would do anything for you. He and I began documenting a lot of procedures, especially when we started to do things like the big-peghead Strats. The headstock angle was slightly different than the vintage peghead, and all these little curveballs and procedures had to be figured out and documented." Steve Boulanger was one of those rare people who not only impressed all who knew him but inspired them as well. Scott Buehl says

Steve Boulanger.

simply: "Steve had a huge effect on my life." Gene Baker: "The guitar playing world is a better place because of him." Steve Boulanger died in 2006.

Greg Fessler: The likelihood that Greg Fessler would one day become a Master Builder might have seemed pretty low back on March 26, 1990, when he joined the gang and went to work on the Kubicki project. "I had never worked in the guitar industry," he says. "I didn't know anything, but John Page had faith in me. I learned everything pretty much on the job." For the Kubicki project, Greg made tuner frames, dressed necks, finished bodies, and did some assembly. After that project he concentrated on neck work for three years or so — fretting, detailing, dressing, and buffing. After four or five years in the shop he was apprenticed to Gene Baker and worked on the Robben Fords, eventually becoming the sole builder of those models. "I was really lucky that a number of Master Builders took me under their wing," he says. "We did the equivalent of what we call the Team Built today, where several builders worked together on limited runs. I got to work on projects for some really neat artists like Joe Perry and Dweezil Zappa. Everything was handmade with unbelievable craftsmanship and a lot of competition among the builders, in a good way. Every-

Greg Fessler.

body was trying to be better than the next guy, and that meant we were all learning from each other all the time, looking over each other's shoulders, picking up tips, getting better."

Pamelina H.: "It was good timing. The year I barged my way into the NAMM show, 1987, was the same year the Custom Shop got started." Artist Pamelina Hovnatanian, better known as Pamelina H., recalls her first meeting with John Page. "I had already painted guitars up in the Bay Area, and clients kept asking for these things, so I took that idea to John. I had painted a guitar for myself, and that's the one I took to show him."

John Page: "She had a backpack and a portfolio of some of her work. She was gutsy and really talented, and I could tell right away that I could work with her. I was always on the lookout for new ways to bring talent into the Custom Shop, and she came along at the right time. People approached me all the time, but other artists' work just hadn't grabbed me the way hers did. Her images were lively and vivid, with a real spark and kind of a whimsical, humorous thing. I could tell that she had a lot of talent, but I could also tell that she was someone I could just turn loose."

Pamelina: "John put me to work right away and gave me freedom. I moved down to Hollywood, and he said, I'm shipping you ten bodies – do whatever you want. John was a real visionary, and he has an artist's soul himself. He told me one time, and this is really true, that he could envision things and somehow I could read his brain and put it down on paper and make it happen in the real world. That was the key to the relationship. Once we had done a couple of projects, there was a real push for those art guitars." Pamelina has worked on some of the shop's most memorable guitars: the Regina Del Mare series, the Velvet Elvis, the

Pamelina H.

Fender
THE KING LIVES!
Elvis Presley

Bird O' Fire, the Harley-Davidsons, the Playboy/Marilyn Monroe limited run, The Jimi Hendrix Monterey Strats, the Crown Royals, and others.

Pamelina H. works as an independent contractor in her home studio in Sunland, California. Sometimes she uses brushes and acrylic paints, creating her designs on 15 x 30" sheets of paper. Other times she works on her computer, accessing templates of a variety of Fender bodies, necks, pickups, and components which she can then manipulate with PhotoShop and other graphics programs. "I can really see what it looks like in 3-D before I submit it," she explains. "I can change colors and make adjustments with just a keystroke and simply e-mail the final rendering to Fender."

Hunka hunka burnin' twang: Pamelina H. recalls, "The Velvet Elvis Telecaster from 1995 was a really fun project, very special. Painting on black velvet, that's just so classic. It's a very interesting process. This is real velvet on the guitar. Fred Stuart was the builder, and I just love Fred and love working with him. This is one of those projects where it's hard to say who came up with what, because John [Page] and Fred and I were all in the room throwing ideas around and we all got excited about it." The body is trimmed in black and gold rope, and the musical notes on the body are the beginning of the "Love Me Tender" melody.

Pamelina sometimes blends hand techniques and semi-mass production procedures that permit her to work on several guitars at a time. While the Hendrix Montereys were entirely brush painted, the Playboys and the Crown Royals entailed a combination of airbrush, paintbrush, and pencil work. Some of her GuitarMania instruments were illustrated entirely with paintbrushes while others were painted with an airbrush and frisket paper, a clear protective sheet with adhesive on one side that can be cut to shape and placed over one part of an artwork while the artist is working on another part.

In Pamelina's case, any project involving frisket paper also entails airbrushing. She explains, "An airbrush is just a little paint gun with an air source. I like to use pressurized carbon dioxide. Great care has to be taken to protect the part that isn't being airbrushed, so the rest of the body is covered in tape and paper. I use an X-Acto knife to cut out the areas intended for airbrushing. I remove the pieces and save them for later replacement. I go through the process, removing other areas of the frisket and spraying different colors. I use these same paints and techniques whether it's a guitar, motorcycle, or canvas. On my projects in general, once I finish the design, the actual painting is done by airbrushing. There's always a concern of keeping the paint as flat as possible and as thin as possible so that a clear coat can be applied easily. A large part of the process is laying down the base colors with an airbrush. I also do a lot with paintbrushes and more traditional techniques, so it's a combination. I'm actually relying less on the airbrush than I used to, but if it's something that needs to be clear coated – like guitars and motorcycles – airbrushing is essential. It's the easiest for applying the clear coat.

"My role and my relationship with the shop has changed quite a bit. In the beginning, John Page was clearly the manager and overseer of every aspect. Everything went through him. I've become very good friends with many of the builders over the years, and we've stayed close. Now I am contacted by individual builders rather than one person acting on behalf of the whole shop. They approach me directly, and I work one-on-one with them. I'm often working on more than one Custom Shop project at a time. For most of the projects, once I design it I continue to collaborate with the builder, and there is a lot of back-and-forth. Sometimes it's hard to say who has the final word, because we all throw ideas around until we agree on what it should look like. It's a very open, free-flowing kind of exchange, which is always the best way to get results in an artistic environment.

"At first, because the Custom Shop was brand new, there was more freedom. Now the shop is very well established, and they're so successful they have their hands full just trying to fill orders. There is just so much demand for their guitars now. In the early days, we were establishing that demand. We were showing people what the Custom Shop is capable of. We were saying to the world, hey, look what we can do."

A rich diversity of influences

J. Black: "John Page brought in a lot of his old friends. He was very good at that. He brought John English in to do the LJ, and Steve Boulanger to do the tooling. Scott Buehl, Todd Krause, and Jason Davis came in from Charvel/Jackson. One guy had worked at B.C. Rich, another at G&L — that whole Southern California thing, so many companies, lots of experience coming in the door, lots of influences. Duane Boulanger, Greg Fessler, Art Esparza, Mike Bump, Scott Grant, Ralph Esposito — each guy was important in his own way."

It wasn't just the Master Builders, sales reps, and marketers who established the shop's reputation for quality and craftsmanship. J. Black: "If somebody just profiles the Master Builders, they are missing an ingredient that is key to how the whole thing worked. Some of us got a lot of attention because we were building guitars for Keith Richards or Eric Clapton or whoever, but all those other guys were in the back working their asses off, and the Custom Shop could not have survived without them. Some of these guys who became Master Builders

The American Girl Stratocaster was built by Todd Krause and painted by Pamelina H. She recalls: "It was Todd's concept. He wanted shot glasses for fret markers, and I incorporated the shot glass in her hand. In the background is an old saloon. I told Todd I liked the idea of letting the wood grain show through in the artwork. I accomplished that and also matched the wood grain on the pickguard so that it continued all the way through. The lettering was especially fun to do with all the intricate whirls and curlicues. The most interesting part was researching lingerie from the period, which I kept accurate."

later were just as important to the Custom Shop when they were tune testers.

"Look at Maria Orduño. You never read about her, but in terms of how Fender became Fender again, she was crucial. She was this young Hispanic woman who eventually became the Custom Shop's lead [production floor supervisor]. She couldn't even speak English when I got there in '89, but she was already the lead on the floor and did a fantastic job. You talk to *any* of the builders — we wouldn't have wanted to try to make it without her. When we went to the Custom Shop price list production [in 1992, Chap. 12], she was in charge of all that on a day-to-day basis, a huge job."

Maria Orduño's hiring on October 28, 1986, actually predated the founding of the shop by two months. Todd Krause: "Maria was the lead for certain projects, the limited runs and [what would later be called] the Team Built guitars. The lead is the go-to foreman-type person, the one who tells each individual, 'I need five of these, six of those' — sort of like a project manager. It's their job to make sure the work gets done on time and everything is right. When you're a lead, you're directing your team."

Freedoms weird and wonderful

Certain members of the early crew became legendary not only for their creativity but also for their commitment to the shop. Fred Stuart's idea for a Telecaster-style 6-string bass/bajo sexto pretty much fell on deaf ears, but instead of abandoning the project he spent his vacation in the shop designing and building the thing. Once they saw it, his colleagues put it into production. J. Black: "What a phenomenal thing to do, to believe so much in a product that he would take his own vacation time to make it happen. And then we all thought, 'Well, yeah, that's the kind of people the Custom Shop should have.' That was an example of the weird freedom we had. Sometimes you had to fight for it or ask permission, and sometimes you just went ahead and did it and asked permission afterwards."

Maria Orduño. "We wouldn't have wanted to try to make it without her," says J. Black.

Coining the "Master Builder" title

In the early days, titles such as Master Builder were vague, and detailed job descriptions were nonexistent. Fred Stuart, for example, was hired as an apprentice, soon became a Master Builder, and was eventually promoted to Senior Master Builder. But despite sharing titles with other craftsmen, he sometimes performed very different functions. As he explains it, the one common assumption was that any person who held the title of Senior Master Builder was expected to handle any task that was handed to him.

Before anyone thought to make "Master Builder" an official title, the builders were referred to as "design engineers." This had to do with in-house accounting as much as anything else; Fender just needed a title that reflected a builder's pay grade. As best as John Page and Michael Stevens can remember, the term "Master Builder" became official during the shop's second year.

This big sharing of ideas

The early builders enjoyed quite a bit of independence. There were exceptions, as when a builder might take on a task somewhat outside of his experience. If someone well versed in building '80s-style shred guitars took on a vintage project, John Page might look over his shoulder. On rare occasions, he'd step in and say, "Something's not perfect here. This isn't Fender. You can't ship it." "Then again," he says, "somebody like J. would come in, and I would never look at his work at all, except to admire it."

Before long, individual builders began to cultivate their own reputations. In fact, some were already well known before coming to the shop. Michael Stevens's reputation preceded him, for example, and clients such as Stevie Ray Vaughan, Jimmie Vaughan, and Eric Johnson would eventually develop longstanding relationships with the shop.

The Resonator Tele: Fred Stuart integrated several influences in this beautifully sunbursted guitar: a Dobro-style single-cone resonator and soundholes, a Telecaster body outline and neck, and full-depth hollow construction. Fred set it up high for playing slide, and you just know it sounds good.

Jason Davis, John Page, and Scott Buehl, with the Phoenix Stratocaster. The guitar was conceived by John Page and illustrated by Pamelina H. John Page: “The concept was, this guitar represents the rebirth of Fender, the whole ‘Phoenix from the fire’ sort of thing.” George Amicay hand-carved the body, Bill Swank inlaid the neck, and Ron Chacey engraved the pickguard, headcap, and neck. The summer 1993 *Frontline* reported that “bidding is currently up to $45,000 and climbing.”

John Page: "When I was interviewing J. and he was asking me whom I had built for, it was clear he had never heard of me. But why would he? I was 'Fender,' that's all. I'd been in R&D designing new products. But now with the Custom Shop there was an increasing awareness of certain names. As people became aware of J. Black, Fred Stuart, John English, and others, that was all part of the prestige."

Each builder brought unique ideas to the mix, and there was much exchange and sharing of techniques. J. Black: "Once again, Fred Stuart is a good example. He would incorporate something into a particular project, but then the rest of us could take a piece of it and maybe reinterpret it and incorporate it in a later project. Everything was building upon the previous work. It all interacted."

A case in point was a modest run of guitars featuring pickups Michael Stevens had developed back in Austin. They came to be called Texas Specials, and were installed in many future models from both the factory and the Custom Shop. One reviewer called them "the pickups that made the Custom Shop famous." Ralph Esposito: "At first we called them 'Calibrated' pickups. Michael designed them to be progressively wound relative to their position — neck, middle, bridge — in order to have the optimum output and to keep the balance from the neck to bridge. The middle pickup was reverse-wound, reverse-polarity to eliminate hum in the second and fourth positions on a Strat.

"Fender had missed out on the aftermarket thing that allowed DiMarzio and Seymour Duncan and those sorts of companies to succeed. We ignored it for so long. Stevens gave me all the specs for the Texas Specials. We had a Tanac, a Japanese winder that's sort of one step up from a sewing machine motor. Our first one didn't even have a digital counter. It had a mechanical counter. In about 1990 or 1991 we dusted the thing off and I started winding Texas Specials by hand. We had a little croc pot upstairs where I dipped those pickups in paraffin wax. The Texas Specials were so important because they were our first aftermarket attempt at pickups, and they came right from Michael Stevens and an individual Custom Shop project." John Page: "Even though some of the limited-edition things didn't seem particularly significant on their own, we were learning from every project, and sometimes a project would have an important offshoot like the Texas Specials."

One of the earliest traditions of the Custom Shop was that you taught, and learned from, each and every colleague. Dennis Galuszka remembers John English: "When you were around John, you'd better put your ears on, because you'd learn a whole world of stuff. He was both amazing and extraordinarily frustrating. There were times when I'd walk into the shop and think, *I am not going to work with this person one more day*. He was very exacting, but that's what made him one of the greatest teachers I've ever had."

Duane Boulanger: "J. Black probably taught me more than anyone else. He is a great guy but very demanding. I knew I was on the right track when *finally*, J. would look at my work and say, 'That's cool.' That's when I knew I had been accepted."

Gene Baker remembers Steve Boulanger: "He always had huge amounts of work to do and was constantly pulling miracles out of thin air. He was a thinker extraordinaire, and I learned a lot of my CNC skills from him. I bounced many ideas off of him and he always gave me useful feedback."

Art Esparza remembers Richard Syarto: "He was a great builder. He actually had several talents — violin repair, for example. I looked over his shoulder whenever I could. We were always learning from each other, all of us."

John Page: "Nobody kept anything for themselves. It was all on the table. Everybody wanted every project to be the best it could be. The builders were competitive but unselfish. There was something magic about that period. It was just this big sharing of ideas, and I think that's one of the main reasons it was so successful."

The traditions of teaching, learning, and mentoring would continue into the shop's next phase, the early and mid 1990s.

The Zeal Stratocaster was built by Art Esparza for Ernie Isley, of the Isley Brothers. Art recalls: "His wife Tracy came to me and drew out 12 roses on a piece of paper, and I picked up the rose motif. She wanted to give Ernie a surprise for his birthday. George Amicay carved the top. I ended up building three guitars all together, over a period of a few years. 'Zeal' was a name that Ernie came up with."

Fender

CHAPTER FIVE

5

Forever Man

Eric Clapton and the Custom Shop

For more than two decades, Fender's Eric Clapton Signature Stratocaster has been marketed as a "factory" model rather than a Custom Shop model. So why profile a factory guitar in a Custom Shop book? As it turns out, that factory guitar was very much a product of the Custom Shop. In fact, *all* of the early artist models — whether cataloged as production guitars or Custom Shop guitars — were developed by Master Builders who worked with R&D's George Blanda and Marketing's Dan Smith.

Regarding the inner workings of Fender, a key realization is that when it comes to R&D, design, marketing, and artist relations, distinctions among departments often melt away. Employees set aside formal job descriptions and pitch in to achieve common goals. A prime example is the Clapton project, which after years of collaboration resulted in Fender's foremost artist signature guitar. Although the guitar's planning was initiated prior to the birth of the Custom Shop, it was the Master Builders who refined the design, built the final prototypes, built Eric's personal guitars, developed the factory's original Blackie model in 1990, and crafted the Tribute Series Blackie Stratocasters in 2006.

As we go to press, the Custom Shop's relationship with Eric Clapton is well into its third decade. His namesake guitar is profiled here in more depth than any other instrument, for several reasons: It is the most significant artist guitar in Fender's history, Clapton's relationship with Fender is unlike that of any other artist, and his endorsement went far beyond selling more guitars; it helped to re-establish the credibility of the entire company at a time when its very survival was at stake. For our purposes, two additional reasons are that the tale of the Clapton model's development illuminates the behind-the-scenes collaborations between the Custom Shop and other departments, and also demonstrates the painstaking efforts Custom Shop craftspeople are willing to make in order to satisfy their artist endorsers, no matter how demanding.

The Eric Clapton Signature Stratocaster

Put yourself in the shoes of Fender's President. It's March of 1985. You find yourself at the helm of a brand new company with a 40-year legacy and a tarnished reputation. You are in desperate need of a jolt of good luck, something — anything — to help you spread the news: Fender is back, we're correcting the mistakes of the past, our best is yet to come. The ultimate prize, the stuff of dreams, would be an endorsement from the most celebrated guitarist in the world, Eric Clapton. (Miami Steve Van Zandt put it this way, in *Rolling Stone*'s 2004 The Immortals special issue: "Eric Clapton is the most important and influential guitar player who has ever lived, is still living, or ever will live. Do yourself a favor, and don't debate me on this.")

Clapton's unofficial association with Fender was already a decade and a half old, and his two main Stratocasters, Blackie and Brownie, were among the most famous electric guitars seen on concert stages and album covers from the early '70s through the mid '80s. And yet "Slowhand's" choice of instrument was a mixed blessing. Blackie and Brownie helped stoke the markets for vintage guitars and perhaps for Fender's reissues, but Fender was not in the vintage guitar business. Fender sold new guitars, not old ones.

Way back in the Custom Shop's first year, soft V neck profiles for the new model were hand-drawn on graph paper.

What if?

But what if Fender could build a new model that would not merely satisfy Eric Clapton but impress him to the point where he would consider retiring his beloved Brownie, and even Blackie, which he described as having "become a part of me"? Such a coup would be among the most valuable endorsements in the history of the industry and would surely jumpstart the Fender revival.

Early signals from the Clapton camp were encouraging. Lee Dickson, Eric's highly regarded guitar tech since December '79, suggested that Eric would be willing to test prototypes and provide feedback. Everyone at Fender sensed the breathtaking potential for a touched-by-God endorsement. Fingers were crossed. Sort of an Apollo moon-launch project for Corona R&D, the high-stakes Clapton collaboration would involve the best efforts of Fender's brightest minds and most skilled craftspeople.

1984 and 1985: Gearing up

Given Clapton's quirky tastes and impeccable standards, not to mention the kind of lengthy, one-on-one communication such an enterprise would require, it was inevitable that prototyping the Eric Clapton Signature Stratocaster and crafting Eric's personal instruments would one day fall to the Custom Shop. But in '85, the shop was still only a gleam in Bill Schultz's eye, almost two years away. Schultz was never one to wait around, so only a few weeks after the acquisition of the company from CBS the project was assigned to Fender's Renaissance man and all-around go-to guy, future Fender Hall Of Famer Dan Smith. He recalls, "I had started on this back in 1984 and spent about a year going to concerts, talking to Eric and to Eric's management about getting a guitar together for him. And I would bring stuff in for him to try. He was very nice to me."

Dan Smith flew to Dallas, where Clapton and his band were rehearsing. He met with Eric on April 5th, 1985 (Dan remembers the date because it was his birthday). He played Blackie for ten or fifteen minutes and got a good feel for the neck: "Eric felt that all I should need is a few minutes playing his guitar and I would know what he wanted. I pushed the issue a little and explained that we wanted to make his guitar with his favorite neck. He told me that, actually, his favorite neck was on the old '30s Martin his grandparents gave him as a child. I had worked on enough guitars to remember that those old Martin necks had a real sharp V in the back. Also, Eric's hands are not all that big, so I knew he wouldn't want a neck that was too big." Over the next two years, the necks on both guitars, Blackie and the Martin flat-top, would serve as starting points for Clapton prototypes.

On that same trip to Dallas, Dan brought along one of the few instruments left in the warehouse after the buyout, a non-trem Stratocaster Elite. Fender had agreed to donate a few Elites as promotional giveaways on the upcoming tour, and Eric wanted to make sure he liked them before autographing them. This chance encounter would have lasting significance far beyond that 1985 promotional campaign, because at some point Eric plugged in an Elite and was quite taken with its active onboard circuit, usually described as a midrange boost. After several modifications it would become the circuit used to this day in Clapton Signature Strats from both the factory and the Custom Shop.

Brownie and Blackie

At the dawn of the 1970s, Eric Clapton had adopted the Fender Stratocaster as his main guitar for both live performances and studio recording. His first Strat, nicknamed Brownie (serial no. 12073), was the sunburst '56 he had played on his debut solo album, *Eric Clapton*, as well as on his epic masterpiece, *Layla And Other Assorted Love Songs*. He purchased it for £150 at Shop At The Cities in London on May 7th, 1967. On June 24, 1999, it sold for nearly half a million dollars at the first of two Christie's auctions of Clapton's guitars.

Brownie was succeeded by Blackie, a "parts guitar" assembled in 1970 from components that came from three of the six Stratocasters Eric acquired in Nashville for about a hundred dollars each. Eric gave the other three guitars to his pals Steve Winwood, Pete Townshend, and George Harrison. (Winwood's own work on the Strat had influenced Clapton's decision to convert from his various Gibsons to the Fender.) Blackie's "donor" guitars were all circa 1956/1957.

After a long and storied career in the hands of Eric Clapton, Blackie was retired in 1985. In the summer or early fall of that year, during the first of Blackie's several visits to southern California, John Carruthers made a copy of the neck using the duplicating machine of his own design. Because the original had been played so heavily for so long, the area between the frets on the neck's bottom edge had worn away somewhat, making it increasingly difficult to keep the guitar in playing condition. John Carruthers: "You'd come off the edge of the neck while you were playing because of those gaps, so on the duplicate we took filler and filled the spaces that had worn away and used that neck to make the pattern for the new one."

Within a month or two after his October, 1985 hiring, George Blanda joined the top-priority Clapton project. Smith and Blanda each retrieved three 21-fret neck blanks from the factory and carved them to different shapes for Eric to try. The profiles ranged from an extreme V like the Martin neck Eric had told Dan about to a much softer V, closer to Blackie's neck.

Early in 1986, Dan Smith went to London for Fender's presentation of the Blanda-built, commemorative Fiesta Red Strat to Hank Marvin [Chap. 3]. It was a good opportunity to continue discussions with Eric Clapton, one of several stellar guitarists in attendance. Smith overheard Eric telling Jeff Beck about his in-the-works signature guitar project: "Jeff was blown away that Eric could figure out what neck he wanted just by touching one, without actually having it on a guitar to play. But that's what he did. He picked the neck that had the sharpest V."

Prototypes and colors

By April 1986, the project was a year old and yet still in its preliminary stages. George Blanda: "Dan and I did the first Clapton Signature model prototypes. During that year, when I was the only guitar guy in R&D, I worked with Lee Dickson. I spoke directly to Eric Clapton, but only a little bit. We took three prototypes to him when he was making that album *August* [recorded at Sunset Sound Studios, Los Angeles, in April and May 1986]. Dan and I had been up late the night before, getting them put together and set up. During the craziness of all that, I suggested we put a cigarette up behind the nut to burn the headstock [as on Blackie], just as a joke. I just was riffing on an old observation from Larry Henrickson that in his vintage shop he could tell the blues Fenders from the country Fenders because the blues Fenders had cigarette burns on the headstocks. Eric laughed and said there's no need for that, I'll do that myself.

"He wasn't really vocal about what he wanted. He talked to Dan quite a bit, and we both talked to Lee quite a bit. From those necks we had sent to England for Eric to feel, we put his two favorite ones on the prototypes we took to the *August* sessions in May."

Esthetics were important, too, for a guitarist whose onstage outfits of jeans, leather vests, aviator shades and Lee bib overalls had been replaced with designer wardrobes by Versace or Armani. For his earliest guitars Clapton picked two colors. One was Ferrari red; Fender would call it Torino Red. The paint actually came from a Ferrari dealer. Clapton reportedly preferred the older, more orangey Ferrari color but approved the new one. He also selected "anthracite," reportedly a Mercedes color that Eric sometimes called charcoal gray. Fender had offered the same color, or a similar one, on the Elite series of the CBS period; Fender called it Pewter.

Later, Clapton requested a third color. Bruce Bolen: "Lee called and said Eric really loved the color on that 7Up can, so I went out and bought a can of 7Up and brought it over to the Custom Shop, and the guys built this 7Up green Strat for Eric. That stayed part of the line for a short time." Officially, the color was Candy Green; in house, they called it 7Up green. (Note: As is the case with many guitar finishes, some of these colors changed over time because of aging or exposure to the elements. For example, the Pewter/anthracite color was noticeably affected by the topcoat yellowing, making it appear somewhat green as it aged. One of the original Clapton protos from 1986, serial no. V000009, had a newer 22-fret neck installed by Mike Stevens on February 23, 1988; one of Eric's favorite stage guitars, it was sold for $95,000 at the 1999 Christie's auction, and by that time the Pewter had acquired a greenish hue.)

Given the several stages in the Clapton signature model's design process, those original 21-fret guitars might be called pre-prototypes. George Blanda explains: "On that first trip [to the *August* sessions], we only had Clapton's two neck choices mounted on [reissue] '57 Strat bodies, which were painted in the Pewter and the red. After we got Eric's general approval, we took these guitars back to Fender and built the *real* protos with the approved necks. Two weeks later these protos were delivered with the blocked trems and active circuits with

Eric Clapton specified "7Up Green" as one of the colors for his signature Strat. This is a modern factory version, the color officially dubbed Candy Green.

hidden batteries [see below]. We also delivered one extra Pewter guitar."

The red prototype had the sharpest of the V necks. Dan Smith: "A lot of people played it and said, 'Oh, this is a V neck like Fender used to make in the '50s.' Well, Fender never made a V neck that was *that* sharp. Eric actually went back and rerecorded some of the solos [on *August*] with the guitars we took to him – that's how much he liked them. And of course, that made us feel great."

For the next year and a half Eric Clapton played the three prototype Stratocasters he had received in the spring of 1986. During that period of near-constant touring and recording, there was little communication between Clapton and Fender, resulting in a postponement of the production guitar's debut. The delay was so lengthy that prototypes were displayed at three NAMM shows stretching over a year and a half before Fender ever shipped a production version. At some point on tour, the red guitar with the sharp V neck "went squirrelly," as Dan Smith puts it, and Eric started playing one of the Pewter guitars, which became his new favorite. Its neck was closer in profile to Blackie's. Dan Smith: "By that time we had already introduced it with the [sharper] V neck, but Eric changed his mind. The neck was the major reason for the delays."

Enter the Master Builders

In early 1987, new arrivals Mike Stevens and John Page were striving to get the Custom Shop off the ground. Although by that time Clapton had approved the Blanda/Smith prototypes and preliminary agreements had been signed with Clapton's management, Page and Stevens had plenty of Clapton-related work to do building the next generation of prototypes as well as sample Clapton Signature Strats for upcoming NAMM show displays.

By early 1988, Eric had inflicted a zillion miles' worth of wear and tear on the three original Strats (plus a fourth one supplied by Smith and Blanda). Blanda recalls that Eric requested three new guitars, and a new neck for one of the Pewter originals: "This was the first time John Page and Michael Stevens [who had already built sample Clapton models for NAMM] built any guitars for Eric himself. In 1988, Lee Dickson was here for several days when Michael, John, and I completed the second batch of Eric's personal guitars."

Michael Stevens remembers: "When I arrived at Fender, the Clapton project was ongoing but still in the tweaking mode. Eric had not signed off on it, as I was told. I set to the task of making the neck shape he wanted. He had already tried to buy an original '57 Strat from Jimmy Wallace, from the Dallas Guitar Show. I had reworked the neck, frets, fingerboard radius, and fingerboard finish on it, so I knew he liked how I set guitars up, even though he had no clue who I was.

"I made some necks, but the specs kept changing and the necks were rejected, so I would make another pair that were correct to the info given me and played great. The first set or maybe two were made in George's R&D shop in Brea and put on recycled bodies George furnished. I made two or three sets and again, rejection! Thrown again to the lions. By then John and I were in Corona. I went ballistic. I'd never been rejected by anybody. I threw a big fit and told Dan that Clapton could go to hell. I was obviously not getting the correct specs or this would be over and done with. This is not rocket science." George Blanda reports that Michael is referring to necks that were perfectly spec'd, except that the edges of the fretboards were somewhat sharp instead of being "rolled over." George Blanda: "This seems like a minor detail in general, but it was major to Clapton. No matter how perfect the rest of the neck was, the round-over was what would make or break Eric's opinion of it."

Mike Stevens continues: "I told Dan, I don't care if he's God, get his ass over here face to face and tell me what he wants! That did not happen, but Lee came over from England with Blackie and delivered it to the Custom Shop and said to me — *like this*. I do not remember making any major changes to those neck specs. Now, I've heard other stories, some of them conflicting, but my story is this: Lee said, 'This is what we want,' and I duplicated that damn neck. I slept with Blackie under my bed and a gun under my pillow until I was done with it and Lee left. As I recall, just about the time I had those necks ready the other components arrived and John, George, and I set to assembly.

"I slept with Blackie under my bed and a gun under my pillow." — Michael Stevens

John routed battery pockets, and George routed the pocket for the active electronics board, a hand-soldered board about the size of a cigarette pack under the pickguard.

"A very curly maple neck, number 1, was put on the Pewter body, and a bird's-eye neck, number 2, was on the 7Up green. I believe these were both new bodies; at least the green was, as it was a new color Eric had asked for. I had delivered a 7Up can to Spartan Paint and they mixed it for us. Bodies were wired, trems blocked, and handed to me for final setup. I made the carving templates and helped get the signature Clapton into production.

"Later, Lee called and asked Dan if I could fix a fret on the Pewter Strat. Dan sent me to the Pacific Amphitheater [in Costa Mesa, Orange County] to fix it. Lee had me switch necks on the Pewter and green bodies, so now the bird's-eye neck went on the Pewter. On the green one, I put in a new first fret and set it up with the curly neck. That green one with the curly neck would later get a black body. When the Pewter Strat was sold in the [first] Christie's sale, it was the fifth highest priced guitar and the only non-vintage guitar to go over $100,000."

Hands on: On one of several trips to the Custom Shop, Clapton's guitar tech, Lee Dickson, right, learned the ropes under the watchful eye of Master Builder J. Black.

George Blanda believes that much of what Michael describes took place between the summer of 1987 and February 1988, when Stevens dated the replacement necks. He recalls, "Blackie was shipped here to Michael and John but was suddenly needed back in England. Both guys were called out of the company's summer picnic to get Blackie ready to ship back the next day. In February '88 the necks were dated and everyone remembers Lee Dickson coming over to pick them up."

Finally: Fender's first artist signature guitar

Fender and the Clapton organization were communicating again by the end of 1987. The signature guitar project entered the next phase, which entailed a new round of prototypes with several experiments: a neck with a less drastic V, a massive increase in the amount of the preamp's horsepower to a roaring 25dB, and a switch from more or less conventional Strat pickups to the new Lace Sensors, which Fender was about to introduce.

The Eric Clapton Signature Stratocaster was unveiled at the summer 1987 NAMM show in Chicago, but Eric changed his mind about a couple of details, particularly the neck shape. Due to that snag, and also due to delays in getting final papers signed, no guitars were shipped until the following year, which accounts for reports dating the guitar's introduction to both 1987 and 1988. George Blanda: "A long damn time after we had the basic guitar finished, the factory version finally became official. We had a major ordeal getting something signed that was needed to actually start production. We were still waiting long after the instruments that Dan and I made were being played to death on tours and recording sessions. [The official introduction] was after Page and Stevens built replacement units which were now in use by Clapton, and after all details were locked down, all papers were signed, and all tweaks were made."

The production Clapton Stratocaster was historic, Fender's first artist signature guitar. It featured Gold Lace Sensors, a TBX tone circuit, the midrange boost (variable up to 25dB at about 500Hz), and a blocked, otherwise stock tremolo. While prototype necks had 21 frets, production versions had 22; the 22-fret neck was relatively new for Fender. Dan Smith: "I had suggested the 22-fret neck because its headstock access for truss rod adjustments made it easier for both production and for adjustment out in the field. In addition, these necks had our Biflex truss rod [yet another feature that had premiered on the Elites]; it had proven to be more dependable than the stock truss rod necks. Since this Clapton neck was spec'd out with a 9.5" radius, it could start out in production using the [then] new American Standard Strat neck blank, which made production much easier on the new manufacturing facility."

Lee Dickson also remembers favoring the 22-fret neck and top-end truss rod adjustment: "I was pretty sure that I chose the 'stepped' [extra] fret, having seen it on another neck when at the Custom Shop. I thought Eric might like it, and I can remember asking if we could have the truss rod more instantly accessible, at the top of the neck." Although based to some degree on Blackie, at Clapton's request the new guitar was not offered in a black finish. Black versions would be released later, with Clapton's approval [see The First Production Blackie, Chap. 9].

J. Black: "Many people ask if Eric has special electronics in his personal guitar. No, his guitar has the exact same pickups and preamp that come in all Clapton models. The neck shapes on Eric's own guitars vary from guitar to guitar and builder to builder, but all of them are a medium V shape; some are just a slightly harder V than others.

"Eric must have hit on something when he designed his production guitar with Fender. Other artists have taken aspects of Eric's guitars and made them their own. Jerry Donahue's Telecaster neck was based on Clapton's. The Buddy Guy model has both the electronics and the neck shape. The first guitars I made for Richie Sambora had both the neck shape and the preamp from Eric's guitar."

Fixed specs, changing specs

The guitars John Page and Michael Stevens built or renecked for Eric Clapton in 1988 marked the beginning of a deep and multifaceted association between Clapton and the Custom Shop. The Eric Clapton Stratocaster designed in 1986, unveiled in 1987, tweaked and officially introduced in 1988, and still sold today has always been an R&D/factory model, but the Custom Shop builds Eric's personal guitars, exclusive limited editions, special instruments for charity auctions or other events, and prototypes which, once approved, are then given to the factory for production. Some of these instruments have been up-market guitars with ash bodies, gold hardware, quilted or flame maple tops, abalone markers, matching headstocks, or pearloid

These slotted neck blanks are being marked for Clapton-spec shaping and fretting.

pickguards. Whether offered through the standard Fender catalog or the Custom Shop, all Clapton models since 1988 have been developed in the Custom Shop.

Aside from the usual differences in overall quality and attention to detail, there is one other aspect that distinguishes production and Custom Shop artist models. More than is the case with factory Fenders, the specifications of Custom Shop versions — particularly the Master Builts — are subject to change, reflecting the musician's growth and evolving tastes. On the various Clapton models, one example is the TBX tone circuit. Todd Krause, in 2009: "The Team Built Clapton had the TBX because Eric was using it back when the model was created. The Master Built does not, because Eric is not currently using it. The Team Built guitar's specs don't change. It has the TBX, and a more current neck profile than, say, the factory model. The Master Built is exactly like Eric's current guitar today. It changes as he changes."

In August, 2007, referring to the Crossroads "Sun Strat," Mike Eldred told modernguitars.com's Tom Watson: "Sometimes [Eric] likes a thinner neck; sometimes he likes a bigger neck. So, over the years, the specs on his personal guitars change while the specs on the Eric Clapton Signature model have pretty much stayed the same. The Signature production model is like a snapshot taken at the time he was using that guitar. What we do in the Custom Shop when we make a guitar for him is we tailor it to what he wants at that time. He might order six guitars with a specific neck shape and then a year later order six more and fatten up the neck. The specs of the Sun Strat are what Eric is using right now."

Many years, many guitars

Sometimes dealers or distributors requested limited runs of Clapton guitars with this or that modification, but because any guitar with the Clapton name was subject to Eric's approval, Fender usually tried to avoid such arrangements. There were exceptions, however, particularly in the early 1990s, when the Custom Shop, with Lee Dickson's permission, crafted limited runs of modified Claptons for distributors such as Yamano. In 1991 Eric agreed to allow his signature model to be offered with an optional rosewood fingerboard. However, reportedly only 94 of these short-lived models left the factory, and the option was promptly dropped.

J. Black: "I made a lot of guitars for Eric, not just the things you see in the catalogs. Eric wants a hardtail. Okay, here's a hardtail. Eric doesn't like his [Gibson] Chet Atkins guitar, can you make a classical electric? Sure, I made him a classical electric. He hated it. They sent it back. We're making some guitars with metal bodies — would you like a Blackie with a metal body? Sure, send it out. He hated it. Eric might call and say that he loves the color on some fancy new car he got — could you make me some Strats in this color? We might make a couple, and Eric says, 'That ain't the color,' so we make some more. There was always a lot of stuff going back and forth, and we were learning all the time. It was like that with a bunch of the artists — Jeff Beck, Richie Sambora, the Stones. Sometimes the ideas would come from us, sometimes from the artist."

As noted, Fender's departmental divisions are often ignored in favor of collaboration. J. Black: "The regular Clapton was always the guitar that Dan, George, Mike, and John did in the '80s, but when Clapton wanted some variation, we built it in the shop and then later marketing/R&D might add the new option to the catalog. The shop wasn't a separate institution. It was a moving, flowing process, never in stone. If the neck shaping template was having issues in the factory mill, we would rework it for them in the shop. We worked with the factory people all the time."

Aside from Page, Stevens, and Black, Larry Brooks and Mark Kendrick have also built guitars for Clapton, as has Todd Krause, who's had the longest association with Eric. Some of Eric's better known guitars are exclusively associated with one builder, but as Black explains, "It's hit or miss which guitars he used at any given time by any given builder. Also, Lee sometimes swapped necks with bodies, so you could have a body from one era and a neck from another."

Several of the Custom Shop's Clapton variations are discussed or pictured throughout these pages. Although the production Clapton Strat features unique details and has evolved over the years, it has been described as, basically, a Blackie reissue with new colors as well as a truss rod and updated electronics borrowed from the Elite. That's a reasonable assessment, but it's only the beginning of the story of a signature Fender guitar that's as distinctive as its namesake. Details follow.

Super Glue

On early prototypes, Dan Smith and George Blanda treated the necks with a Super Glue finishing process developed by John Carruthers. Lee Dickson reported in 2008: "The neck was a big problem, to get that just right. Sometimes they would coat the neck with a high viscosity Super Glue called Zap. [Super Glue and Zap are trademarks of Super Glue Corporation/Pacer Technology, which manufactures several cyanoacrylate-based adhesives under both names.] This stuff was so toxic you had to wear a mask and use it in a well-ventilated area. It would seep into every nook and cranny, and when you rubbed down the neck and got it smooth again it really felt like a nice satin finish. The Super Glue treatment would wear off when you were playing it really hard, but some of the prototypes still have it, and the necks look a little dirty almost, because of this experimental treatment."

> "The shop wasn't a separate institution. It was a moving, flowing process. We worked with the factory people all the time." — J. Black

J. Black was told that Eric wanted a woody feel and also a roadworthy guitar. He reports that the Zap process filled the bill. The substance was thin and viscous, it soaked right into the wood, maintained the woody feel, protected the neck, and helped alleviate the sticky feel that can come from playing many outdoor gigs. J. Black: "Eric loved it. Richie Sambora took to it, too. A lot of our early Samboras were just Clapton copies with Floyd Roses. You would take Super Glue and put it on a rag, and you'd have to wipe it on very fast. The rag would actually flash off, practically catch on fire, because it would create some sort of catalytic reaction. You wipe it on the neck very quickly, and then you sand it back almost to the wood, but it leaves a finish and a sealer on the neck, ultra thin. Zap was nasty stuff. It would burn your eyes, burn your lungs. We always did it outside, if possible. Lee actually mastered the technique himself, so if it wore out he could repair it on the road."

Todd Krause came up with a more durable satin urethane finish. By sanding it a certain way, he was able to duplicate the feel while avoiding the toxicity and high maintenance of the Zap process. Ever since the switch, all of Eric's guitars have had the new neck treatment. Lee Dickson: "I trust Todd implicitly, so when he came up with this new technique, I got the guitar right into Eric's hands and he liked it."

The blocked trem

One of the quirkiest details among all Fender artist guitars is the Clapton model's blocked tremolo. A piece of wood, a bit smaller than a matchbox, is wedged between the trem block and the rear edge of the trem cavity, immobilizing the tremolo and stabilizing the combination bridge/tailpiece. What at first appears odd about the makeshift solution is that Fender has offered non-trem Strats, or "hardtails," since the 1950s; Eric Clapton nevertheless wanted the blocked-trem feature. He has tried hardtails, but even though he didn't use the tremolo there's something about the cavity and springs arrangement that he likes. Lee Dickson: "He can tell the difference. It might be a special resonance from the hollow part, or maybe he can feel it vibrating because you hold it close to your body. So we block that trem, and it stays in tune and gives him the sound he's looking for."

Todd Krause explains that when building Eric's personal guitars he uses all five springs and tightens the clamp all the way against the interior cavity's forward wall. He says, "You can feel that thing vibrating and singing just by picking it up."

Pickups

Unlike the original Blackie, neither the factory nor the Custom Shop versions of the Eric Clapton Signature guitar have ever featured conventional single-coil pickups. The prototypes were fitted with stacked single-coil units handmade by Dan Smith and George Blanda using Schaller humbucker bobbins. Production versions debuted with

Lace Sensors. Although somewhat resembling conventional pickups, Lace Sensors were in fact unique designs intended to capture the sound of Fender pickups while eliminating 60-cycle hum. The first Strat to use them was the Strat Plus, which premiered in March 1987. They appeared on Clapton Strats until the summer of 2001, when they were replaced with the stacked-coil Vintage Noiseless pickups Fender had offered since 1998 on its American Deluxe series.

Lee Dickson: "Around the time *Riding with the King* was about to be released [summer 2000], we switched from the Lace Sensors to the Vintage Noiseless pickups [in Eric's personal guitars]. Eric liked those Lace Sensors and there were different versions — gold, silver, red ones and so on with different sounds. I chose a combination and Eric liked the sound, and they worked well with the onboard preamp, but Todd [Krause] called me one day and said they had some new Noiseless single-coils that sounded good and looked more like a real Fender pickup, so we put those in one of the guitars and Eric liked the sound. It was simple as that. He said, if Fender wants to use these [on production models], that's fine."

The onboard preamp

An irony of the Clapton Stratocaster is that some of the essential features of this wildly successful guitar were borrowed from a previous model that was something of a commercial flop. When Bill Schultz and his associates bought back the company, among the few guitars left in the warehouse were some Strat Elites. These active-circuit models featured many innovations, including an

In 2008, the Custom Shop built 100 examples of the 10th Anniversary of Crossroads Antigua Stratocaster, one of several variations on the Clapton model. See Chap. 30.

The Custom Shop version of the Clapton Strat appeared in 2004 (Chap. 26). The variation shown here, the LTD Eric Clapton Signature Stratocaster, was offered only during 2010, in EC Grey or Daphne Blue.

onboard preamp that boosted the midrange about 6dB and softened the high end. The idea was to make a single-coil pickup sound more like a humbucker — more specifically, to make a Strat sound more like an ES-335 or a Les Paul. Produced in 1983 and 1984, the Elites failed in the marketplace mainly due to their Freeflyte tremolo units, but many players thought the onboard boost was a practical idea.

Lee Dickson: "I absolutely loved those Elites. Tonally, they were just phenomenal sounding. They were among the first active guitars. Fender had bad luck with them. People would complain that they died on stage. Well, you have to change the batteries! But people weren't used to that in those days so those guitars kind of faded out. We adopted the boost idea for the Clapton guitar. When we first started, I think the boost got up to 12dB or so, but it just wasn't enough. It didn't do what Eric was looking for, so we went back and forth many times and gradually got it sorted out. It became a 25dB boost over any pickup combination."

Bruce Bolen recalls that Fender was also tasked with modifying Clapton's relatively modest pedalboard to interface with the in-the-works signature Strat: "On some of those original models the amount of boost in that midrange control was horrendous. You threw that thing into active mode and it was like King Kong [laughs]. Lee came over from England and brought Eric's pedalboard. We were working in Brea at the time. Eric wanted us to modify the board to suit the guitar. We modified [the gain on the guitar] a few times and came up with something that Eric liked and that also worked for the pedals."

The unit is an active, preamp-driven circuit described by Fender as a midrange boost, but because of its sonic effect Eric typically refers to it as an overdrive, distortion, or compressor. Lee Dickson: "Eric always plays with his tone knob all the way up, and sometimes when he's soloing, particularly if the band is really cranking, he just wants a little more, just a bit of a boost to take the sound to the next level, and that's where the idea came from. Eric plays in the neck position most of the time. It really depends on the gig and what he's feeling at the moment. Sometimes the band is just in another world, on its own level, with extra energy. If they are driving hard, sometimes I'll hear Eric dial in that boost. Sometimes he'll play the first part of a solo without it, and then dial it in for the second part. It doesn't do much in the way of volume, but that midrange boost is nice."

The extra switch

The Clapton model was initially intended to have an extra switch that would disable the preamp, converting the circuit from active to passive in case the battery failed during a performance. This version appeared in an ad that was viewed by Clapton or Dickson, and the word came back from the UK: Lose the switch. Bruce Bolen: "Dan Smith's philosophy was, if your battery goes south in the middle of a show, you're stuck, but if you could switch over to passive, you'd be OK. George Blanda came up with the active/passive switch, but Eric wanted the guitar to be active all the time, so we dropped the idea."

No one at Fender can say for sure how many Claptons were made with the active/passive switch, although one showed up at the 1999 Christie's auction. It was one of the rare 1987 prototypes, serial no. V025603, with Lace Sensors and a 7Up Green Metallic finish. It sold for $55,000.

TBX

Factory Clapton Strats have always featured the TBX tone circuit. Like the midrange boost, it was first offered on the Strat Elite of 1983 and 1984. As Dan Smith explained in *The Stratocaster Chronicles*: "'TBX' stood for 'Treble Bass Xpander,' one of those marketing names. It's a stacked control — two pots with one knob on top. . . . At the midpoint — the 5 setting — it was equivalent to a normal control set all the way up, on 10. When you rolled the TBX back toward zero it worked just like a regular tone control except with a short range. When you went back up to 10, it was the equivalent of removing the control altogether from the circuit, and it let a lot more high end through."

The shop's Team Built Clapton Strats have the TBX. At Eric's request, neither his personal guitars nor the Master Built Eric Clapton Strat has it. Instead, along with the master volume and boost knob, they have a standard, passive tone control, which Eric usually or always leaves on 10.

Forever man

George Blanda: "Clapton has always been great, of course, but he was reemerging at the time we started to work with him, and his career was really taking off. It was so great for us to be associated with him. Fender was struggling to reestablish our credibility. There were bad feelings towards our quality because of a lot of the Fenders built during the late '70s, plus there were some really good boutique builders competing with us in the mid '80s and also a lot of high-quality Japanese instruments, so we really had a tough struggle. Clapton was a huge help when he went public with his endorsement."

J. Black: "No one has ever had a relationship with Fender like Eric Clapton's. If any other artist had a problem, it was a thing between the builder and the artist, or the artist's tech. If Eric Clapton had a problem, Bill Schultz knew about it. Bill Mendello knew about it. It percolated through upper management."

Dan Smith: "One thing that Bill Schultz had was integrity. We made some mistakes, but we always kept our integrity. If you worked for Bill, you never lied. If he had a question and you didn't know the answer, you just said you didn't know and you went out and got it. And he surrounded himself with those kinds of people. So our personal integrity and our boss's integrity and the company's integrity were all on the line. Artists felt that, and that is how we got our artists back. Eric Clapton in particular — his involvement was huge."

The most ambitious of the shop's Clapton endeavors was the meticulously reliced Blackie Tribute of 2006 (Chap. 28). Senior Master Builder Todd Krause, shown here inspecting a finished piece, spearheaded the project.

It's in the way that you use it

Lee Dickson reflects on Eric Clapton's long association with the Custom Shop

I get asked a million times, *hey guitar guy, what kind of distortion does Eric use, man, what kind of fuzz?* And I say, 'Nothing, it's just him.' It's in his hands. Occasionally he might have a wah-wah in the signal chain. The other thing is a Leslie ["rotating" speaker]. He's got a control for that. If it's a small club and the Leslie can't fit in, I might put in a chorus if he's going to do "Wonderful Tonight" or "Badge," but the sound is in his hands and the guitar and the amp. That's the way they used to do it, and that's the way Eric still does it. It's like Jeff Beck — you can buy the guitars and the amps and the boxes but you're never going to sound like Jeff Beck. It's the same with an artist like Eric. You have to remember how much of it is in the hands, the fingers, the touch. There's no overdrive in the line, no distortion, no gain switch — you just crank the amp and do it with your hands.

You never know what Eric is going to do, and that's a great thing. He may use the wah-wah on a solo where he's never used it before. Even at this stage of the game, he's still out there playing by the seat of his pants, just feeling it. It's fantastic. To this day I marvel at how lucky I am to be able to work with an artist who still freaks me out every time he goes out onstage. His artistry is mind-blowing to me, even after all these years.

It was enlightening and amazing to go out to the Custom Shop for a few weeks to work alongside guys like John Page, J. Black, Fred Stuart, Alan Hamel, Larry Brooks, the late John English – wonderful guy – Mark Kendrick, Todd Krause, a wonderful guy called Art Esparza, all these great guys. There was John Cruz and a great fellow named George Amicay, who's a master engraver. They're absolutely superb builders and artisans, and I was so lucky to be in the same room as those guys to learn about necks and how the guitars are detailed and put together. They'd sit me down and let me work with 20 different truss rods. I learned how to finish necks, how to refret necks, all sorts of things.

I could not have been in a better place. Before that experience I don't think I could've told a difference of two thousandths of an inch, but John Page would sit me in his office and hand me a guitar and say, "Close your eyes and try this one." And I'd get it.

I don't really have to do anything to the guitars. We get them from Fender, and once I set them up to Eric's preferences they're ready to go, but one thing I've noticed: Eric's had a long relationship with Fender, and many people have built these guitars over the years. They may have the same specs, but they are not stamped out on a mass-production line. The people who build them are highly skilled craftspeople, and they put themselves into each instrument. I was reminded of that when I got all these guitars together to prepare them for the two Christie's auctions [in 1999 and 2004, benefiting the Crossroads Centre in Antigua, a drug and alcohol rehab facility established by Eric Clapton]. We started with Dan, George Blanda, and John Carruthers and then went to John Page and Mike Stevens. J. Black made some and the great Larry Brooks made some. Larry had terrible problems with his hands and so we went to Mark Kendrick, and then Todd Krause has been making them for the last few years.

So I pick up all these guitars and begin to notice very subtle differences. Each one was ever so slightly different, reflecting the interpretation of each craftsman. A general member of the public might not have felt it, but if you're attuned to it, there's a difference. I would imagine the ones they're doing now are more consistent in those tiny details. They have computer programs with very exacting standards. But even then, there's always the human element in everything the Custom Shop does.

In 1996, Mark Kendrick custom built a gold leaf Strat for Eric Clapton to commemorate Fender's 50th anniversary. The gilt finish, applied by George Amicay, had the soft luminescence of a pre-Renaissance painting. Memories vary as to who came up with the concept, and also regarding whether Eric wanted a "flashy" look or an "Old World" look. In any case, as Lee Dickson points out, "The 50th anniversary is the golden one, so a gold guitar made sense, but Eric said to me — 'Not gold paint, though. Gold leaf!'"

John Page recalls, "At the time I was doing some art pieces at home in gold leaf, so it was fresh in my mind. I attempted the first body myself, but I was too impatient with the application of the sizing — the adhesive used to attach the leaf — and I also used an incorrect brush. After my initial attempt I passed it onto George Amicay to perfect the process, which he did."

Mark Kendrick: "The neck plate refers to the 50th Anniversary and has the serial number EC1, which Lee requested on Eric's behalf. Originally, the guitar had all gold hardware, including the pickguard. When first delivered, Eric strapped it on and said that it looked 'army.' He had Lee swap out the pickguard to a white one the following day."

Lee Dickson: "It was a superb guitar and looked awesome. Opinion became divided after a while, into a love/hate thing with the fans, as some thought it too flashy and others found it to be a thing of great beauty because of the way it was done and the fact that it didn't have the uniformity of a solid color. It was always one of my faves." The guitar was later sold by Christie's auction house for a reported $455,000. In 2004 the shop issued a limited run of 50 similar models.

40

FORTIETH ANNIVERSARY TELECASTER

CHAPTER SIX

6

The Great Leap Forward

Spec Guitars and Big Numbers

The 40th Anniversary Telecaster

Filling those custom option orders for 20 or 30 instruments at a time was a step in the right direction, but a few months into the shop's second year, Fender marketing was thinking bigger — much bigger. What if the Custom Shop could produce *hundreds* of examples of a single, unique design? Such an enterprise, if successful, would entail previously unheard-of production efficiencies and might go a long way toward turning around the shop's financial fortunes.

Marketing decided that some sort of Anniversary Telecaster would serve several functions. It would memorialize Fender's first electric Spanish guitar, which in turn would commemorate the history of the company itself. It would also showcase the shop's high level of craft. Finally, it would slot Fender into the high-end market occupied by Gibson's priciest guitars as well as those from relative newcomers such as Tom Anderson and Paul Reed Smith.

Swanky twang: 1988's flame-top 40th Anniversary Tele was not only an elegant re-imagining of Leo Fender's first guitar but also a milestone in the shop's evolving mission and identity. These beautiful examples were finished in Honey Violin Transparent.

Everyone thought that the Telecaster had been introduced in 1948, and everyone was wrong. Mr. Fender himself, along with other principals from the early days, had repeatedly cited 1948 as the birth date of the Tele, or more specifically its short-lived predecessors, the first-generation Esquire and the Broadcaster. Fender even went so far as to picture a "1948" Broadcaster in full-page advertisements. Richard Smith corrected the record in his early *Guitar Player* magazine columns after reviewing original documents that revealed that while prototypes were indeed in the works in '48 the date of the guitar's commercial introduction was actually 1950. But back in the early days of the Custom Shop Fender still relied on the 1948 date, so in 1988 the timing seemed ideal for a 40th Anniversary Telecaster.

Mike Stevens, John Page, and Dan Smith collaborated on the design of a guitar that despite the "anniversary" moniker wasn't any sort of reissue. Instead, they started with an American Standard platform, which simplified production. The new Custom Shop guitar was introduced in June 1988, and it was a stunner, with an ash body bound in celluloid, a bookmatched flame maple top, a curly maple neck with abalone dot markers, pearloid tuner buttons, a grained ivoroid pickguard, and gold-plated hardware. The available finishes were an "Antique" two-color sunburst, natural, and transparent red, each highlighting the dramatically figured maple top.

The Custom Shop crafted 300 of these dazzlers, each individually serial numbered on the back of the peghead (for example, 064 of 300) and accompanied by a Certificate of Authenticity signed by John Page. The craftsmen who worked on them typically wrote their names or initials in the pickup cavity, further personalizing each piece.

By Fender factory standards the 40th Anniversary Telecaster was a modest project, but for the Custom Shop it was epic. Even before construction commenced, simply sourcing high-quality woods in such quantities presented challenges of a magnitude never before faced by the tiny crew. John Page recalls, "Fender announced that we would be making hundreds of these things, and we all thought, wow, *how are we supposed to pull this off?* There were only about a half-dozen of us when we started, although other guys joined during the process." The first guitar was presented to Bill Schultz, who by all accounts was delighted. Although the project was more extensive than anything the shop's builders had previously attempted (or probably even imagined), all 300 instruments sold out quicker than Monkees tickets at a mid-'60s all-girls middle school.

Another milestone: While previous orders came from customers, distributors, or retailers and were therefore guaranteed sales, the order for the 40th Anniversary Tele came from Fender marketing with no guarantees at all. Unlike marketing's previous orders for one or two demo guitars or prototypes, the gold-hardware *über*-Tele was a high-stakes gamble. In house, Fender called it a "spec" guitar; the "speculation" was, we think this is so cool that enough people will want one to make substantial production profitable.

The gamble paid off handsomely. The success of the fanciest guitar Fender had ever produced in quantity hinted at exciting new directions not only for the shop but for the whole company. Fender began to reconsider the Custom Shop's mission, potential, and very identity.

Homer's odyssey: The HLE Strat

After the exhilarating success of the 40th Anniversary Telecaster, Fender wanted to capitalize on the momentum with the release of another Custom Shop guitar, this time in even greater quantities. Bruce Bolen knew guitarist Homer Haynes, who had been partnered with mandolinist Jethro Burns in the country comedy duo Homer and Jethro. During the 1940s, 1950s, and 1960s they were best known for their deadpan, knee-slapper parodies of pop songs and satirical sketches on radio and TV, but both were also sophisticated jazz musicians influenced by Django Reinhardt. "I got to know Homer when I was a freshman in high school," Bolen recalls. "I studied with him. He was a mentor, the one who got me into this business. Without a doubt, he was the finest rhythm player on earth. Guys are still trying to figure out how he did what he did."

Leo Fender had built two Stratocasters for Homer in 1957, a blue one and a gold one, both with gold hardware. They were later acquired from one of Homer's sons by Tom Barnhart, one of Bolen's close friends. The blue Strat wound up in David Gilmour's collection and is pictured in the book *American Guitars*. The gold one became the inspiration for the Custom Shop's

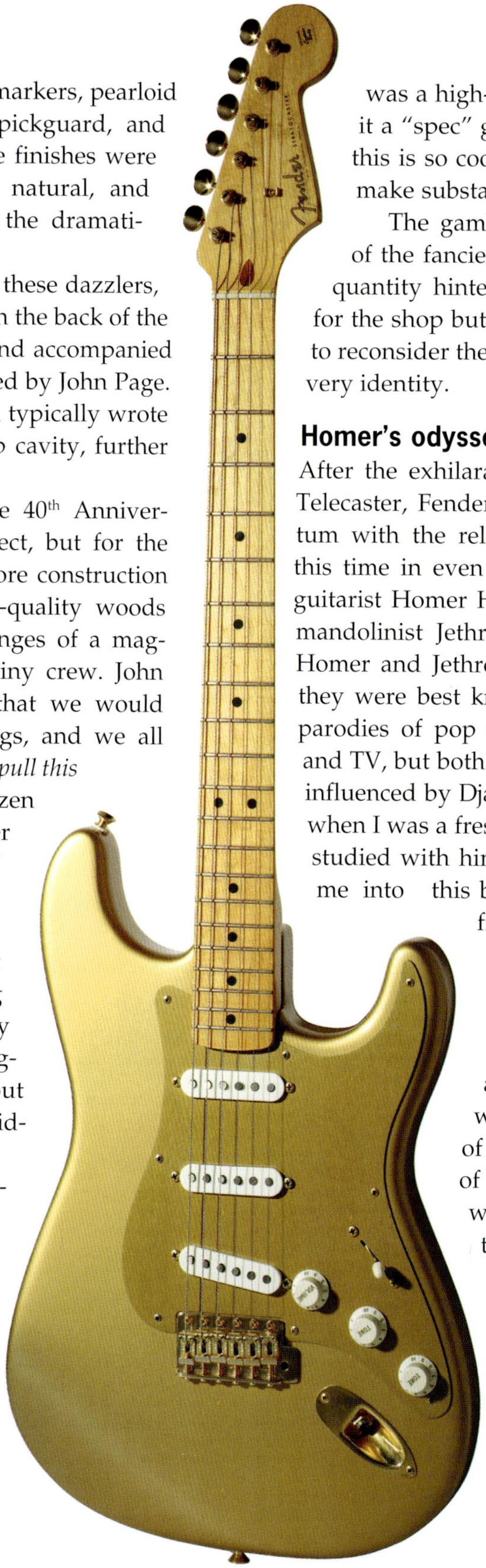

In a project initiated by Bruce Bolen, the shop paid tribute to Homer Haynes with a 500-piece run of the gold-on-gold HLE Stratocaster.

Apprentice Brett Faust was reassigned from the factory to the Kubicki project and worked in the Custom Shop from late 1988 through October, 1991. Here he's assembling an HLE Strat.

HLE Stratocaster. Bruce Bolen: "I had played Homer's guitar as a kid and thought it would be a good thing for the Custom Shop to do in quantity, something that would give us a lot of bang for the buck, where instead of doing one guitar, we could do a whole series, and these instruments would have a musical purpose but be unusual and very special. It was a time when the shop didn't have any big orders to speak of.

"I called Tom and he sent it to me. It was a tri-gold guitar — gold machine heads, a brass-anodized pickguard, and a gold finish. I took it to the shop and said I wanted to do five hundred of these things, and they thought I was out of my mind. But the fact is, we needed bigger orders to support the shop. HLE stood for Haynes Limited Edition, or Homer Limited Edition, but only in-house. Nobody outside the company really knew what the HLE initials meant, not at first; it was just something that warmed the cockles of my heart, a little silent tribute to my mentor."

Built in the shop's "phase two" facility in Fender's fourth Pomona Road building, the 500-guitar HLE series marked another milestone. The 40th Anniversary Tele's entire run of 300 pieces had sold out so quickly that some dealers were miffed because they couldn't get their hands on one — one reason why the order for the HLEs was even bigger. Bruce Bolen: "The HLE was the first bulk order of that size ever created for the Custom Shop, a very desirable guitar, and it kind of put a flame to the shop. I think a good chunk of them went to Yamano, and overall they sold very well. Once we did that Homer model, things got rolling. The shop kicked off after that."

Mike Lewis would one day assume several duties as a key executive at Fender, but back in the late '80s he was a retailer. He remembers, "From the earliest days of the Custom Shop, even back when I was a dealer, they would spec out some guitars themselves and build quantities of them. I had one of those HLEs. I had number 007. When that came in, I thought, *I gotta have this,* with the whole James Bond/Goldfinger thing. I subsequently sold it and kick myself to this day, because it was one of the finest Stratocasters I ever played."

Fred Stuart thinks the HLE project of 1989 might have been premature, too big for the shop's resources at the time. On the other hand, he allows that its magnitude encouraged Fender to once again rethink the shop's mission. The success of the earlier Anniversary Tele was apparently no fluke. After shipping the HLEs — or "Homer golds," as they were sometimes called in-house — Fender considered expanding the Custom Shop with a new urgency.

The shop brought back the HLE Gold finish for 2009's Limited Collection 1950s Telecaster Thinline Relic.

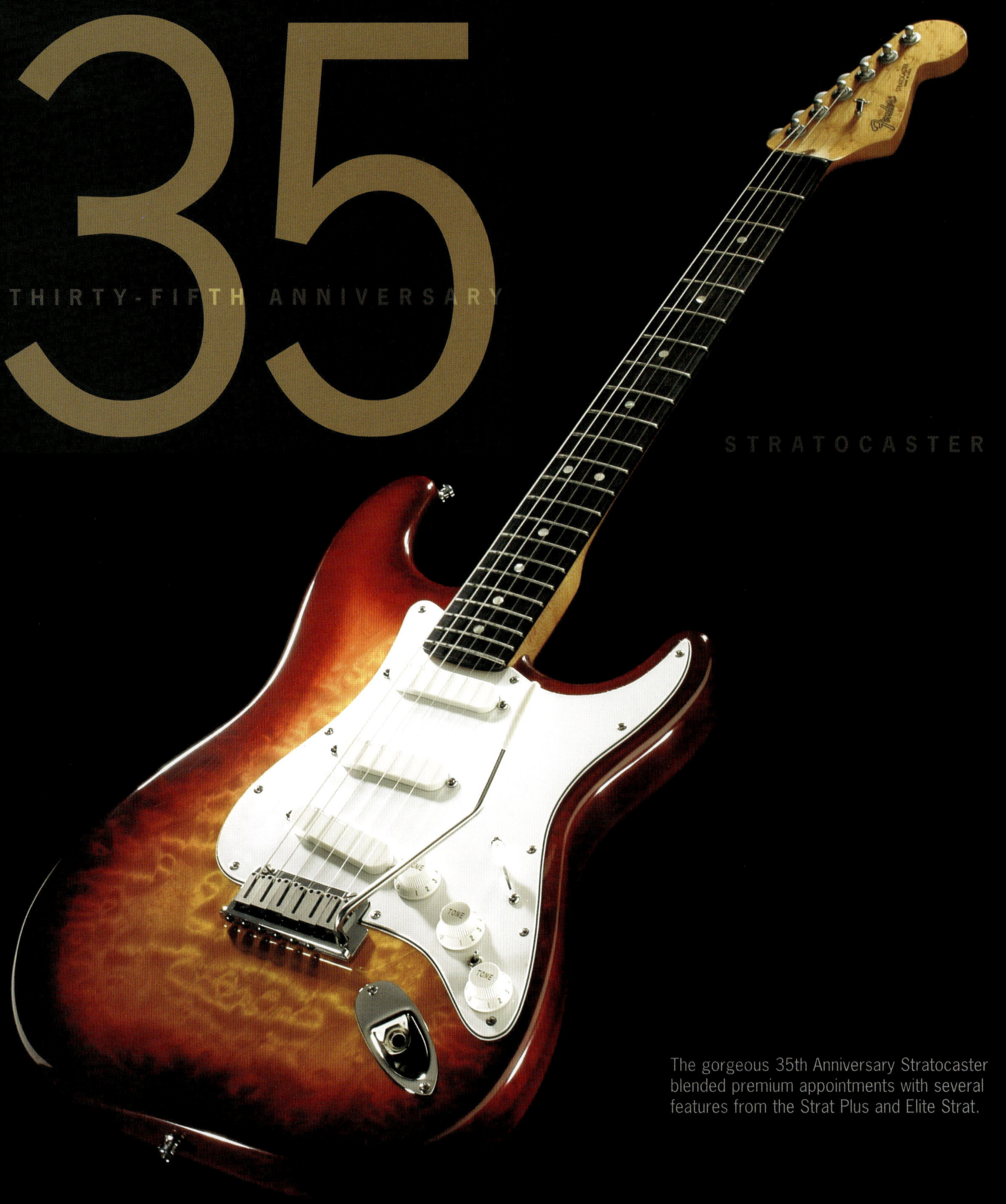

The gorgeous 35th Anniversary Stratocaster blended premium appointments with several features from the Strat Plus and Elite Strat.

The 35th Anniversary Stratocaster

The year 1987 had seen significant developments at Fender, including the founding of the Custom Shop, the unveiling of Lace Sensors, and the debut of the Strat Plus, the factory's new, top-of-the-line Stratocaster. Now it was 1989, 35 years after the Stratocaster's 1954 debut, and given the success of the 40th Anniversary Tele, some sort of anniversary Strat seemed appropriate, perhaps inevitable.

While the Custom Shop builders had maximized production efficiency by basing the 40th Anniversary Tele on the American Standard platform, they patterned the new Stratocaster to some extent after the Strat Plus, which in turn had evolved from a guitar initially intended for Jeff Beck (Beck's signature model would be announced in January 1990, although production was delayed for the better part of a year).

From the Strat Plus the Custom Shop builders borrowed Lace Sensors, locking tuners, and a roller nut designed by Trev Wilkinson. From the late-CBS-era Elite Strat they borrowed the TBX electronic system and the active midrange boost that was also used in one form or another in the Clapton Strat and the USA Richie Sambora Strat. (On the 35th Anniversary model, the mini toggle switch between knobs 2 and 3 bypassed the active electronics; as noted elsewhere, Dan Smith originally intended for the Clapton model to have a similar feature, but Clapton vetoed the idea.) The Anniversary Strat's two-point floating trem dated back to the American Standard.

These functional features were combined with high-grade woods and appointments befitting a Custom Shop tribute to the venerable Stratocaster's 35th birthday. The guitar's 22-fret bird's-eye maple neck was fitted with a fingerboard of ebony (an unusual wood for Fender) with abalone dots. Its stunning figured maple top was somewhat thick because the shop had not yet developed a top-bending capability. A touch of extra elegance was lent by the Lace Sensors' unperforated covers, which turned the pickguard area into a vast expanse of white that was set off against the sunburst finish.

From 1989 to 1991, the shop built 500 35th Anniversary Stratocasters, each individually serial numbered and accompanied by a Certificate of Authenticity. Another of the many examples of the interaction between R&D, the factory, and the Custom Shop: The 35th Anniversary Strat had borrowed from the Elite, the American Standard, and the Plus models, and it would go on to serve to a significant extent as the basis for the factory's Strat Ultra, introduced in 1991.

A lateral move for Bruce Bolen

During the shop's transition in day-to-day management from Michael Stevens to John Page, and soon after production of the HLEs, President Bill Schultz assigned new duties to Bruce Bolen, who relinquished supervision of the Custom Shop. Frankly, he was relieved to have one less responsibility on his plate.

He remembers, "Bill put me in charge of sales, and that lasted for a very short period. Then he made me VP in charge of all the marketing. I wasn't involved with the shop all that long, maybe a year, just enough to get it going. John Page took it over and went from there. It got off to kind of an awkward start, but it got some momentum and the next thing you know they're back-ordered. That's when the pressure *really* got put on. We were very proud of what we were able to accomplish, and I was just tickled pink that we could go from the ragamuffin little concept to what the Custom Shop became. I was happy to be able to play my small part in the early days. Dan Smith should also feel very proud, because he was a hundred percent behind it."

The first big shift

J. Black came on board in June of '89. He sees the evolution from one-offs and a few limited runs to large-scale projects such as the Anniversary Teles, HLE Strats, and Anniversary Strats as "the first big shift, not only in how the Custom Shop operated but also how it was perceived by Fender." He elaborates: "The difference between 1987 and 1989 was significant. There were so many things going on when I arrived. The 35th Anniversary Strat was on the drawing board and about to start production. It was a huge leap from one-offs and occasional limited runs to these much larger runs like the Anniversary Tele and the HLE in the late '80s and early '90s. The change was astronomical, and it was already in full swing when I got there in the summer of '89. The one-offs were important, but the limited runs were the bread and butter of the Custom Shop."

Public reaction to the Anniversary Tele, Anniversary Strat, and Homer Strat brings to mind the old saying "success breeds success." If the Custom Shop could sell 300 flame-top Teles, 500 triple-gold HLEs, and 500 flame-top Strats, why not repeat the formula with other guitars? Fred Stuart: "Projects like the Homer Haynes Strats were a big motivation and impetus for expanding the shop." This self-stoking cycle of success/expansion/success would characterize the Custom Shop for years to come. In Winter 1990, Fender reported that the Custom Shop had 25 employees, including six Master Builders. All would have their hands full in the coming months.

The shop's original oval logo was sketched by Michael Stevens.

Custom Shop logos

For the first year or so, Custom Shop guitars bore one of two decals on the back of the peghead. Although the term "Master Builder" had not yet been coined, Fender wanted a special mark for instruments associated with individual craftsmen. These guitars had a "CUSTOM-BUILT FENDER U.S.A." decal that included the maker's signature. Other guitars carried a decal with a Strat headstock outline and the words "CUSTOM SHOP FENDER U.S.A." Michael Stevens recalls: "They had the signature logo concept happening and laid out — just needing a signature. Dan Smith had me sit down with a young lady, a company artist, and sign my name a bunch of times soon after I arrived. I wrote a bunch of them and gave them to this girl and came back a day later and they had the artwork. Then people said, 'What are we going to put on everything else?' I drew the oval with the Strat peghead on some paper and said, 'How about this?' and off she went. The next time I saw it, we had a stack of them."

The oval logo was simple and elegant, but there was a problem. Bill Schultz had allowed Fender Japan to use an oval symbol on some models. John Page was not amused: "It looked just like our Custom Shop decal. I was worried about confusion in the market, about rumors that we were being made in Japan." Page had already commissioned Pamelina H. to design a different logo for the shirts he had ordered for the crew. That design, with the now-familiar V, was copyrighted in 1989 and soon migrated from the clothing to the instruments.

"I had this funky little pink Chevrolet key rack that hung above my desk," Page explains. "It had the classic V8 emblem on the trunk, and the Chevrolet logo was in chrome script. Electric guitars and the auto industry have had a relationship since the beginning, probably because of the whole rock and roll/hoodlum kind of vibe. I just thought the idea of the Custom Shop fell nicely into a car logo. Plus, part of our job was to reinvigorate the Fender image with the shop. I wanted to do that initially by distancing ourselves from Fender a bit, to boost the image of the shop and have that trickle down into the factory image. That's why I used the Fender 'F' as an identifier, as opposed to the word 'Fender.' I hoped the shop would become its own brand, not because we didn't want to be a part of Fender — I mean, it was the recognizable Fender 'F' — but aside from clarifying that we were *not* made in Japan we were trying to raise Fender up with our own special thing. Anyway, Bill got pissed at it, and [by the late '90s] they merged the V logo with the word 'Fender' instead of the 'F.'"

Pamelina H. remembers that after initial discussions with John Page she began examining old cars in her neighborhood, specifically their chrome nameplates. She wanted a vintage look, but with a modern twist — a "Miami Vice" vibe, as she described it. Her design, as approved by John Page, is entering its third decade as we go to press, having become an icon in its own right. On occasion, Fender will modify the decal — adding "LIMITED EDITION," for example — to distinguish a particular run or series.

Resting at left on John Page's desk is the shop's new logo, designed by Pamelina H. and copyrighted in 1989. Look closely, and you'll see that it's leaning against a wall-mounted key holder modeled after a '57 Chevy's tailfins; that little piece of pink plastic was Page's inspiration for the new design.

"Getting your own decal" signifies a milestone in the career of a Fender Custom Shop craftsperson.

The Kubicki Factor

Former R&D employee Phil Kubicki left Fender in 1971, moved to the California coastal town of Santa Barbara, and started building innovative basses under his own name. Developed over two years and first sold in 1985, the Kubicki Factors were widely considered to be among the most innovative and ergonomically correct basses in the world. Some featured a peghead-mounted lever that lowered the E string to D.

Fender had introduced the electric bass in late 1951 and for more than three decades enjoyed the reputation of being its dominant manufacturer. But times were changing, "boutique" designs were turning heads in the bass world, and the company felt compelled to augment its decades-old Precision and Jazz Basses with fresh designs. Phil Kubicki remembers, "Dan Smith suggested I design a bass for them, but the more we talked, the more it seemed like a good idea for Fender to actually manufacture the basses I had already designed."

In 1988, several Custom Shop employees, among them John Page, Art Esparza, and Fred Stuart, visited Kubicki Manufacturing in Santa Barbara. Some of the Fender folks stayed for several months, observing processes, learning Kubicki's techniques, and building the earliest Fender/Kubicki basses under Phil's watchful eye. Art Esparza: "I went up there first, got a house about a block from the beach, and rode my bike to Kubicki's place every day. It was a great experience. I studied with him for months or maybe almost a year. I learned a lot, a highlight of my years at Fender." Phil Kubicki: "From January 27, 1988 through January 26, 1989, per our Licensing Agreement, we were in the 'Technology Manufacturing Period,' and the instruments were made in Santa Barbara at our facility. Art and Fred came to the Kubicki facility during the beginning of the licensing agreement phase. The basses were produced there for about a year as the Fender production line was being set up. Then, tooling and machines were loaned and shipped to Fender."

Starting in February 1989, and for nearly two years thereafter, Fender built Kubicki basses in a suite set aside for that purpose in the Pomona Road facility's fourth building. Models included the Factor 4, the Factor 4/fretless, the EX Factor 4 extended bass, and the EX Factor 4 extended bass/fretless. According to Phil Kubicki, the Fender/Kubickis are serial numbered from 1287 to 3049.

The Kubicki basses were intended to compete with expensive boutique models. Dan Smith: "Fender could not just 'be Fender' and expect to survive. I firmly believe that Fender would have died off a long time ago if it continued to only offer its core models in their original state."

When J. Black arrived in the summer of 1989, the Kubicki project was the shop's top priority. Given the nature of the market, however, he had reservations about it: "We were supposed to produce 140 or 150 of these very high-end basses every month, which I thought was ridiculous. Tobias was probably making 25 a month. Pedulla was making about 30 or whatever it was. And we're supposed to sell 150 Kubickis at a high-end price point. I think it was a failure only because it had unrealistic expectations from the beginning. That's just my opinion." John Page: "We started out with low production numbers, with a mission to ramp up to 250 a month, as I recall. We got up to about 125 a month and then the warehouse started backing up with them."

Dan Smith: "These [projections] didn't come out of thin air. They were based on the demand for those instruments while Phil was making them himself. He couldn't keep up. Kubicki basses were a hot item, played by a number of top bassists, including Stu Hamm, who was *the* bassist at the time. All indications led us to believe that the numbers were sustainable. What killed it more than anything was that we hadn't been realistic in how long it would take for us to start manufacturing the basses ourselves. This would lead to disagreements over distribution. Sadly, that put an end to the relationship."

The whole point of the Kubicki project was to allow Fender to do something different, but in the minds of some employees, the modernist basses with the body-mounted tuners and active electronics were *too* different. Ralph Esposito remembers: "The amount Fender needed for us to ship was far beyond our means and resources, so it was a losing battle. Speaking candidly, there was a struggle with part of our sales team because some of the old timers really didn't care about the new stuff. A Kubicki didn't look like a Precision, so some of these guys just couldn't get behind it, didn't want to deal with it. Some of the reps preferred to keep their bread-and-butter Fender stuff going."

Dan Smith: "Here's the reality: You can't stagnate. If you want to stay in business, you have to grow. Fender could not just 'be Fender' and expect to survive. History has a bad habit of repeating itself, and there were plenty of times in Fender's history when it was not the in-demand brand. That was the whole thing behind trying to sell instruments that stepped outside our image. But, most often the first line of resistance came from the die-hard Fender people, whether it be our own employees, dealers, or customers. Why should we compete against the boutique guys and other manufacturers? Because that's the business. Don't grow, and eventually our employees don't get paychecks, and our dealers and customers don't get new Fender products. It's that simple. I firmly believe that Fender would have died off a long time ago if it continued to only offer its core models in their original state."

There were production problems as well. Before joining the Custom Shop crew, Alex Perez worked in Fender's Customer Service Department. He recalls, "We got a lot of those Kubickis back. They had some inherent quirks and some problems with these little wheels on the bridge for the tuning. Also, the electronics were always a nightmare. There were no problems in how they were being built; it was just a design issue. I think those basses were probably ahead of their time. And some of the things that we needed in order to make the bass the way it was designed just weren't available."

Although Fender abandoned the Kubicki effort by March 1991, J. Black sees the experience as beneficial: "The Custom Shop gained advantages in tooling and technology it never would have gained had it not been for Kubicki. You could say that it failed for Fender corporate, but it was a success for the Custom Shop because it brought in new people like Ralph Esposito and Art Esparza. It kicked Fred Stuart to a higher level of responsibilities. Scott Grant, who had been a tune tester, got a new position as lead on the floor, which was a good thing. Jason Davis and Dave Nichols were brought in to work on the necks, Steve Boulanger to do the tooling. We had this huge influx of new staff. I think the HLE project had had a lot of support from manufacturing, using factory parts and so on, but with Kubicki the Custom Shop was pretty much on our own. John [Page] took on a lot of new responsibility and pressure with these higher production numbers. The shop grew in a hurry."

To build the Kubickis, the shop acquired NC (numeric controlled) machines. At the beginning, some of the bodies were imported from Japan, but once the NCs were up and running all of the bodies were made in the shop. Fender had NCs over in manufacturing, but the shop wasn't using them much except on special runs. Now that it had its own

At an early trade show exhibit, John Page gets a visit from Albert Lee, who's holding a rare, Thinline "Page-o-Caster." *Guitar Player* magazine retired Albert from the Best Country Guitarist category in its annual readers poll after he won it five times in a row. Eric Clapton recorded and toured with Albert and has been reported as calling him the best guitarist in the world.

Larry Brooks works on a pin router at far left; we can see pin router templates for several instruments on the wall. At far right: a stack of Kubicki bodies.

machines, the Custom Shop could use them from then on for all sorts of projects. In terms of the shop's production capacity, Kubicki was a breakthrough.

Ralph Esposito reported in 2008: "That NC machine we got to do the Kubickis is still around. Kubicki was definitely a good thing for the Custom Shop because it gave us notoriety, especially with the bass players. Stu Hamm played one, and he was very prominent, and that really helped Fender. We really started a new thing. It seemed that everyone started to have a Custom Shop, and not just in guitars. Even in the motorcycle industry and elsewhere, the whole custom shop idea started up. We were the only company doing this kind of thing on that kind of level. We were blazing our own trail, and it was a heyday for us in all respects."

The Kubicki basses represented Fender's first major production of domestic instruments that aside from the oval Custom Shop emblem on the back of the peghead carried no Fender logos. (In this regard they were similar to the LJ models, which bore a Stevens brand; however, only a few dozen LJs were produced; p. 145.) From one perspective, this signaled a new direction for a company that would in the coming years distribute or manufacture professional-level guitars under many banners — Guild, Gretsch, Jackson, Charvel, Taylor, Ovation, Takamine, Tacoma, Hamer, and others. On the other hand, the Kubicki project was viewed at the time as more of a transitional step than any sort of milestone. Once Fender had introduced good quality reissues of its venerable Precision and Jazz Basses, along with new models sporting contemporary features, there was little need to bring other brands of basses in house.

As we will see, guitars were a different story.

While the Kubicki experiment was a failure in some respects, it brought in several new employees and vaulted the shop into a higher level of production capacity and tooling. This machine was set up to slot the Kubicki necks and eventually was used in regular Custom Shop production.

John English at work on a triple-pickup, bound-top Thinline Tele. At right: a similar instrument, ready to ship.

"Here's the reality: You can't stagnate. If you want to stay in business, you have to grow."

– Dan Smith

Inheriting a formidable legacy, the first generation of Master Builders could only dream of a comprehensive line of Custom Shop guitars like this 2010 collection — authentic recreations of the Telecaster and its ancestors. From left: The "snake-head" Tele prototype, single and double-pickup pine-body Esquires, Broadcaster, Nocaster, and Telecaster.

CHAPTER SEVEN

7

Vintage Rising

"The more we refined our Custom Shop product, the more we looked back to the vintage era."

Looking back

When Bill Schultz delivered his charge to Michael Stevens and John Page — "I want to be able to build these artists *exactly* what they want" — we can only speculate as to whether he might have envisioned Fender designs with modern, high-tech refinements. But from the inception of the Custom Shop, many of the clients didn't want high-tech guitars with alien-mothership arrays of gadgets and gizmos. They didn't want tomorrow's guitars, or today's. They wanted yesterday's. They wanted once-stock models that Fender hadn't built for decades — butterscotch, black-guard Teles, blonde Strats with ash bodies and gold hardware, Fiesta Red Precision Basses with anodized pickguards, and other icons from the vintage era.

Okay, so . . . no problem, right? After all, we're Fender. Those vintage guitars and basses were made right here in Southern California. Some of the craftspeople who built them still work here. There must be blueprints and schematics lying around, so let's just build guitars the way we used to. How hard can it be?

Fiendishly difficult, as it turned out. For one thing, Fender had to play catch-up to its archrival. J. Black: "In those early days, it was all about Gibson. I'd go to these vintage shows where they'd have some Custom Shop stuff alongside the vintage guitars, and these well-financed Japanese guys who were representing serious collectors would be buying loads of Gibsons. They hardly looked at Fender's new stuff. Gibson had a head start. They were better financed and had more staff at first, and they had been doing their own art guitars for a while, so people were really noticing them."

Groundwork

It's not as though recreating a classic Fender was a new idea. When the Custom Shop was set up in Corona, the factory's own Vintage Series was in its fifth year (not counting production stoppages during the buyout transition); those reissue guitars and basses both reflected and heightened a vintage awareness among players and dealers. Michael Stevens: "The new guys who had bought the company in '85 were rockin' and rollin' by the time I got there. They had the reissues going. Dan Smith was really going to town. They had a serious production facility going on there, but there was no room in the regular

Scott Grant, left, with Fred Stuart. A key figure in bringing a vintage sensibility to the shop, Fred sometimes blended classic Fender designs and custom features, as seen here on this Tele Thinline. Note the "Gretsch orange" finish with matching peghead, bound body, gold hardware, moto pickguard, and bar markers.

production line for something like a '55 two-color Strat with an ash body, so one of the things we could do in the shop was to address that."

The reissues of 1982 were never intended to duplicate the originals. John Page: "We weren't trying to be exact. It was more, 'Let's *evoke* a '57 Strat, let's get the vibe,' and Dan would say, 'Yeah, but let's go with a more comfortable neck; let's put a few player-friendly touches on there to make it more adaptable to contemporary playing styles.' It made sense at the time, but with the coming of the whole vintage thing, that was no longer the case. Most of these customers didn't want the general vibe. They wanted it *nailed*."

As the prices of original vintage guitars approached federal-bailout levels, pushing them increasingly out of reach, customers demanded more authenticity in their reissues. Another factor was that tastes in music and playing styles were shifting. J. Black: "If you didn't have the resurgence in blues and blues rock with Eric Clapton and Robert Cray and Stevie Ray Vaughan, if you were still back in the heavy metal, hair-band thing, none of this would have happened. But once the market shifted from metal and got back into more traditional stuff, there weren't enough vintage guitars out there for the average guy to afford, so everything changed, and the Custom Shop was able to respond quicker than Fender manufacturing only because we had a smaller operation."

Black acknowledges that the entire Fender team played a role: "Fender's sales reps and the dealers were key in that shift. You had good dealers who had the ear of Bill Schultz and who really wanted their own little custom runs. And the things they wanted, you couldn't do it out of manufacturing. All manufacturing was offering was new colors or gold hardware or those sorts of simple things. So a lot of that fell to us."

If a reissue was the closest thing to a '57 Strat you were ever going to get, then that's precisely what you wanted — the closest thing. Customers increasingly demanded virtual clones, as identical to the original as was humanly possible to build. Some felt that Fender's best designs had all been unveiled by the late '50s or early '60s anyway, so why fix what ain't broken? Consider the reverse curve on a pre-CBS Tele body where it joins the neck on the bass side, or the tummy tuck on a '55 Strat. Who *wouldn't* prefer such subtleties to the cruder contours on some of the oafish clunkers that somehow slipped through Quality Control in the CBS era? If a reissue were to evoke more than a whiff of the original's essence, it had to look, feel, sound, and even smell like the real deal.

Even working musicians who otherwise might have appreciated, say, a flatter neck radius or bigger frets often wanted their reissues to sport vintage specs in every detail. Modern features, more versatile electronics, and even comfier playability were almost beside the point for these customers. They wanted that smaller neck radius, skinny frets, and 3-way switch on their reissue Strat. They wanted three saddles on their Teles, not six (and while you're at it, make 'em out of unthreaded steel, and grind 'em flat on the bottom). The Custom Shop's ability to render such details was only the beginning. Before long, increasingly sophisticated clients forced the builders to re-examine the plating of metal parts, the formulas of finishes, the beveling of pickup polepieces, the sheathing of interior wires, and other details previously considered too trivial to bother with or ignored altogether.

The builders spent years educating themselves, a process that entailed examining each other's guitars (Fred Stuart owned a particularly clean '53 Telecaster) and poring over vintage instruments at helpful Hollywood retailers such as Guitar Center and Albert Molinaro's Guitars R Us. Fred Stuart: "We would look at a vintage Fender and ask, how can we replicate that? The more we tried to refine our Custom Shop product and make it different from the factory, the more we looked back to the vintage era."

Build me a '52 Strat

Part of the learning process entailed fielding occasional curve balls thrown by customers. John Grunder: "We had a guy who wanted a guitar just like Eric Clapton's. J. Black had been building Eric's personal guitars at the time, and he built a beautiful Clapton-style Strat for this guy. But the customer sent it back because he had close-ups of Clapton's guitar, and the new one didn't match the grain patterns on the neck. I explained to him that wood is organic and no two pieces are exactly alike. If anything, the neck on his guitar was fancier than the necks on Eric's guitars. But he sent it back because it wasn't identical. Crazy."

Some of the buyers who thought they were demanding vintage authenticity were actually requesting guitars that never existed (a '48 Broadcaster, a '52 Strat), or specifying combinations of details that had never appeared on any stock Fender. One early client wanted a '52 Telecaster in Dakota Red with a rosewood fingerboard. Original '52 Teles, of course, had maple boards, not rosewood. Another wanted a '54 reissue with a laminated pickguard, a feature not introduced on Fenders until years later.

John English was another builder who pushed the shop toward vintage authenticity. Gene Baker: "He loved to pass on a lot of Fender history and all the stories from the early days. He wanted to bring back a lot of the old-school stuff like the vintage details."

Mixing and matching stock features wasn't necessarily a production problem (attaching a rosewood-board neck was no more difficult than attaching a maple-board neck). In fact, guitars that mixed features from different eras would become Custom Shop staples in the years to come. But some customers wanted it both ways — unprecedented combos of features, and authentic recreations of guitars from Fender's increasingly exalted past. Michael Stevens: "It was a problem because depending on what the customer said he wanted, we might have to move the decal or the holes for the pickguard, and do we use slotted screws or Phillips heads? Where do we put the string tree?

J. Black with Maria Orduño, who along with Scott Grant managed the shop's day-to-day operations.

So we'd send out exactly what the guy wanted, but maybe the guitar ended up in Japan with the decal and the string tree in the place where you'd see them on a '52 but not on a '62, and they threw a fit."

Learning curves

A few customers were astute enough to demand top hat switches and barrel knobs on their Telecasters or pre-CBS contours on their Strats, but the pickier they got the more difficult it became to track down the right parts or to shape original-spec bodies and necks. In the late 1980s, there was nothing like the heaps of printed and online material available today covering vintage guitar details down to the plating on the pickguard screws. The Fender factory might have been sacred ground to vintage enthusiasts, the High Church of the bolt-on creed, but most employees had nowhere near the depth of knowledge required to render instruments with the level of authenticity we now take for granted.

Nor did they have access to some Warehouse That Time Forgot. If Fender craftspeople attempting to recreate a '58 Precision Bass wanted to examine an original, they had to go out and find one like anybody else. (Steve Soest, from Soest Guitar in nearby Orange, remembers lending old neck templates, vintage bridges, tuners, and other parts to the builders to help in their research and self-education.) J. Black: "Back in the '80s Fender didn't really want the Fender legacy. They didn't really want to make vintage guitars. They wanted to make modern guitars. This vintage thing was all new for Fender. I was from the vintage thing and Mike Stevens was from the vintage thing, same with Fred Stuart. So we all had different opinions."

Michael Stevens: "Fred Stuart and one or two other people knew about those nuances, but that was it. Very few others at Fender knew about them, and if we didn't happen to have some old stock lying around, we had to go out and find stuff. And with those paper-feed machines, we had a lot of trouble getting parts to line up. You'd see a Strat pickguard misalign on the horn and that sort of thing. So we would try to fix them with templates that I had made by hand in my garage."

Dan Smith explains the other side of the story: "The perception in the Custom Shop and to some people outside the company may have been that we didn't want to make vintage-based instruments, but that wasn't the reality. Our intent from 1981 on was always to offer high-quality American made instruments that paid homage to our legacy. We never wanted to be in the 'CBS' position of being held accountable for abandoning our tradition. But our manufacturing capabilities in the early '80s [at CBS Fender] and then again as a start-up in the mid '80s didn't allow for the fine details we needed to do it 'collector correct.' In addition, there were a number of products — Jazzmasters, Jaguars, Thin-Line Telecasters and such — that we would have loved to add to the American series but couldn't for those same reasons. Instead, we expanded the already successful Japanese vintage product we'd introduced in the early '80s. Fuji-Gen Gakki had the manufacturing capacity that made it easy for them to accept odd and low-production product.

"If you took a closer look at what we offered during that time, the majority was vintage-based. But with our limited production capacity in those first years, the bottom line for the American-made product was that we wanted to make the best guitars that we could actually sell, and to take the Strat, for example, there was more demand for the American Standards than any other version."

Beyond the custom option approach

The nitpicky complaints coming from Yamano Music often echoed those of individual U.S. customers, but as Fender's Japanese distributor and partner, Yamano was particularly influential. (Dan Smith speculates that, "the highest percentage of Custom Shop stuff over all these years has been sold to the Japanese market.") Yamano's big-number orders and demanding standards were frustrating in the short term but ultimately helpful in pushing the builders to take their reissues to the next level of authenticity. This shift required not only unearthing vintage-correct parts and components, sometimes from the original suppliers, but also rethinking the production process itself. After all, you couldn't assemble stock parts from the factory bins and expect to come up with a '58 Mary Kaye.

John Page: "Yamano would say something like, we want 25 option-program Strats in Burgundy Mist with a slightly different neck contour. So we would make them up and send them over there, but then they'd reject them. Yamano was like [other customers]. It turns out that's not what they wanted after all. They would say, 'The routs aren't right, the contours aren't right,' etc. This went on, frankly, for years. People were gradually becoming much better informed about minute details, which made them gradually pickier and pickier. It was all part of our re-education."

J. Black: "At first, we would look at the photos in the book *American Guitars*, just to see the Fender colors. Andre Duchossoir's book came out [*The Fender Stratocaster*'s first U.S. printing was in 1985], which was more detailed than what we'd seen before. Gradually the general public was getting access to all sorts of information, whereas before if you wanted to find this stuff out you had to go to the vintage show in Dallas and examine these guitars in person."

John Page explained that the demand for increased authenticity was one reason why the option approach went away quickly. It probably lasted only until the end of the second year, at the latest. Even by the end of the first year the crew could see it wasn't working very well. They realized that at least for the immediate future, truly authentic reissues would have to be built one at a time, basically from scratch.

The personal touch: Art Esparza files the nut on a lefty Strat.

The personal touch

Aside from the limited runs, the shop's output was relatively small, which facilitated the kind of personal attention that building period-correct reissues would require. Michael Stevens: "I'd do things like go over to Spartan [one of several paint suppliers] to mix up some lacquers. I found some original jars with Leo's signature on them from 1952 or something. They hadn't been opened and the paint was just fine. So I brought some back to the shop. I could have hand mixed it, but these guys already had it just lying there for all these years. No one had ever asked them for it. So these were the kinds of things we were doing, using old stock when we could find it and building guitars that Fender used to make but people couldn't get anymore."

Yas

Back when used guitars were just beginning to acquire their vintage auras, some of the enthusiasts who assembled the deepest repositories of American guitar lore weren't exactly locals. They lived about as far away from Fullerton as you can get without leaving the planet. Some had never been to America and could only dream of what it must be like to visit the shops and factories where iconic American guitars had been blueprinted and built in decades past. Some didn't even speak English.

Yasuhiko Iwanade checks out a big-head rosewood Strat as John Grunder looks on. J. Black: "Yas tried to bring a vintage accuracy that only the Japanese had at the time. I have to admit that at first we were a little dismissive of it, [but] I have to credit Yas for being about five years ahead of the curve."

They were Japanese, which shouldn't have been surprising. Japan's post-War fascination with American culture — with rock and roll and guitars in particular — was well documented. Such intense interest stimulated an increasingly sophisticated awareness of all things guitar: model details, production processes, parts and components, and more. By the time the Custom Shop was established, Fender had for five years worked closely with wholesalers Yamano and Kanda Shokai as well as Matsumoto-based FujiGen-Gakki, builder of well crafted, bona fide (if not American-made) Fender-brand guitars. In fact, when the new Fender company decided to expand its line of U.S.-built instruments beyond the vintage models, it was Fender Japan whose high-quality guitars raised the bar for their California counterparts.

When it came to increasing the authenticity of Custom Shop reissues, the employee with the single biggest influence was author/collector/builder Yasuhiko Iwanade. John Page interviewed him for a job in December, 1989.

J. Black: "Yas arrived with this new sensibility just when that vintage thing was happening, and he was saying, 'You guys aren't vintage enough.' He instructed us right when we needed it, perfect timing. There was a real serendipity to the way things came together. The yen was getting stronger, the dollar was getting weaker, and the Japanese were buying *crazy* amounts of vintage guitars." (This author remembers one Texas guitar show where Japanese enthusiasts rented a booth not to display anything but simply to have a convenient storage area. They purchased scores of vintage treasures, piling cases on flatbed dollies and stacking them up in their booth in preparation for shipping.)

Michael Stevens: "I met Yasuhiko at the Dallas Show before I came to Fender in '87. He was walking by with a

"At Fender, we were now part of all that we loved."

— Michael Stevens

Fender 12-string neck and a box of parts. We talked for a long while, and he gave me the neck and the parts. At that time he was a full-time repairman in Tokyo and writing for *Player* magazine. Yas was a vintage *freak,* as are many of the Japanese customers, just voracious. They knew *exactly* what they wanted — no ifs, ands or buts. At Fender he was also like me — dumbfounded and proud to be working in an electric guitar Mecca. We were now part of all that we loved."

J. Black: "We were all into old guitars, but it was Yas who made the leap. He was the first one to say, 'You guys are using enameled wire on your vintage Strats, and you should be using Formvar.' It's a different coating on the pickup magnet wire, with a different look and a different sound. Our first reaction was, 'Well nobody is really asking for that.' But he was right. He knew what we needed."

John Page: "I gotta admit, my first reaction was, um, *who is this guy* [laughs]? But my background was in designing new Fender products, not old Fender products. You also have to remember that it wasn't just bits and parts; if we were going to do it right the whole factory mentality had to change. Let's say you want to bevel the top surfaces of the polepiece magnets, give them a little [vintage-style] 45 degree chamfer. If you do it on a machine it won't look right. It'll look too perfect, which looks fake. It has to be hand-turned on a grinder. The reaction was, 'You can't hand-bevel in a factory!' So we had to re-educate ourselves to say, 'Wait a minute. We're not the factory. We're the Custom Shop, and we *will* hand-bevel these magnets — whatever it takes to make it right.'

"So those sorts of little things were a learning process every step of the way. As average guitar players out there were learning more, we were learning as well, right there in the shop. That's one of the reasons why the loose directive we got in the first place from Bill [Schultz] was such a good thing. We needed it to be open-ended because we needed room to grow, to change, to be able to respond to shifts in the marketplace. Wherever the customers took us, we were able to follow."

Dealers were saying, *hey, we're not selling as many graphics guitars and big-hair '80s shred machines; we want traditional Fenders.* And Yamano and Yasuhiko Iwanade were crucial influences on the shop's response. They continued to push for higher levels of accuracy — the correct dot spacing on fingerboards, the precise contouring of V necks, and so on — but meeting those standards was slow going. Processes were refined when the shop got its own Haas and CNC machines, which allowed the builders to perform additional functions independent of the factory. For example, J. Black explains that they could now drill accurately spaced holes for the tuning machines. There was a hard tool in the factory called a multi-drill, and it provided only American Standard spacing, so the shop's earlier vintage guitars had been drilled with American Standard specs. Such details were corrected because of pressure from Yamano. J. Black: "The American and European dealers didn't see it at first, but they benefited from what Yamano did. Yamano got [the higher levels of accuracy] at first, and then dealers like Norman's Rare Guitars picked up on it. The guitars we built for American distribution started to have the more accurate details. It spread."

The bevel on Fender pickguards was another sore point. The pre-'66 bevel was more sloped, revealing a wider stripe, but Fender had been using the shallower, post-'66 bevel for years. Iwanade insisted on the earlier, more correct spec, and also pushed the shop toward using thinner finishes. "He tried to bring a vintage accuracy that only the Japanese had at the time," explains Black, "and I have to admit that at first we were a little dismissive of it. We thought, that's just way too anal, who cares? We felt the public didn't know — or rather, the *American* public didn't know — or the people who did know would be thinking, why should I buy a Custom Shop guitar for $1,200 when I could buy the real thing for $1,500? Vintage guitars were still cheap enough that it made no sense for us to make these sorts of changes, but that didn't last much longer. Yas even detailed out things like decals, the size of the font. We were like — what are you *talking* about? Even the clear coat around the decal and the way it's shaped, Yas would point these things out. We thought, oh god, nobody knows that, and now we *all* know it. I have to credit Yas for being about five years ahead of the curve."

Loaves and fishes for the multitude

Like alchemists, the Custom Shop builders pursued their quest to somehow conjure in a new guitar the ephemeral essence of a vintage treasure — without the sticker shock that would send a typical working musician rolling out of his local retailer on a gurney. (Their endeavor would reach its ultimate expression in Fender's Relic program of the mid 1990s and thereafter; Chap. 16.) In the years to come, vintage-style Fenders would prove crucial to the shop's success. Some designs replicated Leo Fender's originals while others were re-imagined and tweaked by artists and other players, dealers, Fender marketers, or Custom Shop craftspeople. These instruments would eventually succeed in impressing a particularly tough crowd — vintage guitar buffs.

Vintage enthusiasts revere Fender's original designs and are quick to turn up their noses at the slightest whiff of fakery. No detail is too trivial or obscure to escape their scrutiny, not even, say, the font used for the fine print on a headstock decal, or the crosshatch pattern on a Telecaster dome knob. For some of the more extreme aficionados, their persnickety attitude borders on fanaticism, but they help to keep guitar companies honest, their reissues authentic.

Michael Stevens: "The vintage community really responded to the Custom Shop. John and I'd take some of our guitars to the Dallas vintage show, and people went crazy for them. You'd think we were handing out bread and fish. The guys who really knew vintage Fenders were just so happy to see that Fender could still do it right."

The Custom Shop's high-quality replicas were expensive, yet far more affordable than the originals. J. Black: "Once the market shifted from metal and got back into more traditional stuff, there weren't enough vintage guitars out there for the average guy to afford, so everything changed." Shown here: bound-top Esquires in Sea Foam Green (preceding page) and Dakota Red.

"If you didn't have the resurgence in blues and blues rock with Eric Clapton and Robert Cray and Stevie Ray Vaughan, if you were still back in the heavy metal, hair-band thing, none of this would have happened." — J. Black

Let Fender be Fender

The late 1980s and early 1990s were a tough time for Fender, as it reorganized itself, faced shifting tastes and an unpredictable economy, and grappled with complex marketing challenges from traditional rivals as well as a host of impressive newcomers. The Custom Shop was tasked with building the Kubicki basses, helping to design the Heartfields [Chap. 8], and inaugurating the U.S.-built Set-Neck models [Chap. 9], all of which were departures from Fender's comfortable practices and familiar identity.

The vintage reissues, on the other hand, were more than a response to current markets. They were a way for Fender to return to, and to celebrate, the designs and concepts that made it a revered American institution in the first place. John Page reflects on the turbulent marketplace of the early 1990s: "It turns out that what people really wanted was for Fender to be Fender."

The shop would eventually offer almost countless combinations of classic and modern features, such as this vintage-style guitar — an LTD '56 Strat NOS — in Candy Persimmon over White Gold Leaf.

Years after vintage reissues were officially added to the line, the shop intensified the old-guitar vibe with the Relic and Time Machine programs. This Limited Collection '51 Nocaster's sunburst finish would have made it a fluke or a custom order back in 1951; while it seemed to bear the scars of endless hard rockin' gigs, in fact it was brand new in 2009.

Seymour Duncan
Seymour Duncan

CHAPTER EIGHT

8

Unleash The Füry!

Big Hair and Batwings

During 1988 and 1989, the Custom Shop's John Page and his colleagues over in Fender marketing debated strategies, sometimes heatedly. Page felt the marketing guys made too many of their decisions as reactions to other companies' successes. As he puts it, "With all respect, Fender didn't get where it is by following." The other problem, in his view, was Fender's size and inertia. By the time marketing would recognize a trend, conceive a product in response to it, integrate it into their marketing plan, turn it over to R&D, wait for R&D to design and prototype it, send it on to production for trial runs, and wait for feedback, many months could go by.

In contrast to the factory, Page saw the Custom Shop as fast and lean, a place where bureaucracy was much less of an obstacle: "You get feedback and boom, you're out the door. We tried to develop product based on the direct input from artists setting the trends, *as* they were setting them. Then we were able to fast-track development and hit the marketplace while the trend was just breaking."

Marketing's view: The glory days of the '50s and '60s are long gone. We can no longer depend on Strats and Teles alone. Times have changed, and we can either adapt or disappear. We have the best builders in the world, but nothing else matters if you go out of business. Selling guitars to people who already want them is easy, but it's rarely sufficient to sustain an operation of any significant size. New markets have to be researched and developed, and we can't keep selling money-losing Custom Shop guitars, no matter how cool they are.

These tensions escalated as Fender faced one of the biggest challenges in its history: how to succeed in the guitar market of the mid and late 1980s, one that Leo Fender and his sales and marketing chief Don Randall scarcely could have imagined.

The Harmonicats vs. Viking warlords

The mid 1980s saw the rise of "Strat mania," but the one manufacturer that most deserved to capitalize on the phenomenon was hardly in a position to do so, having effectively shut down during the post-CBS buyout transition period. There were plenty of more or less Fender-style instruments on the market; the problem was, many of them didn't say "Fender" on them. In the late 1980s the new Fender company responded to this exasperating state of

affairs with factory Strats, Teles, and basses whose quality steadily improved, and with Custom Shop Strats, Teles, and basses whose quality was exceptional from the outset.

Now, what about the rest of the market? What about all those glammed-out, leather-legged, poodle-haired dudes who preferred what Hartley Peavey called "batwing" guitars? They had scads of instruments to chose from, some loosely based on Fender Strats, some on Gibson Explorers or Flying V's. Many had in-your-face model names such as Destroyer, Warrior, and Striker (Fender's 1965 Marauder would have fit right in). Some featured appropriately menacing Ginsu-cleaver headstocks, ninja-black hardware, and spiky bodies decorated with targets, lightning bolts, spider webs, even bloodstains. Their advertisements and their endorsers' album covers sometimes depicted caskets, evil-eyed skulls, mace-wielding Viking warlords — a far cry from those genteel '50s and '60s Fender brochures picturing the Harmonicats in tweed sport coats, or the '70s catalogs with their trippy flower power cartoons. Fender literature had always included no-nonsense descriptions of the guitars' functional advantages, the fruits of Fender's painstaking R&D engineers. But in some of their competitors' mid-'80s advertisements, the attitude was more Freddie Krueger than Freddie Tavares.

Grover Jackson acquired Charvel Guitars in 1978 and founded Jackson Guitars two years later. At trade shows throughout the early and mid 1980s, few new brands stimulated anywhere near the buzz ignited by Grover Jackson's hard rockin' solidbodies. They were *the* weapons of choice for a whole galaxy of heavy metal and modern rock stars — Eddie Van Halen, Warren DeMartini, Richie Sambora, Jake E. Lee, Randy Rhoads, Vinnie Vincent, George Lynch, and others. Every major manufacturer had more than one marketing meeting addressing the topic of *what to do about Jackson*. Several Charvel/Jackson veterans would come to work for the Custom Shop, including Scott Buehl, Jason Davis, Todd Krause, Stephen Stern, and eventual director of marketing Mike Eldred.

Todd Krause: "Starting in the early 1980s, Charvel/Jackson was the dominant company when it came to innovations, the one that was turning heads and making everyone sit up and take notice. Most of the guitars were individually ordered and built to the customer's specs. Later, even when we had cataloged models, we usually tweaked them to please the individual player. We were building high-end, custom-ordered guitars on a sizable scale before anyone else. A few guys were doing it on a small scale, but Grover Jackson was the person who proved to the industry that a factory could have impeccable standards of craftsmanship — those guitars played great right out of the box — and make a profit with custom-ordered guitars. They were so popular. When you turned on MTV, what did you see? Charvels and Jacksons all over the place. I have

to believe it was Charvel/Jackson that made Bill Schultz look at the whole custom shop idea and say — there's gold in them hills." (Another rising force was Kramer, whose best-selling guitars were often seen in the hands of Eddie Van Halen, Vivian Campbell, Richie Sambora, and others.)

While the guitars of Charvel, Jackson, Kramer, Ibanez, and other brands often sported a brash appearance, it wasn't just about cosmetics. Many of these new instruments revitalized some traditional construction techniques (neck-through bodies, for example) or pioneered a new generation of designs and technologies — locking tuners, locking trems, slick, no-heel neck/body joints, new switching systems, and high-output pickups that screamed louder than a summer camper in *Friday The 13th*. The success of component manufacturers such as DiMarzio, Seymour Duncan, Kahler, and Floyd Rose fostered a mix-and-match, hot-rod-it-yourself craze that further complicated the challenges faced by the traditional companies.

With so many companies offering so-called "Superstrats," the manufacturer of real Strats found itself looking a bit sedate and sorely in need of fresh designs. The blues revival was underway, thanks in large measure to the incendiary Stevie Ray Vaughan, but metal and its various offshoots still ruled. Leading shredheads, some of them indisputable virtuosos, included the astonishing Eddie Van Halen, Joe Satriani, Steve Vai, and the guys in Megadeth, Iron Maiden, Metallica, and hordes of others. Few if any played Fender guitars (Yngwie Malmsteen, his namesake Fender still a couple of years away, endorsed a Schecter Strat copy).

Fender estimated that metalheads and their instruments of choice accounted for a quarter or even a third of the market. J. Black: "There was no clear vision for what Fender should do about it. Kramer was hot, then Jackson took it over, then Ibanez took it over, and Fender hadn't gotten that jolt from the grunge thing or the vintage thing, not yet. The blues revival was beginning to kick in, but when I got there in '89 there was very little interest at Fender in vintage. Artist Relations was still trying to draw on the L.A. big-hair guys. My feeling was, who cares about those guys? We're Fender. But if you turned on MTV, you couldn't find a Fender. All you'd see was a Jackson or a Kramer or those sorts of things."

Heavy metal shred machines weren't the only challengers. Paul Reed Smith's elegant instruments were drawing enthusiastic reviews from all corners of the guitar community, even finicky, hard-to-please vintage enthusiasts. Execs at several companies confided in private that PRS was raising the bar for the entire industry.

The Charvel and Jackson brands are now owned by Fender, but in the 1980s, Charvel/Jackson revolutionized the market with radical designs, exuberant graphics, and technological advances. Todd Krause: "I have to believe it was Charvel/Jackson that made Bill Schultz look at the whole custom shop idea and say — there's gold in them hills."

The two-edged sword

When it came to expanding its market share, Fender's biggest asset became its biggest drawback. As one in-house memo put it, "Why couldn't we sell those other styles of guitars? Tradition. In the dealers' and consumers' minds, Fender means … Strats, Teles, P's and J's. We could tweak them a little here and there, but heaven help us if we went too far. Don't mess with tradition. It seemed like every time we did, we had messed with mom, apple pie, baseball, the flag, etc."

Fender had already marketed the HM series of Floyd Rose-equipped Strats in order to compete with Charvel and Jackson. Some had bubblegum-pink bodies, black headstocks, and graffiti/splatter logos (we can only imagine what no-nonsense old-timers like Bill Carson must have muttered under their breath), but they still looked like Fenders, and when you thought of Fender you thought *music/tone/style*; you didn't think *shred/Spandex/pillage*. Fender had few if any instruments that could take on Ibanez in what might be called the virtuoso rock guitar market. Once it dropped Kubicki, it also had little to offer bassists who preferred high-end boutique instruments such as those from Tobias, Ken Smith, Pedulla, Spector, and the like.

It's not as though Fender had never ventured outside the box with "un-Fender" designs. Consider the ill-fated Starcaster of the mid '70s, a semi-hollow guitar designed to compete with Gibson's ES-335, or the imported Esprit of the mid '80s, a lovely instrument (also intended to compete with the 335) that would evolve into the Custom Shop's Robben Ford guitar. But those were individual models with modest options or limited packages of features and finishes. Now, going up against formidable competitors, Fender didn't need a new model or two. It needed a whole new line.

The Heartfield experiment

Considering all these factors — plus the opportunity to establish a new dealer network, the need to shield Fender in the face of shifting tastes, and the fluctuating value of the yen relative to the dollar — it made sense to import newly designed, shred-worthy guitars and high-end basses made in Japan and bearing a brand other than Fender. Given the creativity and talents churning around in the Custom Shop, it was not surprising that its employees were consulted on the design of these new, non-Fenderish members of the Fender family.

Based in Matsumoto, Japan, manufacturer Fuji-Gen-Gakki had a strong track record in the metal and fusion markets, having built Ibanez guitars as well as Fender's own Contemporary Series (described in catalogs as "slightly more rock oriented") and the original Fender HMs. Fuji had supplied Fender with excellent instruments when the tiny, post-buyout company had no other source, and it even helped to set up Fender's facility in Mexico. Bill Schultz wanted to find a way to keep Fuji in the picture, to return the favor.

Fuji had designed a line of Heartfield guitars for its own market in Japan. They were well made, with innovative features such as clever active electronics systems. Some had set necks; others were bolt-ons. The basses were in the boutique vein, and Fender marketers thought they had particularly strong potential. Fuji agreed to let Fender market Heartfield in the U.S. and internationally, but although Dan Smith and his fellow execs thought the imports would help expand Fender's market share, they still might not

So-called Super Strats typically sported roaring pickups and heavy-duty, multi-adjustable whammy mechanisms built not for gentle wavers but rather for in-your-face dive-bomber assaults.

compete directly with PRS or Ibanez. So, more new models were in order. Dan worked with Fuji's designers on a set-neck Strat with "modern" features (a refined shape, a fancy carved maple top, humbuckers, etc.). Intended to compete directly with PRS, it was dubbed the Elan.

Now, what about Ibanez? Dan Smith: "The hip word of the day was 'synergy,' a word that eventually made me cringe. It was decided that we needed a synergistic design team to work on Heartfield. Jack Shelton was put in charge." The U.S. crew, officially called the Synergy Group, consisted of John Page, J. Black, George Blanda, Bruce Bolen, Dan Smith, Fred Stuart, Larry Brooks, Yasuhiko Iwanade — all of them key Custom Shop or R&D figures — as well as Shelton and Custom Shop Artist Relations manager Mark Wittenberg. They met, conferred, and haggled, eventually coming up with a new model. Called the Talon, it was obviously — too obviously, perhaps — intended to compete head to head with the popular, Steve Vai-endorsed Ibanez JEM.

Heartfield was a burden to John Page, who was tasked with coordinating the design efforts of the U.S. and Japanese teams, but otherwise it put no significant strain on the shop's resources. In most cases the builders merely sat in on a few meetings and acted more as consultants than actual designers. (Dan Smith remembers, "Their hearts never seemed to be in it.") These exchanges did little to alleviate tensions between the shop and Fender management. J. Black: "I walked out of one meeting and went to Kurt Hemrich and said, 'Why are we doing this? We're Fender, for God's sake! Why are we chasing Ibanez?' And he said, 'It's a market share that those guys have already created. If we can take five percent of it, why not?'"

Offered from 1989 through late 1993, the Heartfield imports had superhero/doom-worthy model names — EX, Talon, Prophecy, etc. — as well as the requisite menagerie of features (batwing bodies, "sabretooth" inlays). "Combining the look of yesteryear with the technology of tomorrow," they weren't cheap; Fender marketing characterized them as "upper-middle priced." Some models were later relaunched with the Fender brand, but eventually the entire project was dropped and the Synergy Group disbanded. Smith estimates that Fender's substantial investment of several hundred thousand dollars was recouped, so at best Heartfield might have been a break-even deal.

Exotic woods and multi-laminated necks and bodies were additional challenges to long-held design conventions pioneered by Fender, Gibson, Gretsch, and others.

The historic Fender brand was too iconic to be applied to radical designs, so an entirely new line was created: Heartfield.

Aftermath

After Heartfield failed to sufficiently penetrate new markets, one aspect of that challenge fell upon Page and his crew. While Fender's modestly staffed Custom Shop was in no position to take on Jackson, PRS, or Ibanez, let alone all three, its "lab" function did allow new Fender designs to be prototyped, built in small quantities, and market-tested with relatively low investments and short turnarounds.

Perhaps a more significant consequence was that the Heartfield venture contributed to a restructuring of Fender departments. In addition to his role as manager of the Custom Shop, John Page now wanted to oversee both Fender R&D and Custom Shop marketing. He got his wish, taking over Research & Development for all of Fender guitars and basses on September 13, 1989, a significant move for an aspiring rock and roller who less than three years before had been hired to help Michael Stevens build a few fancy guitars a year. Fender announced, "By combining the computer and manufacturing capabilities of the R&D department with the artistry of the Custom Shop, John is heading Fender into the future with a bullet." Page reflects, "There were other factors as well, but Heartfield was my major reason for pushing for the change." He thinks the move was a good one for all parties. With R&D and the Custom Shop under the same roof, the shop could help Fender to address market needs by fast-tracking prototypes, working with R&D to create the proper documentation, and buying some time for R&D and production to develop and introduce the factory versions.

All of this would demonstrate to the world that Fender was now a quick-response outfit at the forefront of trends. As an example, Page cites the late-'88 Yngwie Malmsteen Strat, the factory's second artist guitar. The Custom Shop prototyped it and made the first 25 or so scalloped-fingerboard necks until the factory employees could be taught the process and the tooling was developed. The Kubicki bass — with its active electronics, bridge mounted tuners, and neck of 32 laminated maple strips — was another design that in Page's view would have been prohibitively complicated to produce in the main factory.

Combining departments also meant that Page could allocate design roles to both R&D and Custom Shop personnel as he saw fit: "R&D was used to taking a long time to develop product, while the shop was used to taking an idea, building a guitar, and shipping it — period. No drawings, no prototyping. So if I wanted something developed quickly, now I could task someone who was used to that quicker style. It did smooth things out, at least from my point of view. We released an enormous amount of new products during those Custom Shop/R&D years. A lot of them were basses, like the Custom Shop P/J Bass, the Urge [the Kubicki's successor], and the American Deluxe Basses. We also did the Telecoustic guitar, some Floyd Rose models, a bunch of artist signature guitars — way too many to remember. So putting the shop and Fender R&D under one roof worked."

The growth of the Custom Shop continued to accelerate over the next five years, with several new artist signature models, new marketing campaigns and promotions, and many one-offs and limited runs that came to be called "art guitars." John Page became overwhelmed with responsibilities and told Schultz and Hemrich that he needed to relinquish supervision of overall R&D. In May 1995, Dan Smith left Arizona and moved back to Corona to reassume supervision of Fender Guitar R&D. Custom Shop R&D remained under Page's direction. Custom Shop marketing was shared by Page and his colleagues in Fender marketing.

Custom Shop boss John Page took over R&D for Fender guitars and basses in 1989. "Heartfield was my major reason for pushing for the change," he says. The factory's American Deluxe Jazz Bass, shown here in an Olympic White 5-string version, was one of many instruments designed during the period when Page headed up both departments.

The expensive, top-of-the-line LJ was a milestone: Fender's first U.S.-made set-neck guitar. It was designed by Michael Stevens, shown here holding an LJ neck. Behind him is a rack of LJ bodies.

CHAPTER NINE

9

The Set-Neck Fenders

"They were the beginning of the 'price list,' the Custom Shop's own product line."

The Stevens LJ models

Michael Stevens was hired for several reasons, one of which was his demonstrated ability to craft extraordinary instruments in the Fender tradition. After all, back in Texas, his clients had included some of the best-known Fender players in the world. But Dan Smith saw another advantage as well: Stevens's potential to take Fender in new directions. As George Blanda explains: "One of the biggest factors in hiring Michael was that his own designs were so appealing. It's funny — Dan's a Fender guy, but he also really liked Gibsons, and he really liked the Stevens LJ model. By the time I got to Fender I was much more into the Fender-style bolt-on thing, but I had built a guitar that was like a double-cutaway Les Paul, and I think both Michael and I got hired because we made good Gibson-style guitars [laughs]. How ironic is that?" (In fact, at the same time Stevens was interviewing at Fender, he was being courted by Gibson for a similar position.)

Aside from the Kubicki basses and some of the more esoteric one-offs, the early Custom Shop instruments were just what you'd expect: either vintage repros or fancy Fenders whose overall look was rooted in the historic design esthetic established in the early 1950s by Leo Fender himself. At a time when the Custom Shop had no from-the-ground-up designs of its own, Michael Stevens conceived and crafted a dazzling single-cutaway guitar that looked like no instrument Fender had ever built. In fact, it didn't look like any other company's guitar, although its Gibsonesque traits were unmistakable.

Fender publicized three versions, each with a pair of humbuckers. The top-of-the-line LJ I ($2,799) was a Custom Shop model. The less expensive LJ II ($1,799) and LJ III ($1,199) were intended to be imports, and although they appeared in the literature they were never put into production. Michael Stevens: "The LJ II was a curly maple top version with a mahogany body. The number III was a very cool guitar, very Fendery sounding. It had a plain maple top on alder with a maple neck." The III was billed as featuring a (relatively plain) rosewood fingerboard with dot markers, while the II's fingerboard was Brazilian rosewood with bar inlays.

Michael Stevens recalls: "The LJ was a design I came to Fender with, blueprinted but not yet produced. Previous to employment I presented nine of my own designs, and that was one of them. They licensed the design from me. Larry Jameson had died by then, but I named it after him because he was the one who led me into guitars. He had good ears, and built everything by hand. When I came along I knew all about tools from woodshop. I was a mechanical engineering kind of cowboy, and I was also in art school. Larry had gone to the California College of the Arts in Oakland, so together we made a great team, and he just taught me so much. The very first LJ prototypes were started in the Pomona Road Shop. The plan was, the LJ I would be built by me, the II and III by FujiGen in Japan. FujiGen actually got theirs built before I finished mine."

Despite never being produced in substantial quantities, the top-of-the-line LJ I was something of a milestone for at least five reasons. Although it was a Michael Stevens creation (John Page considers it more of a "Michael Stevens guitar" than a "Fender Custom Shop guitar"), the Custom Shop nevertheless now had a design all its own. It wasn't a one-off built for an individual, or a limited run dreamed up by a dealer or a distributor, but a model conceived by the Custom Shop's own design guru and offered to the public in official literature.

Second, the new model was not merely a duplicate or a creative reworking of a Tele or a Strat but rather a radical departure from traditional Fenders in all significant respects, with a one-piece mahogany back, a chambered body, a 24.75" scale length that duplicated Gibson's published specs, mother of pearl markers, a bookmatched, gorgeously figured maple top, custom-designed humbuckers, three-on-a-side tuners with pearl buttons, a 12" neck radius (significantly flatter than Fender specs), coil-splitter switching, and Fender's TBX tone circuit.

Third, to say that the LJ I was Fender's most expensive guitar is an understatement. In the late 1980s the U.S. factory's limited-edition, Mary Kaye-style '57 Strat reissue retailed for $1,199, and the Clapton Signature Strat was $1,299. The $2,799 LJ I cost more than those two guitars put together, about $5,000 in today's currency. Another example: The LJ I's list price was more than a thousand dollars above that of the D'Aquisto archtop, which at the time was an import. Aside from its radical design, the LJ's price tag alone proclaimed loud and clear that Fender was willing to shake things up.

Fourth, the LJ incorporated a new construction technique that Fender would apply to certain elite models from then on. A hallmark of the company's traditional approach is the method of securing the neck to the body with wood screws. In 1983 Fender had departed from this familiar "bolt-on" technique with the imported Flame and Esprit, which featured glued-in, or "set," necks. It continued to explore new territory with the Heartfield imports of the late 1980s and early 1990s, some of which were set-neck guitars. Now, the Custom Shop had a guitar that in a way could be seen as the pinnacle of a group of instruments that embraced the Master Series, some of the Heartfields, and the shop's own Set-Neck Teles and Strats. In fact, the LJ was a first not only for the Custom Shop but for Fender in general, the company's first U.S.-made set-neck guitar.

Fifth, and perhaps most significant of all, the peghead didn't say *Fender* on it. It said *Stevens*. (In this regard it was somewhat similar to the Kubickis, but where Kubicki was an existing line that Fender brought under its umbrella, the Stevens guitars were all-new and refined in-house by the Custom Shop's first hire.) More than any press release ever could, the LJ's *Stevens* logo, elite features, and striking originality announced Fender's willingness to depart from

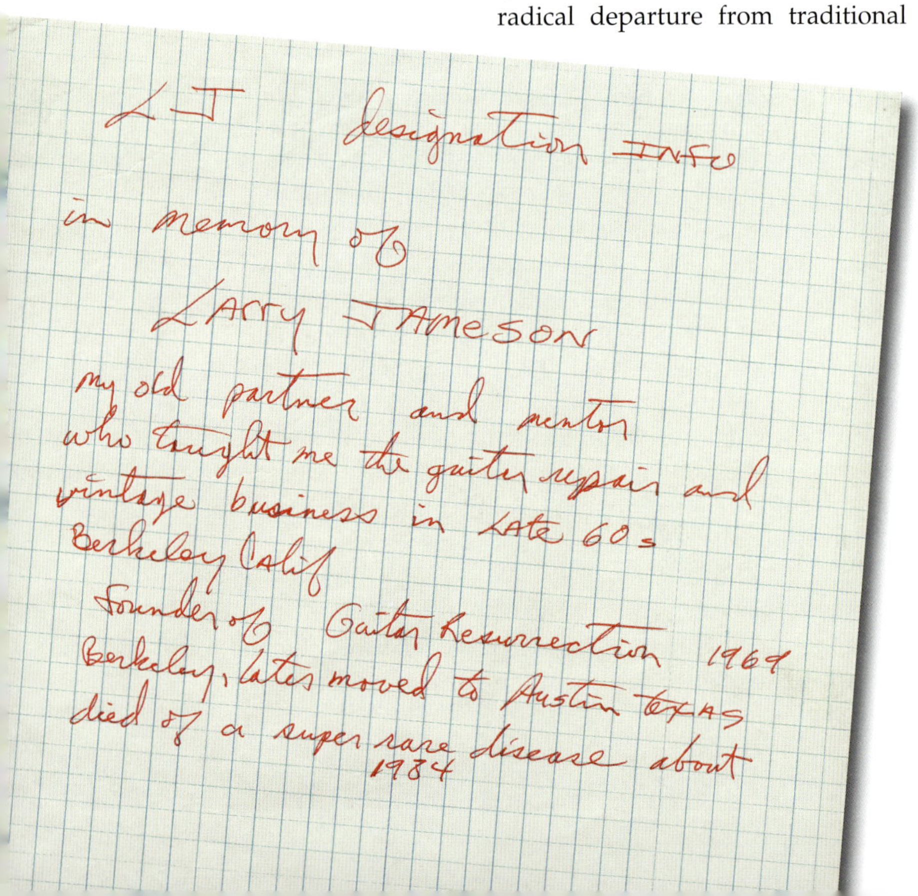

Rendered in Michael Stevens's hand, this note explains how he came to name the LJ after "my old partner and mentor."

the security of familiar designs and more specifically its intentions to take on Gibson and other makers of expensive, humbucker-equipped set-neck guitars.

In this last regard, the LJ meshed with Fender's larger market strategy. J. Black: "You had three things happening in '90 and '91. The first conversation was, how do we get into Ibanez's market share? And that became Heartfield. Then, how do we go into Paul Reed Smith territory? Which also became Heartfield. And finally, how do we go after Gibson? You had Slash coming out with Guns N' Roses, you had Gibson getting hot again, Paul Reed Smith getting hot. The pretty flame-top thing had died off in the early '80s because of the heavy metal guys, but now the Van Halen/graphic/Kramer thing had slowed down and the beautiful flame-top thing was back." Like the Custom Shop's first Anniversary models, the LJ was an early attempt to address "the beautiful flame-top thing" with a handsome, U.S.-made instrument.

Some of the LJ's most distinctive attributes weren't visible to the naked eye. Michael Stevens: "I used a flat strip of ebony as a stabilizer on the mahogany necks. We would put the truss rod in and lay the ebony strip on top of it and then lay the fingerboard on top of that. The function of the ebony was to stiffen up that mahogany neck a little more, give it a little more tension. Some good quarter-sawn necks are fine without it, but some need it."

The model's unconventional design and construction entailed new production challenges. Scott Buehl: "I think I did pretty much everything on that guitar. It was me, Stevens, and John English. John English — what a character! — was real proud of those guitars. I can't remember if anybody else helped on it. We only made 30-something of them, not many at all. We sold a few of them. We had a hard time producing them. Guys said we were 'sticking cash in the case' before we shipped those things. In other words, as expensive as they were, they were still costing us more to build than we sold them for. But gosh, it was just an excellent guitar."

John Page: "Fender has wanted to take some of Gibson's market share all along, just as Gibson wanted ours. The LJ was very Les Paul-ish, and everyone who played it loved it. We used to call it a Les Paul by Salvador Dali, and we meant that lovingly."

Any expensive single-cutaway, maple-topped, humbucking-equipped solidbody (or chambered-body) guitar would likely be compared to a Les Paul, but Scott Buehl sees the LJ as a unique instrument: "I played Les Pauls, and it didn't really remind me of a Les Paul, probably because the LJ had pseudo-chambers. Stevens had DiMarzio custom-wind those pickups. When somebody in the shop would stick a cord into one of those things and light it off, you'd hear the music coming off it, and it was so fat and so nice, such a pretty sound. A really nice guitar."

The LJ I appeared in Fender's November 1, 1989 price list. The blurb did not refer to the Custom Shop or even specify that the guitar was a "Custom Order Only" or "Custom Built" instrument. Instead, it was positioned in the U.S.

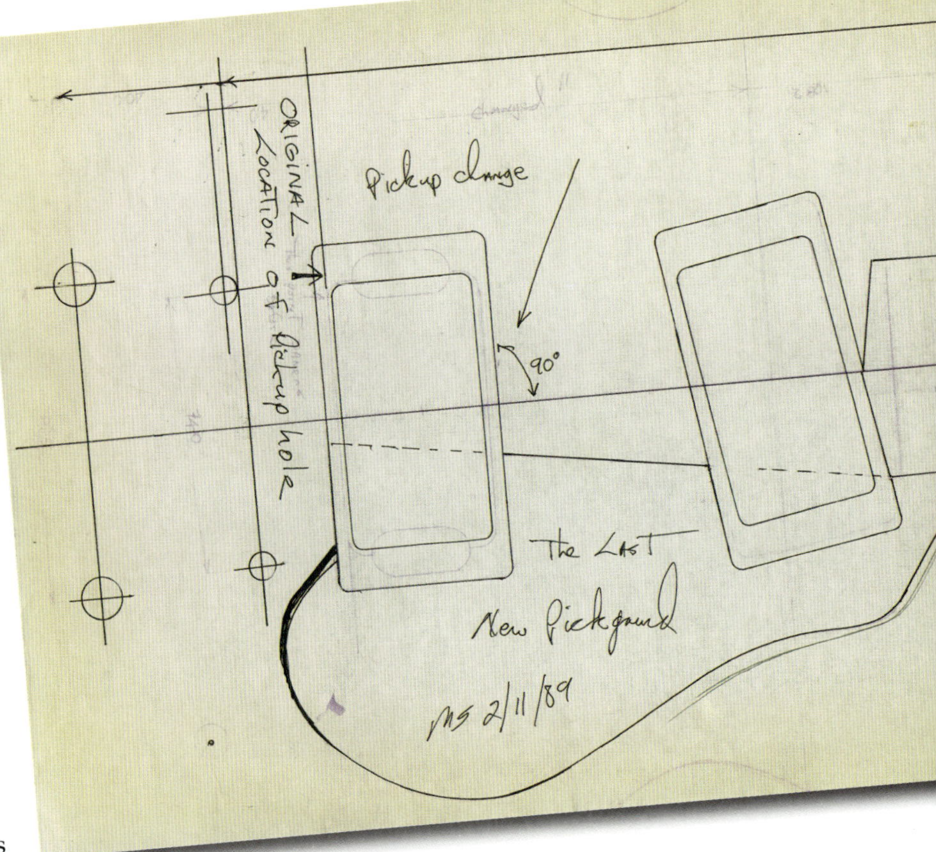

The front DiMarzio pickup's slanted position was only one of the unconventional details on the instrument that Don Mock called "this strange guitar . . . the best thing I've ever played."

Stevens Series along with the LJ II and LJ III. The U.S. Series was itself located within the short-lived Designer Series (later called the Designer/Signature Series). Even though the LJ I was included in that general Fender price list, other Custom Shop instruments — even those produced in significant quantities such as the 40th Anniversary Telecaster and the HLE Strats — were not. This inconsistency may be one reflection of Fender's shifting strategies regarding how Custom Shop instruments would be positioned relative to the factory line.

The Custom Shop's LJ was so radical it didn't even say *Fender* on the peghead.

Despite the "U.S." category, the LJ II and LJ III were actually built by FujiGen-Gakki but never made it past the prototype stage. Michael Stevens reports that only two LJ IIs and two LJ IIIs were ever made, making these guitars perhaps the rarest electric models ever publicized in a Fender price list, even more scarce than the Marauder of 1965. Michael Stevens: "I worked with FujiGen's only custom builder at the time, a Mr. Sukiaki. He spoke no English, and I spoke no Japanese. We had a blast anticipating what the other guy needed. I had not made a prototype LJ yet, but I took the pattern for the top carve and left it in Japan for them to use. They returned it barely in time for me to get a guitar ready for the NAMM show. That is the LJ that Don Mock has."

Don Mock reported on Michael Stevens's website (the following are edited excerpts): "It was at the 1989 NAMM show that I met and played my future favorite guitar. Robben Ford was there promoting his Robben Ford artist model and asked me to play with him at the Fender booth. I noticed an odd guitar sitting in the corner that looked kind of like a Les Paul with crooked pickups. I was basically a Les Paul guy, [so] as a crowd was forming to see us play, I grabbed this guitar and asked what the heck it was. Dan Smith told me it was the first prototype for a new Fender line to be built in Japan. I played one chord on it and quickly told Robben in a relieved tone, 'This will work; let's play.'

"I never like strange guitars when I first play them; every one I have ever owned has been reworked the way I wanted it, but here was this strange guitar and me loving it exactly the way it was. It had a wider than usual fingerboard, it sounded great, and its balance and feel were perfect. It's the best thing I've ever played. I was able to do some head to head comparisons with my old trusty Les Paul, and the LJ simply did everything better."

And in other news: The first production Blackie

A couple of years after the Clapton Strat's long-delayed introduction, Fender decided that a factory/production Blackie version was in order (not to be confused with the Custom Shop's much later Tribute Series Blackie Stratocaster, Chap. 28). The Custom Shop's J. Black was tasked with building the prototypes. George Blanda taught him how to do the critical Super Glue neck finishing process, and Blanda and Mike Stevens provided neck specs. J. Black built two black Strats — serial no. 0194, with chrome hardware, and 0195, with gold hardware.

In July 1990, J. took the guitars to Miami, Florida, to meet for three days with Eric Clapton and Lee Dickson. Aside from checking and fine-tuning all of Eric's guitars (including his Gibsons and Martins), he sought approval of both the new color and the new headstock decal. Black recalls, "I took along some hand-rubbed lettering, and I showed them a 'BLACKIE' label in black Letraset that we had come up with, to go on the headcap under the Eric Clapton signature. Eric just looked at it and said, 'That's fine.' That was the end of it. It was quick. I took the info back to Fender R&D and we made a new decal with the approved style and font, just as I had laid it out by hand for Eric and Lee, no changes."

After Black forwarded the specs to Dan Smith and George Blanda, the Blackie Strat went into production over in the main facility. It was identical to the factory's other Clapton models, aside from the new color and decal. Production stocked two necks in final assembly, one with the signature plus "BLACKIE" for the black versions, the other with the signature alone for the other colors. Although the Clapton model was officially a factory guitar, it was one of J. Black's prototypes that was often seen in the hands of Clapton himself. In a 1990 follow-up memo to Kurt Hemrich, John Page wrote: "As of August 2nd, the 'Blackie' proto with chrome hardware is Eric's main guitar on this tour, with the Pewter one being used as a backup."

The two protos were the first Blackies delivered to Clapton, although they did not have the "BLACKIE" decals. Clapton's first Strat with the decal was built by J. Black and forwarded to Eric in September 1991. This guitar, serial no. 0091, had a drilled hole that could hold a cigarette in the top edge of the headstock. Later dubbed the "Custom Smoker's Model," it was sold at the 1999 Christie's auction for $68,000. According to the auction booklet, "Clapton sometimes referred to 'smoking and non-smoking' versions of his signature guitar."

While the early-'90s Eric Clapton Signature Blackie model was never intended as a Custom Shop product, it provides a good example of how the shop, R&D, marketing, and the main production facility all worked together across several departmental lines.

John Page and Michael Stevens had high hopes for the LJs and discussed the possibility of expanding the line to include mahogany flat-top solidbodies not unlike Gibson's Les Paul Specials and Juniors. But as Stevens puts it, "It just never played out." The LJ II and III were dropped from the literature in 1990, the LJ I in 1991.

Designs of their own

Despite the countless student and intermediate grade guitars made by Kay, Harmony, Danelectro, and others,

Fred Stuart and John English with a pair of Tele C/A models. Among the fanciest of the Set-Necks, the C/A guitars sported bookmatched tops, ebony fingerboards, custom pickguards, and locking tuners. Fred Stuart proudly displays a C/A version of his long-neck bajo sexto design.

and notwithstanding the thousands of fine professional instruments made by Rickenbacker, Epiphone, Guild, Gretsch, and others, when it comes to the modern age of the electric guitar, two names dominate: Fender and Gibson. While both companies manufacture instruments of many styles, Fender, of course, is best known for building solid-bodies with single-coil pickups and screwed-in ("bolt-on") necks. Many of Gibson's most highly acclaimed guitars have humbucking pickups, and all of them have glued-in, or "set," necks. Needless to say, Gibsons aren't the only guitars with humbuckers and glued-in necks, any more than Fenders are the only ones with single-coils and bolt-ons. But those two companies' bread-and-butter models became worldwide icons so long ago that even vaguely similar designs from several manufacturers are often referred to as "Gibson style" or "Fender style."

Starting in 1990, the Custom Shop began to develop a line of guitars that although less radical than the Stevens LJ would nevertheless mark a major departure from Fender's traditions of design and construction. The new line of "set-neck" guitars would position Fender as a direct competitor to its archrival in the prestigious and lucrative glued-in/set-neck category traditionally dominated by Gibson's Les Pauls, ES-335s, and other instruments.

The Custom Shop's first Fender-brand Set-Necks were Telecasters. (The official "Set-Neck" designation appeared with and without a hyphen.) J. Black recalls making a pair of prototypes for John Page in June 1990. Page had requested them for a sales meeting, and within a few months the new Set-Neck Telecasters were offered to the public. They predated the price list [Chap. 12] and were intended more or less to replace projects such as the Kubicki basses and the LJ guitars. Some of the employees who had worked on those instruments were reassigned to the Set-Necks.

Scott Buehl: "I went right from the LJs into the Set-Neck line. John English was my boss, and I don't remember much of a transition. It seemed like the day the LJs were done we were ready for the Set-Necks. It was intense; it seemed we had to get going right away. I was trying to find some guys to help who could work fast and do a good job, and I happened to run into Todd Krause in a dive bar in Upland about a mile down Route 66 from my house. I said,

This worker is using a fixture originally set up to carve the tops on the LJ models and here is being used to shape the neck/body joints on Set-Neck Telecasters.

Binding a Set-Neck Tele body.

Using a CNC machine to cut the Boulanger-designed set-neck heel.

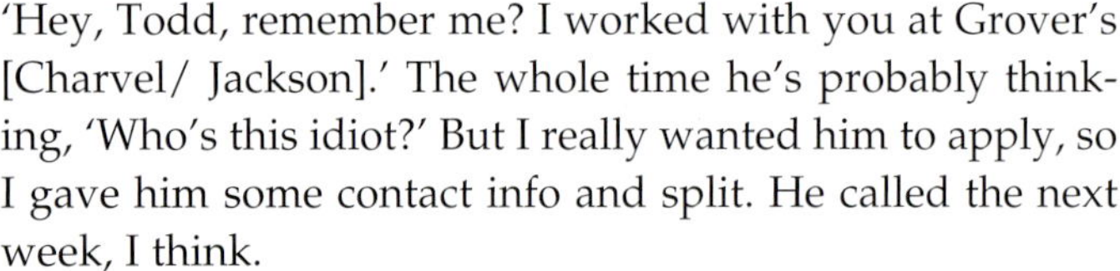

'Hey, Todd, remember me? I worked with you at Grover's [Charvel/ Jackson].' The whole time he's probably thinking, 'Who's this idiot?' But I really wanted him to apply, so I gave him some contact info and split. He called the next week, I think.

"We always tried very diligently to make the Set-Necks better in whatever way we could, and that fostered a competitive atmosphere with all of our egos to be the best in the shop. The Set-Neck Telecasters were much easier to produce than the LJs, although I do remember that the neck joint made it somewhat tough, and we struggled and jumped through hoops till one day we put together a couple of router jigs that would perfectly sync up the glue surfaces on the body and neck. That joint gives no room for error, and when Boley [Steve Boulanger] machined the first ones for us to mess with, it was clear we had to come up with a way to ace them. That joint has two parallel surfaces, a wedge, and two 'crush joints' on either side of the neck that all had to come together perfectly, so our usual tolerance of plus or minus five-thousandths [of an inch] wouldn't do. Those guitars were fun to build and I liked the mahogany; it just shapes nicely. You could glue them up fast with a minimum of clamps, so it made it easy because the fit was so nice."

The creation of that neck joint was a good example of how the shop operated. One of John Page's goals was to create a Custom Shop instrument that could also be manufactured within the main factory. That meant creating a set neck joint that could be fabricated from stock, Fender-style necks. John Page: "I asked Steve Boulanger and J. Black to come over to my place one Saturday to brainstorm. The three of us came up with a unique joint that worked perfectly with the existing Fender neck processes. It allowed us to create relatively large numbers — for the Custom Shop — of non-traditional Fender guitars."

The new design was fundamentally different from the Stevens neck joint. The idea was to permit the continued use not only of stock Fender neck blanks but also Fender body blanks and truss rods. J. Black recalls that Boulanger and Page "cleaned up" the design: "Besides the neck and body mod, the truss rod was still the basic American Standard rod that George Blanda developed in the mid-'80s; its

Prior to gluing, a pin is set that will draw the neck into the body.

Final shaping of the heel with a hand rasp.

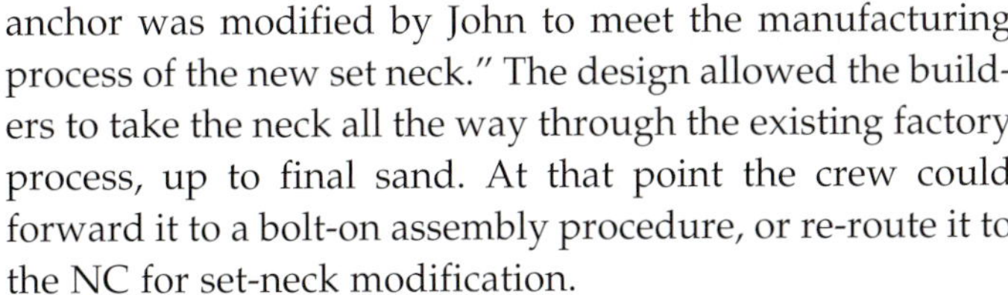

anchor was modified by John to meet the manufacturing process of the new set neck." The design allowed the builders to take the neck all the way through the existing factory process, up to final sand. At that point the crew could forward it to a bolt-on assembly procedure, or re-route it to the NC for set-neck modification.

The Set-Neck design was so distinctive that in June 1991 Fender applied for a patent. It was granted a year later, naming Stephen Boulanger, John Page, and J. Black as inventors. The key innovation is described as: "a set-neck guitar in which the inner neck end has a tongue that seats in and is glued in a pocket in the body and in a protuberance on the body. Corresponding sidewalls of the tongue and pocket are parallel to the center line of the body, while other sidewalls are at an angle thereto so as to create a wedge relationship. A cam and bearing element is provided to force the wedge surfaces together and improve the connection. The underside of the protuberance on the body is carved back, as is part of the neck, to create a generally integral-seeming joint. Crush points are provided to facilitate the operation and enhance esthetics."

By January 1, 1991, Set-Neck Teles were available in either solidbody or Thinline f-hole models. In the fall of that year, more Set-Neck Teles were announced, some with humbuckers and whammy bars. Also new that season was another Set-Neck Tele, the fancy maple-top C/A (also billed as the CA). During the same period, Set-Neck Stratocasters were developed in the Custom Shop. Appearing in the February 1, 1992 price list, these were modern, upscale models with bookmatched tops, ebony fingerboards, roller nuts, and locking tuners. The standard-trem and Floyd Rose-equipped Set-Neck Strats cost the same, $1,999, as did all four versions of the Set-Neck Telecaster.

The early Set-Necks weren't just some random way to round out the catalog. They sent a powerful signal. Ralph Esposito: "At that time Bill Schultz wanted to convey to the guitar buying public that Fender could do anything the world threw at us — we're not just a bolt-on guitar company — and we did that successfully with the Set-Necks and the Robben Fords. It was a new avenue for us in the Custom Shop, and it opened up a new market for Fender."

Cutting the nut for a Set-Neck Tele.

The builders sometimes selected the choicest woods for the Set-Necks and often applied custom finishes. Here, some of the very earliest Set-Neck Teles await the installation of humbuckers.

In fact, John Page conceived these guitars as the first in a series of original designs that would help establish the Custom Shop's own identity. They would balance traditional conceptions of what Fenders were supposed to look like with unique functional aspects that went deeper than mere cosmetics. In later years, descendants of the first-gen models would include the Set-Neck Tele Jr. and some of the Showmasters. (Dan Smith adds that the design's success contributed to Fender's decision to relocate production of the set-neck D'Aquistos and Robben Fords from FujiGen-Gakki to the Custom Shop.) John Page: "The Set-Necks were the beginning of the 'price list,' as we called it. It would turn out to be the Custom Shop's own product line."

Set-Neck Tele Jr.

John Grunder recalls having a hand in conceiving the mahogany-body, soapbar-equipped Set-Neck Tele Jr.: "I wanted to come up with something that would poke Gibson in the eye at a NAMM show, and John Page and I came up with the Set-Neck Tele Jr. Yasuhiko [Iwanade] knew all about Gibsons as well as Fenders, and he said that our 'limed mahogany' was actually closer to the original Les Paul Specials than the [re-issues] that Gibson had in their booth.

"I never intended for the guitar to go into the price list. I just wanted to sell a hundred of them. But at the show we got the orders for all one hundred in the TV finish, and they were gone instantly. I had Ralph [Esposito] go to the printer real quick to print up a hundred more order forms. I figured that the next color that would be big would be the cherry red over mahogany, like you see on an SG or the back of a Les Paul. Well, they all sold before the show was over, so Ralph went back to get *more* order forms. This time we specified a two-tone sunburst. I had no idea the Tele Jr. would be so successful."

Mahogany rush: Available in several finishes, the Tele Jr. featured a body with 11 chambers; some were made with three chambers, but the builders' recollections vary as to whether many of them ever made it out the door. Details: P-90 type pickups, a pau ferro fingerboard, and a flipped-around control plate. (John Page: "I always reversed the controls on my Teles to make it easier to do pinky swells. So did a lot of people.") Pickguards varied. The smaller one is shown here. The shape of the larger version can be seen on the Merle Haggard Tribute, Chap. 10. It was adapted by Fred Stuart from the Tele Thinline in order to show off more wood on some of the figured-top models.

merle
Fender
TUFF DOG TELE

CHAPTER TEN

10

The Halo Factor

Artist Signature Guitars of the First Decade

At your service

Along with the price sheet and the debut of the art guitars, one of the Custom Shop's most significant developments of the early '90s was a modest but vigorous program to design a line of "Signature Series" guitars, instruments whose exclusivity would distinguish them from the factory's own Clapton model and other artist guitars. The earliest examples were available by the summer of 1990 and advertised in the fall of 1990 and the winter of 1991. Although limited in number, they were official, cataloged models, intended for public consumption and typically featuring idiosyncratic details specified by the artists.

Concurrent with these standardized public offerings, the builders continued to craft one-off, personal instruments for the artists themselves. In both cases, they did whatever it took to accommodate their clients' requests. J. Black: "Jeff Beck said, 'I want a double whammy, with an arm on both sides of the bridge.' The Beck models don't have it; this was for his personal guitar. So Scott Buehl took a left-hand bridge block and a right-hand bridge block, cut them in half, and welded them together. We plated it, I made the guitar, and there you are, Jeff. That's how we worked. When an artist made a request, we honored it."

JD Dworkow is a guitar tech who has worked with Peter Frampton, the Rolling Stones, Bon Jovi, Prince, and many others. He also served as Fender's Artist Relations director, East Coast, in the late 1990s, and he set up Fender's New York City showroom. "The Custom Shop guys would bend over backwards for you," he says. "We were constantly ordering stuff, whatever our imaginations could come up with. For the artists, they could skip the shortcuts and protocols you'd have with a typical corporation. I could call Steve Grom with a special request on a Friday afternoon — they were three hours behind New York time — and I'd have a guitar or two when I came into my office on Monday morning. The shop people, including the ones in shipping, were our make-or-break allies."

JD was in the studio working on Jon Bon Jovi's first solo album, *Blaze Of Glory*, released in August, 1990. Bon Jovi brought in Jeff Beck to play solos. "We realized we

Left: From pearl-button tuners to gold-plated output jack, the Merle Haggard Tribute Telecaster is one of the fanciest limited-production Fenders ever.

record a half-step down," says JD, "so Jeff's guitars were all wrong, useless. John Page and J. Black came up, sussed it out, and figured it was actually less of a hassle to build new guitars than to re-set Jeff's guitars for these sessions and then set them back all over again, so they worked all night and built new guitars and set them up a half-step down. We got them in one day. Unbelievable service and dedication — lifesavers."

J. Black: "I assembled three guitars from factory production American Standard and Strat Plus parts, or I may have had some Jeff parts from all the Custom Shop protos we had been trying. I think I had a Beck proto in the works for summer NAMM and may have used some of those parts for the studio guitars. I don't think the signature model had been released yet, so this was also an opportunity to try some new things. We went back the next morning and gave the guitars to Jeff for the session. It was fun to see Jon Bon Jovi directing him in terms of what he wanted to hear. It never occurred to me that you told Jeff Beck what to play. With our backs to Jeff, I swore he was playing with a slide, but when you looked at his hands in the control room, it was just fingers."

J. Black (left) and John Page (right) put together three new guitars for Jeff Beck, literally overnight. JD Dworkow: "Unbelievable service and dedication — lifesavers."

Distinct identities

The first official artist guitar was a $1,900 Stratocaster based Robert Cray's '59 hardtail. It was followed by Telecasters designed in association with Albert Collins and Danny Gatton. Number four was the Jerry Donahue Tele, which appeared in Fender's February 1992 price list. The same quartet reappeared in the first price list devoted exclusively to the shop, published in August 1992.

But the official Custom Shop models and the personal one-offs were hardly the only artist guitars developed by Stevens, Page, and crew. As we've seen, the factory's first artist signature guitar, the Eric Clapton Stratocaster, was refined in the Custom Shop. Working with George Blanda and Dan Smith, the builders also prototyped the factory's Yngwie Malmsteen and Jeff Beck Strats during the shop's first year. Several of these early projects were in development simultaneously. George Blanda: "There was so much overlap in the beginning stages. The Clapton, Yngwie, and Beck guitars were all started in rapid succession but then took varying amounts of time to get finished and released. For example, the Yngwie started with Dan Smith and me, but the first instruments were built by Michael Stevens and John Page in the Custom Shop." The Jeff Beck model was similar, having been initiated as a marketing/R&D effort, brought to fruition in the Custom Shop, and then manufactured in the main factory.

Right: Star-board doubleneck Strats built for Richie Sambora. J. Black did the necks, and Fred Stuart built the bodies. A detail on the 12/6 guitar: The paisley designs continue uninterrupted over the pickups and edge of the pickguard.

Even with respect to the official models, there was no mention of the shop in the Fender literature of the time; the Cray, Collins, Gatton and Donahue guitars were simply described as "Custom Built, Custom Order Only." Over the next two years, three new artist guitars joined the Custom Shop line: the Dick Dale Stratocaster built by John English, the Buddy Guy Stratocaster built by Larry Brooks, and the Clarence White Telecaster built by Fred Stuart.

As the Custom Shop's artist program was getting underway, the factory's own artist instruments included the imported Robben Ford guitar as well as the U.S. made models associated with Clapton, Beck, and Malmsteen. The marketing appeal was clear: All four players were popular not only among guitarists but also among the general public. But while Cray, Collins, Gatton, and Donahue were also esteemed, world-class artists, how did they come to be chosen for the freshman class of official Custom Shop artist guitars? Dan Smith explains that initially the idea was to give those instruments a somewhat distinct identity by recognizing "players' players," artists who might not be household names but who were highly regarded by their fellow guitarists.

John Page adds that most of Fender's signature guitars up to that point were still originated by marketing and then produced by the factory. There were two reasons the Custom Shop would take on an artist guitar: Either the sales quantity was predicted to be too low to justify going through the production line, or the specs were too detailed or complex for factory production. The Cray Strat was a good example of the former; after considering it as a factory guitar, Fender decided that its hardtail feature would make it a specialized, limited-production model better suited to the Custom Shop.

Given their sometimes quirky details, low production numbers, and elite status, the Custom Shop artist guitars naturally cost more (typically a lot more) than Corona manufacturing's artist guitars. For example, in 1992 the factory's James Burton Telecaster listed at $1,399, while the Custom Shop's Gatton and Collins Teles, at $2,499 each, cost almost 80 percent more — for good reason, as we will see.

Teamwork

In the 1990s, ideas for artist guitars came from several sources. J. Black: "Marketing was one place. That's how Eric Clapton got the Lace Sensors. It wasn't like he called us and said, 'Hey, I hear you've got these bitchin' pickups.' Rather, it was Fender going to the artist's representative and saying, 'We've got something we think you'll really like. Please give it a try.' So there was a lot of interaction between R&D, the Custom Shop, marketing, manufacturing, the artist, the artist's management, and sometimes the road tech."

Part of this integrated approach entailed building upon longstanding friendships between the craftsmen and their artist clients. Some of these relationships preceded by several years the builders' arrivals to the shop. Before joining the crew in March, 1987, Fred Stuart had cultivated connections in Nashville. J. Black had worked in New York with amp guru César Díaz and through him had contacts with Bob Dylan and Keith Richards. Mark Kendrick knew Merle Haggard and Buck Owens. Michael Stevens had worked with some of the best known players in Texas.

Mixing it up, round 1

Employees in marketing, sales, manufacturing, R&D, and the Custom Shop often worked across departmental lines with little or no regard for rigid corporate structures. Internally, this was all well and good; such collaboration was essential to Fender's success. But from a public perspective, the catalogs sometimes failed to sort out who did what. For example, anyone attempting to discern which of Fender's artist guitars were made in the factory vs. the Custom Shop would find some of the early and mid-'90s literature unhelpful, to say the least. The Robben Ford models (made in Japan until 1994), the Corona factory's artist guitars, and the Custom Shop's artist guitars were sometimes lumped together in a generic "Signature" category with no clues as to their origins in FujiGen-Gakki's Matsumoto plant, Fender manufacturing, or the Custom Shop.

One example is the factory's initial Stevie Ray Vaughan Stratocaster (not to be confused with the Custom Shop's Limited Edition Stevie Ray Vaughan Tribute Model "Number One" Stratocaster of 2004). The winter '94 Frontline extensively quoted Master Builder Larry Brooks in regards to its development, possibly suggesting that the early SRV was a Custom Shop product. Actually, it was intended from the outset to be a factory model.

But the fact that Fender's literature didn't always distinguish manufacturing's artist guitars from their costlier

Custom Shop cousins merely reflected the company's evolving strategy regarding positioning the shop's instruments vs. the rest of the line. After all, they were all Fenders. It was also a likely result of John Page's parallel duties as supervisor of the Custom Shop and director of R&D for both the shop and factory. George Blanda: "At that time it wasn't just the Custom Shop models that were developed in the shop. The factory's artist models were also developed by the Master Builders, and they went through the shop all the way from initial planning through artist approval. This is always a long process with a lot of iterations, and the Master Builders could turn them around quickly. Once approved by the artist, the Custom Shop prototypes would be passed on to R&D. Our job was to make them production-ready." Other examples included the factory's Richie Sambora Stratocaster and the Stu Hamm Urge Bass, which were prototyped in the Custom Shop by J. Black. He worked with Fender engineer Seiki Goto and George Blanda before turning the projects over to Fender R&D and engineering for production.

Nine guitars

Along with the artist models described in captions here and in other chapters, this section profiles nine representative instruments from the shop's first decade. These are the Custom Shop's so-called '67 Jimi Hendrix Reissue Strat, Robert Cray Strat, Albert Collins Telecaster, Danny Gatton Tele, Jerry Donahue Tele, and Merle Haggard Tribute Tele, plus three Strats designed in the Custom Shop but produced in the main factory: the SRV, the Yngwie Malmsteen, and the Jeff Beck. Together with the discussion of the factory's Eric Clapton Signature Stratocaster and the more recent Tribute Series guitars, these accounts shed light not only on typical processes behind the development of Custom Shop artist models but also on the shop's indispensable role in developing factory versions.

Conjuring Jimi Hendrix

A Jimi Hendrix-inspired Custom Shop guitar was released in 1991, although it hardly qualified as a typical "artist guitar" and was never produced in significant quantities. Various authorities have speculated that perhaps only ten or so were made; Scott Grant recalls that the number was 15. It has been mislabeled the "1967 Reissue Jimi Hendrix Stratocaster," but it was not co-designed with any of the late guitarist's associates or family, was not officially linked to Hendrix's legacy, and did not "reissue" any specific model.

It was instead one of several attempts to evoke the Hendrix mystique for right-handed players. It had a left-hand neck on a standard right-hand body, a platform similar to that of R&D's obscure "top-scoop" Strat of 1979/1980 and also the factory's highly regarded Voodoo Strat of 1998. Details included an Olympic White finish, a large reverse headstock, a transition logo, a 4-bolt neck, and a Certificate of Authenticity signed by John Page. Two later Custom Shop projects, the Hendrix Monterey Strat (Chap. 19) and the Hendrix Woodstock Strat (Chap. 24), were far more successful in all respects.

Cray's hardtail prototype: Cockeyed perfection

Michael Stevens reports that aside from a no-trem tailpiece and a slab fingerboard, Robert Cray specified a certain pickup adjustment for his Custom Shop Stratocaster. "On his personal guitar, Robert had a certain setup that he wanted. He plays with his pickups almost flush with the plastic [pickguard]. Herb Ellis was another player who liked it that way; Herb always figured that if you had the pickup a long way from the string, you'd get less attack and

On Robert Cray's personal Strats, Michael Stevens aligned the strings slightly off-axis over the fretboard. He explains: "It gives you more vibrato room on the treble." This stock, hardtail Cray Strat features gold hardware on an Inca Silver body.

Preceding page: A Frost Gold Danny Gatton Tele, along with the model's original handwritten specs. Note details such as a bent toggle switch, a notched bridge housing, and a neck that's unfinished in back.

Left:The Custom Shop's Danny Gatton prototype no. DG0001 was built by Mike Stevens in 1991. This was Danny's main gigging guitar for two years. As explained in his handwritten note, he turned down a $10,000 offer for it. A relentless experimenter, Gatton himself added the third pickup. (Author's note: Danny handed me this guitar at a gig in the mid 1990s and rather suddenly asked me to autograph it. He was about to go onstage, so I signed it in a hurry the way I autograph my books. Of course, I was thinking, "Why didn't I bring *my* Telecaster for *him* to sign?")

Wacky logic: The Danny Gatton Tele

Perhaps there is no better example of just how far Custom Shop builders will go to recreate an artist's guitar, peculiarities and all, than the Danny Gatton Signature Series Telecaster, a guitar with more quirks than a Star Trek fan club. Ralph Esposito: "That guitar had all sorts of stuff — an extra [22nd] fret, an extra dot on the first fret, Joe Barden pickups. The selector switch spade was bent and the spring was loosened to be able to operate quickly between detents for certain Gatton effects. At the time we also did the two extra holes at the front of the bridge, which actually had Gibson pickguard screws holding down the bridge plate to the top of the guitar; it sat solid and flush so the resonance would come through. Normal Teles don't have that. Another thing, the frets were cut off straight. Danny would push the bass strings over the edge to get a certain effect, so he didn't want any reduction in the fret width. The frets were dressed and polished up, but they were straight on the edge because that's how he liked it.

"It's a good example of all the things we do, and also [an example] of a guitar evolving over the years. The shop makes each artist guitar to the 'T,' just the way the artist's own guitar is. Danny's Tele had that stainless steel bridge with a missing section at the bottom of the bridge plate. I came up with a way to cut it back the way Danny had done it. I used a special cutter on the Bridgeport, which is a metal mill that's kind of what you would have left if you took the computer works out of a CNC; the X axis and Y axis are done with little crank handles. Danny had just filed it down in his garage, but you can't do it that way when you've got a hundred orders, so I went over to engineering and rigged a thing up on the Bridgeport, cut it back, radiused it on a grinder, and feathered it around just like Danny's. Each one was completed by hand.

"We had to find zircons for the little side dots on the neck so you could see everything on a dim stage. I found them because I used to deal with a jewelry supply company in Anaheim. That was part of the fun challenge for us — figuring out how to actually *do* all these things. I helped develop a way to put those markers in. Another thing was that Danny would use his tone pot as a wah-wah. He'd take it out to hammer the shaft and push the wiper down so that it was easier to turn. That was one of my other jobs, loosening up wipers on tone controls. So that guitar was quite an intensive project. It may seem wacky, but there's a logical reason for what the guy did at every step."

Sometimes an artist's specs are *too* quirky, which can hinder the guitar's acceptance among the public. Ralph Esposito: "Some concepts on that Gatton Telecaster were hard for customers to understand, so in order to sell a reasonable amount of products we listened to players and changed a few little things to make it a bit more practical. It used to have a '50s baseball bat neck, and there was no finish on the back. In a sense it was one of our first Relics, if you will. We didn't use that term yet, but on Danny's own guitars he just took all the finish off, so that's the way we did it at first. People had a hard time playing it with the way the frets were done and the chunkiness of the neck. I remember customer concerns that the frets felt 'sharp' or the back of the necks getting 'dirty' because the finish was taken off. We had a similar issue when we introduced the Jeff Beck Strat; the neck was initially patterned after his Les Paul and the public response was that the neck was too uncomfortable. So in these cases marketing made some changes to make the guitars more marketable." The guitar was based to a significant extent on Danny's '53. According to *Gruhn's Guide,* the Custom Shop version was available in June 1990.

Jerry Donahue's happy-accident Tele

The Jerry Donahue Telecaster proved to be one of the Custom Shop's longest-running success stories, no doubt because it offered loads of versatility while still maintaining its *essence de Leo.* "The whole thing was a happy accident, really," Jerry explains. He used to take both a Strat and a Tele to gigs. He spent plenty of time on both guitars, enamored of the Strat's neck pickup and the Tele's bridge pickup. "I started on Strats, but one time I picked up a Tele to demo an amp, and I was just so blown away by the sound of the bridge pickup. I thought, 'I've *never* played a Strat that had that kind of wallop.' For me, the bridge pickup is usually the weakest link on a Strat, and I've always thought that was a function of its relatively low output combined with the reduced string movement at the bridge." It wasn't long before Jerry began to play a Telecaster with a Strat pickup in the neck position, which provided not only the front-pickup tone he was looking for but also, to his ear, a better balance between the two pickups.

But that was just the start of Donahue's sonic journey. His Tele was fitted with a custom-made, Strat-type pickup in the neck position, but due to a convergence of flukes it did not perform as expected. It was better. "It ended up being out of phase," Jerry says. "I usually don't like that sound — too doinky, too nasal, no bass — but in this case I only got a taste of that effect, like a good Strat with the switch in the 2 or 4 position. I couldn't figure out why." He took the guitar to Seymour Duncan, who performed some tests and discovered that the front pickup had a capacitor inserted about halfway through the winding process. In the middle position, that capacitor altered the two-pickup sound from a complete to a partial phase reversal. "It just tilts the sound in that direction," Jerry says. "It hits that sweet spot."

One problem: The Strat-like middle-position sound was cool, but Jerry missed the conventional, both-pickups Tele sound, a classic tone indeed. Seymour came up with a 5-way switch that solved that problem and added a bonus. With the switch all the way back toward the bridge, you get the bridge pickup — "the magic," Jerry calls it; "this is why you buy a Tele in the first place." Next position: both pickups with the capacitor and the Strat-like pseudo phase reversal. The middle position provides the standard both-pickups Tele sound, with no capacitor, no extra phasing. Next is the front pickup with the tone knob engaged as usual; Jerry Donahue: "You can always roll off a bit of treble for a good rhythm sound." Far forward: front pickup, with the tone control removed from the circuit for extra brightness.

"Once I had this wiring finished," Jerry recalls, "I took it to Dan Smith. Fender was really over the moon with this setup, as was I. Dan said, perfect, we'll do it on your guitar. It was the first I'd heard of their plan to do a signature guitar anyway." Jerry had one other request: to move the front Strat pickup about a quarter of an inch further away from the neck.

"I love my guitar," he says. "Some signature guitars are too subtle, like they're going to appeal just to the artist and

The Jerry Donahue Tele sported subtle Stratocaster influences and a unique 5-way switching system developed by Seymour Duncan.

few others. Others are limited for the opposite reason — too radical or unconventional. But mine just brings into play sounds that had been popular for a long time; they just hadn't all been accessible on one guitar. If the switching wasn't enough, it was considered by many to be one of the most beautiful Teles ever, while keeping to the traditional look."

Artist Builder Larry Brooks proudly displayed the prototype of the factory's Stevie Ray Vaughan Signature Series Strat. This version, built in the Custom Shop, had a roller nut and no peghead signature; the pickguard's oversized SRV initials were mocked up on a piece of masking tape. Larry and Mark Wittenberg visited Stevie on the set of *The Tonight Show* and gained approval of the model.

Pride and Joy: the SRV Strat

The factory's Stevie Ray Vaughan Stratocaster was fully developed by Custom Shop Master Builder Larry Brooks in early 1990. Brooks explained: "Stevie called his old Strat 'Number One,' because that was the one he always wanted ready for all his shows. So we built the signature model to closely match that guitar. He loved the old natural wood feel, so we used a Super Glue finish on the back of the neck and then applied steel wool to give it that woody feel. And he preferred the feel and sound of rosewood. He felt maple was too crisp, and ebony too 'bitey.'"

Production was delayed following Stevie Ray's death on August 27, 1990. George Blanda: "At the time Stevie was playing a favorite Custom Shop prototype onstage. Seiki Goto had been given all of the information and had finished developing the instrument for production. Fender was just about to introduce the factory model when the tragedy occurred. The project was put on hold until the family felt it was appropriate to go ahead with the instrument as a tribute."

The shop-built SRV prototypes had the Wilkinson roller nuts Fender was using on the Strat Plus, and Stevie Ray liked the way they performed, but since he had played them in public only for a month or so, Fender decided to retain the traditional melamine nut for the production SRV Strat. Dan Smith: "Stevie's interest in the roller nut came up during his tour with Jeff Beck [fall, 1989]. He tried Jeff's guitars and liked how the roller nut helped with the standard tremolo tuning issues. As much as it would have helped with the promotion of the Strat Plus series, I felt the right decision after Stevie's death was instead to stick with the detail from the guitar he had played for such a long time." (Also see the Custom Shop's SRV Tribute "Number One" Stratocaster, Chap. 26.)

The Malmsteen Strat, production version

Although produced in the factory, Fender's second artist signature guitar, the Yngwie Malmsteen Stratocaster, was another typical example of cooperation among the factory, R&D, marketing, and the Custom Shop. George Blanda set to work on the project in November 1986, a month before Michael Stevens's hiring and two months before Michael and John Page arrived in Corona to begin setting up the Custom Shop. At the time, the American Standard Strat was in the last stages of its design phase and about to go into production.

George Blanda recalls: "Dan Smith had previously met with Yngwie and had started the process. He and I went to an Yngwie show in Long Beach to finalize specs. I took all the notes and measurements from Yngwie's guitars. He liked different features from several '50s and '60s Strats — there were no '70s Strats in the picture at this time. The first thing Yngwie said to me was, 'Let me show you something that you obviously seem to have forgotten!' He showed me the contours of his various vintage Strats — as if I were responsible for changing the contours in the '70s and '80s. I did pay close attention, and we did get the contours as correct as possible — given our hard tooling — for Yngwie's model and for all Strats. Dan also brought one of the first six production samples of the American Standards, which Yngwie liked; this connection was how the American Standard tremolo got included on the first generation of Malmsteen Strats."

Yngwie had a couple of main Strats and several backups. All had scalloped fingerboards, although no two were exactly alike. George Blanda: "Some were scalloped by him while the rest were done by his tech. We discussed which features of the scallops he liked better. Also, he didn't use the middle pickup and had lowered it out of the way on all of his guitars." In January '87, the Custom Shop's first month, all of Blanda's notes and specs were forwarded to Stevens and Page. Michael built the first prototypes, which Yngwie approved. Subsequent editions of the factory/production guitar featured the larger peghead, a vintage-type trem, a different neck profile, and different electronics. In

Like the factory's other artist models, the scalloped-fretboard, DiMarzio-powered Yngwie Malmsteen Stratocaster was developed and prototyped in the Custom Shop.

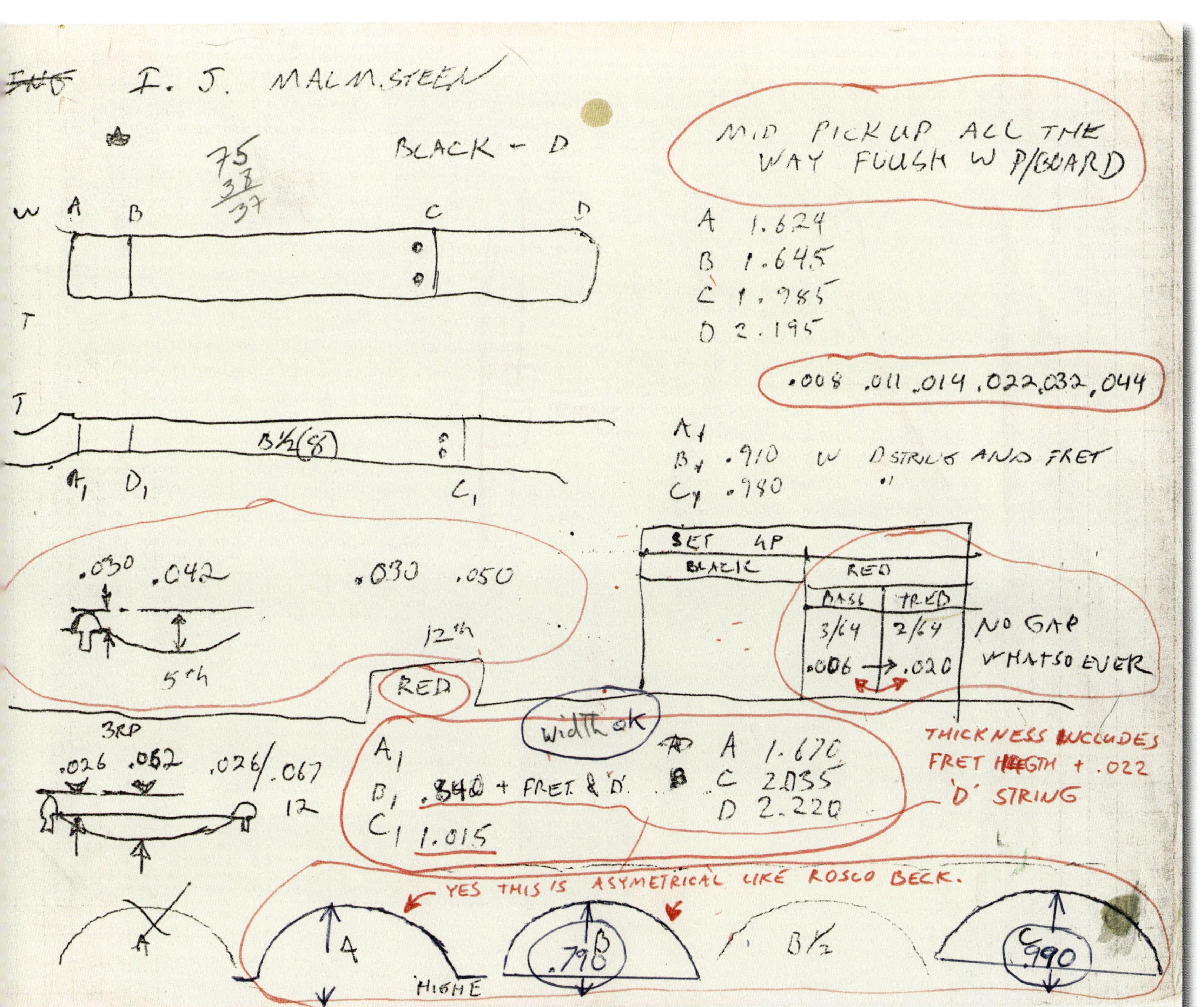

These drawings may look a bit crude, but they got the job done, documenting specifications agreed upon (after many conversations) by Yngwie Malmsteen and Custom Shop builders — neck width, neck depth, pickup height, string gauges, setup, and more. Toward the bottom of the sheet you'll see details regarding the Malmsteen Strat's slightly asymmetrical neck.

late 2008, the Custom Shop introduced its own version, the Yngwie Malmsteen Tribute Stratocaster (Chap. 30).

The Jeff Beck Strat, production version

George Blanda's recreation of Hank Marvin's Fiesta Red Stratocaster (Chap. 3) was presented to Marvin in early 1986. Jeff Beck and Eric Clapton were among the stellar artists attending the festivities, held in a London suburb. Clapton's signature Strat was in the works, and Eric suggested to Jeff that he might be interested in a similar project. As Dan Smith recounted in *The Stratocaster Chronicles*: "But Jeff was so modest — 'Who'd want a Jeff Beck guitar?' Eric tried to talk him into it, and they went back and forth. I did offer to build him a guitar. Jeff liked early-'60s Strats, so I suggested the '62 Vintage reissue. His only requests were a bright yellow, to match one of his hot rods, and 'the biggest neck you can make.' George Blanda built it and left the neck unfinished so we could work on the final shape with Jeff. We took it to a rehearsal, and he liked it so much he insisted he take it on tour to Japan — as is, and [with the back of the neck] unfinished."

As was the case with the Clapton model, several years would pass between initial design work and the appearance of the Jeff Beck Stratocaster. Once again, despite Fender's plan to offer the model as a factory guitar, the Custom Shop's involvement was crucial. Michael Stevens recalls: "John and I put together a bunch of Beck guitars with those big baseball-bat necks. At the time I remember thinking it was extremely cool that he loved the American Standards. That would have been my ad campaign, but nobody listened to me about that. I was at a Beck concert somewhere in the L.A. area, and he played the hell out of them. It gave me pause to wonder about vintage when a guy could do that on brand new guitars."

During the long process of negotiations and trial runs, one of the early Beck protos was evolved into the factory's upscale Strat Plus, introduced in 1987. George Blanda: "We didn't hear back from Jeff for ages and [temporarily] gave up hope on the Jeff Beck Signature model. One of the guitars we had sent had a very rough proto of the American Standard tremolo that we pulled off of the first American Standard prototype, probably in March or April of 1986. It had a Wilkinson [roller] nut and some cobbled-

The factory's Jeff Beck Stratocaster of 1991 appeared along a continuum of design and development that stretched all the way from Leo Fender's early-'60s rosewood-board Strats to the Custom Shop's Jeff Beck Signature Stratocaster of 2004.

up, stacked-coil pickups, like the first Clapton protos. This exact guitar, with the addition of Lace Sensors, became the Strat Plus."

In October 1989, at the direction of Dan Smith and John Page, J. Black built a trio of revised prototypes. One featured a blue finish that matched the guitar on the cover of Jeff's landmark *Guitar Shop* album, released earlier that year. Another was a deep purple Strat with a Brazilian board and triple Gold Lace Sensors; Jeff could be seen with it on the February 1990 *Guitar Player* magazine cover that he shared with Stevie Ray Vaughan. The third guitar was one of several "graphic" prototypes with a hot rod painted on the body. (Beck has been a serious and knowledgeable hot rod mechanic and collector since the 1960s; Pamelina H. recalls painting the image, from a photograph of Jeff's own car. In January 2007, experts commissioned by Ford compiled a list of "The 75 Most Influential '32 Ford Hot Rods," which included Jeff Beck's own 3-window Deuce Coupe. One of his cars was spotlighted on the cover of the March 2000 *Rod & Custom* magazine.) In March 1990, four years after the preliminary conversations at the Hank Marvin bash in the UK, J. Black crafted three additional protos — another purple one, a green one to match a guitar that George Blanda had made, and another graphic guitar.

The Strat Plus was Beck's guitar of choice until the long-delayed Signature Jeff Beck Stratocaster (as refined primarily by J. Black) was finally released, about a year after its official announcement in January 1990. An interesting side note: Beck's modesty was further reflected in his reluctance to see his name on the guitar. As J. Black explains, "Jeff was the first artist who said, 'Do not put my name on the headstock.' He wanted to play a *Fender*, not a Jeff Beck Fender." Beck relented, and the model did appear with his signature, which had been scanned from a *Guitar Shop* poster. The first official version of the Beck Strat sported a deep, U-shaped neck and four Gold Lace Sensors, two of them adjoined to resemble a humbucker. Later editions featured Schaller tuners, an LSR roller nut, Noiseless pickups, and a sculpted heel.

The development of the factory's Jeff Beck Strat and the Custom Shop's own version, unveiled in 2004, provides one of many examples of the intertwining legacies and collaborations among Fender's various departments. To backtrack: The Custom Shop's Jeff Beck Signature Stratocaster was based on the factory's Jeff Beck Signature Series Strat, which was based on the Strat Plus, which was based on a Custom Shop prototype, which was based to some extent on the factory's American Standard and to a larger extent on the '62 Vintage reissue, which was based on Leo Fender's early-'60s original.

The Merle Haggard Tribute Telecaster

Merle Haggard worked with Master Builder Mark Kendrick on the all-new Merle Haggard Tribute Telecaster, a contender for the title of Most Elegant Variation On The Tele Theme Ever. It's a modified Thinline with a laminated, figured maple top, body binding, a highly figured maple neck, overwound Alnico 5 Texas Special Tele pickups, an American Series bridge, gold hardware, pearloid tuner buttons (the same as used on the James Burton Tele), a two-tone sunburst, a very cool reinterpretation of the stock pickguard shape (rendered in ivoroid), a "Tuff Dog Tele" peghead inlay (a nod to Hag's pooch, Tuffy), a Merle Haggard signature peghead decal, and a 4-way selector switch (either pickup, both in parallel, or both in series). Perhaps the most unusual of its many distinctive features is its appearance as a neck-through design. Actually, it's a set-neck, but Mark carved away the heel, crafted a maple centerpiece, and attached contrasting alder body "wings" painted in Dark Salem for a striking neck-through look. The wings have Thinline type chambers, but unlike the Thinline this guitar has no soundhole.

Mark Kendrick began work on the project after meeting with Merle Haggard on January 10, 1996. He completed the prototype in May, and the model was officially introduced the following January. "I was the Artist Builder at the time," Mark recalls. "I'd always wanted to work with Merle in some capacity or another and was stoked to be able to build a guitar for him. They drove the bus right up to the shop's front door. I went out to greet the guys and after some formalities we touched on what we might be looking to do. One of the funny things was, Merle put on a dress coat because he was going in to meet the 'boss man' at Fender. After he noted Page wearing shorts and a work shirt, he sent the coat back to the bus. Page loved it!

"After Merle toured the factory, he handed me his Jerry Jones Tele-type guitar and said, let's start here. By all appearances it was pretty straight ahead, but then I noticed the neck-through design, and it was hollow. Merle had a two-day break in L.A., and that's the amount of time I had to spec it out. I had to figure a way to see what was going on with the construction but could not get at it, even with dental mirrors. My mother-in-law worked in the trauma room at Western Medical Center in Santa Ana. I called her and asked if they would X-ray the guitar. They were like, 'You want to X-ray a *guitar*?' So, I drove over and we did it. His guitar wasn't very Fender-esque inside, and I wanted to do something different. I started with a Thinline idea but figured I'd use a solid top. There was a beautiful piece of Western big leaf maple sitting in a dusty corner, and I got just enough of it to make a beautiful top. It had so much depth, it looked like feathers. Merle thought the top was so stunning he asked what kind of wood it was. When I told him it was Western big leaf maple, he had a tree planted at his place in Palo Cedro.

"Using the set-neck joint that Boley [Steve Boulanger] designed, I tried to make the guitar appear to be a neck-through. I hand-carved the heel really deep. Originally the fingerboard dots and side dots were a faux nitrocellulose tortoiseshell material that looked really nice. It was the only model where we used it, but we had difficulty finding a vendor who could supply it consistently, so Merle allowed us to substitute black micarta.

"I drove down to the fairgrounds in Del Mar to present it to Merle. He asked everyone to leave the bus except for him and me. He opened the case and just paused. When he went onstage that evening, he had the guitar strapped on. That's rare when an artist of that stature will play a new guitar the same evening. They usually have to get to know the instrument better. As it turned out, Merle and I have become dear friends. One of my prouder achievements."

The Haggard Tribute has since been rechristened the Custom Artist Series Merle Haggard Signature Telecaster.

Mixing it up, round 2

One of the Custom Shop's mid-'90s full-color catalogs was so extravagant that Fender put a $20 price tag on it. (This gesture alone helped to highlight the shop's exclusivity.) That publication and an insert that accompanied it further muddied

The strikingly beautiful Merle Haggard Tribute seems to have a neck-through design but in fact employs the set-neck joint patented in 1992 by Steve Boulanger, John Page, and J. Black.

the waters regarding the source of Fender's artist guitars and basses. They specified a diverse array of what were billed as Custom Shop artist guitars but were in fact a mix of Custom Shop and factory guitars. The text made no distinctions between the two groups. The actual Custom Shop instruments included the by-now familiar models (Cray, Gatton, Collins, etc.). These were pictured alongside the factory's Stuart Hamm bass as well as the factory Strats and Teles associated with James Burton, Jeff Beck, Eric Clapton, Yngwie Malmsteen, Richie Sambora, and Stevie Ray Vaughan.

Back then, why would Fender include factory guitars in a Custom Shop brochure? As noted, factory artist guitars were typically conceived in the Custom Shop. The other reason was that many of the artists' personal instruments were built there as well, even if their signature guitars were factory models. To the extent that there was any sort of rationale at all, Fender felt that these associations were sufficient to justify grouping all of the signature guitars together, despite the inevitable confusion resulting from labeling factory guitars as Custom Shop products.

Another issue was marketing's budget. Dan Smith: "We were short on bucks for advertising, as always, and we decided that great photos on high-end paper with little verbiage would give us the most bang for the buck. We listed *all* the artist guitars in that Custom Shop catalog, whether or not they were actually from the Custom Shop. This helped sell the expenditure to Bill Schultz, and without that I doubt the brochure would have been approved." Fender has long since removed any ambiguity; for more than a decade all literature has clearly and proudly distinguished Custom Shop guitars from manufacturing's models.

The Namesakes of 1996

Fender released two matching catalogs in 1996, both labeled Volume 50, No. 1, one for the Custom Shop and one for the rest of the line. The Custom Shop version now grouped the artist guitars under a new category, Namesakes. (The general Fender catalog continued to use "Artist Signature" for the factory's guitars — Beck, Clapton, Vaughan, Sambora, etc. Note that Jerry Donahue was associated with both a Custom Shop artist model as well as the more affordable J.D. Telecaster, which despite its occasional appearance in the "U.S. Signature Series" was imported from Japan.)

Mike Lewis had assumed responsibility for electric guitar marketing in the previous year. He explains: "I started calling the signature models 'Namesakes.' It was just a way to put guitars together that were tied to a name. Most of them were 'artist signature' models, but the D'Aquisto guitars were the exception, associated with the builder rather than an artist. So the more general 'Namesakes' designation seemed to be a better fit than 'artist.' Also, 'Signature' seemed generic. That's what everybody used, so I came up with 'Namesakes' just to set them off."

> "When an artist made a request, we honored it."
> — J. Black

The models included the three D'Aquistos (the Ultra with and without a pickup were listed as separate models), three Robben Fords (Elite, Ultra SP, Ultra FM), continuing Teles and Strats named after Robert Cray, Dick Dale, Jerry Donahue, Danny Gatton, Albert Collins, and Clarence White, along with the year-old Waylon Jennings Tribute Telecaster.

Introduced in the summer of 1995, the Jennings was the first of the shop's "Tribute" guitars. In the coming years, Fender would use this new designation in various ways. At first, it was applied to guitars associated with esteemed Fender players who were known more for their singing or songwriting than their guitar playing, Waylon Jennings and Merle Haggard being ideal examples. For a time Fender also considered invoking the name when honoring artists who had passed away before the builders had a chance to collaborate with them on signature instruments. As we will see in upcoming sections, starting in 2000 the Tribute designation was reassigned semi-consistently to a series of meticulous recreations of the personal guitars of

Muddy Waters, Andy Summers, Eric Clapton, Stevie Ray Vaughan, Rory Gallagher, Yngwie Malmsteen, Jeff Beck, and others.

The halo factor

January 1997 marked the end of the shop's first decade. The Artist Signature series numbered two Strats (the Robert Cray, at $2,199, and the Dick Dale, at $2,699), four Telecasters (the Albert Collins, $2,949; Danny Gatton, $2,949; Jerry Donahue, $2,499; and Clarence White, $3,799), and three Robben Fords (see Chap. 15). In a class by itself, the Waylon Jennings Tribute Telecaster was $3,599.

Like the signature guitars of 2000 and later, the Custom Shop's artist guitars of the 1990s were built with motives other than profits. Mike Lewis: "We keep them in the line even if they are only selling a few guitars. There's the 'halo factor' — the way these things reflect well on the whole line and the whole company — and also it's our way of acknowledging an artist we really admire and care about. We can show we love this artist and we've worked with him to create his particular dream guitar, which translates to: We can create your dream guitar, too. If his guitar is right for you, you can get one just like it. If we don't sell that many, it's okay, because what it's really about is raising the bar and the level of the whole shop. It means these great artists have come to us. They play our stuff, we work closely with them, and we are the only place that can do this. I mean, you look at some of these artist models and think, *who is going to build a guitar like that?* Well, we don't mind if it has unique features particular to that artist's style. In fact, that's the whole point."

John English co-designed and prototyped the appropriately flamboyant Dick Dale Signature Strat and called it "basically a 1960 Stratocaster with three custom vintage pickups." The once and future Surf Guitar King described the sound of the front pickup as "real fat," the middle as a bit lower in volume, and the "saddle" pickup as having a "trebly bite." According to Fender, this Chartreuse Sparkle, reverse-headstock beast has "a special switch that simultaneously turns on the neck and middle pickups to produce the guitar's trademark wall of sound." Note the reverse slant of the bridge pickup, which likely gave even more oomph to Dale's trademark tsunami cascades on the bass strings. Tone knobs? Who needs 'em?

Built by Fred Stuart, the Clarence White Signature Telecaster featured a string-bending device invented by White and Gene Parsons (the two had performed together in one of the greatest American bands of all time, the Byrds). The StringBender, also "B-Bender," works by pressing down on the guitar neck, which activates a strap button mechanism that shifts the B string's pitch a full step for pedal steel effects. Fred Stuart: "We modified the feel of the B-Bender's pull to replicate that of the original." The Clarence White Telecaster had a Custom '54 Stratocaster pickup in the front position and a Texas Special Tele pickup at the bridge.

Announced in the summer of 1995, the floral-motif, double-bound Waylon Jennings Telecaster was co-designed by Jennings and Larry Brooks, based on Waylon's customized '63, and built by the Custom Shop staff. Dru WhiteFeather crafted the "White Rose" leather body inset, and George Amicay inlaid the "Flying W" at the 12th fret. The low E's tuner is a Scruggs peg.

Fender

CHAPTER ELEVEN

11

Art Guitars and the Wow Factor

"It's all about the sky's the limit."

One could argue that Fender's first "art guitar" was the sleek Stratocaster of 1954. Long recognized not only for its functionality and distinctive voice but also for its sensuous curves, the Strat is a museum-quality example of how the great industrial designers of 20th Century America melded art and practicality to produce everyday objects of timeless beauty. Or, how about a '57 Mary Kaye? Or, consider a '62 Jaguar, gleaming in Candy Apple Red paint and armored in chrome like some Best Of Show hot rod? Or for that matter, how about any of the Custom Color guitars and basses of the pre-CBS period? Were these not "art guitars" of the highest order?

But in the early years of the Custom Shop, the term "art guitar" would take on new meaning at Fender. The shop's most flamboyant creations were one-of-a-kind guitars built to showcase the artistry of the shop, to spotlight its individual craftspeople, and simply to boggle minds. While the idea of designing instruments to be anything other than musical tools would have seemed as foreign to Leo Fender as a Village People reunion tour, the spotlight-grabbin' "art guitars," as John Page dubbed them, quickly became the most prominent creations of Fender's rapidly expanding Custom Shop.

The program got underway in earnest in 1992 and 1993, although various art guitars

Surely one of the most elaborately adorned guitars of the 20th Century (or any century), Fred Stuart's Mayan/Aztec Telecaster was displayed in 1995. Fred reported: "Ancient art themes seem to lend themselves to guitars. This instrument is a tribute to the Mayan and Aztec cultures. [Inlay artist] Larry Robinson, working from a rough sketch of mine, added his own creative refinements to the original design." The use of Corian was suggested by the success of the Egyptian Telecaster of the previous year. Fred Stuart: "A guitar like this — I can't even imagine how many hours we had into that thing." The inlays were cut from pearl, plastic, abalone, and various metals. John Page reported that the shop turned down a $75,000 bid for the guitar.

had been built in the shop as early as 1990. In the winter of that year, the shop's modest NAMM show display featured a glitzy Stratocaster with a reverse headstock, an f-hole semi-hollow body, and a silver-flake paint job covering the entire instrument, even the fingerboard. Also in 1990, John Page built an extraordinary, big-body Telecaster to help celebrate a concert to benefit the Nordoff-Robbins Music Therapy Centre in London (see p. 185).

The more or less official art guitar program was to some extent another consequence of the price list of 1992 [Chap. 12]. J. Black: "All of a sudden, the art guitar stuff really blossomed. You've got Fred Stuart out there discovering Corian and putting it on guitars. Most of us reacted by saying, 'Um, sure, Fred. Have fun.' We didn't know what to make of it. But I don't know if that kind of freedom would have been possible without the price list relieving some of the production pressure. It gave us breathing room so we had time to come up with new, very creative things, rather than just trying to keep our heads above water all the time."

Within a year after publication of that '92 price list, the art guitars had begun to spark a significant increase in the shop's public posture, especially at the NAMM trade shows. The builders were encouraged to create whatever they dreamed up and, at first, they were told they could keep the instruments once the guitars had dazzled dealers and other trade show onlookers. George Blanda's Detroit-meets-Fullerton Rocketcaster helped raise the bar, and before long other builders, sometimes working with Pamelina H. and other independent contractors, had risen to the occasion with showstopper creations of their own.

John Page, John English, Fred Stuart, Alan Hamel, J. Black, woodcarver George Amicay, and others collaborated on a seemingly endless stream of astounding guitars. They drew their inspirations from multifarious cultures and traditions, including Cowboy/Western, Native American, Celtic, Egyptian, Aztec, Mayan, Art Deco, the '50s car and motorcycle scene, '60s psychedelia, girlie pinups, comic book art, and tattoo art. Rarely has any guitar company experienced such a supernova of unbounded artistry, as the Custom Shop workers integrated into their craft any number of art forms — woodcarving, metal work, tile work, leather work, bead work, pinstriping, pearl inlay, marquetry, jewelry, drawing, airbrushing, etching, anodizing, painting, and more. Their creations reflected moods and motifs ranging from baroque and formal to cartoony and whimsical. As if to further exalt the instruments and to celebrate the traditions or cultures that inspired them, some of the more regal guitars were accompanied by an entourage of uniquely crafted pieces — leather-bound cases, painted amps, custom clothing, framed artwork, or other accoutrements.

Fred Stuart was one of the earliest and most creative of all the Custom Shop builders. To this day his former colleagues marvel at the originality of his vision and the precision of his manual skills. John Page: "Fred Stuart took it to the limit. He had the wackiest ideas. His trilogy of the Egyptian, Mayan/Aztec, and Celtic pieces were absolutely amazing." What inspired Fred Stuart's daring artistry? He recalls, "Remember those Bo Diddley Gretsches? There was that rocket ship kind of guitar on the cover of that album [*Bo Diddley is a Gunslinger*], and the rectangular guitar that he was seen with in all those photos. That got me to thinking that guitars didn't have to look like L-5's or Les Pauls or Telecasters. They could be fun and really different.

"After I'd been in the shop for just six or seven months I built a guitar we called the Santacaster. It was like a Tele but with a square or rectangular body that looked like a Christmas present, complete with ribbon and some sort of foil decoration. I built it on my own time. I remember

Unique in every way, the "White Buffalo Miracle" was displayed in 1995. Native American craftsman Dru WhiteFeather designed it, several craftspeople contributed to it, and Jason Davis assembled it. WhiteFeather said at the time: "The appearance of a White Buffalo is a sign that prayers of abundance are being heard and the sacred pipe is being honored. To celebrate the recent birth of a White Buffalo, I created this Telecaster from the natural elements of wood, leather, turquoise, and silver."

The White Buffalo on the front was sewn onto the buckskin with tiny glass beads. George Amicay inlaid semiprecious stones into his carvings of the sacred animal on the fingerboard. The sterling silver parts were stamped with traditional native patterns. Details included a beaded elkskin gig bag with a lining made from a Pendleton blanket. George Amicay: "The guitar was stitched up like a tom-tom, with elkskin and sinew." Silver, leather, and beadwork by Dru WhiteFeather; hand-painted Hopi kachina by Sheree Henry.

Fender

Japanese visitors coming through the shop. They see this Santacaster and they're going crazy. Another early one was a black Telecaster with white binding and a clear, very thin Plexiglas pickguard. I cut out a piece of cowhide and put it under the Plexiglas, and we called it the Cowcaster. By the time the next NAMM show came up, I suggested to John that we could do some cool things like that, something no one had ever seen before. It would be a way to show off what we could do. No matter how goofy the idea was, the mantra from John was always, go ahead and build it — but don't let it impact your productivity. I'd say, okay, John, sure, but the fact is, it always *did* impact my productivity [laughs], because there were just so many man-hours going into those things."

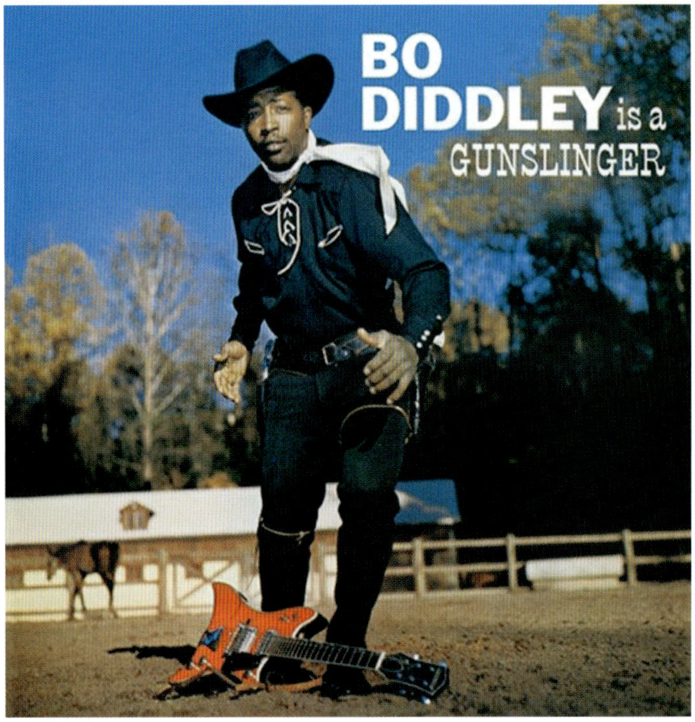

John Page: "Fred has this eclectic creativity, the coolest ideas from all sorts of sources. He took celluloid mirror sets or pens or poker chips and made inlays for fingerboards out of this stuff. I don't think that way, but he does, and he made very cool things." Fred Stuart: "I still use a certain kind of poker chip, a plastic called Harvite. It's a brand name. I've heard it called clay-fill and also abrasive-fill. It's a variation of phenol-based plastic, and it's the closest thing you can find to the original clay dot material [used for position markers on early Fenders], a little like Bakelite. It's kind of an antique or obsolete plastic now, but I go to swap meets and I'm always looking for those poker chips, because the plastic looks exactly right on fingerboards."

George Blanda recalls that a trade show in 1992 marked the first time the shop went all-out with an outrageous display of one-off Master Built guitars. "John had thrown out the opportunity for interested Custom Shop and R&D people to build artistic one-offs for the show, so there were about ten or twelve great guitars in the display. He also had a plan of commissioning well-known artists to create concept guitars. They would be the 'Art Guitar' program, so that term could mean a couple of different things. The open casting call for interested Custom Shop and R&D people was even bigger the following year, but if an instrument generated any orders at the show, then whoever designed it would have to fill those orders." This burden impacted the workloads of some builders so drastically that the program was scaled back and, on occasion, temporarily abandoned. (It continued in fits and starts over the course of the 1990s and was reinstated and reorganized under Richard McDonald's and Mike Eldred's direction in the 2000s.)

Guitars such as Bo Diddley's "rocket ship" Gretsch got Fred Stuart to thinking . . . .

Art guitars displayed in the summer of 1993 included the Robo-Caster, which had an anodized aluminum skeleton and a clear acrylic body; the Lipstick Jazzmaster, which had a translucent green finish and Danelectro-style "lipstick" pickups; a Strat and a Tele, both of which featured abalone and mother of pearl vine fretboard inlays and bodies with quilted maple tops and gold hardware; and the Phoenix.

By incorporating a rich diversity of pop culture themes and by partnering with iconic brands such as Playboy, Disney, and Harley-Davidson, the Custom Shop helped Fender to raise its profile beyond the musical instrument industry, taking its place as a pop culture icon in its own right. The art guitars also served to introduce to the guitar community the creative temperaments and unique skills of individual builders, some of whom would soon acquire their own fans and personal followings.

Aside from the PR advantages, John Page saw the art guitar program as a way to kindle a healthy competition among his builders, one in which they would learn from each other even as they tried to top each other's creations. George Amicay: "John really fostered a lot of this conflict. He felt that tension is sometimes how you break through to develop new ideas. I think he was fostering an attitude to try to get ideas out of us, so it was competitive because we were trying to top each other. And it worked. These people were passionate about what they were doing to begin with, and the more passionate you are, the harder you fight for what you believe in. But ultimately, we were all passionate about Fender. In spite of whatever else is going on, it says *Fender* on the headstock, so the ultimate goal was always the best product. We stood behind the pride that John Page felt, and there was a lot of supporting each other and camaraderie."

It was perhaps inevitable that given the program's success, it would expand beyond the one-offs to include limited runs as well. Fred Stuart: "We put all this time and energy into these guitars, and then we sold them and they would get swallowed into the world and disappear. Some would get shown at one show, and then they're gone. Like my acoustic Tele 12-string with a spruce top — that guitar came out really well, but then it just went to a customer and that was it. Bill Schultz realized early on that we could be getting more mileage out of them, so some of the ones that were designed to be one-offs grew into limited production models, whereas the Playboy, the Harley, the Disney, and so on were designed from the beginning to be limited-production things."

The metal-bodied Harley-Davidson was the first of what might be called the art runs — art guitars built as a set or a limited run, rather than just the single guitar. Before long some of the one-offs and art-run guitars were going on tour in Europe and being displayed not only at NAMM shows and guitar expos but also in some of the Hard Rock Cafés. On one occasion Fender took a collection of Custom Shop art guitars to Nashville and invited prominent guitarists to come see them. It all added up. J. Black: "The shop went from being this funky little thing in a remote corner of Fender to being this phenomenon with incredible buzz." Mike Lewis: "Some of the art guitars over the years were created for a particular customer and got sold, but mainly they were intended for shows and calendars and other displays. It was a way of showing the world what those amazing, creative guitar builders could do."

The art guitars not only dropped jaws and opened wallets, they also sparked imaginations. They reminded players that no matter how many more or less production-type models the Custom Shop might release, the heart and soul of the Dream Factory was revealed in a simple promise: If you can conceive it, we can build it, and we're not just talking about necks and frets and pickups; go ahead and let your imagination run wild. Many an onlooker came away from an art guitar on display or a picture in a catalog or calendar with visions of his or her own unique creation. Richard McDonald: "We need to have a stable of products, an actual line of Custom Shop guitars, which keeps the motor running and gives us the flexibility to go off in different directions and to experiment. As the Team Built thing offered the opportunity to order Custom Shop instruments with organized sets of features on a regular basis, the art guitars showed that we continued to offer limited runs and one-offs that take incredible creativity and artistry. They reminded customers that you can always specify every detail from the ground up, whether it's your own personal take on an otherwise spot-on vintage classic, or something radical that no one ever dreamed of before."

"In spite of whatever else is going on, it says *Fender* on the headstock, so the ultimate goal was always the best product."
— George Amicay

"The mantra was always, go ahead and build it — but don't let it impact your productivity. But the fact is, it always *did* impact my productivity, because there were so many man-hours going into those things."
— Fred Stuart

The art guitars were a response to Fender's competitors as well. J. Black: "Gibson was way ahead of the curve, and Fender was looking at what they were doing with their art guitars. They were at NAMM shows with all sorts of art guitars way before we had anything. Gibson had quite a team, and the stuff they were doing was outstanding. At first our Custom Shop was supposed to be that same sort of thing, but it dawned on us — that ain't Fender. A lot of our customers didn't want a Fender with the Beatles painted on it. They wanted a guitar that looked and played exactly like a '54 Strat, which the factory wasn't offering, so that was always a big part of it, too."

The first-generation art guitars were products of the shop's mid-'90s freewheeling environment. Still, while builders were permitted and even encouraged to create whatever they could imagine — no matter how elaborate, costly, or time consuming — someone had to keep an eye on the bottom line. Mike Lewis: "A lot of these art guitars were not built on the direction of marketing or sales. They were things that the shop just dreamed up and went ahead and did. As Vice President of guitar marketing [from 1995 to 2000], I wasn't really their boss. I wasn't running the shop. I was responsible for marketing, so I knew they were doing this stuff because we'd talk all the time and I would give feedback. Sometimes they took my ideas to heart, and sometimes they went ahead and did whatever they wanted [laughs], and that was okay."

How did Fender balance giving its builders all the creative freedom they wanted while on the other hand running a business and making a profit? Sales chief John Grunder played a key role early on. His tireless networking with dealers lent credibility to the art guitars concept. As one builder put it, not only did the art guitars look cool and push boundaries, but they could also be sold, which further encouraged builders to take risks as they explored their creativity.

Mike Lewis: "The Custom Shop is all about a guitar where the sky's the limit and it says *Fender* on it. At the same time, everybody understands what we need to do. Everybody knows what the basic business metrics are, but then if we want to do something on top of that, we figure out a way to do it. It's possible to be artistic and responsible at the same time. If they are taking months to build a single guitar for one customer, that customer is going to pay for it. It's all part of the program. Other times they are going to build things strictly for the wow factor, but that's part of the plan, too, to raise the profile. Occasionally I'd have to say, you really shouldn't do such and such because we need to channel our efforts into some other project right now, but they would still show up at a NAMM show with something nobody had seen before and no one even knew about, and it would just knock your socks off. It was a lot of fun. It still is."

In that respect, the art guitars continue to reflect one facet of Bill Schultz's original mission for the Custom Shop — to dazzle customers and dealers with artistry and craft. Dan Smith: "That part of Bill's vision never changed. You go to any trade show and there's some unbelievably fantastic stuff that will just knock your eyes out."

Kip Frank was a contractor who did electrical work at the shop's facility on Enterprise. "We did a lot of horse trading back in the day," says George Amicay, "and we did the Father and Son Cowboy Tele Set for Kip to keep down some of our costs for his electrical work." This Thinline Tele duo was built for Kip and his son Sean. The "S" guitar had a three-quarter scale. George Amicay: "The 'F' is for the last name, not 'Father.' I put the kid on the stick pony in the same position as the horseman, because the kid wants to be like his dad. I relief-carved these figures and then took a wood burning tool, sort of like a soldering iron, and scorched them for the black charcoal look." The guitars were built by J. Black and John English. Custom inlays, hide-covered pickguards, and gold hardware completed the set.

Images of many of the art guitars are dispersed throughout this book. This chapter and Chap. 25 present entire galleries.

Bird-O-Fire

Even among the Custom Shop's fabulous art guitars, the semi-hollow, carved-top Bird-O-Fire from 1996 was a standout. John Page was inspired by the extraordinary work of French Art Deco jeweler and glass artist René Lalique, and that influence is seen in the design of this chambered, set-neck Stratocaster. It features pickups specially built by John Suhr, as well as a rosewood centerpiece in the quilted mahogany body. Gene Baker built it, Larry Robinson inlaid the body and neck, Pamelina H. did the painting, John Page built the picture frame, and all four collaborated on the design. For the inlays, Robinson worked with a variety of materials, including mother of pearl, abalone, silver, and copper.

Gene Baker: "Because I was involved with the Set-Necks and carved-top guitars, John Page gave me the Bird-O-Fire. He had found some very special quilt mahogany that I used. To be on the extra cool side, John Suhr made the pickups with no outside height adjustment screw holes. Instead, each pickup

The Bird-O-Fire's richness and coloring, the delicate beauty and intricacy of the inlays, the rendering of a nontraditional Fender logo, the Art Deco vibe — it all added up to a breathtaking piece that during the first decade virtually defined Fender Custom Shop Art Guitar.

has two screws mounted like on a P-90 soapbar that are hidden underneath the metal covers. John had to install them, then adjust their height, and then attach the covers with hot beeswax.

"I think I had the construction done within a month and sent Larry one body and two set necks. That gave us a backup neck in case something went wrong. Larry was given artistic interpretation on the inlay. Fred Stuart was working on the Mayan/Aztec Tele at the time, using a lot of Corian material, and I believe Fred or Page suggested we try replacing Larry's original mirror pieces with Corian. They got some nice pastel colors for the final revision. I made the Corian knobs and switch buttons and the abalone accents around the guitar." John Page reported that the shop turned down a $50,000 bid for the guitar.

The Knebworth Tele

This unique big-body Telecaster was auctioned in 1990 to raise funds for London's Nordoff-Robbins Music Therapy Centre. It sports autographs from Eric Clapton, Jimmy Page, Hank Marvin, Paul McCartney, David Gilmour, and other stars who performed at a June 30th benefit concert held near the village of Knebworth in Hertfordshire, England. John Page built it and fitted it with black and white binding, an ebony fingerboard, and a most unusual peghead that incorporates a hollowed-out variation on the Centre's logo.

John Page recalls: "The concert was going to present the who's who of rock and roll, and I was totally stoked to do the project. Like a lot of these special projects, if I was really into it I would take it on myself, especially if my guys were buried. So I decided to build an oversized, bound Tele, finished in white. I thought it would make the perfect canvas for all those famous rockers' signatures. I also wanted to incorporate the Nordoff-Robbins logo. Just engraving it on the pickguard was easy and obvious, and I wanted to do more. Their logo was a modified treble clef, and I decided to incorporate it into the peghead, but in a unique way. I ended up hand-cutting it out in .050" brass sheet stock with a fine jeweler's saw, which took hours. I then had it chrome-plated, and I inlaid it into the peghead. I also decided to have the peghead open all the way through, in the body of the treble clef. It turned out really cool. It retained the Fender signature peghead and also incorporated their logo.

"This project was important to me for a very personal reason. Paul McCartney was why I wanted to get into music in the first place. I still remember as a kid watching the Ed Sullivan Show in '64 when the Beatles were on. Paul became my inspiration to be a musician and songwriter. Although that part of my career ended in my early 30s, it still led to my life of guitar building and designing. You can imagine my excitement when I was given the opportunity to spend the entire day backstage having the artists sign the guitar. I had dealt with some of them in the past, but the chance to meet and chat with Paul McCartney was one of the greatest highlights in my career. He joked and laughed with me and made me feel quite special because of the guitar. It's always nice when you meet your heroes and they don't disappoint."

The Knebworth Tele, before it was autographed by some of the biggest names in music.

Rock like an Egyptian

One of Fred Stuart's masterpieces was the Egyptian Telecaster, a Corian-covered guitar displayed in the summer of 1994. Stuart reported in an early *Frontline* brochure: "Egyptian art has had a profound effect on modern art, and has been incorporated into everything from architecture to rock and roll. For me, this project came together when I met George Amicay, a very talented woodcarver, who applied his skills to carving Corian, a synthetic stone made by Dupont. The final element was a trip to Las Vegas, just after the Luxor opened their pyramid. I noticed they used Corian in some of the construction, and I thought, 'I see a guitar,' and this is what we came up with."

Fred Stuart added in 2009: "This was relatively late in the shop's [first] series of art guitars. I was increasingly fascinated with Corian, the countertop material. I liked

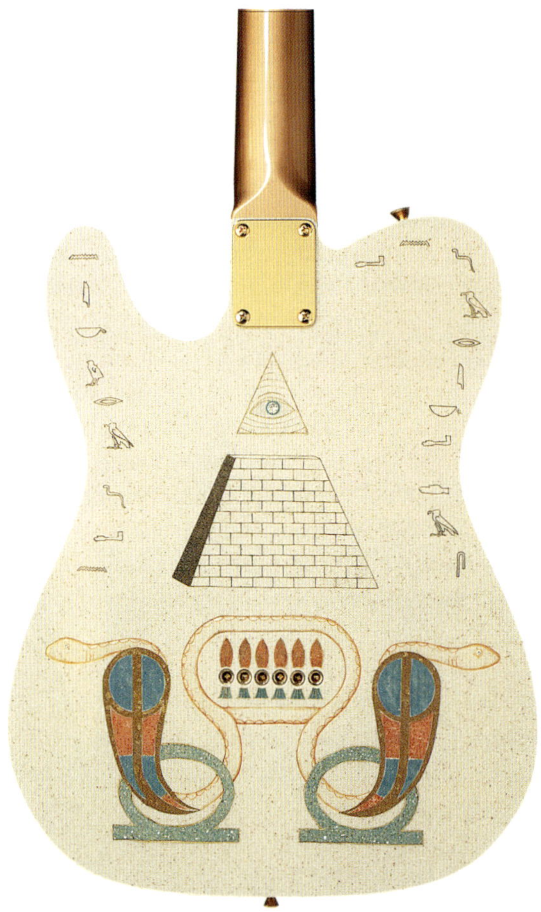

The Egyptian Telecaster.

the way you could work it into a lot of different shapes. I thought I could cut it really thin and cover a guitar and make it look like it was made out of stone. There are so many materials and different techniques that went into this guitar, like the scarab has some abalone in it. For some of the colors we would crush up deep blue lapis lazuli and make dust out of it."

George Amicay: "All the color you see? A lot of it is crushed stone, copper, and other things. On the falcon [upper bout], that's crushed coral, and I relief carved it the same way the Egyptians did. I would carve out a channel after drawing the outline, and we would fill the space with crushed stone and then flat-sand it. It's hard to see unless you're holding the guitar, but on the neck the hieroglyphics spell out the names of Bill Schultz and Kurt Hemrich. Under the falcon, just to the left of the pickguard, it's J-O-H-N, and next to that, on the pickguard itself, it's P-A-G-E. On the right [treble side] of the pickguard, it's F-R-E-D and S-T-U-A-R-T. To the left of the bridge cover the hieroglyphics say *Fender Custom Shop, Corona*, and to the right it's my last name. Underneath are two Egyptian gods. On the back, the green is crushed abalone and turquoise. The hieroglyphics spell out the names of my daughters."

What Sort of Man Plays Fender? The 40th Anniversary Playboy Strat

In 1949, a photographer in the employ of a calendar company took a nude image of an aspiring actress. By the time she posed for the photo, 22-year-old Norma Jeane Baker had changed her name to Marilyn Monroe. Hugh Hefner purchased the rights to the image and printed it in the premiere issue of his new magazine, which he called *Playboy*. It debuted in December 1953, when Marilyn Monroe was on the cusp of stardom. Eventually appearing on millions of calendars, postcards, key chains, playing cards, and the like, the photo, titled "Golden Dreams," is one of the most famous images in the history of American culture.

James Peterson, a writer and editor with three decades of experience at *Playboy*, approached John Page and suggested a collaboration of some sort. Peterson reports: "I realized that Leo Fender and Hugh Hefner had gone into their garage/bedrooms at the same moment to create what became icons. I asked John if Fender planned a 40th Anniversary guitar that I could feature in *Playboy*. He countered with an offer to make a Playboy 40th Anniversary guitar. He had a very short list of companies he wanted to do business with. Harley was number one, Playboy number two.

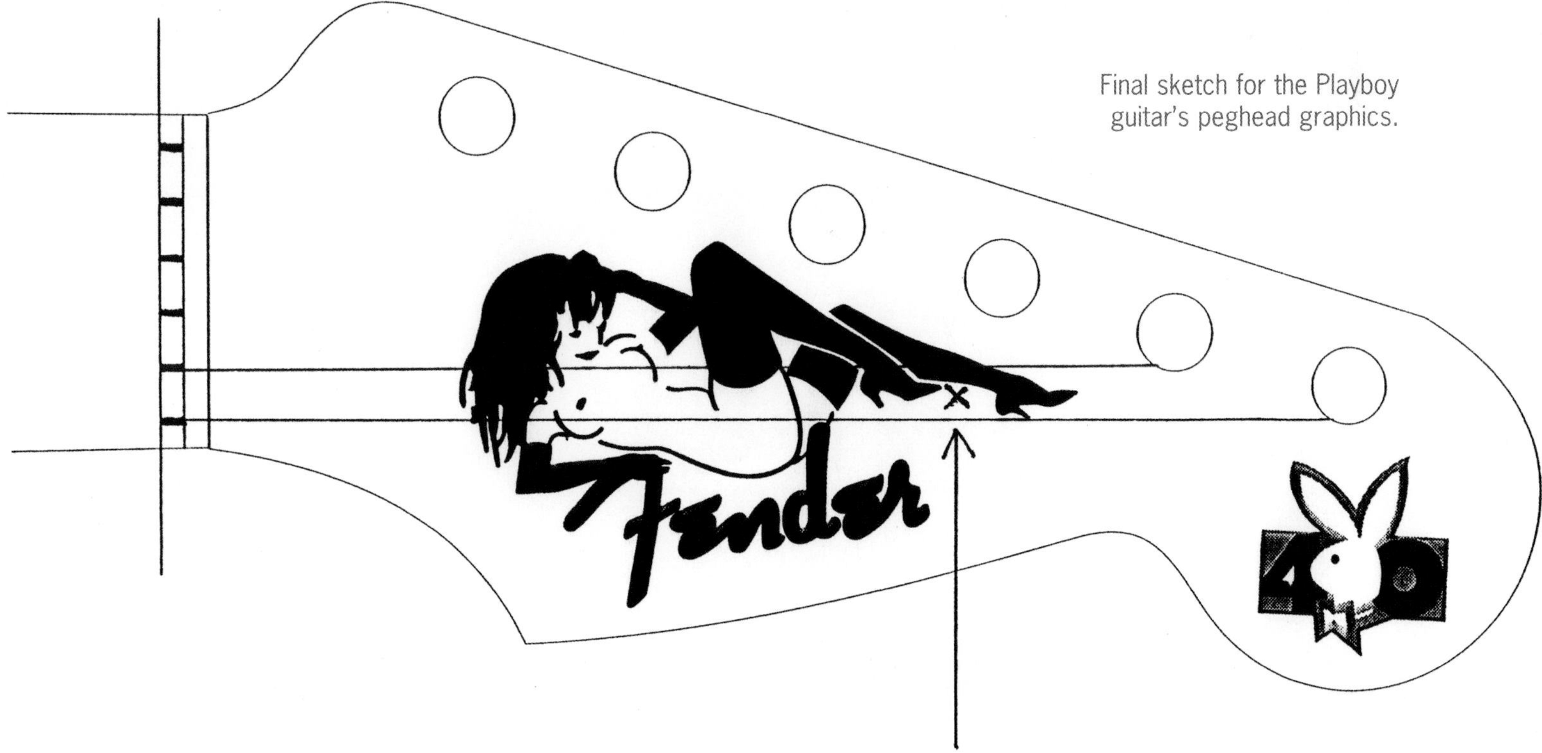

Final sketch for the Playboy guitar's peghead graphics.

"John and I worked on the design. He wanted a vintage look, something like Vargas pinups on WWII bombers. I suggested the Marilyn pinup. I still recall the moment her curves settled into the curves of the Stratocaster. It just seemed so right. The evolution of the design was a delight. John wanted the Femlin; I wanted rabbit heads on the neck — my daughter's idea. John and I had a long and wonderful discussion about working within the constraints of a legend. He compared the Fender/Gibson rivalry to Playboy/Penthouse. There were things our loyal players and readers would not tolerate, things we could do technically but not without killing our identity. I still recall my tour of the Custom Shop, with guitars hanging like bats from the ceiling. I met an aerospace engineer [George Amicay] doing woodcarving that would have been at home in a cathedral. It was without doubt one of the magical experiences of my term at *Playboy*. If I could describe the recognition, the feeling, it was sort of like being knighted, if not by the king, then by a peer."

John Page: "Jack Shelton had come up with the Diamond Dealer program, a way for us to offer exclusive deals to favored retailers. We had done the Harley and were looking for another project, and it all came together perfectly with *Playboy*. I had Pamelina do a pinup girl with a ribbon wrapped around her that said "Happy Birthday," but Hugh Hefner said no, it's got to be Marilyn, so that was

his choice. We brought in the Femlin [the black-gloved, black-stockinged feminine gremlin seen on the headstock] and all the bunnies as iconic characters." James Peterson: "What could have been clutter became sleek, understated, letting just the three symbols — Marilyn, the Femlin, the rabbit head — say *Playboy*. The guitar said Fender."

Each guitar was hand-painted by Pamelina H. She created a master drawing and then Xeroxed several copies that she used as templates for the artwork. She recalls: "That was such a memorable experience. I painted all of them individually, starting from scratch on every single one, and every one went through my studio. There were 175 in the run, plus a few extras. That was all I did, pretty much, for a whole year. Sometimes I would only get a couple done a week; other times I would do as many as 10 a week.

"Frisket paper [a clear, protective sheet] was applied to each guitar. Then the drawing was transferred to the frisket using white transfer paper. The major areas of color were cut out of the frisket. With the Playboys, this was the body and the hair, with sections of the body being cut according to the needs of hard-line shading. I began by spraying the body colors on all ten guitars at a time. Then I added shading on the body, spraying the same color on all ten at a time. The body would be covered up, and then the hair color was sprayed. After this, the parts that were sprayed were covered, and the background was sprayed. Finally, I removed the frisket and painted in the details — the lips, then the eyes, then the hair details, etc. This was the best way to keep a consistency in all the work. The mass-production aspects made all of them consistent and similar, and the hand work made each one unique."

J. Black: "The special red leather case and Playboy strap that came with the Marilyn was a great example of Page following through with all these sorts of cool details and extras that tied into the guitar. Mike Eldred really picked up on that in a very smart and cool way in later art guitars, making the package more than just the guitar itself." J.'s records show that 100 pieces were allocated to the domestic market, 50 for export, plus 23 to Playboy, for a total of 173 instruments, not including an estimated three prototypes.

John Page adds: "One more thing that was wacky-cool. Someone in Scottsdale thought the more conservative dealers, especially in the Bible Belt, might have a problem with Marilyn's nudity and wouldn't hang it on the wall. I ultimately came up with a 'Chastity Bag' that would be like a negligee. I think Maria Torres's mom made them all for us, if my recollection is correct. These were red satin drawstring bags made for each guitar so the dealer could choose whether or not to go 'full frontal' while on display."

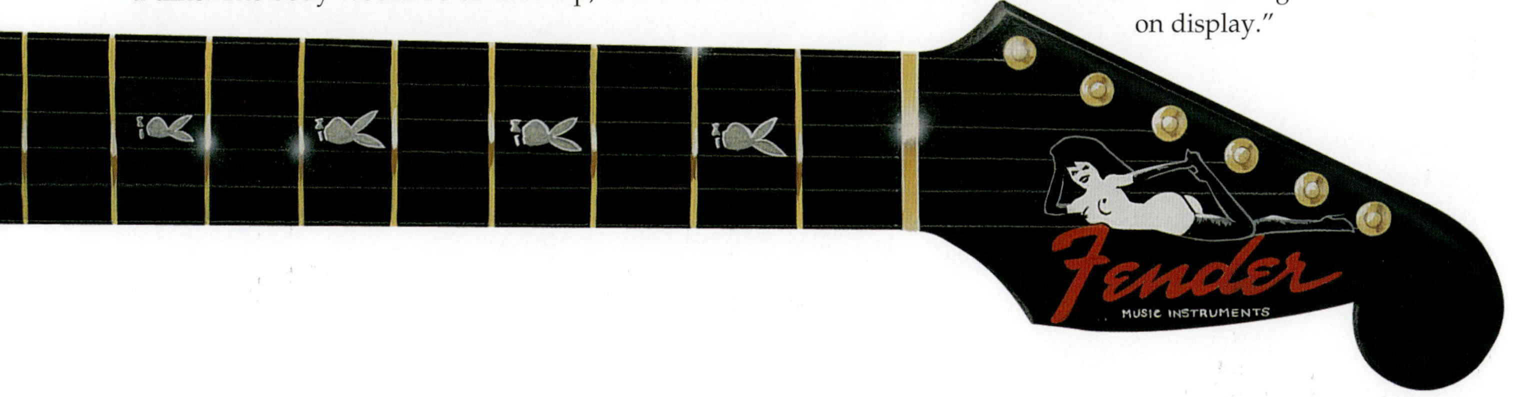

John Page: "I had Pamelina do a pinup girl with a ribbon wrapped around her that said 'Happy Birthday,' but Hugh Hefner said no, it's got to be Marilyn."

PLAYBOY

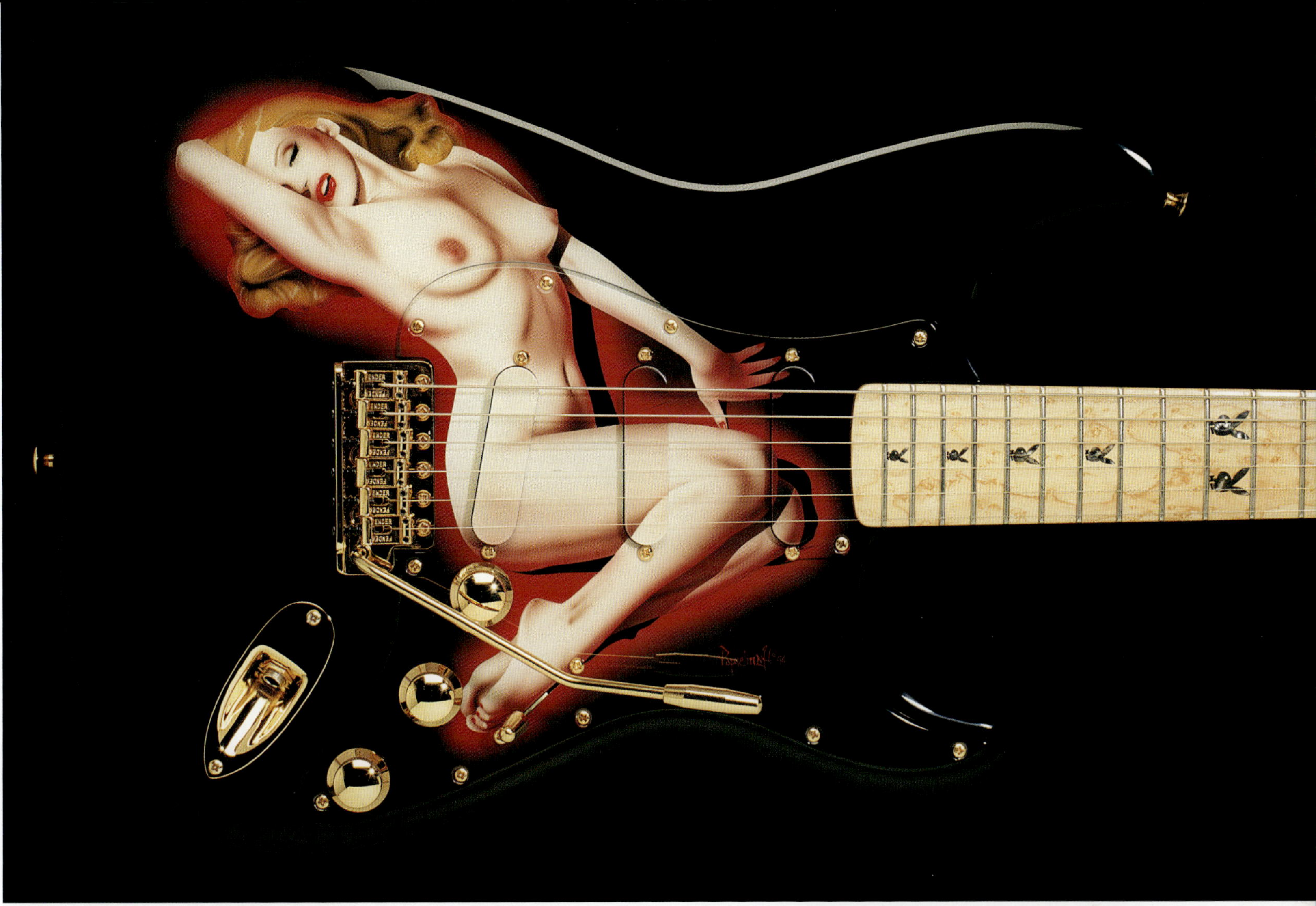

The Playboy guitar, production version. The original "Golden Dreams" photo of Marilyn Monroe was taken on May 27, 1949 and eventually appeared in the premiere issue of Hugh Hefner's new magazine.

Fender
Fender

Alan Hamel's Western Set

Grab Yer Fender, do-si-do! This jaw-dropping set was designed and built by Master Builder Alan Hamel. George Amicay did the carving, Pasadena silversmith Miles Haworth engraved the intricate patterns on the hardware, and Hamel made the silver Concho knobs, strap buttons, and calfskin pickguards. The alder bodies are double-veneered with flame maple over rosewood, and the necks are bird's-eye maple. The pau ferro fretboards sport hand-twisted sterling silver inlays. One particularly inspired detail: Hamel trimmed the body edges in hand-formed, sterling silver barbed wire.

Alan Hamel reported in early 1995: "When I was asked to build a western Strat/Tele matched set, the whole concept came together very quickly. I own a small ranch on which I raise livestock and breed paint and quarter horses for a hobby. My home is decorated with antique western memorabilia, books, and artwork that I used to help create these guitars. Custom Shop woodcarver George Amicay relief-carved the silhouettes on the flame maple tops to expose the alder underneath. We then used a saddle maker's leather stamp to texture the background. The sterling silver barbed wire was inlaid and clinched into the bodies in order not to snag the player."

George Amicay adds: "Most silhouettes are done where the subject matter is black and the background is light, but we wanted to reverse that for this project. The cowboy, riders, and other figures — that's the flame maple. I cut all the wood away around them to set them off against the background, which is rosewood. Then I stippled the background for texture and dyed it black." Note the astonishing craftsmanship and detailing around the edges of the bridge plate and control plate on the string-bender equipped Telecaster.

Woodcarving, silversmithing, and guitar building all went into Alan Hamel's Western Set.

The Rocketcaster

Spectacular yet sublime: Inspired by the exuberant styling of 1950s American automobiles, George Blanda's Rocketcaster was one of the shop's first art guitars (see the full-length photo, Chap. 1). He had read that Gibson's late-'50s Explorers and Flying V's and early-'60s Firebirds had been influenced by Detroit's futurist esthetic, and way back in the late 1970s he began to envision an over-the-top "Edsel" guitar complete with jukebox pushbutton switches. George Blanda: "By the time I actually built it in 1992, my taste in guitar had changed from overdriven distortion to the clean, clear sounds that had first attracted me to electric guitars. I toned down the styling from a parody to a more tasteful homage to the look of classic '50s cars.

"I also re-examined the Jazzmaster and realized that it was a serious attempt to create a solidbody 'jazz guitar.' While it's no ES-175, it does produce tones that are in line with Gretsch guitars, which were my main players at the time. I built the Rocketcaster using the Jazzmaster as the basis so that its sounds would fit a style of music that would also go with the guitar's visual vibe. It was designed and built in about a ten-day period leading up to a NAMM show. Due to a lack of time, the custom-mounted Jazzmaster pickups that I intended to make had to be replaced at the last minute with humbuckers." The chrome trim was hand-formed. Paint by Alfredo Esquivel.

Coolest detail ever: The Rocketcaster's knobs are chopped and channeled cigarette lighters from a '58 Oldsmobile. Vrrrooooom!

What would Liberace play?

Fred Stuart built this guitar. The body, neck, fingerboard, and the cover of the headstock were all done in Corian. The grapes and leaves are rhinestones, even on the output jack receptacle. George Amicay: "I did all the jewel work. Fred went to a lot of pawn shops and swap meets to find this stuff. The vines are relief-carved, and I covered them with 23 carat gold leaf. The position markers are inlaid, but I had to really dig in to get each pit deep enough to set the stone in. I filled it with Super Glue so you could play it without touching the stones. It's a very playable guitar. The theme was wine, women, and song. We thought, if we were to do a guitar for Liberace, what guitar would he play?"

J. Black: "With these sorts of guitars, we were kind of sneaking them in. We weren't necessarily given permission to do all the things we did. This was very early Fred, and it was amazing to see how quickly he progressed, like watching the Beatles going from 'I Want to Hold Your Hand' to Sgt. Pepper's in three years. To see how Fred progressed from this guitar to the others is mind-boggling." We can imagine that Liberace would have approved of the gold-plated lipstick pickups.

The "Liberace" Strat.

La Riata

Fred Stuart reports that this project brought George Amicay into the shop as a subcontractor. Amicay remembers: "My second day on the job, the people from Guitar Center came in. They had about 16 stores. I had just done a guitar for Fred Stuart called La Riata, where I carved rope around the perimeter and carved a cow skull and a cactus and a few things like that. Guitar Center came in and ordered one for each store. I had six months to complete them.

"I had never worked on a project that extensive. Just a little over a year and a half after the first time I ever put a knife into a piece of wood I was doing the Phoenix [Chap. 4], and it sold for tens of thousands of dollars. And now I found myself with an order for 16 La Riata Thinline Telecasters. Actually I did 17. The extra one was serial number 00. They squeezed it in for Larry Thomas, president of Guitar Center at the time.

"That project was like Groundhog Day, that movie [laughs] — the repetition. Every day, same thing. I did the rope on all of them, then the cactus on all of them, and so on, rather than finishing one guitar at a time. It drove me crazy, but one thing it taught me was how to work with people. That was a project from hell [laughs], but I loved doing it, and to see them all together lined up on a rack was amazing." The leather pickguard looks like it could have been cut from some bronco rider's hand-tooled rodeo saddle.

La Riata.

Below: Although the shop provided high-tech power tools, George Amicay preferred to work with his trusty X-Acto knife and his own handmade implements.

First Breath

George Amicay wanted to create a guitar with an environmental theme. He relief-carved the alder body of 1994's First Breath Stratocaster, and renowned artist Wyland painted it. The bird's-eye maple neck was stained a deep-water blue, and the ebony board was adorned with sterling silver insets. Abalone and chrome details completed the guitar. George Amicay: "I was a huge admirer of Wyland's murals of endangered animals, and it was an honor to work together. The guitar shows a blue whale pushing her calf to the surface for the first breath of life. I hand-carved the body and inlaid the neck. Afterward, Wyland painted his original design, and the guitar was finished by the custom shop staff."

The acclaimed marine life artist Wyland painted the First Breath Strat.

Below: George Amicay with the First Breath guitar.

The Disney Strats

One of the shop's most memorable projects was a limited series of late-'90s Disney 75th Anniversary Stratocasters. A collaboration among George Amicay, Disney animator/illustrator Chris Schnabel, and several of the Master Builders, the original hand-painted, hand-carved dazzler depicted some of the Magic Kingdom's most beloved characters. After the initial, ultra-fancy guitar was completed and given away in a contest, the shop built 75 much plainer versions for distribution through Disney galleries.

Magic Kingdom meets Dream Factory: Some of the most memorable characters in children's literature emerge from the white light of an open book on one of the shop's most fanciful creations, the one-of-a-kind Disney Strat of 1998.

Nice touch: Tinkerbell, wreathed in fairy dust on the peghead along with a custom-inlaid Fender logo.

Master woodcarver George Amicay with the original artwork, Master Builder Jason Davis, and Disney animator Chris Schnabel.

Below: George Amicay's relief-carved Strat body awaits its dazzling paint job.

The limited-run Disney guitar was an American Standard Strat with typical features (Bi-Flex truss rod, DeltaTone wiring, 2-point trem, etc.) as well as several unique details: Mickey Mouse appears as he did in 1935's *The Band Concert*, and Tinkerbell is a chrome appliqué. The trem cover [not shown] bore a Disney 75th Anniversary logo. Retail price: $1,495.

The Jaguar XK 50 Strat

In mid and late 1999 the shop collaborated with British luxury car maker Jaguar Cars, Ltd. to produce a 25-piece run of sumptuously appointed Stratocasters. The former owner of the piece pictured here, David Brass, of Fretted Americana, Inc., explains that the project celebrated the 50th anniversary of Jaguar's famed XK dual overhead camshaft 6-cylinder engine, introduced in 1949.

The guitars were co-designed by John Page and Jaguar Design Director Geoff Lawson (who coincidentally had admired one of Page's handcrafted tables at an art gallery in Laguna Beach). John Page: "I was so inspired by Jaguar design over my lifetime, and he was their head of styling. It was a total rush for me, probably second only to meeting Paul McCartney." Page also recalls that the guitars were sent to Ivor Arbiter (1929 – 2005), a giant in the UK music industry and an enthusiastic fan of Jaguar automobiles. Pamelina H. rendered the preliminary artwork shown here, and Steve Stern built the prototype.

Each guitar sported a British Racing Green paint job, gold-plated hardware and inlays, leaping-jaguar logos on the peghead and on the bound walnut fingerboard, and pickguard and headstock veneers fashioned from the kind of burled walnut used on the dashboards of XJS grand tourers. Aside from their walnut construction, the pickguard and backplate were unique in another way as well. Both had maple contrasting stripes and were attached to the body with push-on fasteners that eliminated visible screws; the result was a clean look that further enhanced the Jag Strat's showroom sleekness. Other appointments included an old-school, round string tree and an engraved and numbered JAGUAR XK 50 neck plate. Each guitar was accompanied by a flight case as well as a gig bag fashioned from cream-colored Connolly hides fit for an upscale British motorcar's interior.

It seemed like a cracking good idea at the time, and the guitars were posh indeed, but the builders recall the experience as a bit of a cockup, as they say in the UK, due to the complexity of the detailing and the difficulties of working with the materials supplied by the car maker. Several of the Jag Strats had to be returned to the shop for repair or fine-tuning, but however challenging, the project resulted in one of the most richly elegant Stratocasters ever rendered by the Custom Shop.

One XK 50 hallmark was a walnut pickguard that was unperforated by screws and bordered by a maple strip.

Pamelina H.'s artwork for the XK 50.

The XK 50's bound peghead featured special logos on a walnut veneer.

The metal guitars

Building guitars with metal bodies is an idea that dates at least as far back as the National company of the mid and late 1920s. Given that historical precedent and the let's-try-anything enthusiasm permeating the Custom Shop, it's no surprise that in the early 1990s the builders experimented with metal bodies. What was surprising were the results — some of Fender's most beautiful guitars.

Machinist/fabricator/guitar builder Scott Buehl was a natural choice to help build these groundbreaker Fenders, which had hollow bodies welded in a "clamshell" structure. "Anything that had an aluminum body, I worked on it," he remembers. All of the metal bodies that went into the shop's production guitars — the Harley-Davidsons, the Alohas, the Freddie Tavares models, etc. — were built by Spruce Hill Guitars of Perham, Minnesota. Spruce Hill's founder and master luthier is Marty Schulte. He recalls displaying an aluminum-bodied guitar to Dan Smith in a hotel room at a NAMM Show. Dan brought the idea of a metal-bodied guitar to John Page. "I immediately thought of Harley," Page recalls, "because that hollow clamshell reminded me of a gas tank. It took a couple years of planning and negotiations to pull it off."

Marty Schulte: "We have a set of dies that cost a quarter of a million dollars. We use it to stamp the top and back of Strat bodies. It's the only existing set, and we keep our processes and our special alloys secret. We never even let Fender in here to see it. We make a superstructure — a protected, proprietary design — running the length of the guitar body. It's like you'd see on the chassis of a car, with solid blocks for the bridge and the neck joint. It transfers sustain and makes the guitars really resonant."

Scott Buehl: "I do aluminum sheet metal work on the side, like race car bodies and airplanes, so sometimes I took this stuff home. I'd get on the TIG [Tungsten Inert Gas] welder, drill out the pits, weld it back up, dress out the welds, and polish it up so that you couldn't tell where the seam was."

Plating and anodizing

The aluminum guitars were chrome-plated by Cal-Tron Plating, Inc. in Santa Fe Springs, about 35 miles west of Corona. Scott Buehl: "They still do a lot of our plating. They did great stuff, beautiful work. We'd send a bare aluminum body. They put some copper on it, and then we'd have the copper engraved. Copper engraves very nicely, and when we buffed it out, the detail was still there on the aluminum. Then we chromed it. It would come back to me or Jason

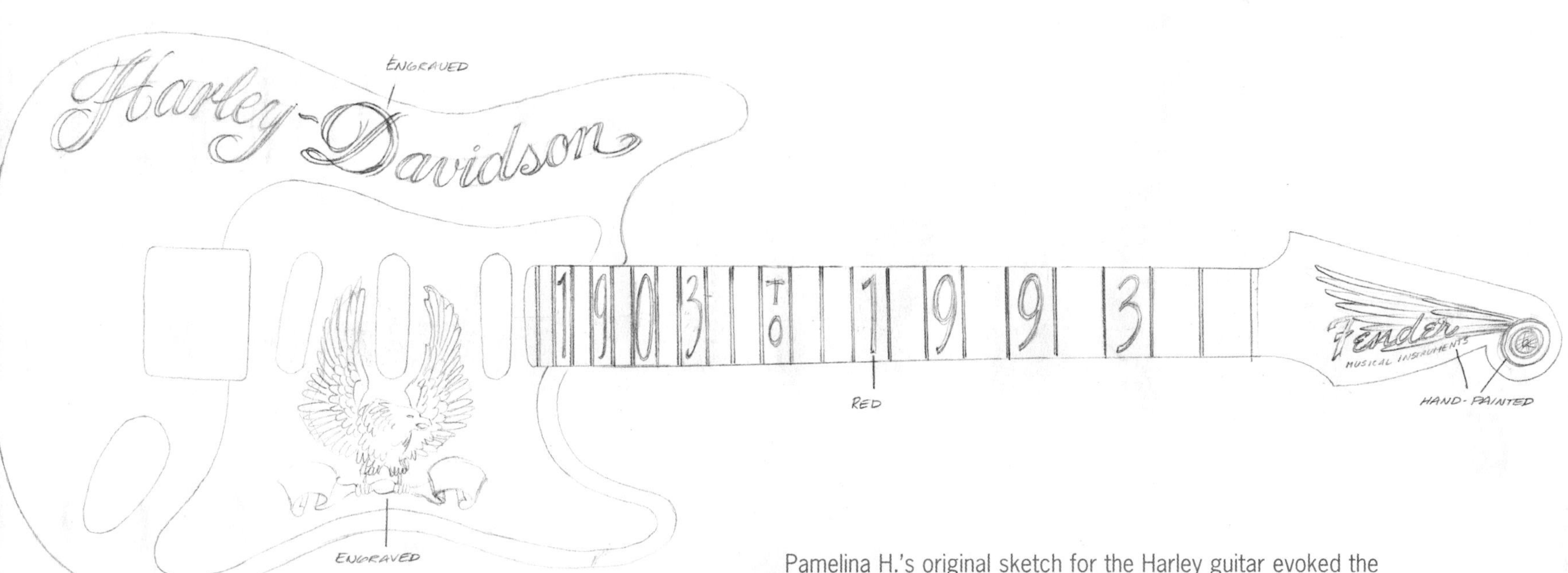

Pamelina H.'s original sketch for the Harley guitar evoked the motorcycle company's various winged logos.

Davis, and we would hand-paint all the detail that was going to be gold with this green rubbery paint that stank like acetone. It went back to Cal-Tron, and they dropped it in the gold tank. We would wash it off with acetone very carefully, and we'd be done. One example of this process was the Harley."

Aside from chrome plating, another treatment was selective anodizing, performed by Peter Kellett of P.K. Selective in Santa Clara, California. He recalls: "I remember reading that Leo Fender liked aluminum pickguards, so in about 1991, I sent to George Blanda about 20 small multicolored, rectangular pieces of anodized aluminum that I had made. Fender made them into pickguards for Custom Shop guitars." John Page gave one of the Harley prototypes to Peter, who anodized the body. Fender ultimately chose a chrome and gold motif for the Harleys, but the project gave Kellett a chance to show his stuff. Page was impressed.

Peter Kellett explains the process: "Anodizing forms an aluminum oxide film that 'grows' into and also on top of the aluminum. So if the oxide is a thousandth of an inch thick, half of that goes into the aluminum and the other half grows on top. Anodizing is the opposite of plating. In plating, you are depositing something. In anodizing, it's an electrochemical process where you reverse the electrical current – the cathode becomes the anode, hence the term anodizing. The piece goes into a big tank with a solution of about 10% sulfuric acid in water. In some pieces the process is controlled, and some are random."

The Harley-Davidson Strat

In the history of all products marketed in America, has there ever been a brand that inspired a deeper devotion than Harley-Davidson? In 1993, the venerable maker of motorcycles celebrated its 90th Anniversary by collaborating with the shop on a gold and chrome-plated Stratocaster. John Page, J. Black, and Pamelina H. designed it (Spruce Hill's Marty Schulte also claims credit for certain details). Pamelina H.: "I've painted motorcycles longer than I've painted guitars. I'm very familiar with that genre and comfortable with motorcycle society, which helped a lot with designing the Harley guitar. Once I rendered the design, I was done with it. It was all done with metalwork and etching after that."

In late 1992 Pamelina H. rendered this preliminary artwork for the upcoming Harley-Davidson Stratocaster. The black-and-chrome motif with the red 90th Anniversary Edition ribbon carried over to the first prototype.

The first Harley prototype, one of two rendered in black and chrome by J. Black. He recalls: "These lipstick pickups were the original concept, but at the time we mocked it up, it just looked too pedestrian. Now, there is something in their simplicity that appeals to me."

Scott Buehl and Jason Davis assembled and set up the guitars, Louis Alegre and Ron Chacey engraved the bodies, and Tim Shimp engraved the 12th-fret inlays (which were set into pin-routed slots) and engraved the pickguards as well. Details included a highly figured maple neck, and stainless steel dots on the ebony board. (Note: Officially, 109 were made, but official numbers for limited runs typically excluded a few prototypes, as well as a piece or two set aside for the Fender Museum or for the collection of Bill Schultz. Such guitars sometimes bore the serial number FM001 or WCS — for William Charles Schultz — 001.)

John Page explains that attaining the required "jewelry finish" for the Harley bodies was sometimes problematical at first, because the mirror finish would reveal even the slightest imperfection. "The anodized metal bodies were a little less demanding because not every tiny flaw would show up. But because the Harley was the first project and the finish was so critical, we had to work out some pops in the welds, for example, with smoothing and polishing. [Spruce Hill's] quality definitely improved over time, and they were essential partners in these projects." J. Black adds: "A lot of people had their fingerprints on the Harley

Every detail of the black-and-chrome prototype's headstock was hand-painted by Pamelina H. John Page: "It's crazy, isn't it? Unbelievable brushwork skill. On the production models, we went with silkscreen versions by Karen and James Kulback."

— Steve Boulanger, myself, and James and Karen Kulback, who did the headcap silk screen. There were several prototypes and just so many different parts and details, but it was Scott and Jason who shepherded the project all the way through on a day-to-day basis.

"This kicked off a new era, where we went from having custom-made one-offs that got a high margin of profit to a series of art guitars that got a *huge* margin of profit. It was a $3,500 guitar, dealer cost, very exclusive, and we told special dealers around the country, 'You've got first shot at this.' A lot of guys within Fender said, '3,500 bucks — we can't sell that. It's too much.' But people wound up paying full pop, so retail was 7,000 bucks. And they sold. I think that's when Bill Schultz went, 'Hey, wait a second. These guys are writing checks for seven grand.' Some of these things peaked out at 18,000 bucks. Jay Leno got one. Travis Tritt got one. So Fender saw the phenomenon of customers bidding against one another, exceeding retail. That's when I think Bill said, 'This art guitar thing can have huge margins.' So we did the Playboy guitar, the 40th Anniversary Strat, the Aloha. The Harley sparked a new way of thinking."

"Goldie" is the only complete guitar of its type in the world, although John Page recalls there might have been a second gold body. "The other Harleys were fancy and cool, but we just wanted to see how far we could push it. It's plated in 23 carat gold, with 10 carat gold fingerboard dots. Ron Chacey engraved the pickup covers, but we decided it was too much information, so we simplified the covers for the production versions."

Harley-Davidson
EST.
USA
1903

Diamond Dealers

Bill Schultz's "new way of thinking" materialized in the Diamond Dealer program, which was put into effect by Jack Shelton, Senior Vice President of Sales. It created an elite class of select dealers who had to commit to ordering a specified number of limited-edition models and were then given exclusive access to them. John Page: "The idea was, these high-dollar guitars like the Harley are so special, we can't just sell a hundred. We have to get more bang for the buck. If we were going to go to all this trouble to come up with a concept and design it, let's do some higher production numbers so it might actually pay for itself. So now, with the Diamond Dealers, all of a sudden, we had to develop some kind of product every six months. It was so successful we were behind all the time."

The Harley-Davidson Stratocaster, production version.

The Aloha Strat

The aluminum-bodied Aloha Stratocaster was designed and built by John English and displayed in 1994. He said at the time, "Guitars of the metal resonator type were built in the late 1920s and are still built today. These guitars were often decorated with elaborate engravings and plated with gold or nickel. With the Aloha, I wanted to go one step further. I have always liked Hawaiian and Deco Art, so I combined hand engraving with state-of-the-art color anodizing."

The body was hand-engraved by Ron Chacey and selectively anodized by Peter Kellett. It featured an exhibition-grade flame maple neck with abalone markers, an engraved and anodized headstock overlay, gold hardware, Lace Sensors, and custom knobs. It inspired the limited run of Freddie Tavares Strats. Officially, 153 Alohas were made, but J. Black suggests: "I don't think we shipped that many. I show 92 shipped." John Page adds that three others were presented to the Tavares family.

Tribute to a Mentor: A Guitar for Freddie Tavares

Announced in the winter of '95 as part of the Diamond Dealer series, the Freddie Tavares Commemorative Aloha Stratocaster was designed by John English, George Amicay, and John Page. Larry Sifel, of Pearl Works, did the inlay, and Ron Chacey engraved the nickel-plated body; both were highly regarded in the shop and turned out to be key collaborators. Note the peghead's twin palms, its signature, and its inlays of the Fender logo and the silhouette of Hawaii's Diamond Head. The staff built 153 of the guitars to honor Freddie Tavares, who was Leo Fender's right-hand man when it came to engineering, R&D, and interfacing with musicians.

The Aloha Strat.

Right: The Freddie Tavares Aloha Strat honored a witty and gentle soul of Hawaiian descent, a talented guitarist, and a busy session musician. After more than 30 years at Fender, Freddie passed away in 1990. He is fondly remembered by all who knew him.

ALOHA

John Page: "When I saw John English's first Aloha proto, I thought we should do a tribute to Freddie. I pitched it to Dan Smith and Bill Schultz for approval. Freddie was my mentor and was like a dad to me. I wanted him to be officially recognized. John [English] knew him as well and thought the world of him. What you see on this guitar is Freddie playing the ukulele for his wife Tamar, who's doing the hula. You also see Diamond Head. Freddie and Tamar bought their first house there." The guitar was accompanied by a custom leather strap and gig bag in Pacific blue.

The Splato Strat

Someone had a great idea in 2004 — let's run a contest with a guitar magazine, and whoever wins gets to design his or her very own Custom Shop guitar. Sounds good. But what if the winner comes up with a design so far out in left field that it pretty much flies out of the ballpark altogether? After winning the "Design Your Dream Guitar" contest in *Guitar World* magazine, Californian Jimmy Stout sent to the Custom Shop a drawing for a guitar whose metal body had several see-through chambers filled with colored liquids. It's the kind of thing school kids doodle on their notebooks all the time. But to actually build such a thing? Who you gonna call?

You gonna call Scott Buehl, the shop's one and only unofficial "über Builder." If ever there was a project that would put that lofty title to the test, this was it. "My boss came to me and said, 'This is right up your alley,'" Scott recalls. "It's a chrome body, all windowed-out, and it's got colored liquid inside the windows. I thought, everything about this thing is pretty nuts."

Scott got to work in January, 2005 and completed the project after 18 long months of experimentation, false starts, and frustrating trial and error. He explains, "I changed a few things. Jimmy had it with a rosewood board, but I thought that would clash with some of the colors. I thought black is so neutral, let's do it with ebony and I'll put chrome dots on the board. I hammered this guitar out of aluminum sheet metal, literally — I did it with my hammer. I beat out a Strat body and welded it together."

The body and headstock are 5052 aluminum alloy. The multiple-strut skeleton was crafted from aircraft-grade 6061 aluminum. Major challenges included formulating some sort of chemical combo for the colored liquids and, for the chambers, finding transparent material that wouldn't corrode. For the liquids, Scott settled on a stew of paraffin oil, distilled water, hydrophobic dye, food coloring, and a biocide ("to ward off impurities"). The chambers were hand-formed of Lexan, a polycarbonate thermoplastic resin. Details: a Seymour Duncan Pearly Gates humbucker and two Fender Noiseless pickups with modified lipstick covers.

Scott's fellow builders are used to his sometimes mind-blowing creations, but some of them were stunned by this trippiest of all Strats. According to Fender, "One person backed away from it in awe." Scott Buehl: "I've done some unusual stuff over all these years, but that thing is just crazy. That thing is the hardest guitar I've ever built in my life."

The "Splato" Strat — "the hardest guitar I've ever built in my life."

1954
1994

CHAPTER TWELVE

12

Jump to Lightspeed

Price Sheets and the Second Big Shift

The balancing act

Going all the way back to the May 1987 press release that heralded the establishment of the Custom Shop, a continuing challenge has been balancing the prestige and high-profile glamour of offering dazzling, one-of-a-kind instruments and, on the other hand, maintaining some semblance of production efficiency and profitability. A unique guitar might entail not only substantial investments of time in design and construction but also the additional burdens of tracking down and purchasing a few non-stock components in small quantities, with neither the convenience nor the discounts that come with bulk orders.

Guitars such as 1994's 40th Anniversary Stratocaster celebrated Fender's legacy and also reminded players and retailers that "price sheet" guitars would continue to be supplemented with limited editions. Fitted with a bookmatched, flame-maple top and limited to 150 pieces (not including an estimated five protos), the guitar was designed by John Page, J. Black, and Pamelina H. Ron Chacey engraved the pickguard, and Larry Sifel crafted the unique 1954 - 1994 12th-fret inlay.

Don't let their hefty price tags fool you — those labor-intensive one-offs may dazzle and delight, but they don't pay the bills.

Another problem early on was that while exuberant gearheads relished the intricacies of sifting through a long list of tantalizing options for a one-off's each and every detail, some dealers and customers who might otherwise have wanted a Custom Shop guitar found the ordering procedure daunting or laborious. Yet another, mundane concern: Compared to factory guitars, one-offs entailed much more in-house paperwork per instrument.

Slim pickin's, but not for long

Some of these considerations were addressed with the custom option program of the late 1980s, in which certain orders could be filled by mixing and matching more or less stock components from the main factory's supplies and then tweaking them to order in the shop. Examples included three new Custom Shop guitars announced in the summer of 1992: a 1960 Esquire in Teal Green Metallic (available in a limited run of one hundred) and two versions of a Set-Neck Strat, one with a Floyd Rose and

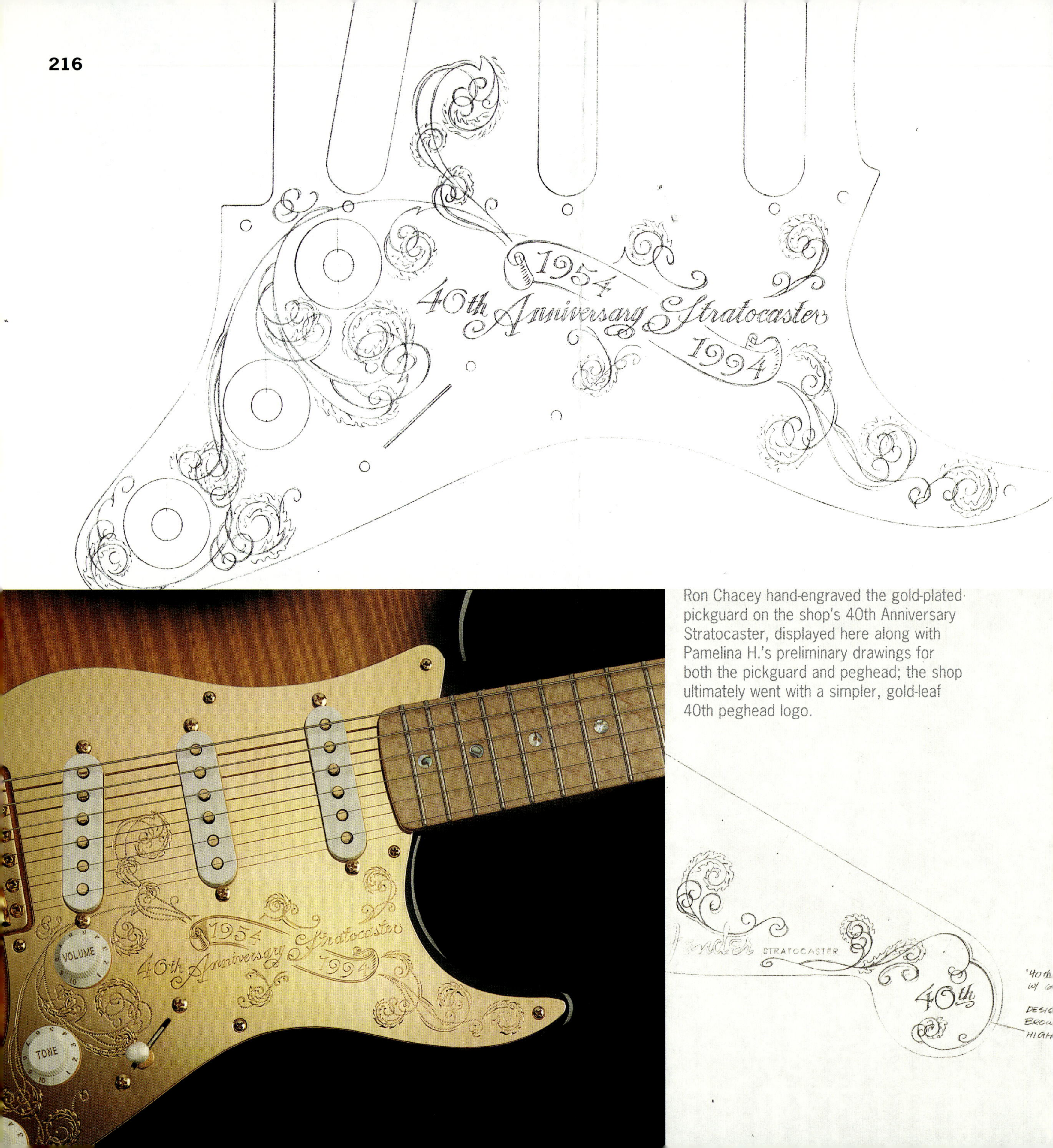

Ron Chacey hand-engraved the gold-plated pickguard on the shop's 40th Anniversary Stratocaster, displayed here along with Pamelina H.'s preliminary drawings for both the pickguard and peghead; the shop ultimately went with a simpler, gold-leaf 40th peghead logo.

Lace Sensors, the other with a conventional trem and a mix of single-coil and humbucking pickups. Otherwise, the Custom Shop's fixed-spec models of that summer included the Set-Neck Teles, the three earliest artist Telecasters (Gatton, Collins, Donahue), and a single artist Stratocaster, the Robert Cray. That was it — no other guitars, and no basses at all.

The price sheet of '92

But during that same time, John Page and Fender marketing were collaborating on a program that would soon take the Custom Shop one step toward a factory structure. The plan was known in-house as the price list, or price sheet. This program's much wider selection of instruments would eventually be matched by a conspicuous marketing effort. The result was a broader and somewhat clearer identity for the shop, and in terms of public perception it happened virtually overnight.

The first extensive Custom Shop price list took effect on August 1, 1992. Published apart from Fender's general literature, it was titled "American Custom Classics, Special Order Only" and sported the shop's "V" logo, designed by Pamelina H. in 1989. Regarding the number and diversity of fixed-spec instruments, this was like something out of *Star Wars*, a jump to lightspeed.

The four Signature Series artist guitars were the same as before: Gatton, Donahue, Collins, and Cray. Interestingly, the least expensive model was the Cray Strat, at $1,949; the Donahue Tele was $2,099, and the Gatton and Collins Teles, each entailing several production quirks, cost $2,499.

Each of the five guitars in the price sheet's Set-Neck Series retailed for $1,999: the Set-Neck Telecaster, the Set-Neck Telecaster C/A, the two Strats (with and without the Floyd), and the Telecoustic Custom, which was a Tele-shaped acoustic/electric with a bound, solid spruce top, pao ferro fretboard, and piezo pickup system. Note that the selection of Set-Neck Telecasters had been slimmed from four models to two.

The biggest news was the Classic series, which embraced *seven* right-hand models ranging from $1,399 to $1,999. There were two year-specific Strats, a '54 and a '60; in a way, they were forerunners of a long list of year-specific instruments of ever more detailed authenticity. They were accompanied by two Sparkle Telecasters (gold and silver); Fred Stuart's Bajo Sexto Telecaster baritone guitar, with a 30.2" scale; and a pair of American Classic Strats ("Custom Shop versions of the American Standard Strat," maple neck or rosewood board, both with Texas Special pickups).

Up to their necks in the Kubicki project since late 1988, the Custom Shop crew had found little time to craft any basses aside from one-offs and dealer-ordered limited runs, but now Fender cataloged the shop's first fixed-spec 4-strings, the Custom Classics. These included the Vintage Precision Custom (with the old Tele style headstock, slab body, and a combo of "P" and "J" pickups) and left-hand versions of the '57 Precision and '62 Jazz Bass. The fact that the price sheet offered lefty basses but not right-hand versions seemed to show that notwithstanding the mainstream appeal of its Strats and Teles, the shop was still considered very much a specialty operation.

Finally, the three other models in the August '92 Custom Shop brochure were left-handed versions of some of Fender's most highly acclaimed guitars, all of them now grouped in the Classic Series: the '52 Tele, the '57 Strat, and the '62 Strat. These guitars and the Custom Classic basses cost $2,099.

Rendering Custom Shop versions of both American Standards and vintage guitars may have seemed like a modest concept, but in fact it marked the dawn of a new era for cataloged, fixed-spec models in which the Custom Shop would offer its own take on Fender's most popular instruments.

Spreading the word

Fender marketing was not about to let such a milestone go unheralded. The next *Frontline* magazine, Fall '92, opened with a splashy two-page spread about "The Dream Factory," highlighting the shop's ordering and production processes in text and full-color photos. A couple of pages later, a full-color ad displayed a dozen Custom Shop instruments: a Set-Neck Telecaster, a Set-Neck Stratocaster, a Set-Neck Floyd Rose Strat with a reverse headstock, two American Classic Strats, a left-handed '57 Strat, a trio of year-specific Strats (two '54s and the 1960), two Vintage Precision Custom Basses (blonde and sunburst), and the Sparkle Tele.

The Set-Neck Series Telecasters sported familiar Tele shapes but were otherwise upscale in most respects, each with a bound mahogany body, bookmatched figured-maple top, a coil-cut mini toggle switch, and the TBX tone

circuit. The Set-Neck Telecaster had a Brazilian rosewood fingerboard, while the Set-Neck Telecaster CA (also C/A) featured an ebony fretboard as well as a Honduras mahogany neck, a custom DiMarzio humbucker in the neck position, a bridge pickup borrowed from the American Standard, and a tortoiseshell pickguard. Like Fender's Robben Ford model (imported from Japan but soon to be relocated to the Custom Shop), these fancy Set-Necks helped Fender escape the constraints of its traditional iconic models and move into the luxury market inhabited by Paul Reed Smith, Tom Anderson, Hamer, and the high-end Gibsons.

Aside from the stunning increase in the sheer number of guitars, another notable price sheet development was the shifting balance of models. Where previous Custom Shop offerings were dominated by Telecasters, the Strat received equal billing in 1992, with a half-dozen Custom Shop variations. The literature from that same year also displayed a Custom Shop doubleneck built for Jeff Cook of Alabama; the "Koacaster," reportedly purchased for $6,000 by Stephen Stills; and a jaw-dropping Fred Stuart Telecaster wrapped all over in black and grey pearloid (or "moto," as it is affectionately if somewhat inelegantly called; "moto" is short for "mother of toilet seat"). Such guitars reminded customers that despite all the fixed-spec models, the shop still produced knockout one-of-a-kind guitars as well.

Some of the year-specific guitars were described as "Custom Shop versions of vintage Stratocasters." While an important step toward the highly detailed vintage reissues of later years, some of these 1992 "recreations" merely invoked the general vibe of the originals rather than duplicating them in every respect. In that regard they were somewhat akin to the factory's reissues of a decade earlier. For example, the 1960 Strat sported Texas Specials rather than vintage-style pickups, and the 1954 and 1960 Strats had 9.5" radius fingerboards, flatter than the 7.25" originals.

The second big shift

The price sheet was based in part on the "spec guitar" approach in which the builders or Fender marketing would design guitars ahead of time and speculate that they could sell them later, rather than building them in response to

A Set-Neck Strat with a maple-on-mahogany body, pearl dots, Wilkinson roller nut, and Lace Sensors: blue (neck), gold, and dual red.

advance orders. The 40th Anniversary Teles, Homer golds, and 35th Anniversary Strats were earlier examples.

The planning of the spec guitars was hardly random. As we have seen, as soon as the Custom Shop was up and running, multiple orders poured in for recreations of Fender's most revered instruments — two-color sunburst Strats, early-'60s Tele Customs, '50s-style P Basses, and the like. Even when ordering non-stock guitars, customers checked the same boxes again and again for certain cosmetic options (custom colors such as Fiesta Red or Lake Placid Blue, gold hardware, etc.) as well as contemporary features such as hotter pickups, locking trems, and bend-friendly jumbo frets.

Inspired by the success of the early Set-Necks, John Page decided to expand the concept of fixed-spec guitars across the Custom Shop's entire range of instruments. He explains: "The idea with the price list was to create a more profitable organization. After we saw so many people ordering the same guitars and the same details over and over, I thought, 'Well, why don't we make this popular guitar or this package of features ourselves, in advance? Let's make it a standard thing, and offer it in a price list.' That would simplify choices for customers and also make it quicker for the dealers who thought the Custom Shop was a pain in the butt. There were dealers like Thoroughbred Music [in Tampa] and Matt Umanov [New York City] who had ideas, but a lot of dealers *didn't* have ideas and really weren't equipped to come up with sensible concepts for one-off Fenders. Now, they didn't have to think about endless options. Just order it from the catalog; we've already put the cool features together for you."

Compared to previous spec guitars, these new price sheet instruments directly reflected consumer demand. Few people thought to request a flame-top anniversary Tele or a gold-on-gold tribute Strat (although once Fender dreamed up the guitars, they sold quickly), but *loads* of people were champing at the bit for a '54 Strat repro or a slab-body P Bass.

Another consideration was bookkeeping. As with any successful company, Fender's expenses are tightly monitored, at least in theory. Every can of paint, every carton of Phillips head screws, every box of resistors is accounted

A baritone guitar from the new Classic Series: the Bajo Sexto Telecaster.

for. Each Fender guitar has what's called a bill of materials, part of a tracking system that's suitable for a high-volume factory operation but less so for a small shop. During the Custom Shop's early years, a dollar actually had a part number. One dollar was Part No. 012-0000-999, so if the shop bought some rock maple for two hundred dollars, it would be documented as 200 units of that number. John Page: "This allowed us to buy parts on a one-off basis if necessary and still review our inventory dollars when we shipped. [For most of the first year], I kept a detailed dollar expenditure for each guitar we shipped. I was able to work out the percentage of parts dollars vs. the wholesale price charged to the dealer. It was relatively accurate but had to be reviewed every year after physical inventory. It was pretty difficult to make it exact, which doesn't go over well in a corporate environment."

Scott Grant agrees that the dollar/part number system worked well enough at first, but because the shop used so many custom parts and purchased them in such limited quantities, the system had to be replaced as the shop expanded. "With the catch-all dollar figure, it eventually became quite impossible to keep track of things," he says. "We had a situation where 50 percent of our inventory was an undefined number."

The complexities of monitoring expenses were multiplied by the Custom Shop's routine of often building only one guitar at a time. On one day the shop might buy one Floyd Rose tailpiece for one guitar, on the next day a Kahler tailpiece for another, and two weeks later, another Floyd. Each of those transactions would require as much documentation as purchasing, say, a crate of tuning keys or a pallet of maple boards. Trying to adapt Fender's system to such practices was described by veteran employees as "suffocating" and "a nightmare." J. Black: "Fender wasn't set up to build one guitar at a time. It was set up to make a thousand American Standards, all with the same bridge, all with the same pickguard, all with the same pickups. That's hard enough. Imagine the challenges when each guitar has a unique set of specs. If somebody wanted a moto pickguard with a hole for a humbucker and one less pot, the builder wouldn't find it in a catalog; he'd have to craft it

The Telecoustic Custom featured pearl-button Schallers, a mahogany body, an oval soundhole, a laminated pao ferro and ebony bridge, and a Fishman Matrix transducer.

from scratch. We were growing fast, and it was killing us to try to track fourteen of this and twelve of that and twenty of this other thing."

The hectic atmosphere of the time also affected the relationship between the shop and Fender Sales. Fred Stuart: "John Grunder was in telephone sales, reporting to Dan or Bruce, whoever was in charge of marketing at the time. Bill Schultz would be saying, *'I want to see more productivity out of there!'* So Grunder would get on the phone with one of the big dealers and say, 'I've got three beautiful Strats here with matching pegheads – are you interested?' He would sell them first, and then we had to scramble around and actually build these things [laughs]." John Grunder: "In the beginning, we often had a hard time filling orders, so in order for the guys to 'make month's end,' they would work until 3:00 o'clock in the morning making spec pieces."

The price list helped alleviate all of these challenges by offering completed, fixed-spec guitars. A significant side effect was that most or all of the builders could now work together on a whole run of instruments instead of having one builder crafting one guitar at a time. This made better use of resources, cut materials costs, and increased output. John Page: "A couple years later, marketing came up with the term 'Team Built,' which was a much better name for the idea."

J. Black: "When John did the price list, that was huge, a major leap-frog forward. The first big shift had been going to limited-edition custom runs as opposed to one-offs. The price sheet was the second big shift. It solved many problems all at once."

The expanded catalog of models allowed players and dealers to order a guitar whenever convenient, rather than having to plan one from scratch or scrambling to get in on some sort of limited run. In that regard, the little shop was now functioning like any big guitar company. It would take years to work out the nomenclature and various glitches in the catalogs, ads, and price sheets, but 1992 was nevertheless a watershed. This seemingly modest reversal in production philosophy — build 'em first, take orders later — was crucial, an early step toward evolving the shop from a strictly custom/one-off facility into a new kind of limited-production factory.

Consequences, intended and otherwise

From the outset of the Custom Shop, the retail costs, quality, and desirability of both the factory and Custom Shop instruments affected each other in a web of complex relationships. J. Black reports that in 1989 the average dealer price of a Custom Shop guitar was $829.00. The official list price would be set at about double that, say, $1,600 or $1,650, although the guitar would typically sell for about $1,200 or $1,300. Compared to customer-ordered one-offs, the models designed in-house and manufactured in quantity could be offered for lower prices, due to economies of scale.

An unexpected consequence, according to J. Black: "Well, Yamano saw these [in-house designs] going into the price list and then it was like, 'Well, now these are too ordinary; they aren't good enough for us anymore. We want to be even more specific, even more exclusive and detailed.' And John's reaction was, okay, but it's going to cost another 200 dollars per guitar, or whatever it was."

So while the efficiencies of the price sheet guitars allowed them to be offered for less money, at the same time those instruments inspired costlier, ever more sophisticated models. These latter guitars further clarified public perceptions regarding the relative exclusivity of price sheet guitars vs. those whose features were specified by customers, dealers, or distributors. They also helped to further sharpen perceptions of the Custom Shop's capabilities vs. those of the factory.

Yamano's relationship with the shop worked both ways. As noted, their reaction to the price sheet resulted in new kinds of orders, but in some cases those new orders affected the next iteration of the price sheet. J. Black: "Yamano was in a league by itself. Their orders were *very* specific and well thought out. If they ordered the same thing over and over, then we had to think, 'This looks successful — let's put it in the price list.' In a way, Yamano was marketing their own idea of what we should be doing, and sometimes we responded."

The price list's success prodded the main factory to step up the quality of its own instruments. While specific details and techniques did "cross over" from the shop to the factory, the most important influence was simply an increase in general quality. Dan Smith: "The biggest thing was raising the bar in terms of overall production,

tolerances, and better specs. The Custom Shop showed the factory: *Look how good these guitars can be.* That's what benefited the factory more than anything else, and then in a way it bit them in the butt over in the shop because the factory started pushing *them*. Some of those price sheet guitars from the shop were very authentic and period-correct, [but] they were also doing good things in the main plant, so we had to ask — now, what *can't* they do in the main plant?

"One difference was that the price sheet guitars could still be much more limited than factory offerings. If there was some tiny little detail that applied only to one year of production, they're not going to mess around with that in the factory. But that's just the kind of thing we can do in the Custom Shop for that handful of people out there who care about that particular detail." With positive influences going in both directions, the shop and factory helped to redefine each other and to increase the quality of all Fender instruments.

Many hats, few heads

Be Careful What You Wish For Dept.: An unrelenting problem throughout the shop's first decade was that an expansion of any kind — in the workforce, marketing, floor space, or product line — never seemed to solve whatever problem it was intended to address, at least not for long. Instead, it only stimulated new stresses and the need for still more expansion.

This perpetual commotion was fueled by public demand for Custom Shop instruments. J. Black: "The impression we got from management was that we were never making enough money. Say we need some more people to catch up. Okay, we get more people, but then we need to make more guitars to pay for the new people. This was a constant cycle; we *never* could catch up. We never could hit whatever the number was for that month. John would come in and say, 'If we don't make this certain number, we're going out of business.' So, we worked *huge* amounts of overtime. Some of the hourly people were being paid double time or time and a half, so we'd get the 83 guitars out, or whatever the number was, but we've just blown our budget on overtime, and these people who have just worked 18 hour days, they're sick now, so they're not showing up for a while. The cycle of pressure never stopped. Chaotic days and nights were typical."

Along with the price sheet guitars and limited runs, the builders continued to craft highly individualized special orders. The Jazzmasterish guitar on the left had a bound flame-maple top on a Thinline body, custom inlays, Seymour Duncan humbuckers, a painted "soundhole," a Floyd Rose, and gold hardware. The pastel green Tele had a painted headstock, pearl dots, and a custom-pinstriped ash body with a DiMarzio humbucker in front. Both were built by J. Black for Yamano Music.

Typical, indeed. During the late 1980s and early 1990s several of the key people at Fender wore many hats, sometimes several at the same time. Dan Smith wore a tower of hats so tall he could have been a Dr. Seuss character. The price sheet provided some relief from all this (at least temporarily), because the Custom Shop crew finally had some givens. They could focus on building a batch of guitars with identical specs rather than having to hash out every detail from scratch with marketing, Artist Relations, a dealer, or a customer. The shop could build 40 identical '54 Strats, send them to the warehouse, and let the sales staff take it from there. Putting price sheet models into continual production evened out the planning, inventories, and scheduling — at least until the next expansion.

Art Esparza: "If the builders didn't make their numbers, John would come around and say, Art, you need to build more guitars because we are not making the budget. There was such excitement about the Custom Shop, but we had to figure out a way to make the financial part of it work out." The price sheet was an essential part of this new financial strategy.

Another reason the price sheet was a milestone was that unlike the custom option instruments, which were often assembled from factory-standard components (with modifications or options provided by the Custom Shop), the price sheet guitars often started with the shop's own hand-selected supplies, a shift that marked another increase in the shop's independence from the factory.

Additional fallout from the price sheet's success included diminishing the shop's role as a sort of test lab or proving ground. Dan Smith: "Ritchie Fliegler came on board and said perfectly what I had been thinking all these years: 'How come you don't do like a Futurama?' He used to go to auto shows and they would have a 'Car Of The Future' concept car. I always thought the Custom Shop should have concept stuff, but now the problem was they were just so busy filling orders. You don't want to over-staff

This is one of three trans-red Custom Tele Thinlines Fred Stuart built for Yamano. It featured a bound body of lightweight ash, a painted faux soundhole, three lipstick pickups in a Strat-like array, and a moto pickguard. Fred went to the Maybelline cosmetics company, sourced actual lipstick tubes, and made the pickups himself. He calls it "quite an adventure, and a great learning experience."

the place, and with so many orders you can't have people sitting around with their feet up, dreaming up futuristic stuff. So that part of it never happened, but the only reason it didn't happen was that they were just so successful in other areas."

Hodgepodge and helter skelter

To fully appreciate the beneficial impact of the price sheet on day-to-day operations, consider J. Black's recollection of how chaotic the earlier working environment was, particularly with respect to artist relations: "Richie Sambora – his knee would jerk: 'Hey, I want a Thinline today.' Okay, make him a Thinline. The Rembrandts have a hit with this new show, *Friends*, so we bring them in: Hey, we want this, we want that. So I make one thing, Larry makes one thing, Fred might make one thing. Travis Tritt comes in: 'Well, I like the 35th Anniversary Strat, can I get one of those?' And I want a Harley Strat.' We didn't make them anymore, but okay. Phil Chen, bass player with Rod Stewart, he wants something. Give me the specs; Phil Chen gets his something. Now Yamano wants a special run of this, and you've also got a sales rep going, 'I want a five-piece run of that.' Then Bill Carson comes along: 'I want a custom run of my own signature.' Tom Nolan [from Nomis Studios, London] comes along: 'We need to do a Hank Marvin — right now.' Next thing I know, I'm making Hank Marvin Strats. I'm too young. Hank Marvin? Who's that? But by the time we get through the history of it, it's like, 'I'm working on Hank Marvin! *Wow!*'

"David Gilmour wants two guitars. Joe Walsh needs a guitar. Here's a little project for Entwistle; get these knocked out. And then the road techs would come: Bon Jovi's in the studio, so Jon gets one, Richie gets one, the producer gets one, the recording engineer gets one. Mike Stevens is doing stuff for Robben Ford, and when Mike leaves, Gene Baker is doing stuff for Robben, then Greg Fessler. This went on all the time.

"Then when John Grunder came over from Brea, all hell would break loose. He'd run in and say, 'I got Matt Umanov on the phone, and they need something special for a show! What can you do for him — *right now?*' I don't know if Fender condoned that sort of thing — I don't even know if they knew it was going on [laughs]. It was such a hodgepodge. Everyone was kind of inspired, a little pissed off, and a little leery all at the same time. There was a lot of competition among everybody, but also a lot of camaraderie. Until John came up with the price list, this pace and craziness is what it was like. It was helter skelter."

Many unique Custom Shop guitars are conceived as "what if?" projects, combining elements from previously existing designs. Wow, how cool would it be if Fred Stuart rendered his bajo sexto design as a custom-inlaid rosewood Telecaster? Here you go.

The astonishing Western Boot Set — guitar, strap, belt, and boots — was designed by Alan Hamel and Nicholas Guiterrez and crafted by Hamel. The guitar's body is covered in multi-colored, hand-stitched kidskin, and the pau ferro fretboard is inlaid with hand-twisted sterling silver and bronze wire. The headstock overlay is sterling silver, as is the engraved hardware. Silver engraving by Miles Haworth; leatherwork by Alan Hamel and Nicholas Guiterrez of Renick's Western Boots of Riverside, California.

CHAPTER THIRTEEN

13

The Cycle Continues

Expanding the Team

During the early 1990s, the growing popularity of Custom Shop guitars fueled demands for increases in raw materials, production equipment, and especially skilled craftspeople.

Todd Krause arrived in March of the shop's fifth year, 1991, after working for a decade at Charvel/Jackson. "Page was running the show," he remembers. "Michael had already gone back to Texas. I started working on the Set-Necks, which were still relatively new. I'd help to prep bodies, glue the pieces together, sand the undercoat, sand the topcoat. Early on I was the model maker in R&D. For any new guitar that is blueprinted, before it goes into production you build the first article to make sure the measurements line up and the blueprints are accurate."

After his stint in R&D, Todd became a Master Builder for Artist Relations, working in the Custom Shop, and then he was reassigned to the Custom Shop proper in '97 or '98. All of the Senior Master Builders have impressive client lists, but Todd Krause's is especially noteworthy — Jeff Beck, Eric Clapton, David Gilmour, Mick Jagger, Keith Richards, Bob Dylan, Roger Waters, and many more.

When **Mark Kendrick** joined the shop on April 30, 1991, he was already steeped in Fender lore. In fact, he is something of a legacy employee. His dad and uncle were touring musicians who played with some of country music's most admired artists — Bob Wills, Red Foley, Marty Robbins — and both worked at Fender in the vintage era. Mark's impeccable craftsmanship and his ability to capture a vintage vibe in a new guitar help account for a client list that includes Eric Clapton, Marty Stuart, Sting, Buck Owens, Merle Haggard, Keith Richards, and many others. Some of his guitars now reside in Cleveland's Rock and Roll Hall of Fame and Museum and Nashville's Country Music Hall of Fame. Mark trained and mentored several of the shop's current Master Builders and apprentices.

Alex Perez started working in Fender's Brea, California, Customer Service department on May 16, 1990. He moved over to the Custom Shop's Enterprise Court facility in 1992. He was an assistant to the Artist Relations director, the late Mark Wittenberg, and also to Artist Builder Larry Brooks, handling phone orders and various administrative chores. Before long he was making pickguards and setting up and

Todd Krause crafted two exquisite Custom "Koicasters," each depicting a serene koi pond setting. The first guitar was completed in late 2003 and featured subtle pagoda reflections rendered by airbrush artist Dan Schultz. The second guitar, shown here, pictured the edge of a wooden deck and was completed in time for the January 2005 NAMM show; the airbrush artist was Dan Lawrence. Both instruments featured inlays by Ron Thorn.

Mark Kendrick.

Alex Perez.

assembling guitars. Eventually he would go on to build signature instruments for John 5, Jim Root of Slipknot, Billy Corgan of Smashing Pumpkins, Tom DeLonge and Mark Hoppus of Blink-182, and Frank Bello of Anthrax.

"Mark Wittenberg was great, just the nicest guy, Alex says. "Everyone remembers him fondly. Whether he said yes to you or no, he was always nice about it, very straightforward, and he had the greatest sense of humor, very quirky. The beauty of my job was that I did both administrative and some building. John Page let everybody have their own accountability. You knew what you had to do, and you were in charge of your own work."

As we go to press, Alex's title is Artist Relations Manager, and he reports to VP of Artist Relations Bill Cummiskey. "Most of our business comes to us," he says, "but on the other hand I do go out to a lot of shows. We deal with artists, their record labels, and their managers. I get a lot of requests from bands who love Fender — can you help us out? Anybody who is looking for a handout, just because it is free, we stay away from. If a band is up and coming and

Mark Wittenberg.

they already play Fender, we might contact them. We're not trying to talk them into playing a Fender; we're dealing with people who are already excited about our guitars, basses, and amps. For us it's all about building relationships. Each Fender artist has their own web page, with their bio, gear, tour dates, whatever they want to promote. And we take care of that. As they grow and get more visibility they might call and say, 'Hey, we're doing Letterman next week — can you get us a bass or a guitar?' We bend over backwards for our artists and make things happen quickly.

"I've worked with Duff McKagan, Mike Dirnt, all sorts of people. I'm here in the shop every day, and I can tell you that we are making amazing guitars. The quality is as good if not better than ever. We have many special and unique processes here. I hope people understand all the fine details that make these guitars so special. That Custom Shop decal means a lot."

Mike Ponce worked at the Custom Shop for seven years, starting in October, 1992. After honing his woodworking skills with Todd Krause in the Set-Neck department, he was apprenticed to Stephen Stern at the outset of the D'Aquisto Deluxe project. Mike recalls, "Stephen and Jimmy [D'Aquisto] and John [Page] came up with the processes, and I did a lot of the grunt work. After apprenticing for several months I was able to build the Deluxes all the way through — the laminations, all the binding, final sanding, some of the paint stages, everything from start to finish, always with Stephen's guidance and supervision. There was constant feedback and help. My workspace was right across from Steve's. He would approve and sign off on every guitar. He was brilliant at the final details, and I learned a lot from him. As a group, I think the D'Aquistos were absolutely the highest quality instruments the Custom Shop was producing at the time. We worked so hard to make every single guitar perfect, and they were beautiful."

Mike also apprenticed with Mark Kendrick, John Suhr, and Gene Baker. He became particularly adept at staining highly figured woods such as quilt maple and flame maple. In late 1998 he was promoted to Master Builder. He left Fender, worked at Rickenbacker from 2000 to 2002, then joined John Suhr's young company. As we go to press Mike Ponce is the day-to-day production supervisor and a Master Builder at Suhr Guitars.

Mike Ponce.

The crew sometimes referred to presentation-grade instruments such as these beauties as "doctor/lawyer" guitars — collectible instruments for enthusiasts who might not be working musicians but had dreams of the perfect guitar and enough money to make it happen. Note the lavish inlays, bound fingerboards, and gold hardware. The clear pickguards and clear "hotdog" control plate on the Tele highlight the deep-quilt tops and stunning cherryburst finishes.

Duane Boulanger joined the main factory crew on November 30, 1992. He worked as a tune tester for just a couple of months before relocating to the Custom Shop. He worked there for five or six years before moving over to Fender R&D for another decade or so, leaving Fender on July 21, 2008. At the shop, he was an assembler and tune tester in the Set-Neck department. "They had two lines for a while, Set-Neck and bolt-on. I was on the Set-Neck team. Scott Buehl was more or less the head of that department, and then Todd Krause pretty much took over. This was all informal. Because there were only about five of us, we all had to do several different things, which taught me a lot in a hurry. After a while they decided to combine the divisions, so some of the girls who were doing the bolt-on assembly were also put to work on the Set-Necks, and I was working with John Cruz, doing a lot of tune test work and examining the quality."

As Steve Boulanger's younger sibling, did Duane ever feel like he was following in his brother's footsteps? "More like in his shadow," he says. "He created big footsteps, not just at Fender but in the industry. I didn't really aspire to get into the CNC stuff because that was Steve's gig. He was great at it, and I felt if I went into the same field I would always be the 'little brother,' so I was more interested in working the wood with my hands, assembling and testing the guitars, and so on. There were always so many tiny details to figure out, just endless. Like when we started the Relics, there was so much energy devoted to treating the woods, which makes sense, but one little thing – how do you age a nut so that its appearance matches the aging of the rest of the guitar? Little things like that, we had to figure them all out."

Duane Boulanger, right, with Dan Smith at Dan's retirement celebration, August 11, 2006.

Alan Hamel came to Fender on March 15, 1993, earning a reputation for craft and creativity that is still talked about today. When applying for the job, he presented impressive examples of his work to John Page. "But I could also tell he was low-key and didn't have a major ego," John remembers, "so I figured he would meld right into the team. That's exactly what he did. He was an excellent builder with a great grasp on vintage trivia and a good eye for 'cool.'" Scott Grant describes Alan as "a soft-spoken, country-boy kind of guy, down home. He was drawn to Southwest motifs. He liked B-Benders."

J. Black explains that while some of the builders had a sense of production and could streamline the execution of a product while maintaining high quality, Alan Hamel simply couldn't be rushed. Another colleague remembers him as "painstakingly slow, but capable of unique artistry." J. Black: "I think Alan's instruments are sought after because he had a great eye for detail. He rivaled Fred as one of the more creative art guitar builders, exemplified by his western theme boot set." Dan Smith: "Alan is amaz-

ingly talented and knowledgeable, meticulous to a fault, with a high degree of mechanical skills and artistry — a rare combination. He reminded me of Michael Stevens and George Blanda in that regard and, like them, he couldn't be rushed. You may have to wait a little longer for a project to be completed, but when done, there was no question that the result was as perfect as humanly possible."

George Amicay had worked for years as an aerospace technician in nearby Anaheim before being laid off in April, 1991. With plenty of time on his hands he began to concentrate on his recently adopted woodworking hobby. He carved up a couple of cheap, swap-meet solidbodies, one of which was a Strat knockoff that came to the attention of Mark Kendrick. The elaborately carved body was paired with a neck that John English had squirreled away for a while, and the resulting guitar served as Amicay's intro to the Custom Shop and Fender in general. He completed a number of freelance tasks for the shop, and when his unemployment income ran out he asked John Page for a job. Page hired him at about thirteen bucks an hour, as George recalls (according to Fender's records, George was hired on May 20, 1993). "I didn't really have a job title. I was doing wood carving and had also studied calligraphy for many years, so I did lettering or whatever they needed – certificates and stuff like that. I started working there in the new facility on Enterprise."

Alan Hamel, who lived on a ranch and bred horses, often incorporated western themes and artwork into his guitars.

George Amicay, with the Carved Floral Stratocaster. The guitar features Amicay's tour de force relief carving. "It's a sheet of flame maple over a mahogany body," he explains, "and I cut it so the mahogany is now the background and the maple is relieved. This is in the Western tradition that I saw on saddle work and other leather work." Details include gold hardware and abalone dots on the pau ferro fretboard.

The Dragon and the Mermaid. George Amicay: "Before I got hired, I did the Dragon/Mermaid guitar — the alder body only — just to demonstrate the sort of carving I was capable of. I thought, if I can get $800 for this, that would be great. John Page thought it was really neat. He asked me how much I wanted for it. I said, 'How about $2,000?' He said, 'Sure.' Later I said, 'You know, John, I would've sold it for $800.' And he said, 'I would've paid you $4,000!' [laughs]." John English built the guitar, and Pamelina H. painted it. Nice touch: The dragon's teeth are mother of pearl; its eye is abalone shell.

George Amicay is nothing if not a fast learner. "Fred Stuart was doing these Telecasters that looked sort of like Gretsch cowboy Roundups with the orange body, and he wanted some block inlays with the cow skulls and that Western stuff. They asked me if I could do engraving. I'd never done it, but I thought I could figure it out. I didn't make any money — just twenty-five bucks a neck, at first — but it helped to introduce my work."

To call George Amicay "old school" only begins to describe his approach to his art. "When I was learning how to carve wood," he says, "these books I bought showed all these tools that cost thirty or forty dollars for each chisel, so I would just use X-Acto knives, or if I had a requirement for a special cut, I would just get a hammer and a nail and I would flatten out the nail and sharpen it the way I needed it, and pound it into the end of a broomstick for a handle. After I was there for a while John told the supply guy to order whatever I needed, so they ordered all kinds of pneumatic engravers and carving tools, but it was stuff for people who didn't build guitars. I tried using them and did some engraving, but it wasn't my forte. I did order some impressive hand chisels for my bench so it would look like I knew what I was doing when people came by on a tour, but after they passed by I would pick up my X-Acto knife and go back to work. Eventually I did get a title, Master Artisan Woodcarver." Before leaving full-time Custom Shop employment on March 1, 2002, George Amicay collaborated with John Page, Pamelina H., and other colleagues to produce some of the shop's most memorable art guitars. He continues to take on occasional freelance projects for the shop.

One of several western-themed collaborations between Fred Stuart and George Amicay, this Tele Thinline features particularly intricate fingerboard carvings. George Amicay: "Don't let the vines and flowers fool you. We made sure every guitar was just beautiful to play." Note the extra detailing on the peghead and around the rim of the pickguard.

Stephen Stern, with one of the six guitars he did for a show in England; the theme was World War II airplane nose cone art. Three of the instruments, including this one, were painted by Dan Lawrence (the other three were painted by Sara Ray, Chap. 25). The guitar is a Gretsch 6120, although Stephen likes to install White Falcon tailpieces because they reveal more of the underlying artwork.

Stephen Stern worked at Charvel/Jackson for about five years. Mike Eldred was his boss, and when Mike left, Stephen took over Mike's lead position in final assembly on the production floor. He later established a cabinet shop where he refined his woodworking skills to a high degree of artistry. "I had heard of the Custom Shop," he remembers, "and it sounded very appealing. In March of '93 I brought down a Les Paul-type guitar I had made, along with my cabinet shop portfolio. I didn't know it at the time, but John Page also does a lot of custom furniture, so we hit it off and had a lot to talk about. My first job at the shop [starting on May 24, 1993], though, was to work outdoors in the parking lot, building a bunch of workbenches for the other builders. That's what they needed me to do, with the understanding that I would soon be building guitars."

Stephen was apprenticed to Jimmy D'Aquisto and crafted Fender's D'Aquisto guitars under the legendary builder's direction (Chap. 15). His promotion to Master Builder was swift. He explains, "John Page felt that building the D'Aquistos was Master Builder work, so for me the process of becoming a Master Builder was fairly quick. Then only a year or two after that they made me a Senior Master Builder, and in my case the duties didn't really change. It was more of a recognition of what I had already been doing since '93, working with Jimmy and building the archtops." Stephen also worked with Bob Benedetto on Fender's Benedetto and high-end Guild guitars, and he later took over the Gretsch Custom Shop, building White Falcons and 6120s. Other projects included crafting the Blue Guitar collection's D'Aquisto Centura Deluxe and several custom archtops in collaboration with the Disney Co. that celebrated the anniversary of the animated classic *Fantasia*. Gene Baker describes his former boss: "Steve Stern is not only a great builder but also a fine teacher, a well versed and eloquent guy." Today he is recognized as the shop's most accomplished archtop builder.

Gene Baker.

Gene Baker joined Fender's Custom Shop in the summer of 1993 after working in Gibson's West Coast Custom Shop and service center for two years. He brought with him a wealth of experience, having worked on a number of different brands and body styles. "At Gibson, we were always talking to the guys at Fender because we traded parts for various projects. Bands would drop off all their gear when they were on the road, so we were working on Gibsons, Fenders, Gretsches, you name it." After coming to Fender's Custom Shop, Gene started in the Set-Neck department. "The shop had about 30 or 35 employees at the time," he remembers, "and the building was going through a lot of changes as they were making way for new projects — more benches, electricity, machinery, etc. The shop was literally draped with extension cords and growing quick. I think it went from 30 to 60 employees in the six years I was there.

"There were just a few of us on the Set-Neck team. The atmosphere was very fun and team-oriented. John Page had high expectations, and he really encouraged and motivated people. They were doing the Tele Jr. and Set-Neck Strats, and I started sanding and buffing. Pretty soon I was being groomed by John Page and J. Black, my other mentor, for the new archtop division headed up by Steve Stern."

Gene played key roles in the Robben Ford project. His apprentice, Greg Fessler, eventually took it over. After gaining experience working on vintage-style guitars alongside Fred Stuart and J. Black, Gene was promoted to Master Builder in January, 1995. He prototyped the Contemporary and Carved Top Strats, built many different Custom Shop models, helped refine the Showmasters, co-designed the John Jorgenson model, was promoted to Senior Master Builder, and trained apprentices Mike Ponce and Mike Bump. He left the shop in January, 1999 and founded Baker Guitars in Riverside, California.

Thought by many to be the finest archtop builder who ever lived, Jimmy D'Aquisto held a unique position among the Custom Shop crew. See Chap. 15.

Left: The Limba Trio. Gene Baker built this matching trio of guitars with necks and bodies of limba, a wood associated with several classic Gibsons. He recalls: "I tended to get assigned this sort of thing because of my past experience with Gibson. These are black limba, really pretty, with a lot of figure. The customer wanted white limba, so we ended up making two sets." Gold hardware and tortoiseshell pickguards perfectly complement the wood's distinctive hue. Note the pearl-inlaid headstocks.

Abigail Ybarra.

John Cruz started working on Fender's main production line on October 23, 1987, in the early days of the William Schultz era. "They were just building a few guitars a day at that point," he recalls, "really a small operation. Everything was tiny. The 'wood shop' was not much bigger than my own work area is now — and it's not a big work area [laughs]. The only opening they had was in the wood shop, planing body planks down, gluing joints together, all that kind of stuff. So my first experience was doing that, and selecting wood. I gradually started working on necks, gluing fretboards on, [installing] truss rods, sanding necks, tune testing. I did the whole process from the beginning up. We had 14 tune testers over on the main line at the time I moved to the Custom Shop. I was probably the top tester over there. I usually had zero fallout, so my guitars were in good shape and they were going through."

Fred Stuart told *The ToneQuest Report*: "When we first started to become more autonomous in the Custom Shop, we went over to the factory and began to identify the really cracking guys that do the most and have the most potential, and John really stood out as someone who is driven to learn new things . . . A lot of guys just wanted to work their shift and go home. John has gone further . . . . he's a hell of a player, too."

John Cruz: "John Page came through the production line, looking for a few people to come over to the Custom Shop. He asked me if I'd be interested, and he said, 'I have to be up front with you, man; we don't always have a lot of work going on, and there are layoffs once in a while.' I needed some assurance of a steady job, so at first I declined, but he called me back a couple years later to be a tune tester. Over in the factory we had specialists who would do one thing like shielding or installing pickguard assemblies, but in the shop it's more common for one person to do several things, and that's one reason I took the job. I could try my hand at anything that needed to be done. And this is the cream of the crop. Everything has to be perfect;

Abigail "Abby" Ybarra is one of the shop's strongest links to Fender's vintage era. She came to work for Leo Fender in 1956, later commenting, "He wore overalls and worked as hard as any of us. Later I learned he was the owner." She worked in the metal shop for a couple of months, grinding frets and doing other chores. Within a couple of years she was transferred to small parts assembly, where she wired up harnesses, assembled components and, most notably, wound pickups. During the 1980s she worked in final assembly, putting bodies, hardware, and necks together. "I started working for the Custom Shop in 1993," she explains. "I mostly wire pickups for the Master Builders and also for some of the Team Built guitars." Her name or initials grace the pickups on some of the shop's most exclusive limited runs.

everything is double checked and triple checked.

"At the Custom Shop I had a really good eye for detail, so at first I was doing QA [Quality Assurance]. I was doing a lot of assembly and tune testing, helping out John English, Fred Stuart, John Suhr, J. Black, other Master Builders, just doing whatever anybody needed. Duane Boulanger was doing a lot of the Set-Neck tune testing, and I was doing the American Classics and a lot of vintage stuff. I worked with Abigail [Ybarra] for a little while, helping to wind pickups, a great experience. I learned so much from all these people. As an apprentice, the first one they let me build myself was a leopard Stratocaster. That was JC 001."

John Cruz became a Master Builder in 2003, helped initiate the shop's own Quality Assurance system, and made invaluable contributions to the Relic program. Some of his noteworthy projects have included the Muddy Waters, Stevie Ray Vaughan, Rory Gallagher, Jeff Beck, and Yngwie Malmsteen Tribute guitars. He has built personal instruments for Ike Turner and members of Whitesnake, REO Speedwagon, Mötley Crüe, Bon Jovi, U2, Guns N' Roses, Aerosmith, and many other bands.

John Cruz, assembling a Blackie Tribute Strat.

John Suhr.

John Suhr joined the Custom Shop crew on September 1, 1994, at a time Fender was exploring new strategies for entering high-end niche markets. Given his background, it was good timing for all concerned. John had grown up in New Jersey and in the early 1980s worked for Rudy Pensa at Rudy's Music Stop on 48th Street in Manhattan. In 1984 he began to establish a name for himself building elegant guitars favored by Mark Knopfler and others. They carried the R Custom brand name, later changed to Pensa-Suhr. He came to California to work with high-tech effects-rack guru Bob Bradshaw in 1991 and after three years moved on to the Custom Shop.

John Suhr: "I was hired as a Senior Master Builder. The only other one at the time was J. Black. I had known him from back in New York, and he was the one who convinced me to come to Fender. I think John Page was able to justify hiring me as a Senior Master Builder right away because aside from building guitars I was also doing electronics and a lot of pickup R&D. I made Jeff Beck's favorite pickups, and some tweed Twins for Eric Clapton. I actually had to build those in my garage because I really had no electronics equipment at Fender. I also made amps for B.B. King and Mark Knopfler, and did the electronics for the first American Deluxe bass." John Suhr made invaluable contributions to the Contemporary Strat and Showmaster projects (Chap. 19) before starting his own company, Suhr Guitars in Lake Elsinore, California.

In 2003, then-apprentice John Cruz built a pair of leopard-print guitars, a Tele and a Strat. Details included paw-print fretboard markers and black hardware.

Fender

CHAPTER FOURTEEN

14

Marketing Evolves

Beyond the Phantom Flagship

It's understandable that Fender's print catalogs have always had a tough time keeping up with its rapidly evolving product line. An additional complication during the late 1980s and early 1990s was that the company had basically started over after the buyout from CBS and was still in the throes of reorganizing. Another was that the Custom Shop was not only a new department for Fender but an entirely new concept. It had many early successes, but because every success entailed new challenges, what seemed to be a scattered, haphazard corporate environment was simply the result of Fender's wrestling with its own volatile growth.

One result of all this was that even though the in-house publicity machine, such as it was, sometimes touted the Custom Shop as the company's pride and joy — the Dream Factory, the flagship — other times it seemed to ignore it altogether. As noted elsewhere, this may have resulted in part simply from Fender's own shifting perspective on the shop's identity and proper role within the company.

In the mid 1990s, Fender ushered in a marketing strategy entailing a more cohesive line of Custom Shop products, more prominent NAMM displays, and an emphasis on art guitars. This was the shop's first metal guitar, displayed at NAMM in 1993. J. Black and Ron Chacey designed it, Black built it, and Chacey did both the Art Nouveau body engraving and the floral neck inlay. J. made four more of them, one of which went to Dave Stewart of Eurythmics.

Aside from its trade show displays, dealer seminars, and advertising in guitar magazines, Fender's primary vehicle for promoting its products and giving players and dealers an inside perspective was its own *Frontline* magazine. It offered interviews, features, tips, and columns, as well as full or partial catalogs of products. The Custom Shop had been founded in early 1987, and early *Frontlines* sometimes featured articles on its builders and instruments. It included ads for Custom Shop products as well as factory guitars that had initially been designed in the Custom

Mid-'90s ads promoted the shop's high level of craftsmanship, demonstrated that guitars could be adorned with highly unconventional materials and designs, and introduced individual builders to the public.

Shop, such as Richie Sambora's HRR Strat. Despite all that, well into the 1990s *Frontline*'s catalog portion, or "Product Index," usually failed to mention the shop at all.

Examples abound. The prestigious LJ was conceived by the shop's chief design guru, Michael Stevens, and was Fender's most expensive model by far; it was also its most distinctive departure from familiar designs — in fact, it didn't even say "Fender" on the headstock — and yet it wasn't designated as a Custom Shop guitar or even "Custom Order Only" in some of the literature.

One confusing detail was that several players — Eric Clapton, Yngwie Malmsteen, Jeff Beck, Robben Ford, and others — were routinely identified as Custom Shop artists, even though their signature Fenders were, at least most of the time, factory guitars or imports rather than Custom Shop models. While in fact there was no inconsistency at all — factory models and imports were sometimes designed in conjunction with and named after artists whose own personal guitars were built in the Custom Shop — it was nevertheless difficult at times to ascertain from the literature whether a model was an import, a USA factory guitar, or a Custom Shop product.

In the *Frontlines*, the Custom Shop's artist guitars were identified as such some of the time; other times they appeared alongside the regular factory guitars and were listed as "Custom Order Only" instruments, with no mention of the shop. On occasion, the same model might be identified on one page of a *Frontline* as a Custom Shop model and elsewhere in the same magazine with the less specific "USA" or "Custom Order Only" designation. In a fold-out flyer from 1992, the year of the price sheet, the shop's artist models appeared without even the "Custom Order Only" designation.

Many such listings continued through 1993, with no mention of a Custom Shop that by then was in its seventh year. The Product Index failed to recognize even the price sheet guitars as Custom Shop models for two years or so after their otherwise conspicuous introduction. For example, the '54 Stratocaster, the '60 Stratocaster, and the American Classics were all tagged with the Custom Order Only designation, with no indication that they originated anywhere other than the main factory. The same was true for the expanded line of artist Strats, left-handed Strats, and Custom Shop basses.

One exception was the listing for the Set-Neck Telecasters. In 1991 these guitars *were* specified to be Custom Shop instruments, even though other Custom Shop instruments were not. Was there some reason for this distinction? Was it because the Set-Necks had somewhat "Gibson style" glued-in necks and were therefore the catalog's biggest departures from conventional Fender designs? Or was it simply the kind of inconsistency that has plagued many companies' catalogs over the years? Probably the latter, but if any guitars were to be singled out as Custom Shop products, the Set-Necks — among the first examples of the shop's own in-house designs — were ideal candidates.

This ad showcased John English's selectively anodized, metal-body Aloha Strat, which demonstrated a level of artistry and creative expression rare among major companies. It also helped to ratchet up the shop's exclusivity by spotlighting a particular builder. Chap. 11 depicts Fred Stuart and George Amicay's Egyptian Tele from 1994, facing page, as well as a different take on the Aloha Strat theme.

John Page speculates that perhaps the copywriters sometimes chose not to identify Custom Shop guitars as such because Fender perceived them, and wanted dealers and consumers to perceive them, as the top end of the main line rather than the products of a more or less self-contained unit. (If so, there was nothing phony about such a strategy; it was simply one way to view the shop and its guitars. In fact, at least during the first several years the "all under one roof" depiction was, if anything, more accurate than the "separate entity" portrayal, given the interactions and revolving doors between R&D, marketing, the factory, and the shop.) Page says, "They saw the line as Squier at the low end, Fender in the middle to the upper end, and the Custom Shop at the top." However, Mike Lewis cautions: "Don't read too much into it. Back then, the shop was redefining itself on what seemed like a daily basis."

One window into Fender's attitude towards the shop: If you were lucky enough to acquire one of its earliest guitars, it wouldn't have said "Custom Shop" on it. The first logos said "CUSTOM-BUILT FENDER U.S.A." along with the builder's name. In this regard, those early logos and the *Frontline* magazines' "Custom Order Only" designations were consistent.

A blurry public profile

Whether downplaying the Custom Shop's identity as a semi-freestanding facility was intentional or, more likely, simply the result of a marketing strategy that had yet to coalesce, it had nothing to do with disrespecting the shop. In fact, the Dream Factory has been described by various principals as "Bill Schultz's baby." Way back in January 1987 — four months before the official announcement in May — Fender was already proudly spreading the word: "A much requested Custom Shop . . . is slated to begin production . . . ."

The shop's early, ill-defined public profile was also due in part to that age-old corporate predicament, the right hand not knowing what the left hand is doing. Dan Smith explains: "Surprisingly, the marketing guys had very little input as to what was actually printed in the *Frontline*. We were pretty short staffed, so there wasn't much time to help out. We'd get asked a few questions and then sometimes we'd be asked to proofread it, but that was generally after it was too late to fix anything, much to our chagrin. The [Custom Shop] numbers were so small at first that we were more concerned with being able to deliver product than anything else."

From the shop's point of view, any lack of departmental communication was sometimes seen as an advantage that fostered the builders' perceived autonomy. Fender management's response was a mix of pride and frustration: At times it seemed as though Fender looked upon the shop as something of an errant, precocious offspring, a brilliant but hard-to-corral stepchild whose role would come into focus only after a decade of shifting strategies, dizzying growth

spurts, and familial wrangling. Ralph Esposito: "There was constant turmoil about the way the Custom Shop was portrayed. Sometimes it seemed like [Fender marketing] wanted to leave us alone, but other times it seemed like they were fighting over who would get control of it."

The ambiguities in the early '90s literature also resulted in part from a policy of not always publicizing the country of origin of Fender guitars in general. Fender was importing guitars from Japan and still grappled with the perception on the part of some players and dealers that offshore instruments were inferior, despite abundant evidence to the contrary. Finally, as Dan Smith explains, "Prior to 1994 or so, there just wasn't enough Custom Shop product for Fender to do a separate catalog or have a separate section in the main catalog."

Marketing evolves

While John Page's takeover of R&D was official, his assumption of his new role as head of Custom Shop marketing was less formal and more gradual. Bill Schultz didn't actually assign him to do it; rather he allowed him to do it. He was never given any sort of "Custom Shop Marketing Director" title, and in a way it seems that aside from his official supervisory responsibilities, Page thought one of his key jobs was to represent his builders' interests. This attitude fostered a sensibility among the crew that the Custom Shop was something of an artists' collective, distinct from conventional top-down corporate models. "I just took on the role during 1992 and 1993," Page says, "and fought with those who would try to push products or ideas against what the majority of the shop's builders or customers thought was correct."

1994: More wham at NAMM

John Page had been dissatisfied with the Custom Shop's NAMM trade show displays for years — how dinky they were, and how they seemed to reinforce the impression that the shop was a segment of the production facility rather than a separate entity. Now, as de facto Custom Shop marketing manager, he could coordinate the exhibits with Fender's highly regarded advertising and promotions

John English built a Thinline version of the Stratocaster for Thoroughbred Music. The bar-marker motif was also used by Fred Stuart on some of his guitars.

manager, Jim Cruickshank. "I always felt we couldn't be the flagship if we were tethered to the rest of the line," Page says. "I would look at the exhibits and say, 'Hey, Jim — what the *hell?*'" Page laughingly remembers one NAMM display where "a couple of Custom Shop guitars were tucked away between some of the Japanese imports on one side and the Korean imports on the other." That was the last straw.

Cruikshank asked Page what sort of NAMM display he wanted. John Page: "My objective was to make it look like a jewelry store or an art gallery. If you want people to believe it's worth more than your other product, you better give it the respect of something valuable when you display it." The Custom Shop began to work directly with display companies, and over the next couple of years the exhibits became much larger and more elaborate. Now, NAMM attendees could hardly fail to notice the shop's dazzling designs and world-class craftsmanship. The new exhibits raised the shop's profile among dealers and competitors alike.

J. Black: "In a way, the history of the Custom Shop is marked by the history of the NAMM shows. They tell the entire story. In '92, it was just John Page, me, Fred Stuart, and John English, and that's when we started showing some of the art guitars. The display was very small, just this little spot. But '94 was huge, by far our biggest display to date, with signs, displays, booths, literature, and T-shirts. By then we were advertising Custom Shop accessories, too — pickguards, straps, gig bags, pickups, and all that stuff. That's how fast this little Custom Shop grew, from only Mike and John to a much larger operation in just a few short years. Everything was growing exponentially, and it was all reflected at NAMM."

Like brothers: working it out

Despite much collaboration and camaraderie, the perceptions of marketers and Custom Shop workers sometimes conflicted. John Page admits, "I pissed a lot of people off. Looking back on it, everyone is going to have a different perspective; I realize that. My perspective is this: I saw the potential for this shop, and if I ran into an obstacle I'd take it to the mat with Bill Schultz and say, look, this guy's in the

Fred Stuart custom-built this ash-body 12/6 Strat doubleneck for Jeff Cook of Alabama.

way. I argued. I thought if I get fired, then OK, I get fired, but I'm not going to pussyfoot around. I kept thinking, if you're going to call us the flagship, then let us be the flagship, let us lead the way. But here's the thing: Dan Smith and I would have these intense arguments, and then it was like, come on, let's go get a hot dog and a beer. Brothers — you know, they butt heads sometimes."

On that point, Dan Smith has the same view: "John wore every hat that you could possibly have for the Custom Shop. There was a lot of passion there, and he fought for what he believed in. Sometimes to the angst of Bill Schultz, John and I would butt heads on occasion, but I have a lot of respect for him, and we loved each other. We were like brothers. I was the older brother, and he was like the kid sometimes. We would tussle, but always with the best of intentions and the proper goals in mind."

J. Black's perspective is that the politics and all the drama at Fender in those days was sort of like junior high school. It seemed important at the time, but at the end of the day the company was moving forward and it was all pretty light stuff. People liked and respected each other. The tensions were likely due in part to the atmosphere at the top filtering down to all departments. Bill Schultz was a taskmaster, a whip-crackin' guy. He wanted results, and he wanted them right now.

As we will see, resolving the debates between the Custom Shop and Fender marketing would help set the course for the shop's evolution into a major, highly acclaimed, semi-independent manufacturer in its own right.

The glory of grunge

The Heartfield project had been similar to the Kubicki experience in one way, in that once again some of the dealers and sales reps couldn't get behind the idea of non-Fenderish Fenders. But the two projects also shared a common advantage: They provided a way for Fender to respond to shifting tastes without having to alter their core designs – Telecasters, Stratocasters, Precision Basses, and Jazz Basses. Ralph Esposito: "At least Heartfield let us try to penetrate these new markets without messing with the standard stuff. Rather than try and adapt the Strats and

J. Black built this Custom Telecaster Thinline for retailer Sam Ash. It featured a bookmatched flame-maple top, a bird's-eye soft-V neck, and gold hardware.

Teles to these new styles, it made a lot more sense to leave them alone. The wisdom of the Heartfield strategy became obvious in '89 or '90 when Nirvana came along and Kurt Cobain picked up Jaguars and Mustangs. All of a sudden guys were playing Duo-Sonics and all those other things that Fender had already been doing."

Alternative/indie musicians typically disdained the look of artists they perceived as being too slick or too glam, favoring jeans and flannel shirts over Spandex, eyeliner, and architectural haircuts. Instead of expensive boutique instruments or Holy Grail vintage treasures, they often preferred relatively obscure, out-of-fashion guitars, including low-end student models and bargain-bin imports. Alex Perez: "Grunge was just huge for Fender because we were already making the guitars that people wanted, and we had been making them for a long time. Kurt Cobain was playing Mustangs and Jaguars. When I came over to the Custom Shop [in 1992], one of the first projects Larry Brooks and Mark Kendrick were working on was the Kurt Cobain guitar. That was a huge thing for Fender. I will never forget seeing the box that he sent to us. We had sent him a guitar, and he took the box it was sent in and cut it out in the shape he wanted after hand-tracing it with a Sharpie or something. He sent that cardboard back, and that's what Larry used to make that Jag-Stang."

Ralph Esposito: "Sales on a lot of our guitars spiked with grunge. Instead of Fender trying to catch up, now the other companies were trying to figure out how to capitalize on the new styles. People suddenly didn't want as much of the Floyd Rose stuff or the spiky bodies and so on, and next thing you know within a year or two those other companies were looking to us and copying what we were doing with Fender body shapes and moto pickguards and all the rest. The tables were turned."

Here we are now

When Kurt Cobain brandished a lefty '69 Lake Placid Blue Mustang in the 1991 "Smells Like Teen Spirit" video, it was perhaps the most prominent image of an artist with

A hybrid of the Jaguar (once the top of the line) and the Mustang (a "student" model), the short-scale Jag-Stang was conceived by Kurt Cobain. This lefty version was custom-built for him, but Fender received news of his death before it could be shipped.

Although commercial versions were imported from Japan, the Jag-Stang was prototyped in the Custom Shop. Each pickup had its own 3-way switch. The Dynamic Vibrato tailpiece was borrowed from the Mustang.

a Fender guitar other than a Tele or a Strat since 1977, when a knock-kneed Elvis Costello posed on the cover of his debut album with his Jazzmaster. Cobain suggested a new guitar that melded aspects of two favorite models, the short-scale, 22-fret Jaguar and the Mustang. The Jag was the top-of-the-line guitar during the later years of the Leo Fender era, although by 1991 it had been out of production for a decade and a half. The $189.50 Mustang was introduced in the summer of 1964 as a mid-line, short-scale guitar a notch above the Duo-Sonic and Musicmaster student models; Fender had recently reissued it, in 1990.

Artist Builder Larry Brooks reported in *Frontline*: "Kurt always enjoyed playing both guitars. He took photographs of each, cut them in half, and put them together to see what they'd look like." The resulting body shape was Fenderish if a bit cartoony, something Leo Fender might have designed if he'd been watching 30 straight hours of *The Jetsons.* Brooks built a prototype for Cobain in 1993. He recalled: "It was his concept, and we detailed it and contoured it to give him balance and feel . . . He was really easy to work with. I had a chance to sit and talk with him, and then we built a prototype. He played it a while and then wrote some suggestions on the guitar and sent it back to us. The second time around, we got it right."

Fender called their new Jaguar-Mustang hybrid, naturally enough, the Jag-Stang. Kurt Cobain was quoted as saying, "Ever since I started playing, I've always liked certain things about certain guitars but could never find the perfect mix of everything I was looking for. The Jag-Stang is the closest thing I know."

After Cobain's death in April 1994, Fender collaborated with his estate to produce the commercial version of the Jag-Stang, which was made in Japan. Released in the fall of '96, it featured a 22-fret rosewood fingerboard, a 24" scale, the unusual Dynamic Vibrato floating tailpiece borrowed from the Mustang, a slanted humbucker in the bridge position, and a Strat pickup in the neck position. While many Custom Shop designs were ultimately produced in the U.S. factory rather than the shop, the Jag-Stang provides an example of a Custom Shop design that was manufactured by FujiGen-Gakki and imported by Fender. Some Custom Shop designs would later be rendered in Fender's Mexico plant.

Kurt Cobain's instrumental preferences helped associate Fender with a new generation of players, new musical styles, and new attitudes toward gear. It also put the spotlight on models other than Teles and Strats.

With handcrafted archtops such as this one, the shop helped redefine the very meaning of "Fender guitar." This example is a custom one-off, #029, built in 1998 for Josep Melo, a luthier based in Barcelona.

CHAPTER FIFTEEN

15

The Designer/Signature Series

Robben Ford, D'Aquisto

The Master Series

Dan Smith knew that if Fender were to manufacture high-end guitars with glued-in necks and humbuckers, it would be interpreted as a signal that the company intended to tackle Gibson on its own turf, perhaps even to beat Gibson at its own game. With precisely that goal in mind — and simply to plan for the possibility that market tastes might someday turn away from Fender's core products — Smith spearheaded the design of a collection of all-new instruments in 1983. Fender called it the Master Series.

With their three-on-a-side pegheads and luxurious appointments, the Master Series instruments looked like nothing Leo Fender had ever designed, or ever cared to design. They included two double-cutaway guitars conceived by Smith himself and designed by Smith and John Carruthers: the alder-bodied Flame and Esprit, each available in three packages of features and trim levels ranging from elegant and simple to elegant and fancy. While they didn't look like specific Gibson models, the Esprit was intended to compete directly with one of Gibson's best and most highly acclaimed guitars, the historic ES-335; and the Flame, although chambered and somewhat larger than a Les Paul, was in fact designed to take on Gibson's flagship solidbody.

The Master Series also included a stunning "jazz guitar" designed by Jimmy D'Aquisto, the premier archtop builder in the country and former apprentice and heir to the legendary John D'Angelico of New York City. It, too, was available in several trim levels. All versions of the Flame, Esprit, and D'Aquisto guitars were initially manufactured in Japan by FujiGen-Gakki and imported by Fender.

From the outset, Fender made no secret of its target market. Its mid-'80s catalog copy proclaimed: "While the only serious competition for Fender's designs was the family of hollow and semisolid guitars utilizing set necks and dual-coil humbucking pickups, Fender saw opportunities for major improvements in this basic design concept and decided to undertake the project. Thus the Master Series was born." Additional literature emphasized Fender's commitment to innovation while at the same time acknowledging its archrival once again in thinly veiled text: "While the new Fender Master Series Esprit and Flame guitars bear a superficial resemblance to other popular electrics, closer examination reveals a myriad of subtle detail refinements . . . ."

The Robben Ford model, Japan

In the late 1970s Robben Ford began to establish himself as a versatile, toneful, and electrifying guitarist onstage and in the studio. Robben's wife at the time worked at Yamaha, as did Dan Smith. Smith and Ford became acquaintances, sometimes going on double dates. Smith recalls: "Robben and I got to be close friends. My wife Sylvia and I made him a part of our family, and the first concerts my kids went to were Robben Ford concerts." (One of those kids was future Master Builder Jason Smith.) Dan thought Robben would be an ideal endorser for Yamaha, but then Smith went to Fender, joining his former boss and new Fender President Bill Schultz.

Dan Smith: "When we were developing the Master Series, I invited Robben along with other L.A. studio guys for product evaluation and development. After a number of pickup swaps and refrets, Robben really began to like the Esprit Ultra. He endorsed it for us, and this became his main guitar from the mid '80s into the early '90s. It was on the majority of tracks he recorded during this period and became part of 'his' sound. All during this period he experimented with other brands and models and had the original Esprit doctored and re-doctored."

In 1987, Smith and Ford collaborated on a new guitar that would elevate Robben's favorite model to the artist signature level. They started with the Esprit Ultra, changed the pickups, and rechristened it the Robben Ford. FujiGen built it, and Fender imported it through 1993. Dan Smith: "The Robben Ford model, as made in Japan, was exactly the same as the Esprit Ultra with the exception of the pickups. The Schaller pickups with their unique shape and mounting method were ditched in favor of a standard humbucking system. This allowed Robben to try a variety of over-the-counter pickups, although he seemed to always come back to a Duncan '59 in the neck and a Duncan JB in the bridge. This guitar had a coil-splitter switch and, oddly enough, Robben most often used only the single-coil mode, very rarely the full humbucker."

The original Esprit/Robben Ford had a maple neck with an ebony fretboard and a chambered alder body with a carved spruce top. Dan Smith: "My inspiration came from the old [small-bodied] Guilds of the '50s — M-75s and George Barnes models — and also from what I had seen Jimmy D'Aquisto do with his little solidbodies. My favorite guitar was the ES-335, but it just wouldn't cut through a Hammond B-3 organ or synthesizers without turning it up. The Esprit/Robben Ford was born out of the desire to have a slightly smaller-bodied version of the 335 that would cut through and also deliver a solid blues and jazz tone."

Designer/Signature Robben Ford

By 1993 Fender had decided to move production of the Robben Ford and D'Aquisto guitars from Matsumoto to Fender's Custom Shop. As before, they were grouped in the same collection, now called the Designer/Signature Series. That series also included the U.S.-made LJ model. (By the Spring of '96 the Robben Fords and D'Aquistos would be moved to the new Namesake Series, along with other Custom Shop artist signature models.) Although initial announcements in 1994 specified two versions of the Robben Ford, the Ultra and the Elite, these early designations were promptly revised. The newer variations, also promoted in 1994, were dubbed the Ultra FM, with a chambered body and a carved flame maple top; Ultra SP, with a chambered body and a carved spruce top; and Elite FM, with a solid mahogany body and a flame maple top. While the original Fuji models had 24.75" scale lengths, which matched Gibson's published measurements, the Custom Shop Robben Fords had 24.625" scale lengths, which matched Gibson's *actual* measurements; scale length is an important contributor to both tone and feel.

Master Builder Gene Baker took charge of the project, in part because of his experience building Gibsons and Set-Neck Fenders. He recalls: "At first, I used Fender Japan bodies to create all the templates I needed, and I'd make changes along the way. We had no CAD documentation on the model for a good while until Steve Boulanger, bless his soul, was able to document it. At that time we cut some templates on the shop's CNC. [CAD stands for Computer-Assisted or Computer-Aided Design; CNC, or NC, refers to Computer Numeric Controlled cutting and shaping equipment.] I began building tooling for the guitars in mid '93, started working closely with Robben in about September,

Greg Fessler on the Robben Ford model, right: "Fender was trying to show that we can step outside the box and do different things. In a way these guitars were our answer to Gibson and to Paul Reed Smith. Fender's new approach was, why limit yourself?"

Fender

and delivered the very first solidbody Elite prototype to him on October 13, 1993. After a lot of experimentation we released the three models at NAMM in January '94. The Custom Shop's Robben Ford model was always completely hand-built using pin routers, a table saw, a pantograph, and hand tools." (A pantograph is a mechanical drawing/copying device dating to the 1600s.)

As we have seen, some Custom Shop projects used the main factory's facilities to one degree or another. Gene Baker saw the Robben Ford project as a "Master's Apprentice-built model," in between the Master Built concept and what would soon be called the Team Built approach. He explains, "What I liked about the model was that the builder could personally do as much of the work as he wanted to control. You could get the help of the paint department or assembly, or just do as much yourself as you desired."

Gene Baker's apprentice was Greg Fessler. After only six months of training, the talented apprentice was promoted to Master Builder in July 1994 and took over the Robben Ford models. This freed up Gene Baker to take on a job that he found even more exciting and challenging: building one-off Strats and Teles. Greg Fessler recalls, "Gene probably made about 25 Robben Fords. He needed some help, and John [Page] thought we could use another Master Builder making Strats and Teles, so they had me helping out. The idea was, I would get my chops up working on the Robben Fords and then once I got really good at it I could move over to Strats and Teles, like Gene. But once Gene did the prototypes and we got all tooled up, the word got out and demand was very high, so I ended up staying with the Robben Fords. We continued to make the three versions, all by hand. The spruce top definitely gives a slightly different sound than the maple, which is a much harder wood with a snappier sound. Most of the guitars that I made for Robben were spruce-top models."

Left: The new models featured choice woods, subtle finishes, multiple body bindings, and the latest incarnation of Fender's glued-in neck/body joint.

As is often the case when art meets craft, some disagreements arose over the design of the Robben Ford models. Gene Baker found himself "in a bit of a pickle, trying to keep everyone happy." Dan Smith: "I thought all the Custom Shop Robben Fords were beautiful guitars, and since we were looking to expand the Custom Shop, why not offer them all? But I did insist that we continue making the first, original model in the style of the Esprit Ultra — not because John Carruthers and I had designed it but because it was the guitar Robben used most often, the one he kept coming back to after swapping out pickups and trying all sorts of variations.

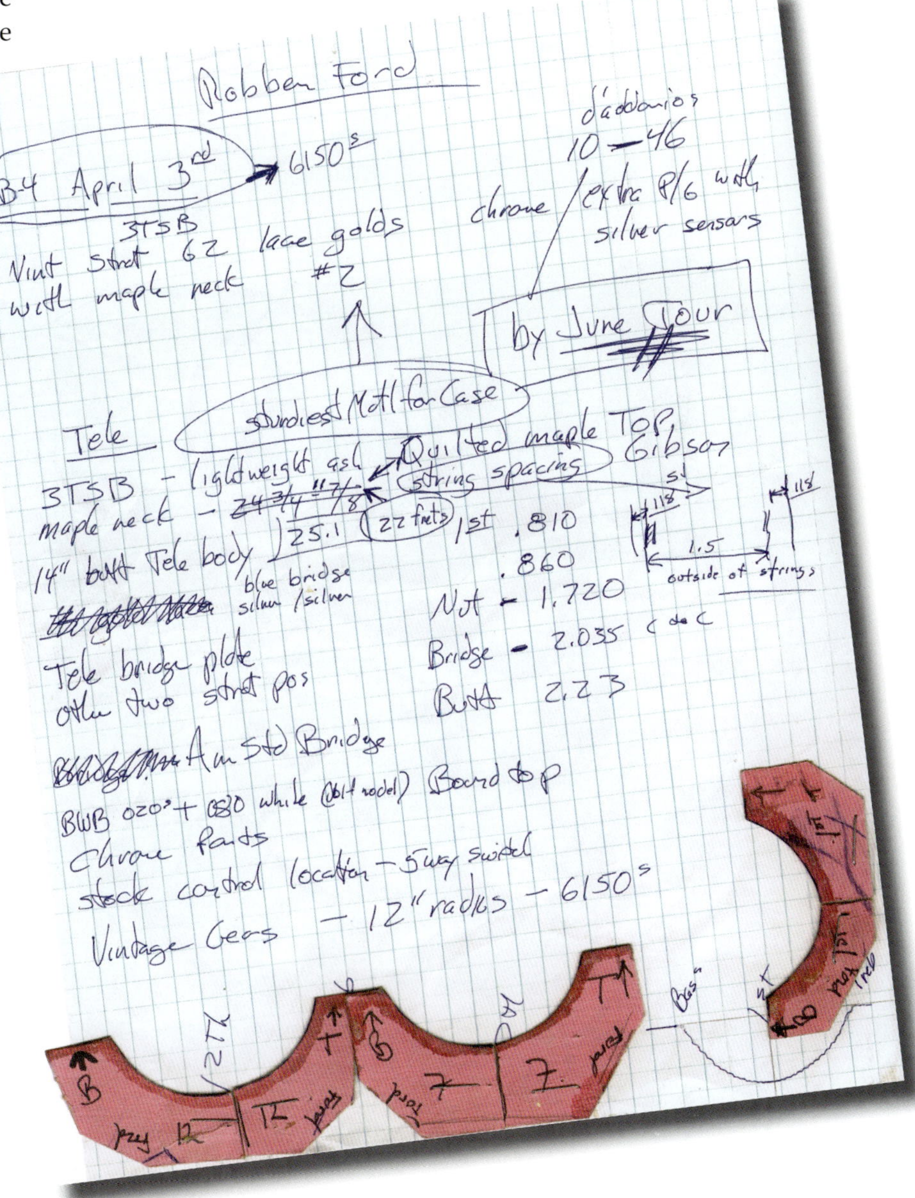

Right: Collaborations between builders and artists were often documented in handwritten notes and sketches; the pink cardboard pieces specify contours along the neck of a Robben Ford model.

"Over the years the shop tried to build Robben a guitar that he felt matched the original from FujiGen but, sadly, it never happened. In fairness, Fuji never built him one that he liked as well, either. It was understandably frustrating for everyone involved, including Robben, who was unbelievably generous with his time. These were not easy guitars to build, but because of Robben's unquestioned talent and natural likeability, everyone felt compelled to put their best effort into getting it right. While some of the guitars had problems, others were truly fine instruments. Sometimes you just come across a magical guitar — one that seems to deliver on every level — and chances are, like it seemed to be for Robben and his original Esprit, you never find another one like it."

Stephen Stern, right, on his mentor, Jimmy D'Aquisto: "He didn't have a lot of fixtures or those sorts of things. He was very intuitive, and everything was done by hand."

The Custom Shop manufactured the Robben Fords until 2002. Greg Fessler: "I love those guitars. They are some of my favorites. They are also a lot of fun to make. Fender was trying to show that we can step outside the box and do different things. In a way these guitars were our answer to Gibson and to Paul Reed Smith. Fender's new approach was, why limit yourself? They were much more successful than everybody predicted, so I worked on them nonstop for six years or more. These were in response to orders from dealers or players; we didn't make them up ahead of time and keep them in stock. We could only make about four per month because they were complicated to build and very labor intensive. I must've built about 300 in all, and I probably could've been working on them nonstop right up to this day. Customers were still ordering them at the time we lost Robben as an endorser and Fender discontinued the model."

Mentor and young master: Jimmy D'Aquisto and Stephen Stern

An association between Fender and Jimmy D'Aquisto might have left purists scratching their heads. After all, Fender is all about Strats and Teles, P Basses and Jazz Basses, bolt-ons and single-coils, rock and roll, country and blues — or so goes the conventional wisdom. But there can be no stronger evidence of Bill Schultz's and Dan Smith's ambition to expand their company's role beyond those constraints — and no stronger evidence of their faith in their own craftsmen — than their bringing the legendary Jimmy D'Aquisto, heir to John D'Angelico, into the Fender family. As Paul William Schmidt wrote in his fine book *Acquired of the Angels: The Lives and Works of Master Guitar Makers John D'Angelico and James L. D'Aquisto,* "D'Angelico and D'Aquisto were not unlike the Amati and Stradivari of guitar makers: brilliant artists who have truly graced the earth with the most eloquent of instruments. D'Angelico and D'Aquisto were perhaps the preeminent archtop guitar makers of the 20th Century, and their artistry will benefit humanity for centuries to come."

Although the Fuji-built archtops of the 1980s were high quality instruments, Fender decided to raise the D'Aquisto guitars' profile by relocating production to the Custom

Shop. The project was assigned to Stephen Stern, who would become not only a Senior Master Builder and Fender's number-one archtop craftsman but also a world-class luthier in his own right, eventually taking on the Fender Benedetto project as well.

When Stephen was interviewing for a job, he told John Page that he wanted to build custom Telecasters and Stratocasters. Page responded that he already had several people who could do that, but he needed someone to take on an especially exciting and challenging project — building archtops designed by Jimmy D'Aquisto. Stephen Stern: "I had never built archtops. I did have my background with Charvel, and I had made guitars in my woodshop at home, but those were solidbodies and neck-through bodies. It was so important for Jimmy to have confidence in Fender, but I was confident that I had all the chops to do it, and John saw that I had the woodworking skill and the necessary experience with tooling, so he offered me the job."

After wrapping up business at his cabinet shop, Stephen joined the Fender team in May 1993, and he and Jimmy started working together that summer. "Fender wanted something to show at the January '94 NAMM show," Stephen reports, "so I had to make all the tooling. First I got blueprints both from Japan and from Jimmy. Fuji's were drawn by a draftsman, very detailed, with everything precisely measured. Jimmy's were quite different. He had drawn up his own blueprints himself, and I don't think there were any actual measurements on them. You know, his way of building would have struck some people as being crude. He didn't have a lot of fixtures or those sorts of things. He was very intuitive, and everything was done by hand."

Gene Baker also helped out on the project. "I had a Les Paul that I had completely hand-built while I was at Gibson," he remembers, "and I showed it to Steve. He could see I was well versed in electronics and hardware, and right away they thought the archtop department would be a good place for me. I helped Steve to do a lot of the tooling for the D'Aquistos."

Stephen and Jimmy began their collaboration on the telephone. Stephen Stern: "Jimmy was always a good listener, and encouraging to me. Because of his reputation and his exacting standards, he could have been intimidating and aloof, but he was very warm. Instead of just giving me orders, he treated me like a fellow builder. He was an uncomplicated person whose goal in life was simply to build the best guitars in the world."

The two builders met in person at that January 1994 NAMM Show in Anaheim, where Stephen had his first Fender D'Aquisto Ultra on display (this guitar, number 001, eventually went to the D'Aquisto family; also unveiled at that show were the other members of the Custom Shop's Designer/Signature Series, the Robben Ford models).

Formulating the design and dimensions of the neck/body joint presents one of the most exacting challenges in constructing a guitar with a glued-in neck.

Jimmy and Stephen addressed the new project without referencing the previous guitars made by Fuji. Stephen Stern: "I don't know what Jimmy thought about those guitars, but he didn't tell me to do anything different. He saw the Ultra I made and told me a few things that weren't correct, but I was on the right track and the changes were minor. For example, the arching on the top on the upper bout needed to be changed a little bit."

After those discussions, the Custom Shop went into "production" — if we can call it that. In fact, all of the high-end D'Aquistos were made to order, so while fixed-spec models did appear in catalogs, the actual ordering and construction processes were typical of Master Built instruments, with one-on-one collaborations between luthier and customer. By the summer of 1994, the project had solidified to the point where Fender was offering distinct models. These were proudly displayed in Fender literature that, with justification, touted Jimmy D'Aquisto as "undisputedly the finest archtop guitar builder in the world."

The top of 1994's two-model line was the 17" Ultra, a solid-wood, hand-carved instrument that by 1997 would retail for $8,799. Its high-end appointments included a maple body, spruce top, ebony fingerboard, ebony tailpiece, multiple binding, and gold hardware. Although it was designed as a purely acoustic guitar, it could be ordered with an optional Kent Armstrong pickup for an additional $225.

The less fancy but still sumptuous Elite had a smaller, 16 1/4" body. Dan Smith describes it as basically the same as the previous Fuji-made D'Aquisto Elite but with a carved solid spruce top (the Fuji version had a spruce plywood top). Its pickup was built into the top, as opposed to the Ultra's optional pickup, which was suspended, or floating. As Smith puts it, "While the Ultra was designed as a top-of-the-line, all solid wood, Gibson L-5 size full acoustic archtop, the smaller Elite was more in the electric ES-175 vein — although its solid spruce top was an upgrade from the [laminated-top] 175, kind of like a Gibson L-4 with a built-in humbucker."

The Elite was soon dropped, although a year or two into the program the D'Aquisto line was augmented by the more affordable Deluxe — "for players who need a full amplification without the overtones of the solid wood presence." Stephen recalls that Jimmy liked the old Guild humbucking pickups made by DeArmond, so Stephen tracked one down and sent it to Seymour Duncan, who spec'd out similar pickups for the Deluxes. Duncan reports that he used the Guild/DeArmonds as a model, but wound the Deluxe's pickups on his own humbucking bobbins. "I wanted a fairly low DC resistance, something like 7.4k," he explains. "Standard Gibson humbuckings are maybe about 7.8k to 8.4k on average, but the Guilds were 400 or 500 Ohms lower, around 7.2k or 7.4k, so you do get a much cleaner sound out of them with the heavier strings that jazz guys like. An 8.4 in there would be too boomy on the bottom end, too thick. With about a 7.4 in the neck position, you get a really nice, clean jazz sound, and then if you want to roll off the high end you can do it with the tone control. You get a nice bottom that's not too muddy or dark."

Stephen Stern fits a maple neck to a blonde archtop body.

Aside from their laminated figured maple tops, Deluxes also had maple bodies, master volume and tone controls, and fingerboards and tailpieces of ebony. Stephen describes the Deluxe as "a very fine, workingman's archtop guitar." In 1997, it retailed for $3,199.

As Stephen Stern was mentoring his apprentice, Mike Ponce, Jimmy D'Aquisto continued to guide and teach Stephen. "Jimmy would come out to the shop," Stephen recalls, "and give me instructions and pointers. I made carving patterns that we could use on a machine. It wasn't a CNC machine, but it was a little bit like a pantograph. I made patterns for it and Jimmy modified them. He dialed them in and got the specs exactly where he wanted them. When we started making the more affordable Deluxe, with its plywood top and back, we used that machine for the patterns, which were sent out to be digitized. Molds were then made for the plywood press that were identical to the pattern that Jimmy made."

Fender offered D'Aquisto guitars for the rest of the 1990s, although the nomenclature shifted around a bit. The models were relocated from the Designer/Signature series to the mid-'90s Namesakes series and finally to the Master Built series (don't get confused by the inauguration of the "Master Built" series — all of the high-end D'Aquistos, not just the late-'90s versions, were custom-ordered, Master Built guitars). Stephen Stern hand-built one or two solid-wood Ultras each month. The Elites were much more scarce; in fact, Stephen's records reveal that he built only four of them (they rival Mike Stevens's LJ IIs and IIIs in rarity). While Fender literature predicted that the shop would produce about 20 Deluxes each month, the builders think the number was likely a bit lower. Mike Ponce: "We never had many Deluxes in stock, but sometimes if we got an order I would build more than one. So if we got an order for a trans red or a cherry or a sunburst, I might build four or five."

The fullest expression of the Fender/D'Aquisto partnership, the Ultra featured a hand-graduated bookmatched top of solid quartersawn spruce, a solid maple body, a maple neck, and an ebony fingerboard with pearl inlays. Jimmy D'Aquisto's touch is particularly evident in the design of the soundholes and ebony tailpiece. This version is equipped with a floating Kent Armstrong pickup.

Of the 50 D'Aquisto Ultras built by Stephen Stern, five had larger, 18" bodies. The impetus for the modification was the Blue Guitar project initiated by the late collector Scott Chinery, who was an admirer and patron of D'Aquisto's. In 1994 he ordered an 18" D'Aquisto Centura Deluxe with a most unconventional finish — a shaded, deep blue color. He then commissioned 21 of the world's leading builders — among them Bob Benedetto, Mark Campellone, Mark Lacey, and John Monteleone — to render their own take on the blue-archtop idea. The result is one of the most stunning collections of innovative, unusual, and beautiful jazz guitars ever assembled.

On this Ultra, note the highly figured wood, pearl inlays, multi-ply bindings, and attention to detail.

As the representative of Fender's Custom Shop and Jimmy D'Aquisto's apprentice, Stephen Stern was an obvious choice for participation. In 1996, he built a blue 18" Ultra in the Enterprise Court facility. As the first Fender D'Aquisto with an 18" body, it was given the serial number 01. In the book *Blue Guitar*, author Ken Vose wrote: "According to Scott Chinery, the D'A Custom Ultra is as much Jimmy's as it is Stern's: 'As soon as you pick it up and play it you know it must be a D'Aquisto. Stern was very successful in translating what was one of D'Aquisto's last designs.'"

In that same book Stephen reflected, "I would say without a doubt that working with Jimmy D'Aquisto was the greatest experience of my career. Jimmy taught me how the archtop guitar works in a way that I can visualize, not in abstract theory but in plain, simple English." Mike Ponce: "It was just great seeing Steve grow as a builder under the mentoring of Jimmy D'Aquisto."

Did it ever strike Stephen Stern as ironic or intimidating that his very first major project at Fender was to craft guitars designed by an artist considered by many experts to be the greatest archtop builder of all time? He puts it this way: "I was struck by how fortunate I was to be in that position. It was luck, but they say luck is when opportunity and preparation meet, and I believe that. I did have 80 or 90 percent of the skills I needed, and Jimmy helped me go that extra distance."

Greg Fessler provides additional insights: "Gene Baker was my mentor on the Robben Fords, and he was very patient with me. He is an outstanding builder, and he took me under his wing and showed me everything. I also had the very great privilege of getting some help when Jimmy D'Aquisto came out. He showed me a lot of pointers and was just a great guy. I was struggling with some stuff, techniques I wasn't sure about. He would say hey, here's how you fix it, here's what I would do. It's okay to do it this way, but not that way. I was learning on the fly, and he was very practical. He had inherited the legacy of John D'Angelico, so as you would expect he had the highest possible standards, but he was never nitpicky just to be nitpicky. It wasn't about that. It was about the guitar sounding right and playing well and looking right. Everything

Archtop elegance meets rockabilly bop: Stephen Stern's one-of-a-kind Classic Rocker prototype featured DeArmond-style pickups, a blueberries & cream paint job, binding from a violin shop, and a through-the-roof Wow Factor.

you did was to achieve those goals. The aesthetics had to be right, but if you had to cheat a little bit here and there to make it play right or sound right, he was cool with it. I was blown away by that. He said to me one time, 'Hey, do you think with all the labor John and I put into those D'Angelicos that when we messed up something or had a little problem we were going to throw it in the trash? We'd fix that thing and make it look right.'

"In the precious short amount of time we had the opportunity to be with him, I learned so much. All he cared about was, did it play right? Did it sound right? People say he was the finest builder in the world, and I agree with that. Bill Schultz never wanted to see Fender pigeonholed into this little solidbody electric niche. He wanted to make the Custom Shop an elite shop for anything and everything. So what do you do? You bring in the best guys in the world. When it came to archtops, that was Jimmy."

Rockin' Classic

Many of the earliest rock and roll guitar solos were recorded with archtop instruments years before the solidbodies later associated with the style gained substantial popularity, in some cases before they were even invented. Because of Stephen Stern's work with the D'Aquisto models, he was the ideal candidate to build a new Fender archtop whose inspiration would come not from the elegance and sophistication of jazz but rather from the swagger and twang of boppin' rockabilly.

The result was Fender's Classic Rocker, a 17" hollowbody guitar with a top, back, and sides of figured maple, checkerboard top binding, a set neck, and two DeArmond 2000 pickups. Crowning touch: a heavy-handled, spring-loaded Bigsby vibrato that looked like it could have been a kickstand on a '59 Harley-Davidson. As was the case with the Gibsons and Gretsches favored by so many pioneers in the 1950s, Fender Rockabilly Cool wasn't cheap. Excluding the D'Aquisto Elite and Ultra's retail prices, the Classic Rocker's $5,799 tag topped that of all other late-'90s Custom Shop guitars.

The prototype was designed as a NAMM Show project in 1998 and displayed in January 1999. It was basically a D'Aquisto Deluxe whose two-tone cream and blue paint job gave it sort of a '55 Bel Air vibe. Stephen Stern: "That first guitar had a 16" body, and I put Grover Imperials on the headstock. I liked those old Kay headstocks, so I was going for a little bit of that look. Alan Hamel or Fred Stuart gave me some really cool binding from an old violin shop, and I put that on. It was just a one-off, but Dan Smith wanted it to be a model, and at that point we turned it into a 17" body. I designed the inlays, and Alan and I worked on their design. I didn't want just plain old blocks. We were looking through a guitar book and I saw these lap steels with closed diamonds and open diamonds connected to each other, so that's where the idea for the pattern came from. It was very limited. We got a few orders, but I only made about ten of them."

Some of my best friends . . .

The Robben Fords and D'Aquistos were never intended to tempt diehard Fender purists to abandon their Strats and Teles. The idea was rather to fulfill the expansionist vision of Bill Schultz. They demonstrated loud and clear that the Custom Shop could meet the needs and tastes of professionals in all styles of popular music, and like the LJs and Set-Necks they proved that Fender's craft and expertise extended beyond its historic bolt-on solidbodies.

Although the Master Series, Robben Ford, and D'Aquisto projects are often associated with Dan Smith, he is quick to share credit: "It started with Bill Schultz, and what he must have learned back at Yamaha for all those years. Fender is a *guitar* company, so he felt that if a guitarist or bassist walks into a music store looking for a particular type of guitar, Fender should at least offer something that would satisfy those needs. He realized we weren't Gibson or Martin, but he felt it was misguided to just rest on our core product and not be willing to broaden our approach. I wholeheartedly supported his wishes. After all, I always considered myself a guitarist, not just a Fender guitarist. I have always had a love affair with a variety of brands; to paraphrase — 'Some of my best friends were Gibsons.'"

As sensible as it sounds, this attitude provoked arguments and sore feelings. Dan Smith: "I did my best to market the Master Series and the subsequent offerings from the Custom Shop, but all throughout that process I was met with opposition, not only from outside the company but from inside as well. For many, Fender is a religious experience. Designing and promoting new styles of Fender guitars, you'd think I was committing blasphemy. It was like living in Boston and rooting for the Yankees."

The other view: For many players Fender continues to mean Strats and Teles, P Basses and J Basses. As one exec put it, "So let's just be the best *Fender* we can be." Besides, given Fender's distribution or ownership of Jackson, Gretsch, Guild, Hamer, etc., it can address a range of markets with no compromise to its traditional designs.

New horizons

After a long history of battling various health problems, Jimmy D'Aquisto died on April 17, 1995 at the age of 59 while on a trip to Fender's Corona facility. As Stephen Stern looks back on their partnership, it's clear that his relationship with the great man was more than a matter of tools and techniques. "He had a wealth of stories," Stephen recalls. "I was back at his shop in New York City in March 1995, just a few weeks before he died. He was building his last guitars. It occurred to me that I was recording all the wrong things. I should have been recording all his great stories. They were just priceless — about John D'Angelico, the day he met his wife, all the great players. Nobody told a story the way Jimmy could. Just so much history."

Stephen still made one or two D'Aquistos per month after Fender relocated to Cessna Circle in 1998, but after conflicts arose over ownership of the D'Aquisto name, Fender discontinued the association and soon began to negotiate with another world-class builder, Bob Benedetto. Taking the designs of an exacting artist and rendering them in woods and metals would once again fall to Stephen Stern.

Stephen Stern estimates that he made only ten or so production versions of the Classic Rocker. On his personal guitar, shown here, he replaced the pickups with TV Jones Classic Filter'Tron-style units.

A blast from the present: This butterscotch beauty is a Custom Shop '51 Nocaster, nestled in its period-correct case.

CHAPTER SIXTEEN

16

The New Old

Relics and Time Machines

When old guitars became cooler than new guitars, you couldn't help but notice that many of those vintage 6-string treasures were dinged up. After all, they had been played hard in the first place because of their tone, style, and durability. To mainstream retailers and customers, a ding on a brand new Strat was a gasp-inducing bummer, like a scratch on a showroom Chevy. But in the mid-'90s vintage market, perceptions were different. Dead-mint guitars continued to command the highest prices, but as the vintage vibe resonated throughout guitar culture, the chips, scratches, and worn areas on old instruments took on a mystique of their own. They lent character. Like a dueling scar or the faded travel stickers on a cracked-leather suitcase, the marks of age and toil on a decades-old Fender hinted of a storied history, memorable journeys on the road, countless hours of inspired music, perhaps even a bar fight or two. Anyone could buy a new instrument, but the owner of a hard-knocks guitar might have suffered or delivered a few hard knocks himself. Or so it seemed. (Try to imagine the vibe of the *Born To Run* album cover if the guitar slung over the shoulder of the leather-jacketed Bruce Springsteen had been, say, a pristine Gibson L-5.)

In January 1995 Fender introduced a series of instruments that somehow looked and felt old and worn. Key distinction: They didn't look like new guitars that had been banged up; they looked *old*. John Page came up with the perfect name, one that suggested ancient artifacts cherished for their iconic significance. He called them Relics. The man who brought the idea to Fender, the Custom Shop's J. Black, is reluctant to take much credit for it. For him, the concept was merely the next step in a long chain of events. Craftspeople in the furniture industry had been aging their wood products for decades. Borrowing some of their techniques, guitar repair people sometimes aged finishes and components, typically as part of a restoration. For example, a repairman installing a new pickguard on a 50-year-old Broadcaster might buff, stain, strike, and burn the edges of the replacement so that it matched the beat-up body. A repairman fitting a new top on a pre-War D-28 might age its finish to complement the look of the well-worn neck, sides, and back.

John Page acknowledges that various Fender employees had discussed the idea of aging parts and instruments years before the Relic guitars were officially unveiled. "It was in my earliest days at Fender, when I was still a model maker, so we're talking 1978 to 1980. Gregg Wilson had me make a UV aging box out of an old Rogers bass drum shell with a sun lamp in it. He was trying to see if we could age the finishes. He also had me try to age some plastic parts [by soaking them] in coffee and stuff. Fred Stuart and John English actually came into my office before J. did with the idea of a beat-up guitar. They told me about some guy in San Diego who was taking new guitars and dragging them behind his truck. I thought the idea was stupid. Years later, after we did the Relic project and credited J. for the idea, I told Fred and John that it was the timing and the way it was presented. It just didn't make sense at the earlier time."

Before coming to Fender, J. Black worked with Roger Sadowsky in New York, and on occasion they distressed a guitar's finish by hanging it in a sunny window or putting it in a freezer overnight. Black remembers Scott Baxendale, who in the early 1980s worked at Gruhn Guitars in Nashville: "He was the first person I saw who took a vintage instrument body and aged it. It was a '52 or '53 Tele. The body had been stripped, and he refinished it, but he burned through the edges to show the white undercoat so the neck, parts, and body all looked to be of the same era."

George Gruhn: "We were not doing any relicing of new instruments to make them look old back then, but it was routine for us when doing repair work to try to make the repairs blend in so they wouldn't look glaringly new on an otherwise vintage and worn instrument." Black also cites the exceptional work of Tom Murphy, who later became Gibson's guru of guitar aging, as well as the brilliant T.J. Thompson, who years before the advent of Fender's Relics was employing lacquer checking, coloration, and other aging techniques in his work on Martin guitars.

An N.O.S. guitar was described as one that had been discovered in a warehouse and showed no signs of wear. Despite a headstock with no model name, Fender considers this mixed-features, Dakota Red example a Tele rather than a Nocaster. Officially, it's the Limited Collection 1950s Telecaster Thinline N.O.S.

Not all of the people who used these methods were ethical. As far back as the early '80s, some cads were intentionally passing off new or somewhat old guitars as much more valuable vintage instruments. George Gruhn: "People were starting to do fake Flying V's, Explorers, and Les Pauls, and I strongly suspect that some of those were being reliced to make it easier to pass them off as originals. There are far too many people claiming to have original V's and Explorers than can possibly be accounted for by the number of real originals."

John Page was sensitive to concerns that Fender's aged-in-the-shop guitars might confuse a market already awash in "vintage" instruments of questionable authenticity. J. Black: "The Relic concept is so accepted now, but we caught lots of flack early on. We were accused that we would degrade or damage the vintage market. John wanted to ensure there wasn't any confusion, so he had metal stamps made up that would emboss the word 'Relic' in the body, and we put the Custom Shop logo on the back of the headcap to prevent counterfeits or confusion."

As always, artist influence was a factor in the rise of battered chic. Some of the coolest players of past and present — Rory Gallagher, Jeff Beck, Stevie Ray Vaughan, Roy Buchanan, Andy Summers — played Fenders that looked thoroughly thrashed and furiously flogged. Danny Gatton insisted on using old-style, Bakelite-like switch tips on his Telecasters; Vince Cunetto, who would relic guitars for Fender from mid 1995 to mid 1999 ("relic" is now a verb), found the original manufacturer and had them reproduced. Gatton also had a template for how he wanted the back of the neck on his Custom Shop guitar to be tinted; rather than a random application, it followed a pattern of aging and wear that retained the guitar's old familiar feel. J. Black recalls a neck from Bob Dylan's '52 Tele, which he received with instructions to copy it in every detail, including the aging. He points to some of Grover Jackson's necks, which featured high-gloss pegheads but very thin oil finishes on the back of the neck; they felt comfy-old and played in. Fender adopted a similar process for the Kubicki project from 1989 to 1991. Black also cites Fender's practice of tinting some necks back in '81 or '82, and Gibson's following similar procedures for some of their custom instruments at about the same time.

Sometimes individuals would take matters into their own hands. Black remembers, "I refinished a body for [collector] Jim Colclasure one time, and he said, 'I'm gonna put this in a gunny sack and tie it to the back of my car and drag it around a field on my farm.' I said, 'You aren't really gonna do that,' and he said, 'I'm doing it — I need it to look old.'"

In J. Black's modest assessment, all of these trends were precursors to the Relics, which he describes as "just an idea whose time had come." But were pre-aged Fenders really that inevitable? It's one thing for a repair person to age a new finish or a replacement component to impart visual consistency to an old guitar. It seems to be a significant leap for a major manufacturer to age a whole series of brand new guitars from headstock to hardware, but to J. Black, "The writing was on the wall. People wanted vintage, and they wanted it to look older. Vintage repairmen had been doing restorations and relic-style work, but it was unique to the nonoriginal component. It was within the context of a repair. Vince Cunetto was aging new pickguards so they looked 50 years old, just beautiful. I had recently used one on a Custom Shop restoration of Ronnie Wood's Broadcaster. That's how Vince came into the [Fender] loop. It just took time for it to develop to the point where an artist like Don Was would say, 'I want an *entire guitar* made to look old.'"

Keith Richards was an early Custom Shop client, but contrary to myth (and to an inaccurate magazine article), he had nothing to do with initiating the Relic concept at Fender. That distinction belongs to bassist/producer Don Was. In 1994, J. Black visited a Rolling Stones recording session on Mulholland Drive in Los Angeles. (He might

As the Master Builders perfected their relicing techniques, they were able to render recreations of iconic guitars with stunning authenticity. One example is this detail on the SRV/Lenny Strat (Chap. 29).

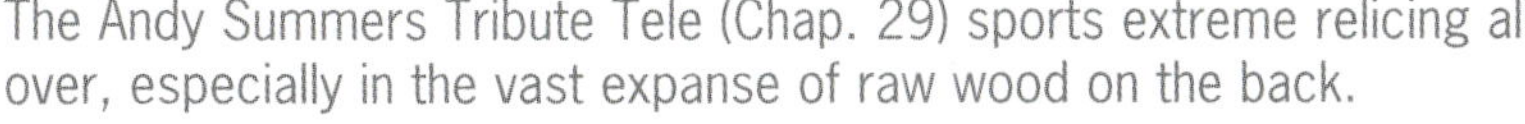

The Andy Summers Tribute Tele (Chap. 29) sports extreme relicing all over, especially in the vast expanse of raw wood on the back.

have been returning a guitar that had been restored at the Custom Shop. He can't remember; the shop did many projects for the Stones.) That night Don Was manned the console, and he asked J. to beat up his new Sadowsky bass. He would be performing with Bonnie Raitt at the upcoming Grammy ceremony and thought the new instrument looked nerdy, too squeaky clean. At first the idea struck Black as an odd one, but then again the Custom Shop prides itself on serving artists, and Black would certainly accommodate Don Was. The more he thought about it, the more he thought the idea of making a brand new instrument look old might have significance for Fender beyond any single artist's request.

Black recalls that when he spoke to Vince Cunetto about the concept of distressing a manufactured guitar, Cunetto informed him that he had already been experimenting in that area. Cunetto sent to Black a Shoreline Gold Stratocaster that he had painted and aged. J. Black: "I knew he messed with parts and did some Tele bodies, but I did not know he was doing complete distressed guitars until he sent the gold guitar. All the parts were aged [and the finish had a patina]; it looked like an authentic vintage instrument, very convincing. That got the Relic idea rolling at an accelerated pace."

J. displayed Cunetto's aged, gold Strat to John Page. In *The Stratocaster Chronicles* (pub. by Hal Leonard), Page recalled the launch of the Relic program: "That was J. Black's inspiration. He nailed it on that one. J. comes into my office one day in '94, shuts the door, and says, 'I've got this wacky idea. These distressed guitars — what do you think about releasing them?' I said, 'Great idea! Let's not tell anyone. Let's do a couple for the NAMM show and put them in a glass case and just shock everybody.' So J. worked with Vince Cunetto and they built a Nocaster and a Mary Kaye Strat. Vince did the paint and aging. We took them to the January 1995 NAMM show. All the dealers said, 'This is so cool for you to honor your legacy by displaying these old classic guitars,' and we said, 'Um, actually, they're spankin' new! *How many you want?*' [Laughs.] We left that show with hundreds of orders, and the Relics

The first Relic Strat was this 1956-style Mary Kaye. Built by J. Black, Vince Cunetto, and the Custom Shop staff, it garnered rave reviews at the January 1995 NAMM show.

became the number one seller in the Custom Shop." Not even Mike Lewis, Fender's new chief of guitar marketing, knew about the project prior to that winter '95 display. "I don't think even Dan Smith knew," he said. "It was something they dreamed up in the Custom Shop, and they just decided to spring it on everybody. It was the first time that anybody at Fender had seen them."

Selling manufactured authenticity — at a premium price, no less? Some people thought this strategy sounded flimsier than a *Baywatch* plot, but Mike Lewis loved the idea. "Of course, reactions were mixed," he says. "Some people didn't understand it; other people thought it was the coolest thing they'd ever seen. I thought it was the coolest thing I'd ever seen. I thought it was genius."

During the time Fender was considering going into production, there was a concern that the company would no longer be able to spray lacquer on a significant scale, due to tough restrictions imposed by the EPA and Southern California's Air Quality Management District. John Page: "For several years we sent components to Vince Cunetto, who did a brilliant job with the painting and aging." As recounted in *The Stratocaster Chronicles*, Cunetto struck a handshake deal with John Page, hired a couple of helpers, and set up Cunetto Creative Resources, Inc. in Bolivar, Missouri. Cunetto and his tiny crew hand-sanded wooden components and finished the pieces with thin, nitrocellulose lacquers and paints mixed to Fender's old formulas. They found a way to introduce subtle finish cracks, and to replicate the look of an aged clear coat. Once painted, the components were nicked, worn in strategic places, scratched, and otherwise cosmetically distressed.

Vince Cunetto investigated many old instruments in order to examine their patterns of neck wear, body wear, scratches, and even rust. "For each guitar we aged," he told this author, "we would actually imagine an individual player with his own style and approach, and everything was done in keeping with that player. Maybe he was a country rhythm guy, so all the finger wear would be in the first positions, with strum wear around the upper frets and pickguard wear consistent with that. There's a real art to it

The other guitar on display in 1995 was this Nocaster. Viewers — including most Fender employees — were surprised to learn that this well-worn, "original" guitar was actually a brand new instrument.

If it weren't for the erosion of the pickup covers on the original, it would be hard to distinguish the 1954 Strat from the 2004 Anniversary reissue. This project (Chap. 26) required Chris Fleming and his fellow builders to take their relicing techniques to the next level.

... The real 'secret' to a convincing aging job is making the aging level of each part consistent with the whole guitar. Before we'd ship a batch back to the Custom Shop, we'd lay out the aged parts, then start with bodies and necks and match parts to each guitar to make up sets."

In recent years, more players have come to recognize the extent to which a guitar's finish can affect its sound. The first sets of necks and bodies that Fender sent to Vince Cunetto were already undercoated and painted. Cunetto told *The ToneQuest Report*: "We tried lots of stuff with the stock paint on them — sunbursts, blondes, butterscotches — but they just looked stupid. Finally I said, 'J., I can't do this. Send me some raw parts.' So he sent me completely unfinished necks and bodies . . . ."

Vince Cunetto opened his new shop on May 5, 1995, and shipped the first batch of unassembled Relic Telecaster components to Fender on June 27. Following the introduction of the Relics, Cunetto and Fender went on to introduce Olympic White '60s-style Strats and a three-color sunburst Jazz Bass (winter 1996); custom-color '60s-style Strats, three-color sunburst '60s-style Strats, and Olympic White Jazz Basses (winter 1997); and two-color sunburst '50s-style Strats (summer 1997). Many other examples would follow as Cunetto's production increased from about 20 sets of components per week to about 30 or 35 sets per week, occasionally more.

Upon receiving the parts from Fender, Cunetto or his assistants would ink-stamp them with date codes revealing the year's last digit, then the day of that year, and finally the number of the instrument within its batch; so, for example, 714219 would identify 1997, the 142nd day of that year, and instrument number 19 in that batch. Toward the end of the Cunetto era some components were stamped with a month/day/year code (041699 = April 16, 1999). Vince explained to *ToneQuest Report* that for custom-order one-offs they used Fender's order number rather than the batch code or date code. He told this author that his company processed about 4,800 Relics of all styles and colors, including catalog items and a few one-offs.

By late 1997 change was in the air. Part of the factory's move to the new Cessna Circle location would entail moving the Custom Shop into the main production facility. John Page soon departed and was succeeded by Mike Eldred. Fender invested millions of dollars in new paint

A real motorcycle jacket and dungarees kind of machine, this tough-looking, black Team Built '68 Strat featured an extreme aging technique that came to be called Heavy Relic. The model was also offered in three-color sunburst and Lake Placid Blue. List price: Five grand.

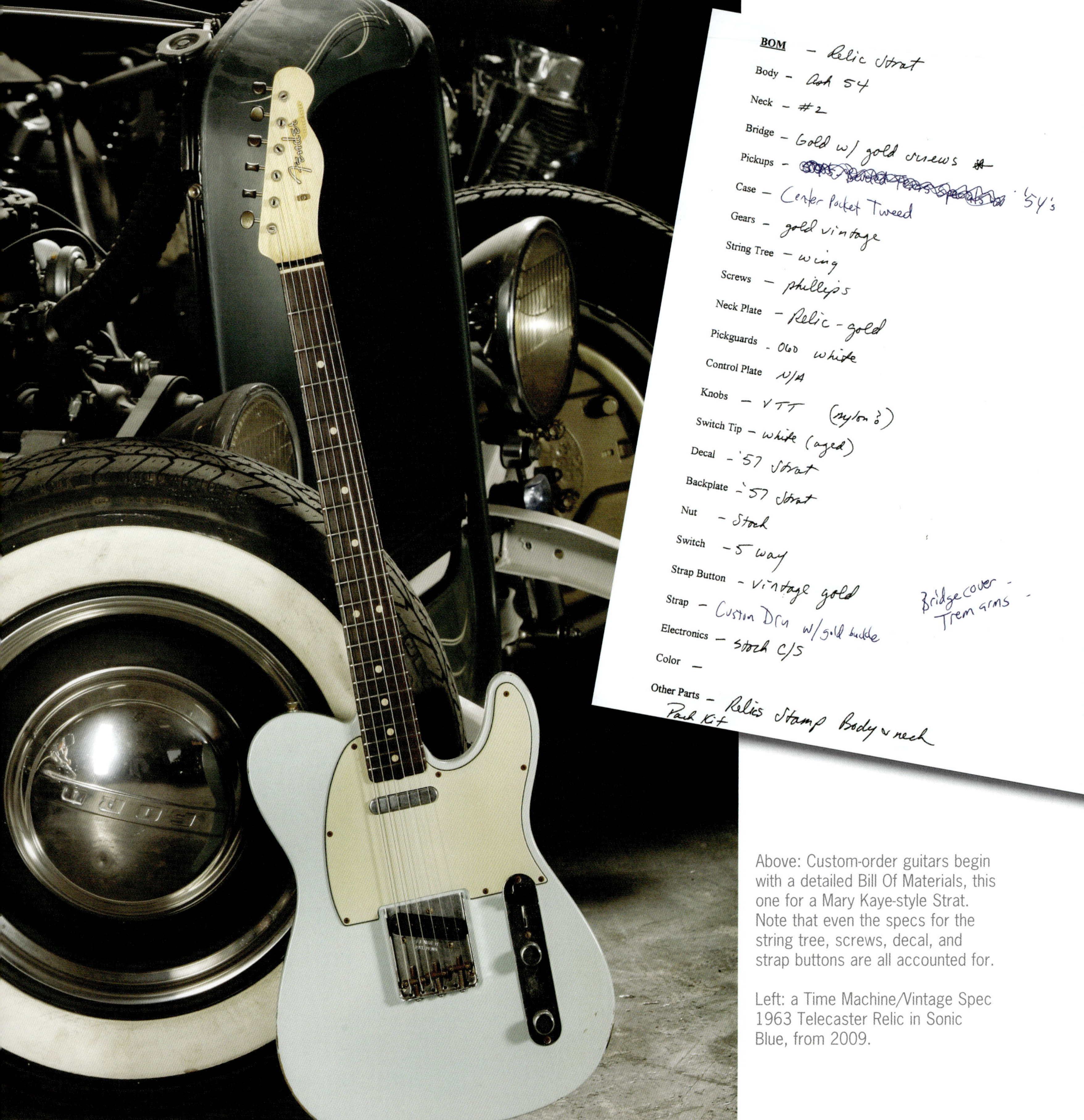

BOM – Relic Strat
Body – Ash 54
Neck – #2
Bridge – Gold w/ gold screws
Pickups – '54's
Case – Center Pocket Tweed
Gears – gold vintage
String Tree – wing
Screws – phillips
Neck Plate – Relic - gold
Pickguards – 060 white
Control Plate N/A
Knobs – VTT (nylon?)
Switch Tip – white (aged)
Decal – '57 Strat
Backplate – '57 Strat
Nut – Stock
Switch – 5 way
Strap Button – Vintage gold
Strap – Custom Dru w/gold buckle
Electronics – Stock C/S
Color –
Other Parts – Relic Stamp Body & neck
Pack Kit
Bridge cover –
Trem arms –

Above: Custom-order guitars begin with a detailed Bill Of Materials, this one for a Mary Kaye-style Strat. Note that even the specs for the string tree, screws, decal, and strap buttons are all accounted for.

Left: a Time Machine/Vintage Spec 1963 Telecaster Relic in Sonic Blue, from 2009.

facilities that would enable the company to apply thin, vintage-correct, nitro finishes while meeting strict environmental requirements (some Fender folks like to say that the air going out is cleaner than the air coming in); in that regard, Vince Cunetto's services were no longer required. Furthermore, Fender would soon begin implementing its own version of the instrument aging process. Finally, on the drawing board was an ambitious plan to expand the Relic concept to a multi-level array of vintage-type finishes. Given these developments, the decision to bring the entire Relic program in-house was no surprise. After about a six-month transition period of having the Relics processed in both places, the last batches of "Cunetto Era" Relics were shipped to Fender, in May or June of 1999.

To this day, some players and collectors value the Cunetto Relics above all others. Travis Egnor, at Gruhn Guitars in Nashville, reports: "There certainly is a buzz about the Cunetto stuff. While a used, non-Cunetto Custom Shop Relic will sell for $1,800 to $2,200, a Cunetto Relic can bring as much as $2,800 to $3,200 or more, depending on the model." A contrasting point of view is provided courtesy of veteran collector/retailer Nate Westgor (also known as Willie), of Willie's American Guitars, in St. Paul. He told this author in 2009: "It strikes me that every time a change is made at a factory the construction details of the previous generation are duly noted and disseminated by the buying public and then given mythical status. It's most always true that if you want people to want something, you just take it away. We call that rule number 1. In my humble opinion, the current guitars coming out of the Custom Shop not only rival the earlier Custom Shop stuff but many times rival the pre-CBS guitars."

Guitar tech and former Fender East Coast Artist Relations director JD Dworkow helped set up the Fender booth at that January 1995 NAMM show, and he was in on the secret. "Everyone who saw the Mary Kaye was convinced it was a real '50s instrument," he says. "Now anybody could own an 'old' vintage Fender. They were period-accurate down to the most minute details, and I believe this helped bring the quality levels up over the entire line of production reissues that were introduced in the following years. The Relics were game changers. I couldn't keep Mary Kayes or Nocasters in stock in my New York showroom. They sold as fast as they came in from California."

Time Machines

Mike Lewis had become marketing chief for Fender guitars in 1995. "Under my direction," he explains, "we changed the Custom Shop a ton. When I started, the shop was primarily doing custom one-offs, so we were looking for different ways to expand, to offer more variety, and to build highly desirable, very special guitars but do it in a more efficient way."

One of the first things Lewis did was to address a question on the minds of more than a few prospective Custom Shop clients: What if you wanted a vintage-style Fender that seemed as authentic as a Relic, but looked as new as one of those legendary, under-the-bed-for-40-years guitars? Or perhaps a guitar that looked worn but somewhat less thrashed than a Relic? In a brilliant move, Lewis worked with John Page and, later, Mike Eldred to formalize and expand the appeal of the Relic concept by launching the Custom Shop's Time Machine array of finishes: N.O.S. (New Old Stock), Closet Classic (lightly aged), and original Relic (heavily aged and well worn).

Fender's catalogs spelled it out: A New Old Stock instrument appeared "as if the guitar was discovered in a warehouse after many years, never played and showing no signs of age or wear." (Dennis Galuszka: "A New Old Stock finish is done the same way we do a brand new guitar; we do not age it. The difference is, we paint it using the *process* they would've done back in the day rather than a modern process.") In the middle was the Closet Classic finish: "Imagine discovering a vintage guitar at a yard sale that's been stashed in a closet. It's worn a bit, yellowed with age, and the finish is slightly checked with hairline cracks that are typical of an instrument that's been exposed to years of humidity and temperature changes." And finally, the Relic: "Shows natural wear and tear of years of heavy use — nicks, scratches, worn finish, rusty hardware and aged plastic parts. Looks, feels and plays like it's taken the punishment of many long nightclub hours."

Mike Eldred: "The Relic thing had taken a nose dive. We weren't selling as many of those things, and we thought, let's take this to the next level. So we picked specific years for the models, and then offered them in these levels of N.O.S., Closet Classic, and Relic." Mike Lewis: "With the Time Machine series it became much more organized. Mike and I came up with the idea to do the three different levels.

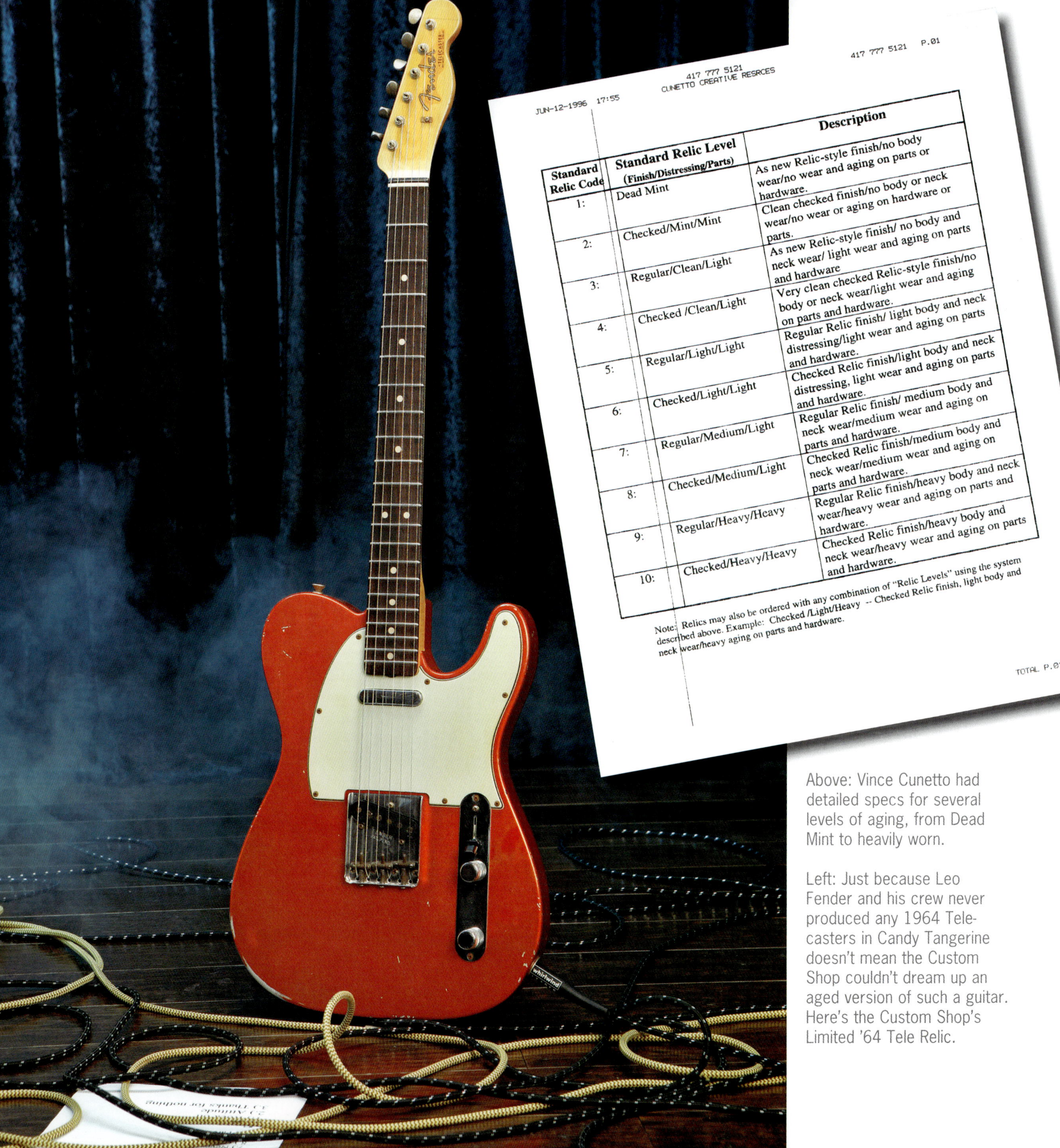
JUN-12-1996 17:55 417 777 5121 CUNETTO CREATIVE RESRCES 417 777 5121 P.01

Standard Relic Code	Standard Relic Level (Finish/Distressing/Parts)	Description
1:	Dead Mint	As new Relic-style finish/no body wear/no wear and aging on parts or hardware.
2:	Checked/Mint/Mint	Clean checked finish/no body or neck wear/no wear or aging on hardware or parts.
3:	Regular/Clean/Light	As new Relic-style finish/ no body and neck wear/ light wear and aging on parts and hardware
4:	Checked /Clean/Light	Very clean checked Relic-style finish/no body or neck wear/light wear and aging on parts and hardware.
5:	Regular/Light/Light	Regular Relic finish/ light body and neck distressing/light wear and aging on parts and hardware.
6:	Checked/Light/Light	Checked Relic finish/light body and neck distressing, light wear and aging on parts and hardware.
7:	Regular/Medium/Light	Regular Relic finish/ medium body and neck wear/medium wear and aging on parts and hardware.
8:	Checked/Medium/Light	Checked Relic finish/medium body and neck wear/medium wear and aging on parts and hardware.
9:	Regular/Heavy/Heavy	Regular Relic finish/heavy body and neck wear/heavy wear and aging on parts and hardware.
10:	Checked/Heavy/Heavy	Checked Relic finish/heavy body and neck wear/heavy wear and aging on parts and hardware.

Note: Relics may also be ordered with any combination of "Relic Levels" using the system described above. Example: Checked /Light/Heavy -- Checked Relic finish, light body and neck wear/heavy aging on parts and hardware.

TOTAL P.01

Above: Vince Cunetto had detailed specs for several levels of aging, from Dead Mint to heavily worn.

Left: Just because Leo Fender and his crew never produced any 1964 Telecasters in Candy Tangerine doesn't mean the Custom Shop couldn't dream up an aged version of such a guitar. Here's the Custom Shop's Limited '64 Tele Relic.

That allowed the Custom Shop to just about double its production and to this day, that series remains a major source of revenue for us."

It took a few years for the Time Machine concept to blossom into full flower. In January 1996, the modest Relic series comprised only three guitars and a bass. Rather than year-specific models, all were more or less generic instruments — a '50s Nocaster, a '50s Stratocaster, a '60s Stratocaster, and a '60s Jazz Bass; these early offerings included no Precision Basses. During that same year, Fender referred to its "exclusive" and trademarked "Time Machine Process," without employing the term as a model name or series name.

In January 1997, the Relics ("cosmetically aged by the Custom Shop Relic aging process") remained the shop's only category of aged guitars. The most expensive piece was the '50s Relic Stratocaster, at $2,799. Although Fender did not invoke the Mary Kaye nickname, the guitar had an ash body, a Vintage Blonde finish, and aged gold hardware. The rest of 1997's Relic lineup duplicated the offerings of 1996.

"The Relics were game changers."

— JD Dworkow

By 1998 the Relic Stratocaster had been joined by the N.O.S. Stratocaster. Both were separate models, as opposed to finish options for any single guitar. The N.O.S. Strat was described somewhat generically as a mid-'60s guitar, although its pickups were specified to be exact replicas of 1965 units. Also in that year, the decade-generic (as opposed to year-specific) guitars and Jazz Bass were joined by a '50s Relic Telecaster. There were no Closet Classics, no P Basses, and no year-specific instruments.

Early the following year, the Closet Classic made its official debut as part of the somewhat ungainly titled N.O.S., Closet Classic, and Relic Series (for a brief period in the literature there was no mention of Time Machines). Another step forward not only provided a new level of detail but also served to more clearly separate the Custom Shop guitars from factory reissues: All N.O.S., Closet Classic, and Relic instruments were now year-specific models. The impressive array included the '51 Nocaster, '56 Stratocaster, '60 Stratocaster, '69 Stratocaster, '63 Telecaster, and Relic '64 Jazz Bass (although officially called the Relic, the J Bass was available in all three finishes).

In the summer of 1999, the program further coalesced on all fronts. The instruments included the six previously noted year-specific models, all grouped under the Time Machine banner and all available in all three finishes. For an extra 200 bucks the '56 and '60 Strats were available with optional gold hardware in all three finishes, and the '69 Strat could be ordered with either a rosewood or maple fingerboard. Sample prices: the '56 Strat retailed for $2,399 in N.O.S., $2,599 in Closet Classic, and $2,749 in Relic. By the end of that year, the Relics, Closet Classics, and N.O.S. guitars were marketed as both Time Machine and Team Built instruments, bringing together the twin master strokes of the Mike Lewis era in marketing Custom Shop guitars (he was also a crucial figure behind the successful revamping of Fender's production guitars and amplifiers).

In January 2000, the Precision Bass was offered for the first time in all three Time Machine finishes. It was a 1959-style instrument, with the gold anodized pickguard. The Custom Shop now offered Time Machine variations on all four of Fender's revolutionary core instruments — Telecaster, Stratocaster, Precision Bass, and Jazz Bass. Including the maple/rosewood option for the '69 Strat and the gold hardware upgrades for the '56 and '60 Strats (and excluding a variety of body color choices), the 2000 Time Machine Series comprised a whopping 30 models, ranging in retail price from the $2,499 P Bass N.O.S. to the $3,199 '56 and '60 Relic Strats with gold hardware.

Some observers couldn't help but comment on the fact that for any Time Machine model, the more beat-up it is, the more it costs. Longtime collector/author/retailer George Gruhn: "I find it ironic that the Custom Shop charges more for the Closet Classic than the N.O.S., more yet for the Relic, and even more for [one-off] models that are beat up beyond a Relic. It is a source of amusement to me that if a player uses an N.O.S. model onstage enough to produce honest wear, its value goes down, whereas if Fender [ages the finish], cuts it, and beats it, the price goes up."

But of course, producing a new guitar that looks authentically old and worn (as opposed to producing a guitar that looks merely new yet abused) requires much skill, hours of hand work, and the application of proprietary techniques and processes. Mike Lewis: "There were mixed reactions to the Relics in the first place. Plenty of people said, why would anybody want something like this? I would always say, imagine you're going to a gig, you're flying in, your gear gets separated, it's five minutes before you're supposed to go onstage, and your guitar hasn't made it. You look around and somebody hands you a Relic Strat and says, here, play this. You'd say, perfect! You'd get onstage and feel absolutely fine, and it would look right and sound right and be just right for any kind of music. In a way the Relic thing took up from the idea of people buying an old-looking, creased leather jacket or a pre-faded pair of blue jeans. It was absolute genius in its initial concept, and the Time Machines drew upon and expanded that original idea."

In 2003 the Time Machine series was augmented with three new guitars. One was the '65 Stratocaster, which duplicated the original's round-lam rosewood board and other specs.

Like the original, the new '59 Esquire reissue was stunning in its stark, bare-bones styling. There's just something about that maple board with the black dots and the pickguard's unperforated expanse of white plastic that says "this could only have come from the mind of Leo Fender." Unlike most Tele or Esquire bridges, the '59's bridge loads the strings through the back edge of the bridge plate instead of through the body.

The third new Time Machine was the 1960 Tele Custom with its single stripe of white binding on the top and back. Back in 1960, this fancified model was the only Tele available with a stock three-color sunburst, and sales chief Don Randall positioned it at the top of the Tele line.

The Time Machines became one of the most successful series in Fender's entire history. Even vintage purists, a hard-to-please bunch, were often quite taken with them. In a major feature on Vince Cunetto, *The ToneQuest Report*'s March 2004 issue recounted players' reactions to a 2001 Relic Strat: "At the Dallas Guitar Show — one of the largest vintage shows in the world — a new Relic created the biggest buzz among the veteran players . . . ." As we go to press, the ingenious Time Machine Series continues to provide a wide array of variables in a conveniently structured array, yet another sensible compromise along the spectrum between a factory guitar and a one-of-a-kind Master Built instrument. In fact, customers who do select a Master Built guitar often use a Time Machine model as a starting point.

A beautiful '65 Strat Relic in Dakota Red.

Angels in the details

As the years go passing by, the Custom Shop delves ever deeper into the minutia of vintage specs. Mike Eldred: "The whole point of selecting a single year of production was to show just how specific and picky we could get. The 1960 Stratocaster is a great example. The original had a smaller truss rod. You know the way Leo Fender worked – they probably ran out of their usual material and he found something else for pennies on the dollar, and they used that for a while. We got the dimensions from an original '60 Strat and couldn't find it from any of the suppliers, but we figured if we were to put a regular truss rod in that guitar the level of integrity would drop, so to this day we take regular truss rods and send them out to a guy who mills them down to the right thickness for that one year of production. This also means that we have to get a custom-made truss rod adjuster and a custom-made anchor. This is the kind of thing you wouldn't even know about unless you cut that neck in half. That's just one example. So the Time Machine concept is still here, but now we plug different stuff into it. What this is all about is making an exact reproduction, making the full commitment with one hundred percent integrity."

Faux and mo' faux

If the faux aging on a normal Relic isn't drastic enough, then more radical treatments are available, sometimes called Ultimate Relic or Heavy Relic. From the builders' point of view, "ultimate" and "heavy" are different terms for the same, extreme level of aging (let's call it "the full Rory Gallagher"). The former has been described as the "been to hell and back" finish. It appeared on a number of Master Built instruments crafted by John Cruz and designed in collaboration with The Music Zoo of Queens, New York. According to the retailer, these finish treatments approximated those of Tributes such as the Andy Summers Tele and the SRV Number One Strat. In 2009 the shop offered several Limited Dealer Select models designed in association with Make'n Music, the highly regarded Chicago retailer established in 1973. These included '50s and '60s Heavy Relic Master Built Strats and '50s and '60s Heavy Relic Master Built Teles.

A '59 Esquire Relic from 2004. What made the original so distinctive and just so, well, *Leo* was not so much a matter of what it had but rather what it didn't have. It's the ultimate among Spartan tools for no-nonsense musicians. Note the unusual bridge-loading of the strings.

This Team Built Custom '51 Nocaster just oozed too-cool-for-school attitude, with its black pickguard over a reliced, wide-grained, sunbursted ash body. It was displayed at a 2008 NAMM show to demonstrate that Nocasters were available in non-stock colors. Public reaction was positive, and limited runs of similar models soon followed.

CHAPTER SEVENTEEN

17

Sorcerers and Apprentices

Master Built and Team Built

Talking of Michelangelo

The advent of the 1992 price sheet, consumer response to Fender's new methods of organizing its products, and evolving marketing philosophies all affected each other, pushing the Custom Shop ever forward toward a bigger, more productive, more efficient entity. The hard truth in the mid 1990s was that the shop would perish without more profits, which in turn would require more floor space, more workers, more production — more of just about everything except man-hours per instrument. Dan Smith figured that Fender's "halfway" commitment to the Custom Shop was no longer adequate: "[We decided] that we were going to stop relying on the factory for bodies and necks, and the standards we had for the factory weren't going to be sufficient for the Custom Shop. We could take some of the stuff that the factory made and use it in the Custom Shop as a starting point, but the momentum was toward more independence for the shop."

Putting the price sheet into effect had entailed a restructuring of the production process. Dan Smith: "A viable custom shop has to be a small factory. You know, Stradivari did the same thing. He didn't sit and whittle violins all day. Even Michelangelo, all the artisans, they had a staff of people who did a lot of work under their supervision, and then the master did the artistic finishing touches." It was precisely that idea that stimulated the next major step in the Custom Shop's structure: the Team Built concept.

The ninety percent solution

Mike Lewis's candid assessment of his role as Vice President of electric guitar marketing helps explain the relationship between marketing and the shop in the mid and late 1990s, one that might be called productively informal: "My involvement was just helping the people in the shop as best I could, and spreading the word to the world that some amazing things were going on in there. I would give them suggestions on things to do, certain combinations of features or models. But you're dealing with creative artists, and there's gotta be ninety percent ownership on their part if they're gonna do their thing. My job was to take that, with some input and suggestions, and then help them facilitate what they were doing, and to encourage and support them. So there was a lot of communication between production and marketing. We would all get on the same page before moving forward."

Team Built

When Mike Lewis assumed his role as marketing chief for electric guitars, Custom Shop production was mostly focused on one-offs and limited runs. The price list concept, although three years old, was still evolving. Lewis would build on that idea, adding new models with fixed combinations of features that he felt players would be likely to want. Within a year or two, this new approach had revolutionized the Custom Shop. Lewis explains: "We were running a business. If you get overburdened and inundated with custom orders — some of these things are very complicated and take a long time to build — you can't just whip these things out. It's a long process. So we were trying to find new ways to make Custom Shop guitars available on a regular basis. We would forecast — we think we can sell so many of this type of guitar and so many of that type — but we were always offering the custom one-off projects at the same time."

Mike Lewis, John Page, and Mike Eldred worked together to reorganize Custom Shop instruments into more definable groups. The new ways of cataloging the products further defined the artisan-guild approach to building them in the first place. The result was the Team Built program, a direct descendant of the 1992 price sheet. Providing more convenience for customers and more efficiency for the shop, it was a brilliant concept located between the lone builder at one end of the production spectrum and a full-blown factory at the other. Team Built guitars would be crafted by a select group of skilled apprentices under the watchful eye — and with the final approval — of a Master Builder.

Jason Smith explains that Team Built projects often entail building guitars with minor variations on existing products, with a level of detail less pronounced than on a Master Built product. "With a Master Built, you are getting the highest level of craftsmanship Fender has to offer," Jason says. Aside from building Team Built guitars, the apprentices are crucial to the shop's success for another reason: They are potentially the Master Builders of the future, learning not only techniques and processes but Fender's storied history as well.

The Classic Relic HBS-1 was a Team Built, Time Machine Strat. Introduced in January, 2009, it sported a Seymour Duncan SH-4 humbucker. This example is the N.O.S. version.

Although Fender literature describes the team as apprentices, Yuriy Shishkov thinks of them in this way: "They're a small group of really talented craftsmen who build some of the Custom Shop's 'catalog' guitars. It's like, if you want to buy a Ferrari, *every* car is pretty much custom built, with a lot of handwork. But then if you want something unique or extreme, then they take it off the line and build it especially for you. That's the Master Built guitar."

Another, in-between category is the Apprentice Master Builder. Paul Waller and two others hold that title as we go to press. Paul explains, "The main difference, besides the money, is the Master Builders have a signature decal and we don't. Fender gives me a free artistic reign. They know I am here to make a career out of this. It's humbling to know they trust me to design and build whatever pops into my little brain. I am, however, at the mercy of my peers. If I create something ugly or not up to par, I'm going to hear about it. The Master/Apprentice relationship is like a marriage in a lot of ways. The pairing has to have the right chemistry. The essential part of the equation is that the customer loves his new guitar. All of the apprentices are capable, experienced builders. We're the next generation."

"Stock Team Built" guitars feature the most requested specs and configurations. Over the years they have included the American Classic Strat, the Classic Player Strat, the American Classic Telecaster, the Vintage Precision Bass Custom, the Set-Neck Tele Jr., the Showmasters, the Time Machines, and the Custom Artist models. Mike Lewis: "Now you could see a Custom Shop offering in a catalog, and they might have one in stock, ready to ship, just the way you wanted it. It was an actual model; it had a part number. The dealer could check to see if they had any in stock or if some were scheduled for an upcoming production run."

Another advantage was that instead of waiting for orders to trickle in, builders could put models into continual production, which evened out the planning and production schedules, just as the price sheet had done to a lesser extent. In 1995, under Lewis's direction, the new system of organizing the instruments was accompanied by a belated coherence in their marketing. Things fell into place in the *Frontline* magazines. The "Custom Order Only" designation was dropped, and the Custom Shop guitars — all of them — were finally identified as such. By the 1996 brochure's release, there were 50 different models, some available with several options. Fender's Custom Shop was now an instrument manufacturing entity of significant magnitude in its own right.

Skilled team members work together to make Custom Shop quality available at more affordable prices. Dan Smith: "Even Michelangelo, all the artisans, they had a staff of people who did a lot of work under their supervision, and then the master did the artistic finishing touches."

"The Master/Apprentice relationship is like a marriage. The pairing has to have the right chemistry. The essential part of the equation is that the customer loves his new guitar." — Paul Waller

Helping hands

The Team Built program offered packages of features that were not only exciting and appealing but also practical. After all, sometimes a customer has a bad idea. Mike Lewis: "When you're doing a menu of options, you try to keep that in mind so that people can't have *too* bad of an idea. It's something we constantly face, but as soon as you give the customer some guidance, the bad ideas go away. If the ideas are really out there, it becomes a Master Built kind of thing. That Master Builder is going to make sure the customer is happy. That final project is going to be beautiful and unique, everything he wants, but it's also going to make sense and be practical. You know, you're not going to make a guitar that has a Floyd Rose tremolo and Scruggs tuners [laughs]. We try to put the menu together in such a way that you can't go too far wrong."

Ralph Esposito adds: "When you order a guitar, you don't want the guy selling you what *he* wants; you want him to sell you the thing you came in for. We don't like to sway our customers towards something they don't really want. It's up to them, not us. However, if something just will not work or won't give them what they are seeking, we'll give them some input. Otherwise it's whatever they want, no problem. People appreciate that kind of collaboration. It makes for a better fit all around, and guarantees satisfaction."

John Page: "We decided early on that we would never put the Fender name on anything that we weren't proud to see out there in the world. But you know, the builders and customers have always gotten together. Leo and Freddie and those guys talked to customers all the time. Sometimes somebody will specify something and you're thinking, no, no, no, and you find a gentle way to talk them out of it, because you know which materials and details are going to give them the sound and feel they want. You may have to provide some samples, paint a few things, or try different pickups, but customers want that; they want help. They don't want to be disappointed any more than the builder does, so there's always collaboration. I built many guitars that turned out to be ten times better than they would have been had we stuck to every detail the customer originally specified, and that's true with the other builders."

As we go to press, Master Builder apprentice Brian Fields has worked at Fender for nearly a dozen years. "It took me five years to get to the Custom Shop," he says, "and three more to make apprentice. Most of my work is in final neck sanding, fret dressing, finish sanding, buffing, polishing, making pickguards, pre-assembly, final assembly, tune testing, and final inspection."

A veteran of Rickenbacker and Dobro, Dale Wilson works especially closely with Chris Fleming, Greg Fessler, and John Cruz. Greg calls him "an outstanding apprentice, a Master Builder of the future."

The Master Built guitar represents the shop's highest levels of craft and attention. This black-on-black model from 2008 got both the Master Built and Heavy Relic treatments.

Master Built

The Stock Team Built idea supplemented rather than replaced the Master Built concept, which continued to be an essential part of the shop's public profile and day-to-day operation. Yuriy Shishkov explains that with Master Built instruments, the paperwork listing the specifications is just the starting point. The craftsman typically communicates one-on-one with the customer, sometimes every day at the outset of the project. Customers often have many questions and want guidance from the builders, although the blend of input from customers and builders varies. Yuriy Shishkov: "We have a dialog. The exception is when somebody says, 'I want a stock '56 Strat,' for example, a perfect replication with no custom aspects. We know exactly what that is and do not need to discuss details."

Master Built instruments are identified by a headstock decal with the builder's name, while Team Built guitars sport the Custom Shop's V logo, sometimes with the words "Limited Edition."

Bespoke guitars: made to order

A Master Built instrument may be pictured in Fender literature or on the website, but that doesn't mean any such guitars are in stock. Alex Perez: "That guitar still requires an order and is going to be built for a particular customer or dealer. The picture on the webpage or in the catalog just shows a collection of features that we are ready to build, but we may not build it until we get an order.

"Let's say you see a photo of a John 5 Tele and you order one of the Custom Shop versions. Well, we are going to build you that guitar from scratch. If you wanted something different about it — let's say you wanted a white one instead of a black one — we would have to get John 5's permission. That's the way it works with all of our signature artists. When we had a D'Aquisto in the catalog, that didn't mean we could just ship you one. It was a very specialized instrument, and there were only one or two guys here who could actually build it, and that's why it was a Master Built. Even though something's in the catalog as a 'model,' a guitar often has to be built by one guy because of the difficulty in the process, and it's going to be built to order for an individual."

Chris Fleming explains that even Team Built guitars are often made to order, despite their appearing in catalogs:

Master Built guitars feature premium components, sometimes including pickups hand-wound, signed, and dated by longtime veteran Abigail Ybarra.

Each Master Builder has his own signature decal and, for some instruments, separate series of serial numbers.

"Unless we announce a limited run ahead of time, we don't stockpile them. Sometimes we will build multiples, but generally it's market-driven. If marketing wants to release a new product, they'll have us make some so we can get them out there and people can see them, but more often a dealer calls up and orders 10 of these or 20 of those, and we then build them to order."

When considering the prestige of owning a Custom Shop guitar, one more dimension is the name recognition of the Master Builders. If the shop is smaller and inherently more exclusive than the factory, then the ultimate in exclusivity is specifying the one individual who will build your personal guitar. You're not just getting a Fender, you're not just getting a Custom Shop Fender, you're getting a Custom Shop Fender built by Todd Krause, or Mark Kendrick, or Chris Fleming, or Yuriy Shishkov, or whoever it might be. It's the same with Custom Shop guitars from the early years. It's not just a Custom Shop guitar — it's a Fred Stuart Telecaster, a J. Black Strat, a Mike Stevens LJ. (Relatively recent Fenders associated with particular builders may one day come to be prized in the same way knowledgeable vintage enthusiasts revere '50s Fender necks shaped and initialed by Tadeo Gomez, or tweed amp chassis signed by Lupe Lopez.) Richard McDonald: "If you could see Todd Krause's file drawer, it would make you drool. Jeff Beck, Eric Clapton, Pete Townshend — he builds for all these guys, and that's a part of the appeal as well. The customer knows, 'Wow, the Master Builder who builds Eric Clapton's guitars built my guitar, too!'"

Color collaborations

One of Yuriy Shishkov's specialties and favorite techniques is staining woods. "Sometimes a customer knows exactly the color he wants but doesn't know how to get it. We collaborate. I like staining bodies. People don't realize that you can pull so much color and flavor out of the wood, things that you otherwise couldn't see. If you know how to use them, stains can bring a guitar to life."

A Master Builder can control whether the finish looks warm, or cool, or anywhere in between. Some stains are natural, earth-based pigments. Others are chemical or synthetic. Some are liquid; some come in a powder or granule form, and the builder decides whether to mix them with alcohol or acetone. Yuriy Shishkov: "Let's say you find the perfect blend for a sky-blue finish the customer wants. Well, if you put it on a piece of maple the color is going to turn somewhat greenish or aquamarine because of interaction with the wood's natural yellowish hue. So you have to know how to bleach the wood first, and get it almost white, in order for that sky blue to maintain its color. With paint it's almost like you put a film on top of the wood, but with a stain, you are penetrating the grain patterns. The way it penetrates soft and hard parts makes some figures more pronounced. The stain is applied with a rag, sometimes with several applications, and you have your little secrets in exactly how you do it. When you think about all the different stains, the ways you can mix them, the application methods, and the ways certain ones react with different woods and grain patterns, you appreciate just how much variety is possible and how much control you have."

Yuriy Shishkov's fully equipped work space is a far cry from the Belarusian root cellar where he began to fashion remarkably functional guitars out of wood scraps and spare parts.

Senior Master Builder

When a Custom Shop craftsman is promoted to Senior Master Builder, it entails recognition of a job well done as well as the assumption of new responsibilities. He works with apprentices and the rest of the team to meet production deadlines, continues to make his own guitars, talks to customers and dealers, comes up with ideas, perfects his specialties, acts as an all-around trainer, mentor and problem solver, and more. Chris Fleming: "Most of the Senior Master Builders are product managers, like the way Todd Krause headed up the David Gilmour Stratocaster and the Blackie, or John Cruz doing the heavy Relic Malmsteen. Even with Team Built projects, a Senior Master builder runs the program, so it's very all-encompassing."

"If you could see Todd Krause's file drawer, it would make you drool. Jeff Beck, Eric Clapton, Pete Townshend — he builds for all these guys, and that's a part of the appeal as well. The customer knows, 'Wow, the Master Builder who builds Eric Clapton's guitars built my guitar, too!'"

— Richard McDonald

BILLY GIBBONS
COURTNEY LOVE
CLINT BLACK
WAYMAN TISDALE
BOB BRITT
BOZZ SKAGGS
HAULIN' OATS
ROSCOE BECK
JAKE ANDRE
GEDDY LEE
DALE PETERS
SAMBORA
JOHNNY LANG
KENNY WAYNE SHEPPARD
DAVID HOLT
ROGER WATERS
ROBIN TROWER

Yuriy Shishkov is not only a Master Builder but also a master colorist. He explains, "If you know how to use them, stains can bring a guitar to life."

The third way: Tweakable Team Built

A third, in-between option further sharpened the balance between giving customers precisely what they wanted while maximizing efficiency. This was the "modified" or "custom" Team Built instrument: Start with a particular features package that the shop has compiled for you, and then tweak this or that detail to your heart's content. Take an otherwise authentic vintage Telecaster reissue but specify a different neck profile or gold hardware, or put Texas Specials or a B-Bender in there. You want a '50s-style bridge, or a '60s-style laminated pickguard, or '70s-style block markers, or an '80s-style locking trem — live it up.

At some point, however, extended tweakage would elevate your order from a modified Team Built guitar into Master Built territory. In that case, your guitar would be built under the supervision of a single Master Builder, who would collaborate with you on every aspect and then carry the guitar through the entire process to completion. That one-on-one relationship and level of attention to detail continues to distinguish Master Built guitars from Team Built guitars.

Aside from individual customers, the dealers and distributors were quick to respond to the new concept, using Team Built guitars as starting points and then specifying a different finish or other detail. Eliminating the need to research and pinpoint every single spec, this approach provided the prestige and Cool Factor of owning a special Fender Custom Shop instrument with a minimum of fuss. Before long, music stores and retail chains were offering their own bespoke editions of uniquely painted, drastically Reliced, or otherwise modified Custom Shop guitars, yet another example of the shop's facilitating new kinds of partnerships between Fender and its dealers.

The lab

Another of the many advantages of the Team Built program was that it allowed the Custom Shop to expand its role as a proving ground or testing lab for the whole organization. The Set-Neck Telecaster and Telecoustic designs — both atypical of Fender — were examples. The shop could build them in limited quantities, and Fender could promote them and assess dealer and consumer reaction with less risk and less of a resource commitment than would be required of a full-scale factory project. John Page: "That's why I wanted to take over R&D as well as the Custom Shop. It was a natural fit. We've got top artisans in the shop trying new things all the time, and we're getting all this direct input from customers, so why not channel that into the factory?" As noted in Chap. 6, because Fender now owns, distributes, or manufactures Charvel, Jackson, Gretsch, Guild, Taylor, Hamer, and other brands, it allows "Fender to be Fender." There's less of a need for the Custom Shop to explore "non-Fender" designs.

Systems old and new

While the different nomenclatures and series names come and go, they all reflect the builders' goal of serving a range of needs among dealers and players. "The 'Team Built' concept has always been employed in the Custom Shop," explains Mike Eldred. "The LJ guitars, for example, were not built by one lone builder but a team of guys." On occasion a term will enter the literature only for a brief period. For example, two versions of the Robin Trower guitar were described not as Master Built and Team Built but rather as Team Built Custom and Team Built. As we go to press, the system of Team Built, Modified Team Built, and Master Built has been replaced by a more streamlined classification of two categories: Master Built and Custom Built; details in Chap. 30.

Custom Classics on the rise

Much of the shop's R&D went into expanding the Custom Classic line, which in the mid '90s included more than two dozen models described as "classic renditions of the legendary instruments that laid the groundwork for the sound, feel, and urgency of rock and roll today." Five models were available in either of two versions — standard or gold hardware. These included the American Classic Strat, American Classic Tele, '58 Stratocaster, '50s Telecaster, and the bound-body '60s Telecaster Custom.

The Custom Classics of '96 also included two other year-specific (as opposed to decade-generic) Strats, a 1954 and a 1960. Both were available in four versions — basic with standard hardware, basic with gold hardware, FMT (flame maple top), or FMT with gold hardware. (One anomaly: The whole idea of the Custom Classics was to offer a vintage vibe with cosmetic and functional upgrades such as abalone dots, Sperzel Trim-Lok tuners, a 2-point tremolo, and so on. In terms of marketing, the strategy made perfect

sense, but including specific years in the instruments' names seemed contradictory — here's a "1954 Strat" with major departures from 1954 specs. Mike Lewis would straighten it out by reassigning the year-specific names to where they belonged, the Time Machines.)

The Custom Classic line was rounded out with the 30.2" scale Bajo Sexto Telecaster, maple and rosewood-board versions of the Telecaster XII 12-string, the Vintage Precision Custom Bass (generally a '50s style instrument with a "Telecaster bass" type peghead), the American Classic Jazz Bass, two lefty basses (a '57 Precision and a '62 Jazz), and three lefty guitars: a '52 Tele, a '57 Strat, and a '62 Strat.

A few notable particulars from the Vol. 50, No. 1 brochure: All five left-handed Custom Classic guitars and basses were detailed, year-specific models rather than decade-generic instruments. The year-specific Strats included a dozen guitars, while the only year-specific Tele was the lefty '52. (It would be several more years before right-handed, year-specific Teles were listed as Custom Shop catalog items.) Offering such a broad selection of year-specific Strats — some of which sported period-correct neck shapes, original dot spacings, vintage style trems, and aged plastic parts — was another step in the shop's evolution toward increasingly authentic reissues.

The American Classic Tele was impressive, but although its third pickup was a versatile addition, few people would have associated that feature, the Schallers, the TBX circuit, or the extra fret with a "classic rendition of a legendary guitar"; rather, this instrument was a conspicuously modernized, high-performance upgrade. Finally, with its natural-finish body, bound neck, and white block markers on a blonde fingerboard, the American Classic Jazz Bass recalled the age of bell-bottoms, fringed vests, and CBS rather than Fender's classic era of the 1950s and early '60s. These quirks are trivial and merely reveal that while the mid-'90s Custom Shop offered an impressive array of models, the nomenclature was still evolving toward the detail and period accuracy we would soon take for granted.

Custom Classic specs have varied over the years. This is a Special Edition, with a 22-fret maple board, a C-shaped neck, 1969 Abigail Ybarra pickups, a 2-point trem, and a thin skin nitro finish in Bing Cherry Transparent.

A pair of Custom Classics, the Tele in Bing Cherry Transparent, the Strat in Cobalt Blue Transparent. The Custom Classics were retired in 2009.

The Schultz-o-Caster was one of many Custom Shop instruments that depended on a ready supply of the highest grades of quilted maple, flame maple, and other woods. J. Black: "We made this tree-of-life guitar for a NAMM show, but before the show Bill Schultz took it to a Sam Ash grand opening and presented it as being the cream of the crop of what the Custom Shop could do. The body was one piece of solid quilt maple, so it had some weight to it. It was serial number 000. Bill liked the guitar and ordered one for each of the sales reps, so we changed it a little. We couldn't get enough quilt to do solid bodies, so we went to quilt tops. We had a clear plexi pickguard, but we took that off for the later ones. We nicknamed it the Schultz-o-Caster because it was the first Custom Shop thing Bill ordered himself."

CHAPTER EIGHTEEN

18

Getting Better All the Time

Quality Control in the Factory and Custom Shop

Having a world-class builder make your dream guitar exactly the way you want it was the cornerstone of the Custom Shop's initial appeal. By contrast, designing Team Built models in-house and then offering them in a catalog seemed to be a one-eighty reversal. Production wise, the shift from "have it your way" to Fender's still-appealing "have it *our* way" sounds efficient, but what does it do to the shop's foundational philosophy, its (pardon my French) *raison d'être*? The shop was still offering spec-it-yourself one-offs through the Master Built program, but regarding its other products, one might ask: If the customer is removed from the design equation, at what point are Custom Shop guitars no longer custom?

To pose the question from a corporate perspective, if the dreamed-up-by-customers distinction no longer separates many of Fender's elite guitars from its less expensive ones, what does? In a word, quality. (Well, two words: quality and prestige.) As long as a discernible leap in quality separated Custom Shop models from their production counterparts, the former would retain their alluring radiance and continue to command big dollars.

The "problem" was that by the mid 1990s players, dealers, and the guitar media all agreed that factory Fenders were getting better all the time, and more consistent than ever. And while the factory was elevating its standards toward those of the Custom Shop (and often incorporating techniques acquired from the shop), the shop was perceived to be a bit more like a factory, offering premium yet standardized models. So if the factory guitars are getting better, and the Custom Shop is becoming more like a factory, what's *really* the difference between the $800 Telecaster and the $2,200 Telecaster?

Discussions comparing the quality of Custom Shop guitars vs. factory guitars go back to the earliest days of the shop. They reflected not only developments within Fender but within the entire industry as well. Dan Smith: "As Fender raised the bar, *everybody* started raising the bar. The Custom Shop was competing with Paul Reed Smith, who had that great reputation, and we were looking at these small companies who were building Fender-type stuff. They had a certain level of fit and finish, and we could not make a guitar that *should* sell for $2,500 given the

Picky, picky, picky: Like the other Master Builders, John Cruz examines every detail, at every step of the fabricating and assembly process.

materials and handwork and then sell it for $800. Fender is like anybody else in that way.

"The flip side is, we can't use the $800 guitar as a standard of quality for the Custom Shop. You can polish it all you want and change a few details, and maybe that might raise it to a $1,500 guitar, but the bar is getting raised all around — our own guitars from Mexico, from Japan. Nowadays guitars coming from China are better and better. One of the earliest solutions was the price list, and then the Team Builts. They [supported] the Master Builders who were getting out the very top-end stuff."

Are Fender execs ever concerned that the production guitars are getting so good they threaten the Custom Shop's exclusivity, or that the shop is getting to be so much like a factory that its prestige is compromised? Let's put it this way: They aren't worried about it, but they do recog-

Jason Smith wouldn't think of assembling this Stratocaster without confirming that every rout is exactly the correct size and depth.

nize that this challenge is never ending. Since the mid 1990s they have responded with an integrated, cohesive approach to the production and marketing of all Fender instruments. The same executive who oversees the imported guitars also oversees the domestic factory as well as the Custom Shop. By monitoring differences in features, materials, and production costs at every level, Fender keeps the categories distinct and fine-tunes a retail price and an appropriate marketing strategy for each instrument, whether it's an entry-level import from China or a one-off from Corona costing thirty times as much.

Mike Lewis: "We are constantly pushing the envelope at *every* level, so the entire line evolves and improves together. If we raise the bar in the production guitars, then in response to that we raise the bar in the Custom Shop, too. These things are never piecemeal. Decisions are made in conjunction with each other, always looking at the entire spectrum of Fender guitars."

An example of this integrated approach goes back to the late 1990s, when the factory evolved its U.S. Vintage Reissue series into the American Vintage series. During the same period, and not coincidentally, Fender created the Custom Shop's Time Machine series with the N.O.S., Closet Classic, and Relic finishes, a level of customer-selected detail that helped elevate these pricier guitars above the fixed-spec American Vintage line. Another example is that while it's not unusual for a model to first appear in the

Custom Shop on a limited basis and then migrate over to the factory, it's less common (although not unheard-of) for Custom Shop and factory versions of the same guitar to be offered concurrently.

Ralph Esposito: "We very closely monitor the quality of the woods and also the weight of the guitars in the shop and also in the factory. Our woods will be cleaner, with fewer mineral stains, for example. Sometimes we decide what to offer based on what the factory is doing. If they are offering '57 and '62 Strats, then we might offer a '60 and a '65 – something they *aren't* making." Scott Grant explains that such painstaking efforts have always characterized Custom Shop operations: "We hand-selected our own wood, not just for figure but for weight, too. When the factory was experimenting with multi-piece bodies, we would do two-piece. We had our own specs for necks and pickups, and put more time into each guitar."

Artist Signature guitars are other examples of Fender's efforts to put distance between Custom Shop and factory models. Alex Perez: "If somebody wants a guitar exactly like John 5's, they would go for the Custom Shop version. But if you just thought that his guitar looked cool and didn't want to spend a few thousand dollars, then the regular production model would be a good choice. That guitar comes out of Mexico. It's a good thing we offer a lower-price version that the average player can afford."

Beyond prestige and provenance

What about the simple cachet of owning a guitar that bears a "Fender Custom Shop" decal? Whether it's a matter of showing off, or guitar-geek chic, or simply an issue of personal, unpretentious pride, wouldn't prestige alone go a long way toward justifying a Custom Shop guitar's price, aside from its presumed superiority as a musical instrument? Richard McDonald: "To be honest, the answer is yes, but only up to a point. I had a realization — if you had two Fenders that are exactly the same, and one of them had a Custom Shop logo and cost $1,500 or $2,000 more than the other, the guy who wants the Custom Shop instrument will buy it just because of what it is and where it came from. But it's not the same customer, exactly, who's purchasing that Custom Shop guitar, and we never take customers for granted. We recognize [the power of the shop's prestige], but at the same time the line has to have integrity. It's really unfortunate if you're in a music store overhearing a conversation and a customer asks the sales person what's the difference between this factory '62 Strat and the Custom Shop '62 Strat and the sales person can't answer. The fact is, there is an *unbelievable* amount of difference between those two instruments, even though they might seem on the surface to be exactly the same."

For example, Fender picked particular years for some of the Custom Shop's vintage style guitars vs. those from the factory, in certain cases specifying a neck profile, construction technique, or other feature that was unique to a single year of original production. Examples have included the '51 Nocaster, '56 Stratocaster, '63 Telecaster, '69 Stratocaster, and Relic '64 Jazz Bass. If both the factory and the shop offered reissues of, say, a '56 Strat (perhaps at different times), Fender would take pains to distinguish the two, even if the differences were subtle. Mike Lewis: "Some of these things are not even visible to the naked eye. You would actually have to take the guitar apart to see them. If the rout for the truss rod was done in a funky way, only in that particular year, then we would do the same thing in the Custom Shop."

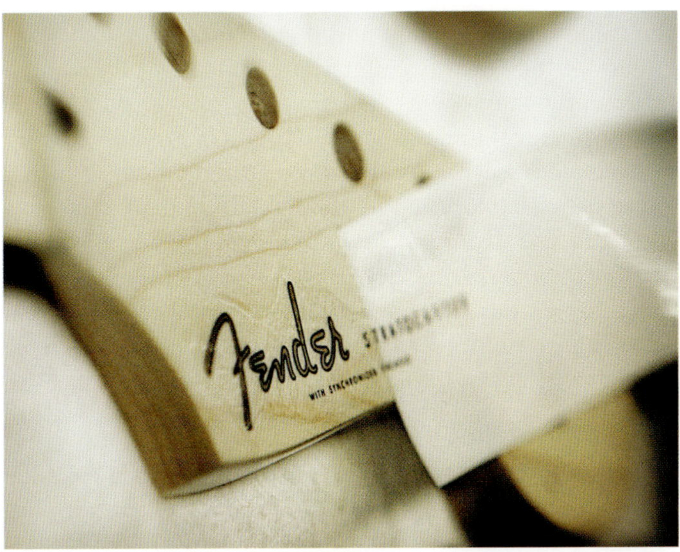

Such differences have less to do with player-centric features than vintage authenticity. Richard McDonald: "They used to rout out the body channels with a drill press, where they would just push the body under the press back in the old days. We do it that same way in the Custom Shop. It looks like it was done with an axe [laughs]. The clay position dots, the materials used, the spread of the wood underneath the paint, the paint that's used, the material in the saddles, the bridge spacing — all of these sorts of things are different, and they all matter to that Custom Shop customer."

This attention to detail is a direct response to the practical needs and sometimes hyper-discriminating tastes of typical clients. The majority of the guitars start with a vintage platform, and in some cases the builders use not only the same types of machinery but the actual equipment that was used in the days of Leo Fender, Freddie Tavares, and George Fullerton. Richard McDonald: "We're using the same machines, whether it's the drill presses from 1949, the original neck tooling from the '50s, a [fret] slotter from the '60s, all that stuff. And in some cases the same people are working on the guitars."

So if you want a nice guitar that looks pretty much like one that Fender made in 1962, you can find it in the regular catalog, but if you want a guitar that was *made* the same way as in 1962, go to the Custom Shop. Richard McDonald: "If you pull the pickguard off a [factory reissue] '62 Strat, you'll see the perfect CNC rout, but if you pull the pickguard off a '62 Custom Shop guitar, you'll see things like the paint-can rings on the underside of the pickguard." (Original pickguards were punched from the same vulca-

Highly figured woods are cherry-picked from several suppliers.

Above: Glued-up spreads are dried in a clamping device. Below: Ready for the neck duplicator, these blanks have been prepped and fitted with truss rods. Code letters indicate details, such as ASBE (American Standard specs, bird's-eye maple), 57F (vintage '50s-style, flame maple), etc.

nized fiber material Fender used for the pickup bobbins. As they were sealed with Homoclad and top-coated with lacquer, they were often set on paint cans or coffee cans so their edges could be coated without the piece's sticking to the work surface. Mark Kendrick adds, "Early on, it was decided to spray them with black lacquer in addition to the lacquer topcoat. After switching to a phenolic pickguard material, Fender continued using the same basic process, buffing them prior to final assembly.")

Win-Win

Dan Smith recalls that he and John Page often argued about the relative quality and the details of Custom Shop guitars vs. their factory counterparts. "One time we wanted to upgrade the brown shell material on the pickguards on our [factory] vintage series. The Custom Shop was up in arms because it was the same stuff they were using. These debates happened all the time, but again, the bar is getting raised all around, and more pressure is piled on the Custom Shop: *What are they going to do next?* It's an ongoing battle to this day, but look who benefits. The guitars get better. Our reputation gets better. Players and dealers have better instruments. It's a good thing all around."

Woods for bodies

In the early days, woods for Custom Shop bodies came from several sources. The factory had excellent supplies of high-quality alder, so the Custom Shop builders hand-picked their alder from Fender's main wood storage area. Michael Stevens: "I recall the ash coming in on semis, like the alder did, and John and I cherry-picking it for one-piece and light-weight planks." On the other hand, the shop's maple — particularly figured maple — was typically sourced from other suppliers, simply because the factory wasn't using it for the tops of bodies at the time.

Solid guitar bodies are typically made from rectangular blocks called "spreads." Through the late 1990s, both the factory and the Custom Shop were buying lengths of wood, sawing them up, and gluing pieces side-by-side to make spreads for guitars and basses. The process demanded many hours of work and the use of expensive tooling and machinery. It also entailed a fair amount of waste, which reduced the cost-effectiveness of the operation.

The late Bill Redman provided high-quality Western maple for fancy tops. John Page: "It was really tough

Woods are meticulously examined not only for their appearance but also for their tonal qualities. Here, Mark Kendrick selects highly figured maple tops for a special run that was exhibited at the 2009 Tokyo Guitar Show. The lead for the Custom Shop mill, Homar Silva, looks on.

because the color varied so much with Western, so Bill went above and beyond, investing in a vacuum kiln to help us get as white a block as possible. When we started with him we were doing the Set-Neck Teles, and we figured we would sell them with mildly figured tops. The market had a different idea and wanted everything to be AAA and better. It was a tough bill to fill, but he did a really great job. Bill supplied wood for the Custom Shop through the end of my tenure." J. Black adds that without Bill Redman, groundbreaking projects such as the maple-top Schultz-O-caster simply wouldn't have been possible.

The factory quit manufacturing its own spreads in the early '90s. The Custom Shop crew inherited some of the equipment and continued to make their own spreads while they were still located on Pomona Road and Enterprise Court. When Fender moved to Cessna Circle in 1998, the Custom Shop was brought under the same roof, and its floor space was cut from 18,000 square feet to about 7,000 square feet. Because there was insufficient room to continue fabricating their own spreads, and for other reasons as well, a new system was established in cooperation with Westwood Lumber, an Oregon-based sawmill operator and a supplier of hardwoods to several industries. As it turned out, the new arrangement had several advantages.

Westwood's representative, Grant Wheeler, explained to Page and his crew that apart from the considerations of reduced space, they no longer needed to cut, plane, and glue the woods for body blanks. Westwood could do all that for them, saving many man-hours in production. Another advantage was that Westwood had so many uses for wood that it could fabricate smaller products from Fender's leftovers, which meant that Fender no longer had to pay to have its waste wood hauled away. Eventually, Westwood set up a wood-processing facility right next to Fender, supplying spreads to both the factory and the Custom Shop.

Halfway between spread and Stratocaster, a jig-mounted guitar body takes shape in the hands of Mike Eldred.

Right: Finished product and raw materials: One of the 20 Sonic Blue Limited Collection La Cabronita Especial guitars rests against a stack of rosewood fingerboard blanks.

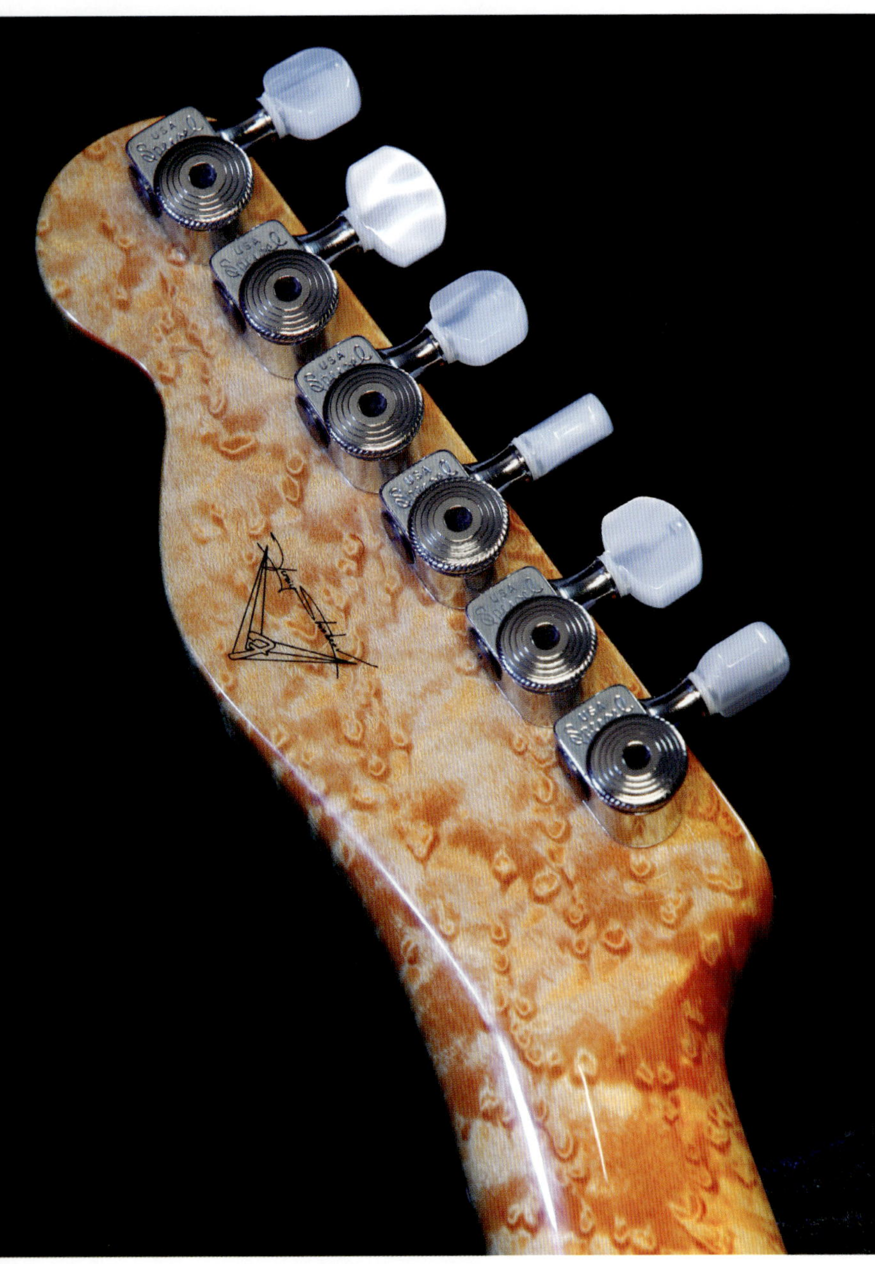

Regarding the ultra-figured maple neck on Keith Urban's Shattered Mirror Telecaster (Chap. 31), Mike Eldred commented: "I had never seen a piece of bird's-eye like that — ever."

J. Black: "We had been gluing up our own spreads and getting a good seam. We got really good at that because we had been doing flame maple stuff for years — starting with the Anniversary Tele back in '88 — and at the time manufacturing was not using those figured woods. When you put two pieces of flame maple together and the seam shows, it ruins the guitar. So John put in a lot of time with the guys to get those details right. The way we refined the process in the Custom Shop later transferred over to the factory spreads. When Westwood came in, we saved all the time it took to process that wood, plus we were able to get rid of a lot of machinery in manufacturing — chop saws, thickness sanders, all the gluing fixtures. Grant Wheeler gets a lot of credit for bringing that kind of quality control to us."

Wood for necks

A woodworker with a longtime passion for bird's-eye maple, Lawrence Berndt is the founder of Yankee Veneer Corp., based in New Hampshire. Yankee saws and mills several types of woods, specializing in plain, figured, and bird's-eye maple. It processes pre-sized pieces for several guitar builders, including neck blanks for Fender's Custom Shop. Lawrence Berndt: "We sent our first pieces of wood out there in 1994. Scott Grant ordered eight blanks, and it grew from there. The pieces are pre-dimensioned, jointed, and planed. Bird's-eye is not flat when it comes out of a kiln, so we take care of that at our end." Lawrence reports that guitar neck blanks typically measure 1" x 4" x 29", or 1.2" x 4" x 29", while bass neck blanks are about 1" x 4.5" x 36".

John Page explains that when he and Mike Stevens started working together, "a guy would pull up the truck and we'd take out six boards or whatever, and that would last us for a couple of months." But the shop grew quickly, and many of the customers were asking for premium-grade woods. Finding high-quality lumber in sufficient quantities became a formidable challenge. John Page: "Some of the suppliers did not have access to the kinds of forests where the wood was hard enough, in our opinion. But Lawrence had access to those forests, and his workers were very protective of the way they cut the lumber. Their wood was rock hard and beautiful. The other thing was that Lawrence was dependable."

Before long, the Custom Shop's demands got to the point where Lawrence Berndt expanded his entire operation to accommodate the new relationship. "At first I wasn't their only supplier, but they told me my wood was extremely consistent in color, dryness, and quality. With some of the other vendors, sometimes they would have things in stock and sometimes they wouldn't. Sometimes the wood would be dry, other times green; sometimes white, other times gray. So it was consistency and quality that led the Custom Shop within six months to make me their exclusive supplier of bird's-eye necks and flame maple necks. John Page really put me to work [laughs]. Before long we were shipping anywhere between 30 and 100 necks a month."

Because several aspects of guitar building are matters of taste, Berndt developed personal relationships with some of the builders. "I would go out and visit those guys," he recalls, "and J. Black would take me aside and show me a piece of wood and say, 'Don't *ever* send me a springy neck like this [laughs].' He'd pull out four or five others and say, 'I want all of my necks to be rigid, like this.' So the builders were very particular, and I knew several of them so well that I would set aside necks and put their names on the wood, or call ahead and let them know that special pieces were coming for one project or another. In the early years those builders could hoard their favorite components, hang onto them until the time was right. Several of the guys had their own stashes of favored woods. They were typical builders, with a driving passion for quality. I worked with all the builders and with 'Red' Dave Nichols, who became their chief wood inspector."

To this day Lawrence Berndt bends over backwards to accommodate special requests, no matter how unusual — an ultra-thin piece of figured maple to be used for a pickguard, for example. In recent years he and Mike Eldred have become good friends, often collaborating on setting grades for wood and other issues. Lawrence explains that all of the wood supplied to the Custom Shop has to be hard and stable. To be used for a top-quality guitar neck, it has several requirements regarding grain structure, dryness, and workability.

A gorgeous solid rosewood neck is marked with its serial number and Master Builder Greg Fessler's decal.

Beyond those high standards, it's the depth of the figure (or, in the case of bird's-eye, the count of the eyes) that determines the grade, from the lowest "A" grade to the highest "5A," or "AAAAA." While those terms are industry standards, their application in practice is anything but uniform. Lawrence Berndt: "There's an awful lot of subjectivity involved in the interpretation, so what might be a AAAAA piece for one supplier might be a AAAA for me. One reason I have this long relationship with Fender is that I'm a fanatic about it. I still personally grade the wood that goes to the Custom Shop, and continue to provide wood to my good friend John Page."

The Danny Gatton doubleneck Tele

Building any doubleneck presents a host of special demands, but working with the late Danny Gatton entailed additional challenges — and joys. This six-pickup, two-headed Tele was designed by Gatton, Fred Stuart, and Alan Hamel and built by Stuart and Hamel. Details: ash body, highly figured maple necks — one standard guitar, one 6-string bass — a gold anodized pickguard, gold hardware, and a tremolo that can accommodate either a right-side or a left-side trem bar placement.

Fred Stuart: "Danny had seen this sort of mother of toilet seat, two-tone black and white guitar that I had done for a NAMM show, one of the art guitars. He just loved it, but it had already been sold. In the process of working with him he came up with the idea of the doubleneck. Alan and I literally hand-made all the parts for this thing. That double-sided tremolo allowed Danny to put the bar on the top side or the bottom side, depending on what mood he was in." J. Black: "This looks like nothing that came out of the shop in the '50s, and yet it's so pure it looks like Leo Fender himself could have designed it."

Perhaps the most unusual feature of the Gatton doubleneck is the guitar's left-hand/right-hand tremolo bridge.

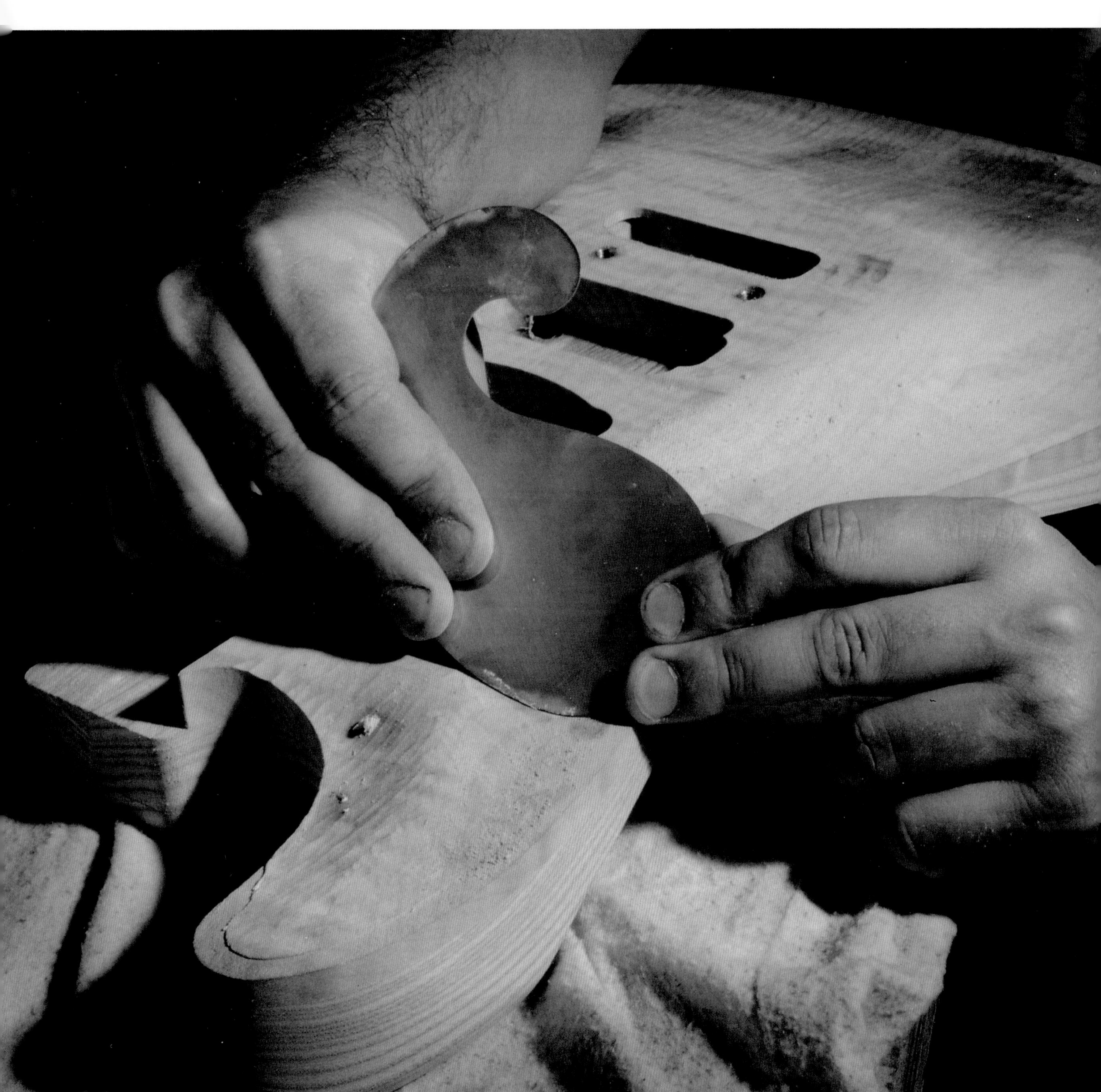

Proto

CHAPTER NINETEEN

19

Late-'90s Set-Necks, Showmasters, the Hendrix Monterey Pop Strat

Set-Neck/Contemporary Series

The Set-Neck/Contemporary Series of 1996 numbered a half-dozen 22-fret guitars. Most were Strats. The lone Tele was the year-old Set-Neck Tele Jr., a chambered Fender for players who love the classic combo of a glued-in neck and a flat mahogany body with twin soapbars, in this case Duncan SP90s.

The beautiful new Set-Neck Strat featured a flame maple top on an ash body, locking Schallers, a Duncan JB humbucker in the bridge position, and two Texas Specials. Despite its upgrades and humbucker, the familiar body shape and three knobs made it a relatively conventional guitar when compared to the other Strats in this new series.

Described as "downsized modern guitars designed for virtuoso rockers," the three Contemporary Strats were later, better, and what might be called truer Fender guitars that targeted the shredder market previously addressed by the HM series and the Heartfield imports of the late 1980s and early 1990s. The basic Contemporary Strat was accompanied by a version equipped with a Fender/Floyd Rose trem, as well as the ultra fancy FMT, named for its flame maple top. All three had slightly smaller bodies with sharper body horns, a pair of Texas Specials, and a Duncan HB. (Although some of the '96 literature specified the conventional three-knob array, the Contemporary Strats actually had two knobs: master volume and master tone.)

The Jimi Hendrix Monterey Pop Festival Stratocaster of 1997 commemorated the '65 Strat that Hendrix himself had painted. The shop added the backstage pass, which incorporated Ed Caraeff's iconic photo of Jimi burning the guitar during the performance.

John Suhr

As noted in Chapter 13, John Suhr built guitars at Rudy's Music Stop in New York before coming to Fender. Those models were favored by several prominent players, including Mark Knopfler. For his Pensa-Suhr models, John sourced guitar bodies from Schecter. Tom Anderson provided necks and, later, bodies. The body shape that John requested was Strat-ish but a little down-sized, more modern, and not as heavy metal looking as, say, Jackson's guitars. "That was the 'dinky,'" he explains. "I think both

Grover Jackson and Tom Anderson had used the term. Tom sent me some smaller bodies, and we tweaked them and used them at Rudy's for the early Pensa-Suhr guitars."

When John Suhr came to Corona, he brought his dinky design with him. "It became the Contemporary Strat," he says, "and that was the first Custom Shop model I influenced. Tom Anderson's success was frustrating for Fender, for good reason, and they wanted to attack guys like that — Tom, Roger Sadowsky, plus the sorts of things I had been doing with the Pensa-Suhrs."

The Carved Top

The other guitar in the Set-Neck/Contemporary Series of 1996 was the Carved Top Strat (flame maple on ash, Texas Specials and a Duncan HB, master volume and tone controls with chrome knobs). Unmistakably Strat-like in silhouette but otherwise an even further departure from classic specs, this no-pickguard two-knobber with the sculpted, premium-grade top was a forerunner of a new series of upscale, outside-the-box Fenders.

The Carved Top was in a way a descendant of the Contemporary. John Suhr had mixed feelings about that development: "John Page said, let's go further with this and do more of the thing you were doing with the Knopfler guitars — carved tops, exotic woods, a different carve on the body horns, and so on. But John and I butted heads on how to carry it out." The problem was that Page wanted to keep the Strat's full body perimeter so as to maintain its iconic identity. Suhr respected that opinion but felt the carved top on a full-size body didn't look right. The regular Strat body has a large radius — the round curve where the top joins the sides. That lack of a corner reduces the size when seen from the front. John Suhr: "To mount a carved top on there, you need more of a corner, but if you reduce the radius and keep the body size, it looks too big."

The Showmaster debuts

There was a bit of juggling when it came to organizing the series for 1997 (the Set-Neck Strat and Set-Neck Tele Jr. were now the only members of the Set-Neck category), but otherwise the lineup of Set-Neck, Contemporary, Contemporary FMT, and Carved Top Strats was unchanged. The Showmaster had yet to appear.

This Carved Top Stratocaster was designed by Gene Baker, John Suhr, and John Page and built by Gene Baker. The combination of a carved top on a full-size Strat body was the subject of debate between Page and Suhr.

The mid-1998 line continued to offer the Set-Neck Strat as well as the maple-on-ash Carved Top Strat, the latter guitar now appearing in two versions — the original HSS model, with a humbucker/single/single pickup array, and a newer HH guitar with twin humbuckers. The new Showmaster accompanied the Set-Neck Strat, the two Carved Top Strats, and the Set-Neck Tele Jr. in the five-model Contemporary series.

In a way, the new Showmasters were a solution to John Suhr's complaint. "They went with a Set-Neck like they were doing on the Tele Jrs.," he explains, "and then they also used my original body perimeter and radius — the dinky — from the Contemporary Strat. In other words, with the Showmasters, they did what I said they should've been doing in the first place." By that time, John Suhr "had one foot out the door," as he puts it. He was frustrated by Fender's failure to replace its old CNC machinery with the new equipment he and Steve Boulanger had been requesting for at least a year. After three years or so at the shop, he left to start his own company, Suhr Guitars.

Although the maple-on-alder Showmaster was similar to the Carved Top Strats, it was labeled simply as the Showmaster rather than the Showmaster Strat, likely a result of its departure from the Strat's conventional body shape. (The Showmaster name sounded like it could have come from the mind of Don Randall, who dreamed up Telecaster, Stratocaster, Jazzmaster, and almost every other name for instruments and amps in Fender's vintage era.) Although its pickup array was nominally different from that of the Carved Top HSS, it did share several features with the Carved Tops: a carved maple top, figured maple neck, Sperzel Trim-Loks, an LSR roller nut, and 22 frets.

Gene Baker spearheaded the Showmaster project, which aside from John Suhr's influence was to some extent inspired by a one-off Strat Baker had built at the shop, working after hours and on weekends. "John Page really liked it," Gene recalls, "and said something like, 'Man, I could sell these things.'" There was still much work to be done, because Gene's proto had a number of complexities — a pitched neck and a tilt-back peghead among them — that would have made it impractical for production.

As the team went to work on designing a production-friendly version, the beautiful instruments coming out of the shop's archtop department further stoked Gene Baker's resolve to pursue the idea of blending a carved top with traditional Fender design principles. His goal had been to craft a slightly fatter body, which he believes translates into bigger tone. He settled on a side profile that below the carve was the same thickness as a stock Strat; the carved top added about a quarter of an inch to the thickness.

"The carve of that top was so important," he explains. "One fond memory is John Page closing his eyes and feeling up the sample carved tops I made up, and he's saying something like, 'Imagine giving your wife a back massage and you're feeling her hips, the waist, into the shoulders, very smooth flowing lines.' It was all about the hands."

In terms of commercial appeal, Baker envisioned a modern version of the Strat with hot pickups and a fast neck, one that could compete with shred machines from Jackson, Ibanez, and others. But he wanted to combine all that into an elegant, "grown up" model that could also compete with the stunning carved-top, set-neck, humbucking-equipped guitars coming from PRS. For example, the new Fender would have a sculpted heel that would give the neck/body joint a smooth and seamless feel. "When John Suhr came onboard," Baker explains, "he'd already had all that experience with designing and building those very contemporary, carved-top Pensa-Suhr guitars, so Page

Virtually obliterating the conventional neck/body joint, the builders extended the smooth-as-silk feel to the part of the guitar where it mattered most — the newly contoured neck heel.

Left: Sporting a variety of finishes, fingerboards, pickups, and bridges, these maple-topped, "modernized" updates of the Stratocaster were intended to compete not only with popular shred machines but also elegant carved-top models from PRS.

saw it as a great opportunity to create something really new for Fender. We were researching new, grain-popping colors, too. Lastly I think we all agreed it needed to have a humbucking Seymour in the bridge and a single/single duo for the middle and neck. There were also some things we *didn't* want, like a sharp-cornered body or headstock that looked too much like an ESP or a Schecter."

After John Suhr left Fender and acquired the software and CNC equipment he would need to make his own guitars, one of his first jobs was to help out his former associates. "The first ten or twelve Showmasters were done by hand, by Mike Ponce and Gene Baker, at Fender," he explains. "Then Steve Boulanger and Gene Baker brought me the Showmaster template, and I drew it and handed them the surfaces, the specs they would need. They were still updating their programming skills, so Steve Smith, a programmer who was my partner, programmed the tops and we actually cut the next 75 or so Showmaster bodies on our own machines at Suhr. Once Boulanger picked up on it and we'd given them what they needed, the Custom Shop took it over. When Bill Schultz found out that a former employee had done the engineering on the tops and cut the first production bodies, he had a fit. The way it was explained to me, Bill said, *well, damn it, get whatever Suhr has, so we can do that stuff here!* Fender finally got the equipment I had wanted them to get all along."

While reporting to John Page, Baker was in charge of managing the project's construction, documenting the procedures, and making some of the tooling, including the carved-top template for the shop's pantograph-type duplicator. "I also worked with Steve Boulanger on the CNC," he says, "prototyping and dialing in the specs. We used hand-operated machines for carving the top, but there was also one custom cutter we had made for the CNC to carve the rear neck pocket contour. It was this really old Cinnimatic CNC, before we had a Haas, and we really depended on Steve Boulanger's skills to run it."

A top-of-the-line, Strat-like guitar with a Tele peghead, the new Showmaster Elite featured revoiced pickups, a flatter fingerboard, and exotic top woods. Mike Eldred called it "essentially a whole new model."

Expanding the line

The freshman class of late-'98 Showmasters joined the Classic Player Strat and Set-Neck Tele Jr. in the Contemporary Series. The three Showmasters were the Standard (bolt-on neck, alder body with a carved top); the FMT (bolt-on neck, carved flame maple top); and FMT Set-Neck (glued-in neck, carved flame maple top, locking trem or stop tailpiece). A 7-string hardtail version was offered by January 2000.

All three of the 6-string Showmasters had alder bodies, carved tops, 22 frets, abalone dots, LSR nuts, Sperzel Trim-Lok tuners, a Seymour Duncan '59 Trembucker in the bridge position, a pair of Custom Shop Fat 50s pickups, and master volume and tone controls with chrome knobs. The Showmaster Standard and Showmaster FMT offered a 2-point trem, a bolt-on neck, and a choice of a maple or rosewood fingerboard. The top-of-the-line Showmaster FMT Set-Neck was available only with a rosewood board but offered a choice between a Wilkinson stop tailpiece and a deluxe locking trem. Befitting its role as Fender's challenge to the high-end guitars of various rivals, the FMT Set-Neck cost $3,599, more than any of the Custom Classics or Time Machines.

Mike Ponce and Mike Bump were apprenticed to Gene Baker at the time, and both helped out on the Showmaster project. Gene Baker: "They saw how good I was with training people and documenting the procedures, so they gave me the task of being the apprentice trainer. Mike Ponce, Mike Bump and I could tag-team so well that it really increased the Master Built output. Mike Bump had come from the wood mill, running the CNC machines, and he was very good with organization. Mike Ponce had been building a lot of necks and was really good, so the three of us were very efficient." Mike Bump often prepped the body woods and operated the CNC, and Mike Ponce helped select the neck woods, worked on necks, and coordinated with Corona production when necessary to use their machinery.

For the 2004 model year, the Standard, FMT, and Set-Neck FMT Showmasters were joined by a new top-of-the-line guitar, the Showmaster Elite. It had a mahogany neck

The Elite's fancy fingerboard inlays evoked sort of a heavy metal/tribal tattoo vibe.

Custom Shop
Fender

(the others were Fender's customary maple), an ebony fingerboard (vs. maple or rosewood), intricate "tribal sun" fingerboard markers (vs. abalone dots), optional exotic top woods such as spalted maple and lacewood and, of all things, a Telecaster peghead — likely the only example of Fender's placing a Tele crown atop the king of a line of more or less Strat-type guitars. "This was essentially a whole new model, not just an upgrade-type mod," explains Mike Eldred. "We changed the top carve and body perimeter, revoiced the pickups, made it the first Showmaster with two humbuckings [also available with a single humbucker], put the new inlays on there and the Tele peghead, and gave it a 12" radius."

The Showmasters were dropped from the catalog after the 2008 model year, marking the end of a successful, decade-long run, but as Mike Eldred explained in 2009, "We don't discontinue stuff. We retire guitars from time to time and bring them back later. We backed the Showmasters out toward the end of last year, along with the '66 Strat, '67 Tele, and others. At some point they may be back."

Richard McDonald adds: "The Showmasters are awesome. I own a spalted flame top with tribal inlays and a single humbucker. In the Custom Shop, nothing is discontinued, only retired or on hiatus. Much like a Paisley Tele or a Blue Flower Stratocaster, there is an ebb and flow in the marketplace. Players get excited — *wow, a Telecaster with wallpaper on it!* — and then the instruments fall back in people's minds. All of a sudden there is a rediscovery, and the pent-up demand reaches an apex. Next thing you know, we put them back into production. Showmasters aren't dead. They're just on holiday."

Gene Baker looks back: "I really enjoyed the project because there was a lot of teamwork and support from the original proto startup to the final Custom Shop release and production. Many builders strived to keep as much production within the Custom Shop as possible, versus using the production line. That kept us self-supportive. It allowed us to react to new ideas quickly — and to put more blood, sweat and tears into our work."

A Showmaster Elite built for speed: Like a Ferrari without cup holders or a radio, this Tele-headed, stripped-down machine sported a racy red body that oozed elegance, a minimally adorned fretboard, and a single Gretsch-style pickup.

Next to your fire: The Monterey Pop Strat

One of the Custom Shop's most artful and memorable creations was the limited-edition Jimi Hendrix Monterey Pop Festival Stratocaster of 1997. Commemorating the 1965 Strat that Hendrix played, torched, and sacrificed during his now mythical June 18, 1967 performance at the Monterey International Pop Music Festival, the run of 210 instruments was built by John Page and his crew. Pamelina H. hand-painted each one, approximating Jimi's artwork and adding a few touches of her own.

Pamelina H.: "It's my favorite Fender art guitar because there is so much personal connection to it in my own life. I was there, at Monterey Pop in 1967. I was seven years old. My mom took me. I grew up in Monterey, and I was such a big, big Hendrix fan, so that guitar has always had a special place in my heart."

After more than a year of research, design, and cooperation among John Page, Jimi's sister Janie, and Pamelina H., the project got underway, ultimately entailing building a run of 1965-style Strats with small headstocks and transition logos, painting them Fiesta Red, covering part of each body with a cloudy swath of white paint (as Hendrix himself had done on his original), and then recreating Jimi's fanciful, leafy curlicues.

Along with the 210 guitars, the shop also built several prototypes (proto Number One has been seen in the hands of John Mayer). John Page: "Some of these projects could have hundreds of hours in development and research before the building ever started. We were always in green-light mode at the shop. Our brains never shut down, and the creative juices were always flowing. We had a video of Jimi's performance, and I worked with a guy who had a gizmo that would let us extract stills from the video, to examine them in a bit of detail. One of the reasons we had something like eight prototype levels with Pamelina — these were completed instruments — was that we kept seeing new things in these individual frames as we discovered more photos."

Pamelina H.: "The story goes that Jimi painted his Stratocaster not very long before he went onstage, so the original didn't exist very long in that state. There were a couple of pictures of him with it, but to get the design correct I watched the video of the performance frame by

Pamelina H. hand-painted each of the 210 Monterey Pop Festival Stratocasters. "It's my favorite Fender art guitar," she says, "because there is so much personal connection to it in my own life. I was there, at Monterey Pop in 1967."

Fender

frame by frame. It took me four hours to do 15 minutes of video.

"The original plan was to copy the paint job exactly the way Jimi did it. The story as I heard it, and I cannot confirm this, was that he used model paints, the kind that come in the little square jars, and those really bad paint brushes like kids use on their model cars and airplanes. He did not use professional brushes. When you see that surviving chunk of wood from the body you can see how crude and sloppy it was, but remember, that guitar had a very short life in that state. It was all very quick. My original version was an exact duplicate, just as sloppy as Jimi did it, but it progressed and got prettier and prettier. John Page told me to 'Pamelina' it. Apparently, I became a verb for that job [laughs]."

Pamelina tweaked and smoothed some of the details from the original's artwork, and also added a backstage pass that incorporated the famous Ed Caraeff photo of Jimi burning the guitar during the performance. John Page reports that the only reason he decided to do the backstage pass was that he felt the white swath of paint was graphically boring compared to the rest of the instrument. Page just wanted to fill that space. "I was looking at it from the hanging-on-the-wall point of view," he says. Cool detail: The number on each pass matches the serial number of that particular guitar.

Unlike the Playboy Strat and some of Pamelina's other art guitar projects, the Hendrix Monterey Strat did not involve the use of frisket paper (p. 189), so it all went relatively quickly. Pamelina says, "I would work on ten bodies at a time. First I'd paint the turquoise color, then the red, and finish with the black. By the time I was done painting all 210, I could practically do it without a template. I believe I was able to paint them at the rate of about three a day."

Each alder-bodied guitar was a right-handed model that was strung left-handed, although a conversion to right-hand stringing was relatively simple. Each was individually serial numbered, and fitted with a period-correct rosewood fingerboard, three-way pickup selector, and three-ply pickguard. The limited-edition package included a flight case, a plush-lined gig bag festooned with appropriately groovy tassels and beads, a custom strap, a laminated backstage pass replica, a leather folder with the Custom Shop Certificate of Authenticity, and a copy of the Caraeff photo. Representing the Hendrix estate, Jimi's sister Janie approved the final design.

John Page: "We wanted to capture the whole mood, so we did the guitar and the backstage pass. Dru (WhiteFeather) beaded all the white suede gig bags with turquoise and silver beads on the fringe to match Jimi's jackets. I had drops of patchouli oil put in the case so when you opened it up it even *smelled* like the '60s." Duane Boulanger laughingly recalls: "The entire shop *reeked* of that stuff the whole time we were building those things."

Venus

Although manufactured in Japan by FujiGen-Gakki, the Squier Venus was another guitar that began life in the Custom Shop. Designed for Courtney Love, it was based on her Mercury brand guitar. Alex Perez remembers: "When the Mercury came in, it came to me. Billy Bush, Courtney's tech, told me they tried to get more guitars from the original builder, but he was out of business." Larry Brooks was Fender's Artist Builder at the time, and he built a set-neck guitar for Courtney that was more or less based on the Mercury's shape; the electronics were designed in the Custom Shop to accommodate Love's request for a basic, performance-friendly system. Alex Perez: "They needed it turned around fast. They were trying to jump on the Courtney and Kurt thing while the iron was hot. Mark [Kendrick] took over and built two bolt-on versions, and then Todd [Krause] took over and built a lot of them for Courtney."

Joe Carducci was marketing manager for Fender's imports at the time. He recalls a visit to his brother's house: "A light bulb went on in my head when he called his family cat's name, 'Venus.' The following Monday morning I sent a message to Fender's Artist Relations man, Del Breckenfeld, with the suggested name." Del Breckenfeld: "I attended a benefit event in Hollywood and ended up sitting with Courtney. I took the opportunity to ask how she liked the name 'Venus' and she said it was 'radical,' which I took as official approval." The production version was introduced in January '97 as part of the Vista series of Squier guitars.

Right: Courtney Love and Artist Builder Larry Brooks came up with a body shape unlike any Fender before or since. Brooks and Mark Kendrick built this single-pickup, no-switch example. Production versions were marketed under the Squier brand for two years. In concert, Love often played custom-built or modified guitars.

Fender

CHAPTER TWENTY

20

The Pirates of Corona

Just a Bunch of Ragtag Guys

The shop's rapid growth provoked inherent complications. Would Fender's growing "flagship" be a department within the factory, an adjunct to the factory, semi-autonomous, entirely autonomous? Custom Shop employees would be part of the Fender clan, of course, but would they be brothers and sisters at the family table, or distant cousins on the outskirts of town? Cooperative grownups sharing household responsibilities, or unruly teenagers holed up in their rooms doing God knows what?

Former Senior Vice President Ritchie Fliegler: "The Custom Shop was always sort of a loose cannon, not just at the beginning but for years and years. A lot of us didn't really know what they were up to half the time. We'd go to a NAMM show and John Page and his guys would show up with some guitars, and we'd go, 'Wow, great,' but we weren't always in the loop and weren't sure what to expect. It would have been better if we had more communication, but there were times when I would just sort of read about it in the papers, if you see what I mean. Rather than functioning in a typical chain of command type of thing, where the shop would report to marketing, it was more of a relationship between the shop and manufacturing."

In several respects a companion to Fred Stuart's Mayan/Aztec and Egyptian art guitars (Chap. 11), the Corian-on-ash and maple Celtic Telecaster is another work of breathtaking artistry and complexity. Fred Stuart and Larry Robinson designed the guitar, Stuart built it, and Robinson inlaid it with various metals, pearl, and abalone. The Celtic-motif decorative gilt was applied by hot rod painter/pinstriper Lil' Louis of San Bernardino, California.

Despite often depending on the factory for components or setup (and in the early days always depending on it for paint), John Page wanted some distance from Fender's management. Fred Stuart: "We were a bit insulated from the business side. To John's credit, he tried not to burden our minds too much with making profits. We would just build these things and put them in Fender's ballpark as far as marketing and selling them."

Dreamsville

John Page got what he wanted — at least some degree of independence — but at a price. There was grumbling

John Page describes the Custom Shop crew of the first decade as "a bunch of woodchucks, a bunch of knuckleheads having a lot of fun by being really, really skilled at what they did and pouring their hearts and souls into the quality."

in the factory about those guys over in "La-la Land" or "Dreamsville" who supposedly just hung out with rock stars, built a few guitars, never punched a time clock, basked in the lights of fawning media, goofed off a lot, and didn't have to worry about quotas or profits like everyone else. Fred Stuart: "A joke in the factory referred to us as The Lazy Club. I don't know why, but they had this image that we were just a bunch of prima donnas who didn't really do anything."

J. Black allows that any resentment on the part of the factory workers was not entirely unreasonable: "The Custom Shop guys, in our naïveté, thought we were protecting a legacy. That's not to diminish what Dan Smith and everybody else was doing, but there was a kind of naïve arrogance that permeated the shop, and that's probably why when John went to Scottsdale [site of Fender's headquarters since 1991], heads would butt. I'm sure from corporate's point of view, the attitude was, 'Hey, we're paying your salary — lighten up a little bit; be on the team.'"

If the Custom Shop crew saw themselves as the true keepers of the Fender flame, it might have been due in part to John Page's having worked so closely with Freddie Tavares. The late Mr. Tavares was Leo Fender's right-hand man when it came to design, a keenly insightful musician/engineer who is revered to this day as the patron saint of Fender R&D. (One of Page's proudest moments was when Freddie toured the shop and told John it reminded him of the atmosphere at Fender in the 1950s.) Other figures from the golden-aura 1950s and 1960s were also much admired in the shop. Michael Stevens went so far as to practice signing his initials with a number 2 pencil so as to emulate the "T.G." that appeared on so many great necks in the 1950s. "T.G." was Tadeo Gomez, a craftsman who worked on many a Fender in the vintage era.

Like J. Black, other Custom Shop veterans freely admit they contributed to workplace tensions. Greg Fessler: "We *were* a bunch of arrogant guys. We thought we were the best thing around. We had a cockiness about us. Maybe they'd be having a problem over in the factory with the necks choking out, so they'd ask me to show them how I do it. I'd spend a couple hours with the guys on the line, but they'd go right back to doing it the same way they were doing it before. Their attitude was, why should we listen to those jerks from the Custom Shop [laughs]? We were cocky kids, man. We were good, and we knew it."

Michael Stevens: "What bugged me were the complaints about the time some things took to get shipped. The factory guys called John and me 'Leisure World' because we came in at 9:00 a.m., and their first shift was there at 6:30 a.m. to 2:30 p.m. When their second shift went off, John and I had a factory full of tools to use, so factory access for us began at 10:30 p.m. Many, many nights I left for home at 2:00 a.m."

From John Page's point of view, the shop's independence and quirkiness never reflected a hesitancy to contribute to the larger organization. Quite the opposite. He reported in Fender's Summer 1998 *Frontline*: "What we wanted to do all along was to pass on things we learned from dealing with artists and professionals. You are seeing products built in the Corona factory and even in Mexico that only the Custom Shop offered a few years ago ... a lot of what gets passed on are subtle details like peghead shapes, fret sizes, certain finishes and hardware specs." "Rolling" the edges of fingerboards was another example.

Scott Buehl: "We were working all the time, sometimes all night, maybe sleep for three or four hours. It was disorganized, creative, everything growing so fast. It was great, totally crazy, just wonderful."

Merry pranksters

Given the shortcomings in interdepartmental communication, it's not surprising that negative stereotypes took root in all three corners — the Custom Shop, the factory, and marketing. Fred Stuart: "Part of this was understandable. One thing, we built our own bodies some of the time, but other times we got them from the factory, sometimes in a clandestine sort of way [laughs]. Let's just say the factory guys weren't always sure where the bodies went. We were robbing Peter to pay Paul, so to speak."

Scott Buehl: "Sometimes we'd go over there and throw a bunch of necks on the fret slotter or do some other operation. We used to go at night — Page had keys — and we'd take whatever we needed. We went on raiding parties, taking bridges, pickups, tuners. I don't think it was that big a deal because I don't think people were keeping track of things all that closely back then. We were just nickel and diming them. After we took stuff, we'd leave little presents for them or maybe pull a few pranks."

Art Esparza: "It's not like they didn't know about it. We were leaving little notes and stuff, like — hey, we took some of your strap button screws — and we would follow up with the paperwork the next day. We would do that because we did not have access to warehouse storage, but we did have access to production. It's not like we were

Tres amigos: Scott Grant, Ralph Esposito, and Steve Boulanger.

messing up their production or anything, because our numbers were so small compared to the factory."

Todd Krause suggests that the shop's semi-independent status likely contributed to misunderstandings. Many factory workers simply didn't know what went on in the shop. "From the factory's point of view, maybe it looked like we were pampered. You know — 'That ain't workin', get your money for nothin' and your chicks for free.' But I have to say, just about everybody we promoted from the factory line over to the Custom Shop had a rude awakening when they got here, because it was like, 'No, you can't do it like that; it has to be perfect.' Everything had to be more precise, and you really had to have specific knowledge about each and every detail on every model. Some of the people who were transferred to the shop begged to be sent back because of the standards, stress levels, and long hours over here."

Biggest hair ever: Greg Fessler polishes up a gleaming gold Thinline Tele for a lucky customer.

Light up the stogies, pop the champagne

Custom Shop workers got tired of being the target of resentment, so on occasion they would taunt the factory employees and throw it back in their faces with a bit of guerilla theater. Ralph Esposito: "Everybody thought we were on easy street, so we would play the role sometimes, go outside in Hawaiian shirts and sit on chairs. We'd drink Martinelli's sparkling drinks in these little plastic martini glasses so it looked like champagne. We'd be sitting out there puffing on cigars and drinking while the first shift was getting off work. As they were driving away, we'd raise our glasses and wave goodbye. Of course, what they didn't know was that after they left we would be working there until 10 o'clock or midnight."

Art Esparza: "A lot of it was misinterpretation. We *deserved* our barbecues and our Custom Shop parties, because we were busting ass. The factory guys would see us standing around outside eating lunch or something, and maybe they would think we were just goofing off, but what they didn't know was that some of us didn't even have to be there at that time. It was our day off, but we were still coming around because we had a deadline. It was pure dedication. Overtime? Hell, yes! I spent the night there sometimes. And not just me — Fred, John, people would sleep in their cars in the parking lot for a few hours instead of going home and then come back in and work some more. Everyone had the same mentality — whatever it takes, that's what we'll do to get the job done."

When asked if some sort of pirate mentality permeated the shop, Ralph Esposito exclaims: "Pirates! Exactly! And we couldn't be touched. That's what they thought. The factory guys thought we could do anything we wanted, and that was part of the animosity within the organization."

Your atmosphere is different from our own

The differences in mission and mindset in the Custom Shop and factory also produced dissimilar working environments. Instead of performing their tasks according to timetables and schedules, through the early and mid 1990s the shop guys would just show up and do whatever John Page thought they should do that day. Fred Stuart: "John wanted self-initiative kinds of people who didn't need marching orders at every step. He wanted us to know what we needed to do, just take care of business. If he thought something was out of order he would let us know, but otherwise we had a lot of freedom."

Ralph Esposito: "This shop was the happening place. Part of it was because artists loved coming here. When they went to other companies they would be met by some guy in a suit, a marketing guy or a sales rep or something. But an artist would visit here, and here's John Page in his shorts [laughs]. We had a lot of camaraderie going on. It was great to be here. Nobody was in a suit, and artists appreciated that. Elsewhere it was very stuffed-shirt, but here they would just hang out. These guys loved to watch us work and learn how to make guitars because we were just a bunch of ragtag guys."

Pride in every guitar

It didn't take long for the Custom Shop workers to forge bonds among themselves based on their admiration for each other's skills and creativity, their renegade/pirates reputation, and the realization that they would all sink or swim together. Fred Stuart: "A lot of the guitars we were building were survival-mechanism instruments. Remember, one of Page's jobs was simply to fight for our existence. We were scraping and scrambling all the time, just to keep it going."

Pamelina H.: "John was very good at recognizing talent, bringing people together, and turning them loose. You had Dru WhiteFeather doing leather work and George Amicay doing the wood carving, and John and these other builders were in there making great guitars, and we all worked together. John collected all this talent and just let us go. It was a golden time, lots of freedom and creativity."

For some of the Custom Shop workers, any reputation as problem employees or outsiders was a badge of honor. Greg Fessler: "John used to call us his vermin, and that's what we were — the vermin [laughs]. [Author's note: The shop's softball team was the Ver-Men.] And we loved that guy. I would do anything for him. There were bad times as well as good ones, and plenty of times we were all worried whether we would have a job the next month, times when we didn't even know if the shop would stay open. Sometimes John didn't have money in the budget to pay us overtime. He would say, 'Look, we need to get this done but I can't pay you; I'll make it up to you somehow.' That's how dicey it all was, but you know what? It was one of the best times in my life, and we worked our butts off for that guy. He was the most inspirational leader I ever worked for and one of the guys I admire most who I've ever met in my life." JD Dworkow: "John was more than a boss. He was like a father figure, almost. I think a lot of their creativity and success came from the guys trying to please him, to live up to the standards he set."

During the first three weeks of the monthly production cycle, workers would tend to their specialties, but during "hell week," as it was called, as deadlines loomed, builders stepped up to do whatever was necessary to complete the shop's assignments, just as Page and Stevens had done when it was only the two of them back on Pomona Road. Ralph Esposito: "We did whatever had to be done. Sure, I'll do the pickguards, I'll wind the pickups, and when I'm done I'll help the other guys. What 'making the month' really meant was that we had to produce enough product to pay for our overhead and cover our costs, and all of us were aware that staying in business was at stake. If we got a call at home because they needed us for something, we would drop what we were doing and come in, no questions asked. We'd stay till two o'clock in the morning without even questioning it.

"We didn't just pitch in on the work. We all contributed ideas, too. We were a small group, and we would synergize things and make plans and figure out how we were going to pull something off. Each of us was hired for a certain talent that we could bring from our past industries. We all had input so we felt a part of the end result. We all took pride in every guitar."

Clockwise from above: A poster for one of the many Custom Shop jam session/potlucks ("Bring your guitar or bass"). Steve Boulanger, John Page, and Scott Grant twist and shout. A man who knows his way around a Telecaster, Fred Stuart. John Page cuts up.

Family ties

Membership in the Custom Shop club spilled over into the workers' private lives. Pamelina H.: "We recognized we had a special place to work in, and we felt lucky to be working for John and to have each other's talents and each other's company. We had Custom Shop picnics, softball games — throw some meat on the grill, meet the girlfriends and the wives and husbands, the kids. You know — family." (Dan Smith: "Bill Schultz always approved of this. He carried this on for all of Fender's employees. We would have a yearly picnic and a gala Christmas party, and Halloween was always a workday costume party. That was all part of the tradition — bowling teams, lunches, and all that. As the company grew it became tougher to do, but in those early days it really felt like family.")

Ralph Esposito: "Tommy Emmanuel — that project was a good example. He had impressed us so much. He came to the shop and played for us. We all got together and made him an early-'60s Tele, but that wasn't the end of it. We went to his show, everybody. We spent the night in L.A., going out afterwards. This was how we did things — as a group. We wouldn't just work with an artist; we would hang out with that person, get to know them.

"The Catalina Blues Festival was another example. It strengthened and cultivated artist relations, always an integral part of the operation. John and Pamelina and a couple others would get together and design a concept for the guitar we made for the raffle or auction or whatever they did, but Custom Shop people also pretty much ran the whole thing — sound, lighting rigs, we even did security. We would get there on a Tuesday or a Wednesday afternoon and meet the rigging guys, get everything unloaded. We'd set up all the lighting, all the P.A., spotlights, everything, working from dawn till dusk. It was a lot of fun but a lot of work, too. We did everything as a team."

Art Esparza: "At first, we didn't even clock in. There was no point, because we were all working so much overtime anyway. We did have to start keeping track because we grew so fast, but even when the time clock came in, people still hung out at the shop. In the off hours people would work on their own projects or just come in to learn, because we were all very hungry to learn procedures, to get better and better. It was the coolest place to be. I remember John English making breakfast for everybody right there in the shop, which was part of the family atmosphere."

J. Black (shown here with the Schultz-o-Caster proto, serial no. 000) helped to improve relations with the main factory. Dan Smith: "He treated those guys in the plant with respect. To me, J. Black was responsible for turning the shop around in the mid '90s."

Tommy Emmanuel picks up his new guitar. Ralph Esposito: "We made him an early-'60s Tele, but that wasn't the end of it. We went to his show, everybody. We spent the night in L.A., going out afterwards. This was how we did things — as a group."

Cooling off

J. Black had arrived in the summer of 1989. Fred Stuart credits him as being just what the Custom Shop needed, not only because of his expertise and enviable clientele but also because of his personable demeanor. Fred Stuart: "He might take a body over to the factory with some special requirements and coordinate all that, and he had a great rapport with the guys over there, which helped overcome that 'Lazy Club' image. He built good relations. He could get the factory guys to do a lot of stuff for him, whereas I might be working on a 12-string acoustic Tele [laughs], and they'd just look at me like I was off my rocker or something."

From Black's own point of view, relations between the shop and the factory crew started to improve in 1989 and 1990. After all, Scott Buehl, Fred Stuart, Ralph Esposito, and several other shop workers had all come over from the factory. They were steeped in Fender factory culture and had good friends there. Black found everyone in R&D and the metal shop to be particularly helpful. "In the metal shop it was, 'What can we do for you? How soon do you need it?' It was carte-blanche, total cooperation. So each department had a little different relationship with the Custom Shop."

Partners working every which way

Dan Smith explains that despite Fender's internal organizational chart, Mike Stevens and John Page didn't actually report to him, not directly anyway: "To tell you the truth, I think Bill [Schultz] always wanted the Custom Shop to report directly to him. Well, as the company got bigger, that became impossible. It's hard to keep track of it all, because Mike and then John officially reported to several people over the years, and so did I. What's more important is this: Bruce Bolen, Mike Stevens, John Page, and I all worked together."

Despite some tensions between workers in the shop and factory, veteran Custom Shop builders agree that the shop never could have survived without production help from the craftspeople over on the main line. "When I got there," says J. Black, "most of the tooling was still over in the other factory. I introduced myself to the night shift guys over there. They taught me how to use [fret] slotters and how to do truss rod slots. Don't kid yourself — if it weren't for manufacturing, we could not have built one-offs." For many Custom Shop guitars, "We would start them and end them in the shop," says John Page, "and in between, they would work on bodies and necks over in the factory."

Another partner was R&D. In fact, there were so many shared activities and so much information going back and forth between R&D and the Custom Shop that several veterans remember the two departments almost as a single entity. George Blanda describes the division as a "dotted line," with plenty of overlap. In fact, Blanda was sometimes pictured in Fender literature as a member of the Custom Shop crew and was described in the announcement of the Muddy Waters Tribute Telecaster as "the Custom Shop R&D man." He recalls: "Unofficially, I was considered a Custom Shop person, even though on the org chart I was in

R&D. I did some CNC work for the shop, and we often collaborated to build stuff for the NAMM shows. Like I helped Fred Stuart figure out the scale length for his Bajo Sexto Tele, which took about ten minutes of my time, not any big deal — just helping out wherever needed. I worked on the first 5-string basses; John and I were building the necks ourselves, but they were factory basses, not Custom Shop basses, so the cross-pollination went every which way."

Alan Hamel and Fred Stuart pick and grin with a custom guitar/6-string bass doubleneck they built for Danny Gatton.

Every which way, indeed. Many Custom Shop projects were viewed as potential factory runs. John Page: "Once we got to the point where it looked like the market needed a thousand guitars a year of some model, or if Fender needed something in a different price range, we always knew that any given project might be handed over to the factory."

One example: The first-generation SRV Strat was never intended to be a Custom Shop item, and yet it was initiated by the Custom Shop's Larry Brooks. Another: The factory's first Blackie Strat was developed by J. Black. He built prototypes in 1990, met with Eric Clapton and guitar tech Lee Dickson, and provided the specs for the factory version. In fact, as noted in Chapter 10, *all* of the factory's early artist models were developed in the Custom Shop.

When asked if the Blackie project was typical of the way the shop interacted with other departments, Black says that it was just one kind of cooperation. There was no single system or structure. "Bill Schultz's vision was to use all of Fender's resources in whatever manner got the job done," he explains. "I carried out tasks requested by John Page, Kurt Hemrich, Dan Smith, and others. The Blackie thing was typical of just one way management used their various facilities." J. Black also worked on the Jeff Beck and Richie Sambora projects with R&D, but as he points out, many projects didn't include the Custom Shop at all. "Marketing would just find the best way to initiate projects, whether it was through AR [Artist Relations], engineering, R&D, the Custom Shop, Mexico manufacturing — whatever the particular project required. Nothing happened in a vacuum. We were a community that worked in tandem."

Good times and madness in the monster garage

George Blanda recalls the early days with fondness: "All in all, that whole early period was a special time. It was hectic and wild, with a lot of creative energy flying around, a lot of hard work, a lot of excitement and a great camaraderie. The factory, the Custom Shop, and R&D — we all communicated a lot, supported each other, and worked together. There were many, many 80-hour weeks leading up to NAMM, trying to get guitars finished. It was sort of like *Monster Garage*, that TV show. A lot of times, in order to make their assigned production, they'd be working crazy hours. But it was a stimulating time. Everybody had a bunch of good ideas, and everything flowed back and forth very easily. It was a collaborative atmosphere, very cooperative and fun. Eventually everything became more compartmentalized, which was necessary and inevitable."

Scott Buehl: "We were working all the time, sometimes all night, maybe sleep for three or four hours, just to make sure we were worth our while to the company. We had to prove our worth and justify ourselves. It was disorganized, creative, everything growing so fast. It was great, totally crazy, just wonderful. We had to blow off some steam sometimes, and there were a lot of pranks just to relieve some of the tension. I used to sleep in a hammock up high in the pallet racks where nobody could paint my nails and stuff. It was hardcore. You know these reality shows they have on TV? You couldn't even put our stuff on TV [laughs]. It was brutal, just great. We played jokes on guys and had nicknames for everybody and drove some of them crazy."

Scott Grant: "People were waving at my truck as I drove by, and for a while I couldn't figure out what was going on. Finally I checked the back of it, and Scott Buehl had put a bumper sticker on there. You can't print what it said. I got him back, though. I swiped his car keys and dumped the kitchen garbage in his trunk. I don't think he noticed it until it *really* began to stink."

John Suhr: "One time I shot a paper clip or something at Mike Ponce, no big deal, but the next morning I came in and every single one of my tools was glued down to my bench — and that was mild."

Gene Baker: "These guys were jokers extraordinaire, constantly pulling pranks on different people, especially new guys. New guys had to go through a bit of an initiation phase, so there were all sorts of stunts going on. John Page was usually at the heart of it."

> "Sometimes John would say, 'Look, we need to get this done but I can't pay you; I'll make it up to you somehow.' That's how dicey it all was, but you know what? It was one of the best times in my life."
>
> — Greg Fessler

Alex Perez: "Some of it was goofy stuff — paper clip fights, rubber band fights, anything to ease the tension, because there was a *lot* of tension. Sometimes they would take a new guy and dress him up in a bunny suit [a white painter's outfit] and make him walk to the other building with a pallet jack, one of those wheeled platforms with a handle on it. They would send him over there with some ridiculous assignment and the factory guys would go, 'What are you *talking* about?'"

Art Esparza: "Around the corner was a turkey sandwich place. One new guy was told to put on a white paint suit with the helmet and everything, and drag a pallet jack all the way over there to the sandwich place to pick up an order. When he came back the whole shop was standing out front, just laughing, and he was so embarrassed."

Scott Grant: "Page really got into rubber bands. You could not walk through that shop without being hit in the head with a rubber band."

Scott Buehl: "We would glue stuff down, glue people to the floor. Big Steve Olson was working at his bench one time. Scott Grant walks up behind him and squirts a bunch of Super Glue around the heel of each boot and then sprays it with accelerator. It takes about two or three seconds to set. Steve sets his guitar down and we're all just watching, and he starts to fall backwards. He caught himself and tried to move his feet. He said, *"Somebody glued my boots down!"* I'll never forget seeing Scott on the floor behind Steve with a hammer and a chisel trying to get his shoes off the floor without destroying them. This kind of stuff was constant. It was a huge part of the shop, the humor and the pranks."

Todd Krause: "When I was the new guy back in '91, I was on the receiving end of some pranks. They were so tough I really wondered if I wanted to stick around. But after you're here for a few years, you just get warped and get used to the madness."

Ralph Esposito: "There were lots of antics and messing with people. There was so much camaraderie it was unbelievable. Some nights we all spent the night here. Scott would be sleeping in his hammock, someone's sacked out in Page's office, piles of pizza boxes all over."

John Page: "Yeah, it was crazy, I'm telling you. In the early days we built the guitars, no sleep sometimes, Fred would get them set up, we'd pile the stuff into this funky '65 Volkswagen van — floor to ceiling packed with guitar cases — and the van didn't have a starter, so we had to push-start it and then drive it to the warehouse in Brea. We did everything, including the packing, the labeling, and even the delivery. We would get there at the last minute of the last hour on the last Friday of the month to deliver these things. It was hilarious."

Alpha woodchuck John Page. Greg Fessler said of him: "We worked our butts off for that guy. He was the most inspirational leader I ever worked for."

Greg Fessler: "With all the pranks and stuff, it's amazing we got anything done. What an inspirational time that was, so much fun. We were all making six bucks an hour, and we didn't care. It was great. It was a golden era. We all have unbelievably fond memories of those years."

Art Esparza: "I grew up there. We all thought it would last forever."

"Mike Eldred *is* the Custom Shop, period. This is his soul, his heart, his friends, his passion." — Richard McDonald

CHAPTER TWENTY-ONE

21

A New Vision

Mike Eldred Takes the Reins

New digs

Fender broke ground on a new 165,000 square foot production facility in September 1997 and made the move late the following year. Located on a 19-acre site not far from Pomona Road, the new plant, on Cessna Circle, housed both the main factory and the Custom Shop. It featured state-of-the-art environmental controls and other advantages. While putting the shop and factory under one roof saved money and, from Fender's point of view, reduced inefficiencies, some of the Custom Shop people thought the disadvantages outweighed the advantages. For one thing, the shop's floor space was drastically reduced. For another, some thought sharing production space with manufacturing would diminish the exclusivity of the shop and the independence of its builders.

Transitions

In the late 1990s the supervision of day-to-day Custom Shop production passed from John Page to Mike Eldred. The transition was, at times, stressful. Part of it had to do with attitudes and perceptions. For starters, let's reconsider this whole pirates thing.

The triumph of the underdog is one of the most compelling narratives of the American saga, recurring throughout literature and pop culture in many forms — the spunky, blue-collar misfits who kick butt on the hockey rink or baseball diamond against the rich kids with their fancy gear and drill-sergeant coach, the folksy country lawyer who takes on a battery of city-slicker attorneys and makes them look like chumps in the courtroom, and countless more. Highfalutin book-learnin' is all well and good, but it's intuition and grit that inspires Americans. Our heroes are not company men (and they're anything but *corporate*). They live by their wits, don't cotton to bosses, make their own rules. They don't need no stinking badges.

The Custom Shop workers from the first decade sometimes saw themselves in a similar mold. They knew they couldn't have survived without the help of their factory counterparts, but still, as we've seen, most look back with affection to their years as members of a feisty gang of talented pranksters who pushed their luck and on occasion bucked the system. Part of that perception springs from actual experience. Part of it may spring from the seductive

In 1998, the move to the vast new facility entailed a major reorganization of the Custom Shop.

311 Cessna Circle.

tendency to drape a golden romantic aura around early experiences of several kinds, around youth itself.

JD Dworkow refers to the Custom Shop's early days as "the ultimate fun zone for guitar heads, the Wild West." From management's point of view, however, the whole ragtag misfit thing was basically a crock of cluelessness. Romanticized recollections are skewed, according to this view, depending as they do on unfounded perceptions of Fender "corporate." Dan Smith: "That word 'corporate' is misleading in the first place. It suggests some big impersonal company [and] bosses who are out of touch. If you want to apply it to CBS Fender in the 1970s, that's one thing, but it didn't apply to us at all. Bill Schultz was never insulated." Bruce Bolen: "The early period of the shop was also the early period of the new Fender. Being considered 'corporate' makes me uneasy. There was no sense of a corporation in those early days. The 'corporation' was one guy, Bill Schultz. Most of the decisions were basically Bill's. Dan and I had to make those decisions work."

Point taken. When the Custom Shop was founded in early 1987, the post-buyout Fender company was not even two years old. Like the Custom Shop, Fender itself was small, scrappy, and struggling. Like John Page, Michael Stevens, and their merry band of talented rascals, several of the management guys were casual in their dress (Ritchie Fliegler once described Fender as a place where a business suit is a Halloween costume), friendly in their demeanors, serious in their commitments, and deep in their love of all things Fender. If the Custom Shop guys and their counterparts in sales and marketing had so much in common, and if most of them liked and respected each other, which by all accounts they did, why are their assessments and memories of events so irreconcilable? As it turns out, and as John Page himself concedes, some of the very qualities that endeared him to his workers drove his friends in sales and marketing crazy.

Version one of the Page/Eldred transition story goes like this: John Page was a brilliant guy who respected the uniqueness and talents of his workers and encouraged their creativity. He wanted the Custom Shop to operate apart from Fender so the builders could craft the best possible guitars, maintain the highest standards, foster camaraderie, and garner loads of positive media attention, all of which would benefit Fender as a whole. But "corporate" (there's that word again) brought in a My Way Or The Highway manager to enforce a new order. Anybody who didn't like it was shown the door.

Version two: John Page was in all respects the brilliant, dedicated guy described above, but if the workers were to continue to take home paychecks, something had to change, and Page was not the one to change it. The new man, Mike Eldred, was actually a lot like his predecessor in several respects. He loved rock and roll and hot rods, was a hell of a guitar player, and had been building guitars since his late teens. He was tasked with putting into effect the new strategy devised by management, which included cleaning up several messes in the Custom Shop. Eldred and his wife were starting a family. He needed a job, something more stable than his previous gig as a rock and roll guitarist. He never wanted to be the boss, but that's the job they handed him.

Employees disagreed about whether the move to Cessna Circle would benefit the Custom Shop. The shop's total floor space was diminished, although its various production areas were now organized under one roof.

In the new plant on Cessna Circle, guitar necks and bass necks await tuner and fret installation.

The reluctant guardian

Mike Eldred started building guitars as a teenager and was Grover Jackson's first hire at Charvel. "I think it was 1979," he recalls, "and Grover took me under his wing and taught me a lot." After Charvel, Mike worked at a violin repair shop in Long Beach and spent another eight or nine years at Yamaha before joining Fender's Custom Shop crew on March 6, 1996, not long before Page's frustration with Fender began to intensify. (The shop was still located on Enterprise Court; it would soon be moving to the new location at 311 Cessna Circle, also in Corona.)

During his years at Yamaha the longtime guitarist recorded three albums with former Stray Cats bassist Lee Rocker. "After being laid off at Yamaha, I worked exclusively in the band for about a year," Mike explains. "But I didn't want to play music on the road for a living. I wanted to stay home with my family, so I left the band and started looking for a job. I didn't want to be in the MI [musical instrument] industry, either. I wanted to get into a different career path that would be better for my family."

But Mike's destiny would take him to Fender, where he would become to the Custom Shop's second decade what John Page had been to its first. J. Black, in 2009: "I see the Custom Shop as John's era from 1987 to 1997 or so, and the Mike Eldred era roughly from 1997 to the present. Each had his own decade or so of influence." Senior Vice President Richard McDonald worked with both men. He explains: "No question, the Custom Shop rests on Mike's shoulders, as it did on John's. Mike is the man with the vision. I just try to keep people out of his way. I've been a huge supporter of Mike's and have fought many a battle for him. Every single one I would do again — times ten — to keep him in the chair and empowered. Mike Eldred *is* the Custom Shop, period. Fender is so fortunate to have him as the shop's guardian. This is his soul, his heart, his friends, his passion. He is never distracted from that vision, never compromised. To quote Mike, 'If it was easy, it wouldn't be so cool.'"

Dan Smith's perspective

Regarding the Page/Eldred transition, no one has deeper insights than Dan Smith. He was inducted into Fender's Hall Of Fame in 2008 (previous inductees have included Leo Fender, Don Randall, and Freddie Tavares). The induction tribute proclaimed: "In Dan's twenty five years at Fender, he played a pivotal role in almost every department, leaving an imprint on virtually every instrument . . . . His influence, contributions and vision were an integral part of the music industry's greatest comeback." Mike Lewis: "Dan Smith had more to do with all the groovy stuff that happened at Fender than anybody on earth. If it weren't for him, who knows where'd we be? He is part of the DNA of Fender." Dan retired in August 2006.

Former Senior Vice President Ritchie Fliegler: "Bill Schultz and Dan had a very special relationship that went beyond that which Bill had with anyone else. He confided in him things he wouldn't to anyone else. He praised Dan behind his back in a way that he never did in person. That was Bill's way; we all understood that. Dan was not only Bill's confidant and occasional drinking partner, there was also a very special Hell that Schultz reserved only for him. Dan was the innermost person in the innermost circle. For years he was the *only* guitar guy in management. One man's opinion here — as brilliant as any of the other cast of characters may or may not have been, their brilliance would never have shone if they didn't have actual guitars to sell, manufacture, or market. And without Dan, there were no guitars, *period*." With that background, and as supervisor to both John Page and Mike Eldred, Dan Smith is uniquely qualified to lend perspective to accounts of the Page/Eldred transition.

The following comments address the Custom Shop's internal operation in the late 1990s. They are excerpted from interviews with Mike Eldred and Dan Smith conducted in 2009. Their insights are interspersed with brief observations from John Page, Dennis Galuszka, Chris Fleming, Greg Fessler, Scott Grant, Richard McDonald, and Todd Krause. Italic questions and comments are the author's.

What was your perspective of the relationship between the Custom Shop and Fender?

Dan: Fender wasn't the "parent" organization; the shop was one department, like sales or marketing. I was right in the middle, the conduit between the shop and Bill Schultz, so I heard all about it going both ways. Sometimes the shop guys were mad at me because I was telling them what Bill had mandated, and going the other way I had Bill screaming at me because the shop wasn't pulling its weight.

What's wrong with fostering the mentality of the Custom Shop as an independent entity with its own culture and standards?

Dan: I actually supported that. I love and respect John Page. He's one of the most talented people I've ever met, and he was a hard worker with many good ideas. He fought for that Custom Shop, but those guys were out there on their own little island doing their own thing. They were great builders. They were artists and should be treated as artists, but John had insulated all these talented guys from reality, and the reality was, the place had to make money. We were a business, and no one has to apologize for that. You have to meet a payroll. You have to pay the bills. The demand for the product kept growing — the guitars were great, and no one disputes that — but the shop couldn't meet its obligations. Something had to give.

The twin identities of the Custom Shop — showcase and profit center — seemed to be at odds for years.

Dennis Galuszka: When I got hired, Dan Smith explained that the Custom Shop is sort of like a racing program for a car company. It puts the company in the forefront, in the public eye, but it's not necessarily to make money. I arrived in 1999, so even that late they were still talking about the shop as a sort of showcase.

Chris Fleming: The culture was in transition when I arrived in 2000. Mike Eldred was trying to standardize things and get it to function a little more professionally. In the early days the Custom Shop was sort of its own island, but it got to the point where it needed to mature, which necessitated having more structure. Previously the numbers were small and it wasn't making money, so the shop was more of a halo effect for the whole company.

Greg Fessler: If we had an idea for something really cool, John gave us an unbelievable amount of freedom to just go ahead and build it and not worry about selling it. Just be creative and enjoy your work; get it out there so everybody can see what we can do. We always sold everything we had. Now we're a big corporation, no longer small and struggling, so it's a little different but still fun.

Do you think some of the Custom Shop folks thought there was an advantage to the distance between the shop and

Fred Stuart's Custom Shop career extended into the early phases of the new facility. Here he proudly displays one of his doublenecks, in this case a 12/6 Telecaster no doubt capable of unleashing torrents of righteous twang.

Fender management?
Mike: I never took that us vs. them approach. I *wanted* the factory to know what we were doing. Besides, the "corporate" thing — that was really just two guys, Bill and Kurt.

You didn't see Fender as this colossal faceless entity?
Mike: Not at all. It was mainly those two guys. They weren't guitar builders, so they needed us to let them know what we were up to. I'm just not one of those people who builds those sorts of barriers. The factory was a huge *asset*. Part of the reason Bill Schultz came up with a Custom Shop in the first place was to *help* the factory. That is absolutely part of my responsibility, and I totally grab onto that. Some of the guys had that attitude of — that's them, and we're us. But how does that attitude serve the 15-year-old kid who can't afford a Custom Shop guitar? Can't the shop play a role in serving that customer, too?

What's an example?
Mike: Look at the Road Worn Fenders [introduced in 2009], which came right out of the Custom Shop Relic project, descended from it. That's beauty, man. That's the synergy that was part of Bill Schultz's original vision and also in my opinion part of the original design from Leo Fender, the idea that everybody works together.

Richard McDonald: Mike and I did not approve the Road Worn idea for years because we didn't want to dismantle what the Custom Shop had done, but we can do it right, and this is a good example of a Custom Shop process that has come down to the production line. These are mid price-point Fenders, imports. The relicing that these guys started in the Custom Shop has carried over to guitars that don't cost $4,000.

What's an example of the shop's independence turning out to be an obstacle?
Dan: A lack of communication is never a good thing. I had spent *months* in Japan with Fuji designing set-neck Strats and Teles for Fender. I wasn't even told about the Custom Shop Set-Necks, but I show up for the June [NAMM] show and here they are. A lot of work and effort and money had been expended by myself and by Fuji, who was our partner. Remember, Fender couldn't have survived the 1980s without them. We owed them a great deal, and now I had to go back with my tail between my legs and apologize, because the Custom Shop had their own Set-Necks. That's just one example.

Mike, one of the first things you did was to reorganize the shop's neck department.
I sat with John and discussed the way that whole department was laid out. It wasn't as organized as it could have been, so I asked if I could move some stuff around. He said yes, so I came in the next week and started tearing walls down. I jumped right in on it.

You were the new guy, and you were already tearing down walls?
Mike: I started working on necks, but very early on we were talking about me becoming the supervisor. There were some things going on out there on the floor that needed to be reeled in a little bit. Some decisions had to be made, and they were tough ones. Fender wanted a supervisor to take care of that sort of thing, which made it hard for me as the new guy, as you can imagine. I think I started at something like eight bucks an hour, and my title was just Custom Shop worker. My attitude was, bring me up [to supervisor] if you want to. John didn't want to be the tough guy, and I didn't either, but my wife had just had a kid. I needed a job, so I said, tell me what you want and I'll do it.

John Page: No, I didn't need a bad guy. I had laid guys off, fought battles with Kurt and Bill, tooth and nail, all the time. I made lots of tough decisions. I'd put it this way: I saw Mike as the right guy to take over when it became clear in late 1997 and 1998 that Bill and Kurt wanted the shop to morph with the factory. I needed someone who had more of that attitude.

Dan: John was like a father figure to a lot of those guys he hired. Some of them were real projects in the personality department, and he turned them not only into first-class builders but first-class people. But sometimes in those situations people take advantage of you. That makes it hard to do what needs to be done. Fender needed someone who could do what had to be done to keep the shop from going under.

In this photo from 2004, Master Builder John English checks an instrument in his workshop. A Fender veteran since 1970, he passed away at age 57 in 2007. His guitars remain highly prized.

MOE'S TAVERN
Fender

Left: Alongside photos and other mementos, prototypes of the Jeff Beck Tribute Esquire, the Rory Gallagher Tribute Strat, and the SRV Number One Strat all reside in the place where they were created, John Cruz's work space at Cessna Circle. Cruz calls the SRV project "probably the highlight of my career at Fender."

Right: Posing this '68 Heavy Relic Strat with another high-performance machine was one of the countless examples of how under Mike Eldred's direction the shop expanded its long association with car culture.

Was there really a danger that the shop might fold?
Dan: Absolutely. Look, Bill Schultz was an elderly guy. He had lived through the Great Depression, his friends had invested in the company, and there was a real question about whether he could ever pay them back. It ate at him. He didn't sleep much. He would look at the figures from the Custom Shop, and believe me, he had every reason to be worried. We were living on the edge. Many days we didn't know if we were going to make payroll. And this was not all John's fault. Part of it was simply because the Custom Shop went way beyond what it was originally intended to be. By the late '90s the shop was doing higher numbers in annual sales than some entire companies who were Fender's competitors were doing.

Mike, after you had been there for a year or two, was there a general recognition that you were assuming more supervisory capacities?
John was swamped with bureaucratic things like marketing, paperwork, and personnel, and he was getting less involved with day-to-day stuff. He became more interested in the Fender Museum, and eventually he took that over [John Page left the shop in November, 1998]. Maria Orduño, Scott Grant, and myself were working together to organize day-to-day production, to make sure we had met our obligations at the end of the month.

So at least unofficially you were a supervisor, or a co-supervisor. What was it like, your new role?
It was tough. I got a note from John one time, and I still have it. It says, come see me first thing tomorrow morning so I can kick your ass.

John Page: I don't doubt it. It sounds very much like me.

Mike: I don't remember why he sent it, probably something to do with wanting more production. The whole Custom Shop thing was lumped into one ball, and if the Master Builders didn't get their guitars out, it made that ball deflate. The non-Master Built stuff — the bigger runs and so on — was pulling its weight, but John would lean on us about production when we were having some problems with some of the builders getting stuff done.

Todd Krause: The workloads weren't evenly distributed. Somebody like J. Black worked his *butt* off — right next to a couple guys who did very little. They developed a way of monitoring and tracking your hours and productivity. They didn't want to tell us what to do; they just wanted to know. If the answer was, well, I'm out there researching materials for this guitar I'm about to make, their attitude was, that's fine — we just want to know, that's all. Some people were not used to the idea of, hey, you want to know what I'm doing? You're going to look over my shoulder? There was resistance, but my feeling was, if you're not doing anything illegal, what have you got to worry about? Mike Eldred succeeded. Things improved, and the workloads were more evenly distributed. Fender's point of view was legitimate. All Fender wanted was an honest day's work for an honest day's pay.

When John moved over to the museum, was that a clean break? Did the day come when he just said, I'm gone?

Mike: There was a long overlap, but the day came when it was just — I'm gone, clean break. It was right about the time we moved to Cessna, so there was a whole lot of stuff going on. Dan and I were now running the shop, John had left, and we were moving into a new factory all pretty much at the same time.

So that period was a watershed.
Mike: It was major.

Was there ever a day when a formal announcement was made: From now on Mike is going to be the supervisor?
Mike: Not until I'd been there a couple years. To be honest with you, I didn't want to be the supervisor. I didn't want to be that guy. I just wanted to go to work and make a difference and help. I never wanted to be the boss. I *still* don't want to be the boss. I'm a team guy. My attitude was, let's get somebody else to be that guy. But there was really nobody else being that guy. Fender needed a supervisor. So I'm doing all this stuff, and John is further and further out of it, and finally he went to Kurt and Bill and said, I want out, I want to do the museum. We had a lot of meetings, and then Kurt came in and made an announcement that I was going to run the Custom Shop with Dan Smith.

When Herbie Gastelum came to Fender, the Jaguar was still on the drawing board. Beginning in 1961, he worked alongside Leo Fender, Bill Carson, Freddie Tavares, and other key figures from the company's storied past. Like Abigail Ybarra, he is admired not only for his practically legendary work on guitars but also as a veteran who brings Fender's proudest traditions of craft and customer service into the present.

Dan, you were already running Fender R&D.
Yes, so the Custom Shop was on top of those other duties. John Page had been doing both things, but back in the end of May or first of June in 1995 I took Fender guitar R&D off of John's hands. R&D had to grow. Back when [the new] Fender started in 1985, we were only getting a few guitars out the door every day, but now, more than a decade later, the factory was doing hundreds every day. Many of us were chronically overworked, and frankly I was happy to leave Scottsdale and return to California.

How did R&D's restructuring affect the Custom Shop?
Dan: Now we would have our own model shop for guitar R&D rather than relying on the Custom Shop.

What was the division of labor between you and Mike Eldred?
Dan: Mike was responsible for day-to-day Custom Shop manufacturing, but he reported to me, and I was responsible for the entire operation: manufacturing, marketing, pricing all the products, sales, inventory, everything.

Mike: I often said to Dan, tell me what you want. Dan, being Dan Smith, would always seek out my opinion and other people's opinions. He's very inclusive, not a dictator. He knows how to encourage people, and the biggest thing about Dan Smith was the level of integrity he brought to the Custom Shop.

Integrity in what regard?
Mike: The first day they handed it to us, we sat down with the people who do the internal stuff and began going through the budget line by line. Every single item was examined. Like we had a whole bunch of plastic tuners left over from the snake-head Anniversary Tele project that we were never going to use. Tons of wood had cracks and stains; they didn't know what to do with it so they kept it on the books. The warehouse was overflowing with unusable stuff, and Dan and I went through it. It took weeks, and every day he and I would come back filthy because we were going through everything in that warehouse.

So you felt there was a lot to clean up?
Mike: Not just me. There was a lot to clean up, period, and that's not a rub on anybody. It's just what it was. Bill and Kurt wanted a better picture. They really didn't know what was going on, and that made it harder for them to do their own jobs.

John Page spoke with pride about fast-tracking projects with no drawings, no prototypes.
Dan: The final releases out of R&D were always up to standard professional practice — drawings, parts lists, costing, etc. But when Mike and I took over, one of the biggest shocks was finding out that there was almost no documentation for the Custom Shop products. For a lot of them, what you needed to build them — wiring diagrams, for example — was scribbled on scraps of paper or sometimes just part of one Master Builder's memory bank. I'd check on why a group of instruments was not shipping as promised and find out they couldn't be built because the one person who knew how they were to be wired up was out sick. This may have worked when they were shipping a few guitars a month, but by the time John left they were trying to build 20 or 30 guitars a day with upwards of 50 people. While there was some very simplified documentation, for the most part it was sketchy. That seat of the pants, "little shop that could" mentality was insufficient for the expansion that was taking place. To be fair, once they started using CNC machinery they at least had software programs for cutting out the wood components, but even today much of the product is generated off of handmade templates, and you have to have backup documentation.

Scott Grant: Everything was sort of pinwheeling out of control for a while. Mike and Dan moved me over to inventory control. Documentation and inventories were the big problem. We didn't even have computers, and didn't have access to Fender's mainframe, so everything was done pretty much by hand. There was tremendous pressure to get everything completely documented and everything assigned its own part number. Plus the inventory was lousy — we were in short supply, so the boom came down from corporate to clean stuff up.

In this work space, Mark Kendrick has crafted personal instruments for Eric Clapton, Sting, Buck Owens, Merle Haggard, Keith Richards, and many others. In his two decades with Fender, he has also mentored a new generation of apprentices and Master Builders.

The new factory may be jammed with computer-controlled fabricating machines and other high-tech production gear, but plenty of decades-old equipment from the golden age is still in use, such as these toolings for Telecaster hardware assemblies.

John Page and Dan Smith had felt for years that the shop should be more independent from the factory in terms of making bodies and necks.
Mike: Maybe people forget how much stuff John and I agreed on. I wanted to continue that, but it took time, and these things would change as the shop started making different kinds of guitars. Some of the Master Builders were making bodies, but when I arrived in '96 the bulk of the stuff was being made on the line. We would give them specs for 50 ash Tele bodies or whatever, and the line would do them. Sometimes the specs would be right, and sometimes the specs wouldn't be right.

Did you start to make more of your own necks?
Mike: Finally, yes, which took a little longer than the bodies, probably a good two years. We were able to make the bodies sooner because we bought a Haas for the Custom Shop. It's a single-head CNC machine, but you can change the heads. You can do an operation and then replace the bit and do the next operation and so on. Steve Boulanger and I would sit down with Mark Kendrick, who was very helpful. Even though Yasuhiko [Iwanade] didn't work there anymore, he helped, too, bringing in original bodies. I think Mark brought in an original '65 Strat body and Boley [Steve Boulanger] and I started mapping everything out. Boley made templates to put on the Haas. We finally had our own real accurate machine, which was a big thing for us.

Early on, what sort of shape was the tooling in?
Mike: I went out to use one of the pin routers one day, and the table was tilted. I looked underneath and there were metal shims in there to make corrections because the angle was off, which meant sometimes the angles in the cuts were off. I wanted to fix that. There was another pin router, and it had problems, too.

Why was the Haas a step forward from using pin routers?
Mike: Making a body on the pin router ain't no big deal; anybody can do it. But you make ten or twenty of those things and guess what — sometimes that pin can get bent, or sometimes the table goes crooked, and the cutters always have to be re-sharpened, and every time you do that you're taking a couple thousandths of an inch off a piece of metal. These things are going to make a difference in the cut. And when you have a dull bit you'll get all this chatter around

Spanning the generations: The first guitar player to work full-time for Fender, soft-spoken George Fullerton signed on in early 1948 and became one of the company's most admired and best loved figures. He visited with Mike Eldred and Abby Ybarra in the mid 2000s.

1951 Nocaster Relic, from 2009. Only 50 were made in Dakota Red.

the edge of the body, all these little bumps, and now you have to sand that out to compensate and correct it. So all these things needed to be tightened up.

People have built great guitars using pin routers.
Mike: Sure, but when you're working with some sizable numbers, those pin routers need a lot of maintenance, and they weren't always getting it. The Haas was a much better fit, more workable, so after a couple of years — by 1998 or so — there was a step forward in quality.

Any other changes?
Mike: I told them they had the Daphne Blue paint in the Sonic Blue can, and vice versa. They told me, no way, so I had to bring in a DuPont color chart. You had people like Mark Kendrick and J. Black and of course Fred Stuart; those guys knew that vintage stuff inside and out, but except for those few guys there wasn't a lot of vintage awareness. When I came in and started changing a lot of stuff, John gradually began to feel more comfortable with it.

What were other examples of tightening up the procedures?
Mike: We were buying paint from Spartan, out in Downey. I was living in Downey at the time and went over to their facility and was blown away by how old-school everything was. It was right out of the '50s, stuck in the '90s, and they knew their card was up. They had to either clean up or go out of business. Sherwin-Williams was there; Lawrence-McFadden was there. So we'd buy some Sonic Blue from Spartan, some Sonic Blue from Sherwin-Williams, lacquer from McFadden, all these different sources. One time we did a whole tree of guitars in Candy Apple Red. We shot them, and the next day they looked like iodine. We said, what the heck happened? And it was because they used something like gold from Sherwin-Williams, red from Spartan, and a clear coat from somebody else, so these guitars blushed out. We ended up selling them as a special run [laughs], but you see the problem?

What did you do about it?
Mike: I told John, let's get it down to one supplier. I got Fender's original color codes from DuPont. They had all

the formulas, so if you found out the formula for Sherwood Green, it would come up as a Ford Motor Company color. Nobody in the Custom Shop had done that for a long time, so we got those codes, and I had quart cans of all of the colors made up. I took these little blocks and sent a set to Spartan and a set to Lawrence-McFadden. Spartan couldn't go near it because they were going out of business, but Peter Beck, who was a salesman at Lawrence-McFadden, just nailed it. That guy is the best, and he really knows his stuff. He said, I can do all the paint, the urethane, and the lacquer. He still supplies our paint. I was able to go to John and say, okay, we've got our one paint supplier. Another thing, there were no computers in the Custom Shop.

Tracking orders, monitoring inventory — you weren't doing that sort of work on computers by the late 1990s?
Mike: No, so I brought in my old Macintosh SE from home. I still have it. Fender could see the necessity. When guys are bringing in their own stuff it's sort of a red flag — maybe we should get a computer [laughs]. I would sit down with Abby [Abigail Ybarra] and also J. [Black], who helped me immensely. We went through every pickup and documented every detail and put it all into a spreadsheet. This stuff had never been logged into computers. I used FileMaker Pro and made a book with all of the specs. Like a Texas Special Tele pickup: how many winds, what kind of wire, which magnets — everything.

What was the effect?
Mike: A higher level of consistency, so if you ordered a Texas Special you got a Texas Special and not somebody's interpretation of what that pickup might be. The whole purpose of increasing control was just to reduce the time-wasting and increase the consistency, which would be better for the guys in the shop, better for Fender, and better for the customer. That's always our goal — better for that guitar player.

This hybrid mixed features from Strats and Teles, along with exotic woods, a bridge humbucker, and gold hardware. Yuriy Shishkov built it. "I made a lot of Strats with flame maple pickguards," he says. "The tops and pickguards usually come from different pieces of wood, but I match them as closely as possible."

What were the major projects during your first couple of years?
The Set-Neck thing had come and gone by the time I got there. We would make some, but as a major catalog thing the Set-Necks were no longer our focus. The major projects included the Hendrix Monterey Strat. Except for some of the Master Built projects and one-offs, that was really the first guitar where we made our own necks. Pamelina did the painting, and we sprayed patchouli oil inside the cases.

You what?
Yeah [laughs], when you opened the case you'd get that whole experience wafting out — it *smelled* like the '60s. That was the beauty of John's vision. He would think of the whole picture, with all these aspects and how the pieces fit together. He had such a knack for that sort of thing, for making the purchase of a guitar much more than just the guitar itself. Roman Ramirez and I packed a lot of those guitars ourselves, so we would both go home at night smelling like patchouli. In my first few years we were also doing a lot of stuff for Yamano in Japan and for Arbiter over in the UK. The Relics were really starting to take off. They had not yet evolved into the Time Machine series.

How did the move to Cessna change the way the Custom Shop functions?
Before the move we had tons of square footage, which seems like a good thing, except we were spread all over the place. The new area was quite a bit smaller, inside the main factory, but we now had better control over what the heck we were building because the departments and stations and offices were all together. The communication got a lot better.

Under the direction of Mike Eldred and Richard McDonald, the shop reinvigorated its art guitars program. Dave Newman, who adorned this Western-themed guitar, was one of several collaborators.

What about the actual guitar construction?
It got better. Before, the Haas CNC was in a different building, just to give you one example. How do you get necks from there over here for assembly when it's pouring rain and there's no roof or no hallway? How do you build things consistently when one room is heated but another room isn't? So now, you could sort of see everything in one line of sight. If you had a problem in final [assembly], all you had to do was walk back down the line to the Haas and let them know the adjustments you needed. There was a unity, and it helped with integrity, quality, and consistency. Not so piecemeal.

Moving out of your own dedicated space must have diminished the shop's independence.
It was the opposite, really. We had been using some of the labor from the regular production line, but now we were self-contained. That was the biggest difference. We had our own standards, and people were working exclusively on Custom Shop products, so it really helped us to consolidate the vision. The builders could see that they had to rout things differently and sand differently and paint differently for the Custom Shop.

Hadn't that been true since the beginning?
It's a process. In theory, Custom Shop stuff was done separately from the factory. In reality, there was overlap — sometimes a lot of it — and the amount of overlap changed as time went on, and changed depending on the particular project.

Dan relinquished his Custom Shop duties on March 6, 2002. What was it like after he left?
For me, there were some dark days. Marketing was fine, but other people came in to oversee the whole production thing. There was a new influence over the shop, and they started pulling me out of the production side and having

me do more of the marketing. Some sort of split was necessary because somebody really did need to do the marketing full-time.

When you were pulled out of manufacturing, did somebody take over day-to-day management of the shop?
There were several people. It was chaotic there for a while, around 2002.

As marketing director, Mike Lewis had been working with John in the mid 1990s, right before you came on board.
Yes, and Mike understood what it was about. He totally got it. He was followed by Richard McDonald, and he was the same way. Richard and I worked very closely. When Mike was succeeded by Richard, there weren't any fundamental changes in the operation from my perspective. The attitude was just, don't overdo it; keep the numbers down so you can maintain the integrity and quality.

One of the marketing employees confided that he never wanted the Custom Shop to get as big as it did.
None of us did. That's when we had those problems with some of the new people overseeing production. Their attitude was — *up, up, up.*

Another piece by Dave Newman, who is profiled in Chap. 25. As he puts it, "What could be more Americana than Fender guitars?"

Were you ever tempted to quit?
I did quit, three times. The first time was back in my first year, 1996. I left for one week. Jackson had offered me more money anyway, and I had just about had it with the way things were going at Fender. They gave me a guitar and a farewell party and I was out the door. One week later, John called and said Kurt wants you back. So I returned, and I gave them the guitar back. They thought for sure I was going to keep it, and I said, no, I can't do that. [John Page adds: "I fought for him to come back. I went to Bill and Kurt and said, Mike is the guy I think I should hand it over to when I leave."]

Why did you quit the second time?
Problems with upper management. I was really frustrated and just didn't want to put up with it anymore. They basically talked me out of it. The third time, the problems had to do with a production person. They talked me out of it again.

Did it get better?
Oh, yes, much better.

What happened?
Dan Smith. He had that level of integrity I was talking about. He calmed me down and showed faith in my judgment. It was a combination of Dan, Richard McDonald, and Ritchie Fliegler. Richard and Ritchie understood the Custom Shop deeply and completely. They knew what it was, and what it could be, and what it was supposed to be. Richard backed me up a hundred percent. He said, look, Mike is the guy; we should listen to what he's saying and value what he's doing. Let's give him some freedom and see what happens. Give him the ball and let him run.

How did your job change when you relocated from the factory in Corona to Fender headquarters in Scottsdale?
My title changed to Director of Marketing, Custom Shop. Several people have dealt with the manufacturing side since I left Corona. I make lots of trips back to the factory to keep in close contact with everyone.

Why did you move in the first place?
Around early or mid 2006, Richard McDonald told me I should think about moving to Arizona, even though the shop was in California. He didn't want my influence to pull

out of the Custom Shop in terms of day-to-day operation, but the bigger picture was, he knew it would be a better career move to come to Arizona. He was looking out for me. There was a lot of stuff going on at Fender in the upper echelon, some changes in upper management that brought on a new calmness. People were listening. People were doing the right things, and I was getting freedom and most of all a level of confidence I never had before.

And you attribute this to —
Ritchie Fliegler. Richard McDonald. To this day I tell them how grateful I am that they backed me up at a time when I needed it. One time in Scottsdale, Richard brought me into his office and said [at this point an emotional Mike Eldred takes a moment to compose himself] . . . he said, we want you to move here, because what you do brings so much to everything else at Fender. We want that influence on a larger scale. We really need you so badly.

Beyond the Custom Shop.
Beyond the Custom Shop. That level of confidence really meant a lot to me. Matt Janopaul was President and Chief Operating Officer at the time. He was fully supportive, and I knew then I was going to move, and that it would be the best thing for my family and the best thing for Fender.

The best thing for Fender in what regard?
This is where it gets hard for me to put into words, but see, I'm a humble guy, and they had told me that all the stuff I had gotten done and the way the Custom Shop was looking now — they wanted me to have that influence on other people at Fender. Richard was saying, you can help in many other ways by being here. It was overwhelming to me, because like I keep saying, I don't like to be the boss. I don't like to be that guy, but I know that this is what I'm supposed to do. I don't know if you can understand that, but this is what I'm supposed to do.

Not because of your job description, but you mean in the larger sense of why you were put here, your destiny.
I've been building guitars since I was 18 or 19 years old. I've dealt with so many different artists, and there's a level of experience there that's hard to find, so it was just overwhelming to be valued and put in this position. All I ever wanted was to have a nice job for my family, but I've been able to accomplish so much. I look back at this body of work, and that means something. I have the privilege of contributing. This is what I'm supposed to do.

Postscript

Seymour Duncan: "I've been around the Custom Shop for a long time. In the '80s I wound pickups for Mike Stevens and played guitar with Bugs Henderson and Jimmy Wallace down in Texas, before Mike Stevens even came to California. He and I collect old cowboy Winchester rifles, spurs, and stuff, and he would take me to museums when I visited in Austin. One of his very first Custom Shop guitars was my red Esquire — ash body, a translucent cherry finish, sort of like you'd see on the back of a Les Paul. Mike filled in the grain with a dark filler, so it really shows through. The serial number is 1056, which was the number on the Jeff Beck Esquire. So I've known the Custom Shop guys since the beginning.

"Mike Eldred has been a great thing for the shop. He and I worked very closely together on the Jeff Beck Tribute Esquire and my own signature Esquire. He's a great player, and he understands what a guitar needs to do in the hands of the player. He knows the right feel, and he knows the right sound. He is really on the ball with respect to that. He pays attention to the market and knows the kinds of guitars people want. He listens very closely and has a lot of good ideas. It's so hard to be that corporate kind of person, especially in tough economic times, but Mike can balance these things because not only is his head in the right place, his heart's in the right place, too."

In the coming years, Mike Eldred would have his hand in every significant development in the Custom Shop, including the Tributes, a new generation of art guitars, new partnerships with other companies, new artist models, the Master Designs, the Builder Selects, the Limited Editions and various other limited collections, and more.

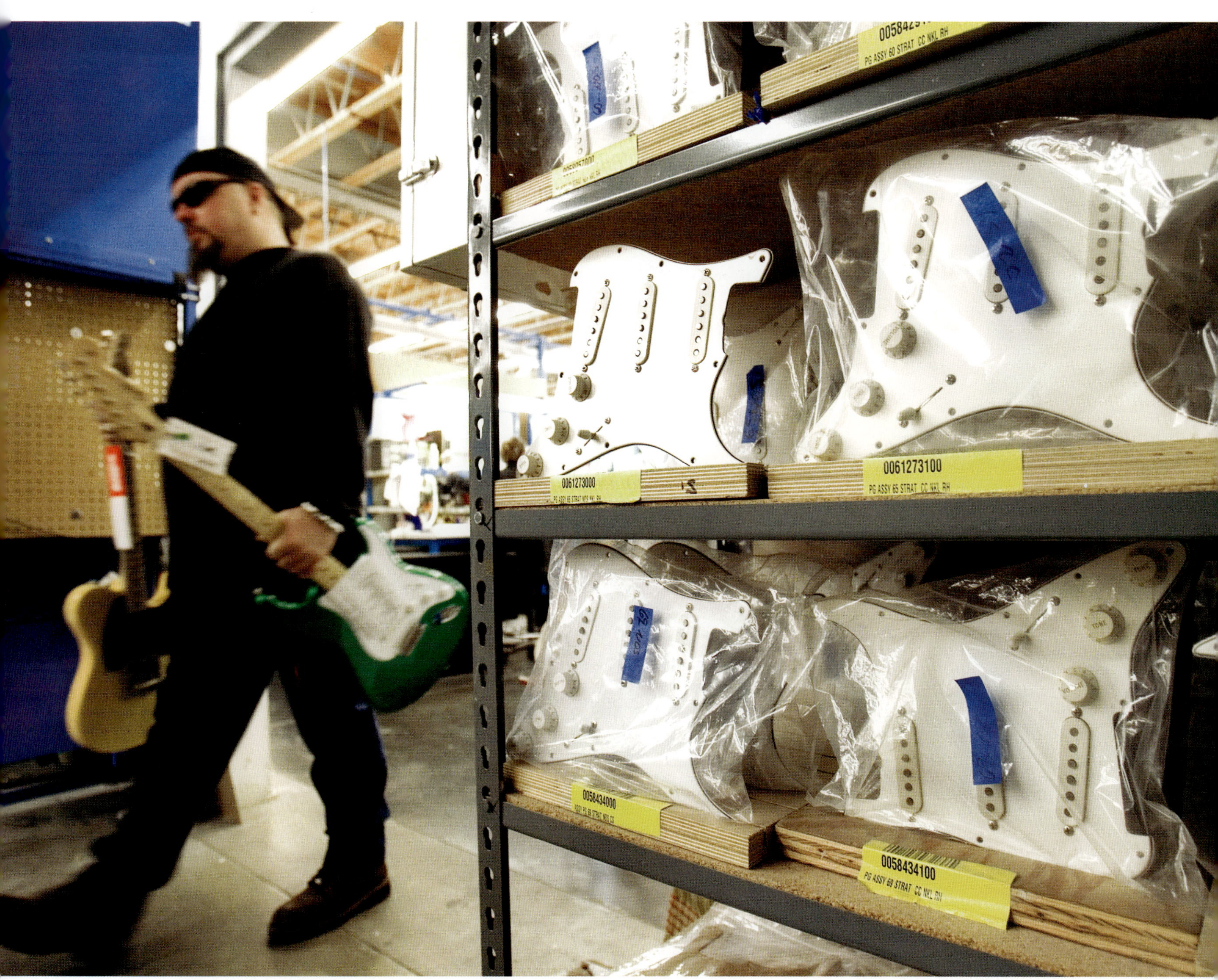

At the end of the line, packer/shipper Fred Connor totes a Tele and a Strat, tagged up and ready to ship.

CHAPTER TWENTY-TWO

22

New Arrivals, New Energy

Team Building, Post-'95

Jason Smith grew up in rock and roll. Accompanying his dad to concerts, he met some of the world's most esteemed guitarists and bassists while still a youngster. His dad? Fender Hall of Famer Dan Smith. As Ritchie Fliegler says elsewhere in this book, "Dan was the innermost person in the innermost circle. For years he was the *only* guitar guy in management . . . . without Dan, there were no guitars, *period*." With his pop playing such a key role in the company's success, it's no wonder that Jason Smith seems to carry some sort of familial Fender DNA.

Still, merely having a revered company veteran for a dad doesn't bestow talent or imbue your instruments with any sort of magic. Legacy or not, Jason Smith had to prove himself like any other aspiring Master Builder. He joined the shop on January 9, 1995 and worked in various capacities before entering into an intensive internship with John English. One of the many projects he worked on was a pair of double-neck Strats built for Dean DeLeo of the Stone Temple Pilots. After five years under English's mentoring, Jason was promoted to Master Builder. He worked on the Yngwie Malmsteen and Andy Summers Tribute projects, crafted a double-neck standard/baritone Telecaster for John 5, and built a trio of striking art guitars painted by his sister in law, L.A. artist Lysa Provencio.

Jason is a bass player. "Whenever I build things for NAMM shows, I always try to do at least one bass," he says. "I know it's a harder sell. The Custom Shop market for bassists has always been a little slow because they don't seem to be quite as picky as guitar players. If it's a Precision, then for a lot of players that's just fine, whether it's made in the shop, factory, or Mexico. But regardless of what you build, there's always one guy out there who wants it. You've just got to find him."

Jason Smith's assessment of the Custom Shop's evolution reflects a perspective that is literally lifelong. "When I started, it was smaller," he explains. "There was a lot of

The gang, early 2000s. From left, top row: Alan Hamel, George Amicay, Yuriy Shishkov, Stephen Stern. Next row down: Todd Krause, Chris Fleming (with Guild guitar; Fender acquired Guild in 1995), Dennis Galuszka. Bottom: Art Esparza, John English, Jason Davis, Greg Fessler. Lower right: Fred Stuart.

clowning around, sort of like being in a high school wood shop class — a lot of fun, semi-disorganized, and with a much smaller product line. We had more free time on our hands, and that can be a good thing if you use that time for creativity. I think John Page wanted it to stay somewhat small. Remember, the whole thing was started as an artist shop and an image thing. There was no intention of turning a profit, but as interest in the shop grew they realized they could turn a fairly large profit on a small amount of product. It may have been too much too fast, and maybe it got a little too big."

A future Master Builder and a future Fender Hall of Famer tour the shop: Young Jason Smith and proud papa Dan Smith.

Jason said in 2009: "Right now we are scaling it back, which is a good thing to me. It's more creative than it was a few years ago. Now we have time to dream things up and more time to spend with each customer and each instrument. It's a good blend now between the freewheeling/good times kind of thing and the more practical, 'let's stay in business' kind of thing. We think about it all the time and try to strike the perfect balance."

"I knew I wanted to build guitars ever since I was a little kid," says **Louis Salgado**. He got his wish, joining the shop on June 26, 1996. "I'm a good example of what they say here, that you can work your way up from the bottom. That is exactly what I did. At first I packed up guitars, worked in shipping and receiving, subassembly. I learned how to sand correctly, with the grain. I buffed bodies, fretted necks, learned how to true fretboards, learned CAD systems on the computer. They let me help with the Set-Necks, which were some of our more complicated guitars to build. I became a 'Master Builder coordinator.' I wasn't really programming yet, but I learned how to operate the CNC machine, so I could make a lot of different necks for the Master Builders. The neck would have the frets, truss rod, and basic shape, and the Master Builder himself would do the final neck shape. That's how I got really good at making necks, and I just kept bugging them to make me an apprentice."

Like everyone else who worked with Steve Boulanger, Louis has high praise and fond memories regarding his former teacher. "When Steve was our CNC programmer, he was so helpful and became very dear to me," Salgado says. "He was a real mentor. He said to me one time, 'You know, everyone always says to me, what you're doing is really cool. You are the only one who ever said, what you're doing is really cool — *how do you do it?*' He advised me to go to school to learn AutoCAD. Gene Baker was working with us, and he taught me how to build my first guitar. I was very straightforward. I said to Gene, 'What do I have to do to be a Master Builder?' And he told me the same thing Steve did: Go to school. I went to school at night and learned AutoCAD, Advanced AutoCAD, and Solid Works, which is a 3D solid modeling program. I built a guitar at the shop after work on my own time, just to teach myself all the processes and to show them I had potential. Gene helped me every step of the way.

Right: Jason Smith with an Esquire that he built for a Western-themed guitar show at famed Abbey Road Studios in St. John's Wood, London; the chambered body was hand-painted by Austin, Texas-based tattoo artist Briza Buscemi.

SL-2HMAH

"I started at the very bottom, and now I'm a Senior Master Builder. Dreams do come true."

— Louis Salgado

"They let me apprentice under Todd Krause for about five or six months, and Yuriy Shishkov. Finally Yuriy said, dude, you're ready. At first they gave me the orders nobody else wanted [laughs], like maybe a Bass VI or a 7-string Showmaster, crazy wiring things, stuff out there on the fringe. My first NAMM show guitar was a one-pickup hot rod with a Floyd Rose and a trans green finish.

"Jason Davis was another builder who helped me. John English, too. I remember John so well. He and I used to harass each other. I was working on one of my [shredder] guitars and he said, 'What are you doing? You're stuck in the '80s,' and I said, 'Hey, you're stuck in the *'50s* [laughs],' but he was right in one way, because I had the freedom to build guitars that I would play myself. I actually endorse Jackson now, as an artist." Louis went on to do the programming and design work for the Frank Bello Signature Bass, and he helped out Alex Perez with the Mike Dirnt/ Green Day Precision Bass.

Mike Eldred promoted him to Master Builder in 2001. (Louis's family framed and still possess a copy of the announcement that Mike sent to dealers.) Becoming a Master Builder was a dream come true, but it was short lived. Because Louis is an expert craftsman who can also program and design on a computer, Fender executives thought R&D would be the best place for him. "Around 2002 they asked me to make the move," he says. As we go

Left: Louis Salgado: "This was my first NAMM show guitar, where I could build whatever I wanted, so I built a shredder I would play."
Right: Dennis Galuszka, with one of his ultra-versatile, über-Relic Andy Summers Tribute Telecasters (Chap. 29).

to press, Louis works more for manufacturing and R&D than the Custom Shop, alongside George Blanda, Michael Frank-Braun, and Seiko Goto. "One of the things I was able to do was to speed up the prototyping of new models, using the CNC," he says. Louis was promoted to Senior Master Builder, and although he is a Project Engineer and reports to R&D, his pals in the Custom Shop still consult him on various projects. "I worked hard for that decal," he says, "and I did keep the Master Builder title."

Dennis Galuszka was a cabinetmaker for more than a decade before joining the Custom Shop crew on August 6, 1999. He had done some guitar repair and built acoustic guitars and flight cases. He was playing drums for Fred Stuart and working for John Page at the Fender Museum, running its drum instruction program. He started bugging Fred for a job in the shop, and when he got it he started working with Steve Stern and Greg Fessler, helping with the Robben Fords in the morning and the D'Aquistos in the afternoon. Gene Baker had just left, and Greg was building the Robben Fords exclusively.

Dennis Galuszka: "Some of the first things I did was to wire up a ton of wiring harnesses and do some sanding, and I started doing the chambers for the Robben Fords and some assembly work. At the time, the Robben Ford was the most back-ordered model in the shop, so they needed some help. Then if Steve didn't need me, they would put me out in the middle of the shop so I could learn the systems from the ground up. I had never used a pin router before, for example, so I learned how to use one to make pickup cavities, body chambers, and those sorts of things."

Did it strike Dennis as ironic that his first job in the Custom Shop was to work on Fender's most expensive models — instruments that had been designed by Jimmy D'Aquisto, the foremost designer and builder of his era? "Not only did it strike me as odd, but it struck some of the other guys as odd as well. I don't think they'd ever really hired someone off the street to come in and do that level of work. But it's not like I begged for that particular assignment. Mike Eldred and Dan Smith offered me the job, and I took it."

Double whammy: You could *rule* your local surf guitar scene with this twin-trem, twin-neck twang goliath. Drawing features from Jaguar, Jazzmaster, and 4-switch Bass VI designs, it was crafted for the Winter 2010 NAMM show by Dennis Galuszka, a surf guitar enthusiast (see Chap. 25). It is shown here in template, subassembly, and finished form. Note the extra (middle) pickup cavity on the Bass VI side. Dennis Galuszka: "It was easier to follow the original template and use the extra rout as a place to install the ground lugs. I figured they left the Tele routs in the Esquire, so I might as well do the same."

After eight months or so Dennis had demonstrated that he could take a guitar all the way through to completion, so Dan and Mike made him a Master Builder. "It happened pretty quickly," he says. "Again, it's not something I went after, but they offered it. I was perfectly happy being an apprentice, which in a way I think is the best job in the shop [laughs]. You get to do all this great stuff without some of the worries the Master Builders have. The whole idea of an apprenticeship here is to work to where you can build an entire guitar on your own, and Greg and I had gotten to the point where we were pretty much building them side by side. I am so thankful I started with the Robben Fords, because you really have to learn everything to build those guitars.

According to legend, Wild Bill Hickok was holding two pair — aces and eights, all spades and clubs — when he was murdered during a poker game in a Deadwood saloon on August 2, 1876. The artwork on the Dead Man's Hand Telecaster was one of several Custom Shop collaborations with Jan and Barry Lowe. Jan draws and woodburns the designs (the process is called pyrography). She then paints the guitar, and Barry applies numerous coats of a special finish to give the piece an aged appearance. The artists report that a single guitar can take weeks to complete. The Dead Man's Hand Tele was crafted by Dennis Galuszka (a second example was ordered by one of Yuriy Shishkov's clients); on the back is a collage in the style of an old Western movie poster.

"When the Robben orders slowed down and they put me on traditional stuff like Strats and Teles, they were sort of throwing me into the ocean to see if I would swim or drown. I chose to swim. I thought, hey, a bolt-on neck guitar — this will be a snap compared to what I've been doing, but I found enormous pitfalls that I had to overcome to build Strats and Teles properly." Dennis built the surfboard-inspired Fenders, a champagne-sparkle Jazzmaster and Jaguar, the reverse proto "top-scoop" Strat, the Builder Select Zero Fret Jazz Bass, the Andy Summers Tribute Telecaster, and G.E. Smith's Jazzmaster "prototype," all of which are profiled in these pages.

He also built a pair of Dakota Red Strats for Andy Summers, based on the '63 Strat in the "Every Breath You Take" video. "He loved that particular Dakota Red Strat," Dennis says, "and he gave me his guitar to copy. I ended up putting the preamp in there, which was kind of cool. Todd Krause gave me this idea, to solder the mid-boost pot onto the last tone pot, back to back, and drill a hole in the back of the guitar for access, so it's kind of a set-it-and-forget-it type of thing. The front of the guitar looks straight-up vintage – Volume, Tone, Tone — but it's got that little bit of a boost on all the time, and if you want a little more you can stick a screwdriver in the back and access the pot. Andy loved the Dakota Red Strat so much he sometimes ended up playing it more than his Andy Summers Telecaster. By the way, I went to see the Police in concert, and Andy was just all over that tremolo, like it was a Floyd or something. He never touched a tuner, so anybody who says that a vintage trem can't stay in tune, they're wrong. Andy made it happen. From there I went on to make a pair of hollow P Basses with f-holes, one for Mike Dirnt and one for Paul McCartney. Mike ordered one for himself and one as a gift for Paul."

Yuriy Shishkov built this semi-hollow, top-bound Custom Tele, which he calls a "jazz box-inspired" guitar. "I like the Bigsby tremolo," he says. "It has a natural vintage feel and also gives a unique look. Having a humbucker at the neck provides more of a jazz-bluesy tone, almost like the mini-hums on jazz boxes. My favorite materials are here — bird's-eye maple neck, and a flame maple top on ash with a classic burst finish. I love this guitar!"

Yuriy Shishkov spoke no English when he emigrated from the Soviet Union to the U.S. in 1990. "As soon as I arrived I could see America was even better than I expected," he says. "It's a great country to live in and work in."
At Right: Yuriy's big-head, gold sparkle Stratocaster had an alder body, a bird's-eye neck with 22 frets, an American Standard trem, an LSR roller nut, and a Duncan humbucker at the bridge. He calls it "very modern, a straightforward player."

Back in the USSR, **Yuriy Shishkov** built and repaired guitars in a root cellar/hideout so tiny that in order to lay a long-scale bass on the work bench he had to open the door. His hometown was Gomel, a city in Belarus that dates to the 1100s. He started playing guitar at about 12 years of age. "For some reason, the Soviets made acoustic 7-string guitars," he recalls. "We all just took off the one string, but the neck was really wide. I joined a rock band in our school, 13 years old. The electric guitars we had in school were made in East Germany and Czechoslovakia, and they weren't bad compared to the Soviet Union guitars. The Soviets made absolutely horrible guitars, almost deliberately it seemed, like they wanted people to hate them. Now they are collectible because they are so bad [laughs]. The electronics — they would use the same switch as a light switch on the wall."

Yuriy never saw American guitars in person. Only a few government-approved musicians had access to good-quality instruments. Gibsons and Fenders were very scarce, and although Yamahas, Ibanezes, and the like were available on the black market, they were prohibitively expensive for typical musicians. Yuriy realized that if he wanted a good guitar, he'd have to make it himself, from scratch.

"People would bring me a picture from a catalog and say, I want a guitar like this," he remembers. "A real one on the black market would cost a fortune, maybe 4,000 rubles, probably double or triple the annual income for many people. I sold mine for 2,000 rubles, so still very expensive. That was equivalent to one hundred dollars at that time.

"My first guitar was a copy of a Stratocaster, which I made from pictures only. I never saw one. I found a picture of somebody playing one, and they were holding their hands up in the picture, and the angle was right, so I took a snapshot of the picture with a 35 mm camera, made a slide, projected the slide, and traced it. This is how I got my dimensions and measured the scale. I got some pickups and spare parts from some East German guitars for my own guitar. It was a great instrument. I tried to make it look like a Stratocaster, and when people saw it, they wanted one. This grew like a snowball rolling down a hill, and I did this for four years.

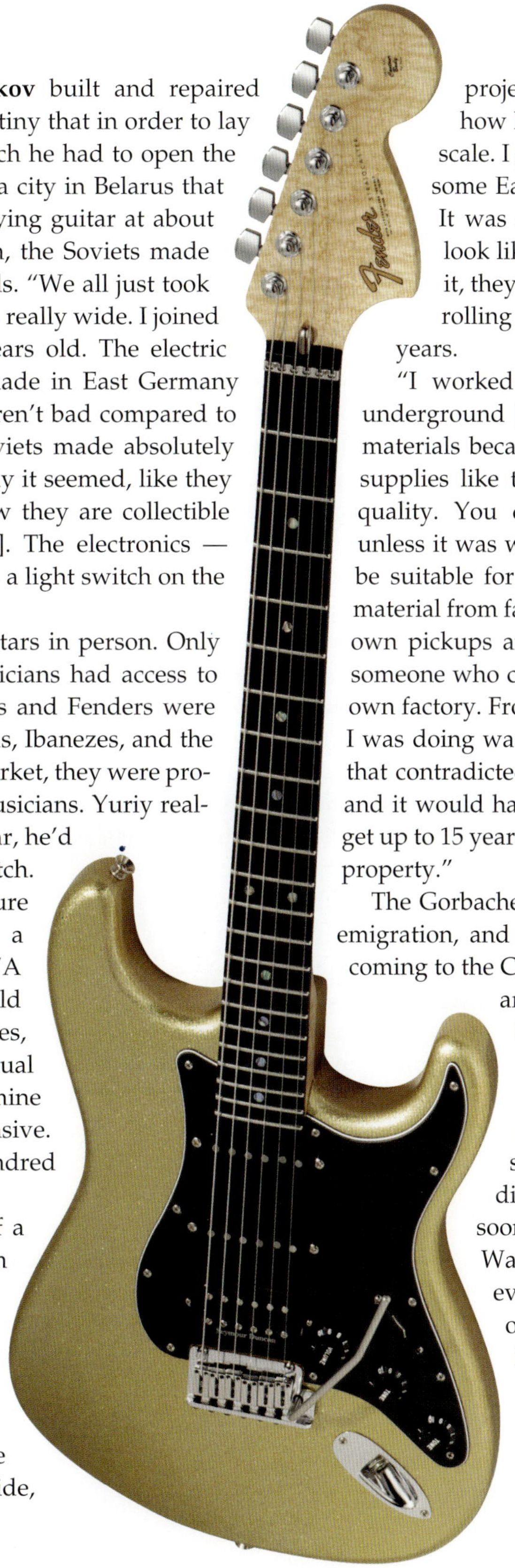

"I worked in a little root cellar. It was truly underground [laughs]. I couldn't buy guitar-making materials because they were not available. Primitive supplies like tools were available but in very poor quality. You couldn't sell materials to the public unless it was waste from the factories and would not be suitable for making anything good. I'd get scrap material from factories that made furniture. I made my own pickups and hardware. Sometimes I could find someone who could make components for me at their own factory. From the government's perspective, what I was doing was illegal. It was private enterprise, and that contradicted Soviet doctrine. This was capitalism, and it would have been punished severely. You could get up to 15 years in prison, with confiscation of all your property."

The Gorbachev regime allowed narrow windows of emigration, and Yuriy seized an opportunity in 1990, coming to the Chicago area in December. "As soon as I arrived I could see America was even better than I expected. I saw right away that a lot of what they said in the Soviet Union wasn't true. It's a great country to live in and work in. I spoke no English when I came. Neither did my wife. I became a U.S. citizen as soon as I could." Yuriy went to work for Washburn in May or June of 1991, and eventually collaborated with a number of well-known artists, including Jimmy Page, Robert Plant, Nuno Bettencourt, Robin Zander, Dimebag Darrell, and Paul Stanley.

He joined the Fender Custom Shop crew in 2000. "At first I thought

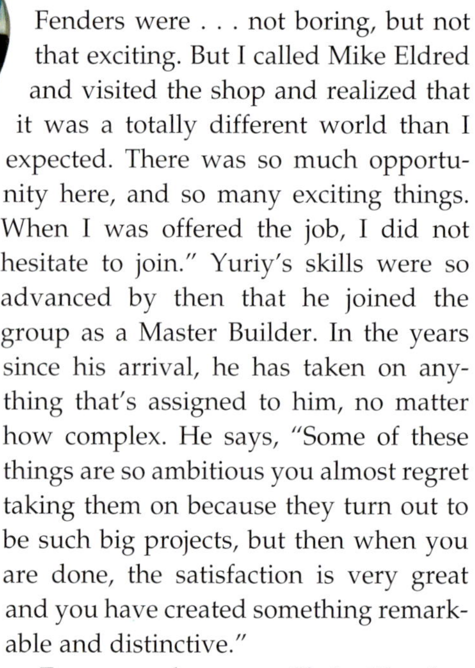

Fenders were . . . not boring, but not that exciting. But I called Mike Eldred and visited the shop and realized that it was a totally different world than I expected. There was so much opportunity here, and so many exciting things. When I was offered the job, I did not hesitate to join." Yuriy's skills were so advanced by then that he joined the group as a Master Builder. In the years since his arrival, he has taken on anything that's assigned to him, no matter how complex. He says, "Some of these things are so ambitious you almost regret taking them on because they turn out to be such big projects, but then when you are done, the satisfaction is very great and you have created something remarkable and distinctive."

For several years, **Chris Fleming** restored, repaired, and built instruments for retailer World of Strings in Long Beach before coming to the Custom Shop in 2000. When he applied for the position, he brought along some of his Gibson-type instruments rather than Fender-style designs. One was patterned more or less after a double-cutaway Les Paul Junior, and another was similar to a "George Gobel," thinbody L-5 archtop. Hired by Dan Smith and Mike Eldred, Chris started as an apprentice, with the bare-bones job description of "guitar builder." "They knew the Guild project was coming up [Fender acquired Guild in 1995 and managed Guild's Westerly, Rhode Island, factory before relocating production to Corona]. They wanted someone with experience in building acoustic instruments.

"I worked in the neck department for four or five months just to get the hang of what was going on," Chris remembers, "and then I became a Master Builder apprentice for John English, Alan Hamel, and Fred Stuart all at once. It was interesting, learning from different perspectives." He spent eight or nine months as an apprentice and then became involved in moving the Guild electric guitar project from Westerly to the Custom Shop. For a couple of years he coordinated production for Guild acoustic instruments, and in 2003 he was given a choice of jobs — marketing manager for Guild, or Custom Shop Master Builder. He chose the latter, eventually collaborating with artists Kid Ramos, Joe Wood, Dave Newman, Kit Carson, Sara Ray, and Nevena Christie. He designed, built, prototyped, or supervised production of the 50th Anniversary 1954 Stratocaster, the Builder Select Tele/Strat Hybrid, the Special Edition 1950s Tele Thinline, the Baja Tele, the Tele/Pro Jr. Relic set, and the Shelby GT Strat, all of which are profiled in these pages.

Chris Fleming worked officially as a Master Builder until early 2007 or so. "I've worn a bunch of hats since then. I've been a special projects coordinator, and production manager for the Jackson Charvel group. I go to Mexico, I go to Tacoma a lot [Fender acquired Tacoma Guitars in October, 2004]. I have a lot of projects in manufacturing and R&D, and I also help with marketing. I have been fortunate because Fender allows me to do a lot of different things." As we go to press, Chris's title is Senior Master Builder and Project Manager for the Gretsch, Guild, Jackson, and Tacoma brands, and he reports to Vice President of Guitar R&D Keith Chapman. Former Senior Vice President Ritchie Fliegler: "You've got all these great classical composers, but there's only one Mozart. The Custom Shop has a bunch of really talented builders, but for me Chris Fleming is the Mozart. He's the guy."

Chris Fleming worked with several artists to create some of the shop's most striking and valuable instruments. Inspired by the pop-culture lore of America's most fabled highway, the Route 66 Tele was a collaboration between Chris and artist Dave Newman.

Chris Fleming with a 50th Anniversary 1954 Stratocaster; one of his proudest achievements was directing the project (Chap. 26). Ritchie Fliegler: "There are good guitars, really good guitars, great guitars, and then once a year, or every two years, something crosses your path that stops everybody in their tracks. This is one of the most insanely good guitars ever, just one of those 'what, are you kidding me?' kind of guitars. It's everything you could ever want."

CHAPTER TWENTY-THREE

23

Wrapping up the Late 1990s

Classic Player Strat, Artist Guitars, Artist Builders

In 1995, Dan Smith left Scottsdale, Arizona, where Fender's corporate headquarters are located, and moved back to Corona, California, site of the factory and Custom Shop. He took over Guitar R&D at the end of May, allowing John Page to refocus his energies on the ever-expanding Custom Shop. That same year, Mike Lewis assumed responsibility for Fender guitar marketing. He reports: "When the guitar marketing torch was passed to me, the Custom Shop came with it. Together with John Page and then Mike Eldred [who joined Fender in 1996], we organized the products and services into more definable groups."

Lewis's modest description of his efforts only hints at the depth and the crucial importance of his tenure as the Custom Shop's marketing chief. His reorganization brought a much-needed clarity and structure to the growing line of Custom Shop instruments. Over the next five years, these efforts would include expanding and then streamlining the Custom Classics, regrouping the artist guitars under the Namesakes umbrella, evolving the Relics into the Time Machines, expanding the remnants of the price list concept into the Team Built program, gradually replacing the decade-generic vintage reissues with more detailed, year-specific models, and adding basses to the Time Machine collection. As noted in Chap. 16, by the time Mike Lewis handed the marketing reins over to his pal and colleague Richard McDonald in 2000, the Time Machines alone numbered 30 different models, an extensive line in itself.

Mike Lewis's contributions are discussed in the sections addressing the Relics and Time Machines, Late-'90s Set-Necks and Showmasters, the Team Built program, the second-generation art guitars, the Namesakes series, quality control in the Custom Shop and factory, the Custom Classics, and other topics. This chapter investigates a few of the programs and instruments of the late 1990s, but most of the major developments are addressed in those other chapters. Regarding additional late-1990s matters, please also see the section on the D'Aquistos and Robben Fords

In 1999, the Custom Shop pursued the idea of recreating an individual artist's iconic instrument — quirks, scratches, and all. Before long, the concept blossomed into a revised and expanded Tribute program. One of the first pieces, and also the shop's first signature bass, was the Jaco Pastorius Tribute Jazz Bass.

(Chap. 15), and on the transition from John Page's to Mike Eldred's supervision of day-to-day production (Chap. 21).

Trickling down, crossing over

During the late 1990s the Custom Shop served as a proving ground for techniques and processes that eventually filtered their way over to the main production floor. Mike Lewis: "A lot of things were tried there first or implemented there first. The pickups, the guitars' body perimeters, body radius, the way we did the headstocks, the rolled edges on the fingerboards, the round-lam fingerboards, the volutes behind the pegheads — all these are examples. When we revamped all the American guitars in the 1990s, starting with the American Deluxe, we went back to all the original specs on those instruments. As years go by, there's something called 'spec creep.' All these different people are making the stuff, and the way things get sanded can change, the radius changes a little bit, the templates wear out. These are minute differences, but they do matter, and they do add up. We made a lot of new tooling. We went back and made sure we were using the *exact* proper details. That was all discovered and first implemented in the Custom Shop."

The "Master Builder" category

In January 1997, the Namesakes were joined by the Merle Haggard Tribute Tele. In 1998 the 15 Namesakes instruments included the John Jorgenson and Will Ray models (see below), named after the fine solo artists who were also Jerry Donahue's partners in the Hellecasters. In the summer 1998 *Frontline*, the Custom Shop offered eight Namesakes Teles (Jennings Tribute, Haggard Tribute, Jorgenson, Ray, Donahue, White, Gatton, and Collins), only two Namesakes Strats (Cray and Dale), as well as the D'Aquistos and Robben Ford models. Within a few months, the literature began depicting the Custom Shop's new Ritchie Blackmore Strat as well as the Jaco Pastorius Tribute Jazz Bass, which

Duplicator neck templates, several of them made by John Page, Mike Stevens, and J. Black. Most were for Custom Shop instruments, although some were made in both the factory and the shop. Also, sometimes an artist with a factory signature guitar would have his personal instruments made in the shop, so on occasion templates and blueprints went back and forth between the two facilities.

Right: On January 15, 1996, Fender announced the 50th Anniversary Limited Edition Guitar and Amplifier set, intended to duplicate the look of some of Leo Fender's first instruments. Reportedly only 50 sets were made. Recreated in the Custom Shop, the pine-body "snake-head" guitar is a reproduction of the 1949 prototype Esquire/Broadcaster/Telecaster, while the amp is a replica of a 1946 Professional. Fred Stuart and John Page built the guitar. Bruce Zinky, Bill Giles, John Page, and Steve Murillo collaborated on the maple-cab amp. Form-fit case by Jerry Germain/G&G; flight cases: Bob Morris/Holmberg Cases.

FENDER®

in the summer of '99 was called the Jaco Pastorius Relic Jazz Bass (see below).

In early 1999 the Robben Ford and D'Aquisto models were reassigned to a new "Master Builder" category, despite the fact that Master Builders designed or built all of the Custom Shop's artist guitars. (What really set the Fords and D'Aquistos apart was their non-Fenderish design, set-neck/contoured-top construction, extra handwork, and limited production.) By mid year, that category's name was changed to "Master Built Guitars," and the Robben Fords and D'Aquistos were joined by the new Fender Classic Rocker (Chap. 15).

Despite the potential for confusion arising from isolating only a few of the Master Built guitars in the "Master Built" category, in another respect the new name actually clarified things, in that the designated "artist" guitars now included only models that were indeed named after players. For these instruments, the Custom Shop went back to using the Artist Signature Series designation in early 1999. Mid year, the name changed again, this time to Custom Artist Models.

Italian Stallion Strats

In some circles, Nick Mason may be almost as well known as a collector and driver of Ferraris as he is for his other gig. He has been the drummer for Pink Floyd since the band's founding in 1964. In 1997, he commissioned the Custom Shop to build six Ferrari Strats. As one might imagine, the Italian supercar company allows its name and prancing-horse logo to be used only for very special projects, but after two years of planning and negotiations, the Strats were built. They delivered everything you'd expect in a Fender/Ferrari collaboration — high performance, sleek musculature, hair-trigger responsiveness, and ultra-exclusivity.

Located in the heart of London, Theo Fennell PLC is renowned as one of Europe's finest jewelers. Fennell made the guitars' fingerboard inlays, volume and tone knobs, tremolo arm tips, and pickup selector tips, as well as the Fender and Ferrari logos, all in solid silver. Pink Floyd's longtime equipment tech, Phil Taylor, worked with John Grunder on the planning; Jason Davis and George Amicay crafted the instruments. The paint? Ferrari red, of course. The components were black or silver, including an ebony fingerboard and a mix of sterling silver and nickel-plated parts. The pickguards and trem covers were made of Kevlar.

Phil Taylor: "Nick is a very astute collector of Ferraris, deeply knowledgeable. He has a longstanding relationship with Ferrari, and that was essential in gaining permission for the project. The Ferrari Stratocasters turned out to be just stunning."

Classic Player Strat

By the late '90s, Fender was becoming even more responsive to niche markets. A good example was the particularly intriguing Classic Player Strat. Here was a generally vintage looking Custom Shop Stratocaster (black versions even came with a nifty gold anodized pickguard) with a choice of either a V neck or a C neck and an alder or ash body. Despite the retro details, the performance features were modern all the way. "Subtle upgrades to accentuate the positive" included Sperzel locking tuners, Noiseless pickups, and a 2-point trem.

In 1998 and 1999 the Classic Player Strat moved back and forth between the Custom Classic series and the Contemporary series. In the summer of '99, it cost $2,249 — 500 bucks more than the American Classic Strat and 150 bucks less than the N.O.S. versions of the year-specific Strats in the Time Machine series. (This original Classic Player Strat is not to be confused with the Classic Player series announced in the summer of 2006, which offered Custom Shop-designed guitars manufactured in Fender's Ensenada, Mexico plant.)

Left: The late-'90s Classic Player Strat was an example of the shop's combining a generally vintage look with modern features. One of the coolest-looking Strats ever was the black version with a gold anodized aluminum pickguard.

Above: The shop would go on to build Classic Player guitars in one form or another for years. In one of many nods to the vintage era, this Strat was offered in Sonic Blue, which dated to 1960 and was the lightest of the three original blues — Sonic, Daphne, and Lake Placid. As with other original Fender colors, Sonic Blue was borrowed from an automobile, in this case a mid-'50s Cadillac.

Three Jazz Basses

In the summer of 1998 the Custom Shop's only cataloged Jazz Bass was the decade-generic Relic '60s Jazz Bass, with a stock pickguard. In 1999, that model was replaced by the year-specific Relic '64 Jazz Bass, also with a pickguard (it was actually available not only in the Relic but also in the Closet Classic and N.O.S. finishes). The other Jazz Bass that year was the new Jaco Pastorius Tribute, a replica of Jaco's fretless instrument, without pickguard. Listing at $3,449, the Jaco model was an early example of the shop's recreating an iconic personal instrument, with all its attendant scratches and dings; the other early example was the Muddy Waters Tribute Telecaster of 2000. These two instruments were the vanguard of the Custom Shop's new approach to the Tribute series.

Fender sometimes called the Jaco model the Jaco Pastorius Relic Jazz Bass (instead of the correct "Tribute"), but it should not be confused with the '64 Relic. Both instruments were offered concurrently — the fretted '64 Relic with a pickguard, and the fretless, no-pickguard Jaco Tribute.

Corona korina: The John Jorgenson Telecaster

Jerry Donahue's signature Telecaster had been a staple of the shop's artist line since the early 1990s, and in 1998 it was joined by two Namesake models designed in conjunction with Donahue's bandmates in the Hellecasters. One was the John Jorgenson Signature Custom Korina Telecaster (not to be confused with the made-in-Japan, black-sparkle Limited Edition John Jorgenson Hellecaster model). Gene

Baker was the point man for the project. He recalls: "I built the prototype and some of the first production guitars in 1998. Jorgenson got pretty involved because he was in the area doing a lot of Hellecasters stuff. It was a fun project but also a wild guitar in many respects, complicated and time consuming."

Korina, or African limba, is a highly acclaimed tone wood most often associated with classic Gibsons such as the original Flying Vs and Explorers. Jorgenson picked korina for his guitar's body, and also specified side-by-side single-coils in a dual humbucker configuration, a modified Tele bridge, a sparkle pickguard, Sperzel Trim-Loks, and custom 5-way switching. The guitar was available in Black, Champagne Sparkle, and Silver Sparkle, and it retailed for $3,870.

Gene Baker: "John really wanted korina for the body, and he was asking for a lot of stuff where we had to really scratch our heads and figure out how to pull it off. It required a lot of hand tooling. We had to design new coils for the side-by-side Tele humbuckers, and I was sketching schematics for days to get the 5-way switch and fairly elaborate electronics to work right. John Suhr was involved in a lot of the pickup R&D. We also needed a custom tailpiece with a longer tray to accommodate the wider pickups, and Scott Buehl had to handcraft some of the metal pieces. For the sparkle finishes, I was ordering Gretsch drum covering from a drum parts supplier in L.A."

Gene Baker describes the Jorgenson guitar as "a Tele on steroids," due to its custom wiring. The goal was to achieve vintage tones while maintaining hum-canceling properties in all five switch positions; starting from the bridge position, they were:

- bridge pickup/humbucking/series;
- the inner coils of the neck and bridge pickups/humbucking/series;
- both pickups/humbucking/parallel;
- the outer coils of the neck and bridge pickups/parallel, with an inductor added to match the series positions' output;
- neck pickup/humbucking/series.

In 1999, the shop extended the year-specific concept to basses, replacing the decade-generic Relic '60s Jazz Bass with the Relic '64 Jazz Bass, which was actually available in all three finishes.

Gene adds that he designed the circuit, Fender pickup specialist Bill Turner made the pickups, and Scott Buehl made the bridge. "We learned a lot on that project," he recalls, "dealing with those pickups and the longer bridge plate. John wanted the metal bridge to affect the final pickup tone versus using a stainless bridge like on the Gatton Tele. We began with standard Tele coils and assembled them as humbuckers, but they squealed like pigs, so we ended up shortening the coil height and using less wire, which brought them down to a PAF-type output. The neck pickup covers had to be soldered together; otherwise, they created microphonic issues.

"We also added small screws to the bridge plate, like on the Gatton Tele, to reduce any plate vibration. The drum covering for the top reduced some paint time and looked cool, while the white moto binding detailed the edge for a nice transition between the front sparkle colors and the rear solid or natural colors. That was a fun project. John a pleasure to work with, very involved, a great guy and extremely talented."

The Will Ray Telecaster was an even greater departure from standard Teles than its outlandish appearance would suggest. Fred Stuart designed it in collaboration with Will Ray.

Will Power: The Will Ray Telecaster

Designed by Fred Stuart, the Will Ray Tele of 1998 was the third in the series of signature guitars associated with the Hellecasters, and like the other two it had a corollary in the made-in-Japan Fender line, the Will Ray Jazz-a-Caster. Sort of a Tele with Jazzmaster pickups, a Strat neck, and a zany voodoo vibe, the Custom Shop's version was officially called the Will Ray Telecaster, sometimes the "Mojo" Tele. At first glance it may have appeared to be little more than a conventional guitar with a mish-mash of Fender features and gotta-wear-shades cosmetics (23k gold leaf over Cadmium Orange!), but it was a well thought-out, versatile, and unique instrument that didn't sound quite like any other Fender.

Details included Custom Shop "Jazzmaster" pickups (a different configuration than original Jazzmaster units), a very flat 15" radius fingerboard (well-suited to Will Ray-style sliding and bending), a white-shell pickguard, a stock 3-way switch plus a custom-wired rotary tone modifier, 23k gold leaf appliqué on the body, sort of a psychedelic/zebra paint job, and pearl skulls on the fingerboard. Fred Stuart: "The rotary switch had a couple of inductors that it added into the circuit, and it would also cut out one of the coils in the pickup — they were humbuckings."

Not a guitar for introverts, the Will Ray Tele was offered in the aforementioned Cadmium Orange as well as Ultra Marine Blue and Lime Green. Over its lifespan it retailed for about \$3,700 to \$4,100, or about \$4,000 to \$4,400 for the version equipped with a Hip Shot string bender.

Wrapping up the Mike Lewis era

Reflecting several trends, a new strategy had been put into effect by the summer of 1999. The Custom Classics had been severely pared back to only four basic guitars and a bass: the American Classic Stratocaster, American Classic Telecaster, Classic Player Strat, Set-Neck Tele Jr., and the Vintage Precision Bass Custom. After this downsizing, the nomenclature was more cohesive. The Custom Artist models were more numerous than ever. The Time Machines had practically exploded and now embraced more than two dozen instruments.

This time around, the American Classic Strat and American Classic Telecaster were accurately described as Custom Shop versions of the American Standards. While those models might not have offered each and every "classic" feature, players and dealers on the lookout for more authentic, vintage-based models could find plenty to choose from in the late-'90s Time Machine series, a much more extensive and detailed collection than the decade-generic Relics of the mid '90s. Each of the Team Built Time Machines was available in N.O.S., Closet Classic, and Relic finishes, and each was a year-specific model: the '51 Nocaster; '63 Telecaster; '56, '60, and '69 Strats; and the Relic '64 Jazz Bass. The only survivor from the mid-'90s Set-Neck/Contemporary Series was the Set-Neck Tele Jr., now relocated to the Custom Classic line. The three Contemporary Strats were gone.

Technically, the Carved Top and Set-Neck Strats had been dropped as well, but the high-end/carved-top concept lived on in the three-model line of upscale, Team Built Showmasters. They incorporated a number of features associated with other high-end brands while maintaining an unmistakable Fender identity (Chap. 19). Similar to the Robben Fords in their departure from typical Fender construction and styling, the "outside the box" Showmasters were otherwise distinctive in that they were designed by Fender alone rather than in association with any particular artist. In other words, Fender itself was calling the shots and expanding its move into new territories.

The exclusivity and workmanship of the shop's late-'90s instruments, particularly the artist models, is reflected in their prices. In the summer of 1999, the Custom Classics included among others the American Classic Stratocaster at $1,749 and the chambered Set-Neck Tele Jr. at $2,599. The Showmaster Series included among others the Showmaster FMT at $2,869. The Time Machines ranged from the $2,399 '56 and '60 Stratocaster N.O.S. models up to their $2,949 Relic cousins with gold hardware. Among the dozen Custom Artist models only the Cray, Dale, and Donahue retailed for less than $3,000. The heaviest price tags dangled from the $4,149 Clarence White Tele and the $4,799 Merle Haggard Tribute Tele.

As Fender looked forward to the year 2000, it offered a diverse array of basic Custom Shop models: five Custom Classics, three Showmasters, six Time Machines (each available in all three finishes), three Custom Artist Stratocasters, eight Custom Artist Telecasters, the Jaco Pastorius Jazz Bass and, from the Master Built group, the Classic Rocker, the three D'Aquistos, and the three Robben Fords. Taking into account neck shape, fingerboard material, trem vs. stop tailpiece (on the Showmaster FMT), the gold hardware option on the '56 and '60 Time Machine Strats, the Blackmore Strat's "Roland Ready" option, and the Will Ray Tele's Hip Shot string bender option (and excluding all of the color choices), the 1999 Custom Shop line numbered a whopping 65 models in all, far more than many companies' entire catalogs.

Each of the year-specific, Team Built Time Machines of 1999 was available in the N.O.S., Closet Classic, and Relic finishes, including this '63 Telecaster in Lake Placid Blue.

The Ritchie Blackmore Strat

A stock Fender Strat with two pickups? That's the Custom Shop's Ritchie Blackmore model. The veteran of Deep Purple and Rainbow reportedly received a Stratocaster as a gift from Eric Clapton. It took him a while to convert from his Gibson ES-335, but during the 1970s the Strat became his instrument of choice. In one of the seemingly numberless ways in which artists have modified the Stratocaster to suit their quirks and tastes, Blackmore lowered the middle pickup as far as he could because it got in the way of his right hand. Reflecting this preference, the Custom Shop's Custom Artist Series set-neck Ritchie Blackmore Stratocaster (appearing in late 1998, officially introduced in January 1999) featured a most unusual pickup array — *two* Gold Lace Sensors. Instead of worrying about how far they could lower that middle pickup, the builders just eliminated it altogether. The selector switch provided three pickup choices: front, both, or rear. While this arrangement may seem less versatile than the standard setup, it did allow for the third knob to be a bridge-pickup tone control, a useful feature most Stratocasters lack.

Not to be confused with Fender's made-in-Mexico and made-in-Japan Blackmore models, the Custom Shop's version featured a set neck, a bullet truss rod, a lightweight premium ash body, a large, '70s-style headstock, locking tuners, a custom oval neck shape, a 2-point trem, and a scalloped rosewood fingerboard with a 7.25" radius. The Blackmore Strat retailed for $3,819. An optional, $4,269 version came with a Roland GK-2A pickup that allowed it to be used as a synth controller.

Ritchie Blackmore didn't use that middle pickup. In fact, it just got in his way, so it was removed from the Ritchie Blackmore Stratocaster, the shop's only stock two-pickup Strat.

The Marty Stuart Tribute Tele

Mark Kendrick was the logical builder for 1999's Limited Edition Marty Stuart Tribute Telecaster project, having already collaborated with Merle Haggard, Buck Owens, and Dwight Yoakam on their respective Fenders. Still, this one was particularly challenging. Marty Stuart is not only an award-winning country singer and multi-instrumentalist, he's also a serious collector. Several of his guitars are historic in every sense, having belonged to Clarence White, Carl Perkins, Lester Flatt, and Mick Ronson; his 1947 Martin D-45 was previously owned by both Hank Williams and Johnny Cash. Not surprisingly, when he collaborated with Mark Kendrick on his Tribute Tele, he had very specific demands and took a hands-on approach.

Mark Kendrick: "Marty brought in three of his guitars: Don Rich's silver sparkle Tele, Clarence White's 10/56 Tele with the B Bender, and Mick Ronson's vintage Esquire. I get chills just thinking about opening up those cases and seeing those guitars all at once. We sat down together and he scribbled out the details on a napkin. He took features from each guitar, but the challenge was that these things weren't a hundred percent compatible, so it was a tall order. For example, the biggest challenge was to capture the tone that Marty had in his head. He wanted the tonal characteristics of both the Ronson and the Clarence, but that Clarence guitar has all that metal in it from the B Bender, and the Marty Tribute wasn't going to have a B Bender unless the customer ordered it that way."

If anyone can conjure vintage tone in a new guitar, it's Mark Kendrick, but as he explains, "You have to remember that those Fenders of his are a half-century old. Back then, [the lumber industry] would go into old-growth forests, and that's where Fender got our maple. Today, old growth forests are protected, as they should be, and maple is farmed in planned forests. In my opinion, it makes a subtle difference in the sound. I ended up using a stock ash Telecaster body. For the neck profile, we started with the Ronson Esquire — which had a Tadeo Gomez neck — but during the collaboration we gradually moved toward the Clarence Tele. Marty wanted to capture that whole Nudie suit/Buckaroo/sparkle thing, that country voodoo vibe, and the checkerboard binding and sparkle finish were inspired by Buck Owens's original '63 gold sparkle Tele and Don Rich's '67 silver sparkle Tele."

A feature most closely associated with vintage Rickenbackers, the checkerboard binding was particularly challenging. As Kendrick explains, when German luthier Roger Rossmeisl came over to Fender from Rickenbacker in 1962, he brought along a stash of this distinctive black and white trim. However, it was no longer available, so the binding on the Stuart guitars was handcrafted by Fender veteran "Red" Dave Nichols. The guitar's exuberant whoopee-ti-yi-yo appearance was further enhanced with a moto pickguard, a dazzling ice blue finish that Fender called Brilliant Stratosphere Sparkle, and intricate cowboy-motif fingerboard inlays.

Mark Kendrick personally built about a half-dozen Marty Stuart Teles, and at one point Fender outfitted Marty's whole band with blue sparkle instruments. Aside from Kendrick's protos, all Stuart Teles were Team Built. As is always the case with such guitars, once the Master Builder has collaborated with the artist, finalized all details, and built the prototypes, he is deeply involved in training the team to craft that particular model. Details: a one-piece maple neck, Broadcaster-type pickups, wiring based on Clarence White's Tele, nickel-plated hardware, and brass saddles. Fender announced that the custom strap would be made by the Edward H. Bohlin Company, saddle makers to golden-era Hollywood cowboys, but the project proved too costly so the straps were crafted instead by Long Hollow Leather in Franklin, Tennessee. The strap buckles were custom made by Bohlin.

Mark Kendrick: "I worked on the project both in Corona and in Nashville. Marty was very savvy, very hands-on and involved. He would drive down two or three days a week to collaborate while I was a building the prototype. We were both frustrated at times, trying to get it just right, but we worked together and over the process became good friends."

The Artist Builders

As noted in Chap. 4, Larry Brooks was a Master Builder who worked in the Custom Shop, but he reported to Artist Relations director Mark Wittenberg. Brooks was succeeded in the "Artist Builder" role by Master Builders Mark Kendrick and then Todd Krause. Mark Wittenberg, who died in 1995, was succeeded by AR directors Del Breckenfeld and later Alex Perez, both of whom oversaw budgets and ordering systems separate from those of the Custom Shop.

Prior to inaugurating the Artist Builder arrangement, Mike Stevens or John Page handled the assignments of artist projects, taking into account the builders' existing relationships with artist clients. J. Black: "When I worked for the Stones or Bob Dylan, that was due to my relationship with [amp tech/guru] César Díaz with Dylan, or [guitar tech] Pierre DeBeauport from the Stones. I kept those relationships when I came to Fender. John Page was connected to Bon Jovi and the Cars, Mark Kendrick knew Buck Owens, and John English knew Dick Dale. Mike Stevens knew Danny Gatton, Robben Ford, Eric Johnson, and lots of others, so all these relationships were independent of what was coming through Artist Relations, Mark Wittenberg, or Larry Brooks and the later Artist Builders."

During the shop's first two or three years, professional musicians often ordered instruments through local dealers and then waited several months or even a year for delivery. The Artist Builder arrangement was intended to bypass those channels so that endorsees and other artists could benefit from quicker service. Artists often made requests to the shop at a time when they were enjoying peak popularity, so getting guitars into their hands as soon as possible not only made for happier high-profile customers but also provided extra exposure for Fender. Having a separate system further allowed the shop to avoid having to backburner dealer requests in order to accommodate unexpected inquiries from artists. Finally, it allowed the AR director to take the initiative in cultivating relationships with artists, particularly up and coming ones.

The Artist Builders and the Custom Shop's Master Builders were differentiated mainly by paperwork, accounting, and corporate structure rather than skill levels or status. As was typical, job descriptions and chains of command were ignored whenever necessary. J. Black provides an example: "The Jeff Beck relationship was with Ralph Baker, Jeff's manager. Dan Smith would get requests and they sometimes bypassed Artist Relations and came directly to us at the shop. The rules changed from situation to situation." All of the builders, regardless of official titles, were willing to help each other and do whatever was needed to get great guitars in the hands of players — artists and non-artists alike.

Artist Relations Manager Alex Perez explains: "The early Artist Builder system wasn't super formal. Larry Brooks reported to both John Page and Mark Wittenberg. We had a builders' meeting every week, and Larry always attended that, but on a day-to-day basis he reported to Mark, and his orders came through Mark, not the Custom Shop. It was a separate channel." Todd Krause describes the arrangement as "a paperwork/accounting thing more than anything else."

By the early 2000s, Fender had decided that the Artist Builder arrangement had outlived its usefulness. Bill Cummiskey: "We never changed the goals, but we changed the way we go about it. We don't have one specific go-to guy anymore. Because we have a lot more builders now, and there is so much talent in that Custom Shop, we can go to any of the Master Builders. If a particular builder is swamped and unable to take something on without a long wait, we'll find another one who's caught up and can turn it around. These orders can come in through any of our artist reps, our dealers, or directly from the artist. Then the sales department writes up an order. If the artist requests a particular builder, then we accommodate that, but otherwise the order goes to the person who's best suited to the project and the one who can turn it around and make that artist happy."

Alex Perez: "The artists are the only ones who can begin the process by dealing directly with the shop, and they do that by personal contact with the builders or through Artist Relations. All other customers go through a dealer. John Mayer is a perfect example. If he's in town he'll come to visit. He's a real kid in a candy store. If he sees something he likes, he'll go to John Cruz or Dennis Galuszka and say, 'Oh, that's great — can you build me one of those?' And of course we will, and we can turn it around quickly. The whole idea is to do what's best for the artist, to get him the guitar he wants and needs and dreams about, without having to wait too long."

John 5 with a guitar built for a Rob Zombie tour, one of the first pieces crafted by Jason Smith after becoming a Master Builder. The top neck is a John 5 Signature guitar neck in standard tuning; the bottom neck is a 27" Sub-Sonic tuned B to B.

In the early years of the new decade, the shop recommitted to collaborating with independent artists, including Dennis Ricklefs, the renowned hot rod pinstriper. Ricklefs painted this beauty, as well as a pink/tan Esquire.

CHAPTER TWENTY-FOUR

24

Mojo Workin' in the New Millennium

Tributes, the Woodstock Strat, Highlights 2000 – 2003

Shifting strategies

In the late 1990s and early 2000s, Fender executives reexamined the Custom Shop's mission and charted a new course that would, in Senior Vice President Richard McDonald's words, "get the mojo back." One problem was that the shop's managers were vexed by the rising costs of materials and supplies. Labor was another issue. The NAMM guitars and art guitars called attention to the shop and allowed the craftsmen to express themselves, but when dealers and players responded by ordering more of the same sorts of high-profile/low-profit instruments, it diminished the shop's ability to produce the more mainstream products that shored up the bottom line. J. Black: "One project Alan Hamel was doing — he showed two guitars at the show and was supposed to build four, and it ended up being twelve, and when you looked at what it cost to keep him as an employee versus what people were paying for these very scarce art guitars, the numbers weren't working out. Manufacturing's attitude was, 'Hey, you gotta get back to making [more mainstream] guitars, because this art guitar thing has kind of run its course.'"

The philosophy behind the evolving price sheet strategy and the Team Built program steered the shop's mission further away from "build whatever you like, and it'll sell." J. Black: "Starting around '96, we went from making whatever we wanted to the attitude of — look, these things have to be pre-sold before we can make them. It was a shift, a plateau. The limited runs, NAMM things, art guitars, and traveling exhibits started to taper off, with a few exceptions like special guitars for Disney."

The arrival of Richard McDonald

Former full-time professional rock guitarist Richard McDonald has worn many hats at Fender — parts representative, telemarketer, executive. He became Marketing Manager of Pro Audio in March 1997, and Marketing Manager of amplifiers a couple of months later. The Custom Shop came under his supervision when in 2000 he succeeded Mike Lewis as Vice President of Marketing for Electric Guitars. He was promoted to Vice President of Marketing for both electric guitars and amplifiers in 2002, and Senior Vice President of all Fender product marketing in 2004.

Having already served in so many capacities, he was ready to hit the ground running when he assumed responsibility for the Custom Shop. He recalls: "Just as Mike Lewis had revamped the line when he took over, I did the same thing. One thing that had changed was that the concept of the Custom Shop as an idea pool [for the larger organization] was diminishing, and it's been much less significant since the early 2000s or so. By the time I came around that was less of an issue because under Mike all the specs had already been corrected and all the workmanship and processes had been elevated.

"But I did have concerns. When John Page left and Dan Smith and Mike Eldred took over, this was an opportunity to expand and evolve the Custom Shop. To tell you the truth, my biggest concern was, had it lost its mojo? I thought, we're producing a lot of these New Old Stocks, but where is the Mayan guitar? Where is the Harley guitar? Where are the Tony Lama boots that go with the leather-covered guitar and all that stuff? So I wanted to fire up the art guitars again.

"The next issue was, the price-list items had been sitting there for years and were kind of stagnant as the core selection of Custom Shop offerings. Despite the different levels in the Time Machine series, those guitars are also where everybody starts when they order their one-offs. It's like, I want that Time Machine Closet Classic '65 Strat, but I want it in Lake Placid Blue. That's good, but I wanted to revamp the nature of the core models. Working with Mike Eldred, we created some new series. One of them was the Master Design series.

Richard McDonald vowed to revamp the core models, spotlight the individual Master Builders, and "fire up the art guitars again."

"The third concern was leveraging the Master Builders and taking them out of the shadow and bringing them forward, letting people know their names and talents and personalities, so we did bios on them with their pictures and put them in *Frontline* so you could meet the guys and get to know a bit about their specialties."

As we will see, Richard McDonald achieved all of these goals, and more. Upcoming sections provide overviews of some of the shop's programs, strategies, and instruments during the first several years of his tenure as marketing chief, beginning in 2000. Many models and series are covered in the next few chapters; please also see the separate sections on the passing of the production torch from John Page to Mike Eldred, Relics & Time Machines, and Art Guitars, the Second Decade.

Highlights 2000

The Custom Artist Series of 2000 included three Robben Fords, the Ritchie Blackmore Strat, the familiar Cray, Dale, Collins, White, and Gatton guitars, and three Tributes: the Waylon Jennings and Merle Haggard Tribute Telecasters, and the year-old Jaco Pastorius Tribute Jazz Bass.

The Team Built Time Machine Series embraced many variations of six basic instruments, all available in all three finish options. The '59 Precision Bass reissue was added to the Time Machine series in all three finishes. (What's the best-looking bass ever? The 1959 style P Bass with a 3-color sunburst and gold-anodized pickguard, or the same model in White Blonde? Take your pick.)

The Showmaster Series continued to offer three instruments (four if you count the trem/stop tailpiece option on the Set-Neck), along with a brand new 7-string Showmaster equipped with a pair of custom-width Seymour Duncan '59 humbuckers.

The Custom Classics included the Custom Classic Strat, Classic Player Strat, Custom Classic Tele, Vintage Precision Bass Custom, the unique Set Neck Tele Jr., and the new Strat-bodied Sub-Sonic, which had a 27" scale and was tuned B E A D G B. The shop continued to offer several non-standard limited-production Fenders — the three D'Aquisto models, three Robben Fords, and the Classic Rocker.

The Tribute Series

Back in the 1990s, Fender had invoked the "Tribute" designation for several Custom Shop artist guitars. Some were associated with musicians who were better known for their singing or songwriting than their guitar playing; examples included the Merle Haggard and Waylon Jennings Telecasters. Another conception of the term is offered by former Senior Vice President Ritchie Fliegler: "I'm a strong believer in rules and consistency, which is a challenge for Fender because we have endless variations on the Stratocaster and so on. At first the concept was simple and easy to grasp. A 'Signature' guitar would be a collaboration with a living artist who then lent his signature to the instrument as an approval. The 'Tribute' guitars would be those where we worked with the estate and paid tribute to artists who had passed away. That's it." (Fender also used the Tribute name for a guitar that wasn't a Custom Shop model at all but rather a factory guitar, the "mirror image" Jimi Hendrix Tribute Stratocaster of the late 1990s.)

Some Custom Shop Tribute instruments were "dream" guitars that were designed from the ground up and bore only superficial resemblance to stock Fenders; examples include the aforementioned Haggard Tele as well as the Marty Stuart Tribute Tele. The Mary Kaye Tribute Strat — a recreation of an unmodified, cataloged factory guitar — fell into none of these categories.

One of the best-looking basses of all time, the '59 Precision — complete with gold anodized pickguard and 3-color sunburst — was recreated and added to the Time Machines in 2000.

Under Mike Eldred and Richard McDonald, the name has been invoked more consistently. Since 2000, it has been applied to spot-on, ding-for-ding recreations of individual, personal instruments that attained iconic status in the hands of acclaimed artists. Built in limited runs, these Tributes reflect the Custom Shop's most meticulous work and deepest level of detail. Mike Eldred explains the characteristics that distinguish the newer generation of Tributes: "We start with an iconic guitar, one that people know. We've heard it on classic recordings that mean a lot to us. We've seen it in photos. It has a story. Then there's a whole new level of involvement and partnering with the artist — more cooperation, deeper discussions about all the details that make the original guitar special and unique. The production is more complicated and thorough than ever. Finally, we get into all the extra things that go along with the guitar, to make it even more special and memorable — a showpiece and collector's item."

Like its competitors' products, Fender's vintage reissues have been subject to increasing scrutiny over the years and held to ever higher standards of authenticity. Mike Eldred: "A lot of things we had done before weren't vintage correct. We might have built a '54 Strat, and it was good, but the magnet structure of the pickups wasn't correct, or maybe the headstock was close but not

The 7-String Showmaster demonstrated the shop's continuing commitment to innovation and its responsiveness to new styles.

perfect. But when we did the 50th anniversary '54s in 2004 [p. 458], those were dead on. We replicated materials for the knobs and switches, all the parts, everything. Remember the white, snake-head Tele, the repro of the prototype Broadcaster/Esquire that George Fullerton had originally worked on with Leo [p. 377]? I think that was the first one I experienced where it was really close and accurate. This gradual increase had taken us to a new level of authenticity that shows up in our Tributes."

These challenges are compounded by the fact that some of the original artist guitars were thoroughly worn out or even abused over decades of hard use. Some were modified backstage or in hotel rooms by the players themselves; a few of these operations were essentially battlefield surgeries performed without anesthetic. Stevie Ray Vaughan's chewed-up Number One, Rory Gallagher's stripped-to-the-raw-wood Strat, and Yngwie Malmsteen's battle-scarred "Play Loud" guitar are examples of once stock Fenders that were not only subjected to the most strenuous playing conditions imaginable but also were reconfigured, sometimes crudely, to meet the tastes and special needs of highly original artists. Reproducing these idiosyncrasies presents some of the most formidable production challenges ever faced by Fender or any other company. Every detail has to be just right. As Jason Smith puts it: "Our goal is to make the Tribute in such a way that compared to the original, the artist himself couldn't tell them apart."

In some cases, Fender's repros so precisely duplicate the originals that would-be crooks are tempted to defraud buyers by passing them off as actual vintage guitars, but in the case of the Tributes it hasn't been a problem. As true icons, the originals are often locked away in vaults or on public display in museums or other venues such as a Hard Rock Café, the Rock And Roll Hall of Fame, or the Experience Music Project in Seattle. The sale of such a guitar would be a well publicized and highly scrutinized event. Fender is nevertheless sensitive to issues of fraud and forgery, and puts the builder's signature decal on Master Built Tributes, and standard Custom Shop decals on the Team Built versions. (Jason Smith: "I have heard of guys trying to pass off their Relic Fenders as real '50s or '60s guitars, but as long as you know what to look for, it is easy to tell vintage guitars from replicas. On the Jaco bass, for example, since the neck has no finish on it, we *stamp* the Custom Shop logo on the back of the headstock.")

The deeper partnership between Fender and the artist or the artist's family results in a number of accoutrements that accompany each Tribute. Far beyond the typical "case candy" of cords, tags, and straps, these items are intended to further evoke the artist's personality, conjure the mojo of a particularly heady period of creativity and excitement, and enrich the experience for the customer. Such items may include a special certificate, a road case, boxed sets of CDs or DVDs, a repro of a personalized strap or gig bag, photos, books, posters, and more. "There's so much work and time going into each guitar," says Mike Eldred, "but then we get to do the whole package that goes along with it. It helps to make the instrument a real trophy piece, and that's a fun part of the process."

Tributes typically sell out quickly, in some cases within a day or two of their announced releases. Some are built by a single Master Builder. In other cases several or all of the Master Builders work together to finish the limited run. Team Built Tributes are built by skilled apprentices who work under the guidance and supervision of the Master Builder who prototyped the model.

Fender charges high-roller list prices for these things, so they must be making a killing, right? Actually, no. The Tributes are not big money makers. Some of them do carry price tags with an extra zero, but they're expensive to produce as well. Fender must take into account the costs of extra planning, traveling to meet with the instruments' caretakers, extra hours spent measuring and documenting the original guitars, even researching and perfecting new production techniques. Then there are all the extra hours required to recreate the guitars one at a time by hand, plus special marketing and advertising costs, and finally agreements under which artists or their estates receive a portion of the income.

Mike Eldred: "Fender doesn't get all that money, just a piece of it. Drain out the dealer's portion, all of our costs, R&D, all the man-hours we spend getting everything just right, buying special materials or whatever we need, the Web content — we build a site for each Tribute — plus the costs of replicating all the swag that goes along with each one . . . . With all that, it's not about making a lot of money. It's about acknowledging an artist who created a huge body of very influential work and used a Fender to do it. Nobody's getting rich off these things. The artist's family probably gets more money than Fender does, and we think that's fine. What's cool about it is the high level of integrity, and it's our way of paying tribute to artists who have meant so much to us, not just as a company but as devoted fans of the music. We're in business, yes, but we're players, too, and we get a huge kick out of these things because we respect these great artists so much and love their music. Another thing, when a consumer buys an Andy Summers guitar or a Crossroads Strat, that guy has a real collectible and it can go up in value, and that's key. That's why when we do a Tribute we'll sell maybe a hundred guitars. They have availability, but it's limited. It's a way for the player to partner and invest in Fender's rich tradition and legacy."

> "It's not about making a lot of money. It's our way of paying tribute to artists who have meant so much to us, not just as a company but as devoted fans of the music." — Mike Eldred

	A	B	C
	rument	SEYMOUR W. DUNCAN-**Signature Model**	
	IDER ESQUIRE	**Specifications: Sunburst Esquire**	
	pecifications:		
	hickness	Stock Fender Vintage Specifications	
	ieces	2 Piece Alder for 2 tone sunburst finish-D&G joined	
	Material	2 Piece Alder	Optional Ash
	Length	Stock Fender Vintage Specifications	
	Width	Stock Fender Vintage Specifications	
	Solid/Hollow/Semi-Hollow	Solid Body Electric	
	Finish	Nitrocellulose Lacquer	
	Color	Vintage Two Tone Sunburst Nitrocellulose Lacquer	Optional Blond
	Features	Esquire with Telecaster Body Rout	
	Weight	**Will get info for approx. weight and wood**	
	y Radius on edges	**Will get spec information...sharper than re-issue 52**	
	ctronics		
	nber of Pickups	One Multi-Tapped Seymour Duncan Custom Shop Pickup	
	e of Pickups	Single Coil with Rod Magnets-Vintage looking	
	w Mounted	3 Point Mounting using Ferrous Bridge Plate	
	itches	3 Way-1452 ElectroSwitch	
	lume Controls	250K Audio Taper with custom wiring circuit	
	ne Controls	250K Audio Taper using .05 mfd. 50v Cap. On Master Tone	
	eck Specifications:	Hardrock Maple-Esquire neck with Clarence White Specs	
	eck Finish	Nitrocellulose Lacquer-thinner	
	eck Color	Aged look	
	eck Material	Hardrock Maple-Esquire neck with Clarence White Specs	
	ingerboard Material	Maple	
	Fingerboard Inlay	Traditional Position Markers-Phenolic?	
	Fingerboard Radius	11"	
	Fret Specifications:		
	Fret Width	Vintage Specifications	
	Fret Height	Vintage Specifications	
	Fret Length	Length measures the same as neck fingerboard width	
	Original Frets	Vintage	
	Frets Dressed	Dressed slightly and polished	
	Binding	No	
	Neck Width:		
7	Nut	C Neck	
8	5th Fret	Traditional specifications	
9	8th Fret	Traditional specifications	
0	12th Fret	Traditional specifications	
11	15th Fret	Traditional specifications	
42	21st Fret	Traditional specifications	
43	Total Frets	21	
44	**Neck Thickness:**		
45	Headstock	Tapered traditional specifications	
46	Nut	Traditional specifications	
47	5th Fret	Traditional specifications	
48	8th Fret	Traditional specifications	
49	12th Fret	Traditional specifications	
50	15th Fret	Traditional specifications	
51	21st Fret or Last Fret	Traditional specifications	
52	**Neck Mounting:**		
53	Solid Mount	Traditional 4 Bolt Neck	
54	Screw Mounting	Yes-4 oval head/slotted	
55	Neck Depth	**.125" deeper than Traditional**	
56	**Screws:**		
57	Tuning Keys	Vintage style Kluson Deluxe & Ferrules	
58	Truss Rod	Traditional Vintage Specifications	
59	Neck	Traditional Vintage Oval Head Slotted Wood Screws-slightly shorter	
60	Pickguard	Traditional Vintage Oval Head Slotted Wood Screws	
61	Bridge	Traditional Vintage Oval Head Slotted Wood Screws	
62	Pickup Mounting Springs	Vintage Ambar Surgical Tubing	
63	Pickup Mounting	Round Head Slotted Machine Screws	
64	Jack Plate	Traditional Cup	
65	Strap Buttons	Traditional # 6 x 1" Wood Screws-Oval Head slotted	
66	String Retainer	Vintage Round String Tree using Oval Head Slotted WS	
67	Control Plate Screw	Traditional Vintage Specifications-Oval Head Slotted WS	
68	**Misc. Information:**		

Every detail of each Custom Shop instrument is spec'd out to the max, right down to the control plate screws.

"My one old guitar"
The Muddy Waters Tribute Tele 2000

The artistry of McKinley Morganfield, better known as Muddy Waters, had an incalculable effect on American culture in the last half of the 20th Century. In 1943, the native of Rolling Fork, Mississippi, took the Illinois Central up to the teeming urban environment of post-War Chicago and within a few years recorded his first sides for the Chess brothers. Over the next four decades Muddy Waters would acquire many nicknames and credits, among them The Father of Chicago Blues, The Man Who Invented The Modern Rock Band, The Hootchie-Cootchie Man, and the Mannish Boy (I spell M . . . .). In 1983 this author interviewed Muddy Waters for *Guitar Player* magazine, with Johnny Winter sitting in on the conversation. Muddy explained that he had acquired his famous red Telecaster in 1957 or 1958.

Johnny Winter: "That's Muddy Waters's guitar, and it won't let anyone play it but him. You pick it up and it just says, 'No!' You can't believe the action. My own action stays real high, but it's nothing compared to Muddy's."

Muddy Waters: "Yeah, I got a heavy hand. Everyone says, 'Oh man, the strings are too high! What are you doing [laughs]?' A lot of guys want to squeeze and bend their strings up, like B.B., so they have the strings real low. My strings are heavy, like a .012 or a .013 for the first one. I don't need to worry about bending, because I can slide so high up there."

Johnny Winter: "The heavier the strings, the better your chance of getting a good sound, definitely."

When asked which tunings he used, Muddy replied: "Mostly standard, 'cause it's tough if you're waiting in between songs to tune to G or A. And I'm too lazy to carry two or three guitars around like Johnny [laughs]. He's still a young boy. He can pull that stuff around. What would I look like with two or three guitars like these kids? I don't need to be bothered with that. I got my one old guitar."

For the first "icon" guitar of the revised Tribute series, the Custom Shop borrowed Muddy's Tele from the Rock And Roll Hall of Fame and Museum in Cleveland. It is a unique Fender. As Muddy told this author: "In the '50s a guy in Chicago made me a neck for it, a big stout neck with the high nut to raise up the strings for slide. I needed to strengthen it up because of the big strings, and I think that the big neck has a lot to do with the big sound." The knobs were replaced with Fender skirt-style amp knobs. Otherwise, the guitar's features are mostly stock, but of course its deep, inexpressible mojo reflects decades of music and toil under the "heavy hand" of Muddy Waters.

George Blanda took measuring tapes, gauges, and calipers to the guitar. He remembers: "It was an incredible experience where I felt the weight of the responsibility of examining the 'artifact,' as the staff called it. A quick example — the first thing a tech would do to check out the details of a guitar would be to cut off the strings and pop the neck. It became crystal clear that the strings on the artifact had not been disturbed in the 20-plus years since Muddy had played it. I was sweating bullets, hoping that one of them wouldn't break as I carefully unwound them."

Blanda forwarded the specs to John Cruz, who recalls: "The Muddy Waters was one of the very early ones I was involved in, before I was a Master Builder. I think I probably got those early ones like the Rory and the Muddy because I had had success with the Relic process. There was no Master Builder in charge of the Muddy project. It was basically my baby. I made the first proto, then trained the Team Built side of the Relic department on how to get the look. So this was one of the first Team Built custom runs. There were only 40 pieces made. I did a few, and the team did the rest." (A more affordable, made-in-Mexico version soon followed the Custom Shop's original run.)

As it turned out, duplicating the nonstock color was one of the thorniest challenges. The finish had been applied by someone other than a Fender painter, perhaps a former owner. It had a primer coat underneath the red, which further complicated the task. John Cruz: "We came up with a custom version of Candy Apple Red that we darkened up a little bit. The thickness of the paint, the primer coat — all these things had to be considered before we even began to relic it and duplicate the worn areas. We had several different paint samples we went through, but by the end of the process I think we pretty much nailed it.

Right: Fender amp knobs, a nonstock red finish, and replications of the wear and tear inflicted under the heavy hand of the Mannish Boy — the Muddy Waters Tribute Tele 2000.

8 7 6 5 4 3 2
8 7 6 5 4 3 2 1

"I won't lie to you. Even before you start work on something like this, there is so much planning — the measuring, the experimentation. You have to figure out how to recreate something that's several decades old and has been in a particular person's hands for so long and has been treated a certain way and exposed to certain environmental conditions. It takes a lot of hard work and many, many painstaking hours to get these details right."

The Muddy Waters Tribute Tele 2000 came with a Mojo Accessory Kit, including a slide, a capo, a thumbpick and fingerpicks, a copy of *The Lost Tapes* CD, and a signed and framed poster of Muddy by noted Chicago blues photographer Raeburn Flerlage.

The R&D Master Builder

Another example of shared activities between R&D and the Custom Shop is that as we go to press, R&D has its own Master Builder, Mike Bump. He explains: "I believe I was the first Master Builder dedicated to R&D, and that became official in 2000. I am a Master Builder, but I don't have a decal and don't get all the glory that comes along with Master Builders in the Custom Shop. I'm sort of a stunt man [laughs], working directly for the plant itself, rather than for an individual customer. A lot of the guitars that you see in the catalog were put together by us in the R&D model shop for the *Frontline* photo shoots."

Mike Bump cites several other tasks performed in R&D that parallel or duplicate former or present assignments in the Custom Shop, such as crafting instruments for NAMM show displays and building prototypes for production. An example of the latter is the Eric Johnson Stratocaster. Despite Johnson's long association with the Custom Shop, Mike Stevens in particular, the Eric Johnson Strat was developed in R&D. Mike Bump: "There was a *lot* of labor in that one. Eric is just so particular. It happens to be one of our best-selling models."

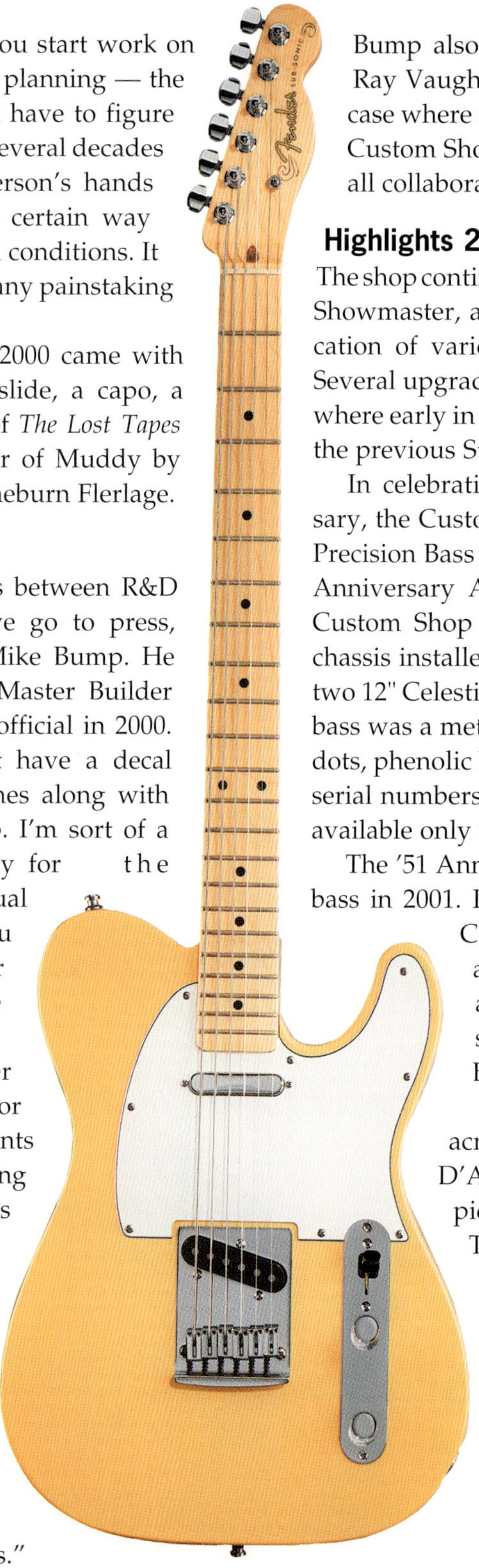

Bump also cites Fender's early work on the Stevie Ray Vaughan Tribute Number One Stratocaster as a case where executives such as Richard McDonald, the Custom Shop's John Cruz, and R&D's George Blanda all collaborated.

Highlights 2001

The shop continued to offer the Time Machine, D'Aquisto, Showmaster, and Custom Artist Series, with some relocation of various models from one series to another. Several upgrades appeared in the Custom Classic series, where early in the year the Sub-Sonic was offered in both the previous Strat incarnation and a new Tele version.

In celebration of the Precision Bass's 50th Anniversary, the Custom Shop premiered the 1951 Anniversary Precision Bass (not to be confused with the factory's 50th Anniversary American Series P Bass), along with the Custom Shop Bass Breaker amp, basically a Bassman chassis installed in a 2x12 lacquered tweed cabinet with two 12" Celestion Vintage 30 speakers. The Custom Shop bass was a meticulous recreation, with fiber fingerboard dots, phenolic bridge saddles, and a chipboard case. The serial numbers started at A001, and the instrument was available only through 2001.

The '51 Anniversary Precision wasn't the shop's only bass in 2001. It was joined by five others: the Custom Classic 4 and 5-string Jazz Basses, each with an 18V onboard preamp; the Jaco Tribute; and two models from the Time Machine series — the '59 P Bass and the '64 Jazz Bass.

Custom Shop instruments were offered across a wide range of retail prices. The D'Aquisto Ultra with a Kent Armstrong pickup topped the 2001 price list at $15,529. The D'Aquisto Deluxe cost a fraction of that figure, at $3,279. The Robben Ford Ultra FM and SP models cost $6,029, while at $5,029 (another 400 bucks for the Roland option) the Blackmore Stratocaster topped the line of Team Built

Long necked and low down: In early 2001, the shop served up the colossal twang of the Sub-Sonic in a new Tele incarnation.

Strats. Among Teles and Strats, the most expensive Custom Shop guitar was Mark Kendrick's handmade Haggard Tribute Tele at $5,779.

Highlights 2002

The familiar series — Time Machines, Custom Classics, Custom Artists — were continued. The Custom Artist series was augmented with 4 and 5-string versions of the Reggie Hamilton Jazz Bass; details included a modified Jazz Bass body, sculpted heel, unique pickup combos, block inlays, and active/passive electronics.

In a further refinement of the Team Built concept, players and Custom Shop Master Dealers were now encouraged to participate in the new Custom Team Built program. It both responded to and furthered the trend of using Team Built models as starting points for personalized one-offs or limited runs. This strategy would remain a cornerstone of the relationship between the shop, dealers, and players up to the present day.

Reflecting Richard McDonald's intent to bring Custom Shop craftspeople into the spotlight, all of the builders were pictured in the 2002 *Frontline*: Senior Master Builders Stephen Stern, Jason Davis, John English, Art Esparza, Mark Kendrick, Todd Krause, and Yuriy Shishkov, and Master Builders Louis Salgado, Greg Fessler, and Dennis Galuszka. A partial list of each builder's star clients was included. Ralph Esposito: "Now, people come to us with a request for a particular Master Builder. It's like anything else — a painting, a drawing. It's going to be totally you, and that's the way these guitars are. Something about you is going to be in that instrument, and each one of these builders has a different genre. They come from different places and have different art forms, and all that comes out in their guitars."

The year 2002 saw the introduction of Jazz Basses designed in collaboration with Reggie Hamilton, whose artistry has graced the music of Tina Turner, Randy Newman, Aaron Neville, Bette Midler, Gladys Knight, Whitney Houston, and many others.

The Jimmy Bryant Tribute Tele honored one of the company's earliest endorsers and one of the slickest, fastest players to ever strap on a Fender.

The Jimmy Bryant Tribute Telecaster

The white blonde, ash-bodied Jimmy Bryant Tribute Telecaster of 2003 honored one of Leo Fender's earliest and most important endorsers. In *The Stratocaster Chronicles*, George Fullerton described the influence of Bryant's endorsement at the dawn of the company: "That set the thing really rolling, because everybody wanted to play like Jimmy." Of course, no one did. The late country jazzer could thrill you with a white-knuckle speed ride that felt like a careening roller coaster threatening to leave the rails, all while rendering sophisticated melodies, seemingly without effort. His recordings continue to drop jaws to this day. Even Chet Atkins once said, "I could never get in his league." Also billed as the Jimmy Bryant Signature Telecaster, the Bryant Tribute had a 9.5" radius that might have felt a little flat to Bryant (who knows?), but many modern players prefer it to the vintage Tele's 7.5. Details included Nocaster pickups, a tooled-leather pickguard overlay, and a price tag of about $3,200.

The Seymour Duncan Signature Esquire

It might strike some folks as ironic that a person who designs and sells pickups for a living prefers to play a guitar with only one of them, but Seymour Duncan, a terrific guitar player, loves his '50s-era Esquire. (Who wouldn't?) That instrument has a 1954 body and a 1956 neck, and it served as the basis for the Custom Shop's Seymour Duncan Signature Esquire, introduced in January, 2003. Seymour himself specified and personally oversaw every detail, from its tapped pickup design to the 100% nitro lacquer finish. "I'm an Esquire kind of guy, a one-pickup guy," he says. "I like the simplicity of it, the way you can manipulate the volume and tone controls for wah wah effects or volume swells. I always loved Jeff Beck with the Yardbirds, and I thought it was so cool that he was doing all that with one pickup. There was something authoritative about it. I always wanted to do the same sorts of things and have some fun with it. Mike Eldred did a whole wall of custom color Esquires that he showed me at a NAMM show. He was real proud of

Influenced by his idol, Jeff Beck, Seymour Duncan selected the one-pickup Esquire for his signature Fender.

More than 200 hours of labor (much of it by Todd Krause) went into the Target Grand Prix guitar, whose release coincided with the 225-lap Grand Prix at the Chicago Motor Speedway. The race was sponsored by the Target retail chain. The guitar's body was virtually a scale model of the Target racing team's CART champion race car. It was painted by Troy Lee, well known for his racing helmet paint jobs.

them, and they were just so cool. I was so honored when they told me I could have my own Signature Esquire."

Evan Skopp, Seymour Duncan's Vice President of Business Development, was involved in the project from the outset. He explains that the guitar's neck is set an eighth of an inch deeper into the neck pocket than normal, which lowers the neck relative to the body: "Seymour likes to use beefy brass saddles, and he's noticed that if you set the height-adjust screws low, you'll get better mechanical coupling. By lowering the neck, you can lower the saddles and bring the strings closer to the pickup."

Seymour Duncan: "You get more of the tone from the pickup's magnetic field. If the strings are too high, you don't get the mids I wanted, and too much of the sound comes from the strings. It's too twangy. Also, the 3-way switch gives you a lot of tone possibilities. The full pickup is 7.6k, which is a DC resistance of 7,600 Ohms. During the winding I run a wire out and continue winding, so I have two outputs. I tap the pickup at about 6.3k, and then in the [switch's] neck position it's that 6.3 but with a tone capacitor that rolls it off a little bit to make it jazzier."

Fender and Duncan sent several necks back and forth during prototyping, but most were actually Strat necks. Seymour selected a neck with a 1962-ish Strat neck contour, but with a Tele/Esquire headstock. He winds the pickups himself, and his company also makes up the wiring harnesses for the Duncan Esquire. "Every single one of those guitars I've gotten my hands on has played just fantastic and sounded great, too," Seymour says. "I got a call from a guy who had bought one, and he was so pleased with it. You know who it was? James Taylor. He's such a great acoustic player. I think this might have been his first electric. He just wanted to call and say he loves it and is really stoked. He plays it all the time and is proud to have it. It was so great to hear that."

The Woodstock Strat (Slight Return)

Now with about 50 Master and apprentice builders, the shop was well positioned to explore new designs and strategies. One of the most memorable projects of 2003 — or any year, for that matter — was Mike Eldred's personal recreations of the Jimi Hendrix Woodstock Stratocaster.

If you had to pick one instrument to rightfully be called The Most Famous Electric Guitar Of All Time, the white 1968 Stratocaster played by Jimi Hendrix at Woodstock in 1969 would be a credible contender. With this guitar, Jimi Hendrix radically transformed "The Star Spangled Banner," not to mention popular music in general. High-tech tycoon Paul Allen purchased it in 1991 for $325,000. He put it on display at the Experience Music Project in Seattle, the interactive museum that he founded in 2000.

By 2002, Ritchie Fliegler was a seven-year Fender veteran and Senior Vice President for Market Development. A major component of his job was to establish and nurture creative partnerships. "Steven Sather was my counterpart at the Experience Music Project," he explains. "Although it was founded by Paul Allen, the EMP operates as an independent entity and needs to raise money like any other nonprofit. It's a good cause, and I wanted to get Fender involved.

"We came up with this idea to reproduce the Jimi Hendrix Woodstock Stratocaster – every dent, ding and iota. It wasn't going to be just a passable replica. The level of detail was going to be insane, and that was the plan from the very beginning. This project was a landmark for Fender because it was the first time where we brought this ridiculous level of detail to the project. It took reams and reams of notes and photographs, lots of video, and endless hours of research and labor to pull it off."

Mike Eldred: "Ritchie called me into his office and said, 'Look, we're going to *clone* this guitar. It has to be exact in every way. This is going to be a new level for Fender.' After that, we all knew — it was *game on*."

Anybody who would take on the formidable task of recreating this icon among icons would likely have no shortage in the self-confidence department. It was Mike Eldred who stepped up. In fact, he fairly begged for the assignment. "I'm a huge Hendrix fan," he says, "and as soon as Ritchie laid it out, I looked at him and said, I want to build them all myself. I'll work after hours, I'll camp out, I'll work on Sundays, whatever I have to do. Instead of business and marketing, it would allow me to concentrate on guitar building again, which is why I'm here in the first place, and on a really personal level it would be my way to honor Jimi Hendrix. Ritchie said okay."

Right: "Mike says, 'You know what that is, right?' The EMP people say no, no idea. He says, 'That's sweat.' So that was one of those moments — Jimi Hendrix's actual sweat, still on the guitar, right in front of them."

Fender
STRATOCASTER
TONE
TONE
VOLUME

Mike Eldred and George Blanda flew to Seattle. EMP's curators shut down the Hendrix exhibit, and the two Fendermen spent hours poring over the Woodstock Stratocaster. George Blanda: "Mike had done massive research on this guitar prior to us going. He had unearthed incredible detail, knew its serial number, the previous owners, and so on."

"This had to be a white-glove sort of deal," explains Ritchie Fliegler, "practically a scientific dissection, in order to get it right. Those guys were all over that guitar, and the level, the depth at which they picked it apart – just insanity. Mike starts with his rulers and measuring stuff, and then he pulls out a screwdriver. The EMP guys go, 'What are you doing?' He says, 'I'm taking the guitar apart.' And they say, *'What do you mean?'*

George Blanda: "They were dead set against us doing any disassembly. There was a film crew there to document the event — and probably to prove any liability if we did any damage. Mike was masterful in his negotiating and debating with the curator. This was just after we'd done the Muddy Waters Telecaster. Mike leveraged the fact that I had taken apart the Muddy Waters guitar at the Rock And Roll Hall of Fame to persuade the EMP to allow us to disassemble the Hendrix Strat. They reluctantly allowed us to do it."

Ritchie Fliegler: "So there was a moment when the caretakers had to grasp that this guitar was going to be disassembled, but there was no other way to do it, no way to absorb its vibe without getting inside it. So, much to their terror, Mike started to take the guitar apart."

Mike Eldred: "It was hushed. They just watched, no one saying anything."

George Blanda: "Mike did the disassembly, and I mainly took notes and video. The guitar itself was one of those stock Strats where everything happened to be done right, pretty rare in '68. It was not at all bashed. This was a guitar that Jimi especially liked as a player, and it was always taken care of. The smashing, burning, and bashing was done to his less favored Strats. This one had a great medium C shaped neck and just great fit and finish. Everything inside was completely stock and undisturbed and really neatly done. Where things got strange was looking at the wear marks. Of course, all the wear patterns were reversed due to his being left-handed and playing a righty. It was very clean, but when you looked close it was just covered with these very odd indentations, very slight, but hundreds everywhere, made by beads that Jimi had worn. The neck had an even, light dusting of tiny dents from the many rings that he wore while playing."

Ritchie Fliegler: "If you remember, there was a period when Strats had that sheet of aluminum underneath the pickguard for shielding. On the Hendrix guitar, there was a green strip underneath it, up against the body, where it had turned color. Mike says, 'You know what that is, right?' The EMP people say no, no idea. He says, 'That's *sweat.'* So that was one of those moments — Jimi Hendrix's actual sweat, still on the guitar, right in front of them." Mike Eldred: "It's like that Strat was alive. In all my years of working with guitars, I have never held anything that had so much vibe to it."

The experience was, in a way, an intimate one, a different kind of glimpse into the life and music of Jimi Hendrix. After the examination, EMP curators put the white Strat back in its alarmed display. At that moment, Mike Eldred recalled: "I felt this overwhelming sadness because no one would ever do that again."

The Custom Shop followed up with a limited-edition project, more limited than usual. Mike Eldred personally built only four replicas, signing each one on the inside of the tremolo cover and initialing each one on the headstock. Fender and the EMP wanted them fairly quickly, and Mike estimates that he completed the work in a month or two, concentrating on little else during that period.

All the painstaking research paid off. While many Custom Shop guitars radiate extraordinary quality, there's something special about a guitar that comes from the hands of a single builder. Ritchie Fliegler: "This wasn't the kind of thing where you have a team of guys building guitars and each one has his own interpretation. You've got one guy, and he's putting his heart and soul into it, and he knows every single detail of each of those replicas. Let me tell you something: These five guitars – the original plus the four clones – are *indistinguishable* from each other, and I do not say that lightly. The colors were correctly aged, and the output of the pickups and the neck dimensions were matched. This is why all that deep research was necessary. Like the separate components on each guitar — a particular part would not only look exactly the same, it would *weigh* the same."

This project was not about making money for Fender. In fact, all four guitars were either given away or auctioned off in 2003. Paul Allen got one for the EMP. The Fender Museum, which operates independently from Fender Musical Instruments, got one; Mike Eldred and Bill Schultz presented it to John Page. Jimi's sister Janie received one for the Hendrix family. In 2003, one was sold at London's Cooper Owen auction house to raise money for the EMP. It sold for a less-than-expected figure, reportedly under $11,000. It has since changed hands at least twice, selling for several times its original price.

To this day, Mike Eldred's Jimi Hendrix experience remains a career high point. "Just to hold that guitar," he reminisces, "a feeling came over me. I can't put it into words, but there was so much great art created on that guitar, and I was standing there with so much history cradled right there in my hands. I'll never forget that moment."

The John 5 Telecasters

Two J5 Telecaster models were designed in association with John 5 and unveiled in 2003. They differ in bridge type (fixed vs. Bigsby vibrato), pickups, and controls. Their three-on-a-side paddle headstocks are stunning departures from one of Fender's most recognizable assets. Other details include a flashy chrome pickguard and a rosewood board with a relatively flat 12" radius. While the massive chrome plate surrounding the Bigsby version's rear pickup and bridge may appear to be another non-Fender detail,

The paddle-head John 5 Tele, Bigsby version.

Above: one of John 5's personal guitars, a three-pickup Tele with a mirror pickguard, handcrafted by Yuriy Shishkov and pictured on Yuriy's workbench.

in fact it duplicates Fender's stock Bigsby-equipped Telecaster of the late 1960s. On the hardtail, the two knobs are both volume controls. The prices: about $3,300 for the hardtail, about $3,600 for the Bigsby version. John 5 said the color combo of black, white, and chrome reminded him of a motorcycle.

Mudflaps and Flat Heads

The builders introduced no less than a half-dozen guitars in 2003 that continued to reflect their passion for blending guitar design with the esthetics and raunchy excitement of fuel-burning vehicles. They collaborated with the So-Cal Speed Shop to unleash a Tele and a Strat designed to match high-performance So-Cal street rods. They also displayed a gorgeous pink/tan Esquire pinstriped by famed hot rod striper Dennis Ricklefs. The Trucker Strat Special (also called the Maximum Overdrive) had a diamond-plate pickguard, strap holders fashioned from lug nut bolts, and 12th-fret inlays that recalled those improbably endowed babes often silhouetted in chrome on big-rig mudflaps.

Named after their flat tops as well as a fabled internal combustion engine type that made history powering Fords, Harleys, and other vehicles, the Flat Head Showmaster and Flat Head Telecaster shared several features: a flat-top alder body, a relatively flat 12" radius, flat black hardware, and a crossed-pistons inlay rendered in showroom-shiny nickel silver at the 12th fret. (It was likely no coincidence that at first glance the Fender F logo and crossed pistons could be mistaken for a skull and crossbones.) There were no other fingerboard markers, which stoked the badass quotient of the asphalt-black ebony fingerboard. The new humbucker

In 2003 the shop revved up a fleet of car-inspired guitars, including cataloged Flat Heads and a unique So-Cal Speed Shop Strat. The So-Cal Speed Shop was founded on March 3, 1946, in Burbank. During the same period, a 45-minute drive to the south, an ambitious radio repairman established the Fender Electric Instrument Manufacturing Company.

SO-CAL
SPEED SHOP
SO-CAL
SPEED SHOP

SO-CAL
SPEED SHOP
SCSS est. 1946

was named the Enforcer, which sounded like a Top Fuel dragster. Described as "no-nonsense, industrial-strength guitars," these one-pickup, one-knob, hardtail bad boys may have conjured the vibe of a stripped-down street rod more than any other Custom Shop tone machines. On a gig with a Flat Head, instead of a break between sets, you might pull in for a pit stop.

And in other 2003 news . . . .

The Strat-bodied Sub-Sonic had disappeared, but the Tele version remained in the line. Appearing in the summer of 2002 and officially premiering in January 2003, the 55 Precision Bass recreated the second-generation version of the venerable P Bass. Available in all three Time Machine finishes, it featured top and back contours on an otherwise slab body, a Tele type peghead, string-through bridge, two saddles, a single-ply white pickguard, and dome style Tele knobs. John English built the NAMM show examples in Teal Green, Fiesta Red, and other custom colors. Nice touch: The painted thumb rest matched the body color.

Also displayed in 2003: a sunburst Telecaster built by Alex Perez for Jeremy Popoff of the California band Lit; it featured a diamond-plate pickguard. Master Builder Louis Salgado crafted a striking quilt-top Showmaster with a transparent green finish, ebony board, single black humbucker, and a Floyd Rose.

Left: Spade tuners, a machine-turned top that looks like a 1930s sports car dashboard, custom inlays, racing logos, and a wolfy cartoon hipster — all part of the Custom Shop/So-Cal esthetic.

Right: A pretty-in-pink Precision, '55-style, built by John English.

Years in the making, the Bonecaster Esquire was built for Billy Gibbons by Chris Fleming, with artwork by Kit Carson.

CHAPTER TWENTY-FIVE

25

The Mermaids of Avalon and Other Tales

Art Guitars of the Second Decade

During the shop's second decade, Master Builders continued to craft art guitars of their own design. Another smart way to increase the production of art guitars without overwhelming the Master Builders was to partner with graphic artists whose involvement went beyond the roles of some of the earlier collaborators. Previously, a single instrument might entail contributions from several contributors — a wood carver, an inlay specialist, a painter, an engraver, etc. In recent years, however, a Master Builder has often given a body and neck to a single artist, letting him or her take it from there, sometimes in a carte-blanche arrangement. The result: some of the most elaborate, memorable, and expensive guitars ever to bear a Custom Shop decal.

Reappearing in this section are some familiar names — Pamelina H., George Amicay, and a few of the Master Builders. Several of the independent artists are mentioned briefly (Dan Lawrence, Ron Thorn, Kid Ramos, Shag, Dennis McPhail, Kirsten Easthope), while others are profiled in some depth, including Dave Newman, Sara Ray, Nevena Christie, Kit Carson, and Joe Wood. The point is not to include every artist and art guitar — for every instrument pictured here there are others, equally stunning — but rather to profile some of the artists and artworks that during the shop's second decade exemplified the extraordinary talents of the Master Builders and their creative partners. Additional art guitars from the second decade appear in other chapters.

The Song of the Road

Ever since Huck Finn lit out for the territory, the American spirit has been infused with wanderlust. That urge to getcher motor runnin', get out on the highway was particularly intense in the age of Kerouac's *On The Road*. Whether sightseeing with the fam in a Buick Roadmaster wagon or some tailfinned heavy cruiser, or embarking on a voyage of self-discovery in a souped-up jalopy or maybe straddling a roaring Harley, countless Americans hit the road in the 1950s and 1960s. It was all part of the grand tradition in which generations of travelers were pulled west by the promise of new beginnings, the unexpected sight up around the bend, the adventure in the next town.

The Eisenhower Administration had overseen a massive expansion of the country's highway system, and

SUCKER
PUNCH
SALLYS
OLD SCHOOL CHOPPERS
YOU BETTER BE READY

Here's a fabulous motorcycle and a Custom Shop guitar to go with it. Or is it the other way around? In any case, this set was a collaboration between the Custom Shop, artist Sara Ray, Triumph motorcycles, and Sucker Punch Sallys, a builder of hand-assembled, old-school motorcycles based in Scottsdale, Arizona.

The bike is a Triumph Thruxton, sort of the Fender Esquire of the motorcycle world. As the Triumph company puts it, "All that's really needed, for many, are an engine, two wheels, a seat and a pair of handlebars. The Thruxton captures that spirit." This particular example was described as being "fitted with custom parts and paint to make it look like a vintage Isle of Man Café Racer." The original café racers — the term applies to both bikes and riders — were rambunctious British bikers who loved '50s-style rockabilly music and fast, stripped-down cycles. The retro vibe fits perfectly with the dungarees & ducktails esthetic celebrated in so many of the Custom Shop's projects.

The bike, the Fender Esquire, and the accoutrements were all painted by Sara Ray. She reports: "The back of the guitar shows a Union Jack with a racer's skull, and the skull is repeated on the bike. I worked with Mike Eldred from Fender, a Triumph owner and lover who collaborated with Christian Clayton at Sucker Punch. The only detail I was given was that they wanted something vintage that paid homage to the Isle of Man races and the Ace Café-era racers. The girl on the guitar is also on the top of the Triumph's tank, and I created her for this set. I also created 'patches' that were painted on the bike and jacket, including a '90 MPH Face Sliders' patch for Mike Eldred, who had recently been in a motorcycle accident."

Lower right: Sucker Punch Sallys' owner, Christian Clayton, is pictured with Mike Eldred.

along with the endless miles of new roads and thousands of filling stations came a new kind of inn, the motor hotel — or "motel" — which catered to weary travelers after a long day behind the wheel. In the big-sky country there was plenty of room for roadside attractions and jumbo signs with neon gas coursing through their veins, their colors ranging from pastel pinky-oranges to lurid purples. Out on the plains in the clear night air, you could see them blinking and buzzing from a mile away, which of course was the whole idea. Along with conventional diners, soda fountains, roadhouses, cafes and coffee shops, travelers could break up their trips with stops at Navajo trading posts, motel cottages shaped like wigwams, or a restaurant wrapped in a whimsical concoction of stucco that looked like a pioneer wagon, a two-story cactus, a spaceship, or a cartoon doghouse.

Fender, of course, was founded in the same region that helped spawn any number of automobile-related trends — hot rods, sports cars, drag racing, convertibles, drive-in malt shops, drive-in movies, "Drive-Thru" bank tellers, and more. In Southern California, it was all about the car. Fender's embrace of cool autos goes back to Bob Perine's catalog photos of the early 1960s; he sometimes included his own sharp-finned '57 Thunderbird alongside kids and guitars in those classic oceanside scenes. Some Fender models shared the names of popular autos (Mustangs, Jaguars), and back in the late 1960s some of the guitars even sported racing stripes.

The Custom Shop's V logo was inspired by retro automotive insignia, and to this day an entire series of Fenders might evoke an exuberant, hot-asphalt vibe — Road Worn, Highway One, Flat Head, Hot Rod guitars, Hot Rod amps. If you buy a set of Samarium Cobalt Noiseless pickups from Fender's Mod Shop, the package doesn't picture a guitar; it pictures a fuel-injected engine from some monster dragster (the letters "O" in "MOd" and "ShOp" are spinning tires). The automobilia even extends to fashion; some of the shirts in Fender's official, logo-adorned line of clothing could have been worn by a Texaco crew somewhere out on Route 66 back when Leo Fender was dreaming up the wide-panel tweeds.

Nowhere is Fender's love of fuel-burning, tire-smokin' vehicles more evident than in the Custom Shop. Consider its collaborations with Harley-Davidson, the So-Cal Speed

Shop, Ferrari, Ford/Shelby, Mattel/Hot Wheels, Toyota Matrix, the Target Grand Prix, and Sucker Punch Sallys. Visitors to the shop's NAMM exhibits in recent years have seen everything from guitars displayed inside replicas of vintage gas pumps to an entire Custom Shop layout that was a virtual shrine to an auto junkyard, complete with retro hubcaps, truck bumpers, dented car doors with faded commercial logos, and piles of rust-caked parts that long ago ran fast, hot and greasy in the guts of internal combustion engines. It's no surprise that some of the graphic artists with whom Fender has worked in recent years have deep roots in the automotive community, or that some of their work reflects a retro/hot rod esthetic.

Dave Newman's jigsaw journeys

Based in Prescott, Arizona, artist Dave Newman works in collage, metal, wood, acrylic paint, and silkscreen. He spends plenty of time scouring antique stores, swap meets, and garage sales, looking for pieces of found art that might find their way into one of his multimedia creations, perhaps alongside an image from one of his many photographs or a ripped-out picture from an automobile ad or a guitar catalog. Sometimes he'll spot something by the side of the road. It might be a discarded item most people would call junk, just some throwaway, but Dave may see potential in it, something evocative. Next thing you know, it's integrated into a one-of-a-kind 6-string work of Fender guitar art.

Dave Newman's influences range from Van Gogh and Matisse to Andy Warhol and Robert Rauschenberg, not to mention Stevie Ray Vaughan and Los Lobos. He is a keen observer of, and aficionado of, post-war American consumer culture, particularly from the 1950s and 1960s. All of these influences show up in the guitars, amps, and cases he paints and collages for Fender. "We usually leave things pretty loose and open," he explains. "We get a general idea, like — let's do a road trip piece — and then they turn me loose and the process is spontaneous from that point. The two main ingredients I use are acrylic paint and collage. I do a lot of sanding and use a lot of different layers.

"I'm basically self-taught, although I've read a lot about art. [Early 20th Century German painter/collagist] Kurt Schwitters was an influence. Picasso was another pioneer. Warhol and Rauschenberg were big influences. I respond to all sorts of visual stuff, like signs and advertisements. I do a lot of photography and sometimes I cut out pictures I see in magazines, or I'll use vintage postcards, old sheet music, wallpaper, a little of everything."

Some of Dave Newman's Custom Shop guitars seem to evoke a jumble of fractured memories from a lifetime of honky-tonking, bowling, road trips, drive-thru meals, high-stakes poker, swigging Lone Star longnecks in pool halls, and watching late-night television in some lost-highway one-nighter motel. "I take bits and pieces," he says, "and put them together to tell, or hint at, a story of some kind, something that people might relate to in their own lives. I'm very big on running just a partial picture of something, a fragment, rather than the whole image. That's just the way I think about things. I'm dyslexic, and things are very fragmented." While individual details are fun to pick out, it's through their interplay that Dave Newman conjures his magic. "My pieces are kind of like jigsaw puzzles, where it may look random at first but the more you look at it the more you see how balanced it is. These things are actually quite orderly."

Dave estimates that he has painted about two dozen guitars for the Custom Shop, most of them built by Chris Fleming. He usually works on a number of different projects at a time, so it's hard to say how much work goes into each guitar or amp. He says, "When I get into them they are so consuming that they just sort of take over everything. I'm so intent on it and think about them and talk about them all the time. I may spend two or three weeks just on one guitar. It's been so great working with Chris Fleming, Dave Brown, and Fender and to see how their views and mine can come together. I mean, what could be more Americana than Fender guitars?"

One of Dave Newman's most striking collaborations with Senior Master Builder Chris Fleming was the Travel Master Esquire. It was paired with a Pro Jr., displayed at the January 2005 NAMM show, and offered at a price of $15,999.

Fender
VACANCY
HOTEL
STILL 15¢
look for the trade mark
CAFE
COCKTAIL LOUNGE
FOUNTAIN SERVICE
PASTRIES
CANDIES
744 SOUTH HILL ST.
WILSHIRE at DETROIT
Los Angeles
TRAVEL
CLUB
COAST
TO
COAST
TOUR
FENDER
BAGGAGE
Just arrived in New York
The Wonder City
SAN BERNARDINO
CALIFORNIA
A LEADER AMONG THE SANTA FE FLEET OF STREAMLINED TRAINS
EL CAPITAN
10 CARDS 15

Also called the Art Deco set, the $15,999 Memorabilia Set is a 1956 Relic Strat built by Chris Fleming and fitted with antique hardware, along with a Pro Jr. amp. Dave Newman covered the pieces in fragments of vintage advertisements and other print memorabilia. "I mixed in some images from the old Fender catalogs they gave me," he says, "but I also worked in some old music ads — those 'learn how to play guitar' things. The arrows and lines came from some old dress patterns, which are very thin paper so they meld right in."

Dave Newman: "This is the Nash Vegas set, which evokes that period when country music was getting a lot more glitzy. The whole Nash Vegas thing is a mix of horses, Las Vegas, and Nashville, and somehow it all fits together."

"What could be more Americana than Fender guitars?"

— Dave Newman

Left: A Dave Newman/Chris Fleming Tele with antiqued hardware and a highway-nightlife theme.

Below: Chris Fleming and Dave Newman's Route 66 Tele; the front of the guitar is pictured in Chap. 22.

Sara Ray

Painter, illustrator, and photographer Sara Ray of Long Beach describes herself as having been "born in Southern California into a family of artist pro surfers and wandering hot rodders." Inspiration for her own creations comes from influences as diverse as custom surfboards, flamboyantly painted street rods, Día de los Muertos iconography, playing cards, dice, the kind of girlie pinups painted on the flanks of WWII-era B-17s, and vehicle machinery and components of all kinds — olive drab Jeeps, motorcycles, pistons, mag wheels, teardrop gas tanks. Clearly, she is a Fender Custom Shop kind of artist. Sara Ray: "It's like an addiction, because it ruins my life [laughs]. Right now I have a 1942 Army Jeep, a 1939 Cadillac, and a 1953 Buick. I had been taking prints of my art and selling them at car shows for a long time before I was associated with Fender, a lot of rockabilly and car-related stuff. I have so many old cars it's ridiculous, and some of that carries over to the Fender work."

In 2004 Fender began commissioning Sara Ray to paint a series of guitars, several of which are spotlighted here. While some either have automotive themes or were inspired in part by cars, others reflect Sara's fascination with history, specifically the World Wars. In her imagery, she goes to great lengths to ensure that the iconography is accurate and period-correct. "I'm crazy that way," she says. "I went to a lot of antique shops in Europe, and I shipped a lot of books home. I probably have 10,000 books on World War I alone. It's totally nuts. And the World War II books — I've lost count."

Sara Ray was "born in Southern California into a family of artist pro surfers and wandering hot rodders."

The King Custom Esquire was built by Chris Fleming. Sara Ray: "This was one where Fender specified that they wanted a hot rod theme. We do see a lot of the same images in this sort of thing, so I wanted to come up with something a little bit different."

The King Custom Esquire. Sara Ray: "In the studio I actually set up a real still life that you see on the back of the guitar, with the skull and the spark plugs and the pistons, which are from a '53 Chevy I used to have."

The Victory Song

Perhaps Sara Ray's best known guitar and certainly one of the instruments with the deepest personal meaning for her is the Victory Song Gretsch, a tribute to America's storied 8th Air Force (Fender has marketed and distributed Gretsch guitars since 2002). At one time the greatest air armada the world had ever seen, the "Mighty Eighth" was instrumental in defeating Nazi Germany and was home to a long list of heroic, highly decorated pilots. Also known as The Victory Guitar, The Victory Song was built by Chris Fleming, displayed at the Summer 2004 NAMM show, and offered along with a Blues Jr. amp, also hand painted by Sara Ray, for $15,999. The set was purchased by Fred Gretsch and placed on display at the Mighty Eighth Air Force Museum near Savannah, Georgia.

Sara Ray: "All the branches of my family fought in the war on different sides, so we had deep connections with those veterans. One of my grandfathers was in both Pearl Harbor and Iwo Jima. One of my great uncles was captured at Dunkirk, and I had another great uncle who was in Stalingrad. And there were others.

"The Victory was the very first guitar I ever painted for Fender. Chris Fleming just dropped it off at my house and said do whatever you want. There was no specified subject matter or anything. I don't think anybody really expected a guitar like the Victory. They probably expected a hot rod theme or a rockabilly thing, because I do a lot of that, but it was getting close to the anniversary of D-Day. I went over to Europe for the anniversary, which was pretty intense, and I happened to finish the guitar on June 6th, 2004, the actual 60th anniversary of D-Day." At the time it was unveiled, Sara explained, "The guitar is meant to look like a relic from the war, a trophy that has been sitting for 60 years in a basement, well worn and dusty, forgotten, like a pilot's once treasured flight jacket, painted with his missions completed, his plane, and his girl back home, the jacket now folded up in a box."

The guitar depicts a B-17 Flying Fortress bomber, an 8th Air Force shoulder patch/insignia, and an American Eagle. The rows of bombs recall the typical way of marking a warplane's successful missions on its fuselage, and the knobs were crafted from the buttons on an American officer's uniform coat. The banner reads "The Sound Of Freedom 1939 - 1945." The buxom blonde riveter, rendered like a painting on a WWII bomber, represents the girlfriend back home, an iconic pinup, and also the thousands of American women who joined the armed forces or went to work in munitions factories in support of the war effort.

The Iron Cross appearing on the headstock was a German decoration awarded for exceptional bravery in combat. It's a particularly sensitive touch, as explained by the artist: "The Iron Cross represents not only the war trophies brought home by Americans but also the thousands of German pilots who lost their lives in World War II. Airmen were a special breed of men, and they were the first to step beyond barriers after the war to become friends with their fellow pilots who were once their enemies. Forever may their songs be heard."

The Victory Song. In rendering the image of a '40s-style pinup gal brandishing a rivet gun, Sara Ray evoked a multitude of archetypes that would resonate with a World War II flyer — the pinup painted on the fuselage of his warplane, the girl he left behind, and the many women who rolled up their sleeves and went to work in support of the war effort.

The Red Baron

German fighter pilot and aristocrat Manfred von Richthofen, also known as the Red Baron, was World War I's most successful ace, officially credited with 80 air combat victories. His exploits inspired Sara Ray, who painted this Gretsch 6120. "Fender gave me the hollow body," she explains. "They were expecting another type of Victory guitar, but I ended up doing the Red Baron instead. It took me three months of solid painting, just crazy. I had planned a trip to Europe anyway, and I went to where they had some of the Red Baron's things. I have a lot of original pictures of him and his planes. Von Richthofen was always somebody who I liked when I was little, being German myself and needing a type of hero who wasn't a total villain." Manfred's brother Lothar was a skilled pilot himself, credited with 40 air victories in World War I. Sara Ray: "I put the Red Baron's brother on the back of the guitar because he was a pilot in the same squadron, and a lot of people don't know that." The knobs were made from the buttons on a German uniform coat from World War I.

SYNCHRO-SONIC BRIDGE
GRETSCH
SYNCHRO-SONIC BRIDGE

Below: Red Baron, rear body detail. Sara Ray's artistry is reflected not only in the soul and vision of her concepts but also in her rich colors and emotionally evocative details.

The Hell's Angels AVG Set

The 1st American Volunteer Group (AVG), better known as the Flying Tigers, was a legendary band of World War II fighter pilots known for their shark-nose Curtiss P-40 Warhawk airplanes, their daring "dive and zoom" aerial combat tactics, and their success against the often superior numbers of the Imperial Japanese Army Air Force. Prior to Pearl Harbor, the Flying Tigers were attached to the military forces of the Republic of China. The third of their three squadrons was nicknamed Hell's Angels.

Having already completed the Victory Song and Red Baron guitars, Sara Ray designed the Army-green "Hell's Angels AVG" Esquire and amp set because she wanted to pay tribute to American forces who fought in World War II's Pacific Theatre of operations. Details include several red-sun flags of the Japanese Army, which appeared on the sides of American warplanes to signify combat victories in the South Pacific. The nudie cutie is rendered in the style of the iconic pinups often painted on WW II-era aircraft.

On the back of the guitar, the shark face and the P-40 are painted over a "blood chit," which was a printed notice carried by pilots. If a pilot were shot down and survived, he would show the chit to any locals he might encounter. As seen here, the chits distributed to the Flying Tigers depicted the flag of the Republic of China, a red banner with a 12-point white sun set inside a blue rectangle. Below the flag, the Chinese characters read: "This foreign person has come to China to help in the war effort. Soldiers and civilians, one and all, should rescue, protect, and provide him medical care." The official Flying Tigers insignia, as seen on Sara's hand-painted amp, was designed by the Walt Disney company.

The Outlaw Gretsch

The $16,999 Outlaw is a '50s-style Gretsch White Falcon built by Chris Fleming. It was displayed at the January 2005 NAMM show along with a companion Pro Jr. amp. Sara Ray, who painted both pieces, recalls: "A friend of mine is a big collector of all things historic, and he found a weird classified ad online from a guy who said he had a car that belonged to Johnny Cash for sale in Kentucky. My friend didn't have the money, so I sold a painting to somebody who had always wanted it and came up with the cash and sure enough, the car's title was signed 'June Carter.' It was a '65 Cadillac in real bad shape — no mufflers, no plates, and no mirrors — but it did run. I picked it up myself at the Port of Long Beach and actually had the Gretsch with me when I picked up the car, so I put it in the back seat. The whole episode inspired the theme of the guitar. The knobs are shotgun shells shot off on a rainy day by the train tracks in Redlands." The figure on the back evokes Hank Williams, who died in 1953 of a drug and alcohol-related heart attack in the back seat of his baby blue Cadillac. He was 29. The words on the scroll are lyrics from Hank's "Lost Highway" and "Ramblin' Man."

The Memento Mori Gretsch 6120

A Latin phrase meaning "Remember, you shall die," Memento Mori refers to a tradition that runs through centuries of visual artistry, from pre-Christian paintings to modern photography. The idea is to remind us of our mortality. "Chris Fleming and I talked about doing something tragic for a change," says Sara Ray, "instead of the usual hot rod/rockabilly stuff that we were seeing a lot of."

The Memento Mori guitar was built by Fleming. The artwork is in part Sara's tribute to the American actress Jayne Mansfield. Although she received a Theatre World Award for her work on Broadway and a Golden Globe for her film acting, Mansfield is best remembered as a breathy, voluptuous starlet who helped define the blonde bombshell of 1950s Hollywood. She died in 1967 when her car crashed into the rear of a tractor-trailer.

Sara Ray: "The guitar was loosely inspired by the myth surrounding her death. There is some common misinformation about it. It was very sad and tragic, and I thought it would be interesting to immortalize her. That's a bit of her image on the front and back, although I changed it. You would not expect a somber subject on a Fender or a Gretsch — maybe on a Jackson or a Charvel; those guys seem to enjoy the blazing skulls and flaming demons — but I liked the unusual juxtaposition of Death, the Maiden, and a wrecked Cadillac convertible on a beautiful '50s-style guitar."

Left: The Memento Mori Gretsch 6120

Right: The Outlaw Gretsch

GRETSCH
GRETSCH

One of the reasons Fender's partnerships with various artists work so seamlessly is that the raucous, rebellious side of rock and roll reflects perfectly the thrillseeker themes and devil-may-care attitudes explored by the artists. Much of the iconography pictured in this chapter evokes the late 1940s and 1950s, a time when American youth culture — and Fender — began to assert itself so powerfully.

Hubba hubba: The $17,999 Master Built Girls! Girls! Girls! set of 2005 paired a Gretsch 6120 built by Chris Fleming with a Pro Jr. amp. The artwork was rendered by Kirsten Easthope, a widely published artist specializing in '40s and '50s-style Sin City sex kittens, pinup girls in leopardskin pedal pushers, nudie cuties, and the like. Nevena Christie: "Even though we have never met, Kirsten and I are like best buds. I saw some of her work and just called her out of the blue and said, 'You don't know me, but I have to tell you, your art rocks!'"

Hawaiian Love Song: Nevena Christi's Artful Leathers

The Leather Hula Esquire set featured a '50s-style Esquire, a Blues Junior amp, and a guitar case, all covered in leather that was custom-cut and hand-tooled by artist Nevena Christi. The guitar was crafted by Master Builder Chris Fleming and features a decidedly nonstock solid rosewood neck that harmonizes with the set's South Seas theme and rich colors. The coverings on the guitar, case, and amp were carved to simulate the look of woven bamboo and rattan. Complemented by a hand-tooled leather strap adorned with tiki gods and totems, the set was offered at the Summer 2004 NAMM show for $25,000.

What do Dwight Yoakam and Mitt Romney have in common? Both are clients of the Rocketbuster outfit in El Paso, makers of the highest quality custom boots. Nevena Christi is Rocketbuster's co-owner, although as it turns out, leather carving is just one of her family's passions. "We are just total crazies," she says, "and we collect vintage travel trailers. We live in an old movie theater and have something like 18 trailers in our back yard."

A quirky artist with a passion for vintage vehicles and the culture of a bygone era seems like a perfect match for a Custom Shop that in recent years has collaborated with the likes of Sara Ray, Dave Newman, and Kirsten Easthope. "In the work we do crafting custom boots, there are a lot of techniques and arts involved," Nevena explains. "Chris Fleming may have seen some of our boots and could appreciate this amazing level of craftsmanship. He thought a partnership with Fender might be fun. I'm just a nut case for crazy projects, so I said yes.

"The idea to go Hawaiian was my idea. At the time I was working on a 1940s Pearl Harbor-ish trailer with a Hawaiian theme. Inside this trailer, I had done a paint-by-numbers table with the hula girl you see on the guitar, so by the time Chris called I was way into hula-girl mode. I have a lot of hula art, but that girl on the table is special, really my girl, and she was the inspiration for the Fender project. As soon as I got started I had all sorts of ideas, like doing the case to look like it had travel stickers on it."

After Nevena drew the image of the girl on the leather, she carved it and stained it with rich jungle-plantation greens and subtle Waikiki sunset oranges. Then she antiqued it. "We used transparent dyes that soaked into the leather," she explains, "and then I went back with a little bit of opaque finish that sits on top of the leather. The stain absorbs into the leather, and then there is a very messy, special sort of antiquing process to make it look old. Then I usually go in with paint on top of the antiquing to highlight — to bring out the whites in someone's eyes, for example. I did have some help from one of our Rocketbuster guys on some of the carving, although I did a lot of it and I always do the faces myself. I mean, a pinup girl can't look ugly [laughs]. It's either really cute, or nothing."

The tooled leather covering for the amp was also rendered entirely by hand, and carved to simulate the look of rattan. "I did not have a pattern to fit the amp," Nevena explains, "so simply making the pattern was a project in itself. I graduated from school in fashion design, and from that training I learned pattern making. In a way, the amplifier was not only an artistic project but also an upholstery project. They just sent me a wood box. I made the pattern, cut and carved the leather, all by hand, and glued it onto the box with a dry-mount process, so there were a whole bunch of different talents and skills involved." Nevena sent the covered amp cabinet back to Fender, where the electronics were installed.

A remarkable artwork in its own right, the hand-stitched case covering maintains the Hawaiian motif, the rattan color beautifully contrasted with end pieces of bright green leather. Its travel "stickers" are actually carved into the leather and hand-colored to look like the stickers on a valise that might have been stashed behind the pilot's seat in a South Seas Flying Boat.

When asked how long she spent on the entire Leather Hula Custom Shop project, Nevena Christi bursts into laughter: "For-friggin'-ever! This project took a ton of carving. It took me months just to get up the courage to tackle something so new and so complicated, and then once I finally got started, it still took forever. There was so much work involved I swore to myself, 'Well, I'll never do that again,' but wouldn't you know it, just when I thought I was out of hot water, they sold it and came back and said there's somebody who really wants one and would you please make another? So I made a second one. My problem is, I have a hard time saying no to people [laughs]."

Fender
Fender Custom Shop
HAND MADE
Rocketbuster
ORIGINALS
FENDER

Kit Carson

Artist, jeweler, engraver and sculptor Kit Carson lives near Phoenix in the Arizona desert. His work is influenced by the southwest environment where he was raised and where he lives and works, and also by Art Nouveau, the Arts and Crafts movement, and Day of the Dead iconography. (And yes, he is indeed related to the legendary frontiersman of the same name — third cousin, twice removed.) Carson's collaborations with Chris Fleming have resulted in some of the most creative and stunning instruments ever produced by Fender or any other company. Chris Fleming: "When I became a Master Builder I decided I wanted to collaborate with a lot of different artists, and I had all sorts of wild ideas. I met Kit Carson through Dave and Donna Newman. Dave also does a lot of work for us. I went out and visited Kit and discovered one of the most talented and creative people I've ever worked with."

Kit Carson: "I like to use a lot of found objects. I just make them fit, but I don't 'fix' them or paint them or anything. The whole point is to use them as is. Like the 'Butter' sign on the back of the Green Esquire is just one of a kind, a fragment of an old enameled sign. I use rivets, brass nails, precious stones, metalwork, all sorts of tools and arts. I'm also a professional hand engraver. I use a tool that is simply a razor sharp piece of steel in a little wooden handle. It's the old style of engraving, the real deal, like people used to use to engrave the backs of watches."

One of Carson's particularly intriguing processes is called lost-wax casting. "I get a block of wax," he explains. "Let's say I'm creating a little skull. Using a hand tool, I carve away everything that doesn't look like a skull. So my master is in wax. Then I encase the master in liquid plaster. When that dries, I bake it in an oven, which melts out the wax — that's the 'lost wax.' Now, inside that plaster is a hollow air cavity. I shoot in molten silver, and when it cools I break off all the plaster and there's the rough silver casting that I polish up and finish.

"For all of these guitars, I do the initial concept in a full-scale color rendering, all of the metal work and jewelry and some of the other work. I send my plans to Fender, and other artists do the inlay and painting. On the Día de los Muertos guitar, for example, I could not believe how accurate the other artists were in following my design, down to the half-millimeter. Dan Lawrence did the air-

PAINT CHART
THIS SKULL SILVER
Pick gaurd is modified on this line only It's lower.
is inlay
ton
NLAY
KC

brushing from my Prismacolor sketches, and he got the colors perfect, right down on the line of my 0.50 mechanical pencil. He is an unbelievable painter and pinstriper. Ron Thorn did the inlay; again — perfect, just uncanny. I always distress everything so that any new parts look worn, to match the old tobacco cans or coins or the metal from old car bodies that I use for the rest of the work."

Collaborators Kit Carson, left, and Chris Fleming knock 'em dead at the 2004 NAMM show with one of their stunning creations, the "Skele Tele."

Tone to the bone: Kit Carson's Day Of The Dead Telecaster

Nicknamed the Skele Tele in-house, the first Chris Fleming guitar to come through Kit Carson's studio was built for a NAMM show in 2004. The sterling silver skulls and crossbones on the top were handmade with the lost-wax process and fitted with eyeballs of semi-precious stones. Carson hand-engraved the bridge cover, pickup covers, control plate, and the skull on the body's upper shoulder. The six tuners were ground down to resemble vertebrae. The neck's side markers are rubies in 18 karat gold settings. Other details include a red die selector switch and custom paint by Dan Lawrence. Fender manufacturing engineer Tom Arndt followed Kit's design to laser-etch the pick-guard, and Ron Thorn inlaid the dancing skeleton in pearl. Another skeleton appears on the back alongside the words "Tone to the Bone!"

The Day of the Dead symbolism has a special place in the artist's heart. "It's all about the memories of loved ones who have passed away," Carson says. "It's benevolent. It's positive. It's about gratitude and humor. In our culture the skull and crossbones has always meant danger, keep out, poison. There is a lot of design work using skulls these days which is all about fear — the faces are mean and the eye sockets are scary and the message is violence. Fear death! This is the total opposite of all that. Death is coming, you can't escape it, so let's be grateful and party now, and when our loved ones do pass on, let's remember them fondly and party some more. Look at the skeleton on this Telecaster – he's playing maracas."

Chris Fleming: "We were all a bit nervous at the shop as to whether this guitar would end up being a very expensive white elephant. It was six months in the making. Thankfully it went over well and was purchased. I believe it was one of the most expensive instruments, if not the most expensive, the shop had produced up to that time. I think some of the other builders thought I was crazy with this one. They were probably right. It plays and sounds great, by the way."

Kit Carson's Day Of The Dead Telecaster.

Kit Carson
LIVE
to

The Green Esquire.

The Green Esquire

A skilled landscape artist attempting to capture the shifting colors of green rivers and Arizona sunsets could hardly have rendered more subtle shadings than the colors on the metal face of this guitar. Although reported to have come from a tractor, it was actually cut from the wall of a shed where that vehicle was parked. It took the eye of an artist like Kit Carson to see a beautiful guitar top in the side of a rusted, weather-beaten outbuilding.

Carson recalls, "I do a lot of work with rusty found objects, and Chris just said, do something on your own with your rusty metal sculpture idea." Decorated with toys, badges, and assorted found objects, the Green Esquire is occasionally referred to as the Barbed Wire Esquire (Carson sometimes calls it the Texas Tele). George Amicay actually carved the "barbed wire" into the wood, and Dan Lawrence painted it to look metallic; he also painted the top and back woods to match the inset metal pieces. Note the sculpted edges of the hot dog control plate. Details include a solid rosewood neck.

Good for all night: A tone machine for the Rev. Willie G., Esquire

A feast for the eyes and, according to Billy Gibbons, for the ears as well, the Fleming/Carson "Bonecaster" Esquire — also called The Billy — was created in 2008. Chris Fleming reports that the guitar was the result of a two or three-year creative process. "Mike Eldred asked me to cook up something special for Billy Gibbons," says Chris, "and I knew Kit would be perfect. The story we heard was that Billy used it on some work he was doing with Ronnie Wood, and they ended up fighting over the guitar — they both wanted it [laughs]."

Carson explains: "I had some red metal from the hood of a 1987 Ford LTD, and Chris Fleming gave me the go-ahead to 'do something in red metal.' I took it from there. I knew about Billy's collecting of cars and guitars, so when I found that oil can that says 'Motor Rythm,' with some big Stevie Ray eighth notes, I knew it would be so cool for this guitar. I flattened the can and put it on the back. You can see some of my hand engraving on the steer skull and on the skull heads on the knobs. One of the knobs even has Billy's hat that he always wears, with the little dangles all over it." The skull on the selector switch and the skull and crossbones mounted on the turquoise piece on the bridge cover were crafted using the lost-wax casting process. (Detail photos: p. 13.)

Kit Carson: "On the neck plate in back is an old coin that says 'Good for all night,' like an old whorehouse coin. I found it in an antique shop. Around the rim of the guitar I've got repeat motifs of black hearts and red diamonds; I made them out of automotive metal and nailed them into the wood.

"Here's a story that'll blow your mind. Under the strings is the Velvet tobacco can. I got it from my friend David Newman, who also has done a bunch of guitars with Chris Fleming. He gave me that can years ago and just said, here, you might use this some day. We give each other stuff. So I'm getting ready to work on The Billy, and I cut that can open, and inside was a mining claim paper. This is not uncommon in those cans. Miners would put their papers inside them and then put the can in a stone cairn to mark their property out in the desert so other people would know not to overstep the claim. Now get this: I pull the paper out and it's registered to the Kit Carson Mining Company. Pure coincidence. Dave didn't know that. That can was rusted shut, and no one had ever opened it, even when it sat around for years in a junk shop.

"I cut off the bottom of the can where it said 'BURNS COOL AND SWEET' and put it under the two knobs — one cool, one sweet. Then I ground down the tuners to look like vertebrae. I did that on the Skele Tele as well. Hanging off the back of the guitar is a little Virgin Mary, a Mexican good luck piece, and also a little plastic skull; when you open the mouth of the skull the hole in the side becomes a naked lady — one of those trick, double-design things. The 'Custom' is off of a Ford pickup. The Texas Longhorn has a garnet, and the neck has 18 karat gold and garnet dot indicators.

"One of the things that is so great about working with Chris and Fender is that they give me free rein. They send me all the parts — body, neck, tuners, and so on. I pre-drill everything, where the pieces are going to go, and in some cases I install them myself and in others I'll send them to Chris so they can be installed after inlay or painting. After the electronics go in, I send photographs of how it comes together to make sure each piece goes in the right place. And then Chris sets them up to play like a dream."

Billy Gibbons chimes in: "Ah, yes, the Chris Fleming/Kit Carson guitar is stunning! Everyone who happens across a view of this thing is instantly and totally stoked. A real work of art that actually plays and performs with a pleasing delivery."

Joe Wood

Musician/artist Joe Wood has performed as a front man, singer, and songwriter since 1979, first with the early L.A. punk bands the Hated and der Stab, and then from 1981 to 1996 with the better known T.S.O.L., the True Sounds Of Liberty. He released three albums with his roadhouse blues trio Joe Wood & The Lonely Ones (described by the *L.A. Times* as "a cross between Howlin' Wolf and Stevie Ray Vaughan"), and he has been invited to perform with many blues greats such as Muddy Waters, John Lee Hooker, B.B. King, and others. He is also a respected painter whose work has been displayed in sold-out gallery shows all over Southern California.

As a youngster, Joe Wood drew pictures "to quiet the busy mind of a kid in school," as he puts it. In his early teens, he drew in pen and ink. "And (at times haunting) family experiences have been depicted in many of my paintings," he says. "Even today, I am inspired by day-to-day life or early life experience. Still, I am mostly inspired and curious about other artists. So, I study documentaries and read books about classically trained and untrained

The Delta Gentleman. Joe Wood: "This is an image I first completed on canvas with acrylic paints. I love the imagery of the Delta. This gentleman seemed like a natural fit for the Fender guitar collection. In the early juke joints of 'the Blue Belt' and the South, the blues guys dressed formally in suits and hats, more gentlemanly."

Right: Day of the Dead Telecaster. Joe Wood: "I love the Mexican holiday and have always admired the artists who depict the whimsical dark beauty of this celebration." Guitar by Chris Fleming.

FENDER
PAT. PEND.

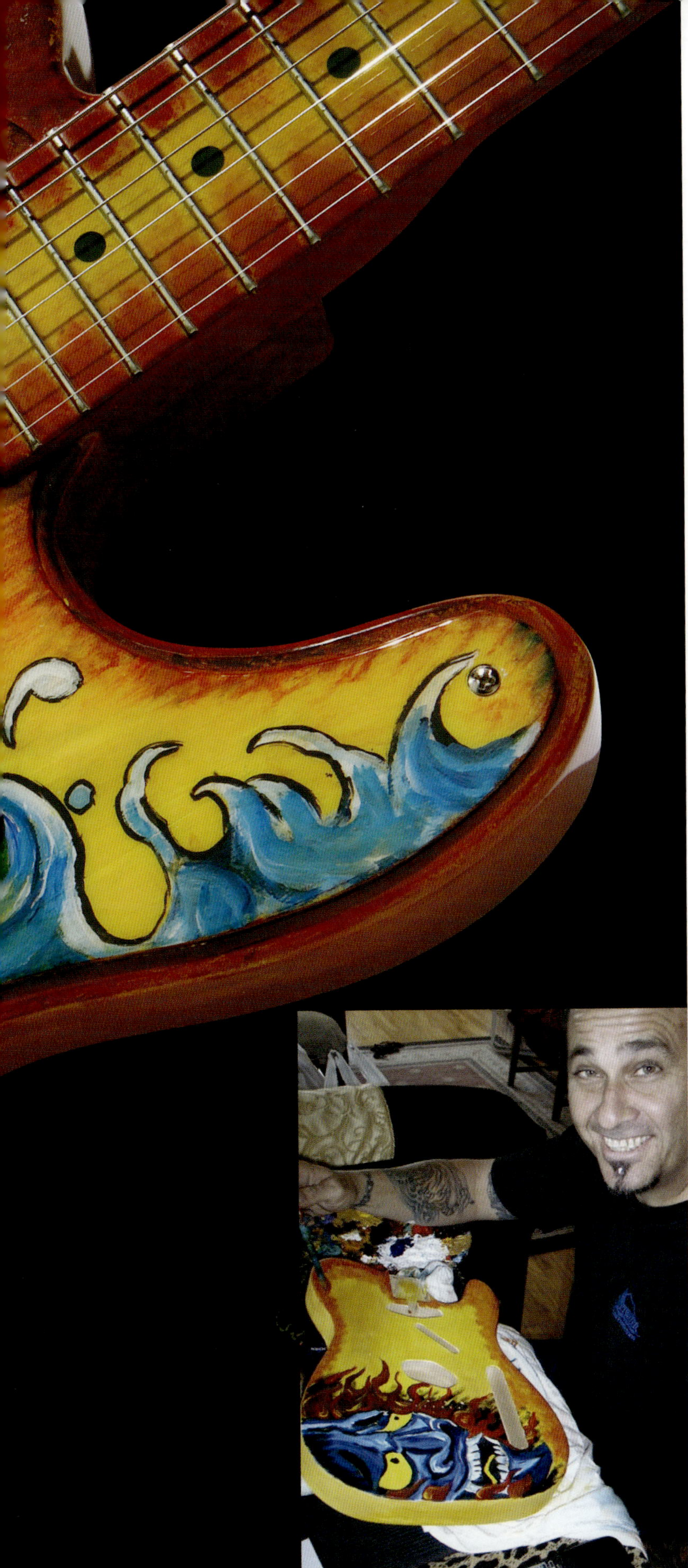

artists of our time. No matter what else I paint, I always have five to ten paintings going at once. Each is inspiring me in a different way. I still paint and write to quiet the noise in my head."

Mike Eldred is a lifelong friend. In 1980 he hired Joe to be a design team member at Charvel. When the Fender Custom Shop's art guitar program was re-energized in the early 2000s, Mike invited Joe to paint guitars and amps for NAMM show displays. Joe reports: "The materials I use for the Fender projects are consistent with my paintings of acrylic on canvas. I always have interesting music playing. I hand-draw the image first on paper. Around the same time, I begin to sand and get a feel for the amp and guitar.

"Each project is unique. Once satisfied with the texture of the sanding and the hand drawing, I use a primer to coat both. I use acrylic paint pens to draw the image. I then layer acrylic paint, outlines, and clear coat, creating five to seven layers of depth and color. [Regarding collaborations with the shop] I trust the judgment of any Master to choose what best suits the final piece. The results are a guitar and amp that can be played regularly as opposed to being just showpieces. That's very important to me."

The Hannya Telecaster Set.
Noh, or Nogaku, is a form of Japanese musical drama that has been performed since the 14th century. The Hannya mask represents one of the best-known figures from Noh traditions. Legend has it that the Hannya was once a beautiful woman who fell in love with a holy man. Her unrequited love turned her into a demon whose horns, wild eyes, fangs, and maniacal grin have come to represent the fury of a woman consumed by madness and jealousy. Chris Fleming built this guitar for the January 2004 NAMM show, and Joe Wood painted it and a companion Blues Jr. amp; it is one of two Hannya sets Joe painted for Fender. Joe Wood: "Many men have this image tattooed on their arm, including me."

Joe Wood at work on one of the two Hannya guitars he painted for the Custom Shop.

Custom Shop
USA

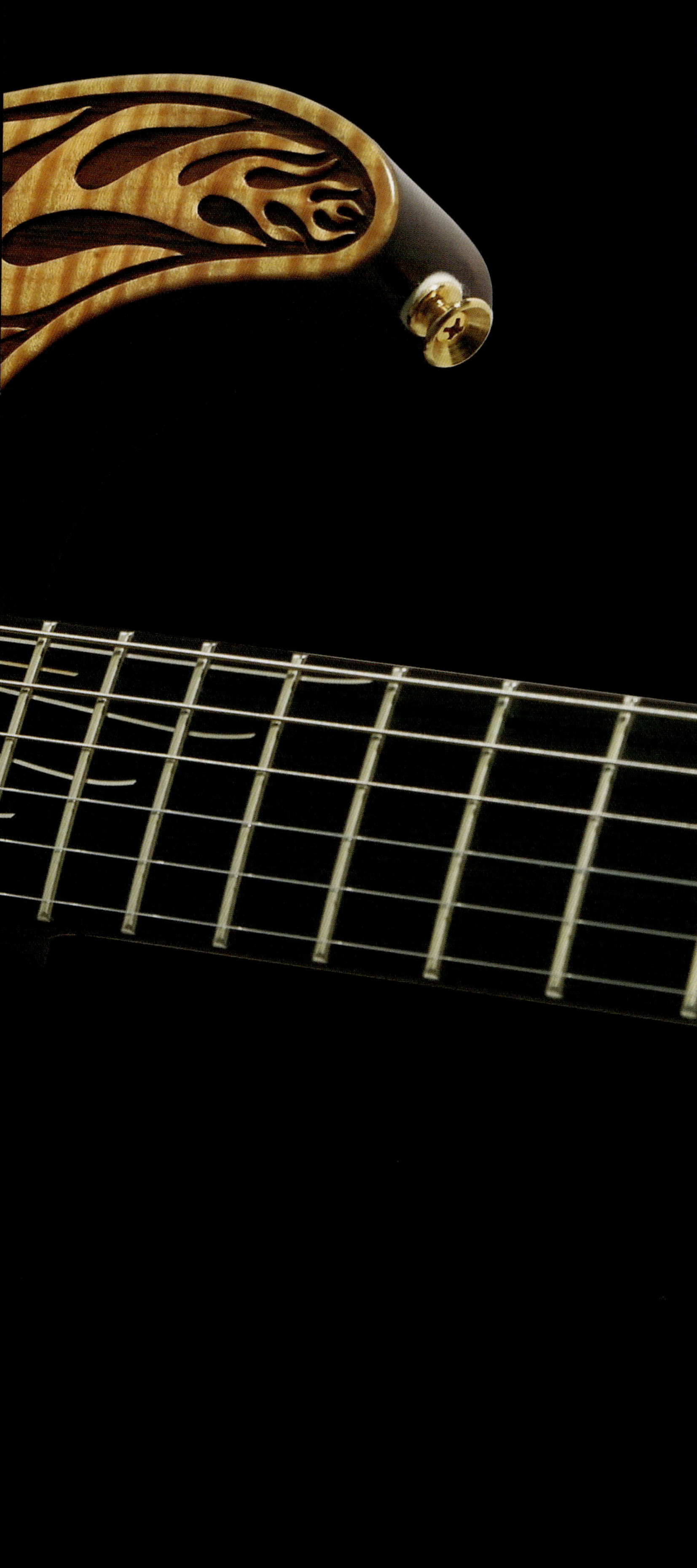

The Carved Phoenix Stratocaster

This beauty was a collaboration between Yuriy Shishkov and master carver George Amicay, who rendered a Phoenix in the style of an Austrian imperial eagle insignia. The Strat's three-layer body is bookmatched flame maple over rosewood over alder. Yuriy Shishkov: "George carved through the maple all the way to the thin rosewood layer, which gave the carving a good contrasting background. To make the guitar more uniform, the body and neck were painted with a dark mahogany color, kind of matching the carving's background. I added some artwork by inlaying the fingerboard with sterling silver wire and mother of pearl. It resembles a wing pattern and gives the neck a touch of personality. I picked gold hardware and pickup covers to give the guitar more attitude. They contrasted well with the chrome pickguard." Details include an ebony fingerboard on a maple neck, and a Custom Shop logo engraved on the pickguard. Note the maple ridge surrounding the pickguard.

The Laguna Beach Esquire

Another Master Built project that entailed a whole set of trappings was Yuriy Shishkov's memorable Laguna Beach Esquire from 2006, built for the January 2007 NAMM Show. Its player-centric features and cosmetics (a 1959 style body, C neck, 7.25" fingerboard radius, gold hardware, etc.) only begin to tell the tale. Yuriy considers it perhaps the most unusual Fender he's ever built — so far. "This was my mad NAMM show idea," he laughs. "I glued a piece of canvas on the body, and then with oil paints I created a scene from Laguna Beach. The painting style is impasto, where your hand movements with the brush or knife are visible because the paint is so thick and dimensional. This guitar's neck is like the artist's palette where you dab the different colors of paint. The guitar came with an actual framed painting on canvas, and the case is very unusual, something an artist would take out into the country with an easel, paint, brushes, and so on. When you open it you have a special easel for the painting, and the easel's legs detach and fit into the case. You also have a palette, actual jars of paint, and so on."

Sometimes the shop's NAMM-display instruments change hands through a raffle. Whoever wins doesn't get the guitar — just the opportunity to buy it. Yuriy Shishkov: "Many people don't know this, but as soon as the show opens its doors, dealers come to the booth and submit their names. Some of these guitars are in such demand that it's not even a matter of first come, first served. The prices are fixed, so there's no bidding. They just need to win the raffle in order to get a chance to specify what they want to buy. I believe the Laguna Beach Esquire set sold for $25,000."

Stoked: Dennis Galuszka's Surfin' Fenders

Leo Fender preferred slacks and yachts to wetsuits and longboards, but 15 years or so after he founded his company, Fender became associated with surfing, more specifically with surf music and a vibrant, idealized version of Pacific Coast culture. Like Fender itself, the instrumental surf music craze was a local Orange County phenomenon before the rest of the world caught the big wave, and in a sense the Fender/surf connection was part of a continuum, given Hawaiian music's earlier influence on the evolution of electric instruments, especially among the Southern California companies.

Don Randall and photographer Bob Perine capitalized on America's fascination with surf culture in a series of early-'60s Fender ads and catalogs picturing attractive California kids on local beaches with their surfboards and guitars. Master Builder and Southern Californian Dennis Galuszka thought it only natural to celebrate that golden time with a set of Fenders whose designs were inspired by the glossy, laminated look of surfboards. Although deeply experienced in building Telecasters, for this project he turned to the Stratocaster, the Jaguar, and the Precision Bass, thanks to their having been adopted by the Beach Boys, the Surfaris, surf guitar tiki-god Dick Dale, and others.

Prior to the 1960s, surfboards were typically constructed of Ecuadorian balsa wood waterproofed with sealers, so Dennis used clear-coated balsa for the first round of his surfin' guitars. He tells the tale: "The surf guitars with the stripes — or 'stringers' — were my idea, one of my very first NAMM projects. The stripes were all done with different woods. On the first run, the top is a thin veneer of balsa with redwood stripes over a regular body wood like alder or ash." The factory usually shuts down for a few weeks for maintenance during the Christmas season, but sometimes the Master Builders don't get that time off because they're finishing up their NAMM projects for January. Dennis Galuszka: "For the first run I built a Strat, a Jaguar, and a P Bass during the shutdown, but we had a break-in and somebody stole the surf bass. It never turned up."

Orders started coming in after the first surf guitars were displayed at NAMM's winter 2003 convention and also in a Custom Shop calendar. Dennis typically gets a couple of orders every year, and he tries to make each instrument unique. "They all have the laminated look with the stripes," he explains, "but I'll find some vintage surfboard to copy so that each guitar is a one-off. I don't use balsa anymore because I found when I was assembling the first run that it was a little too soft, so for the tops I use spruce, and we just use a regular clear coat over it."

Most of the orders in recent years have been for Stratocasters, some with pickguards and some without. Although Fender's legal department understandably guards against nonstock renditions of the Fender logo, on these guitars it is often recast to evoke the logos of classic surfboard companies; Dennis credits Fender's Clay Lyons for the logos' design. Aside from their totally bodacious appearance and veneered tops, most of these guitars tend to be conventional Fenders, with stock woods and electronics. One exception is a guitar that Dennis describes as sort of a Jaguar in Stratocaster clothing. "This was an idea I stole from Dave Wronski of the band Slacktone," he says. "The neck, bridge, tailpiece, 24" scale length, and pickups are all Jaguar. Otherwise, I only made the one bass and a couple of Jaguars, which did not have regular Jaguar circuitry — just volume, tone, and a 3-way, no rhythm circuit. The rest are Strats."

Dennis Galuszka describes this guitar as sort of a Jaguar in Stratocaster clothing. "This was an idea I stole from Dave Wronski of the band Slacktone," he says. "The neck, bridge, tailpiece, 24" scale length, and pickups are all Jaguar." The after-market Buzz Stop on the tailpiece base helps to stabilize the strings.

Coolest Guitar Ever? Cool is a matter of taste, of course (maybe the coolest guitar ever is a stock '53 Tele), but for sheer fun, the jaw-droppin', eye-poppin' Strat Rod Deville of late 1999 was tough to beat. The custom-wired, four-pickup guitar was a collaboration between Alan Hamel and R&D Project Engineer Michael Frank-Braun. Several of the amp's operations — on/off, standby, channel switching — could be controlled via a patent-applied-for wireless system on board the guitar; note the antenna poking up from the amp's hind quarter, and the even cooler, Jetsons-style transmitter recessed into the guitar's top. According to Fender, "Louvers on the amp glow green when the amp is in the clean channel and red when in the overdrive channel." Machinist extraordinaire Scott Buehl fabricated the knobs, which are replicas of automotive pistons. The classic hot-rod artwork was created by car customizer, tattoo artist, poster artist, and graphic designer Dennis McPhail, a one-time associate of the legendary Ed "Big Daddy" Roth.

This Tele Thinline evokes Shag's take on an Afro-Caribbean music/voodoo/rum theme.

Shagadelic! Southern Californian Josh Agle, or "Shag" (Jo*sh* + *Ag*le), is an artist and designer well known for images of slinky, wasp-waisted women and suave, tuxedoed men socializing in space-age bachelor pads amid beatnik sculpture, abstract art, amoeba-shaped coffee tables and swanky modernist furniture. Favorite motifs also include a jazzy, early-'60s take on tropical iconography — tiki masks, bongo drums, jivin' witch doctors, and the like.

Shag collaborated with John English on the design of three Custom Shop Fenders, one of which was an Esquire Thinline completed in 2003. Here, Shag proudly displays the work in progress. The beautiful flamed koa body features scenes from a jungle jubilee. The finished guitar sports tribal-mask position markers crafted in green malachite and inlaid by Ron Thorn.

Bleached skulls, a blazing sun, barbed wire, birds, and booze bottles adorn this Shagified, natural-finish Tele Thinline built by John English.

The Catalina Island Blues Festival, co-sponsored by Fender, was an annual event held from 1997 to 2001. Each year, the Custom Shop created a commemorative "Regina del Mare" Stratocaster that was designed by John Page and Pamelina H., carved by George Amicay, and painted by Pamelina. The designs were inspired by the tile artwork at the entrance to the ballroom of the Casino, the 1929 Art Deco landmark that dominates the harbor of Avalon. (The original art was created by five artists working under the direction of John Gabriel Beckman, the acclaimed muralist and the set designer of *Casablanca* and *The Maltese Falcon*.) The first event was held in August, 1997. According to *The Music Trades*, that year's inaugural Regina del Mare ("Queen of the Sea") guitar was sold for an estimated $70,000. Although the subsequent instruments also featured the island's iconic mermaid mistress, each was a unique artwork, and all five were accompanied by festival posters created by Pamelina H.

Known as La Florita, this hardtail Strat was built by Chris Fleming and painted by guitarist Kid Ramos, a veteran of Roomful Of Blues, the Fabulous Thunderbirds, and several solo projects. The Mexican blanket motif of the Blues Jr. amp, also painted by Ramos, perfectly complemented the heritage and iconography celebrated in the guitar's artwork. The guitar's neck is one piece of rosewood. In 2005 the set was priced at $14,999.

A very appreciative Buddy Guy holds his 80th birthday present, a Custom Shop Stratocaster built for a 2003 NAMM show by Art Esparza and painted by Jim Doody, a watercolor artist based in Costa Mesa, California.

Below: Muddy and Buddy: This Tele pictures Muddy Waters set against a South Side street scene. It was built by Art Esparza and painted by Jim Doody, who specializes in stylized portraits of blues artists. The Buddy Guy Strat shown here and this Tele were part of a Chicago Blues set commissioned by the shop. Jim Doody: "Every graphic element painted on those guitars has a story behind it. The buildings in the background, neck graphics, and fret dots draw upon elements of the lives and times of these two giants and are part of their history. Having grown up on the South Side of Chicago, I felt like it was part of my history, too."

Fender's longest-running artist guitar is the Eric Clapton Stratocaster, which was refined in the Custom Shop but produced in the factory. With 2004's Eric Clapton Signature Stratocaster, the Custom Shop rendered its own, elegant take on the model.

CHAPTER TWENTY-SIX

26

2004

50th Anniversary, Rory Gallagher and SRV Strats; Master Designs

The shop offered anywhere from about 40 to 60 models in 2004, depending on whether we count options such as trem vs. hardtail bridges. Once we start counting maple vs. rosewood boards, gold vs. standard hardware, and the three Time Machine finishes — not to mention specialty options such as spalted maple or lacewood tops on some of the Showmasters — the number approaches the 100 mark.

The models were arrayed in four familiar series — Custom Artists, Time Machines, Showmasters, and Custom Classics — plus the relatively new Limited Release category, whose sole occupant for part of the year was the 50th Anniversary 1954 Stratocaster, one of the most impressive guitars ever produced by the Custom Shop or anyone else.

The brand new Clapton, Beck, and Trower Signature Strats joined the senior members of the Custom Artist series, the Cray and Dale Strats. The other Custom Artist Strats were the stunning new Rory Gallagher Tribute model and the six-year-old Ritchie Blackmore Strat (the Roland Ready version's $6,002 list price was second only to the Haggard Tele's tag, now up to $6,256).

The Custom Artist Teles included some models that went back to the shop's first three years (Albert Collins, Danny Gatton), as well as the pair of year-old John 5 models, the Merle Haggard, and the year-old Jimmy Bryant Tribute. Other Custom Artists included the year-old Seymour Duncan Esquire, the Jaco Pastorius Jazz Bass, and the two Reggie Hamilton Jazz Basses. (Officially, there were no Precisions in 2004's Artist series.)

All Time Machines were offered in all three finishes, and all were year-specific, vintage-based models: four Strats, two Teles, two Precisions, the '64 Jazz Bass, the '59 Esquire, and the '51 Nocaster. Counting the various options and excluding color choices, the Time Machines alone accounted for 42 models. Other series included the Showmasters/Flat Heads and the still-popular Custom Classics.

The shop's Clapton Strat featured Vintage Noiseless pickups. This deep Mercedes Blue example rests on one of Eric's favorite amps, the iconic tweed Twin.

The 50th Anniversary 1954 Stratocaster

In 2004 the biggest news for the Custom Shop and indeed for all of Fender was the 50th anniversary of the Stratocaster. What better way to commemorate the first five decades of the world's most exciting electric guitar than to bring it back to life? Fender had already released several anniversary Strats, including 1994's 40th Anniversary model, intended to be a fairly authentic repro of the 1954 original. But now it was 2004, the venerable Strat had reached the half-century mark, and some sort of tribute was in order. Internal discussion addressed whether a 50th Anniversary guitar might undermine the collector's value of the 1,954 40th Anniversary Strats sold a decade earlier, but Fender decided that a new guitar was appropriate so long as it was distinguished in meaningful ways from the previous model. While the 1994 version had been convincingly realistic, the 2004 model would mark another leap in authenticity. Each and every detail would virtually clone its original counterpart. As Dan Smith puts it: "Basically, we started all over."

A justifiably proud Chris Fleming displays an original 1954 Stratocaster (left) and its virtual clone, the prototype of the 50th Anniversary version.

The task to exceed all previous standards was handed over to the craftsmen who were best able to pull it off, the Custom Shop crew. Chris Fleming, then just getting ensconced in his new role as Master Builder, was given the weighty assignment to direct the project. As is often the case, initial planning was a joint Custom Shop/R&D effort. Collaborating with their peers in marketing, George Blanda and Chris Fleming worked on two versions. The Custom Shop's Limited Edition 50th Anniversary 1954 Stratocaster would basically attempt to bring an intact 1954 guitar into the present, while the factory's 50th Anniversary Edition American Deluxe Stratocaster would replicate the original's 2-color sunburst but otherwise would be fitted with modern features. As the company put it, one guitar would acknowledge Fender's past; the other would look to the future.

The first question Fleming had to ask was: Which 1954 Strat should we reproduce? Given the amount of handwork that went into the originals, not to mention Leo Fender's incessant fussing and improvements of his products (sometimes with no official announcement of alterations), even pristine original '54 Strats can have noticeable differences. Chris Fleming: "If you took several 1954 Stratocasters, each one in some small way would have its own thing, so sometimes it's just about impossible to say that this original, unmodified Strat is more 'authentic' than that one."

The guitar the builders used as a model was the '54 belonging to Richard Smith, author of *Fender: The Sound Heard 'Round The World* and curator of the Leo Fender Gallery at Fullerton's Museum Center. (The same guitar was brought out of its glass case a decade earlier when Fender planned the factory's 40th Anniversary Strat.) Chris Fleming and his colleagues kept the guitar for a month or two, and while it was the only '54 in the shop during planning and prototyping, the builders did examine other '54s later in the process.

Chris Fleming on the Anniversary Strat: "This is a 1954 guitar, with 1954 parts and details, and to the extent that it's humanly possible, we built it the way they built them in 1954."

The Anniversary Strat was cradled in a 1954-style "poodle" case, flat on one side, thick with red plush lining, and sporting a 50th Anniversary medallion.

Richard Smith's guitar isn't just any '54. It might be called the *Ur*-Strat. It bears serial number 0100 and is dated 4/54 in the body cavity, making it *very* early, even for a '54; to Richard's knowledge the neck has never been removed. He adds: "The channel between the pickups and controls under the pickguard is hand chiseled, making more room for the bundle of wires off the pickups leading to the controls; others have noted this in early '54s, I believe. The body is at least three pieces of ash. Everything is factory original."

The guitar was purchased new in July 1954 at a music store in El Monte, only about 14 or 15 miles from where it was built. The records of plant supervisor and later Vice President Forrest White indicated that Fender Sales didn't field orders any earlier than that date, so Richard concludes that the guitar was likely a salesman's sample obtained directly from the factory and sold to the store, along with another Strat, serial number 0101. "Salesmen sold their samples all the time to generate cash flow," he explains. "The original owner was told that the two Strats were the first and second sold by Fender. Forrest thought this was a very plausible scenario."

Selecting a particular guitar to clone was just the beginning. Even if the builders could agree on what constituted "original spec" standards for the materials, dimensions, weight, and production techniques, they could, and did, disagree on how to replicate those details. Chris Fleming: "Dan Smith determined that we were actually going to try to match the pickup outputs, the pickup windings, all the materials, and the tonal characteristics, so we all started on the same page, but we are all artists here, and these are handmade instruments, and sometimes the hand of the individual builder is evident in one detail or another. There are things you can measure and weigh, but others come down to personal taste. There were a few disputes in the process, but that's probably inevitable when you have knowledgeable people who are also passionate about the subject matter."

One bone of contention was the rendering of the 2-color sunburst. All of the guitars' light areas were finished with a paint the shop calls simply "yellow shader." Fender's traditional Dark Salem was used for the outer, darker portions. Chris Fleming prefers a slightly lighter, deep chocolate brown on the outer edges, rather than the blacker hue favored by some of his fellow Master Builders. The prototypes and first dozen or so guitars to leave the shop were all built by Fleming (he would build many more over the course of the next year). The paint on those early guitars was formulated by the shop's "paint lead," Jesus Andrade. At Fleming's direction, Andrade concocted a blend with a slightly different opacity in order to give the outer edges on those protos and early production guitars a slightly lighter hue; the distinction is so subtle that you might need to see examples side by side to notice it. Chris Fleming:

"Jesus tweaked it until I liked it and then mixed it up as I did batches. There was no official difference — they were all 2-tone '50s sunbursts. I believe our paint supplier at the time was Lawrence-McFadden. The other thing I asked for that was different was to grain-fill with a darker than usual brown paste filler; it accentuated the grain and looked very much like the original guitar we used as an example." No one should mistake such minor differences as flaws; in fact, they better reflect the variations among original '54s than would a group of cookie-cutter, utterly identical finishes.

Leo Fender once confided that he was surprised the Telecaster remained so popular, given the availability of his later creation, the Stratocaster. He saw the Strat not only as a separate model but also as the more refined iteration of "the Fender guitar." The Strat itself evolved over time, of course, with several alterations over its decade-long lifespan in the pre-CBS era. Was the Custom Shop ever tempted to incorporate some of those refinements in the anniversary guitar? Chris Fleming chuckles at the question. "No, we don't think that way in the Custom Shop. Fender is always looking forward, but when it comes to updates, that's what the [factory's] American Deluxe version was for. Our guitar was about: This is a 1954 guitar, with 1954 parts and details, and to the extent that it's humanly possible, we built it the way they built them in 1954." Examples of this approach are evident throughout the instrument, particularly in the shape of its U neck and headstock, its spread (the block of wood from which the body is shaped), its plastics, and the aging of the parts and finish. Chris Fleming did most of the initial woodworking, paying particular attention to the headstock volute, the thickness of the headstock, and the rounding of the fingerboard's edges.

The original Strats featured parts fabricated from a somewhat brittle material often mislabeled as Bakelite. Dan Smith reports that Fender tracked down pieces of original pickup covers and knobs and sent them to a lab for composition analysis. The builders were a bit surprised by some of the results. The pickguard was made of a PVC vinyl with a high styrene content, a formulation that was no longer available. The thickness was .070" — which the builders used for the '54 — as opposed to Fender's typical .060" spec. George Blanda: "The old single-ply pickguards always seem stiffer than our current material, and the slight extra thickness was part of the reason. They also typically

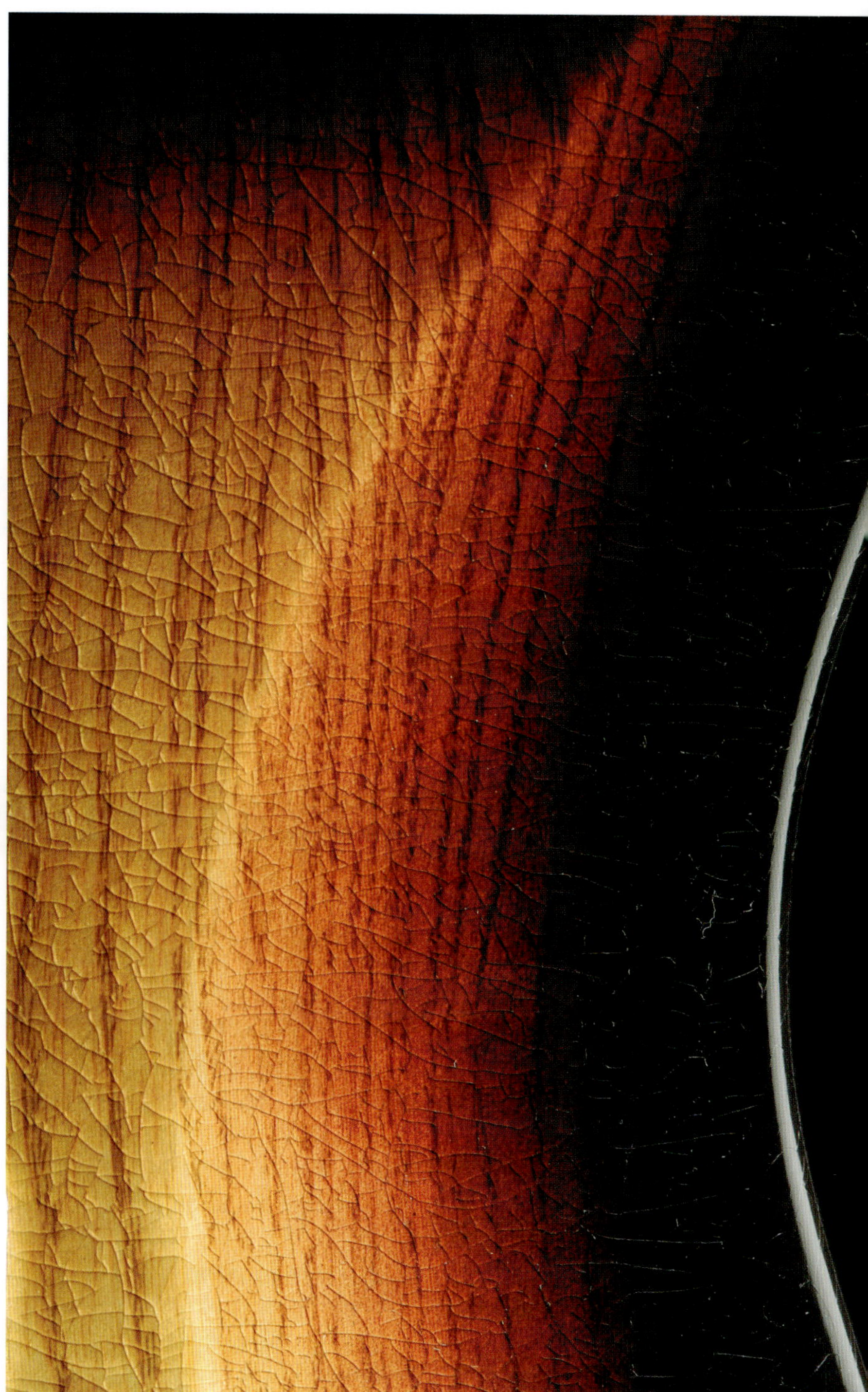

With its finish cracks and subtle hues, the 50th Anniversary guitar's painting process was a particularly complex challenge.

don't yellow like the celluloid 3-ply guards, so finding out they were PVC made sense." Lab results showed that the 1954 knobs were made of acrylonitrile-butadiene-styrene plastic, or ABS. Like the pickguard material, it had a high styrene component. For the Anniversary guitar, the shop used the closest available blend obtainable on the modern market.

Dan Smith: "We did complete specifications and CAD drawings for the [pickup] covers and knobs from actual components. We then spent the money to tool up for those parts — not cheap. We bought injection molds that made the covers and knobs so that they duplicated the originals. That included the rounded edges of the pickup covers, the knobs' narrow skirts, and the details of the knobs' lettering and numbering."

The holes on the tremolo cover plate in back were round in 1954, but by the following year Fender went to oblong holes because it facilitated changing strings. Once again, the 50th Anniversary project was all about authenticity, so the cover plate's holes are round. The Master Builders were committed to recreating Leo Fender's first Stratocaster, not one of his later ones.

Fender even oiled up some of the old machines to make these guitars, including one of the big presses to fabricate some of the hardware, and stamping machines from the early days for the bridges and saddles. As on the originals, serial numbers were stamped not on the metal neck plate but rather on the plastic tremolo cavity cover plate. Pre-CBS employee Roger Centeno used the original die for the numbering. (Todd Krause adds: "The serial numbers are not necessarily in any order. We did not want the number order to place 'extra' value on any particular guitar.")

Although the CTS brand potentiometers on the originals had solid shafts, the Custom Shop guitar was fitted with split-shaft units. Chris Fleming: "The plastic was brittle to begin with, and then they would ram those knobs on the solid shaft, which is the other reason why they sometimes broke or cracked and fell off. We used a slightly newer version with a split shaft, which is designed to flex or give just a bit. It's also got a knurl on it so it holds better." Other details of the Anniversary model included aged nickel hardware and a bone nut. The guitar came in an original style form-fit brown case.

Beyond the authenticity of individual features, the 50th Anniversary Stratocasters were significant in several ways. Chris Fleming explains that each guitar has a two-piece body with an off-center glue joint, or "side seam." "It might have been done previously in the Custom Shop in sort of a onesies/twosies kind of way," he says, "but to my knowledge this was the first time where the specifications for the ash spread actually called for a side seam. We found that generally the seam [on the originals] is on the lower side, where the pickguard covers much of the glue joint. Some people who bought Anniversary guitars thought they had one-piece bodies, but the spec called for a two-piece with the off-center seam. That started a new protocol for how we do vintage stuff. You'll notice now that most of the vintage stuff that comes out of the Custom Shop has that side seam, which is something I decided to do on the '54s.

STRATOCASTER® 50TH Fender ANNIVERSARY 1954 - 2004

"This was also one of the earliest cases where the project was developed by one Master Builder, in this case myself, and then handed over to all the other Master Builders, the way we would later do with Blackie and others. Finally, instead of being available only to Custom Shop dealers, the Anniversary Strat was available to the much wider network of Fender dealers in general."

One of the unexpected consequences of offering the guitar to retailers who were not used to working with the Custom Shop was that some of them were unfamiliar with the Time Machine guitars. A few recipients of the Anniversary Strat opened up the case, saw the guitar's lightly checked Closet Classic finish and aged parts, and complained that they had received a damaged instrument. "It's understandable if they hadn't seen one before," says Chris. "In most cases, once we explained that these were designed to replicate guitars that had been used, they were fine with it.

"The other thing was that on occasion one of the plastic parts would crack or chip, just like on an original '54 that had been out in the marketplace for a few years — and for the same reason. After all, we were using the same materials. That's why Fender went to more durable vinyl instead of that styrene stuff. Maybe a screw was a little tight on the pickguard, so there would be a tiny crack. We might have to explain the concept — this isn't just a new guitar that looks like an old guitar; we're trying to *recreate* the old guitar — and then usually the dealers were okay with it, but if they insisted, we would replace the knob or pickguard or whatever it was." (Some people prefer the authenticity of those '50s style parts. Mike Eldred: "I *still* get hammered for those parts. People really want them.")

Chris Fleming: "Another cool feature was that we went to great trouble to stamp the saddles with the 'FENDER PAT. PEND.' like the originals. The slots in the saddles were longer and allowed the strings to go through without resting against the front edge of the slot as in the current saddles. I like this feature a lot. These are very sought after and impossible to get now."

George Blanda elaborates: "The slot in the saddle that the string goes through is back toward the intonation screw so that in some cases the string rests on the forward edge of the slot before it rests on the intonation point of the saddle. The string touches at three points: where it exits the inertia block/bridge plate junction, the forward edge of the saddle, and the intonation point of the saddle. Most Strats after the PAT. PEND. ones have the three contact points. Fender had this right on the original '54 but at some point changed the design. On the Anniversary we improved the slot position so that this bridge would only contact the string at two points, like the originals. The two-point is a better design, and some players do get that particular over details."

The 50th Anniversary Strat set high standards of authenticity yet at $5,400 was more affordable than many Master Built models. Orders were taken from January 15 through December 31, 2004, and although Fender doesn't release sales figures, the model was by all accounts very successful.

Looking back, Chris Fleming recalls: "The project was challenging, difficult, and to be honest it was frustrating at times, but it was one of the most meaningful Custom Shop projects, for me personally. First of all, I was born in 1954.

Before creating the new model's parts, Fender sent 50-year-old pickup covers and knobs to a lab for a chemical composition analysis.

This was one of my first major projects as a Master Builder, and it was one of the first times I built personal guitars for well-known artists. I built '54 Strats for Ron Wood, Joe Walsh, David Gilmour, and a bunch of others."

Mike Eldred: "The level of detail, the amount of R&D that Dan put into the parts, the saddles, the right contours — all those things made it a really cool project to be involved with."

Dan Smith: "Everything possible was done to accurately replicate those original Stratocaster guitars. One of the main differences was in the original pickups; they had larger-diameter — not stock — Alnico 3 magnets, and we duplicated all those things. A lot of effort was made in research, planning, and construction to get it perfect. After the debating stopped and the dust had settled, what followed was probably the most accurate reproduction to ever come out of the Custom Shop."

Coda: With Mark Kendrick's help, Ritchie Fliegler inventoried Bill Schultz's dazzling guitar collection — the prototype or first production guitar of almost every model Fender had built since 1985. Ritchie happily obliged, working on his own time. Afterward, to show his appreciation, Schultz told him to pick a guitar for himself. Ritchie declined, but his boss insisted.

Ritchie Fliegler: "I picked the first handmade Chris Fleming prototype of the 50th Anniversary 1954 Strat. We play guitars every day at Fender and see a *lot* of them. There are good guitars, really good guitars, great guitars, and then once a year, or every two years, something crosses your path that stops everybody in their tracks. In my life I've been lucky enough to have some extraordinary guitars. I have to tell you, even if you're not particularly a Strat guy — if you're just a *guitar* guy — this is one of the most insanely good guitars ever, just one of those 'what, are you *kidding* me?' kind of guitars. It's everything you could ever want – it's bassy, it's bright, it's fat, it hangs onto a note. Everybody in the Custom Shop signed it and it's the first one, so it's historic and all that, but because I am the way I am, I play it all the time [laughs]. It does *not* sit in a glass case."

Right: The prototype for the Rory Gallagher Tribute Strat was sent to Rory's brother, Donal, caretaker of the original. John Cruz: "The story I heard was when he opened up the case his first reaction was just to gasp because it was so real, and that meant so much to all of us."

Diary of a journey: The Rory Gallagher Tribute Stratocaster

Richard McDonald called Rory Gallagher's tattered, battered 1961 Stratocaster "an open book, like a diary of the journey his music had taken him on." At one time it was a stock Strat with conventional features of the period — an alder body with a 3-color sunburst, a "C"-shaped maple neck, a rosewood slab board with a 7.25" radius, and a white 3-ply pickguard. It was reportedly left in a ditch for several rainy days after being stolen, and its finish was further assaulted by Rory's highly acidic sweat, which his brother Donal once compared to paint stripper. With scars, wounds, and corrosions acquired over four decades of rockin' road campaigns and multiple impromptu mods, this Fender virtually defines "battle axe."

Because the late Irish blues-rocker is practically worshipped in various quarters of the Custom Shop, the Rory Gallagher Tribute Strat became a project of special importance and emotional resonance. In 1997, Mike Eldred met Donal at LAX airport, took possession of Rory's famous Fender, and promptly went home and played it, letting its powerful mojo seep under his skin. "It was a big honor just to hold something that such a great artist had played so much blazing music on," he says. Prior to his becoming a Master Builder, John Cruz was tasked with creating a series of new Gallagher Strats that could somehow evoke the same magic. "It was so cool," he recalls, "because we actually had Rory's guitar here. One night after everybody went home I plugged it in and just really cranked it. What a great experience to play that guitar. The next day, John English took it all apart and everything got measured and weighed and documented. There was some weird wiring, and a lot of modification to the wood under the pickguard. It was beat-up in there. John would find some cool detail and would holler over, *'Cruz! Come here! Take a look at this!'* Everything on that guitar was just mangled, and looking over John's shoulder I learned a lot."

In 2004, John Cruz crafted 40 Rory Gallagher Tribute Stratocasters for the European market. "I did them completely by hand," he explains. "On the prototype, it took me two or three days just to peel the paint off and do all the relicing. It was a lot of fun to work on but such a pain to do. To be honest, Rory's Strat wasn't the easiest guitar to play. You could tell he had to bear down on it to get it to perform

VOLUME
TONE

just the way he wanted, and that was part of his amazing sound and part of the guitar's charm and why it was worn so much. On the Tributes, though, I made the necks really easy to play. Those guitars played like a dream and sold like hotcakes."

Like Gallagher's original, the Tribute's details included a mismatched tuner — one Gotoh amid five Sperzels — and a white plastic dot replacing the original "clay" marker on the treble side at the 12th fret. John Cruz: "I had to figure out ways to do all this on some sort of scale, so for those 40 I made up some templates out of thick plastic that had little holes and spaces where some of the relicing would be applied, and that helped with the consistency. Because the demand was so great, those guitars became the basis for a Team Built version that I supervised. I helped train the team so that we could do a certain amount each month. We started out with a very low number and weren't going to increase production until we had everything just perfect. This was typical. A lot of the Team Built projects morph out of things the Master Builders do by ourselves on a small scale. The Master Builts are received so well that we make them into a more affordable thing so more players can enjoy it. Originally we built the Rory guitars with the 5-way switch but later went to the 3-way and just included the 5-way in the case. Rory's original had a 7.25" radius but had been refretted so many times it flattened out quite a bit. We decided to go with a 9.5, and it was close to that spec anyway.

"When we finished up the prototype I felt really good about it, so Mike packed it up and we sent it to Donal. He represented the family and signed off on the Tribute. The story I heard was when he opened up the case his first reaction was just to gasp because it was so real. He told us we had done a great job, and that meant so much to all of us because of our love and respect for Rory's music."

Tribute to a Texas legend: SRV's Number One

One of the most storied of all electric guitars is Stevie Ray Vaughan's main instrument, the battered Stratocaster he called Number One. On that guitar, the great musician helped revitalize electric blues in the 1980s. In so doing, he became one of the most admired and beloved artists to ever come out of Texas. Few guitarists of any style have inspired so many, so deeply.

On September 8, 2003, Richard McDonald, Mike Eldred, and George Blanda went on a guitar safari to Austin to meet Jimmie Vaughan, caretaker of Number One, and to dissect, analyze, and document each and every detail of his younger brother's legendary Strat. (Often reported to be a 1959 guitar, Fender revealed it's actually a '63 body with a '62 neck.) The pickups' outputs were measured, as were the tensions of their copper coils. Each component was meticulously sized and weighed, every contour duly noted. Most challenging of all was documenting the guitar's multiple gouges, scratches, and worn areas. Instruments that have suffered this level of abuse rarely survive in playable condition (the underside of the treble body horn couldn't have been much rougher if it had been gnawed by beavers). Just holding this guitar was a memorable experience for all concerned, and every man there knew he had touched history. Just before nestling the guitar back in its case, Richard McDonald played it, hard, for several minutes. "It was just crying out to be played," he said. "It's what it knew. I can't explain it."

The team's investigation provided specs for the Custom Shop's Limited Edition Stevie Ray Vaughan Tribute Model "Number One" Stratocaster, unveiled in January 2004. Approved by the Vaughan estate, the series was restricted to one hundred pieces (Fender promises it will never again recreate the guitar). As any fan of Stevie's original Number One would expect, the Custom Shop edition features heavy strings, a thick neck — Stevie Ray's guitar was once described as a "bucking bronco" to play — a flatter than usual 12" radius, jumbo frets, a lefty trem, gold hardware, Gotoh tuners, a black single-ply pickguard, and the familiar SRV letters and reflective stick-on *Custom* tag.

John Cruz was tasked with the SRV project, and he calls it "probably the highlight of my career at Fender." He had already worked on both the Muddy Waters and Rory Gallagher Tribute guitars, both of which had Relic finishes, so he was deeply familiar with the requisite aging processes. "Deadlines were approaching," Cruz explains, "and they needed a guitar for photos and to show Jimmie. Stevie Ray Vaughan was one of my favorite artists. He changed the way I play, so when they asked me to get involved I was more than happy to do it. It was an honor to be a part of it.

Number One: John Cruz prototyped the Stevie Ray Vaughan Tribute Stratocaster by hand. He called the project "probably the highlight of my career."

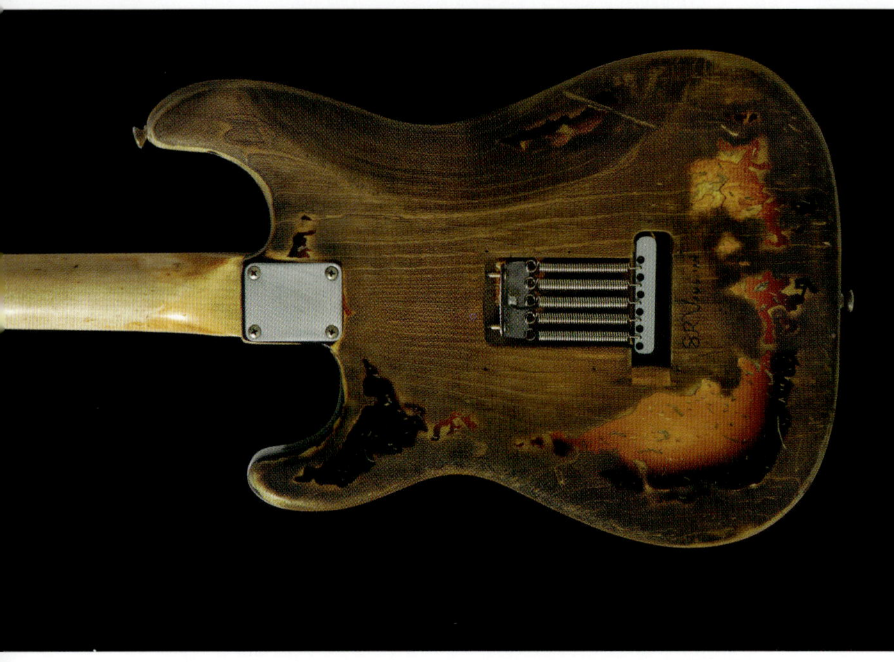

Among Number One's many distinctive touches were a somewhat mangled tremolo cavity, a lefty trem with a brawny, five-spring feel, gold hardware, a black single-ply pickguard, Stevie's initials, a reflective *Custom* tag, and brutal wear and tear.

"George, Mike, and Richard came back from Austin with all that data and made copies for me. I watched the tapes diligently, over and over. I completely absorbed myself, very deeply, in every detail of the tapes, photos, notes, and specs. I really had to think about how we would get that finish to look just like the original, and that is where my experience with the Gallagher project really came in handy. That guitar was worn and mutilated as well.

"All the prototyping for the SRV I did by hand, and it took me forever. It had unusual challenges, like the rout for the tremolo bridge, which looked more than anything like it was the result of a mistake and a subsequent patch job. A lot of people are under the impression that Number One had a huge neck. On my original notes, that really was not the case. It was only slightly larger than a typical #3 oval 'C' style neck. It was not only really worn, but it had been refretted more than once, too. The Tribute SRVs all had very dark Indian rosewood fingerboards that were hand-picked to mimic the look of Stevie's original. We finished the prototype and got it to Jimmie, and he signed off on it. He was the family's representative.

"In production I had to figure out a way to make the process somewhat manageable so that players and dealers could get these things in their hands, so I did each one by hand, but I made a template to help me with positioning the marks and scratches. I built those guitars myself, all one hundred of them, and it nearly put me in the ground [laughs]. It was *so* labor-intensive. It probably took six or seven months, and even toward the end I was still completing only a few each week. It was one of the quickest sell-outs we ever had, very successful. Customers were telling dealers they couldn't wait to get their hands on them."

According to *The ToneQuest Report,* all one hundred SRVs were pre-sold at $10,000 each. The package included a flight case, a red gig bag patterned after Stevie's bag, a repro of Stevie's distinctive black strap with white musical notes, a certificate signed by John Cruz, a copy of 1983's *Live At The El Mocambo* DVD, and a Custom Shop DVD documenting the team's inspection of Number One. Mike Eldred: "This was a great example of how the shop can partner with people. With the SRV Number One, Jimmie really got involved. He really wanted us to include the *El Mocambo* DVD performance. He said, 'That's where Stevie's *just flat gettin' it!*'"

Jeff Beck's relationship with Fender predates the founding of the Custom Shop, and during the 1980s he worked with Fender employees not only in the shop but also in marketing and R&D to create his first signature Strat, a factory model. In January 2004 the Custom Shop introduced its own alder-bodied Jeff Beck Signature Stratocaster as a member of the Custom Artist Series. Available in Olympic White and Surf Green and retailing for $2,391, it featured a somewhat slimmed-down C-shaped neck rather than the Louisville Sluggerish maple block found on the prototypes and early factory models. In a simple and sensible reworking of the tone and volume controls, the three knobs are Volume, Tone for the front pickup, and Tone for the middle and bridge pickups. Other details: a rosewood board, a contoured heel at the neck-body joint, dual-coil ceramic Noiseless pickups, an LSR roller nut, stainless steel saddles, and staggered-height Sperzel tuners.

Guitars with stories: The Master Designs

In the early 2000s, Richard McDonald reexamined the entire line, redid all the option menus, and recalibrated all the prices relative to each other. But in his view, the most significant effort of all was working with Mike Eldred to develop the Master Design and Limited Edition series. As noted, Richard thought the Time Machine models had become a bit lackluster. The Master Design idea was a way to create a sense of urgency among players and also to explore a middle ground of models between existing Team Built guitars and the very expensive and exclusive instruments at the top of the line. Inaugurated in 2004, the new series would borrow a page from the Tribute playbook to add some excitement, diversity, and collector value. "It brought the collateral-material, value-added approach to a new awareness," Richard explains. "We were looking for 'guitars with a story.' This is still a mantra. Without a story, an old guitar is . . . just an old guitar.

"So I went to each builder and said, 'There's a guitar in your life, some Fender in your collection, or one that you had, or one that you always wanted to make that's special, just for you. Go ahead and make it, in a very limited number of Master Builts — maybe just ten, maybe more — and they will sell for 6,000 or 7,000 dollars or whatever it is, and then we'll do another 50 or 75 regular Custom Shop versions for 5,000 bucks apiece or whatever.' So Mark Kendrick says, I've got a '65 Strat with a bound fingerboard and block inlays that I'm crazy about. Okay, so he does that. He keeps all of his notes, all of his thoughts and ideas, we get all the drawings, and let's make a DVD, talk to Mark about it, what's special about it, and we put all that collateral stuff together. So I go to the next guy, and the next one, and we do maybe three a year. And they would have a collectability because they were so limited and also there was a timing urgency — if you want one, better get it now."

The new program would serve additional goals that McDonald had set for himself and for Fender, such as shining more of a spotlight on the Master Builders, and intensifying the training of apprentices. "This would be a way to develop the Master Builders of the future," he says. "We would take the best builders off the floor and move them into the Custom Shop. They would work with our Master Builders as their mentors on these very special, limited-edition Master Designs. In a way, it was a succession plan. After an intensive apprenticeship, they would become the next generation."

The Builder Select models are similar to the Master Designs in one respect, in that the idea comes from the builder himself rather than from a dealer, Fender marketing, an artist, or a customer. Mike Eldred: "Like the Master Designs, the Builder Selects are chosen and designed by the Master Builder. The difference is that a Master Design guitar is based on something that's more personal to him. It could be something from his past, a favorite old guitar. He builds maybe 10, and then we take the specs and Team Build maybe up to 100, with the Master Builder overseeing it. The [Master Design] package includes a DVD interview with the builder, his bio, reproductions of his original notes, drawings, and specs, all in a nice leather binder. There is a special case and certificate, also."

Mark Kendrick's Master Design Strat

Back in 1965, keen observers noticed something odd about the Stratocaster lying on that wicker stool in the Fender catalog's photo. The neck had white binding along the edge. It was a feature previously associated with higher-end Gibsons, Martins, and others, but it had never seemed necessary on a Fender before. It was comfy, though. Plenty of players prefer a bound neck, and Fender made a relatively small number of bound-neck Strats for two years or so.

When Richard McDonald came to Mark Kendrick in 2004 with his challenge to build a guitar that was "special, just for you," Mark responded with a recreation of one of the rarest of all vintage Fenders, in this case a beautiful bound-neck, 1965-style Stratocaster in Lake Placid Blue over Olympic White. Details included a round-lam Indian rosewood board, Closet Classic aging, a Texas Special at the bridge, two Fat '50s pickups, a '65-type decal, and an L serial number. Mark Kendrick wrote up the spec sheet on October 30, 2003, and the guitar was unveiled in 2004. The guitar came in a special Master Design case and was accompanied by a certificate and Mark's comments and notes preserved in a leather binder.

Mark Kendrick: "The guitar that inspired the Master Design came to the attention of my friend Tom Reiser of TR Guitar in Tustin, California. It came to his shop in the back of a Toyota pickup — no case, nothing, just skittering around in the back of the truck. The guy asked Tom if he could get it in working order for his son to play. Tom worked out a deal where he would build the guy a new guitar in trade for the 'beater.' It was in pretty rough shape, but the Lake Placid Blue over Olympic White color was wonderful, and the neck felt great. That was my inspiration. I loved the look of that guitar."

Below: Mark Kendrick recreated one of his favorite guitars, the rare, bound-neck Stratocaster. Released in limited numbers, the shop's first Master Design guitar was finished in Lake Placid Blue over Olympic White and came with a bounty of collateral goodies.

The Robin Trower Strats

The Custom Shop's Robin Trower Stratocasters of 2004 resulted from collaborations between Trower and Todd Krause. Published reports delineated the differences between the Signature version and the $3,799 Tribute; several of these reports were inaccurate. Todd Krause sets the record straight: "When we made the Tribute, we couldn't model it after Trower's original, because that guitar didn't exist anymore, so we made a stock '73/'74 Stratocaster, just like the one Robin Trower played on *Bridge Of Sighs*.

"The *Signature* was completely different. It had a 4-bolt bullet neck with Sperzel keys, abalone inlays, and a slightly sleeker back shape. It had a Custom Shop '54 neck pickup, a reverse wound/reverse polarity '60s pickup in the middle, and a Texas Special — not a Tex-Mex — in the bridge."

The Tribute was available in a limited run of 100 pieces, and only in Arctic White. The Signature was available in Arctic White, black, or Midnight Wine Burst. At the time, Fender was using the term Team Built Custom for the Tribute, and Team Built for the Signature, the former indicating a deeper level of personal attention.

The big-head, bullet-rod Robin Trower Strat came in two versions — Signature (shown here) and Tribute. You can almost hear this '70s-style tone machine through a dreamy, slo-mo Uni-Vibe — *glanng . . . anng . . . anng . . . .*

NAMM 2004

The Custom Shop's display at the Summer 2004 NAMM Show was so extensive that it merited a separate brochure. It specified 35 Master Built guitars and another 30 Custom Built guitars. A few of the many highlights included a 1956 Relic Gold Strat with gold hardware, a gold anodized pickguard and a soft V neck (limited run of 100, $4,631); a 1960 Relic Gold Strat in Gold Metallic with a gold anodized pickguard, matching gold peghead, and gold hardware (limited run of 100, $4,534); a 1965 Relic Gold Strat with the all-gold treatment (Gold Metallic paint, matching peghead, pickguard, and hardware; limited run of 100, $4,678), and the 1957 Melody of Cleveland Relic Strat, hand-painted by Pamelina H. ($7,000).

And in other 2004 news . . . .

The shop premiered the Tye Zamora bass built by Senior Master Builder Jason Davis; its uniquely shaped, multi-lam body and bubinga fingerboard marked a clear departure from familiar Fender bass designs. Two new Time Machines appeared: the '66 Strat and the '67 Tele. Several new Showmasters featured tops made of exotic woods such as spalted maple and lacewood. 2004 was also the year when the shop displayed its beautiful collaborations with artists Joe Wood, Sara Ray, Nevena Christi, and others (Chap. 25).

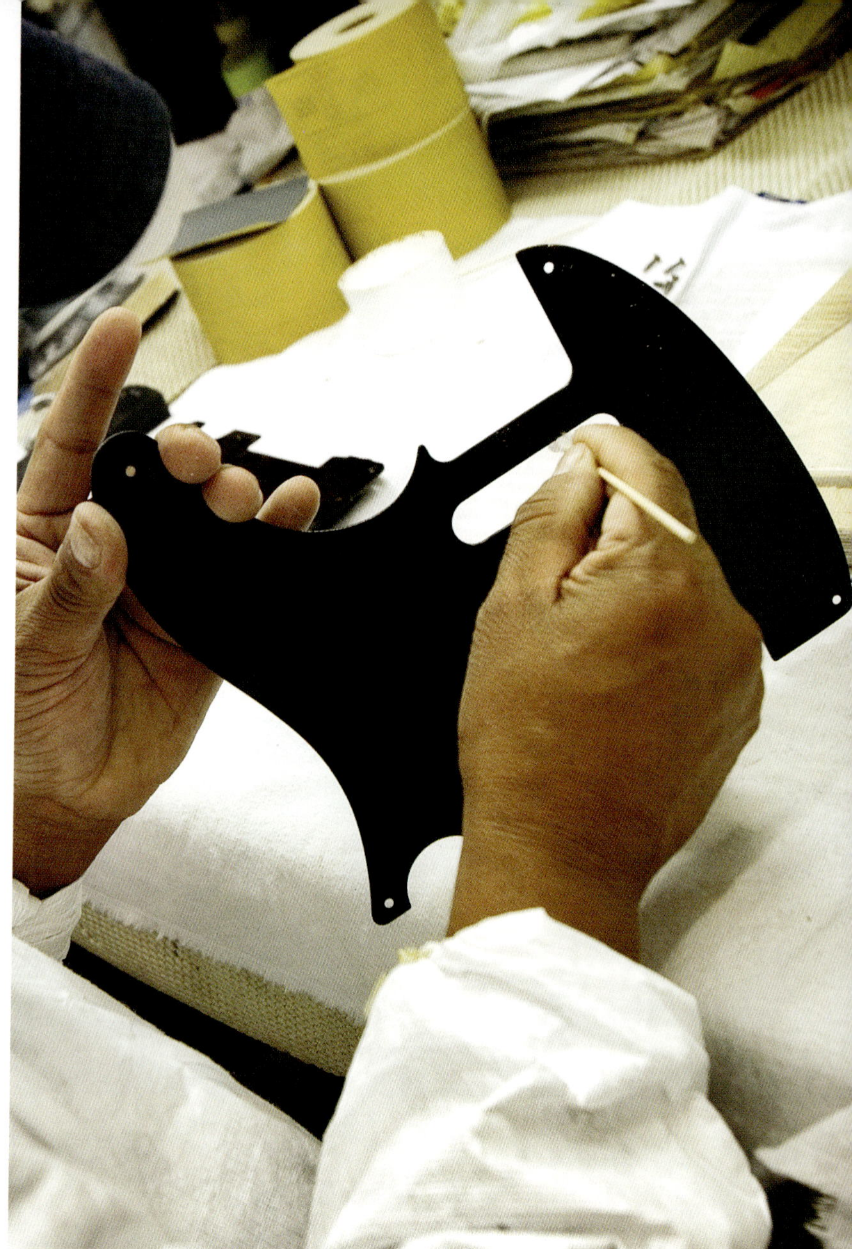

Recreating old guitars with new methods

While the basic designs of many iconic guitars have changed little over the past half-century, the process of making those instruments in quantity has been revolutionized by advances in machinery, particularly Computer Numeric Controlled (CNC, or NC) cutting equipment. Three facts are sometimes overlooked by self-styled purists who tout the presumed superior quality of old-fashioned hand techniques. First, NCs perform their tasks not only with more speed but in some respects with more precision as well. Second, some of the machines from the vintage era are still around and still get used, at least at Fender. Finally, Custom Shop guitars produced with modern equipment still entail plenty of handwork. (One more point: It seems inconceivable that Leo Fender would have failed to employ NC machines had they been available in the vintage era.)

As we've seen, concerns for vintage details approach fanatical levels among some customers, but still, shouldn't today's craftspeople use these updated technologies to correct past "imperfections"? It depends on what the player wants. Some Custom Shop instruments offer refinements of every component from tuners to tailpiece, but others are all about vintage authenticity. "It's always a challenge," says Senior Master Builder Chris Fleming.

"Do we build in all the 'shortcomings' just to make it authentic? Well, yes, unless it's really functionally nonsensical. Most of those little odd quirks were minor oversights. Like on nearly all Telecaster bodies, the neck pockets weren't angled to match the angle of the neck. From the base of the heel to the nut creates an angle, but the pockets were square, so up towards the top of the pocket it sticks out, and you get that little shelf or ledge on the pocket. Nobody really thought it mattered to tidy it up and shape the pocket to match the neck. In the '60s they started to match the two angles so that it was even, but in the '50s and even into the early '60s that pocket had an overhang. When we reproduce a vintage guitar in the Custom Shop, we generally leave those things in."

Sometimes the builders program their NCs to cut some of the basic blanks so that they look like they were done with a pin router. Chris Fleming: "The pin routing was done in two separate operations, on two levels, and you can see a line, a little rim around the inside of the rout that separates the two cuttings. So even though it's done on an NC, we can make it look like it was done on a pin router, and you can see that little line where it looks like the old method."

Dennis Galuszka created a '62 Jazzmaster and a '62 Jaguar in Champagne Sparkle for display at the Summer 2004 NAMM show. Each was offered at $6,400. Dennis reported in 2009: "I made them as a set, and oddly enough, they didn't sell for a couple of years. They finally sold, and then over the last couple of years I've gotten a fair amount of interest in recreating them." Extra-cool detail: maple boards!

In 2004 the shop partnered with Mattel to produce a limited run of Hot Wheels Flat Head Showmasters. The custom paint job was created by Larry R. Wood. A former General Motors designer, Wood joined Mattel in 1967, eventually acquiring the nickname "Mr. Hot Wheels."

Obey
ROCK AND ROLL
ROCK AND ROLL
ROCK

CHAPTER TWENTY-SEVEN

27

2005

The Mary Kaye Tribute, Limited Releases, the Top-Scoop Strat, a New Master Design, Builder Selects

The Custom Shop line of 2005 was another collection of impressive variety and craftsmanship. In the Winter 2005 NAMM brochure, the Custom Shop listed a staggering 97 models in all, 33 of which were Master Builts. The Time Machine, Custom Artist, Custom Classic, Flat Head, and Showmaster series were continued. The second and third Master Design guitars were unveiled — Yuriy Shishkov's Bigsby-equipped '63 Telecaster, and John English's '59 Strat Relic in Sonic Blue — and the Mary Kaye was added to the Tributes. The Custom Artist series included five Telecasters: a pair of John 5 models, the Bryant, the Gatton, and the Haggard (formerly called a Tribute). It also included a quartet of Strats: the Gallagher (formerly a Tribute), Blackmore, Dale, and Cray.

Left: Warhol, fascist poster graphics, street-art chic, social commentary, beauty, irony — and twang: It's all there in the Custom Shop guitars adorned by Shepard Fairey. This page: John English's Sonic Blue Master Design '59 Strat Relic.

Greg Fessler built the Mary Kaye Tribute Strats of 2005, recreating what might be called Fender's original, unofficial "artist guitar."

The Mary Kaye Tribute Series Stratocaster

Mary Kaye was a legend, but she didn't know it. She told this author in 2003, "I didn't even know about that until about four years ago. They told me my name was in all the magazines and books." It all started with a photo published in the 1956 Fender catalog. It pictured a beautiful, dark-haired woman in an evening dress with two tuxedo-clad men, posing with a white Strat and a tweed Twin. The top of the line Fender at the time, the guitar was special indeed — a Stratocaster sporting a thin blonde finish and 14 carat gold hardware. While sunburst Strats retailed for $274.50 at the time, the factory-stock white/gold model cost $330, entailing a hefty twenty percent increase.

Descended from Hawaiian royalty, Mary Kaye was born Mary Ka'aihue. She changed her name because mainland folks couldn't seem to pronounce it, and also because when music fans saw "Ka'aihue" on a marquee or playbill they assumed she played Hawaiian music. In fact, she was an accomplished jazz artist (she once told this author, "I know chords nobody else knows"). On gigs, she played an archtop that John D'Angelico had built for her, but she did on occasion use a Fender amp, and at Don Randall's request she agreed to pose with the Stratocaster for a promo photo. (Now in the hands of a private collector, the Stratocaster Mary was holding is serial number 09391. Its body, still in good condition, is dated January '56. The original neck was replaced at the factory with a neck dated 9/56.)

Flash forward three decades. As players, dealers, and collectors began to pay attention to vintage instruments, any pre-CBS white Strat with gold hardware acquired the nickname it retains to this day: Mary Kaye. The Custom Shop filled orders for one-off Mary Kayes for years. In fact, in John Page's opinion, the very first "true" Custom Shop guitar was the lefty '57 Mary Kaye he built for Elliot Easton back in early 1987 in the first Pomona Road facility.

In January 2005, the Custom Shop unveiled the Mary Kaye Tribute Series Stratocaster. Its figured ash body was highlighted by a semi-transparent White Blonde nitrocellulose finish that was given the mildly checked, Closet Classic treatment. Other details included a soft V neck contour, aged plastic parts and, of course, gold hardware. The pickups were hand-wound by Abigail Ybarra, who came to work in 1956, the same year the now-famous Mary Kaye trio photo was first published. Orders were taken only through 2005, and the guitars retailed for $7,400.

Greg Fessler personally built all of Tributes in the 60-piece run. "I could complete anywhere from five to eight per month," he recalls, "and the whole process took a year. I picked straight-grain ash for the bodies, straight-grain maple for the neck, and used vintage fret wire on the 7.25" radius maple neck. It's basically a straight-up '50s guitar. Abby did such a great job on the pickups."

Since the rebirth of Fender in 1985, dozens of instruments have born the names of official endorsing artists, but the Mary Kaye is the only well-known example of a Fender guitar acquiring an artist nickname exclusively through word of mouth. In that loose, unofficial sense, the original Mary Kaye Strat might be called Fender's first "artist" model. Fittingly, the Custom Shop version was likewise unique. Falling in neither of the primary Tribute categories (a new model with unique features, such as the Merle Haggard and Marty Stuart Teles; or a recreation of a personal, iconic artist guitar, such as the SRV Number One), the 2005 Mary Kaye was instead the only Tribute that replicated an unmodified, factory-stock guitar.

Limited Release: Master Built '58 Strat

A Fender price list of 2004 had used the term Limited Release in reference to the '54 Anniversary Strat, but that model was more often called a Limited Edition. The Limited Release nomenclature was invoked again in 2005 in reference to Mark Kendrick's recreation of a '58 maple-neck Strat, one of the most coveted and most beautiful stock Strats to ever leave the Fullerton factory. As described the following year, Limited Release instruments have an historical significance based on "certain years, features, or innovative aspects . . . . It could have been a prototype or test market guitar. Regardless, there are not many originals, and these models are destined to become collector's pieces themselves." The reissue's 3-color sunburst had plenty of red and yellow, and the outer edges were "dark chocolate," not unusual among '58s but otherwise ever so slightly lighter than the more common black.

Details included a small C neck shape, '58-style pickups, and a reverse wound/reverse polarity middle pickup that provided humbucking operation in the second and fourth positions. A final detail: While stock Strats typically have no tone control for that bright bridge pickup, on the Master Built '58 the middle knob is a tone control for the front *and* middle pickups, and knob number three is a tone control for the bridge pickup, arguably a sensible arrangement for all 3-knob Strats.

The Top-Scoop "Hendrix Reverse Proto" Strat

Years before the Custom Shop was founded, Fender produced a few oddball instruments intended to conjure the vibe and voodoo of Jimi Hendrix. The design was the brainchild of sales manager Mudge Miller, and John Page built the guitars in the R&D model shop. These "Hendrix Reverse Proto" guitars were white Stratocasters all right, and they were fitted with a reverse headstock that more or less evoked the look of Jimi's upside-down, right-handed '68. Beyond that, however, the Hendrix connection was a stretch at best. For that matter, the "prototype" designation was a stretch as well, as we will see.

Aside from appearances, the lefty neck arrangement was noteworthy for other reasons. The Reverse Proto Strat had the much-preferred, pre-CBS type 4-bolt neck attachment, unusual for CBS-era Strats. And its reverse headstock, with the treble E now having the shortest rather than the longest string length, no doubt affected the feel of the guitar and perhaps its tone as well.

But the large, CBS-style reverse headstock was hardly the model's most idiosyncratic feature. Aside from its regular "tummy tuck" contour in back, the guitar featured an extra scoop on the *top*, of all places, as well as an extra arm carve — on the back. Neither of these contours served any function whatsoever, but at least they made the guitar rare and distinctive.

Another quirk: The rear surface of the headstock bore a "Prototype" stamp, even though these models were "prototypes" of guitars that Fender apparently never produced and almost certainly never intended to produce. Tom Watson, of the online Modern Guitars Magazine, has communicated with several owners who confirm that the wording of the stamp reads in full: ORIGINAL PROTOTYPE NOT FOR RESALE Fender MUSICAL INSTRUMENT. (Note the word "Instrument," as opposed to "Instruments.") Tom Watson: "It's really a jerry-rigged looking stamp, nothing like the stamps seen later from the Custom Shop, even the early Custom Shop stamp." If the guitars weren't prototypes of production instruments, what was the real function of the stamp? It might well have been simply a convenient way to alert dealers and buyers: These are *not* official models.

Speculation abounds regarding these non-prototype prototypes, perhaps a result of ascribing to the whole project more logic than it deserves. The reverse headstock often causes the guitar to be included among Hendrix-inspired Strats, which is reasonable. Still, there's no way a serious attempt to design a Hendrix model would include those extra scoops, which might be described in charitable moments as "eccentric." Rather than an official Fender model that would have undergone typical planning and at least somewhat consistent catalog descriptions, this was an impromptu, one-shot deal that was foisted on R&D by a headstrong sales manager with little regard for marketing considerations or coherence. Frankly, John Page resented the assignment. "I was supposed to be building one or two models or prototypes," he says, "not entire limited runs."

How many were built? Estimates vary. As recounted in *The Stratocaster Chronicles*, some reports put the number at about 25, but that figure likely comes from John Page's published recollections, which he has since revised down-

Dennis Galuszka's "Hendrix Reverse Proto" Strat brought back to life one of Fender's rarest and most idiosyncratic guitars.

ward. Dan Smith thought it was a smaller number. He says, "I found one in the customer service storage cage when we were clearing out the Fender building on Valencia in Fullerton and getting ready to move to the offices in Brea. My understanding is that there were about 15, one for each territory or something to that effect. That was the story that was relayed to me by [head of customer service] Ken Young."

After all this time — this was a good seven or eight years before the Custom Shop's founding — John Page is understandably uncertain about some details. "I know that 25 was the run size that Mudge wanted," he explains. "It was a long, long time ago. Whatever the number, I did indeed make all of the parts that were unique to this run — the body and pickguard, at least. I can't remember if I made the necks or not. I also did the final assembly, as I recall. Mudge wanted an 'M' with a circle around it on the ball of the peghead, which I don't think we ever did. He said it was supposed to stand for 'Modified,' but we knew it stood for 'Mudge.' He sold them all to dealer buddies he had in Texas." Tom Watson narrows down the number just a bit: "By the end of 2005, I could account for about ten of the prototypes, but still no production model had surfaced."

Whether the originals numbered ten or 25 or somewhere in between, Master Builder Dennis Galuszka recreated the Reverse Proto Strat in 2005. He says, "The earlier ones were one of those weird things that happens when you let a marketing guy design a guitar [laughs]. Mudge Miller had this idea to make sort of a Jimi Hendrix guitar, although it was never official. Because Jimi had flipped it over, the idea here was to do some reverse stuff, and they came up with a funny interpretation of it. The cutout on the top of the body is shallower than the regular one on the back. Also on the back, for whatever reason, there is an 'arm' cut on the bottom; because of its location it's sort of a knee cut. It makes zero sense."

There was a fair amount of interest in this unique guitar, so the Custom Shop replicated a hundred of them. Dennis Galuszka made them all personally, which took two years. Other details of the Custom Shop's Reverse Proto Strat included a two-piece alder body, a Closet Classic finish in Vintage White, a one-piece maple neck, '70s-style *F* tuners, a '70s-style cast bridge with cast saddles, three '69 grey-bobbin single-coil pickups, and an early-'80s *F*-stamp neck plate with a black plastic gasket. One off-kilter detail was the positioning of the right-side-up decals on the upside-down headstock. Another: The Certificate of Authenticity reportedly calls the model a "79 Reverse Proto Stratocaster," although other Fender literature refers to the originals as 1980 models.

The success of the $8,000 Master Built remake might seem surprising, although some people do like the feel of reverse-headstock Strats. Dennis Galuszka: "I very much believe that string length is everything. Some argue that there is no change in string tension from nut to bridge, but I do not agree. With the reverse head you have longer string length on the low strings and shorter on the high strings, so the longer low E would be

more piano-like with more tension, and the high E would be easier to bend. I have no scientific data to back this up, but I believe in the principle."

Still, players who wanted a Jimi Hendrix-inspired Fender could choose from other Strats with right-handed necks on right-handed bodies, or left-handed necks on right-handed bodies, or left-handed necks on left-handed bodies, all with higher Voodoo Quotients than the top-scoop Strat. There's the Jimi Hendrix Tribute Stratocaster, the Voodoo Strat, the Reverse Headstock Stratocaster, and more. Given those impressive options, why would anybody choose one of the odd-duck Strats with the extra scoops? Was it novelty alone, plus the guarantee of Master Built quality?

Dennis offers two additional reasons: "First, there's a photo of Stevie Ray Vaughan playing one. Second, for a while there John Mayer was trying to find and buy up all of the originals. The one that I spec'd out for the Custom Shop version was one I borrowed from John. So between SRV and John Mayer, it catapulted the popularity of the original." Mike Eldred: "The reason we did that run was because of a discussion between John Mayer and myself. He had just bought one and wanted me to look at it, so he brought it down to the shop and I went through it. I told him we should do a run of them, and he agreed. That's when I brought in Dennis, and he built them."

Dennis Galuszka: "The Master Builts were just like the originals, although mine did not say 'prototype' on the back of the headstock, like the originals did. The press release said that the Custom Shop ones did say 'prototype,' and that was probably the original plan, but that was a typo that never got corrected." Despite published reports that a few of the earliest Master Builts might have borne the stamp, Dennis Galuszka reports that none did. He adds: "The tooling was a little weird back when they did the originals; like there was a tooling hole in the face of the fretboard — stuff that we wouldn't normally do now — but we reproduced all those things, everything except the stamp."

Yuriy Shishkov's Master Design Telecaster

Following on the heels of Mark Kendrick's bound-neck '65 Stratocaster came the shop's second model in the Master Design series, the Yuriy Shishkov Master Design '63 Telecaster of 2005. "I like the shape of the Stratocaster, how sleek and timeless it is," Yuriy explains, "but I like the simplicity and the sound of the Telecaster. I used a '63 Tele pickup in the bridge, and a Twisted Tele at the neck, which is a fuller pickup with much more winding. It was developed in the Custom Shop by Alan Hamel. I like the combination. I like to have a tremolo, too, but I stay away from the Floyd Rose, so a Tele with a Bigsby seemed to be the perfect instrument for my Master Design guitar." The Bigsby is a B5 model that entails an extra metal plate surrounding the rear pickup. It was custom made for Fender and features the *F* logo. Mark Kendrick had a "new old stock" version from way back in 1972 and generously gave it to Yuriy so that he could finish his prototype on time.

There were 50 of these heavy-hardware Teles in the initial group, all hand-built by Shishkov and all featuring his personal decal. They retailed for $7,167. That series was followed by a 100-piece Team Built run. The shop's director of manufacturing operations, Alex Nicholas, explains: "The main specs were the same, but the detail work on Yuriy's are what delineate them — all of the personal touches that represent his building style. Yuriy worked very close with the Custom Shop team, to emulate the vibe and spirit of the original ones that he built himself."

Utilitarian retro: Yuriy Shishkov conceived his Bigsby-equipped Master Design '63 Telecaster as a "working guitar."

The point of the Master Designs is that the builder himself gets to call the shots, but that doesn't mean he works in a vacuum. Yuriy: "You get to pick something special according to your own tastes, but it is smart to consult with the marketing people because you don't want to come up with something that is not really hot or popular. You don't want to build a totally '80s guitar if that era is behind us and hasn't come back yet. So we work together with marketing. This guitar reflects my taste, but I wanted it to be popular and suit the market, too."

The two-piece, premium-grade ash body has a lightly reliced nitrocellulose lacquer finish. The one-piece, AA-grade, C-shaped flame maple neck has a vintage tint, a vintage-spec 7.25" radius, and no separate fingerboard (the frets are mounted directly to the neck). Yuriy adds: "The guitar was really fun to work on. I picked white blonde for the color, and with the Relic finish you can take it on the road and take it on the gig and not have to worry about it. I wanted it to be a working guitar."

In August 2005, Fender opened The Custom Shop Lounge in Düsseldorf, Germany, calling it "perhaps the finest guitar showroom ever built." Designed to emit the vibe of a big-city bar or men's club, it houses nearly a million dollars worth of instruments. Ralf Benninghaus-Fliedner, sales and marketing director for Fender GmbH, said at the time: "We would like to give dedicated Custom Shop dealers and their customers a very special shopping adventure. The Custom Shop Lounge is a dedicated showroom filled with a huge selection of Team Built, Team Built Custom, and Master Built Fender instruments." Gernold Linke, product manager for Fender Europe, explained what players and dealers could expect: "They can come in, get a cappuccino, and look at the guitars. The guy can play it, and he will be treated like a king."

Fender
STRATOCASTER
CZ502876
LIMITED EDITION
Fender
Custom Shop
Fender
STRATOCASTER

White Gold: the Master Salute Strat

In 2005 the shop crafted a run of 250 Limited Edition Master Salute Strats in white gold leaf. Details included a two-piece alder body, a modern C-shaped neck, a 9.5" radius, medium jumbo frets, Custom '50s pickups, and an engraved Limited Edition neck plate. Each one shipped with a Limited Edition certificate, a Limited Edition hardshell case, and a Custom Shop mirror ("perfect for your den or living room").

John Cruz built the prototype, which was displayed at the NAMM show in January. Then, several of the Master Builders were given a certain number to build. John Cruz: "On the Master Salutes, we applied the gold leaf with a varnish. The leaves were housed in a little square box with tissue paper in between each leaf. They were smaller than cocktail napkins and very thin. The whole process was very exacting and time-consuming."

George Amicay is another craftsman with experience in the fine art of gold leaf. "You cover the body with a substance that's like a varnish, using a very fine brush so there are no streaks. You wait about three hours for it to set up, and then when the tackiness is the perfect consistency you lay on these pure gold leaf sheets that are about 4" x 4". You have to be so meticulous — if you touch the leaf, the oil from your finger will cause it to stick, so you use a squirrel [roller] and brush to pick it up and lay it over the varnish. There's a real trick to it because the stuff is so thin and fragile." The Master Salute Stratocaster retailed for $8,226.

George Amicay perfected the time-consuming, centuries-old art of gilding. "You have to be so meticulous," he says. "If you touch the leaf, the oil from your finger will cause it to stick. There's a real trick to it because the stuff is so thin and fragile."

Its body gilded in hand-laid white gold leaf, the Master Salute Strat was issued in a run of 250 Limited Edition pieces.

Obey
OBEY
ROCK
OBEY
SAVE

Big Bro is watching you

Among the most unusual and memorable Fenders introduced in July 2005 were the Limited Edition Telecasters and Stratocasters painted and signed by Shepard Fairey. As of this writing he is the most famous of all the artists to be associated with the Custom Shop and the only one whose work infuses iconography with layers of implied commentary on both historic and contemporary political themes.

Each of these Relic guitars received unique treatment in the hands of the artist, although in general they reflected motifs from Fairey's global, multifaceted Obey Campaign. In explaining the Orwellian vibe, Fairey has said, "Because people are not used to seeing advertisements or propaganda for which the motive is not obvious, frequent and novel encounters with Obey propaganda provoke thought and possible frustration, nevertheless revitalizing the viewer's perception and attention to detail."

There were 25 Shepard Fairey guitars, 12 '50s-style Strats and 13 Teles, and Todd Krause built all of them by hand. The Strats had 10/56 "Boat Necks," while the Teles had '50s-style, U-shaped necks. Each model had a premium ash body with a reliced nitro finish, '50s-style pickups, a distressed aluminum pickguard, and a maple board with vintage-style frets and a vintage-spec 7.25" radius. No two were alike. (Squier versions were introduced the following year.)

Gonna party like it's 1984: Iconic designs by Leo Fender, immaculate guitars by Todd Krause, provocative art by Shepard Fairey, paranoid/overlord vibe by George Orwell.

The John Cruz Builder Select 1962 Stratocaster Relic LTD

In late 2005, John Cruz introduced a 100-piece run of his Builder Select Strat, which incorporated many of his favorite features. "The '60s era is my favorite with Strats," he says. "The '61 is my all-time favorite, but I love the Sonic Blue color in '62, so we called this one a '62. Sonic is the lightest of the blues. John English had done a couple and they turned out really well, so I thought I would do a heavier Relic version in a light Sonic Blue with a specific neck shape and a certain kind of neckwear on the back. This all came from an early-'62 Strat I fell in love with."

John specified a lightweight alder body and a slab-board neck, as opposed to the round-lam. "I also wanted to do a limited-edition bit of hot rodding," he says, "although we weren't using the term at the time, so I used some pickups that Abigail and I had come up with." Details: nitrocellulose lacquer finish, mint-green pickguard, C-shaped neck, a 9.5" radius, three John Cruz Master Built Strat pickups with S-1 switching, and an American Vintage trem.

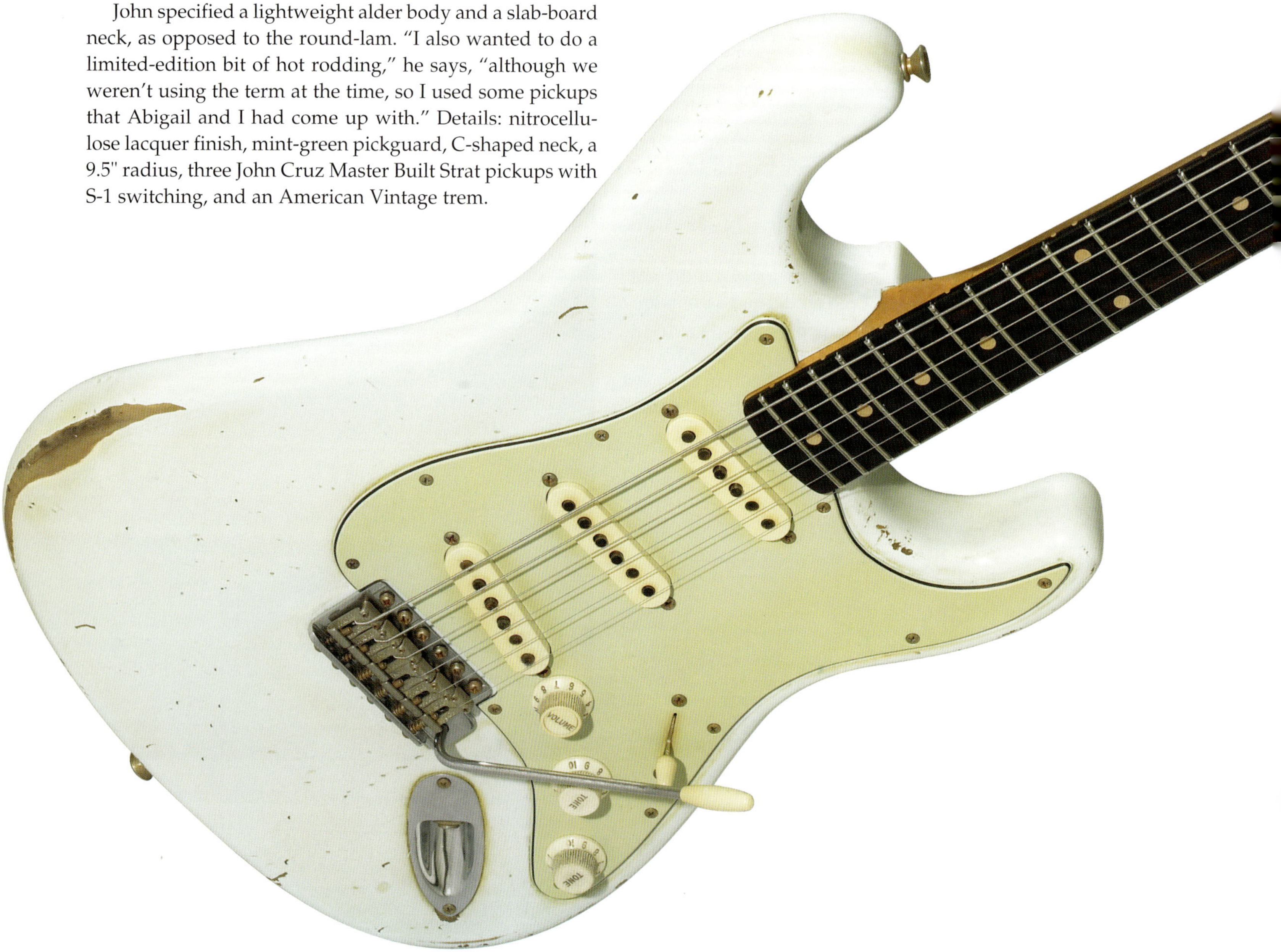

Chris Fleming built two "Mando-Strats." While this one evoked the mid 1950s (two-color sunburst, maple fingerboards), the other one had an early-'60s look, with a three-color sunburst and rosewood boards.

Michiya Haruhata is the virtuoso guitarist and chief songwriter for TUBE, for many years one of the most popular bands in Japan. The Michiya Haruhata BWL Stratocaster of 2005 was offered in two versions: a Master Built run of 12 guitars by John English, and a Team Built Custom run of 60 guitars. All were adorned by master silversmith and leather artist Bill Wall of Bill Wall Leather (BWL), Malibu, California.

Right: A body detail of the leather-covered Master Built guitar.

Below: The Team Built model featured hand-engraved metal parts, a hum/single/single pickup configuration, and a "Malibu/BWL" Iron Cross.

This historic-themed Tele is called Texas Past and was one of two designs ordered by a Guitar Center in the Lone Star state. The other, Texas Present, depicted a city skyline and other modern symbols. Guitars by Todd Krause, artwork by Pamelina H.

And in other 2005 news . . . .

Additional 2005 highlights included Nevena Christi's Leather Hula Esquire, Joe Wood's hand-painted Telecaster, Dave Newman's Memorabilia set, and other art projects. Many of these art guitars are profiled throughout these pages. Limited Editions from 2005 also included the 1966 Stratocaster in Firemist Silver Metallic (Closet Classic, 200 pieces, Team Built, introduced in July); and a 1955 Strat Relic in two-color sunburst (100 pieces, Fat '50s Strat pickups).

Fender

CHAPTER TWENTY-EIGHT

28

2006: Moving Away From The Price List

Beck and Blackie Tributes, More Limited Editions, Strat Pro

The year 2006 marked Fender's 60th anniversary. The Custom Shop rose to the occasion in a big way, crafting the special commemorative Stratocaster profiled here. But while the shop offered from 50 to almost 60 cataloged models, the total varying throughout the year, Mike Eldred's and Richard McDonald's plans actually called for a gradual shift away from the open-ended availability of most models — that is, a departure from the price list idea — and a reorganization of the guitars into ever more specialized collections.

Back in 2004, only one instrument had occupied the Limited Release category, the 50th Anniversary 1954 Strat (that guitar was also called a Limited Edition). But by 2006's mid-year price list, a whopping 17 instruments were assigned to the Limited Edition category: nine Strats, three year-specific Teles, three Esquires, the 1970 Jazz Bass, and the 1958 Precision. All were listed as "new," which was relatively accurate (some were carryovers); by any standard they marked a massive rollout of debut models.

Left: The Blackie project of 2006 would prove to be the Custom Shop's most anticipated endeavor to date.

Most were limited in production to 100 pieces. The exceptions were 2005's '66 Strat in Firemist Silver and the '67 Tele in Firemist Silver (200 each), and the year-old Master Salute Strat (250). As was typical, Fender combined categories in various ways. Among the Limited Editions, for example, one could find the Master Salute Strat, Team Built Master Designs, Master Built Master Designs, and Builder Selects. One could also find guitars that carried "Relic" or "Closet Classic" as part of their official names but were not included in the Time Machine category.

Among 2006's Limited Editions and Special Editions:

- the Strat Pro (see below);
- the Tele Thinline in the three Time Machine finishes ($3,700 – $4,170);
- the '64-style, 3-color sunburst Bass VI (see below);
- Yuriy Shishkov's Builder Select 1964 Strat in Olympic White: 100 pieces, Closet Classic, Custom Fat '50s pickups, 3-way switch, vintage-spec 7.25" radius, introduced in January, $7,500;

This time it's personal: Chris Fleming recreated his own 1955 Telecaster in White Blonde. It was paired with a tweed Pro Jr., then turned over to the team for production.

- Todd Krause's Builder Select 1959 Strat Relic in Desert Sand: 100 pieces, Custom Fat '50s pickups, slab maple board with a vintage-spec 7.25" radius, $7,750;
- a Special Edition 1960 Strat Relic with a Brazilian rosewood board, Fat '50s pickups, a 7.25" radius, introduced in January, available in 2006 only, $8,999;
- a 1956 Strat Relic in Taos Turquoise, 100 pieces, with a 10/56 "boat neck" and Custom Mark Kendrick Design pickups;
- a '50s Strat Relic in Sonic Blue over a 2-color sunburst, 100 pieces, three Texas Specials, soft V neck;
- a '60s Strat Relic in black over a 3-color sunburst, with aged parts and three Texas Specials, introduced in January;
- Chris Fleming's Master Design set: a recreation of his personal 1955 Telecaster in aged White Blonde, accompanied by a lacquered tweed Pro Jr. amp, both Relics, Team Built, introduced in July;
- John English's Builder Select Heavy Relic Esquire in Vintage Blonde, 100 pieces; at $9,500 it was the most expensive cataloged instrument in 2006.

In living colors

Aside from sheer numbers, the Limited Editions were fairly bursting with exuberant colors — Chris Fleming's Tele/Strat Hybrid in Candy Apple Red, the Master Salute Strat in white gold leaf, other Strats in Gold Sparkle, Desert Sand, and Firemist Silver Metallic, Telecasters in Black, Firemist Silver Metallic, and Copper Metallic, an LTD Esquire in HLE Gold (recalling the shop's early Homer Haynes Strat), and a Jazz Bass in Natural. The Time Machines also offered a flashy array of colors, including the rare Charcoal Frost Metallic.

Speaking of colors, back in the vintage era a particular Fender might be sprayed with a couple of different finishes before leaving the factory. If a sales rep wanted a Fiesta Red Esquire and none was available, a craftsman might grab a ready-to-assemble blonde body and apply the red over the existing finish. Or if a mineral stain, bad seam, or other flaw were discovered in a guitar body with a natural, burst, or other transparent finish, Mr. Fender's solution was simple: Paint over it with something opaque — Sherwood Green or Lake Placid Blue or whatever was needed at the moment. Such refinishes typically remained undiscovered unless the guitar was disassembled or dinged up so deeply that the original color showed through the overcoat. In yet another step toward the ultimate in authenticity, the shop offered several show-through, multi-finish instruments in 2006: Sonic Blue over a 2-color sunburst, black over a 3-color sunburst, and Fiesta Red over Desert Sand.

Other categories, 2006

The Custom Artist group included six Strats (Dale, Clapton, Gallagher, Beck, Trower, and Cray). Although it did not appear in a separate category, the Gallagher was a Tribute, and its $3,929 price tag was anywhere from about six hundred bucks to a thousand bucks higher than the others. The Custom Artists also included the Seymour Duncan Esquire and five Teles (the Merle Haggard, formerly in the Tribute series; the Collins, the Gatton, and the two John 5 guitars). These models ranged in list price from the $3,295 basic John 5 to the ultra-fancy $6,256 Merle Haggard.

The Custom Artist basses were the Jaco Pastorius Tribute Jazz Bass, the two Reggie Hamilton Jazz Basses (now in their fourth year), and the brand new, top-of-the-line Pino Palladino Precision, featuring a Fiesta Red paint job over Desert Sand and a $4,500 price tag.

In some of the literature from 2006, the only Tribute-category instrument was the brand new Jeff Beck Esquire, a recreation of Beck's iconic Yardbirds/Rave Up guitar (see below). The Time Machine series continued to provide a broad array of models, with five year-specific Strats ('56, '60, '65, '66, and '69), the '59 Esquire, '51 Nocaster, '63 and '67 Teles, two Precisions ('55 and '59), and the '64 Jazz Bass, now in its seventh year.

The Flat Heads were assigned to the Showmaster category, along with several variations on the Showmaster Elite. The Custom Classics had been streamlined to one Strat, one Tele, and one Jazz Bass.

This photo recalls one of the most memorable NAMM show exhibits ever — a Custom Color rainbow of Esquires.

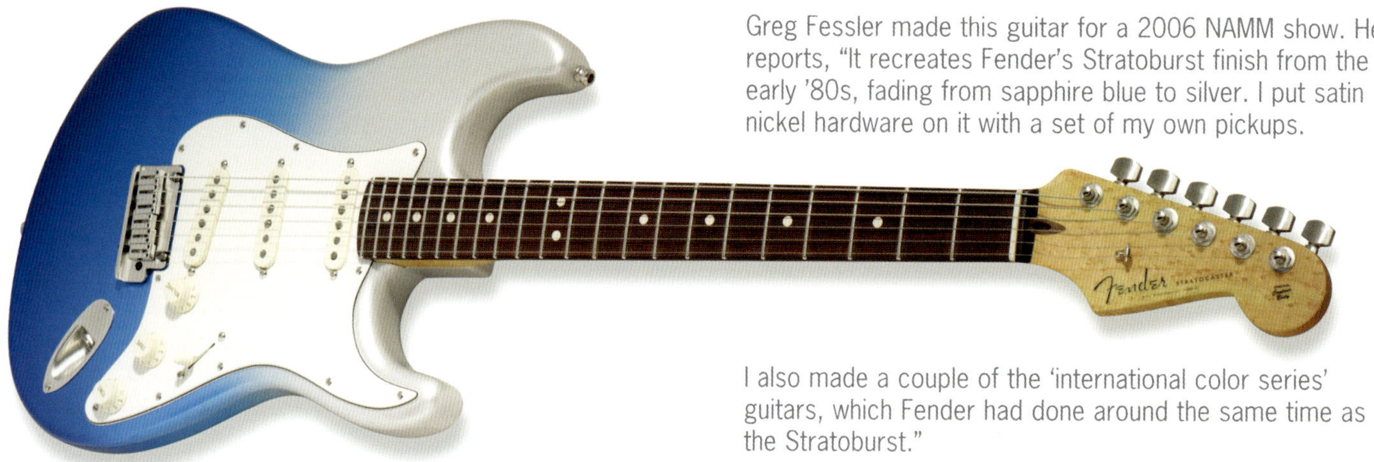

Greg Fessler made this guitar for a 2006 NAMM show. He reports, "It recreates Fender's Stratoburst finish from the early '80s, fading from sapphire blue to silver. I put satin nickel hardware on it with a set of my own pickups.

I also made a couple of the 'international color series' guitars, which Fender had done around the same time as the Stratoburst."

The cat's whiskers: The Jeff Beck Tribute Esquire

David Gilmour called Jeff Beck "the most consistently brilliant guitarist over the last 25 years," and few would argue. Not surprisingly, Beck's choices of instruments have turned heads and influenced trends throughout his career. His blonde '54 Esquire, for example, is one of the great album-cover guitars, along with Buddy Holly's *Chirping Crickets* Strat and Eric Clapton's *Layla* Strat. Beck's Fender appeared back in 1965 on the cover of the Yardbirds' historic *Having A Rave Up*. Featuring "I'm A Man," "Still I'm Sad," "Heart Full Of Soul," and "Train Kept A-Rollin'" (back to back, no less), the LP, one of the punchiest and most innovative records of the entire rock era, is credited with presaging heavy metal, psychedelia, and even art-rock. Seymour Duncan recalled, "I used to stare at the *Rave Up* album cover and wonder what it would be like to see Jeff's Esquire or, better yet, to hold it." Seymour got his wish when in late 1973 Jeff gave him the guitar. Duncan called the gift "one of the highlights of my life." He adds that when he got the guitar it had been gutted, so he installed a wiring harness from one of his own guitars, a '50s Esquire.

In the spring of 1965, the Yardbirds toured with the Walker Brothers. John Maus, a member of that band, possessed a '54 Esquire which he had heavily sanded to impart some Strat-like contours. Beck acquired it for $60 or $70 (recollections vary), and it promptly became a favorite recording and performing guitar. He replaced the white pickguard with an early-'50s style black one, later recounting to *Guitar Player*'s Steve Rosen, "Because it had a blonde neck and a black scratchplate, it was just one of the most sought after guitars in England . . . I was the cat's whiskers again." Referring to Beck's impact on American guitar players, biographer Annette Carson wrote in *Jeff Beck: Crazy Fingers*, "In contrast to their ultra-modern Jazzmasters, Beck's 11-year-old Esquire, with its single pickup, must have raised quite a few eyebrows — as did the way he ferociously wielded the instrument, lunging and brandishing it like a weapon."

In 2006, the Custom Shop issued a faithful, Master Built recreation of the guitar, the Limited Edition Jeff Beck Tribute Esquire. To kick off the 150-instrument project, Mike Eldred visited Jeff at his ancient countryside home, a Tudor mansion dating to 1591. After getting over being a guest in an historic estate that dates to Shakespeare's time, Eldred got down to business. "We sat down and really got into details," he recalls. "A lot of artists don't want to get

Right: Quick — what's the single baddest, toughest electric guitar ever made? One contender: Jeff Beck's iconic, beat-to-hell '54 Esquire, meticulously recreated in the Custom Shop in 2006.

Fender
ESQUIRE

into it that deeply, but Jeff was very willing to speak to us about that guitar. We had a video camera and we talked a lot about every detail. That got us started. Seymour owns it now, and he put it in the Rock and Roll Hall of Fame in Cleveland, so we also went out there to go through it in person. Seymour was a part of the process, too, so that was a lot of fun. To have Seymour sit down and tell you about Jeff Beck and that Esquire — you might as well just turn the video camera on and go get lunch [laughs]. He's got so much to say and so many great stories."

Upon returning to Corona, Mike Eldred called on John Cruz, who remembers: "Mike said, 'We need your help on this,' and I said, *'Gimme it!* Let me run with it.' Jeff is one of my heroes, so I jumped at the chance." Cruz reports that Seymour Duncan continued to provide helpful insights: "He went with Mike out to the Hall of Fame to dissect the guitar. He got his own set of pictures and took his own notes, and he shared all that with me, and all the history of it. I spent a lot of time with all that information before we even started on the project."

Aside from its most obvious quirks — the brutal wear and tear, and the Strat-ish body contours — the Esquire sported several other distinctive details. Beck had replaced its rusty steel bridge saddles with brass saddles from a '52 Telecaster he owned. The rhythm pickup cavity is routed for a neck pickup, as is typically the case on Esquires; the lack of mounting holes suggests that the guitar was never fitted with a front pickup.

The original's face is as scarred as the boards on a Depression-era roller derby speed rink, but let's remember that this guitar was once a stock Fender product. The extra body contouring was performed not in 1954 but years after the once-shiny guitar left Fullerton. To accurately replicate the original, Cruz and the other Master Builders first built factory-stock bodies that were shaped, sanded, painted, and buffed like conventional Esquires or Telecasters. Only then did they begin to duplicate the contours of Beck's gig-scarred original. John Cruz: "There might have been an easier way to do it, and some people might not have been able to tell the difference, but if we had masked it off or used some other procedure, the really detail-oriented people might be able to tell, so the whole idea was to arrive at the finished result just the way it was on the original, and that meant starting with a stock ash body with a factory paint job. That is not something we are used to doing here, so that presented us a different kind of challenge, but that's what's cool about these Tributes. Every one is different, and they all have their own kinds of problems to solve. The Beck Esquire came out just right."

The neck on Jeff Beck's original had been replaced with a '55. Although Fender literature refers to the Tribute's "57-style neck," Cruz explains that that description refers only to the general contour. "The Beck Tribute has a soft V for the first few frets, and then it starts to 'C out' a little bit as you get up towards the 12th fret. The V dissipates. I almost want to say it's more like the 10/56 neck that we are pretty famous for here." (Mike Stevens adds: "The 10/56 neck template was made from an October 1956 neck Jimmy Wallace sent to me to duplicate for a guitar, a Strat in trans red over ash. A lot of us loved it and it was used a bunch.")

Beck's guitar is very light, so Cruz and his fellow Master Builders hand-selected the spreads to make sure they were all appropriately weighted. Fender literature refers to a Nocaster pickup design, but as Cruz explains, "The Nocaster magnets are more flat. The Beck Tribute has the raised G polepiece, typical of the '56 and '57 pickups that I've seen. Abigail Ybarra custom-made these pickups for the Tribute, and the design came right from Beck's guitar."

All the pieces fell into place. Seymour Duncan, who knows Beck's guitar as well as anyone on earth, said, "It's amazing how faithful their replica is." Once John Cruz was satisfied with the prototype, he sent it to Jeff Beck for approval. Jeff Beck later said: "I thought it was the original one. . . . I thought, 'Oh, this is my original guitar back.'" John Cruz: "That blew me away. I was really nervous about him getting the prototype because I was afraid he might rip it apart, but he was happy with it and played it quite a bit and decided not to give it back [laughs]. It was just for him to sign off on, but the story I heard was that he liked it so much he ended up keeping it. I think the combination of the ash, the maple, the light weight, Abigail's pickups — it all makes for one of the best sounding Fenders I've ever heard. The cool factor on this guitar is just immense. I mean, this was the Yardbirds guitar. *It was Jeff Beck's.*"

Despite the five-figure price tags, the entire run of Blackies sold out on "Black Friday," 106 of them in the first two minutes.

Reincarnating an icon: The Blackie Tribute project

On June 24, 2004, Christie's auction house in Manhattan held the most significant sale of electric and acoustic guitars in history, Eric Clapton's personal collection. This was the second Clapton auction, the first having been hosted by Christie's five years earlier. This time around, 88 lots were offered. All were sold, raising well over seven million dollars (note: discrepancies in reported dollar figures are accounted for by auction house fees and commissions). Proceeds benefited the Crossroads Centre. Founded in 1998 by Eric Clapton and located on the island of Antigua, in the West Indies, Crossroads is a non-profit facility for the treatment of addictions.

Characterized by ferocious bidding and what a Christie's representative described as "outbursts of devotional excitement," the tense, two-hour event attracted deep-pocketed enthusiasts from all over the world. Actual sale prices invariably exceeded the estimates, often by a factor of ten or more. In fact, the prices were every bit as astounding as the instruments themselves. A 1939 Martin OOO-42 sold for $791,500. A 2004 Custom Shop Strat built by Todd Krause and painted by Crash sold for $321,100. Even among such 6-string celebrities, the belle of the ball was Blackie. The bidding on Eric's old "parts guitar" was particularly frenetic, and when the dust had cleared Blackie had been acquired by the Guitar Center retail chain for $959,500.

Guitar Center was represented by David Belzer and Drew Berlin, well known in vintage circles as the Burst Brothers. Aside from Blackie, they purchased three other notable instruments that day: a 1966 Martin OO-21 that George Harrison had given to Clapton, the Stevie Ray Vaughan Strat known as Lenny, and Eric's red, Cream-era Gibson ES-335. Journalist Cheryl Brewster reported: "When Blackie made its appearance, there was a roar in the room. 'Dave and I just sat back and took it all in, as the excitement and tension rose,' said Drew." The rate of the bidding was mind-boggling, accelerating from $100,000 to $800,000 in scarcely twenty seconds.

Drew Berlin: "By the time the price hit $800,000, it was completely silent. Then Dave just nodded his head and bid $850,000. We were holding our breath." "It was the longest minute of my life," said Belzer. "When that hammer came down with a '*Sold!*,' all chaos broke loose, with a standing ovation that lasted several minutes." (David Belzer adds that the difference between the bid and the total selling price was accounted for by Christie's premium, which was donated to the Crossroads organization.) All four of the instruments acquired by Guitar Center were purchased with the intention of recreating them in limited editions. Their projected sales figures dictated Guitar Center's bidding strategies.

After Guitar Center commissioned the Custom Shop to build multiple, spot-on Blackie clones, Clapton's guitar arrived in Corona on October 24, 2005. Over a period of several months the Master Builders handcrafted 275 Tribute Series Blackie Stratocasters, 185 of them for the American market. They meticulously recreated the original's many dings, quirks, scratches, and cigarette burns, even the worn areas that came from Clapton's own hand over years of rugged roadwork. The guitars went on sale on a first come, first served basis on "Black Friday," November 24, 2006, at precisely 10 a.m. EST. Each instrument was accompanied by a Certificate of Authenticity signed by Eric Clapton and an artificially aged duplicate of Blackie's "Duck Bros." road case, complete with the London phone number — 01 486 8056 — stenciled on the side. (The Duck Brothers were Eric and his pal, one-time bandmate, and fellow duck-caller enthusiast Albert Lee.) The manufacturer's suggested retail price was $24,000; Guitar Center's "Guaranteed Lowest Price" was $20,000. Despite these lofty sums, the 275 guitars on the global market sold like new Harry Potters. All were grabbed in a single day, 106 in the first two minutes. Portions of the proceeds benefited the Crossroads Centre.

Senior Master Builder Todd Krause had already built several guitars for Eric Clapton and was the logical choice to spearhead the Blackie project. Here he recounts how the reincarnation of an icon took months of painstaking work, plenty of TLC, and a bit of CSI — Custom Shop Investigation.

How did you get started?

The first thing was to get the real guitar here to take photos and measurements and lots and lots of notes about its idiosyncrasies — and there were plenty of those. All we needed was one day with Blackie the first time around, to get all the photos and documentation.

John Cruz examines a Blackie neck. One of the builders' many challenges was to recreate the look of cigarette burns and dirt-infused wood grain, plus the feel of worn-off finish and excessive fingerboard wear — all while crafting an eminently playable instrument.

The works: Each Custom Shop Blackie was accompanied by a duplicate of the "Duck Bros." road case containing a Certificate of Authenticity signed by Eric Clapton, a leather presentation folder, a Crossroads DVD, and assorted Ericabilia.

Hello old friend

Todd Krause: "Our relationship with Lee Dickson was already long-standing by the time we started working on the Blackie project. Guitar Center brought it over, and we brought Lee in to talk about the guitar. It was the first time he had seen it in a few years, and you could see him getting visibly choked up to see Blackie again and putting it away for the last time."

We've duplicated things enough times now that we have a process. We know pretty much how much time we need to spend with an original and how many visits it needs to make. On the first prototype I worked from photos, and then by the start of the actual project each Master Builder was outfitted with a computer at his bench. We had the photos on a file that all Master Builders could access.

What was it like holding a million dollar guitar?
It didn't feel like a million dollar guitar. It was just *the* guitar. The dollar value was not what I felt in it. What I saw and felt was the history, and the kind of personality you get in a guitar when the same person plays it for so long.

Was Guitar Center involved in the construction?
No, except during the process [Director of Purchasing] Mike Doyle from Guitar Center brought Blackie over several more times so we could check to make sure we were on the right track. It was mainly between me, Lee Dickson, and the guitar.

Did the fact that Blackie was a composite guitar in the first place complicate your challenges?
That was just the beginning, really. It's hard to say what was truly original on that guitar. Blackie had been taken apart and reassembled with parts from different guitars, not just when Eric first did it but again and again. The neck had been refinished, and the guitar already had some replacement details on it. Throughout the years, nobody had the idea — "Hey, don't take that screw out, that screw's gonna be worth something in a few years." It was more, "Hey, that screw's rusty, put a new one in." I think the body may have been refinished, because it didn't seem to have the right kind of undercoating you would expect on a Fender.

To build accurate clones, did you have to reconstruct Blackie's past?
Yes. Mike Eldred calls it "guitar forensics." You had to imagine — what has this guitar been through to get to this point? Maybe the fingerboard was refinished and there wasn't enough finish on there, and that's why it wore off the particular way it did. And yet there was still quite a bit of finish on the back of the neck. You could see where dirt had gotten into the grain, but then someone had sprayed over it, and it left these marks that I call whiskers, so we needed to figure out how we're going to duplicate these things — the excessive fingerboard wear, the cigarette burns, all this stuff. The one thing I thought they would never go for in legal was that the Fender logo had been partially destroyed, but we ended up recreating that as well. We had to put the spaghetti logo on, and then wear off and break off the parts that were missing on Blackie.

Even back in '86, when John Carruthers made the first copy of Blackie's neck, it already had significant wear and tear.
Blackie's problems were mostly from the neck being refinished and resanded. The butt end would sort of tip or tilt in the neck pocket [because of reduced width caused by repeated sandings], and the high E was about to hang off the edge of the fret. After having a few fret jobs, the edges of the neck had been rolled over and rounded so much that the actual playing surface was getting narrower and narrower. It didn't play badly, and some spots were better than others, but if you touched the high E string wrong it would fall off the edge.

Did you ever discuss whether to recreate Blackie in every detail, including the shortcomings in playability?
Yes, we had that discussion. On the Tribute, we did not make the neck so narrow, because we aren't going to sell somebody a guitar with a string hanging off the edge. We did everything with the right size and the right fit to fix a couple of playability issues. I mean, how would you feel if you paid extra money for a limited edition and the strings are hanging off the neck?

How many builders worked on the Tributes?
We all did, so the total production was divided between eight or nine Master Builders. We had several months to work on them before the world even knew they were coming.

What was your role?
I built the prototype. I sent it to Lee and Eric, and they were completely enthusiastic about it. It was just a preliminary thing to make sure I was on the right track and hadn't gotten anything wrong. There were still some techniques I needed to perfect in order to get this thing to look right, but both Lee and Eric were very pleased with the prototype. Being the project lead, I had to ride herd and make sure everything got done. Once Eric and Lee signed off on the prototype, the Master Builders went to work.

How could you afford to put all the Master Builders on one project?
We schedule these things so we can really concentrate on them. You have to juggle other things around it. We all pretty much devoted ourselves to the Blackie project, and we kept it very secretive. We were well along in the process before anyone even knew about it. Every time we do a Relic or one of these Tribute Series recreations, we learn new techniques. It improves our abilities to go further each time.

Most of the Master Builders worked on the Blackie Strats (Steve Stern did not; he was spearheading the Benedetto project at the time). Pictured here with a rack of finished guitars, from left: Dennis Galuszka, Jason Smith, Custom Shop manager Alex Nicholas, John Cruz, Todd Krause, Mark Kendrick, and Yuriy Shishkov.

The Master Built versions of Greg Fessler's Master Design Strat retailed for $8,000. "I wanted my instrument to feel like an old friend," he says, "yet look like something with a bit more flash."

Greg Fessler's Gold Sparkle Strat

Two years into the Master Design program, the shop unveiled the fourth member of the series, Greg Fessler's gold sparkle Stratocaster of 2006. "I happened to be looking through the *Galaxy Of Strats* book," he remembers, "and I saw this gold sparkle '64. I thought it was a neat, flashy guitar, so I went with that and it turned out really well. I put my own set of custom pickups in there, and it had the transition decal and the round-lam fingerboard. I handmade a hundred of them, and supervised a run of Team Built versions." The 100 Master Builts retailed for $8,000, the 100 Team Builts for $5,000.

While the gold sparkle paint job would get you noticed on any bandstand, the heavy finish cracks softened the impact and warmed up the overall look. All in all, this unique guitar combined some modern features, a bit of vintage vibe, and what might be called subdued pizzazz. Details included a 9.5" radius, American Standard frets, and aged nickel hardware. For the pickups, Greg installed a Texas Special in the bridge, a Fat '50s reverse-wound, reverse-polarity pickup in the middle, and a '69 Strat unit in the neck. He reported at the time that he liked the sound of each pickup in its respective position. "I also like the feel of the worn-off lacquer finish on the back of the neck," he said. "I wanted my instrument to feel like an old friend, yet look like something with a bit more flash."

The Zero-Fret Jazz Bass

For his Builder Select instrument, Dennis Galuszka chose a bass instead of a guitar. He started with Fender's classic Jazz Bass, a design that dates back to early 1960, and added a twist. "During the mid-2000s, I was listening to some of the gripes of bass players," he explains. "One of the things they always complain about is that an open string sounds totally different than a fretted note. I got the idea from Mike Dirnt of Green Day. He was talking to Alex Perez about doing a tilt-back headstock with a nickel nut to alleviate that problem, and I thought, why not just put a zero fret on there and be done with it? So I put a zero fret on my Jazz Bass, showed it to Mike at a NAMM show, and he dug it. It makes the open string sound different because the string is actually sitting on that fret; in that case the only thing the nut does is to maintain the string spacing. The open strings now sounded the same as the fretted notes, which is a great thing. This project was a big one for me. Every bass player who tried it loved it. It was really cool. I made them all myself, and they all sold."

Dennis also installed a Fender preamp, although he specified a reduction in output from 18 to 9 volts. He selected a satin, no-gloss finish in one of Fender's most subtle colors, Ice Blue Metallic. Although published accounts specified a production run of 100 (which may have reflected Fender's original plan), Dennis reports that he completed only two or three dozen examples of the zero-fret Jazz Bass because Fender needed him to return to guitar building. To this day it remains the only zero-fret instrument in Fender history.

Strat meets Tele: All 300 pickups for the 100-piece run of Limited Edition Builder Select Hybrids were personally hand-wound by Chris Fleming.

Doing the Strat thing: Chris Fleming's Builder Select Tele/Strat Hybrid

We've all done it — imagined the perfect guitar as some sort of best-of-both-worlds combo. A Strat that sounds like a Tele, or a Tele but with P-90s, or the neck from this guitar plus the electronics from that one. Jerry Donahue's Custom Shop Signature Tele and the Music Zoo "No-Neck" '60s Strat are good examples. Chris Fleming's Builder Select Closet Classic Tele/Strat Hybrid was another. Fleming explains that he wanted "a Tele — my favorite Fender configuration — that did the Strat thing."

Introduced in 2006 as a member of the Limited Edition series and built in a run of 100 pieces, the $8,000 guitar is a Strat that looks more like a Tele (or vice versa?) the longer you stare at it. It features a 1965-style Strat C neck, a round-lam Indian rosewood board, a 9.5" radius, a trio of Strat pickups, a Candy Apple Red nitro finish, and comfy Strat contouring on the front and back. Extra-cool detail: the matching Candy Apple Red headstock. The controls appear to be lifted from a stock Strat, and do indeed operate in that fashion, until you depress the discreet button in the center of the volume knob. Fender calls it an S-1 system, but here it operates differently than on, say, an American Deluxe Strat. On the Fleming Hybrid, the S-1 turns the bridge pickup on and off, providing a choice of all three pickups, as well as the neck and bridge pickups together to approximate that classic both-pickups Tele sound (the neck/bridge combo is unavailable on a stock Strat, even one equipped with a conventional S-1).

Chris Fleming: "Strats and Teles do different things, and I'm comfortable with both guitars. I wanted to get an ideal blend for that player who likes both and appreciates a wide range of tones. The first one was a custom one-off for a NAMM show. John Mayer bought it from a dealer online. He has since used it onstage for particular songs in an alternate tuning. His affection for that instrument led to my designing and specing the Mayer production Strat. It also inspired us to do the Hybrid in a limited run. These Builder Select projects cost less than a one-off that we build for a single customer, but more than a Team Built guitar. It's priced in between."

Contrary to published reports that Abigail Ybarra wound the pickups (which was likely the original plan), Chris Fleming wound all 300 pickups himself, by hand. He says, "To my knowledge, I am the only builder to hand-wind pickups for production." By the way, if it's neither a stock Tele nor a stock Strat, what should it say on the headstock? *Fender*, that's all.

Nocaster meets Thinline

The Nocaster/Telecaster/Esquire line of 2006 included Chris Fleming's brand new Special Edition 1950s Tele Thinline, which combined features from early-'50s Nocasters and late-'60s Thinline Telecasters. "It's basically a Nocaster but in a Thinline version," Chris explains. "At first it was just a NAMM show thing. It was one of those things that seemed goofy at the time. Some of the guys in the shop thought I was nuts and the guitar was dumb, and it never existed back in the old days, but it turns out to be really good sounding guitar. A lot of customers liked it, so it became a Team Built model." In January 2009, the single-soundhole model migrated to the Limited Collections and appeared in an N.O.S. version.

Corona Six-O: A new wrinkle on "vintage"

Fender was founded in 1946, and to celebrate its sixth decade the Custom Shop took the wraps off the Limited 60th Anniversary Presidential Select Stratocaster, introduced in July. The 100-piece run was one of the more unusual Custom Shop offerings of recent years. Each guitar was accompanied by a six-bottle case of Fender 60th Anniversary Presidential Blend wine, which was selected from several candidates after dutiful and comprehensive wine tastings by Mike Eldred, Fender President Matt Janopaul, and renowned restauranteur Mark Tarbell. (Fender reports that the wines were sampled in a "blind test," which refers to the anonymity of the entries and in no way signifies the final condition of the tasters.) A product of the Hill Family Estate of California's Napa Valley, the wine was a blend of cabernet and merlot. The six bottles were boxed in a unique case crafted of tone woods and decorated with abalone, rosewood, maple, and ebony. The Hill Family Estate is apparently the Fender Custom Shop of wineries; Mike Eldred speculated that anyone lucky enough to buy a bottle of Fender Presidential Blend would likely spend about a grand.

The guitar featured gold hardware, a AA maple neck, mother of pearl dots, and a large, pearl-inlaid 60th Anniversary logo on the fretboard. Putting a new wrinkle on "vintage" guitars, its AAA flame maple top was hand-stained with grape must from the Hill Family Estate. (*Guitar Player* magazine's review said the tone of the guitar carried strong notes of roasted plums and raspberries, and was "assertive yet not pretentious, at once compliant without being obsequious." Not really.)

Here's to Fender's 60th Anniversary — Clink!

The Strat Pro

One of the year's major developments was the arrival of the Strat Pro, which in a way was a direct descendant of the price sheet instruments of the early 1990s in that it combined "the most requested modifications that the Custom Shop has offered over the last 20 years." While most or all of its features had indeed appeared on other Strats, the Pro's combination of details was not only unique but also, once you thought about it, a slap-your-forehead no-brainer. In fact, if you had to pick one Strat to get the maximum number of players with the broadest range of tastes through the greatest variety of gigs, the Strat Pro would be a good choice. It is simply one of the great workhorse guitars of all time.

Developed by Bill Lawrence and fine-tuned by Lawrence and Fender, the Pro's Samarium Cobalt Noiseless pickups had been used on the factory's American Deluxe guitars for years but never on a Custom Shop model. The guitar's big peghead was "popular due to the increased mass and effect on the overall sustain of the guitar." The neck had an LSR roller nut, American Standard frets, a relatively flat, bend-friendly 12" radius, and a non-stick satin finish. Other details included locking tuners, a contoured neck heel for increased access to the upper registers (previously available on the Jeff Beck Signature Stratocaster), the two-point, milled-steel trem originally designed for the Custom Classic Strat, the Greasebucket Tone Circuit ("eliminates the usual gain loss when utilizing the tone control"), and a nitro lacquer, Closet Classic finish. A later version of the Strat Pro would get the Relic treatment and a relocation to the new Limited Collection category.

Mike Eldred: "There is a lot going on with this guitar. It's very intense, and it's one of my personal favorites. Usually, this sort of combination of features would be a Master Built, but we wanted to make it affordable, so we took a lot of features that some of our artists requested and put them all together. Some people are now starting to see the big headstock as a vintage-type detail instead of a later-period thing. These Samarium Cobalt Noiseless pickups are my favorites right now, and they really are punchy; you can tell they're Strat pickups, but they have more volume and depth. With a milled, cold-rolled steel bridge and milled stainless steel saddles, it sounds a little different than an American Standard bridge. With the LSR there is no binding at the nut and no need to clamp it — besides, a clamp changes the sound. The locking tuners are staggered, so there's also no need for a string tree. It stays in tune."

"The Pro Series is a vehicle where we can release certain features and new things, so consumers can try them out or get an up-close look at newer designs. We will continue to use this platform to release Strat and Tele Pros as test models." — Mike Eldred

Among the seemingly endless tweaked and retweaked Stratocasters that Fender has produced for more than five decades, the Custom Shop Strat Pro is one of the most versatile of all. It poses here alongside the Relic version of its stablemate, the Tele Pro.

The Limited Release Rosewood Telecaster

This reissue recalled one of the few truly collectible Fenders from the CBS era. An example of the ultra-rare original was seen most famously in the hands of George Harrison, both in the film *Let It Be* and in footage of the Beatles' unannounced farewell concert on the rooftop of London's Apple Records building. Introduced in 2006 and offered through the end of 2007, the Custom Shop's own Rosewood Telecaster featured a solid rosewood body in a "sandwich" construction, with a thin sheet of contrasting maple between the top and bottom pieces. The hand-selected rosewood was beautifully set off with a black pickguard. A '63-type pickup was installed at the neck, a '67 at the bridge. Each guitar came with a Limited Release certificate, special blonde case, and engraved neckplate.

Spread the love: The Baja Tele

The year 2006 saw an expansion of Custom Shop designs to the Mexico production facility. As Mike Eldred has pointed out, one of his goals was to take the Custom Shop's repository of accumulated knowledge and skills and put it in the service of the first-time buyer on a budget. Chris Fleming and Sergio Villanueva, Fender's Vice President of Manufacturing in Ensenada, Mexico, found a way to do just that. It was a generally '50s-style guitar called the Classic Player Series Baja Tele. Details included an ash body, a soft V neck, a black pickguard, a three-saddle bridge, and the versatile S-1 switching system, configured to provide a phase switch.

"The configuration is something I had done as a Master Builder for quite a few customers," Chris explains. "The

The Rosewood Telecaster's gorgeous body has a thin sheet of maple between the top and bottom pieces.

idea was to introduce features that were like a Custom Shop guitar but to make it more affordable. The neck shape is like the 10/56, which I really like, and a lot of players like bigger frets and a flatter 9.5" radius. Alan Hamel designed that Twisted Tele pickup a while back, which is my favorite Telecaster neck pickup. We have a Broadcaster pickup in the bridge, but I like them with fewer winds so they're a little sweeter, not quite so brash. It's got a 4-way switch, plus the S-1, so you can get series/parallel. I also put in a phase switch so you can get that T-Bone Walker nasal sound, but you can also get the out-of-phase effect in series, without the big volume drop. It's six distinct sounds in a very comfortable, versatile, and affordable Tele. Those Classic Players are absolutely great guitars, and just such great values."

Other Master Builder-designed guitars in the Classic Player series included the '50s Strat designed by Dennis Galuszka, and the '60s Strat designed by Greg Fessler.

The Bass VI

"Built with both the guitarist and bassist in mind," as Fender put it, the original Bass VI of the early 1960s had a 30" scale length that was shorter than Fender's standard 34", and its six strings were tuned one octave below a standard guitar. Those specs were intended to position the instrument as a rival for Danelectro's 6-string bass, introduced several years earlier and popular for its "tic-tac" sound on many a hit recording. Fender's Bass VI appeared in 1961 with three selector switches and a Jaguar-style layout that actually predated the top-of-the-line Jaguar guitar, introduced the following year. A later version of the VI, which added a fourth switch, served as the model for the Custom Shop's $3,600 reissue. Fender specified a 30.3" scale for the reissue.

Chris Fleming recalls that both Fred Stuart and Mark Kendrick had made quite a few of these unconventional instruments. "Fred had just left when I joined the shop, so I became the guy who made a lot of weird stuff. I made mandolins, and a double-neck Strat/mandolin that was very cool. I had made quite a few Master Built Bass VIs. We still have a lot of the steel tooling from the '60s originals, so we used that. Then Mike Eldred decided to put it into the line for a year. He does things like that where he will pick an historic instrument and put it into production for a limited time. The Custom Shop version was just like a '60s-style Fender Bass VI. The only thing that wasn't exactly the same was the bridge, because the original tooling was gone. It's actually a really versatile instrument. It can be an octave bass, right in between an electric bass and a regular guitar, but it can also be a baritone guitar, depending on how you tune it." Plans to make it available only in 2006 were abandoned.

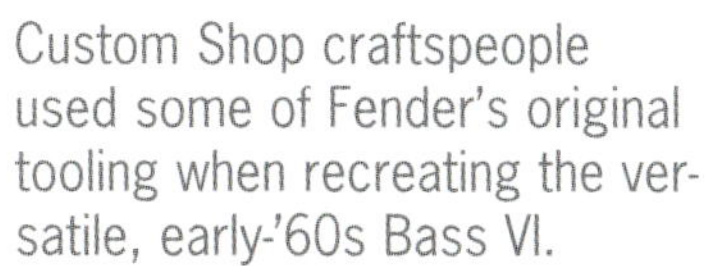

Custom Shop craftspeople used some of Fender's original tooling when recreating the versatile, early-'60s Bass VI.

The shop celebrated two decades of stellar craftsmanship with the 20th Anniversary Master Built Stratocaster, shown here in Closet Classic/violin amber.

CHAPTER TWENTY-NINE

29

2007

20th Anniversary Strat, George Fullerton, SRV/Lenny, Andy Summers, G.E. Smith, Crossroads Sun Strat, Builder Selects, Heavy Relics, Crash

20th Anniversary

Fender commemorated the shop's 20th birthday with the LTD 20th Anniversary Master Built 2007 Stratocaster. Like the Strat Pro and others, it combined a number of frequently requested features. Details included a lightweight ash body, big headstock, special engraving on the neckplate, a Closet Classic finish, a '65 C neck with a 9.5" radius, slab rosewood board with rolled edges, and an interesting complement of pickups: a 1969 Custom Shop neck pickup, a 1969 reverse-wound/reverse-polarity middle pickup, and a Texas Special at the bridge. Most or all of the Master Builders worked on the project.

While this guitar was a worthy anniversary model, the entire Custom Shop catalog of 2007 was another way of celebrating the shop's rich history. There were few if any changes in the Custom Artist series, the Custom Classics, the Showmasters (although the Flat Heads were retired, for the time being, anyway), or the Time Machines (although in '07 the shop dropped the '65 Strat). But the Limited Editions and Limited Releases were expanded and now included several instruments from 2006 — the Rosewood Telecaster, the 60th Anniversary Presidential Strat, the '55 Tele and Pro Jr. set — as well as the new '60 Closet Classic Strat, the Andy Summers Tribute Tele, the '57 and '62 Heavy Relic Strats, and the Builder Select '61 Relic Strat, all of which are profiled in these pages.

Remembering George Fullerton

After several invitations, George Fullerton went to work for his friend Leo Fender on March 2, 1948. One of the young company's earliest employees, he assumed an important role in the development of the iconic Telecaster and Stratocaster. After leaving the company some two decades later, he and Leo founded G&L. He authored the book *Guitars From George & Leo* and over the years kindly sat down with many writers and authors, patiently explaining details of his work and the contributions of his colleagues.

A genial man with many friends and admirers, George Fullerton passed away on July 4, 2009. Author Richard Smith said, "I think the key to George's success was his ability, in the shop, to translate Leo's ideas into products. I don't think it's a coincidence that George was a noted artist . . . I'm fairly convinced, although this has never really been confirmed, that much of the shape of the

Eyewitness to history: The late George Fullerton was the first guitar player to go to work for Leo Fender and a contributor to several classic designs, starting with the prototype Telecaster. In 2007, he was honored with the limited-run 50th Anniversary 1957 Stratocaster and Relic Tweed Pro Junior set.

Telecaster was George's interpretation. I think George's strength was of the hands-on variety in the factory — his ability to use the machines and his talent as a craftsman."

In November 2007 Fender honored Mr. Fullerton by releasing the Limited Edition George Fullerton 50th Anniversary 1957 Stratocaster set. The 150-piece run included a Relic Tweed Pro Junior amp. According to its press release, the company picked 1957 because the three-year-old Strat "hit its stride" in that year, after receiving several refinements. Mark Kendrick, who supervised the Fullerton Strat project, said, "To me, George was the artist." Referring to the contours of the Strat, Mark said: "While the bottom line was Leo, and he made the final call, it was George who brought in the French curve that determined a lot of the Fender look . . . He brought passion and an art to it."

The Master Built Fullerton Strat's pickups were handwound by longtime veteran Abigail Ybarra, who no doubt wound some of the originals back in '57. The guitar was painted with an authentic 2-color sunburst, fitted with a commemorative neck plate, and came with a certificate signed by George Fullerton.

Love story: The SRV Lenny Tribute Stratocaster

It's hard to imagine a deeper connection between a player and his instrument than the affection and esteem that characterized Stevie Ray Vaughan's relationship with the 1965 Strat he nicknamed "Lenny." The 3-color sunburst Fender had endured an amateurish dark natural refin and also sported a flowery inlay that could have adorned a Venetian troubadour's mandolin in a previous century. The guitar was named after Lenora Bailey, Stevie Ray's wife from 1979 to 1988.

Still undiscovered outside the Texas music scene at the time, the young Stephen Ray Vaughan came upon the guitar in an Austin pawnshop and was immediately drawn to it but couldn't handle the $350 price. Lenora reported, "I went out and found seven people with fifty dollars, and they all put their money in and we got the guitar." Lenora and Stevie's other benefactors presented the Strat to Stevie on his 26th birthday, October 3, 1980, at a party at Steamboat Springs, an Austin Nightclub on 6th Street. That night, as his wife slept, Stevie wrote the beautiful, lilting "Lenny." He played it for her in the morning. "How can you stop loving

As we go to press, Stevie Ray Vaughan is the only artist to be honored with two Tribute Series guitars, both Stratocasters. The Lenny was named after Stevie's wife and the poignant song he wrote for her.

anything like that?," she said. Over the years to come, "Lenny" would take its place alongside "Little Wing" and "The Wind Cries Mary" as an evocative guitar piece forever associated with the Stratocaster.

Until the 1990 accident that took his life, Stevie regularly played the song in concert on the guitar his wife and friends had acquired for him, setting aside his Number One Strat for the occasion. Billy Gibbons: "All of a sudden,

On top, Stevie Ray Vaughan's well-worn Lenny Strat; below it is the prototype of the Custom Shop's Tribute.

this somewhat of a throwaway, haphazard guitar became a really heartfelt instrument that he dedicated to only two songs, 'Lenny' and 'Riviera Paradise.'" Double Trouble's drummer, Chris Layton, said, "He had a lot of guitars, but most of them were stored away and he never played them because they didn't mean anything. But that guitar, and Number One, by the fact that they were always with him, spoke volumes about what they meant to him."

Stevie Ray replaced the original rosewood-board neck with a thicker maple neck made by Charvel and given to him by Billy Gibbons (as we will see, this non-Fender neck had a Fender connection after all). Billy reported, "Stevie just absolutely loved it." At about the same time, Stevie etched his name into the neck plate in back. According to Fender, sometime in 1986 he stuck the reflective initials on the pickguard. Guitar tech Rene Martinez reports that he modified the trem so that Stevie could pull up as well as push down on the bar, facilitating the breathtaking roller-coaster whammy bends often heard in the closing moments of the guitar's namesake song.

One of the guitar's coolest and quirkiest details came about after Vaughan performed "The Star Spangled Banner" at the Astrodome in April, 1985. Lenora remarked to the stranger standing next to her, "You know, he didn't know how that went. I had to hum it to him on the way here." The stranger replied, "Yeah, it's a hard song." He then introduced himself: "My name's Mickey Mantle." After a somewhat astonished Lenora introduced her new acquaintance to her husband, the legendary Yankee superstar autographed the Lenny Strat.

On June 24, 2004, at the same auction where it purchased Blackie and other famous instruments, Guitar Center acquired the guitar for $623,500. On October 8, 2007, Fender announced that it had been commissioned by Guitar Center to reproduce a limited run of Lenny Tribute Stratocasters, 185 for the US market and 50 more for international distribution. The model was unveiled on December 12, 2007, at a retail price of $17,000.

Master Builder Jason Smith honchoed the project. He tells the tale: "I took apart the original and built the prototypes. I believe I went through three or four revisions before Guitar Center signed off on it. It had many special challenges, such as recreating Mickey Mantle's autograph on the back, duplicating Stevie's signature etched on the

Jason Smith took the lead in recreating the SRV Lenny Strat, which as it turned out had connections not only to Stevie and his wife but also to Mike Eldred, Billy Gibbons, and Mickey Mantle.

neck plate, and finding a prism sticker pattern for the SRV initials. The body had also been severely over-sanded, with many dips left in some areas. Each one of these Tributes was sanded as close to the original as possible, with all the over-sanded edges and dips. The material behind the bridge is an inlay, and finding the right material for it was a challenge. It's ivoroid, and on top of the ivoroid is an extremely thin nitrocellulose tortoiseshell material. The strap button on the upper horn was an aftermarket diamond shaped button that had long since been discontinued from production; we had to machine a prototype button and send it off to have it duplicated. The original aftermarket bridge saddles were made in the '80s and are chrome-plated solid brass."

On the original Lenny, other quirks were revealed underneath the pickguard. The original, pre-refin sunburst paint was visible. There was a crude rout for a humbucker — in the middle position, which itself is an oddity — and a haphazardly wired control pot assembly that left the tone pots mounted in reverse. All of these details were carefully recreated in the Tribute. (Despite several published reports that the cigarette burns were duplicated with Stevie's own brand of smokes, in fact no cigarettes were used.)

No Team Built versions were offered. All of the Lenny Strats were crafted by Master Builders with the assistance of apprentices and under the supervision of Jason Smith. He explains: "Each guitar was overseen by me, to insure that the integrity of the prototype was matched in every way possible."

Mike Eldred recalls: "Lenny was interesting because it had a neck that I had previously made for Billy Gibbons. When we took the guitar apart, I thought, *wait a minute — this is a Charvel neck*, and on the butt end was an inscription to Billy Gibbons. It was in my handwriting, and that was kind of cool.

"It was so great to get together with Lenny. She signed the certificates. She had some great stories and it was nice going to Austin and dealing with her and getting to know her. She brought down a box with photographs, little snapshots and stuff I'd never seen before. One of the coolest things was a little square cocktail napkin where Stevie had written out a set. We replicated that and put it in the case with a couple of backstage passes and things like that. That value-added stuff really makes it special, and we like for the family or the artists to feel like they've touched the project a little bit when we do these Tributes."

The heavy-duty flight case had HURRICANE painted on one side, STEVIE RAY VAUGHAN on the other; its interior was adorned with "Stevie Ray Vaughan" beautifully embroidered in gold on black. Other accessories included the *Live From Austin, Texas* DVD, a repro of Stevie Ray's white strap with black musical notes (not to be confused with his black strap with white notes), repros of backstage passes, the set-list napkin, and more.

Versatility plus: The Andy Summers Tribute Telecaster

Back in the early '70s, Andy Summers paid a couple of hundred bucks for a thrashed and modified Telecaster Custom, which he went on to use on a long list of monster hits with the Police — "Roxanne," "So Lonely," "Walking on the Moon," "Message in a Bottle," "Don't Stand So Close to Me," "Every Breath You Take," and many more. It's a special guitar. In his 2006 memoir *One Train Later* Andy wrote: "When I start to play it, something stirs within me . . . ."

In late 2007, the Custom Shop released a 250-instrument Limited Edition run of the Andy Summers Tribute Telecaster, which replicates the many quirks of the bound-body, three-color sunburst original. For example, the front pickup is a Seymour Duncan '59 humbucker. The bridge plate is brass rather than the standard chrome-plated metal. The rear pickup is mounted directly to the wood rather than to the bridge plate, which further affects the tone. The extra mini-toggle switch on the alder body activates an onboard preamp, while the mini-toggle on the control plate is a phase switch. Other details include a slim maple neck, standard Fender frets, Schaller tuners, brass saddles, and a worn-to-the-wood, run-over-by-a-bulldozer finish that might be called *über-relic.*

Then there's that third knob. Master Builder Dennis Galuszka, who spent months prototyping the Summers Tele, explains: "It's a gain knob for the preamp. I grew up just in love with the Police and was pretty nervous about having to figure out all these crazy electronics. Like that extra knob — it's located on the wood rather than on the hot dog [control plate]. As Andy described it to me, whether he throws on the preamp just depends on how many people he wants to piss off [laughs]. It's so much more powerful when you throw that switch. It's obnoxious, but in a great way. Mounting the bridge pickup in the body is really for the phase switch more than anything. If you mount it in the plate you get a nasty buzz when you switch the phase because the ground wire from that pickup becomes the hot lead."

The hot-dog knobs are the stock master volume and master tone. The phase switch works only when the stock 3-way selector is in the middle position and both pickups are on. With all these various ghosts in the machine, this guitar just may be Fender's most versatile Telecaster ever, providing a vast range of sounds from a delicate, hollow, non-preamped out-of-phase tone, through the Telecaster's already multivoiced sonic palette, to just a taste of the preamp's effect, to the roar of the humbucker on full turbo.

Multiple electronic quirks make the Andy Summers Tribute Telecaster unique among Fenders. The third knob, for example, is a gain control for the onboard preamp.

(One cool combo, among many: out of phase, but goosed with the preamp.)

Dennis Galuszka: "The original was already modified when Andy got it, so some details of how it got this way are more folklore than anything else. It's fairly common that when you ask an artist what a particular switch does they don't really know. They just love the sound they get, and that's what counts. I don't expect them to be able to explain it unless they're nerdy like us. But Andy was very involved in the Tribute Tele, and he is a great guy to work with, a really funny guy. He just makes you feel nice and comfortable, which I appreciated. We did a lot of our work together in a studio in Venice, California.

"Originally, the shop was going to do a hundred, and I was going to build all of them and just take as long as I needed, but marketing realized that there was going to be more of a demand, so we went to 250 when the Police went back on tour. It's a Master Built guitar, not a Team Built, but several Master Builders worked on them, so it's sort of a 'Master Built Team' project, as opposed to our normal Team Built thing, where apprentices do much of the work under a Master Builder's supervision. The Andy Summers Telecaster was an awesome project. I love that guitar."

Accompanying loot included an Anvil road case with ANDY SUMMERS on the side, a DVD interview with the Police man himself, a boxed retrospective set of the Police's music, and an autographed copy of *One Train Later*. Andy took the first Summers Tribute Tele on the road when the Police reunited in February 2007.

Synchronicity: Andy Summers and Dennis Galuszka collaborated for months on Andy's Tribute Tele.

John Cruz's Builder Select '61 Stratocaster Relic

Sheesh. How many ways can the Stratocaster be modified? Hasn't its sonic potential already been maxed out? Apparently not. Following up on his '62 Strat of 2005, John Cruz took the wraps off of a 100-piece run of his versatile and unique Limited Edition, Master Built '61 model. "That's my favorite year, the '61," he explains, "and this one's definitely a hot rod. I wanted to cater a bit more toward the rock and roll player, so in the bridge position I put a DiMarzio Tone Zone, one of my favorite rock humbuckers. I was making a lot of one-offs at the time and getting a lot of orders for the JC Ltd./Master Design single-coil pickups that I designed with Abigail [Ybarra]. I used them in the neck and middle positions. I did the S-1 switch, which coil-tapped the Tone Zone, and I disconnected the last tone pot and put in a fader pot; it worked as a blender, so you could blend in the humbucker and the neck pickup and really get the best of both worlds. The S-1 split the humbucker, so you get just the one coil, and that gives you a whole multitude of versatile sounds.

"Lots of people have tried to hot rod a Strat, and that was my take on it. I like a somewhat wider neck, like an early Charvel. The whole idea was, this is my take on doing a hot Strat with a wider nut, which a lot of people were requesting from me anyway on my one-offs. I did a 1.75" nut, really wide, and not traditional for a Strat. We used a four-ply pickguard that we called the pepperoni guard."

Details of this 2007 guitar included a two-piece, offset-seam alder body, a compound-radius neck with a dark rosewood fingerboard, and a distinctive 3-color sunburst. John Cruz: "It's faded, and what I call a wide burst, which I love, with the wider red, and really black on the outer edge. The red was stained to be kind of an orangey color with heavy arm wear. I was really into my heavy Relics at that point. The guitar was received very well, although it took a little bit longer to sell because it was so unconventional."

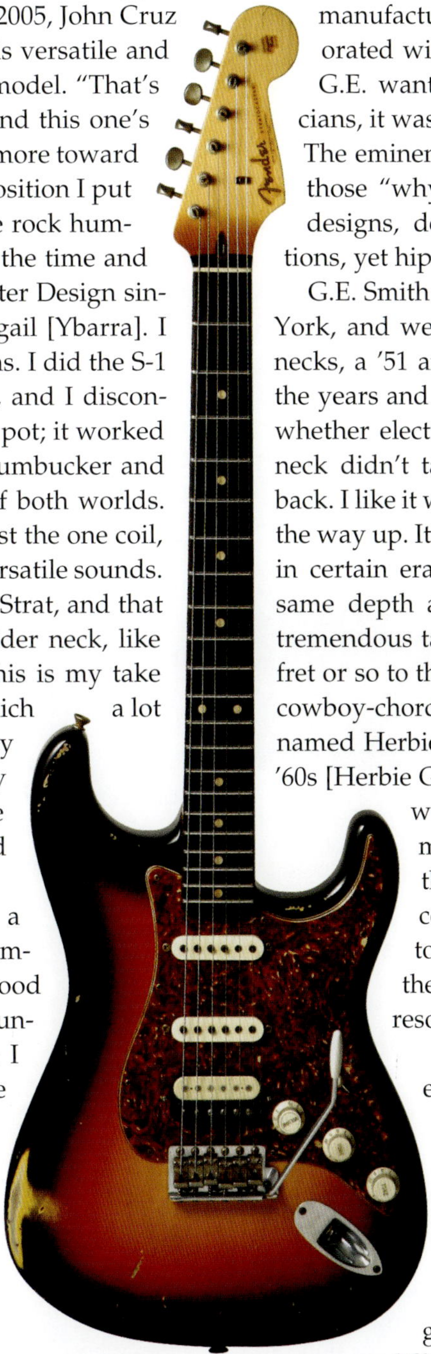

"Definitely a hot rod," the John Cruz Builder Select '61 Stratocaster Relic.

The G.E. Smith Signature Telecaster

The G.E. Smith Signature Telecaster, introduced in January 2007, is another example of how the shop and Fender manufacturing work together. Mike Eldred collaborated with G.E. to design the guitar, but because G.E. wanted it to be affordable for typical musicians, it was forwarded to the factory for production. The eminently sensible model is also another one of those "why didn't someone think of this before?" designs, deeply rooted in Fender's earliest traditions, yet hip and modern as well.

G.E. Smith reports: "Mike Eldred visited me in New York, and we examined a couple of my favorite Tele necks, a '51 and a '52. I've played lots of guitars over the years and the ones with the best sound to my ears, whether electric or acoustic, were the ones where the neck didn't taper very much in depth from front to back. I like it when the neck is almost the same depth all the way up. It seems that for both Fenders and Gibsons, in certain eras, they made some where you had the same depth all the way and others where there's a tremendous taper and it gets shallower from the third fret or so to the headstock, which I guess is nice for the cowboy-chords people. Mike told me there was a guy named Herbie who used to work on necks back in the '60s [Herbie Gastelum joined Fender in 1961], and they would see him really lean on the neck and make a very pronounced taper in the first three frets, really shallow down in the cowboy-chords area, and that detail came to be nicknamed the 'Herbie dip.' But to me the big-neck guitars sound fatter and more resonant. They sustain more."

Regarding the birth of Leo Fender's first electric Spanish guitar, the Broadcaster/Telecaster, this author wrote in *The Stratocaster Chronicles*: "Whereas Gibson adapted its first electrics from the fine acoustic arch-tops it had been building for decades, Leo had no such experience; in fact, he didn't particularly like acoustic guitars. He had been building an utterly different instrument, a lap steel, with a small, solid body and a singing treble tone (lap steels are played

America's rock and roll bandleader, G.E. Smith. Having backed up or directed everyone from Eddie Van Halen and Eric Clapton to George Harrison and Bob Dylan, he brought decades of experience to his signature Tele project. The result was an extension of Leo Fender's fundamental design principles.

flat on the lap, as opposed to the conventional 'Spanish' or upright position). That type of guitar, and that sound, and the way the instrument interacted with its essential but underrated partner, the amplifier, were his starting points."

G.E. Smith went all the way back to Leo Fender's fundamental principle: "I am just so sure in my heart that Leo looked at his Fender Champion lap steel, and in his mind he just grew it into the Telecaster. His idea of mounting a pickup directly into the wood was something I had seen way back in the '60s. Roy Buchanan had done that, and I'm sure Roy Buchanan was no stranger to a Champion lap steel. It makes a huge difference, not just in the single-string solo stuff but in chords, too. The response on the bass strings in particular is strong, and you get a really nice upper midrange warmth." Aside from the big neck and the direct-mount bridge pickup (which entailed a half-size bridge plate), the third key factor was the array of old-style fingerboard markers, available on no other contemporary Fender. If fingerboard markers could talk, these might say, "Barn dance, 1951."

G.E. Smith: "Mike's very first prototype has no finish at all on the great big neck, just raw wood. It's not even number one. It's number zero [laughs], no number. Mine happens to be butterscotch with a black pickguard. We picked a honey blonde for the production guitars. The inlays come right off the Champion lap steel, which is why it looks right — it came right out of the mind of Leo Fender. I play it all the time. It's here in the hotel room right now. I'll play it at the gig tonight."

Passion project: the Crossroads Strat

In July 2007, Fender took the wraps off of the Custom Shop's Master Built Eric Clapton Crossroads Stratocaster. It was promptly nicknamed the Sun Strat because of its sun-face graphic, based on a drawing by Eric himself. The limited run numbered only 100 guitars, 50 of them priced at $20,000. The other 50 were paired with a specially badged, sun-faced Crossroads '57 Twin-Amp and priced at $30,000. No dealers or middlemen were involved, and 100% of the proceeds went to benefit The Crossroads Centre, the addiction rehabilitation facility founded in 1998 by Clapton and

Left: Routed Crossroads Stratocaster bodies are carefully inspected before assembly.
This page: The "Sun Strat" is one of two associated with the Crossroads Centre. The other (Chap. 30) commemorated the 10th anniversary of the facility.

located on the Caribbean island of Antigua. Mike Eldred said at the time, "At its essence, this is a passion project that allows Fender to support the Crossroads Centre, Antigua, and to show our great love and appreciation for Eric."

Heavy Relics: '57 and '62

Back in 1982, Dan Smith spearheaded Fender's American Vintage reissue project. For the Stratocasters, he picked the years 1957 and 1962 because they represented the guitar's classic maple-neck and rosewood-board versions. (He also chose 1957 because "it was just a cool *year* . . . when people talk about cars, for example, look at 1957 — the coolest. Seven's a cool number." He chose '62 because "1962 was just a good year in general. People had good memories of it.")

Those same years were selected in 2007 for the Custom Shop's Limited Release Heavy Relic Strats. Both guitars combined a vintage look with a few modern touches. The soft V maple-neck '57 had a Custom Shop 1969 pickup in front, a Custom Shop Fat 50s pickup, and a Texas Special at the bridge. The C-neck '62 had a three-ply mint green pickguard, a round-lam rosewood board, and Custom Shop 1969 pickups.

High performance: Strat meets 'Stang

In 2007 the Custom Shop partnered with Ford to produce a matched set of American icons: a 325-horsepower black Shelby GT coupe and a companion black Shelby GT Stratocaster built by Chris Fleming. Although the original idea was to celebrate a natural pairing of high-performance machines, the project wound up with a deeper significance: raising money, lots of it, for a worthy cause.

Initial estimates put the combined value of the Strat and the 'Stang at about 50 grand. As it turned out, the pair was auctioned for more than ten times that amount at the January 2007 Barrett-Jackson Collector Car Event in Scottsdale, Arizona, also home to Fender. The car was displayed first. According to official reports, "When bidding stalled at $500,000, auction staff opened the trunk and took out the matching Stratocaster, wowing the crowd and

Reflecting occasional customer requests for extra-intense relicing, Fender made it official with the '57 (left) and '62 (facing page) Heavy Relic Strats, shown here in White Blonde and Lake Placid Blue.

Fender

jumpstarting the bidding." A few minutes later, businessman, philanthropist, and car collector Ron Pratte took the pair for $600,000. The proceeds were promptly donated to the Carroll Shelby Children's Foundation, which offers financial aid to kids who face life-threatening illnesses and supports research into organ transplantation and related medical fields.

The guitar's matching black headstock was graced with a custom silver treatment of the Fender script nameplate as well as a Ford Mustang pony logo. Aside from the racing

The Limited Release '60 Closet Classic Strat featured racing stripes, a specially engraved neckplate, a round-lam fingerboard, and '60s-style pickups. Available only through the end of 2007, the guitar was offered in many original Fender finishes, including rare colors such as Ice Blue Metallic, Shell Pink, Sherwood Green, Dakota Red, Daphne Blue, and Burgundy Mist Metallic.

On G.E. Smith's "prototype" Jazzmaster, the extra piece on the tailpiece base is an after-market Buzz Stop. G.E. Smith: "It's basically like the roller bar on the front end of a Bigsby. It puts downward pressure as the strings pass over the bridge, preventing them from popping out of their slots, especially the low strings."

stripes and Ford/Shelby body logo, details of the hardtail Strat included Schaller tuners, a single Enforcer humbucker, a single So-Cal Speed Shop billet volume knob, pearl dots, and a matching case. Nice touch: The back of the guitar was fitted with a recessed Vehicle Identification Number plate that matched the VIN of the car. A second Strat/Mustang set was given away to Virginian Tim Whittaker, who in January 2008 won Fender's Play Loud/Go Fast Sweepstakes.

The Jazzmaster prototype that never was

G.E. Smith once owned a 1959 Jazzmaster that was so terrific he still regrets letting it go. "The best Jazzmaster ever," he calls it. In the mid 2000s he got the urge to replace the guitar and called Mike Eldred. "Mike told me, make up the Jazzmaster of your dreams," says G.E., "so I pretended I'm Leo Fender, it's the summer of '57, and I get the idea for the Jazzmaster. My idea was to imagine what a prototype might have looked like, so it's got a big V maple neck, not the newer rosewood board like they ended up using, and the body is ash, with that white see-through finish like you'd see on a '55 Tele. The pickguard is also like a Tele — single layer, white, not the tortoiseshell.

"Way back, César Díaz gave me two 1962 Jazzmaster pickups. I thought, 'What? What do I want with these things?' He said, 'Some day you'll need them, man,' and he was right, so they're on there. Dennis Galuszka built it; he's a real craftsman, and it's just beautiful. Being as it was a 'prototype,' I had him put a toggle switch on there, and a volume and a tone. It doesn't have the extra circuit, none of that business up on top. And it's gotta have the Jazzmaster bridge and the tremolo with the locking slider button. So it was sort of a creative whim, with me asking, 'What if Leo did it this way?,' and you know what? It's one of the best guitars I've ever played."

A classic from the CBS period was reissued in a run of 100 pieces: the Team Built 1970 Jazz Bass LTD. Its natural-finish ash body, glossy-finish neck, white neck binding, maple board, and white pearloid block markers fairly hollered "'70s Fender." Details included vintage-style reverse tuners and a 7.25" radius. According to Fender, the bridge pickup was located 1/4" closer to the bridge than normal.

Fender Showcase Tokyo.

Custom Shop Japan

Atsushi Ohata is the Product Manager of the Fender Custom Shop in the Overseas division of Yamano Music Co., Ltd. As we go to press, he is a 15-year veteran with Yamano, and he has worked with the Custom Shop since 2003. He describes his job as bridge-building between the shop and its Japanese dealers and customers. "Mike Eldred calls my job 'sewing,'" he explains. "It is not only [working with] the instruments but also Fender's brand value, the staff's humanity, policy, and dignity of the Fender Custom Shop."

Fender has what it calls Showcase dealers, where Custom Shop instruments are displayed. As we go to press, seven dealers are represented in 16 stores throughout the country, and since September 2007 a central showroom has been located in Shibuya-ku, Tokyo. Fender Showcase Tokyo is not open to the public; it is reserved for artists, music periodical publishers, and others working in Japan's music industry. It consists of two rooms. One is the Custom Shop Lounge, where about 50 Custom Shop instruments are exhibited, and the other is called Studio 1946, where other Fenders are on display.

Atsushi Ohata: "Our typical Custom Shop customers fall into two groups: professional musicians, and enthusiastic amateur musicians who can afford to buy Custom Shop instruments. Both groups have had the same dreams since they were young, that they wanted to own their favorite Fender guitar some time in the future. While the major group is males in their 40s and 50s, there have been increasing numbers of customers in their 20s recently.

"Custom Shop guitars are highly recognized here as the top of the line in Fender, an iconic legendary brand. Most of our customers are serious guitar players who surprisingly know much about the history of Fender and the detailed features of their instruments. Master Built guitars are particularly high-valued with their authentic quality. Even the Master Builders themselves are highly respected by our customers. When we started marketing Custom Shop products, the vintage-spec models were the most popular; in recent years we find an increasing number of customers preferring more playability-oriented guitars."

Three limited-edition models have been released exclusively to the Japanese market: the Michiya Haruhata Stratocaster (60 pieces, 2002), the Michiya Haruhata BWL Stratocaster (12 Master Built guitars crafted by John English and 60 Team Built Custom guitars, 2005), and the Takanaka Stratocaster (100 pieces, 2007).

The Telecaster Pro

The Tele Pro was added to the line in 2007. A worthy companion to the Strat Pro, it offered a classic look with high-performance features such as the Greasebucket circuit, a stainless steel bridge with compensated brass saddles, a front Twisted Tele single-coil pickup, a rear Samarium Cobalt Noiseless Tele pickup, and a 4-way switch: neck, both in parallel, bridge, and both in series. A Relic version was introduced in January 2009 as a member of the Limited Collection series.

Crashocasters

John "Crash" Matos, a New York artist and pioneer of the graffiti/street art movement, crossed paths with Eric Clapton in February, 1997. After discussing the possibility of a collaboration for a couple of years, Crash painted several Stratocaster bodies for Eric. All of the guitars were built in the Custom Shop by Todd Krause. Lee Dickson nicknamed them Crashocasters.

Lee was the go-between, facilitating cooperation between the Clapton camp, Fender, and Crash. "I knew Eric liked graffiti art," he says, "and I got Fender to send Crash a body, which he painted. The great Todd Krause built the guitar, with the standard soft V neck and appropriate pickups for a Clapton guitar, and when the very first one came in, a gift from Crash, I kept it in the case and put it out on a table where we would be taking a lunch break during a recording session in Los Angeles. Eric came in and said, 'Oh, what's this?' I just played dumb — 'Something for you, I don't know.' He opened it up and recognized right away — 'This looks like Crash's work!' I said, 'There you go, you know your stuff.' Eric loves all that graffiti art. He didn't know it was coming. I wanted to surprise him, and he loved the

The Crash project began with a few guitars for Eric Clapton and eventually entailed guitar/amp combos like this special NAMM set.

guitar. Crash works in acrylic, and it had sort of a lemon-peel feel to it, so I sent it to Todd and he put a clear coat on it to protect the art and make it feel like what Eric was used to."

One of the later guitars, Crash-3, as it was called, featured a pickguard/top plate designed by Mark Kendrick, who recalls: "I plagiarized a bit of George Fullerton's control-plate Stratocaster and incorporated it into the Crash design." (George Fullerton's personal 1954 Strat featured a nonstock metal top plate that housed the three knobs. Fullerton made the template for the part himself. The Crash guitar's top plate is similar to the one fashioned by George Fullerton in 1954.)

The Crash-3 Strat was sold at the June 2004 Christie's auction. Lee Dickson: "I was privileged and honored to be in the VIP room upstairs above the auction stage with Eric and Crash and just a few others. We were gobsmacked at the prices. Crash is just such a sweet guy, so modest and spiritual, and he was just freaking out with the bidding going crazy like that. 'Oh my god, I don't believe this! — a hundred thousand! *Two* hundred thousand! *Three* hundred thousand!'" The winning bidder took it home for $321,000.

At the winter 2003 NAMM show, Fender displayed a Crash guitar that was a one-off approved by Eric Clapton for the show only. At that time, no Crash Fenders were available to the public. Mark Kendrick later encouraged Crash to come up with a concept of his own for a limited run. The prototype for that edition was displayed at the Winter 2004 NAMM show, and Crash spent more than two years painting 50 Strat bodies for the project.

Todd Krause hand-crafted all 50 of the one-off Custom Crash Stratocasters, which were completed in early 2007. He emphasizes, "The Crash guitars I did for Eric had nothing to do with the run of 50 Crash guitars. They are two completely different instruments. The 50 guitars were Crash guitars, *not* Clapton models." While Eric's personal guitars were based on the Clapton Signature model, the 50 limited-run Custom Crash Strats featured the Fullerton/Kendrick-type top plate in black anodized metal, black anodized trem covers, Ceramic Noiseless pickups with black covers, *Todd Krause* and *Fender Custom Shop* decals, and a specially engraved neckplate with Crash's signature. The Crash-painted Telecasters were Custom Shop guitars as well.

The art of twang: another Crash set, this time with a Tele.

Left: From a 50-piece run of control-plate Strats painted by Crash.

Referring to the Strat and amp, p. 535, Todd Krause explains: “Some people didn’t get what Crash was doing with the guitars, so I had an idea. Let’s place a guitar and an amp on a big white canvas, maybe 6’ by 6’, and have him paint an entire artwork on it and go right over the guitar and the amp. When we lifted up the guitar and amp, you could see the white spot where they had been. We brought the whole display to NAMM. It looked really cool and illustrated the big picture.”

Ragged glory: Despite the lack of a model name on the headstock, Fender calls this recreation of a 1957 guitar a Tele rather than a Nocaster (perhaps because Nocasters had come and gone by '57). Officially, this battered beauty is a 1957 Yuriy Shishkov Master Built Heavy Relic Telecaster, from 2008; MSRP: $7,800. Yuriy built others that year, but most had black pickguards.

CHAPTER THIRTY

30

From Catalogs to Limited Collections

2008: The Black Strat, Crossroads Antigua Strat, Heavy Relics, Yngwie Malmsteen Tribute

If you were to pick one term to describe the Custom Shop's evolving strategy from 2000 to 2010, "limited collections" might be a good choice. Although the shop's earliest guitars of the late 1980s often used at least some components from the factory, they were built to order for one player at a time. To offset the low profits from those labor-intensive, expensively produced instruments, the price sheet of 1992 and thereafter offered cataloged, fixed-spec models. As we've seen, customers who didn't know exactly what they wanted or who balked at planning every detail could choose from popular packages of features assembled by the Custom Shop crew.

Although the '90s-era price sheet worked well, Mike Eldred and his colleagues gradually steered the shop away from that approach over a period of years. To this day, Mike doesn't particularly like the catalog concept. In fact, he doesn't even like the word. "We don't *want* a catalog," he explains. "That word sounds weird to me. When I hear it, I sort of shudder. We have to publish a list of guitars and prices, so we still have a 'price list' in that sense, but the whole mindset is different now. We have *collections*. We get ideas from artists, other players, Master Builders, and dealers, and we put together guitars with the coolest, most versatile features. They're more affordable, and you can get one right away."

You can get one right away, but you might have to move fast, and that's the difference between the old and new approaches. Having guitars with fixed specs may sound like the old price list, but now their availability is limited, sometimes severely. For years the price list guitars were marketed like other instruments from Fender and other companies: Models were designed, crafted, cataloged, and priced in an open-ended way, meaning they stayed in the line until their retirement, perhaps after several years.

Now, however, the shop's collections are limited in availability from the get-go, either by the number of pieces or by the window of time when they are offered. Global availability of a particular model may be restricted to as few as ten pieces. "I was talking to some dealers," Mike Eldred recalls, "and I said a particular model was going to be limited to 33 pieces, and a guy raised his hand and said, 'That's not enough.' I said, 'Exactly.'"

As we go to press, the shop offers a revised Custom Collection each January. After the inventory has been exhausted or the time period has ended, the models are retired to make way for new offerings. Mike Eldred: "When they're gone, they're gone. This makes the instrument much more valuable on the secondary market, and allows the artist/consumer to 'partner with and invest in Fender's rich legacy and history,' which is what we have mandated as our promise."

While Fender offered scores of cataloged Custom Shop models in the mid 2000s, the limited-edition concept actually went back to the previous decade. Mike Eldred explained in 2009, "Internally, we have been gradually eliminating the open-ended 'price list' mentality since 1997. It's a *custom* shop, so lately the price list has been shrinking every year, and last year [with the limited collections] we finally have a more defined model for what we want the shop to be."

Limiting the guitars' availability went hand in hand with streamlining their production. Mike reported in 2009 that the shop was more streamlined and actually had fewer employees than it did when he was hired more than a decade earlier. "And I guarantee you we have more hands-on procedures than we did in the old days. You know, a lot of those early guitars were built using components from the line. Now we're more independent."

Custom Built and Master Built

In 2008, the continuing shift away from the price list toward the limited collections was accompanied by a change in nomenclature. The term "Team Built," which had served Fender well, was dropped. The new categories: Custom Built and Master Built. Fender describes the Custom Builts as the "first level" of instruments offered by the shop. They are crafted by the entire team of Custom Shop staff, which includes some of Fender's finest craftspeople and apprentices to the Master Builders. Apprentices typically aspire to become Master Builders and serve in many capacities. Mike Eldred: "They are sometimes pulled in closer to the Master Builders and learn from several guys. Sometimes they stay there, and sometimes they go back to tune-testing or whatever their main job was. They never build runs of guitars by themselves, only as part of the team. Each Custom Built instrument is inspected, set up, and signed off by the staff, insuring that the customer is getting the absolute best Fender can build."

As has always been the case, the Master Built program offers Fender's deepest level of personal attention. Consumers, dealers, or artists can direct a Master Builder on how they would like their instrument built. Every detail, no matter how exacting, can be addressed one-on-one with the individual Master Builder who has the sole responsibility to craft that customer's personal dream machine.

The year in brief: 2008

Several of the most interesting guitars of recent years were introduced in 2008, all of which are profiled here: the long-awaited David Gilmour Black Strat, the 10th Anniversary of Crossroads Antigua Stratocaster, the '68 Heavy Relic Stratocaster, the '58 Heavy Relic Tele, and the Yngwie Malmsteen Tribute Strat.

Counting fingerboard options, top-wood options, the three Time Machine finishes, hardtail and trem-equipped Strats, and both 4 and 5-string basses, and excluding color choices, the Custom Shop in January 2008 offered 84 instruments in all. The only Showmaster was the Elite, available in several versions (the series would soon be retired). Several models were dropped, at least for the time being. Others were renamed or shuffled to new series; for example, the '64 Bass VI was relocated from the Limited Releases to the Time Machines.

The Black Strat

In May 1970, David Gilmour bought a black Stratocaster from Manny's Music in New York. Aside from its fairly rare maple-cap fingerboard, its details were typical of a late-'60s CBS guitar — an alder body, a white pickguard, and a 4-bolt neck with a large headstock, a '68 style logo, a top-loaded truss rod, and F-stamp tuners. Over the next several decades the guitar would be modified so many times and used in so many concerts and on so many historic recordings (*Dark Side Of The Moon, Wish You Were Here, The Wall,* and many more) that it would take a whole book to document it all. Such a book could only be written by one person, Pink Floyd's equipment supervisor and David Gilmour's personal guitar tech for more than 35 years, Phil Taylor. It's called *Pink Floyd: The Black Strat — A History of David Gilmour's Black Fender Stratocaster* (160 pp., Hal Leonard).

The guitar became not only David's instrument of choice for many years but also a mobile experimental lab

The Black Strat is a recreation of David Gilmour's main guitar for many years. The project was especially challenging because the original's parts and features had been replaced, repaired, restored, and modified so many times. The prototypes were built by Todd Krause, who points out, "No other Fender has this combination of features."

of sorts. Its pickguard, volume knob, neck, neck plate, tremolo, and tuners were all replaced, some several times. David tried 21 and 22-fret necks, maple and rosewood fingerboards, stock string nuts and locking units, stock and custom wirings, and standard and dropped D tunings. The guitar's half-dozen necks were fitted with Fender, Schaller, Kluson, and Gotoh tuners. An XLR socket was installed on the lower edge of the body, and a switch was added to the pickguard; this arrangement was intended to drive an outboard fuzz unit (the jack and switch were later removed). The Fender trem was replaced with a Kahler, which in turn then that David Gilmour's favorite guitar acquired its nickname: the Black Strat.

David Gilmour has on occasion referred to it as an OK guitar, just a (once) stock Strat, and yet in his hands this instrument has given us one of the electric guitar's most compelling voices ever. Despite all the surgeries and component switcheroos, something about it continues to draw David Gilmour to it. In his book Phil Taylor wrote: "If you have a rack full of the same model guitars and you pick them all up and play them, one will stand out. The Black Strat is like that."

was replaced with the original unit, so there is some visible routing and repair work on the top behind the bridge.

A mini toggle was added that allowed the connection of the neck pickup to either or both of the other two. A patent-number Gibson humbucker was added (later removed) between the middle and bridge pickups, which entailed a rewiring of the extra toggle; a later version of the toggle once again allowed the addition of the neck pickup to the other two. The Fender bridge pickup was replaced by a DiMarzio, which in 1978 was replaced by the Seymour Duncan pickup that remains in that spot. Perhaps the guitar's most recognizable mod was the black pickguard, which was installed back in the summer of 1974. It was

In October 2006, Mike Eldred and Senior Master Builder Todd Krause met in the UK with Phil Taylor to initiate a replica project. It was a reunion of sorts. More than 20 years earlier, during his time with Charvel, Mike had built several guitar and bass necks for David; one of them, a beautiful bird's-eye maple neck, spent a fair amount of time on the Black Strat. Mike recalls: "When we went to spec out the Black Strat, Phil Taylor started pulling out all this stuff — Strat necks, Tele necks — and asked me if I remembered them. They still have them — with my handwriting on them!"

Many challenges were in store for the Custom Shop crew during the design and prototyping stages, not only because of the original Black Strat's numerous quirks but also because of a Catch 22: Phil Taylor insisted on replicating many of the details just so, but David Gilmour insisted on making the guitar relatively affordable. At the end of the day a balance was achieved that satisfied all parties — especially the players who had been waiting years for this model to appear. On September 22, 2008, after years of discussion, planning, and negotiating, the Custom Shop introduced Relic and N.O.S. versions of the Custom Artist Series David Gilmour Stratocaster.

Todd Krause: "On the original, where the humbucker used to be, it's all kluged out under the pickguard. It looks like someone routed it out with a sharpened screwdriver and a hammer. The hole where the XLR jack used to be was filled, using the old glue-and-sawdust trick. If this was a $20,000 Tribute we would replicate all that, but then all the extra man hours and Master Built production would bump up the costs, and David wanted this to be a player's guitar, not a trophy piece that was so valuable you'd never actually play it.

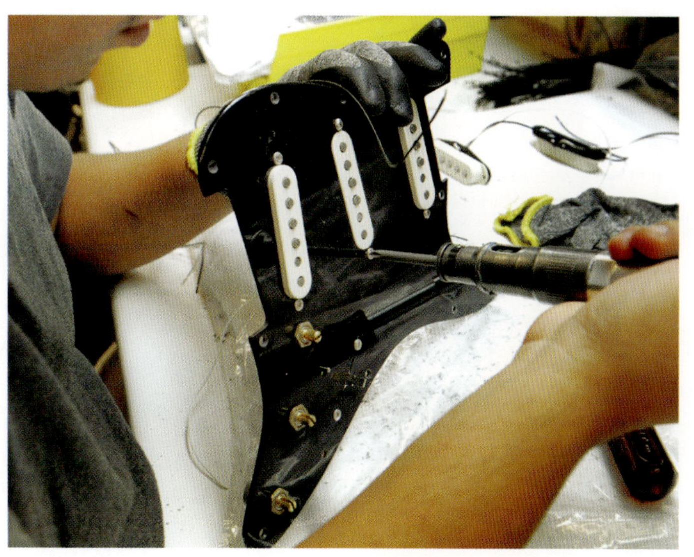

"So the balance is, this is a Team Built guitar where we duplicate all the player-oriented things from David's guitar — neck shape, the shortened trem bar [about 4.25"], the extra toggle switch/pickup selector, and the 7.25" radius. We nailed the tonal character of the pickups — a '54 in the neck, a gray-bobbin 1969 type in the middle, and a special Seymour Duncan bridge pickup. The Relic version looks a lot like David's guitar, but we don't do the maniacal level of detail you see on a Tribute, where we duplicate every microscopic scratch and ding. We do replicate some redundant grounding and also the nonstock copper shielding — somebody had made it for David or it was some kind of after-market thing. We duplicate anything that would affect the tone and playability."

While the Gilmour Strat isn't officially a Tribute guitar — and at about $4,800 for the Relic, $4,000 for the N.O.S. it certainly isn't priced like one — it does have a few bonus features that make it unique. Like Gilmour's original, it has late-'60s CBS body contours. On the original, the factory's black lacquer was applied over a three-color sunburst, and that detail is recreated on the Relic. Todd Krause adds: "We don't duplicate the actual process where the hole for the XLR had been filled, but we do scribe it on the Relic version to approximate the look of the original, again keeping the customer's price in mind while evoking the look of David's guitar.

"Phil pointed out that the plastic we were using for the prototype's pickguard wasn't the right shade of black. At first, my attitude was, hey, we don't make the plastic; we order it, and this is what we get. But Phil was so persistent that we ended up sourcing out an acrylic material and yeah, it definitely does have a certain look to it and greatly improves the appearance of the guitar, so I am really glad that Phil didn't back down on that. It's not as easy to use in manufacturing, but we make the effort because it looks so right. We don't offer that kind of plastic on any other guitar."

One of the most interesting features is the Signature guitar's neck. It duplicates the current neck (as of this writing, anyway) on David Gilmour's original. Officially, that neck was a Dan Smith-designed 57 reissue Strat neck; David had "swapped it in" from his 1983 cream-colored reissue Strat. Here is where it gets a little tricky: The neck on the Custom Shop guitar is an authentic replica of Gilmour's 1980s style 57 reissue neck, which was not a detailed reissue of the 1957 original. An actual 1957 Strat neck would have a soft V shape, but the mid-'80s reissue neck was more rounded, although it did have the period-correct skunk stripe. As

Previous pages: The Black Strat comes together in the Custom Shop.

Above: Black Strats, ready for shipping. Note the tremolo arm, which is not only shorter but also bent differently than stock units. Some players find it particularly touch sensitive.

John Page explains elsewhere in this book, the idea behind those first-generation reissues was to capture the general vibe of the original guitars but also to offer some player-centric details that were suitable for then-contemporary styles; a somewhat rounded neck on the early-1980s U.S. Vintage 57 Strat was one example.

Regarding the Custom Shop model, Fender literature helpfully specifies a "thin-shouldered 'C' neck shape," with a .790" to .870" taper. Todd Krause: "On an actual '60s C neck it's .930" at the 12th fret, with more of a change in taper as you go up. On the Gilmour, the .790 to .870 is more like the 'modern' '80s style where guitar players all wanted that slim, fast-feeling neck with little or no taper."

The shorter trem arm is a nice touch, and practical. It has less flex, and people who try it seem to like it a lot, feeling that it provides a bit more control and accuracy. Could anybody get the same effect simply by snipping off the last couple of inches of a stock Strat trem bar and replacing the tip? Todd Krause doesn't think so, because the bar on David's guitar isn't just shorter; it is also bent differently than a current, stock unit.

The neck and middle pickups are wound by Abigail Ybarra, who began winding pickups for Leo Fender in the 1950s. The bridge pickup is a Seymour Duncan SSL-5 Custom Model, which duplicates the pickup Seymour personally wound for Gilmour more than 30 years ago. (Then-designated the SSL-1C, the original unit became the prototype for the modern SSL-5.)

Other details include a black nitrocellulose lacquer finish on the alder body, a "Thin-Skin" Dark Tint nitrocellulose lacquer finish on the neck, and Gotoh tuners. Available in both like-new N.O.S. and hard-giggin' Relic versions, this unique, David Gilmour-approved reissue of the historic Black Strat costs a lot less than a Tribute, yet it has all of the original's player-oriented features plus many of its cosmetic details as well. (Fender even goes so far as to bevel the corners of the trem block's flat underside. As on David's original, the corners are now angled rather than curved.)

Todd Krause built several prototypes in mid 2007, and final versions were approved a year later. "I made about six of them in duplicate sets of two," he explains, "so that at each stage Phil and I could be communicating about identical details. Phil was very persistent and demanding, but in a good way. Frankly, there was a lot of haggling with trying to draw that balance between an expensive, really detailed replica and an affordable version, but it was all with the best of intentions and served a good purpose. I really have to credit Phil. I don't think it could have turned out so well without his efforts. No other Fender has this combination of features. When it was all said and done, it ended up being a great guitar at a great price."

In 2005, it was suggested to David Gilmour that he once again pick up the Black Strat, long since retired. Phil Taylor wrote: "David's guitar sound instantly ascended to what can only described as 'another level.' His body language changed, becoming animated and interacting with the guitar as if he had just discovered an old long-lost friend." Perhaps one day a player with a soulful artistic sensibility will find the same magic in a Custom Shop reincarnation of the Black Strat.

Eric Clapton 10th Anniversary of Crossroads Antigua Stratocaster

Back in the late 1960s, CBS Fender proclaimed: "Fender's latest color dimension, the Antigua, puts elegance in the spotlight. This inimitable new finish is a rich, antique white with a halo mist shading that produces a subtle feeling of depth and dimension." For some viewers the feelings were somewhat less subtle — "Fender's latest color dimension" was perhaps the most controversial finish in the company's history — but there's no denying its inimitability.

The year 2008 marked the tenth anniversary of the Crossroads Centre, the nonprofit addiction treatment facility founded by Eric Clapton. The Centre is located on the island of Antigua. Sam Ash Music CEO Richard Ash approached Custom Shop managers and asked if they were interested in producing a guitar that would be unique, collectable, and supportive of a charity. He reports: "I asked Fender if they could get the Clapton people to approve a special model that would incorporate a defunct finish from back in the late '60s, the Antigua. I picked the Antigua because it was unique and had a history."

The shop made 100 pieces, each priced at $5,000 and built to the specs of the Custom Shop's Clapton Stratocaster — with an active mid boost, a soft V neck, a blocked tremolo, etc. They were numbered from 1 to 100. Richard adds: "The originals and also the Custom Shop versions

CBS Fender called the original Antigua finish "antique white with a halo mist." In 2008 it reappeared on a special run of Eric Clapton Strats commissioned by Sam Ash Music. A portion of the proceeds benefited the Crossroads Centre, founded by Clapton and located on Antigua.

This big-head Strat is a '68 Heavy Relic in Dakota Red. Once dismissed by purists because of a perceived CBS taint, the large headstock has in some quarters come to be accepted as a legitimate "vintage" feature.

actually have the pickguards painted to match the bodies. It was great because the Custom Shop guys duplicated this unique '60s finish exactly, down to the black plastic parts. The guitars have numbered certificates of authenticity signed by myself and my brother Sam. I offered to donate $1,000 for each guitar to the Crossroads Foundation, $100,000 in all." It's not surprising that the finishes were perfect; Jesus Andrade, who painted the originals back in the day, is still at Fender and painted the Custom Shop versions in 2008.

'68 Heavy Relic Stratocaster

The Limited Edition '68 Heavy Relic Stratocaster of 2008 was the brainchild of Custom Shop sales manager Joe Reynoso. It featured a quarter-sawn maple neck, which produced a particularly stiff and stable neck and also changed the sound a bit. The neck featured a U profile, a 9.5" radius, and 6105 frets, and its finish was removed in back; all of these features were designed to enhance comfort and playability. Details included a lightweight ash body, a big headstock, a round lam fingerboard of particularly beautiful dark Indian rosewood, and a chewed-up Heavy Relic finish (official announcements specified a cigarette burn on the headstock, but after viewing the prototype the builders scrapped the idea). The 1969-type pickups were made in the Custom Shop; Mike Eldred described them as "very rich, very defined." The middle pickup was a reverse pole/reverse wound type, placing it in humbucking mode to eliminate noise in the 2 and 4 positions.

'58 Heavy Relic Tele

Back in the late 1990s, Mike Eldred collaborated with four Master Builders in a quest to find a better pickup for the Telecaster's front position. He wanted something brighter than the stock pickup's sound, which he found muted, or "clouded." "The builders came up with four designs, and then we all sat around and played the different pickups," Mike recalls. "It was a blind test. None of us knew which pickup was which, and we all ended up picking the same one. Its bobbin is a little taller, which gives a bit more clarity. Instead of a typical chrome-plated brass cover, which has a little darker sound to it, this one is nickel silver — really bell-like." This unit became the Twisted Tele. Sounding a bit like a good Strat front pickup, it was a key feature on the shop's Limited Release '58 Heavy Relic Tele of 2008.

The neck pickup is a hot, flat-polepiece Nocaster unit; Eldred points out that it's very similar to pickups found in Fender lap steels and also in the G.E. Smith model (Chap. 29). Other details of the lightweight ash '58 Heavy Relic Telecaster include a soft V neck, a 9.5″ radius, 6105 frets, a vintage bridge with threaded steel saddles, and through-body stringing.

After a blind listening test of pickups, Mike Eldred and several Master Builders selected a somewhat Strat-like unit that came to be called the Twisted Tele. It's an essential attribute of this Limited Release '58 Heavy Relic Tele.

Full shred: The Yngwie Malmsteen Tribute Stratocaster

November 2008 marked the official unleashing of the Yngwie Malmsteen "Play Loud" Stratocaster. It's a meticulous recreation of the Swedish rocker's well-worn 1971 Olympic White Strat, which he purchased at age 15 in 1978. In 1984, two years after arriving in the United States, Malmsteen reportedly found a sticker in the mastering suite of L.A.'s Record Plant Studios and stuck it on his guitar. It says "Play Loud." He did, performing his neoclassical/heavy metal sorcery on that Strat until its retirement from grueling roadwork in 1992.

Fender's relationship with Yngwie goes back to the dawn of the Custom Shop. In 1988, Master Builders put the finishing touches on the first official Malmsteen Strat, which was forwarded to the factory for production (Chap. 10). Over the next two decades several versions appeared, differing in production location (U.S. vs. Japan), headstock size (original '50s-style vs. larger '70s-style), pickups, switching (3-way vs. 5-way), trem (American Standard vs. vintage), tone controls (standard vs. TBX), the depth of the fingerboard's scalloping, etc.

By the mid 2000s, with their increased abilities to analyze every aspect of a heavily used guitar, and having perfected their in-house relicing techniques, Custom Shop craftsmen were ready to raise the bar with a new Malmsteen Strat that was worthy of the Tribute moniker. John Cruz, by now a Senior Master Builder, crafted the prototype and directed the other Master Builders who also worked on the project. All told, one

hundred alder-body, maple-neck Malmsteen Tribute Strats were built.

After John Cruz and Mike Eldred visited the flamboyant metal virtuoso at his home in Miami to spec his well-worn, scratched, bitten, burned and otherwise disfigured guitar, John set to work on the prototype. Yngwie himself had scalloped the original's fingerboard, removing wood so as to leave scooped-out areas between the frets. (Reportedly, he discovered scalloped boards after encountering a 17th-Century lute that crossed his path while he worked in a guitar repair shop.) Master Builder Jason Smith crafted some of the Yngwie Tributes, and he recalls: "Yngwie's Strat was one of the most beat-to-crap guitars I've ever seen in my life. That thing had seen a *lot* of abuse. I had no idea how he did the original scalloping. Some of it was kind of crude, but it was hard to tell because it had been played so much the scalloping had worn in and was smoothed out a bit."

Why scallop a fingerboard in the first place? Jason Smith: "It lets the notes sustain longer because there's nothing underneath the note. You're basically just holding that string against the fret, not against the board. Scalloped fingerboards are a little strange and take some getting used to, but for the people who play them it's natural and advantageous. You need a light touch. If you're heavy-handed, it's easy to inadvertently bend that string and get some intonation problems."

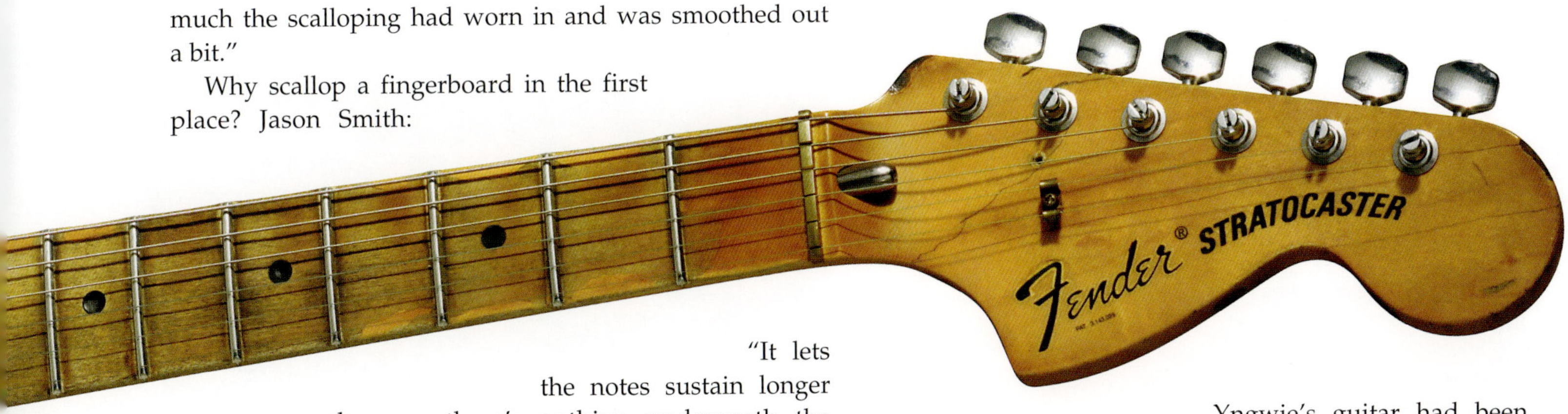

John Cruz adds: "Some of Fender's earlier production Malmsteen Strats had more of a deeply cut, U-shape flute to the scallops, but on Yngwie's own guitar it was very light, not deep, and it was crude, not too pretty. For the Tribute I copied the exact depth of the original, including all the file marks and scattered sanding that came from his own hand." Jason Smith: "If there are places on that fingerboard where it's uneven and worn, we duplicate it on the Tribute. We are not trying to make this a perfectly symmetrical fingerboard. That's not what this Tribute is about. It's about duplicating for you, the customer, Yngwie Malmsteen's personal guitar."

Other details of the heavily reliced Tribute include a pair of DiMarzio HS-3 stacked humbuckers, a middle-position Fender Standard Vintage 1970s-type single-coil pickup, a 7.25" fingerboard radius, a brass nut, American Vintage trem, Fender/Schaller *F* style tuners, one master volume knob, and a 3-way switch. Although the model was officially reported to have No-Load pots, in fact it has stock 250k units, which are disconnected, by the way, as on Yngwie's personal guitar. John Cruz adds: "He liked the direct signal from the jack to the pickups, just like Neil Young did [on his 'Old Black' Les Paul]. I did this to one of my own Strats, and I *love* it."

Yngwie's guitar had been converted from a 3-bolt to a 4-bolt neck attachment, and the Tribute duplicates the original's re-drilled, doweled-up holes. John Cruz: "The Oly White finish had yellowed over the years. The biggest challenge was getting the finish to look right, with the color match, the cracks, and all the detailed dings, bite marks, even burns. It was a normal-spec neck, but it had been refretted a number of times and was switched to [Dunlop] 6000 fret wire; recreating the neck's dings and repairs was tough. The Yngwie was by far the most challenging project I have ever been a part of, but it was really satisfying, too. I took my proto to the Musikmesse trade show in Frankfurt to show Yngwie, alongside with the original. He was blown away, and signed off in record time."

Showcase Italy: Bellissima!

The year 2008 saw the opening of the Custom Shop's Showcase Italy. Located in Bologna, Showcase Italy is the shop's third international facility, joining the Custom Shop Lounge in Düsseldorf and the Fender Showcase in Tokyo. It displays an extensive array of Master Built instruments, as well as the personal collection of M. Casale Bauer, Fender's Italian distributor for more than 40 years.

The grand opening was held on September 21. More than 400 music industry professionals and VIP guests attended the festivities, which included a concert featuring Fender stalwarts Greg Koch and Reggie Hamilton and renowned drummer Dom Famularo. Mike Eldred said at the time, "M. Casale Bauer has really pushed it up a notch with this one — from the stunning guitar display, to the immense sliding panels with artwork by Bob Perine, to the inner lair with hand-stitched Italian leather couches and even more high-end guitars and basses. It is amazing to see it, and the job they have done is unbelievable."

The Custom Shop's third international showroom is the sumptuously appointed Showcase Italy, located in Bologna.

The artwork of photographer/painter Bob Perine illustrated Fender catalogs, literature and advertisements from 1957 to 1969. Some of his work appears in the Custom Shop's Showcase Italy.

SUPER SONIC
Deluxe

Alex Perez reimagined the Fender Jazzmaster in this single-knob, alder-bodied guitar, which he built for Slipknot's Jim Root in 2009. Arty and elegant in its purity of design, it features a standard 3-way switch and EMG active humbuckers — an 81 at the bridge and a 60 at the neck. Gorgeous flame maple was selected for the fingerboard and quartersawn neck.

CHAPTER THIRTY-ONE

31

2009: Themes and Variations

Limited Collections, Limited Editions, Custom Deluxes, Limited Dealer Selects

One can't help but be struck by Fender's seemingly endless variations on a few basic designs. It's as if Leo Fender managed to deliver to the customers of his day several instruments now considered masterpieces — the pre-CBS Telecasters, Stratocasters, and basses — while at the same time bequeathing to his heirs a short stack of templates and sketches that await fleshing out and reinterpretations inspired by fresh insights, evolving tastes, and new technologies.

There was no more potent testimony to the legitimacy of these variations than the Custom Shop's diverse and functional instruments of 2009. The line included eight series of guitars. As we've seen, these series come and go, which in part explains discrepancies among versions of any given year's lineup as it appears in catalogs, price sheets, ads, and web sites. Still, the trend was clear. While the Custom Artist, Tribute, and Time Machine series remained in the line, the Custom Classics — which in 2008 had accounted for four Strats, two Teles, and four Jazz Basses — were retired, as were the Showmasters. All of the other series reflected the new philosophy of limited availability: Custom Deluxe, Limited Edition, Limited Dealer Select, Limited Collection, and Special Edition. (In some of the literature, Fender divided its Limited Edition category into three subgroups. The first was also called Limited Edition; the guitars were produced in limited quantities. Limited Release guitars were available only during the year of release, or until sold out. The third Limited Edition subcategory was the Master Design series.)

At first it might have taken some investigation to discern the differences among, say, the Special Edition, Limited Edition, and Limited Collection guitars, but the categories were generally cohesive. They made sense. One example: The two Teles and two Strats in the Special Edition series were Time Machine guitars that mixed vintage looks and neck profiles with modern electronics, including the versatile S-1 circuit.

Limited Collection

In this group, all four Strats and the Nocaster were Relics. Most of the Teles were Relics as well; the sole exception was the 1950s Telecaster Thinline N.O.S. What the 11 instruments in this group had in common was production limited by the number of pieces. Examples included the

The LTD 1964 Telecaster Relic had a Twisted Tele pickup at the neck and a Broadcaster pickup at the bridge. The Aged Lake Placid Blue finish appeared in the latter half of 2009.

1956 Stratocaster Relic (50 guitars in 2-color sunburst, 50 in Desert Sand) and the 1960 Stratocaster Relic (100 each in 3-color sunburst and Dakota Red). Production for the Limited '64 Telecaster Relic and the Limited '64 Stratocaster Relic was restricted to 50 each in black, aged Vintage White, and Chocolate 3-color sunburst.

For the Stratocaster Pro Relic, production was limited to 20 each in 3-color sunburst with a maple board, 3-color burst with a rosewood board, Sonic Blue with maple, and Sonic Blue with rosewood. For the Telecaster Pros, all of which had maple-cap boards, it was 20 each in 3-color sunburst and Sonic Blue. The shop crafted a mere 10 each in black and Shoreline Gold of the one-pickup La Cabronita Especial, 20 each in the same colors for the two-pickup version.

Limited Editions, Custom Deluxes

Previous "Limited Edition" guitars were described as "customized instruments with modern features that were briefly offered by the shop and then retired for a time." Examples included some of the Tributes, Strats from '54, '55, '57, '61, and '66, art guitars designed in association with Shepard Fairey, and a variety of other models. That same term was applied to very different guitars in 2009. Some were designed at the outset to be true collector's pieces, as likely to be found secured in an alarmed display case as leaning against a blackface Deluxe at an outdoor wedding gig. They included the 60th Anniversary Presidential Select Stratocaster introduced in 2006, and the Master Salute Strat from 2005. The third Limited Edition Strat was the George Fullerton model from late 2007. The Limited Editions also included the Tele/Strat Hybrid LTD, the '55 Tele/Pro Jr. set, and the '50s Top Bound Esquire Relic.

The updated guitars in the Custom Deluxe line were "designed for the working musician." The Custom Deluxe Stratocaster had a 1965-style C-shaped neck, locking Schallers, and an interesting pickup array — a '69 type grey-bobbin neck pickup, a hum-canceling reverse-wound/reverse-polarity '69 grey-bobbin middle pickup, and a Texas Special bridge pickup. The similarly positioned Custom Deluxe Telecaster had a 1952 U-shaped neck, locking Schallers, a Twisted Tele neck pickup, and a Hot Nocaster bridge pickup.

Yuriy Shishkov started with about 600 individually hand-cut, hand-ground 1/16" thick mirror pieces and then assembled 160 or so to make the top of Keith Urban's Shattered Mirror Telecaster. He arched the top a bit to increase the already extreme dazzle factor under stage lights. Urban applauded the guitar's "intricate craftsmanship in every little detail." Yuriy estimated that the glass work alone consumed a month's time. Note the ultra-figured bird's-eye maple used for the neck and fingerboard.

The Limited Collection's LTD 1964 Stratocaster Relic featured Master Built Overwound Fat '50s pickups. Practical touch: The third knob is a tone control for both the middle and bridge pickups. Only 50 guitars were finished in black.

Time Machines, Custom Artist instruments

For 2009 the shop reorganized the venerable Time Machine collection, dividing it into two groups: Vintage Spec and Classic. The former included a severely pared-down array of familiar instruments: '64 Jazz Bass, '51 Nocaster, '63 Tele, and '56, '60, and '69 Strats. The '66 Strat, '67 Tele, and '59 P Bass were retired, at least for the time being, and the Closet Classic finish option was dropped. Compared to the 2008 Time Machines, and not counting color choices, these two changes slashed the Time Machines by about 40 percent, helping to make room for the expanding limited-availability groups. Mike Eldred: "These things come and go, and reflect natural market fluctuations. We don't 'drop' models, but we might retire them for a period and bring them back when the time is right."

The Team Built Classic HBS-1 Stratocaster (also listed among the Special Editions) mixed vintage and modern features: a 1957-style soft V-neck profile, a Thin Skin nitro lacquer finish, a 1959-style mint green pickguard, and vintage tuners and hardware; it also had a 9.5" radius fingerboard, the S-1 switching system, two single-coils, and a humbucker.

Its companion, the Classic S-1 Tele, offered a C-shaped neck with a 9.5" radius, a '60s-type Tele bridge pickup, a Twisted Tele neck pickup, the S-1 system, staggered tuners, a three-ply mint green guard, a vintage-style bridge with three threaded steel saddles, and a nitro finish.

The artist instrument lineup of 2009 included seven Strats (Gilmour, Cray, Gallagher, Dale, Clapton, Beck, Trower), five Teles (Haggard, Gatton, Collins, and the two John 5's), the Palladino P Bass, and the Hamilton and Pastorius Jazz Basses.

Limited Dealer Select

Fender has long been willing to make special runs of instruments for favored dealers. The Custom Shop's Limited Dealer Select program takes that idea to a new level. Mike Eldred: "We partner with a lot of our showcase dealers. We sit down with them and their customers and their staff and ask what sorts of things they would like to see in a guitar, maybe a combination of features we haven't seen before. The first one we did was called the Wildwood 10."

Steve Mesplè, at Wildwood Guitars in Louisville, Colorado, worked with Fender on the inaugural project. "I

The brain trust: Several of the Master Builders are shown here at a NAMM show with some of their creations. From left: Todd Krause, Greg Fessler, Jason Smith, Mark Kendrick, Dennis Galuszka, John Cruz, Stephen Stern, Yuriy Shishkov.

Left: From the Limited Collection: The Strat Pro and Tele Pro Relic shared modern features such as a bend-friendly, 12" radius fingerboard. Note the Strat's CBS-style headstock and LSR roller nut.

Leo Fender and his associates from the 1950s would have recognized many of these neatly arrayed hand tools, which are still in use at the Custom Shop. They also would have recognized this Custom Tele Deluxe's Sonic Blue paint job, and likely marveled at its flamed maple neck.

approached Mike some years back and expressed some of my own frustrations. I had been a 'Gibson guy' but always loved Fenders – I just couldn't get them to play the way I wanted them to. I struggled, particularly with bending strings. I played for years before anybody ever mentioned the importance of string length to playability, but if you addressed playability by changing the string length, it's my belief that it might not sound like a Fender. So instead, Mike and I looked at fingerboard radius and fret profiles. We settled on a 10" radius because that would be noticeably flatter than the vintage 7.25, but not too flat. I learn so much from my customers, and for some of them, if they pick up a guitar with a 12" radius, they say, nope, doesn't feel like a Fender. So we thought a 10 would be just right, and 10 is also sort of a magical number that implies perfection. With the flatter radius and bigger frets, these guitars feel and sound and look like Fenders, but they play like a dream. We also specified lightweight woods and faded finishes that would give you that nice patina like on those old Fenders that we love so much."

The first run, its delivery starting in late 2005, was 200 guitars in four models: a '52 Tele, a more or less generic '50s maple-board Strat, a 1960 Strat, and a '65 Strat with the chunkier neck and round-lam fingerboard. All were Team Built Relics. They were so successful that Wildwood ordered another run with different models, specifying a mix of Team Built and Master Built guitars. Other Wildwood 10 Relics have included '56 and '59 Strats and a '59 Tele.

Steve Mesplè is genuinely excited about these collaborations. "I have no shortage of pre-CBS Fenders in my personal collection," he says, "but I bought three of these Wildwood 10s for myself. I'm going to put them away, and when the time is right I'm going to give one to each of my grandkids. I treasure these guitars and trust that my family will treasure them also. Mike Eldred and the Custom Shop crew get the credit for making what I think are some of the finest guitars Fender has ever made. For me it's been just great to play a small part in Fender's rich history." (Details regarding Limited Dealer Select models designed in association with the Music Zoo and Make'n Music appear elsewhere in this chapter and also in Chap. 16.)

The 3-color sunburst option became available for the LTD '64 Jazz Bass in the latter half of 2009.

From the Time Machine series: The Team-Built Classic S-1 Tele features the S-1 switching system, which on this model provides series and parallel pickup combos at the push of a knob. The additional sound is musical and very useful.

The Team-Built Classic S-1 Tele Relic put the S-1 circuit in an aged body of lightweight ash. Like the N.O.S. version, it was offered in black and 3-color sunburst and featured a Vintage '63 pickup in the bridge position and a Twisted Tele at the neck.

27 new models

The entire Custom Shop line of 2009 included two Esquires, three Nocasters, 25 Telecasters, and 35 Strats. Of those 65 guitars, a whopping 27 were brand new: two Custom Deluxe guitars, 10 Custom Shop Limited Dealer Selects, four Custom Shop Special Editions, and 11 Limited Collection guitars. These weren't one-offs, mind you. These were new models, more than two dozen of them introduced in January 2009 alone. In fact, those 27 models were just starting points, as several were offered with multiple combos of colors, finishes, and in some cases different pickup arrays, neck profiles, Team Built vs. Master Built, necks of quartersawn, straight-grain, or AA flame maple, and other options.

Despite the wealth of choices, for the new guitars of 2009 it was all about playability. While nine of the new models were somewhat vintage-based and year-specific (e.g., the Limited 1964 Stratocaster Relic), and several others incorporated designs from a particular decade (e.g., the 1950s Telecaster Thinline N.O.S.), *all* of them had contemporary fingerboards, flatter than the vintage-spec 7.25". Each "10" model had a 10" radius, and the Stratocaster Pro Relic and Telecaster Pro Relic had wide/flat 12s. All others had the comfy 9.5" radius.

Does the shop really need to continue mixing and matching details from vintage models and then updating them with new features? Haven't we already heard of every sensible combo? Well, consider: The 1951 Nocaster neck felt great and had a Tele headstock, a maple board, small frets, and a 7.25" radius; it had never been put on a Strat before. Strats from the early 1960s had small Strat headstocks and rosewood fingerboards. Contemporary players often prefer larger frets and a flatter board. Now, pick and choose from among these ingredients, blend carefully, add a pinch of a Master Builder's personal style, season to taste, and *voila!* — savor the zesty Music Zoo "No-Neck" '60s Strat, a Limited Dealer Select guitar introduced in 2009 and built exclusively for retailer Music Zoo of Little Neck, New York. It combined that Nocaster neck profile with a Strat headstock, rosewood board, and a 9.5" radius. It was available in a variety of vintage colors and either N.O.S. or Relic finishes.

One of the most modern of 2009's new guitars was the Limited Collection Stratocaster Pro Relic, inspired in part by some of the personal instruments built for endorsing artists. It had a C-shaped maple neck with a round-lam board and a flat 12" radius, 22 medium jumbo frets, three Samarium Cobalt Noiseless pickups, the Greasebucket circuit, deluxe two-point trem, staggered Sperzel Trim-Loks, an LSR roller nut, and a contoured heel. (More on the original Strat Pro of 2006 in Chap. 28; the Telecaster Pro Relic shared some of its features.)

Fender described the Limited Collection's La Cabronita Especial as "probably the nastiest little guitar we've ever made," and it was easy to see why. A Telecaster is hardly a frilly guitar to begin with, but this guy looked like a Tele that escaped into the wild and went feral. It had one big-sounding TV Jones Power'Tron pickup, a one-piece neck, a bone nut, two knobs, a Relic finish, rusty hardware, aged plastic parts, and a decided lack of ornamentation, not even a hot dog control plate. Unlike "normal" Telecasters, La Cabronita Especial had a one-ply custom pickguard whose shape recalled the one Leo Fender put on his snakehead Tele prototype way back in the late '40s. The two-pickup Cabronita Especial had an S-1 circuit. It's guitars like these that convert a reaction of "What — yet another variation on the Strat/Tele?" to "Um, cool. How much?"

This Vintage Blonde '52 Tele Relic was one of the first of the LTD Dealer Select Wildwood 10s. A key feature of all guitars in this series: the 10" fingerboard radius.

The single and double-pickup versions of the alder-bodied La Cabronita Especial feature TV Jones pickups — a Power'Tron in the former and a pair of Classics in the latter; both pickup designs are based on the classic, twangy Gretsch Filter'Tron. The two-pickup model has the push-knob S-1 circuit, this time providing a high-end rolloff in all three switch positions.

Start me up: This 2010 '52 Tele Time Machine Relic in Nocaster Blonde has a front humbucker, courtesy Seymour Duncan, one of the most popular Tele mods. The handwritten scrap on the workbench notes the string spacings and saddle measurements.

CHAPTER THIRTY-TWO

32

The Golden Age

After a complicated birth and an exhilarating but sometimes unruly adolescence, the Custom Shop has settled into an intense yet more stable middle age. The long conflict between building world-class guitars and making a profit has been balanced in such a way as to benefit both sides of the equation. The shop's builders and managers are well educated about running a business, with closer communication among sales, marketing, and production staff. They pay closer attention to inventory.

Yuriy Shishkov: "We are more modern in our management. Things flow more smoothly. You can do these things without any compromise to quality. For example, when I came here [in 2000], we did not have computers. Also, each builder did not have his own phone, so you would have to leave your work space to go talk to a customer or dealer on the phone. Communication with customers and dealers is important here, so improving all these things adds up. The environment continues to get better, constantly. What hasn't changed is the focus on quality. Attention to detail is the most important thing, getting that guitar to the customer exactly the way he wants it."

One continuous thread running throughout the shop's history is passion. John Grunder looks back on the early days: "I gave my heart and soul to that company for a lot of years. For most of those years, they almost wouldn't have had to pay me to come into work. I felt that way because we were trying to do something special. It meant a great deal to all of us." John Cruz in 2009: "Whether our customers are famous or not, when they tell us they're going crazy for how great their guitar is, that makes us feel really good and makes us want to try even harder. Twenty-two years into it, I still have the passion, which is not easy to say for a lot of people in a lot of jobs. We're all players here. Some days, even after I've been working on guitars all day long, I can't wait to get my hands on my own guitar and just play."

Big One

As we have seen, scores of builders, marketers, sales reps, artists, dealers, and managers have contributed to the shop's success. Let's remember where it all started. Ritchie Fliegler offers an insightful and eloquent perspective, citing an observation quoted by John F. Kennedy in 1961:

Success has many fathers, but failure is an orphan. "The more time I spend out on the ponder-osa with this thing, the more I think the root is in that quote. At the end of the day, the Fender Custom Shop is unique, different from all other seemingly similar shops in that it combines the utilitarian ethos of Leo Fender with Bill Schultz's desire to be cast in the same light as those more precious instruments from Gibson, Martin, PRS, and the like. Players of all stripes with wildly varying amounts of money and differing desires can see their dreams brought to life there. Be it a simple Burgundy Mist American Standard, or a recreation of a rock star's workhorse, or a $50,000 hand-carved Tree of Life Strat, any and all are welcome, and each instrument and player is given his/her/its due.

> "As an artists' cooperative making some of the coolest, most bitchin', bad-ass, rockin' stuff, the Custom Shop has no peer."
>
> — Ritchie Fliegler

"There have been struggles, ego clashes, and mayhem — think of the Beatles with a dozen or so Johns and Pauls. Sometimes you get 'A Day In The Life,' and sometimes you get 'Revolution 9.' At all times the fur is flying and the pot is boiling. A success? Financially, not so much. But as an artists' cooperative making some of the coolest, most bitchin', bad-ass, rockin' stuff, the Custom Shop has no peer. Who wouldn't want to be the genius responsible for it all? But alas, there can be only one, and that one is, as Mike Lewis and I called him: Big One. Schultz.

"Like JFK, Bill was in the hot seat. Other people got to second-guess, but he had to 'first-guess.' And like JFK, history and his absence have allowed any number of 'Russian historians' to fill the breach. Their comments and recollections may or may not have suffered or benefited from the passage of time. It's all irrelevant. Each story has its merit; each is a window into the teller's personality, perception, and place in the puzzle — and they all would have been sitting on their hands were it not for Bill Schultz."

Independence and handwork

The shop's current structure reflects John Page's original vision of a separate operation. In fact, the builders operate with more independence than ever. But the evolutionary updates initiated by Dan Smith, Mike Lewis, Richard McDonald, Mike Eldred, and their colleagues — better internal communication, clearer marketing, an improved integration of systems, tighter controls of inventory — have provided a more stable working environment for all parties.

The Custom Shop has a separate area, separate tools, separate processes, and separate workers. "It would be difficult to have the factory do something for us," explains Dennis Galuszka, "because our processes are so different. We have our own staff, and they work exclusively for us, separate from manufacturing. When you have one guy putting in frets all day, he gets very, very good at it. On some guitars, for some processes, we know we can rely on Custom Shop staff to do a great job and meet our standards. If you ordered a [Custom Built] '56 Strat from me with vintage frets, I would be perfectly comfortable with our staff fretting it up for you. On Master Built projects, we take everything upon our own shoulders."

The shop also has its own supplies of woods, the spreads already glued side-by-side in most cases and often pre-separated by weight according to the builders' exacting standards. The wood has to be clean — no mineral stains, no knots, very high quality. "But not everybody wants a lot of figure, either," says Galuszka. "Some people might want a traditional look with a bit less figure like you might see on just a good honest Telecaster from the '50s or '60s. Not every guitar is intended to be a knockout, visually. So we can take care of all these different tastes." The shop also has its own paint facility. Finishing is such a personal process that the painters eventually learn the quirks and tastes of each builder. Dennis Galuszka: "As soon as they see my initials on the body, they know just what to do."

And although the builders have more access to high-tech tools than ever before, they still rely on handwork for many of the procedures, not only for final adjustments and finishing but sometimes for initial steps as well. Dennis Galuszka: "Sometimes, even if we could do something on the CNC, I think it's just better not to have to worry about writing up a program and scheduling a machine. Instead,

Nothing is more important to Fender's legacy than the know-how of its employees. As we go to press, Abby Ybarra is well into her sixth decade at the company. One of her biggest admirers is Seymour Duncan, who addressed her technique on the pickup winding machine: "It's all in the timing, how fast you go back and forth." A glance at Internet chat groups turns up comments such as, "Whatever mojo she's got, it is special," and, "Definitely and by far, she handmakes the best pickups ever made by Fender."

I might make a template and go over to the pin router and do it by hand."

Better than they ever were

The question on everyone's mind: Are today's Custom Shop guitars as good as yesterday's? Sometimes they are at least as good, often they are better, and they are certainly more consistent. Greg Fessler's perspective is rooted in his two decades as a fulltime Custom Shop builder. "Fender is now big and strong, more secure," he says, "but the atmosphere is still very creative, still a lot of fun, and the builders here are as good as *anybody* we had back in the old days. Don't forget that. The guitars are better than they ever were."

Dennis Galuszka agrees: "If anything, the guitars are way, way better than they used to be. You get better as you go. The guitars I made even two years ago aren't quite as good as the ones I'm making now. We're learning all the time — new machines, new technologies, plus we still have to do so many things by hand." Alex Perez: "I'm here in the shop every day, and I can tell you we are making amazing guitars. The quality is as good if not better than ever. High quality is not a problem; it's a given. The concern is about marketing. We need to educate our customers, more than

you would think, because they don't necessarily know the trouble we go to, all the extra procedures. We have many unique processes here. This isn't some factory. That Custom Shop decal means a lot. I hope people understand all the fine details that make these guitars so special."

Even the most acclaimed builders from the shop's first decade tip their hats to the current crew. J. Black: "Some people tell me the new ones aren't as good as the old ones. Maybe they think they're supposed to say that, but I don't know what they're looking at. I've seen recent guitars by Jason Smith, John Cruz, Steve Stern, and others, and they're extraordinary. Back in the old days, you might get a body from your own stock one day, and the next day you'd get a body for the same model from manufacturing. One guy might do the necks one day, a different guy the next day. It's much more consistent now, and as far as I can tell the work is exceptional."

What is the definitive comparator here, the ultimate standard? Which guitars have to be equaled or surpassed in order for the Custom Shop to deserve the mantle as the finest entity of its kind in the world? Would anyone go so far as to say that Custom Shop instruments are not only as good as any company's new guitars, or the shop's early instruments, but also as good as the storied icons from Fender's vintage era? Well, yes. Herbie Gastelum should know. He's been building Fender guitars since Leo Fender's top-of-the-line Jaguar was still on the drawing board. His specialty is neck shaping. He said, "Some people say the necks in the '50s and '60s were better than they are now. But in my opinion, I think the necks — even the entire instruments — are a whole lot better now. Believe me, I've seen the work, and it's a lot more detailed and a lot more critical than in years past."

In a career spanning more than three decades, Nate Westgor, of Willie's American Guitars, in St. Paul, has bought and sold more than 1,000 vintage Fenders and examined or repaired perhaps another 3,000. When it comes to Fenders from the 1950s and 1960s, there's nothing he hasn't seen, examined, played, or heard. As he says elsewhere in these pages: "The current guitars coming out of the Custom Shop not only rival the earlier Custom Shop stuff but many times rival the pre-CBS guitars."

Left: "I've been using this pickup winding machine ever since I started working in the Custom Shop," explains Abby Ybarra. "In the old days I used a machine that Mr. Fender made himself. It was like a little sewing machine motor with belts like rubber bands. But this machine is the only one I've ever used in the Custom Shop, and it's very nice and consistent."

Perhaps the ultimate in elemental electric guitars: a bare-bones Limited Esquire Relic in basic black.

Partnering and investing in a rich legacy

As we go to press, the mission of the Custom Shop is generally the same as it was when Dan Smith and Mike Eldred assumed their supervisory roles in the late 1990s. Mike Eldred: "It's been a matter of growing and refining that vision rather than any major shifts. It's important that everybody — not just the builders, but everyone in the shop — gets on the same track, and deeply understands the vision. It's a simple mandate: to build the very best Fender can build, and to provide a vehicle for artists and consumers to partner with and invest in Fender's rich legacy and history. That's it. That's all we're supposed to be."

The prototype for the John Mayer Black 1 Strat. As we go to press, John Cruz is in the midst of building all 83 guitars himself. Not surprisingly, the Mayer model was influenced by the shop's SRV Number One Tribute Strat. Its neck specs are similar although not identical. The Mayer has custom-wound, '60s-style pickups, stock wiring, and a standard vintage trem in gold. One very interesting detail: The peghead was drilled out for vintage tuners; those holes were plugged and Schaller-style tuners with pearl buttons were installed, as if they were replacement keys. John Cruz: "I'm selecting the wood very carefully, so the weight and the grain are similar to John's own guitar, and I'm tone-tapping each body for tonality."

As an example, Mike recalls a visit from one particularly enthusiastic fan, John Mayer. John wanted to see how the Master Builders craft instruments. Mike gave him some safety glasses, took him out on the floor to the stock of alder wood, and told him to pick a spread. "I said, 'You're going to build a guitar.' I showed him how to make a body, how to align a big Plexiglas template, how to avoid any knots, how to do the radius along the edge of the body with the router. This thing is going like 20,000 rpm, and you can't stop because you are deep into the wood, so you have to pull it through at a very consistent rate, nice and slow, and keep your fingers away, make a nice round edge on that body. I told him, John, don't mess up because if you do, we're both out of a job. He did the sanding, and then I took him into paint. He did this horrible paint job [laughs], with runs in it and everything, and I said okay, this is your guitar. John Cruz reliced it up for him, and that's the black Strat he plays all the time. Now, do you think he plays it because it sounds better than all the other Fenders he has? He plays that guitar because, like I said, he partnered and invested in the Fender legacy. Right there, that shows what we're supposed to do. We can't bring every customer in here and go through that same process, but that's how we partner. It's a great example of who we are."

The long view

Dan Smith's perspective is informed by his unparalleled experience. As Mike Lewis says, "Dan Smith had more to do with all the groovy stuff that happened at Fender than anybody on earth . . . He is part of the DNA of Fender." Dan's view is that the Custom Shop's historic significance extends well beyond its own instruments: The shop restored confidence in the entire Fender brand.

Dan joined Fender in 1981, and for a decade or so, a small group of die-hards regularly called him with questions about Fender arcana. "They came from all parts of the country," he says, "with a variety of job skills and lifestyles. They would call to authenticate some old guitar, or ask if I knew what day this or that screw was used . . . you get the picture." For years, none of these folks ever bought or even considered buying a Fender guitar made after 1965 or so. Dan Smith: "A couple finally bought one of the [factory] reissues — begrudgingly, and only because they didn't want to take their 'real' Fenders out of the house."

Leo Fender didn't play guitar, so from the beginning he depended on professional musicians for crucial feedback. Continuing one of the company's oldest and proudest traditions, enthusiastic patron John Mayer visits the Custom Shop.

Longtime company veteran Dan Smith explains that the shop's impact reaches far beyond its own guitars, continuing to foster consumer faith in the entire Fender brand.

But a year or so after the shop was established, the calls took a different drift. "Now the same people asked if I thought the Custom Shop stuff was really that good — I'd gained their trust — and if so, where could they see it? Instead of asking about the old stuff, the same people wanted to know what model the Custom Shop was going to do next, and how they could get on the list to get one."

As we've seen, another aspect of the shop's long-term influence can be seen in guitar-building improvements that were transferred to Fender's main domestic and international production facilities. G.E. Smith takes a back seat to no one when it comes to a combo of vintage savvy and high-profile gigging with vintage and new Fenders on stages all over the world. He says, "The quality of Fender Custom Shop guitars is fantastic, and so is the quality of the guitars coming off the main production line. The Mexican stuff, too. Fender is on a roll."

Things to come

The future looks good. More people have more guitar-building skills than ever before, and many of them aspire to work in the Custom Shop one day. Todd Krause: "I used to hate the word 'luthier,' because it conjures up images of a guy with a mallet and a chisel. But look where we've come. Now we have a Senior Master Builder title, and people in high school are getting trained in their shop classes, and they're saying they want to be a Master Builder in Fender's Custom Shop. The guys coming up through the ranks possess not only the woodworking and engineering skills but also metalworking and CNC. They can make every single thing on the guitar. They could make the screws if they had to."

The builders continue to think big, to ask — what's the coolest thing we could do? As we go to press, several projects are in the works. The year 2010 marks the 60th Anniversary of the world's most historic solidbody guitar, the Telecaster, and the Custom Shop will celebrate it in big and small ways — big in terms of ideas, but limited in terms of the guitars' availability. Five Anniversary guitars will be released in sequence: A recreation of the snake-head Telecaster Prototype; a one-pickup, pine-body Esquire; a two-pickup pine Esquire; then what Mike Eldred calls a "real" Broadcaster — meaning its routing, maple plug, skunk stripe, decal, and pickups will be spot-on, authentic recreations; and finally a Nocaster. Only 60 pieces of each model will be built. (If a two-pickup Esquire sounds historically inaccurate, actually it's not. Before sales/marketing guru Don Randall came up with the Telecaster name — even before "Broadcaster" — both one and two-pickup versions of Leo Fender's first solidbody Spanish guitar were briefly called Esquire.)

The 2010 lineup also includes Jim Campilongo and Nile Rodgers artist guitars; several '52 Telecasters with neck humbuckers; Heavy Relic '59 Strats; '63 and '65 Strats in three-color sunburst, Dakota Red, and Black (N.O.S. and Relic versions); a '59 Precision Bass in Relic and N.O.S.; and several Quarterly Release Strats and Teles. New colors are available for some extremely limited Strat Pros and Tele

This version of the Limited Esquire Relic recreates Fender's very first two-pickup guitar and is one of several Tele-bration instruments marking the Telecaster's 60th anniversary. Like the original, it has no truss rod.

Pros, several La Cabronitas, and Custom Deluxe Strats and Teles.

Another project replicates the black Stratocaster that John Mayer built under Mike Eldred's tutelage. It's to be called Black 1. Its limited availability — 83 pieces — is in keeping with the shop's evolution toward increased exclusivity. Mike Eldred: "We don't have a catalog anymore. We have special collections. Much of what we're doing is limited either by the number of pieces or by the time. We will ask, what's your idea for the next six months? What about the six-month period after that? A lot of these things are limited, and then we go on to some other new thing, so it's exciting. We've pared our dealer network down, too, so it's also very selective. Even when a model is successful, I prefer to mix it up, change it around, stay on our toes. Whether it's an Andy Summers guitar, a Crossroads thing, or some other Custom Shop guitar, the buyer has a collectible, and very few people are going to have it. It can go up in value, and that's key. Like the Tributes — nobody at Fender is getting rich from doing them, but that's not what it's about. It's about partnering and investing in the Fender legacy."

Jim Campilongo's signature Telecaster blends several custom-tailored features with a deep respect for Leo Fender's original design. It's based on Jim's '59 Tele, a key feature of which is its top-loading bridge. Some people feel that having the strings anchored at the rear of the bridge plate rather than running through the body imparts less unwanted edge to the tone and an easier, slinkier playing feel — "more compressed in the sound, a bit more rubbery," as Jim puts it. The pickups are full-bodied and warm, less high-endy than typical Tele units. Jim Campilongo: "My goal was to have a woody, full bodied sound while retaining the character of a great Telecaster." Jim adds that his Custom Campy pickups feature reverse polarity and ultimate shielding. On the "Campy Toploader," the bridge plate's "sidewalls" have been shaved down; in Jim's opinion they get in the way of traditional right-hand plectrum technique. Other details include: deep-dish peghead contouring to facilitate those behind-the-nut bends, jumbo frets, '63-style knobs, a thinner finish on the body and neck for improved resonance, and a tall, top hat pickup selector for easy switching.

Full Circle

Its design going all the way back to 1949, the pine-body LTD Limited Snake Head Tele recreated the prototype of the world's first commercially successful solidbody electric Spanish guitar. There's so much history here. The original prototype drew on Leo Fender's lap steel designs from the mid 1940s. Its neck was built by George Fullerton, and its pickup design, when refined, unleashed a tone that would forever change the sound of popular music.

Full Circle

The Golden Age

Having worked in a fun, hectic, exhilarating, and sometimes wacky/Wild West environment, some of the early employees will always look back to the shop's first years as the golden age. The other view: Today's guitars are better than ever, so the golden age is right now. Mike Eldred says simply, "The shop today is the very best it's been." By the way, it's not like working at the Custom Shop is no longer fun. Consider this description: "There's something funny about throwing a bunch of creative and funny guys into one room. We are some sort of dysfunctional family that tries to make the best out of the worst through jokes and pranks. There's a lot of laughter going on all day — and it could be about you. Besides the typical male hijinks and shenanigans, you can expect a quickly written song depicting your sexual orientation, or some creative Photoshop work on a personal picture. It makes for a great atmosphere to reduce the stress that is constantly on us with deadlines and the need to produce these flawless instruments." Although they sound like they could have been uttered in, say, 1990, these words are from an account by Paul Waller in 2010.

As noted, Greg Fessler's career spans both decades of the shop's history, as does Mark Kendrick's. Greg Fessler: "It's easy to get this image in your mind of the good old days, when everything was perfect and golden. Mark and I were laughing one time. He was saying, I remember a Stratocaster I made six or seven years ago. I was super proud of it, and the guy sent it in for a repair or something, and I couldn't wait to check out this great guitar. I got it back and I was like, my God, this isn't as cool as I remembered [laughs]. Isn't it funny how that happens? It's human nature to romanticize the past, but we didn't have CNC machines. It was all pin routers and templates and soft tooling, so things weren't as dialed in. Everybody had their own templates, so Fred Stuart's might not match up exactly with John English's. It's standardized now, which makes everything better and more consistent. We still add our own touches to these guitars, to make them ours, but

Another Tele-bration model from 2010, the LTD Limited Nocaster reproduces the short-lived, no-name version of the Tele built between its 1950 Broadcaster phase and early-'51 official Telecaster incarnation.

Some Custom Shop guitars are limited to a single year of production; this one and a few others are limited to a single quarter. Behold the 2010 Limited Collection 1st Quarter — or LTD/Q1 — 1958 Stratocaster Relic. A gorgeous guitar, it's finished in Candy Apple Red over a gold undercoat. It sports a gold anodized pickguard and features pickups handwound by Abigail Ybarra.

the instruments are definitely much nicer than they used to be back in the old days."

So, some will tell you the golden age was in the late '80s and '90s, and others will look to the accomplishments of the new century's first decade. But is it possible that neither view is correct? Todd Krause: "Everyone has their own opinion, but we have consistently gotten better with every year we operate. We are regrouping, gearing up for big things. We have great ideas and are focused on thinking further ahead than we have in the past. We are developing new techniques, not just new products. The apprentices we have now are amazing. They will be tomorrow's super builders. Anybody who asks about the golden age, I would say to them:

Look ahead. The golden age of the Fender Custom Shop is still to come."

PHOTO CREDITS

The author is indebted to the many people who took or supplied photographs. In a few cases, the word "courtesy" is used here to credit a person who contributed an image (perhaps an old snapshot) whose photographer is unknown.

The legend: DM = Dave Maddux, FMIC = Fender Musical Instruments Corp., FS = courtesy Fred Stuart, JB = courtesy J. Black, JP = John Page, MS/AS = courtesy Michael and Alice Stevens, MY = Matt York, PH = Pamelina H., SG = courtesy Scott Grant, SP = Pitkin Studio/ Steve Pitkin, SS = courtesy Stephen Stern

Cover: SP

Front: Page 3 MY, 4-5 John Peden, 6 Gregory Burns, 9 SP

Foreword: Page 10 Rick Gould, 13 SP

Introduction: all photos SP

Chapter 1: Page 22 SP, 24 FMIC, 25 MY, 26 courtesy the late Bill Carson, 27 MY, 29 DM, 30 SP, 31 MY, 32-33 DM, 34 SP, 35 MY, 36 MS/AS, 37 MY

Chapter 2: Pages 38-40 MS/AS, 41 SP, 42 courtesy JP, 43-45 MS/AS, 46-49 DM

Chapter 3: Page 50 Matt Tapp, 53 SP, 54 Matt Tapp, 55-56 MS/AS, 57-61 courtesy JP, 62 SG, 64 MS/AS, 66-67 FS

Chapter 4: Page 70 SP, 72 MS/AS, 73 FMIC, 74-75 SP, 76 top JB, 76 bottom MS/AS, 77 JB, 78 SP, 79 top JB, 79 bottom MY, 80 SP, 81 top courtesy JP, 81 bottom SP, 82-83 JB, 84 SP, 85 courtesy PH, 86 SP, 87 PH, 88 DM, 89 right SP, 90 SP, 91 courtesy JP, 93 SP

Chapter 5: Page 94 Jill Furmanovsky, 96 SG, 98 FMIC, 100-102 DM, 105-108 MY, 109-111 SP

Chapter 6: Page 112 Justin Spargo, 114 SP, 115 left MS/AS, 115 right MY, 116 FMIC, 118-119 courtesy JP, 120 FMIC, 121 courtesy JP, 122 JB, 123 courtesy JP

Chapter 7: Page 124 MY, 126 FS, 127 courtesy JP, 128-129 JB, 130 left FS, 131-134 SP, 135 MY

Chapter 8: Pages 136-138 SP, 139 bottom FMIC, 140-141 SP, 142 FMIC, 143 MY

Chapter 9: Page 144 guitar DM, 144 Michael Stevens MS/AS, 146-147 SG, 148 headstock DM, 148 diagram SG, 149 FMIC, 150 FS, 151-154 JB, 155 Mansons Guitar Shop UK

Chapter 10: Page 156 FMIC, 158 JB, 159-162 FMIC, 163 diagram SG, 163 guitar FMIC, 164 John Peden, 166 FMIC, 167 JB, 168 FMIC, 169 SG, 170-172 FMIC, 174 SP, 175 left FMIC, 175 right SP

Chapter 11: Pages 176-179 SP, 183-184 SP, 185 courtesy Tony Bacon, Jawbone Press, London, 186 SP, 187-189 courtesy PH, 190 SP, 191 top and lower right SP, 192-195 SP, 196 left SP, 196 right courtesy JP, 197 left DM, 197 right SP, 198-200 SS, 201 Dustin Jack/ Fretted Americana, 202 PH, 202 bottom Dustin Jack/ Fretted Americana, 203-204 PH, 205-207 JP, 208-213 SP

Chapter 12: Page 214 SP, 216 bottom left SP, 216 top and bottom right PH/JB, 218 FMIC, 219 courtesy JD Dworkow, 220-224 FMIC, 225 DM

Chapter 13: Page 226 SP, 228 top left MY, 228 bottom and right SP, 229 DM, 230 top JB, 230 bottom SP, 231 FMIC, 232 DM, 233 FMIC, 234 SP, 235 FMIC, 236 MY,

237-238 SP, 239 FMIC, 240-241 MY, 242-243 SP

Chapter 14: Pages 244-245 SP, 246-247 FMIC, 248-250 courtesy JD Dworkow, 251 SP, 252 FMIC, 253 Robert Sorbo

Chapter 15: Page 254 SS, 257-258 SP, 259 SG, 260 SS, 261-262 SP, 263 SS, 264-267 SP

Chapter 16: Page 268 FMIC, 270-271 top MY, 271 bottom SP, 272-273 SP, 274-275 MY, 276 guitar MY, 276 chart SG, 278 guitar MY, 278 chart SG, 280 MY, 281 FMIC

Chapter 17: Pages 282-284 MY, 285 DM, 286-287 top MY, 287 bottom FMIC, 288-289 MY, 290 FMIC, 291 MY, 293 DM, 294 MY, 296-297 FMIC

Chapter 18: Page 298 SP, 300-301 MY, 302-305 DM, 306-308 MY, 309-311 SP

Chapter 19: all photos SP, except 325 Courtney Love © Robert Matheu/Retna Ltd US

Chapter 20: Page 326 SP, 328 and 329 top courtesy JP, 329 bottom JB, 330 JB, 332 top left courtesy Ralph Esposito, 332 top right and bottom left courtesy JP, 332 bottom right FS, 333-334 JB, 335 FS, 337 SP

Chapter 21: Page 338 MY, 340 top DM, 340 bottom FMIC, 341 MY, 343 FS, 345-351 MY, 352-353 DM, 354 MY, 355 DM, 356-357 Dave Newman, 359 MY

Chapter 22: Page 360 SP, 362 FMIC, 363-367 DM, 368-369 SP, 370 MY, 371-372 SP, 373 MY

Chapter 23: Page 374 FMIC, 376 DM, 377 SP, 378-381 FMIC, 382 Doug Crouch, 383-384 FMIC, 385 Russ Harrington, 387 DM

Chapter 24: Pages 388-390 SP, 391 left FMIC, 391 right SP, 395 SP, 396 FMIC, 397 DM, 398 FMIC, 399-401 SP, 402 FMIC, 403 right SP, 404-407 SP

Chapter 25: all photos SP except 410 MY, 432-434 courtesy Kit Carson, 441 inset courtesy Joe Wood, 451 FMIC, 455 Buddy Guy FMIC

Chapter 26: Page 456 FMIC, 458 MY, 459 FMIC, 460-462 SP, 463 FMIC, 465-468 SP, 469-471 FMIC, 472 MY, 473 FMIC, 474-475 MY, 476 SP, 477 FMIC

Chapter 27: Page 478 SP, 479 FMIC, 480 SP, 481 FMIC, 483-484 SP, 485 FMIC, 486 SP, 487 FMIC, 488-492 SP, 493 right DM, 494 SP, 495 DM

Chapter 28: Pages 496-501 SP, 503-505 MY, 506 FMIC, 507 SP, 509 MY, 510-511 SP, 512 FMIC, 513 SP, 515 MY, 516-517 FMIC

Chapter 29: Page 518 MY, 520 DM, 521-523 MY, 525-526 SP, 527 FMIC, 528 left SP, 528 right MY, 529 main SP, 529 inset MY, 530 FMIC, 531 MY, 532 FMIC, 533 John Peden, 534 FMIC, 535-537 SP

Chapter 30: Page 538 MY, 541 SP, 542-546 MY, 547 FMIC, 548-549 SP, 550-551 FMIC

Chapter 31: Pages 552-556 MY, 557 top FMIC, 557 bottom MY, 558-561 MY, 562 SP, 563 MY

Chapter 32: Pages 564-570 MY, 571 DM, 572 DM 573-577 MY

Page 592: SP

INDEX

Note: Rather than having scores of listings under Stratocaster and Telecaster, instruments are identified by specific model names, such as: Limited '64 Tele Relic, and La Riata, both listed under L. If a guitar model's designation includes an artist's or a builder's name, it is listed first name first. Examples: Jimi Hendrix Tribute Stratocaster, and John Cruz's Builder Select '62 Stratocaster Relic LTD, both listed under J.

Page numbers in *italics* indicate photos.

Following page:
Displayed at the January 2011 NAMM show, the Birdflower Telecaster was the most challenging inlay project ever undertaken by Yuriy Shishkov. A mere glance at the instrument suggests the complexity of the task, but as it turned out the biggest hurdles were neither the elaborate design nor the number of individual pieces. Yuriy Shishkov: "Most of the work was done on the top, which is claro walnut, and there is nothing more complicated in inlay art than to do clean work on a material lighter than ebony. Making perfect inlay work on wood like this — by hand, without filler showing around the shells — is nearly impossible. That's why these tasks today are assigned to a CNC machine that can do it with digital precision. My goal was to accomplish 'digital accuracy' by hand, and even do something these machines cannot."

The claro walnut top was glued to a body of aged ash. Master Grade bird's-eye maple was used for the neck, ebony for the fingerboard. The bindings on the body and neck were fashioned from ivoroid, and the pickups were hand-wound by Abigail Ybarra. With virtually zero tolerance for miscalculations, Yuriy cut the ornamental pieces with a jewelry saw and then cut the pockets for them by hand, using a special hand-held mill and a knife. Silver and copper cloisonné wire, only 0.009" thick, was hammered into the wood to complement the inlay. Larger pieces of silver were incorporated with white, gold mother of pearl, blue, pink, and green abalone. The hardware was custom-engraved, and an ultra-thin finish was applied over the body and neck.

Some of the processes required a touch so light and deft that only the most meticulous of artists could accomplish them. Yuriy: "Just cutting a channel for the wire with a special tool sometimes requires doing it in between your heartbeats." Because of his other obligations to the shop, it took Yuriy nearly three years of painstaking, on-again/off-again labor — hundreds of hours in all — to complete the guitar. The name "Birdflower" reflects his vision of a mystical "bird" blossom rising up from a branch of flowers.